MW00824937

What the Researchers Are Saying

Christopher O'Brien is one of those rare researchers who leave no stone unturned in his search of the truth. *Stalking the Herd* is a monumental work demonstrating that mysterious cattle and animal mutilations are deeply embedded in human history, with some very strange and shocking twists. O'Brien sets a new bar on the subject, lifting it beyond the ufology arena that has confined it for too long. There are still UFO connections aplenty here, but much more. This is a superb work, and O'Brien has done an amazing job pulling together a mountain of information.

—Rosemary Ellen Guiley, author, *The Djinn Connection*

Finally, we have the definitive study and expose of the disturbing phenomenon of animal mutilations. Informative, eye-opening, unbiased and terrifying in its implications, *Stalking the Herd* is not just recommended reading, it's absolutely vital reading. After digesting its pages, you may never want to eat another burger again.

—Nick Redfern, author, *The Real Men in Black*

I so respect and admire Christopher O'Brien for his decades of exploring the cattle mutilation enigma in many "mysterious valleys." His excellent *Stalking the Herd* is a highly documented, totally fascinating research report. Carefully, painstakingly, he analyzes every theory for the phenomena—E.T's, Satanists, mad scientists, natural predators, and scavengers with preternatural skills. The solution O'Brien offers in conclusion may leave the readers somewhat startled as he explores a dark closet of American culture.

—Brad Steiger, co-author, *Real Encounters,
Different Dimensions, and Otherworldly Beings*

Christopher O'Brien has been investigating the strange mystery of unexplained animal mutilations for a long time and *Stalking the Herd* is the culmination of his years of research. While reading this fascinating book, I was amazed at how comprehensive it is, how meticulous its attention to detail, and yet how engaging. I could not put it down. This is the definitive book on the subject, showing how the simple dismissals don't fly, how strange these mutilations really are, and how intelligent public policy is needed to deal with this problem."

—Richard Dolan, author, *UFOs and the National Security State*

Other Books by Christopher O'Brien:

Secrets of the Mysterious Valley
Stalking the Tricksters
Enter the Valley
The Mysterious Valley

STALKING THE HERD

Unraveling the Cattle Mutilation Mystery

Adventures Unlimited Press

Stalking the Herd

by Christopher O'Brien

© 2014
Christopher O'Brien

ISBN: 978-1-939149-06-0

Published by:
Adventures Unlimited Press
One Adventure Place
Kempton, Illinois 60946 USA
auphq@frontiernet.net

www.AdventuresUnlimitedPress.com

Portions of "Mute Testimony" by David Perkins have previously appeared in *UFO 1947-1997 Fifty Years of Flying Saucers*, edited by Hilary Evans and Dennis Stacy, ©1997, John Brown Publishing, London, England

STALKING
THE
HERD

Christopher O'Brien

Stalking the Herd:
Unraveling the Cattle Mutilation Mystery:

Acknowledgments:

Stalking the Herd would have been impossible to research, write and produce without the help of many people. First and foremost, David Perkins, who put in hundreds of hours chasing down leads and helped immeasurably with my analysis, thinking and writing of this book. I could not have written *Stalking the Herd* without the guidance, patience and expertise he has graciously provided me for over 20 years. Thanks Izzy for all you've done since that 1975 mute case where you were the chief suspect. And for your perfect Introduction and all those great images from back-in-the-day.

Also *muchas gracias* to: Greg Bishop for his Foreword and important Bennowitz/ Dulce work. Researchers Tom "The Godfather of Mutology" Adams and his Project Stigma; Tommy Blann, Ted Oliphant, Philip Hoyle, Thomas Peay, Gail Staehlin, Jean Bilodeaux, Fern Belzil, and the indomitable Linda Howe and her earthfiles.com—without all of their decades of tireless investigative work, documentation and research, this mystery would have faded off into history and this book would not have been written. Special thanks to Dr. Colm Kelleher, veterinarian pathologist George Onet and the National Institute for Discovery Sciences team. Shout outs to: Nick Redfern and Greg Valdez for their kind input and research materials; George Knapp and those few courageous mainstream investigative journalists that have been willing to cover this subject.

I also want to thank those involved in this book's production: Jeanne Ruppert and Jennifer Bohm for their editing expertise and attention to detail; *The Paracast's* host/executive producer and "forum Super-Hero" Gene Steinberg for the Quark layout process and putting up with my demanding nature; Suzan Fisher for all the countless weeks of transcriptions, article typing and her monumental patience and support on all levels; Mark Brabant/www.hoveringobject.com, for suggesting better book cover typefaces and for polishing my design savvy; Ricky Poole for the pending index; Ro, Brad, Rich and Nick for taking the time to read the manuscript and provide advance reviews of my work; David Childress for coyly suggesting I dust off my research and finally write The Book. Oh well, it took 16 months to write, polish and publish but I did it!

A big thank you to the Don Hard family for the King/Lewis photographs; Scott Corrales/*Inexplicata*; Jeff Rense/rense.com; George Filer/*Filers Files*; thecid.com; the various photographers who contributed images; MUFON and their intrepid field investigators. And a big THANK YOU goes out to the countless ranchers, witnesses and law enforcement officials who had the courage to come forward on-the-record.

Stalking the Herd

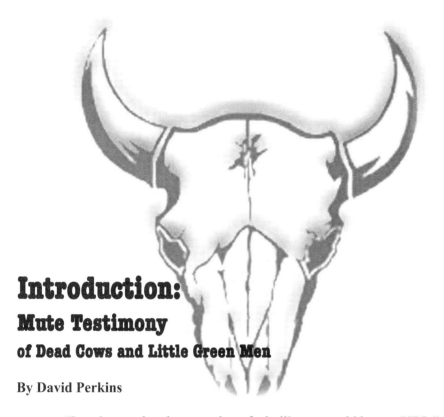

Introduction:
Mute Testimony
of Dead Cows and Little Green Men

By David Perkins

"I can't see what the attraction of a bull's ass would be to a UFO."
Toronto Star (12-17-79)

"We're looking for humans doing these things [cattle mutilations] not UFOs or
little green men." *Edmonton Journal (11-26-79).*
Both quotes by Corporal Lyn Lauber, Royal Canadian Mounted Police.

"If little green men are responsible for the mutilations,
I'll bring them in by the ears."
Ex-FBI Agent Kenneth Rommel, Project Director of Operation Animal Mutilation,
statement to Albuquerque TV Station KOB (5-26-79)

W hile RCMP Corporal Lauber and ex-FBI agent Rommel were cracking
"little green men" jokes in 1979, thousands of ranchers throughout the
American West and Canada were demanding answers from their politicians and law enforcement officials. Who or what was mutilating their animals
and when was it going to stop? Local lawmen were describing the situation in their
communities as "near hysterical" or "total panic" or "somebody's going to get killed."

The cattle mutilation phenomenon had simmered up from the American Heartland in the early 1970s. By 1973 Minnesota, Oklahoma, Wisconsin and Kansas had reported similar incidents. In most cases there appeared to be a consistent pattern. Ranchers reported finding their animals dead, with sexual organs removed, blood drained, and missing some combination of ear, tongue, eye, udder, or patch of skin. Rectums were frequently described as "cored out." In the so-called classic "mute" (for mutilation) case, the incisions were often described as being performed with "surgical precision." In addition, the animal would show no signs of struggle, no tracks or evidence would be found at the scene, and common predators were said to avoid the carcass.

Initially, the seemingly senseless crimes were seen as the work of vandals or pranksters. By the autumn of 1973, however, the situation was reaching near-epidemic proportions. In a six-week period, Kansas lawmen received 44 mutilation reports. Some authorities speculated that the cattle killings were the handiwork of cultists who needed the blood and body parts for their rituals. Local ranchers armed themselves and took to patrolling the back roads in continuous shifts.

By the end of 1975, the phantom surgeons had struck in virtually every state west of the Mississippi. Mutilation reports were numbered in the thousands and losses were being estimated in the millions of dollars. Governor Richard Lamm of Colorado called it "one of the greatest outrages in the history of the Western cattle industry." Newspapers fueled the explosive situation with sensational headlines such as:

"BOY SAYS UFO LANDED, LEFT BLOODY COW BEHIND"

"BORED RICH CULTISTS BLAMED IN CATTLE DEATHS"

"INTROVERTS BLAMED FOR MUTILATIONS"

"MUTILATIONS PRELUDE TO HUMAN SACRIFICES?"

Most theories centered on the litany of saucers, Satanists, or the CIA. Many communities divided into four camps: (1) Those who believed the mutes were the work of space aliens in flying saucers, collecting cow parts for reasons unknown. (2) Those who felt bloodthirsty cultists were responsible. (3) Those who thought that some branch of the U.S. government was responsible, perhaps clandestinely testing chemical/biological weapons. (4) Those who were certain that the so-called mutilations were the work of common predators such as coyotes and buzzards.

It was against this strange backdrop that U.S. Senator from New Mexico, Harrison Schmitt, convened the first multi-state mutilation conference in Albuquerque on April 20, 1979. The already existing network of mute investigators was puzzled. Why would Senator Schmitt, an Apollo 17 astronaut who had walked on the moon, extend his neck in such a politically risky move? According to Schmitt, the mutilation problem was one of the first issues with which he was confronted by his constituents upon taking office. As he told the conference: "There are few activities more dangerous than an unsolved pattern of crime. Such a pattern…is the mutilation killings of thousands of cattle, horses and other animals over the past several years throughout many states. The economic losses suffered by individuals probably have reached 2.5 million dollars or more."

For reasons unknown, I was to be the first speaker. The tension in the auditorium was so thick you could have cut it with a scalpel. As I looked over the crowd, I pondered: What other topic could possibly draw this motley crew into one room? A moon-walking astronaut, FBI agents, state police, sheriffs and local police from around the country, Indian pueblo governors, tribal police chiefs, Los Alamos scientists, veterinarians, New Agers in robes, hippies, news media, politicians, spooky agent types, dusty ranchers in beat-up cowboy hats, independent researchers and, of course, ufologists of all stripes and colors.

I told the diverse assembly that I was a Yale-trained sociologist with an interest in the study of cults, mass delusions and belief systems that lie outside the mainstream. I went on to say that I'd been researching the mutilation phenomenon since 1975, after incidents had occurred in my neighborhood in the mountains of Southern Colorado. What I didn't say was that the first reported mute in my county had happened a short distance down the road from my house. The only evidence at the scene was a few drops of blood leading toward my home. I learned later from my local sheriff, that since I was a relative newcomer to the area, I was briefly considered a suspect. I had my doubts that the audience would appreciate the humor and irony of that scenario.

As the attendees fidgeted in their seats, I told the group that I had amassed a considerable amount of information on the mutilations, which I would be glad to share with anyone interested, and that I'd "never run across a phenomenon which has presented more of a challenge to the rational mind." After more general remarks and exhortations, I asked that the group seriously consider the possibility that so-called UFOs and mutilations were related phenomena.

What followed was a parade of speakers who filed to the podium to regale the audience with UFO/cattle mutilation correlations. At one point, Senator Schmitt reminded the group that although this was "not specifically a UFO conference, it is an issue that has been associated with the cattle mutilation incidents from the beginning." The Senator also related a case from his files involving the disappearance of a calf after a helicopter had been heard at 4 a.m.

On the same subject, Texas researcher Tom Adams gave a summary of "mystery helicopter" cases involving over 200 incidents where unmarked, unidentified helicopters had been observed in the vicinity of mutilation sites. The expanded report was published as *The Choppers – and the Choppers: Mystery Helicopters and Ani-*

mal Mutilations (1980). Adams also edited the *Stigmata* newsletter, the flagship mute publication of both lawmen and the independent research community.

Local lawmen weren't sniggering at the mention of mystery helicopters and UFOs. Their files contained reports of the same admixture of bizarre aerial phenomena. As Colorado Sheriff Lou Girodo later told me: "It's possible that these mutilations are being done by creatures from outer space. Maybe the strange helicopters are really spacecraft camouflaged as helicopters."

A report from the files of Sheriff C.J. Richards of Cochran County, Texas read: "The people all tell the same story. It [the UFO] is about as wide as a two-lane highway, round and looks the color of the sun when it is going down and has got a blue glow around it. When people see this thing, in two or three days we hear about some cows that have been mutilated... It sure has got everyone around here uptight."

Sheriff 'Tex' Graves of Logan County Colorado had also been frustrated in his attempts to apprehend the elusive mutilators. Graves, whose county suffered 72 mutilations between 1975 and 1977, noted tripod marks near some mutilated animals. In 1977 his department expended considerable time and effort pursuing an unidentified craft they referred to as "Big Mama." The large UFO would park itself over Logan County and disgorge "a baby UFO" which would fly off and "disappear." Undersheriff/pilot Jerry Wolever and news reporter Bill Jackson took several distant photos of Big Mama and her baby but their attempts to get a closer look from the air were futile. Wolever reported at the time: "We can never get close to her because she plays games. She always paces us, just so far away, or disappears altogether."

Perhaps the most bizarre files of anyone at the conference belonged to Captain Keith Wolverton, a deputy sheriff from Cascade County, Montana. During the mute onslaught of 1975 Wolverton had been assigned full-time duty investigating the incidents. In a slight departure from cases elsewhere, many of the incisions appeared "serrated." Some of the neat, bloodless cuts seemed "burned' or "cauterized," leading Montana lawmen to speculate that a form of "laser surgery" might be involved. Between August of 1975 and May of 1976, Wolverton recorded over 100 mutilation incidents. During this time he also logged 130 reports of mysterious helicopters and/or UFOs. Many of the anomalous events centered around Malmstrom Air Force Base and the string of ICBM Minutemen missile bases strung out through the neighboring counties. Military personnel had reported similar "incursions" into sensitive Malmstrom air space in both the spring of 1966 and the spring of 1967.

The cult theory received a brief boost with the discovery of a "ceremonial site" near Butte, Montana. A fellow lawman theorized to Wolverton that the cows were being tranquilized with PCP (a hallucinogen). The "witches" would then remove the blood and "trip out" on the strange brew. In 1978 the lab at Oklahoma State University found mescaline, another hallucinogen, in the pericardial fluid of a mutilated Arkansas cow.

As Wolverton's investigation wore on, reports coming into his office gave new meaning to the term "high strangeness." Two young women reported an encounter with a seven-foot-tall "creature" with a face that was "dark and awful, not like a human's." One of the young women fired a .22 rifle into the air in an attempt to frighten the critter. The beast fell down, theatrically pulled itself along the ground and then stood erect again. The women fled in a blind panic.

Another man reported spotting a "tall, hairy creature" carrying an object about the size of a bale of hay with what appeared to be "a piece of dark plastic" flopping from the ends. Perplexingly, reports of Bigfoot-type creatures during mute/UFO waves are not uncommon.

Still, despite the wide range of details presented, Schmitt's conference did not have the desired result of getting the FBI actively involved. Citing "lack of jurisdiction" unless the crimes happened on Federal or Indian land (which they sometimes did), the FBI claimed to have no authority in the matter. The political hot potato was then picked up by District Attorney Eloy Martinez in Santa Fe. Martinez applied for and received a near $50,000 grant from the federally funded Law Enforcement Assistance Administration to finance a yearlong probe into the mute problem to begin in May of 1980.

Kenneth Rommel, who had spent 28 years with the FBI, was hired as Project Director of Operation Animal Mutilation. Senator Schmitt and the mute investigation network were skeptical. Many doubted the motivations and objectivity of Rommel and Martinez. The District Attorney told visiting journalists: "We were out to discredit each of these theories [UFOs, cults, etc.]. Our goal was to put to rest once and for all the extreme ideas about cattle mutilations."

In a breakfast meeting with Rommel, I offered him the use of my files. He had no interest in seeing the files or talking to any of my sources. "But what about solid evidence of cult involvement from Iowa, Montana, Idaho, Arkansas and Canada?" I pressed. "Listen," Rommel said, "the only cult activity comes from people like you... people who need aspects of mystery in their lives."

"Yes, I'm a naturally curious person," I admitted, "but what about the evidence of clamp marks and broken bones that have been reported?" Rommel retorted that the death throes of sick animals can be quite violent and that "someone might have slipped into the pasture to apply the clamp marks as a joke." He confided that his main concern upon taking the job was that panicky ranchers would start shooting at helicopters again as they had in 1974-75. Rommel gleefully added that his final report would "screw a lot of people to the wall, including some very high public officials."

When Rommel's report came out in June of 1980, he claimed to have personally investigated 15 "so-called mutilations," concluding that all had been the work of natural predators. The notion that ranchers couldn't tell the difference between natural and unnatural animal deaths was "simply not true." Senator

Schmitt called the report "not definitive," saying that "apparently Rommel had reached his conclusions before he began his investigation." Even Rommel's counterpart in Canada, Corporal Lyn Lauber of the RCMP (who was still hot on the trail of the cultists), remarked that Rommel's report "appeared to have an ulterior motive." Lauber told one reporter, "I'd like to see him write off our confirmed cases as predators."

From a public safety point of view, Rommel's probe and its "findings" were entirely understandable. *Newsweek* (September 30, 1974) reported that over-anxious vigilantes in Nebraska had fired two shots through the canopy of a utility company helicopter and that the National Guard had ordered its pilots to fly at higher altitudes to avoid being fired upon. Yet the Rommel report was not generally well received by the rural ranchers and lawmen caught up in the mute maelstrom. The cowmen, many from generations of ranching families, were insulted that they were being accused of being so ignorant that they couldn't tell the difference between the work of a coyote and a scalpel. "We ought to get out of business if we can't," one rancher told me.

Mutes were temporarily knocked off the front pages of newspapers. Oddly enough, the main thrust of the phenomenon moved to the western provinces of Canada during the year of Rommel's investigation. As in the U.S., the strategy for dealing with the mutes was blame the media, whittle down the actual numbers involved, downplay the situation, and hope that it goes away.

The Colorado Bureau of Investigation took a similar approach to the numbers game. Of the 203 reports recorded by the CBI during 1975-76, 35 had actually been examined by Dr. Albert McChesney and his staff at Colorado State University's College of Veterinary Medicine. Of the 35 cases, 11 were determined to be "real" mutilations. According to McChesney's summary: "Most affected cattle died from some natural cause… Subsequent to death, some carcasses were mutilated and parts were amputated by unknown persons using sharp tools." Again, the animals were already dead before they were mutilated, so what's the problem?

Just for the sake of discussion, let's play our own numbers game. Assume that the proportion of "real" to reported mutilations indicated by McChesney's findings (roughly one-third) holds true with the total number of reports (203). In other words, one-third of the 203 were demonstrable anomalies, say about 70.

Using the one-third proportion against the total number of reported mutes during the 1970s and early 80s (my tallies show a very low-end number of 2,500) we get a total of roughly 850 "real" mutilations. Just for the record, my files show closer to 400 mute reports in Colorado during the period the CBI claimed 203. As in Canada, that is double what the official sources claimed. If the actual number of cases across the board (as opposed to the number reported through official channels) is roughly double, we're now looking at about 1,700 real cases.

This (low-ball) number is not insignificant. The conclusions of the CBI and the RCMP could hardly be considered comforting to the public-at-large. Don't worry folks. It's only some blood-sucking, scalpel-wielding weirdos lurking around your pastures in the middle of the night, surgerizing cows that had already died of natural causes.

Regardless of how anyone plays with these numbers, local lawmen and independent investigators had good reason to mistrust the findings of state agencies and their government-sponsored laboratories. Sheriff George Yarnell of Elbert County, Colorado related a revealing story to me. During the wave of 1975, he had meticulously taken samples from mutilated cows and sent them to the College of Veterinary Medicine lab for testing. The results always came back: predator damage. To test their accuracy, Yarnell took his own knife, cut a section from a dead cow and submitted it. "Hell, I was really obvious about it. I even cut little notches in it," the Sheriff said. The report came back: predator damage. "I called 'em up to chew 'em out," Yarnell said. "The lab guy just laughed and said, 'We're human too. Everyone makes mistakes.' "

Sheriff Leroy Yowell of Lincoln County, Colorado had a similar tale to tell. In 1975 he had fruitlessly chased mystery helicopters in a plane. Yowell's personal theory was that chopper pilots from the Army base at Fort Carson were doing the mutilations "just for a lark." The Sheriff's theory was bolstered when a blue government-issue valise was found containing a bloody scalpel, soiled plastic gloves, a cow's ear and part of a cow's tongue. The day before, a CBI agent had investigated a nearby mute. In the agent's opinion, the animal had been mutilated "with a sharp instrument after death." Trouble was, the cow parts in the valise didn't match the mute, or any other animal reported mutilated during that time.

Yowell submitted the satchel to the CBI criminology lab technicians who were unable to obtain any fingerprints from the items. Incredibly, the crime lab was unable to determine even what species of blood was on the scalpel.

Carl Whiteside, Deputy Director of the Colorado Bureau of Investigation, candidly told one journalist that the study of mutilations was "like trying to nail jelly to a wall…. It's like chasing a phantom, a ghost….Everybody who has gotten involved with the mutilations has come away more confused than when they went in, including us." He accused the "UFO contingent" of taking over Senator Schmitt's conference "to use cattle mutilation reports to prove that UFOs and space aliens visit the earth."

Mutes and UFOs were strange bedfellows indeed. By the mid-1970s, the major U.S. UFO groups were actually scrambling to *dissociate themselves* from the macabre mutilation phenomenon. In 1974 writer/researcher Jerome Clark, a protégé of America's pre-eminent ufologist, Dr. J. Allen Hynek, began corresponding with a federal prisoner who claimed first-hand knowledge that the mutilations were the work of a nationwide Satanist organization.

Clark took the prisoner's dubious information (later totally discredited) to Donald Flickinger, the Minnesota-based special agent of the Treasury Department's

Bureau of Alcohol, Tobacco and Firearms. In 1975 Flickinger launched an investigation into the supposed Satanist network. His subsequent widely leaked "confidential" report stated that the mutilations were the responsibility of a nationwide "religious occult."

Shortly after the Flickinger Report was leaked, Hynek, a respected astronomer and former Air Force UFO consultant who had recently founded the Center for UFO Studies (CUFOS), issued his own statement: "The press has speculated that UFOs are in some way responsible for cattle mutilations…. Not one documented report exists in which a UFO sighting is directly connected to a cattle mutilation. Research has been done…and a confidential government report has found that a Satanic cult is responsible."

The Aerial Phenomena Research Organization (APRO), which had initially endorsed the UFO/mute connection in the famous 1967 Snippy the Horse case, issued their own statement, which cleared away "the suspicion of UFO involvement in the grisly mutilations…. Our study has provided a glimpse into a Satanic organization…which has grandiose plans of bringing about a 1,000 year reign of terror and darkness." Mainstream ufology, in its continuous struggle for scientific legitimacy, clearly did not want to alarm the skittish American public about murderous aliens, or further muddy the turgid waters of UFO research.

However, ufology's efforts to keep its orphan stepchild at arm's length during the 1970s ultimately failed. In 1980, the mutes came home to roost, at least for a while.

A seminal event in the metamorphosis of the mutes was a UFO/abduction case investigated by Albuquerque businessman and APRO investigator, Paul Bennewitz. A Cimarron, New Mexico woman, Myrna Hansen, and her son consciously recalled seeing UFOs and two white-suited "men" who were "working on" a bellowing cow near Cimarron on the evening of May 5, 1980. A four-hour period of '"missing time" followed. Bennewitz called in Wyoming hypnotherapist Dr. Leo Sprinkle (who had worked with numerous abductees) to regress Hansen. In a hypnotic state, Hansen revealed that she and her son had been taken aboard a craft manned by small gray beings and tall hairless humanoids. Hansen further recalled the aliens mutilating a live cow and being taken, herself, to an underground cavern near what she thought was Roswell, New Mexico. After enduring a painful vaginal procedure, she saw a vat of red liquid in which she observed a floating humanoid figure and what she assumed to be various animal parts. Hansen and her son also stated that '"They [the aliens] mean to control the earth."

A similar story of a Texas woman who claimed to have been abducted into a UFO with her daughter and witnessed a cattle mutilation performed by aliens was reported in the documentary film *A Strange Harvest*. Again, the information was retrieved under hypnosis by Dr. Sprinkle.

A Strange Harvest, produced by Linda Moulton Howe with CBS-affiliate

KMGH TV in Denver (first released in May 1980), was probably the single most influential piece of media coverage ever presented on the mutilation subject. Howe had contacted me in 1979 when she was beginning work on the project. I provided her with copies of my files and lists of contacts, and also traveled with her for much of the filming of the show, appearing in two different segments (but not mentioning UFOs).

The documentary received wide national exposure and MUFON, the world's largest UFO organization, enthusiastically embraced Howe's UFO/mute connection and made her a sort of unofficial spokesperson concerning the topic. By the time the film was aired, my own research was leading me away from a strict UFO/mute correlation. To my mind, the mute myth had become an infinitely complex equation. Even the exotic Extraterrestrial Hypothesis provisional theory could not adequately explain *all* of the evidence surrounding the phenomenon to my satisfaction.

Meanwhile, myth and manipulation became curiously intertwined. In a follow up book, *An Alien Harvest* (1989), Howe gave considerable space to the ideas of ex-Naval petty officer Bill Cooper, who claimed that a "secret government" controlled the country. According to Cooper, this shadow government had signed a treaty with the aliens allowing them to mutilate animals and abduct humans to obtain the necessary blood, enzymes and genetic materials they needed to survive. In exchange, the government supposedly received advanced alien technology. Cooper appeared to have gotten much of his information (if it could be called that) from John Lear, an ex-airline pilot with an alleged CIA background.

When I first met Lear, he provided me with documents of dubious provenance purporting to show the interior of an underground alien/government base near Dulce, New Mexico. There were drawings of large vats with "pale meat" floating in them and chambers where "hybrid embryos" were in various stages of development. According to Lear, the aliens were using genetic material taken from abductees and cattle organs to create "almost human beings." The documents alleged that the aliens put their hands in cow blood for nourishment: "It's not just food they want, the DNA in cattles [sic] and humans is being altered."

The Lear/Cooper paranoid, conspiratorial vision came to be known as "the Dark Side Hypothesis." Lear picked up many of these ideas from Paul Bennewitz, who had been deeply influenced by the Cimarron abduction case, and who claimed to be in contact with the aliens on his computer. Beginning in the early 1980s, an Air Force Office of Special Investigations (AFOSI) officer named Richard Doty, based at Kirtland Air Force Base in Albuquerque, had fed Bennewitz a steady stream of apparently bogus documents and other inducements to reinforce the Dark Side Hypothesis. In what appeared to be a classic disinformation campaign, Doty and his military intelligence cohorts drew in Linda Moulton Howe and several of ufology's most prominent researchers. Bennewitz was driven to the brink of insanity, and eventually hospitalized with a massive nervous breakdown.

In his history of the UFO phenomenon, *Watch the Skies!* (1994), Curtis Peebles claims that by the early 1980s the "flying saucer myth" consisted of three distinct components – crashed saucers, abductions and mutes. Gradually, these three threads were interwoven to make a new mythology, which he calls "the alien myth." According to Peebles, "It was from the mute myth, with its images of death, dismemberment and conspiracies that the alien myth would first emerge. In the end, the alien myth would itself become submerged in a witch's brew of fascist conspiracy theories, hate and paranoia."

Peebles, a UFO skeptic, uses the word myth to mean something imaginary, fictional or unreal. I prefer Joseph Campbell's definition in *The Hero With A Thousand Faces* (1949): "Myth is the secret opening through which the inexhaustible energies of the cosmos pour into human cultural manifestations. The prime function of mythology is to supply the symbols that carry the human spirit forward, in counteraction to those other constant human fantasies that tend to tie it back." As psychologist Carl Jung reminds us: "The most we can do is dream the myth onwards and give it a modern dress."

The question is, does the modern myth of animal mutilations appeal to our fear-based instincts, or "the better angels of our nature?" Oddly enough, it seems to do both. Ultimately, is the mute myth as Macbeth puts it, "a tale told by an idiot, full of sound and fury, signifying nothing?" Or, are the mutes a form of communication, a statement, an invitation, a glimpse of an alternate reality where our survival and the Earth's future hangs in the balance?

One might wonder how a macabre cattle mutilation could have any *positive* implications? Consider this: Every year humans slaughter and eat millions of cows and that is generally thought of as a good thing. Many thousands of animals are killed in the name of scientific research to find cures for our most vicious diseases. Again, this is generally considered acceptable, even desirable.

In the interest of unbiased productive inquiry, it might be best to withhold our judgments and opinions on the malevolent/benevolent issue. All too often researchers have adopted a "Ready. Shoot! Aim." philosophy. Frequently the process has been: (1) Pick your favorite "unusual suspects" and motives and (2) Garner as much evidence as possible to support your theory, while disregarding the evidence that doesn't fit that conjecture. An inconvenient fact can thus be categorized as "an outlier" or "anomalous data". In addition to these pitfalls, researchers must somehow avoid the age-old trap of "escalating hypotheses". It's good to remember Sherlock's old adage: "There is nothing more deceptive than an obvious fact."

I'm constantly amazed that serious, (reasonably) intelligent researchers can look at the same evidence and come away with totally different conclusions. That should be a clue as to the nature of the phenomenon and an indication of why it has been so devilishly difficult to decipher. As Carl Jung said: "It all depends on how we look at things and not how they are themselves." Apparently it would help to be some sort of Zen master to even consider the topic.

We should also remember Sherlock's most famous detective dictum: "When you have eliminated the impossible, whatever remains, however improbable, must be the truth." Fine, but in this age of seemingly endless possibilities, who can say that anything is truly impossible? What did Sherlock know about quantum physics and its Alice in Wonderland world of "observer effects", hidden dimensions and parallel universes? There appears to be a bit more to the mute "crime" than: "Who killed the butler in the pantry with a candelabra?"

I have long maintained that the sheer theatricality of mutilation-related events seems designed to *demand* our attention. In this tricksterish Theater of the Absurd production, there is a fine line between horror and hilarity. Where do each of us stand in the spectrum ranging from "suspended disbelief" to harsh criticism? How do these attitudes reinforce our self-images? On what do we *really* base our opinions? Our fears? Our needs? Our expectations? No matter where one stands on the issue, the mutes seem to cry out for our response and visceral participation. Right now, in some remote eerie pasture there is quite possibly a mutilated cow bearing mute testimony to our unwillingness or inability to step up and come to grips with this exceedingly strange situation.

Back in the Heartland, mutilations are still being found, though infrequently reported. "Why bother?" the cowmen say. Ranchers' reactions to these events vary wildly. In one case, I arrived at night to investigate a mutilation report in Colorado only to find the rancher furiously at work burying the carcass with a backhoe. His wife intercepted me and quickly escorted me back to my car. "Please go away," she implored. " My husband thinks this is the work of the devil."

While pondering another Colorado mute with a grizzled and laconic old rancher, I asked him, What do you think did this to your cow?" He chewed, spit and shrugged his shoulders: "I dunno…I guess somebody needed some parts. It's just the cost of doin' bidness."

The flip side of this coin was my visit to Elsberry, Missouri in 1978. The whole town was seeing "your traditional flying saucers," mutes were dropping like flies, mystery helicopters prowled the hills, 55-gallon drums rose up out of the Mississippi River and flew in formation, Bigfoot creatures picked through the dump and little people wearing "glowing suits" were seen at the lake. Someone had printed up T-shirts saying: "Elsberry Missouri—Mutilated Cow Country." The iconic image on the shirt showed a cow on its back with one leg missing. A flying saucer hovered over the cow containing a grinning little alien holding a bloody knife.

At night the roads were jammed with parked cars. People had driven from miles around to watch for the saucers. With binoculars in hand, folks sat in lawn chairs, drank beer and sodas and ate picnic meals. Children frolicked and dogs cavorted. At first, the scene struck me as rather pathetic, the epitome of folly.

After surveying the situation for a while, I started warming up to the scene. Maybe it was the smell of hamburgers and hot dogs cooking on tailgate grills. Maybe it was the sound of someone playing the Byrds' song "Mr. Spaceman" in their car. Gradually my skeptical outsider persona began to melt away. There was something oddly comforting about this all-American vignette. Maybe it was the illusion of safety in numbers or the enveloping protective aura of the human herd.

In the old days good folks like these would gather for quilting bees, barn dances and church socials— now it's "Welcome the Saucers" parties. What could possibly be next in this progression?

I wondered, how could these people be so content and fearless? How did they know that the little knife-waving saucer people weren't going to return and cut off *their* legs? Whatever fears they had were apparently overcome by the hope and promise offered by the saucers and their occupants – the hope for at least a momentary respite from an often grinding daily existence and the promise of being able to someday "slip the surly bonds of Earth" and go "out there". Whatever it was, eventually I wanted to see the saucers too.

Alas, the saucers did not show that night. In fact they didn't show again until the night after I left town. Hmm. People didn't seem too disappointed though. They seemed to "know" how capricious and unpredictable the ufonauts could be. Maybe they knew this from movies. As one kind elderly lady explained to me: "They've got their reasons."

We all have our reasons, but how are we ever to make sense of a phenomenon that has no readily apparent rhyme or reason? Enter the indomitable investigator Christopher O'Brien and his new book *Stalking the Herd*.

Chris presents for the first time ever, comprehensive documentation of this baffling and seemingly intractable conundrum. Always looking for clues, Chris takes the long view in hopes of answering the basic question: Do the mutes represent an ancient myth in "modern dress" or are they truly something new under the sun? He starts by analyzing 30,000 year-old cave paintings and traces the long, fascinating history of the special relationship between humans and animals of the bovine persuasion.

As he painstakingly tracks the mute myth or meme down through the ages, we are witness to one of history's most thrilling mysteries unfolding. At last the mutilations have been put in their larger historical and cultural context. By the sheer volume and weight of the evidence presented in *Stalking the Herd*, Chris has firmly established what researcher Tom Adams has called "the extra-mundane legitimacy" of the phenomenon. The evidence is quite clear—something very unusual is going on.

So hang on to your hats cowpersons. This is one wild ride. The end result is a unique view of what the mutes say about our society, ourselves and quite possibly our future.

David Perkins on the trail of the mutilators in Australia.

Foreword You will find what you expect to find.

This rule applies very well to the study of the paranormal and anything else currently residing outside of easy human understanding. The study of UFOs is populated by many who have ready explanations for unknowns. No matter that the answers are neither reproducible nor provable to the vast portion of humankind. A foregone conclusion is lodged so firmly in place that any new ideas or legitimate criticisms are treated as blasphemy. Those who expect to find nothing but hoaxes and misidentifications stay comfortably in their belief systems as well. They can conceive of nothing that can't be explained by current knowledge or at least easily extrapolated from known and tested concepts.

As for the subject of mysterious livestock deaths, one group expects to find evidence of extraterrestrials at every turn, and the other believes that mistaken conclusions and cult activity explains all. Those closer to the events—those who own and care for the animals and those who are called to investigate when an out-of-the-ordinary death is discovered have been on an open-ended quest from the beginning. A few long-time researchers like Christopher O'Brien continue to ask questions which fall comfortably into neither camp. This should be interesting to the intelligent and truly curious, since a closer examination of all the evidence falls decidedly into areas that none of those yelling the loudest about this subject have dared to consider.

In the late 1970s, the North American public was just becoming dimly aware of the phenomenon, which would become known as mysterious livestock deaths or cattle mutilations. Many ranchers, stockmen, and law enforcement people were already wearily used to this baffling crime wave. A few independent researchers like David Perkins and Tom Adams began to document the strange deaths and pinpoint them as more than simply due to natural causes and scavenger action.

In 1979, A surprising cross-section of people showed up at Senator Harrison Schmitt's mutilation symposium at the Albuquerque Public Library, including UFO and mutilation researchers, as well as law enforcement, cattlemen and media reps. New Mexico State Patrolman Gabe Valdez (who had by then investigated countless cattle mutilations in the remote town of Dulce, New Mexico) was there, and so was Paul Bennewitz, who would soon become a central figure in one of the most famous UFO/ disinformation stories ever uncovered. Strangely, a UFO witness and possible "abductee" who Bennewitz would soon meet would tell him that she witnessed a cow lifted up into a UFO during a close encounter on a lonely road in northeastern New Mexico, as detailed in Perkins' introduction.

The conclusion of the Rommel report that all apparent livestock mutilations were the result of misidentified routine deaths and scavenger activity stunned researchers and ranchers alike. The report stained the subject forever and framed the culprits (in

the mind of the public at least) into three distinct and restrictive camps: ETs, wild animals and cultists. Indeed, the online Skeptic's Dictionary derisively discusses the "alien" angle and quotes the Rommel report as "the most thorough examination of so-called cattle mutilations." Rommel apparently went into the field to look at a few cases, but during the period of the investigation, there were little or no other reports of strange livestock deaths in the US. Echoing the thoughts of many, Gabe Valdez later told me, "The closest that Rommel ever got to a cow was a steak in a New York restaurant."

During research for my book *Project Beta*, I met and became friends with Valdez and his family. They have a generosity and loyalty that is rare. What Officer Valdez found, and later showed me in person, was evidence that UFOs and aliens were probably last on the list of suspects. Items left near mutilation sites included a gas mask, possible parts of powerful lasers, apparent radar chaff, and other man-made artifacts. Some UFO proponents insist that ETs leave the objects around anomalous bovine death sites to make us think that humans are responsible. What this amounts to is an unprovable supporting an even more remote unprovable.

Valdez and Dulce area livestock owners hard-hit by the strange deaths also found surveillance bugs installed on telephones and in various other locations in their homes. His son Greg, now a police officer himself, recently wrote a book on the history of mutilations and many other strange happenings in the Dulce area when he was growing up, utilizing his own experience as well as the extensive files of his late father. It is uniquely informative, especially for those familiar with the subject.

In a 2005 interview that I conducted with a researcher, we discussed the supposed radar chaff found by Officer Valdez. He claimed that a sample of the material was sent to a lab and the results were unexpected and startling. The final report indicated that the pieces of strange stuff were in fact coated with a paraffin-like substance and were further covered with a thin coating of metal on one side. Their conclusion was that the pieces were once part of an electrical capacitor, which is used to temporarily store often large amounts of electricity for quick discharge (such as might be used to power a directed energy weapon, or a laser, among other things) They speculated that the capacitor had been blown apart in some way, leaving the pieces scattered over the pasture where they were found.

There was also the experiment by Sandia Labs scientist Howard Burgess that was conducted on cows from a ranch hard-hit by the mutilators. The cattle were run through a chute at night beneath differing wavelengths of light. Large patches glowed on the backs of some of the cattle when they passed beneath an ultraviolet bulb. Why aliens would use such a primitive method for marking victims is an important question. The materials and wherewithal to do such things were well within the capacity of current technology by even the mid-20th century, let alone the latter 1970s. These questions continued to bother me and others who looked more closely at the mystery.

Members of the Jicarilla Apache tribe that live in and around Dulce are quite reluctant to talk about the strange goings-on that still crop up with some regularity. There are clues pointing to the status of reservation lands as sovereign nations where the federal and local laws are loosely policed and applied, which leaves the door open for private dealings with shady contractors or others who may wish to conduct business or research away from prying eyes or law enforcement. Kenn Thomas and Jim Martin's 1996 book *The Octopus* details similar events on the Cabazon tribal lands in Southern California.

Over the years, Gabe Valdez cautiously began telling me about the results of his research and that of others who he felt were closer to the truth of the mystery. Due to evidence that he was at least occasionally being watched; he would only give me the info in person. He was convinced that the core of the story involved the beef industry and some sort of pathogen that had been accidentally released into the wildlife population. This was a disease that might have been genetically engineered and would spell the end of the US cattle business. To me, this theory was the only one that fit most of the data, although there were still some unexplained facets to the mutilations that did not fit comfortably into this scenario. Many of these alternate avenues have been examined by Christopher O'Brien.

By 2005, I thought that a book outlining the disease theory would be a great project, but to my surprise, I received rejections from at least four publishers who were known for books on the paranormal. "Too disturbing" was a common reaction. Chris says he encountered this more than once while shopping his ideas to potential editors and publishers. Bestsellers tend to fall into two categories: They are either about some horrible menace, or they delve into a subject that people know a little about, but present new information that changes a popular view. The mutilation mystery had all of these elements. In my query letters, I tried to point out that as a rule, people not only like being scared, but it would also make them question where their steaks and hamburgers were coming from. Chris and I both wondered if the trepidation we encountered was more of a fear of the beef industry and the ensuing lawsuits.

There is no reason that any theory on cattle mutilations cannot include elements of many of the theories proposed to explain them. If we discount "aliens," how do we explain the strangely moving lights (and even higher strangeness) that seem to hang around mutilation areas? If our pet theory is natural deaths and scavengers, how do we ignore the strange substances (such as anticoagulants) found in and around many dead cows? What about cultists? How do they control all of those UFOs and how do they afford the equipment used to lift the carcasses into the air? If we latch onto the secret operations/ disease theory, how do the mutilators cause UFO sightings of lights that move like no aircraft we know of? The problem is multifaceted and whatever or whomever is responsible may be using elements of all these issues to mask their intentions and identity. Likewise, if there is more than one group or force at work here (to me the most likely scenario) they may play off the methods and evidence left by others to add to the confused perceptions of victims, police, and researchers.

Stalking The Herd is the only full-scale examination of the cattle mute phenomenon. It (and the in-depth interpretive volume to follow) should be the only books you will ever need to read on the subject, at least until new evidence is uncovered or the mutilators themselves decide to 'fess up. Christopher O'Brien is uniquely positioned to report on this phenomenon. Although he became a resident in one of the epicenters of activity and investigated many incidents firsthand, that is not what makes his situation unique. Chris is one of those few individuals who refuse to let one theory dictate his research. He expects nothing and discounts nothing, and lets the evidence lead where it may, even if it leads nowhere. This is the hallmark of a person with a deep sense of equity, which is rare, especially in the small community of researchers of the strange. With no preconceptions, he leads us down paths that most of us have not even considered before.

Greg Bishop
Los Angeles, January 2014

Chapter 1
Holy Cow

C attle. If you live out West in the country like I do, it's virtually impossible to avoid them. Herds dot the hillsides like flies and they always seem to be grazing blissfully in their surroundings, chewing their cud, swishing their tails, oblivious to their all-too-certain fate. Over the years thousands of animals (mostly cattle) have been reported "mutilated" with no apparent cause for their unfortunate death and disfigurement. Although cattle make up around 90 percent of mutilation reports, I will also examine purported mutilations of other warm-blooded animals—including humans.

Over 20 years ago, I innocently embarked on a personal investigation to solve the mystery of "cattle mutilations." This book will attempt to illustrate why I've come to believe that this closet subject lurking within Western Culture has deeply profound, perhaps frightening implications for steak and hamburger lovers around the world. I have personally investigated about 200 potential mutilation cases, researched historical texts, collected case histories, and conducted interviews with ranchers, law enforcement officials, and scientists about this subject since my first case in early 1993. I honestly feel that I'm at least a few small steps closer to figuring out this seemingly imponderable mystery. I have elected to emphasize (in italics) facts and descriptions throughout the book. I intuit that these particular details may provide us

with important clues as we attempt to unravel the cattle mutilation mystery.

I should stress, however, that a major part of my process of discovery and deeper knowledge has a result of my examination of humankind's ancient, deeply intertwined relationship with livestock and how humans have utilized cattle for religious and dietary purposes for thousands of years. I suspect that this forgotten connection is inexorably linked to any potential answers to this blood-based "paranormal" mystery. In general, I present the information gathered in this book methodically in a chronological timeline format, both historically and in terms of my involvement in the cattle mutilation subject beginning in the nineties. In order to fully research and investigate the "mutes" (as we handful of investigators sometimes call them) and thus begin to understand the cultural context in which they have taken place, we would be advised to start with the beginnings of the human-cattle relationship and follow its development through changing historical contexts up to our own time. Along the way I'll present sketches of the various roles that cattle have played in human culture over the past 12,000 years. But first we need a sense of the vast extent of present-day cattle populating the planet.

According to the *Iowa State Research Center for Development of Agriculture and Rural Areas,* there are approximately 1.37 billion cattle on the planet today, and the area of grazing land that livestock herds occupy amounts to about 25% of the Earth's landmass. Depending on the quality of the grazing land, it can take up to 180 acres of land to support a single head of livestock for one year. Most statistics concerning the current cattle population might surprise you. For instance: there are 40 percent more cows than people in Australia. In South America, cattle are as numerous as humans, and in Uruguay and Paraguay, cattle actually outnumber humans.[1] In the United States, almost 30 percent of the land-mass of the country is devoted to livestock grazing lands. The McDonald's Corporation is the largest purchaser of beef at over one billion pounds per year.

As of January 1, 2013, the United States officially had 29.3 million beef cattle 9.2 million dairy cattle, and 13.4 million head of cattle and calves were being fattened up in feedlots, readied for slaughter. Americans have slowly reduced their per capita beef consumption over the past 50 years, as this was the lowest yearly number of US cattle since 1952's total of 88.1 million head for a human population of 267 million people, according to USDA statistics. We will dig into the impact of cattle on our fragile environment in Chapter 12. According to beef industry figures, beef consumption peaked at 94.4 pounds per person in 1976 and fell to 57.5 pounds in 2012. The number of cattle in the U.S. peaked in 1975 and has steadily declined ever since. Isn't it interesting that 1975 was the peak year for cattle mutilation reports?

Where did all these cattle come from? The answer is surprisingly simple in its complexity: Cattle are among the earliest domesticated animals and there are presently more than 940 distinct breeds divided into five separate groups according to their use: beef, dairy, draft, sport, and dual usage cattle used for two or more of the above types. Our ancient paleo-ancestors are responsible for beginning the process of selective breeding and our beef-obsessed Western Culture may not be able to continue using beef as a protein source at current levels as we move further into the 21st century.

Bovines, or cattle, are a subfamily of the *Bovidae* family of mammals. The term *cattle* was derived from the Middle English *catel* meaning "personal property" and the Medieval Latin *capitále* or "wealth." The word's meaning is similar to that of today's term chattel, or "moveable personal property." Prior to their domestication by humans, there were three prevalent types of wild cattle: *Bos Primegenius*, or aurochs, a now extinct type of wild ox; *Bos Taurus,* which grew to ten feet high at the shoulder, proto-European cattle; and *Bos Indicus,* cattle breeds such as the zebu found on the Indian subcontinent. These distinct types probably evolved in what is now Northern India. (figure 2) These surviving cattle-strains can be crossbred with other closely related species including bison, yaks, buffalo, and musk oxen.

Cattle are considered undulates referring to their unique four-stomach digestive system. Cattle are able to digest otherwise marginally nutritious plants by regurgitating and re-chewing their 'cud', thus obtaining a maximum of nutritional benefit from available sources. The re-masticated cud is re-swallowed and further digested by their complex compartmented stomachs. Cattle belch or pass methane into the air on the average of once every two minutes and, at over 80 million metric tons of methane produced yearly, cattle are the second largest naturally-producing source of ozone-depleting gas.[2] With their uniquely-adapted digestive tract and the ability to eat and gain nourishment from forage such as grass, which is inedible to most animals, this amazing adaptation that enables them to thrive on available forage such as wild grass is unique to cattle species. Undoubtedly, early paleo-man marveled at bovine species' ability to adapt to the inhospitable terrain they shared with humans. And the psychotropic *cubensis* mushrooms that grew in their manure must have had quite an effect on them as well. (figure 3)

The development of shamanic practices and proto-culture may have received a jump-start by early man expanding into the verdant grasslands and exploring new potential food sources. Terence and Dennis McKenna have devised an ingenious theory that may help explain the robust development of shamanic culture in regions where cattle and other undulates were found:

> At its fullest, shamanism is not a simple religion; it is a dynamic connection into the totality of life on the planet. If…hallucinogens operate in the natural environment as message-bearing molecules, exopheromones, then the relationship between primates and hallucinogens signifies a transfer of information from one species to another. The benefits to the mushroom arise out of hominid domestication of cattle and

hence the expansion of the niche occupied by the mushroom. Where plant hallucinogens do not occur, cultural innovation occurs very slowly, if at all, but we have seen that in the presence of hallucinogens a culture is regularly introduced to ever more novel information, sensory input, and behavior and thus is moved to higher and higher states of self-reflection. The shamans are the vanguard of this creative advance.[3]

Taming the Wild Aurochs

How long have cattle been domesticated and where were they first captured, contained and tamed? We find a probable answer in the results of a genetic DNA study from ancient proto-cattle bones discovered in present-day Iran. Scientists studying this DNA have recently published surprising facts that we will address in a moment.

Ancient man barely succeeded in domesticating these animals, having had little margin for error. It appears that all of the cattle extant on the planet today have descended from a single herd containing as few as 80 animals. These cattle were domesticated from wild oxen approximately 10,500 years ago, a period shortly after the development of proto-agricultural farming practices in the region.

Until recently, cattle were-thought to have been domesticated in today's northern Turkey at Çatalhöyük, a 9,500-year-old prehistoric village that has been established as one of the most populated Neolithic settlements yet discovered. Located on the Konya Plain, the site was discovered in 1958 and is thought to have been a home to upwards of 8,000 people at the height of its 1,000-year existence. This impressive settlement featured the first mud-brick, timber, and stone buildings and some of the earliest evidence of the domestication of grain. But still-earlier evidence of cattle domestication has recently been unearthed and dated there.

Çatalhöyük is where we find the first cattle cults and there appears to be some ambiguity as to which gender was dominant within the belief system. Both cows and bulls appear to have had equal status. Sheep also played an important role in the society that developed over millennia. One recently unearthed burial site featured a human male with a sheep buried next to him in the same grave. That must have been one special ram! (figure 4)

> At its height the cult at Çatalhöyük represented the most advanced and coherent expression of religious feeling in the world. We have very little evidence upon which to reconstruct the nature of the cult acts performed, but the sheer number of shrines in relation to the total number of rooms bespeaks a culture obsessed with religious observances, We know that this was a cult of totemic animals—the vulture, the hunting cat, and always preeminent, the bull or the cow. Later religions in the

ancient Middle East were bull worshipping in spirit, but we cannot assume this for Çatalhöyük. The sculpted heads of cattle that protrude into the cattle shrines at Çatalhöyük are sexually ambiguous and may represent bulls or cows or simply cattle generally...It is impossible not to see in the cult of the Great Goddess and the cattle cult of the Late Neolithic recognition of the mushroom as a third and hidden member of a kind of shamaic trinity. The mushroom, seen to be as much a product of cattle as are milk, meat, and manure, was recognized very early as the physical connection to the presence of the Goddess. This is the secret that was lost some 6,000 years-ago at the eclipse of Çatalhöyük.[4]

By the time we see the rise of Çatalhöyük in 9,500 BC aurochs had evidently been domesticated for almost 1,000 years. As mentioned, recent DNA studies have uncovered an astounding scenario that will probably be difficult for some people to wrap their heads around.

A team of scientists from the *Centre National de la Recherche Scientifique* (CNRS), the National Museum of Natural History in France, the University of Mainz in Germany, and University College London (UCL) in the UK recently analyzed DNA from the bones of these barely-domesticated cattle In Iran and published their results in the March 2012 issue of the *Journal Molecular Biology and Evolution.*

Team scientists ascertained how "small differences in the DNA sequences of those ancient cattle, as well as cattle living today, could have arisen given different population histories." Using computer simulations they found that the DNA differences could only have been present if a small number of animals, approximately 80, were domesticated from wild oxen—aurochs [Bos primigenius]. Aurochs developed as a species around 20,000 years ago in what is now Northern India. Slowly spreading south into Asia and Eastern Europe, herds of aurochs ebbed and flowed with the spread and retreat of the glaciers and were actively hunted and then domesticated by humans.

In a recent study, lead author Dr. Ruth Bollongino of CNRS, France, and the University of Mainz, Germany, explained the difficulty faced by scientists engaged in collecting Near-Eastern DNA samples:

> Getting reliable DNA sequences from remains found in cold environments is routine... That is why mammoths were one of the first extinct species to have their DNA read. But getting reliable DNA from bones found in hot regions is much more difficult because temperature is so critical for DNA survival. This meant we had to be extremely careful that we did not end up reading contaminated DNA sequences from living, or only recently dead cattle.[5]

5

University of Mainz scientist Joachim Burger, who participated in the genetic study, was understandably surprised at the results of the testing:

> Wild aurochs were very different beasts from modern domestic cattle… They were much bigger than modern cattle, and wouldn't have had the domestic traits we see today, such as docility. So capturing these animals in the first place would not have been easy, and even if some people did manage to snare them alive, their continued management and breeding would still have presented considerable challenges until they had been bred for smaller size and more docile behavior.[6]

Bio-archaeologist and coauthor Dr. Jean-Denis Vigne explained why the study results are important in ascertaining how these wild bovines were first domesticated:

> In this study genetic analysis allowed us to answer questions that—until now—archaeologists would not even attempt to address. A small number of cattle progenitors is consistent with the restricted area for which archaeologists have evidence for early cattle domestication ca. 10,500 years ago. This restricted area could be explained by the fact that cattle breeding, contrary to, for example, goat herding, would have been very difficult for mobile societies, and that only some of them were actually sedentary at that time in the Near East.[7]

Dr. Marjan Mashkour, a CNRS archaeologist working in the Middle East, explained why the results of the regional study has global implications:

> This study highlights how important it can be to consider archaeological remains from less well-studied regions, such as Iran. Without our Iranian data it would have been very difficult to draw our conclusions, even though they concern cattle at a global scale.[8]

We now are fairly certain that cattle have been under the yoke of human control and selectively bred for at least 10,500 years, which makes them one of the original domesticated species raised for end-use consumption. Science is telling us that all current 900-plus breeds of cattle are direct descendants from a *single Iranian herd*. Given the human tendency to form permanent social groups and to solve problems as a group, it appears that the domestication of cattle originated in local collective efforts that might then have led to the development of agriculture and the first permanent human settlements eventually leading to the rise of urban culture in Mesopotamia.

Dogs, sheep and goats had effectively been domesticated by this time and the art of selective breeding techniques were being realized. These smaller animals were easily managed, but wild aurochs were another matter. With their massive horns and wild dispositions, they must have been daunting to the smaller humans of that time. One can imagine hunters and wranglers needing to be emboldened by some berry wine, or maybe beer, before matching wits and athleticism with the rampaging behemoths. Next would come the task of somehow selective breeding of these creatures for desired traits.

The strategies developed almost certainly would have involved ritual and belief. The selected "goddess cow" would be adorned and presented to the ideal bull in an endless trial and error process of selective breeding. It is probable that a sophisticated ritualized shamanic practice of *un*natural selection was developed and only success bred success. Shrouded in ritual, this emerging understanding of genetic breeding developed into flourishing herds of hearty stock.

The DNA study noted that the type of bovines apparently first domesticated were a species of wild aurochs. Aurochs were among the largest undulant herbivores during the post-glacial years of the late Pleistocene, and aurochs remains found in India have been dated to two million years ago. Descendants of these original wild herds have resulted, through selective breeding, in Indian cattle breeds such as the distinctively humped zebu, the Brahma, and the Spanish fighting bulls bred for their aggressiveness and stamina on the Iberian Peninsula of Spain.[6]

One of the first written descriptions of the mighty aurochs was given by Julius Caesar in his book *The Gallic Wars*. The book details Caesar's military expeditions from 58 BC until 50 BC. In his journeys through the primordial forests of northern Europe, Caesar encountered the aurochs and the tribesmen who hunted them. He described the animals as "a little below the elephant in size." He marveled at "their great strength and speed" and noted that "they spare neither man nor beast once sighted." Caesar was also impressed by the bravery of the "hardened" young hunters of these enormous creatures.

The Earliest Depictions

Perhaps the earliest European artistic depictions of bovines were discovered in the Chauvet Caves. (figure 5) This cave system, located in the cliffs overlooking the Ardèche River in the Ardèche region of France, was first explored in 1994 by a group of three speleologists. This important archeological site now bears the name of one of them, Jean-Marie Chauvet. The cave walls are covered with the images of a wide variety of now-extinct Ice-Age fauna and possibly the earliest artistic drawing of a human. And the Chauvet caves also contain some of the earliest renderings of the ancient paleo auroch (now-extinct), drawn at least 30,000 years ago, although images found in the Altimira Caves may be older. (figure 6).

Along with cave bears (which were far larger than grizzly bears), the lions, mammoths, and rhinos account for 63 percent of the identified animals, a huge percentage compared to later periods of cave art. Horses, bison, ibex, reindeer, red deer, aurochs, Megaceros deer, musk oxen, and an exceptional image of the lower body of a woman was found …Oxen, panther, and owl are also represented. [9] [Chauvet and a cave in the US are the only known examples of white owls found in paleo cave art.]

Some of the earliest cave paintings depicting hunting cattle are also found in Somaliland in the Laas Gaal cave complex, located near the town of Hargeisa. Beautiful stylized images of cattle are depicted in herds and individually, and several artistic depictions indicate that early humans in Africa 20,000 years ago venerated these animals as well as hunting them for food. (figure 7) Curious details from Laas Gaal also show cattle in ceremonial robes accompanied by humans, and around the necks of some cows are decorative plastron, or ceremonial beaded collars.[10] (figure 8)

Are these suggestive artistic depictions the result of wishful thinking on the part of the shamans who painted them? Or perhaps the artists were projecting their desire to tame and domesticate these huge animals?

Of course there is the possibility that depictions of clothed and adorned animals were indications that they had already been tamed almost 25,000 years earlier than the UCL DNA study suggests and that the paintings reflect existing human control over at least one bovine species. The paintings leave little doubt that humans had a spiritual fascination with the early proto-cattle species and this relationship would evolve into important African belief systems—spanning entire cultures—surviving even today.[11] We will discuss the importance of this emerging culture on the Tassili-n-Ajjer Plateau in a moment.

First, what happened to Aurochs and when did they go extinct? For thousands of years the aurochs, or *Bos* that blanketed the steppes of Eurasia, had been slowly dying off from over-hunting, loss of habitat and a host of domestic cattle diseases.

By the 1500s they were found wild in Poland. As their numbers diminished toward extinction, edicts were passed in an attempt to protect their dwindling numbers and they were brought under the protection of Polish royalty. But a 1564 survey of royal gamekeepers indicated that only 38 aurochs were thought to remain on the protected reserves. The last of them died of natural causes in 1627 in the dark Jaktorow Forest of Poland.[12]

By all accounts, the aurochs would have gone extinct much earlier without the care and concern of the Polish monarchy. In return for protecting the animals, the local villagers were exempted from paying taxes. The penalty for hunting aurochs was death. According to the gamekeepers' records, the herd had dwindled to one male and one female in 1620. In that year the bull died. Its horns were encased in metal and sent to the Polish king Zygmunt. The female was then left to wander alone for another solitary seven years—the sole survivor of a long and noble lineage. But even in death her journey was not quite over. In 1655 Sweden invaded Poland in what came to be called The Deluge. During that especially vicious conquest and occupation, some 40 percent of the Polish population died and 188 cities and towns were destroyed, including Warsaw. Among the most prized pieces of booty hauled back to Sweden by their army was the skull of the last aurochs. Today the skull reposes at the Royal Armory Museum in Stockholm.

Aurochs, along with mammoths, are on the short list as target species for controversial genetic experiments that could bring them back from extinction. Scientists are planning to first obtain genetic samples from bone and teeth fragments gathered from specimens found in museums and private collections. If enough genetic material is obtained, they will try to recreate its unique DNA sequence. Using DNA matches to modern cattle, researchers will then attempt to create a selective-breeding program to bring them back from extinction. Cool, another exciting Professional Bull Riding division!

Donato Matassino, head of the Consortium for Experimental Biotechnology in Italy, is one of the scientists involved in the project. He told *Time* magazine in February 2010, "Everything will be put together in a genetic mosaic. Once we have all the roads, we'll try to follow them back to Rome." Rome indeed—home of the bloody, bull worshipping Mithra cults that will be discussed shortly.

Holy Cows and Sacred Bulls

Bovine worship undoubtedly extends back into prehistory before the first herd was domesticated more than 12,000 years ago, as cave paintings and other artifacts would suggest. It should be noted that two of the earliest forms of bovine worship evolved where the earliest domesticated herds were found: Persia and India. So when these early cowboys became able to tame them, what did they do besides milk, slaughter, and selectively breed more of them? They institutionalized worship of the bull and the cow as representations of a marriage of the solar/bull and lunar/cow aspect.

And they had help. As mentioned, the psychoactive mushrooms that grew in cattle dung undoubtedly factored into the formation of belief systems that evolved around a sacred perception of cattle.

How did religious belief around cattle evolve in the first urban centers of Mesopotamia and later in India? Archaeologists have uncovered evidence that ancient peoples practiced a form of divination utilizing cattle entrails—much like the Suri people in East Africa, even today. In ancient Rome and in the Celtic countries, sheep's livers were used in this fashion.

It appears to me that the early divine aspects ascribed to cattle initially reflected equality between the bull and the cow, but this began to change. The divine

Goddess aspect of the cow appears to have moved east toward India, while the Solar/Bull cults moved west into what is modern day Iraq. Vestiges of Goddess/cow worship in Egypt did survive, but the bull began to become predominant.

Ancient Sumerian beliefs concerning the sacred bull, in particular, have survived through the ages in one of the earliest known written texts, the *Epic of Gilgamesh.* Early in this high adventure we find evidence of the oldest written reference to divine bovines yet discovered. Dating to about 1800 BC, the oldest of the tablets on which the epic was transcribed introduce Gilgamesh, King of Uruk, and describe his friendship with Enkidu and their journey to the Cedar Mountains (probably today's Lebenon) to defeat Humbaba. Here is where the plot thickens. There the goddess Ishtar becomes enamored of Gilgamesh and he spurns her advances. In anger, she sends down "the bull of heaven" (what we call the constellation Taurus) to destroy the crops and turn the people away from Gilgamesh.

The heavenly bull is normally controlled by Ishtar's father, Anu, the sky god, but Ishtar convinces him to relinquish control over the bull. As with most "tragic hero"/trickster tales, the bull is promptly stalked and slain by Gilgamesh and Enkidu, but then Anu and the gods are angered and they agree to sentence Enkidu to death as a punishment for killing the bull. (figure 9) Enkidu becomes sick and dies a tragic, untimely death, and Gilgamesh is then forced to continue alone on his epic journey without his antagonistic friend at his side. The epic recounting of Gilgamesh's life is probably a version of ancient predecessor stories that emerged from prehistoric oral traditions.

During this Sumarian time-period, about 4,000 years ago, Aryan tribes including the Mitanni began expanding south and east from the steppes into present-day Iran and further east into northeastern India. They found that both cultures already sacrificed cattle to the gods, so they introduced their own bovine-inspired symbol, Mitra—"Lord of the Contract." Mitra, or Mithra, is considered by some to be the first *moral* deity. The unifying of regional cattle worship in Eurasia would evolve for two thousand years and mirror sacred *Bos* rites in the Minoan and Egyptian cultures.

> Like the Indians, the Iranis sacrificed cattle to Mithra…They associated him with fire. And like both Indian and Roman worshippers, the Iranis concluded contracts before fires so that they might be made in the presence of Mithra. Like Mitra, Mithra saw all things. The Avestan Yast (hymn) dedicated to him describes him as having a thousand ears, ten thousand eyes, and as never sleeping.[13]

To Hindus, even today, cows are a symbol of the earth that provides for us all. They are worshipped but they are not considered deities; like the Earth, cows give us much: milk, curds, butter, mushroom-adorned dung, and like the Earth, cattle ask for nothing in return. It is considered good luck to feed a cow in India. No cow can be harmed. They still wander around the cities and in rural areas wherever they like, and when they get old and sickly, they are taken in by local monasteries who then act as surrogate cattle nursing homes. Today, orphan calves are wet-nursed if necessary. (figure 10)

In India, the bull is also held in reverence. Madurai's Nandi bull shrine and the Shiva temple at Mahabalipuram are two of the most important sacred bull temples and attract millions of worshippers. And the Indians are serious about this. Non-Hindus are barred from entering the 500-year-old Bull Temple in Bangalore. (figure 11) Maybe this reverence for cows would have come back to bite them when they offered to take in all six million head that were about to be slaughtered because of the devastating outbreak of "mad-cow" disease in UK cattle herds. The offer fell through, but more on those "mad-cows" later, we're talking oblivious Indian cattle.

It is thought that the cow initially became important in India in the Vedic period (1500-900 BC) as a symbol of wealth, and that a fully realized sacred tradition ascribed to them had yet to be developed. Slowly over time, however, cows assumed a place at the heart of Hindi religious sacrifices—but not as blood sacrifice as in other ancient belief systems.

> Cows represent sacrifice. Without them, there can be no sacrifice… Cows are guileless in their behavior and from them flow sacrifices…and milk and curds and butter. Hence cows are sacred... In the Vedas the water-dripping clouds of heaven are constantly compared to cows. According to occult Hindu symbology, they are linked with the primal principle of humidity, a flowing out of the 'stuff of creation.' The rain that falls upon the earth can be seen as a form of milk, and many Hindu allegories describe the battles waged by the gods to secure the rain cloud cows from the demons who try to steal them. These myths provide a model for the worldly 'soldier' who 'fights about cows'. That the moon is also linked up with moisture only substantiates the symbolic link frequently recognized between the moon and the cow. Lunar goddesses of many traditions wore horns on their heads and acted as links between the moon, the sun and the earth. These are the Heavenly Cows who graze in the celestial fields of Indra's [the lord of heaven, the god of rain] heaven. The mother of Indra [a deity] is depicted as a cow, and Indra in his bull-form freed the cows which were held fast within the stone cave in the ridge of 'The Encircler.' As a bull, Indra fertilizes the waters of heaven, which are cows. Rescuing them from the grasp of the demons, he brings them back from the South each year in the form of the monsoon rains….

Shiva is also intimately linked to cows. As Rudra, he was the god of cattle and his violent aspect was reflected in the fact that he exacted from his worshippers a sacrifice of cattle. The seven holy rivers of India that break through the matted locks of Shiva's hair have their source in Gomuckh Cave—the 'Cow's Mouth' …Shiva manifests in the world of duality the infinite unity of Aditi. The shrines of Shiva are guarded by statues of him in his bovine aspect, just as his human form is adorned with the horns of the crescent moon. Both symbolize the mysteries of initiation.[14] (figure 12)

This Vedic sense of sacredness around the cow holds true today. Ghee or clarified liquid butter made from processed cow's milk is a mandatory element in modern Hindu ritual. Ascetics still wander around India today with a paste of ashes from cow dung fires smeared all over their bodies, and this ancient practice is mirrored in Africa by the Neur people.

McAloo for You?

I'm often asked if there are any McDonald's restaurants in India. For decades they were barred, but lately that's changed. There are 271 (all beef-free outlets) in the second most populous country on the planet. That's 271 out of a worldwide corporate juggernaut franchise fluctuating total of around 33,000 restaurants. In India, McDonald's quietly sticks to chicken, fish, lamb, and vegetarian options for their menu. Local favorites include: McAloo Tikki–a deep fried cake of spicy mashed potatoes and McSpicey Paneer—an Indian spicy cheese snack. Too bad fast food joints don't serve these dishes here in the USA; sounds better than ammoniated "pink-slime."

As India slowly moves further toward modernity, attitudes about beef are slowly changing, and one indication of this is the rise of cattle rustling. Called "lifters," gangs of Hindus are using old dump trucks outfitted with ramps to kidnap stray Brahman cattle roaming the streets late at night. These sacred animals are being sold on the black market to feed a growing beef eating population. A recent story in the New York *Times* looked at this emerging trend:

> Behind the cattle rustling is a profound shift in Indian society. Meat consumption—chicken, primarily—is becoming acceptable even among Hindus. India is now the world's largest dairy producer, its largest cattle producer, and its largest beef exporter, having surpassed Brazil last year, according to the United States Department of Agriculture.
>
> Much of that exported beef is from buffalo (India has half of the world's buffalo population), which are not considered holy. But officials in Andhra Pradesh recently estimated that there are 3,100 illegal slaughterhouses in the state compared with just six licensed ones, and a recent

newspaper investigation found that tens of thousands of cattle are sold annually for slaughter from a market in just one of that state's 64 districts. Killing cows is illegal in much of India, and some states outlaw the possession of cow meat…Beef from cattle is also widely consumed by Muslims and Dalits, among India's most marginalized citizens. Indeed, meat consumption is growing the most among the poor, government statistics show, with overall meat eating growing 14 percent from 2010 to 2012…

But the demand for beef keeps rising, many here say, and with it the prevalence of cattle rustling. Last year, the police in Delhi arrested 150 rustlers, a record number. This year, arrests have continued to surge…[15]

It would appear that the sacred cattle of India are losing some of their luster and status as more and more Indians discover the pleasurable allure of rich, bloody-red beef.

Apis and Hathor

Meanwhile, to the west of India, as cattle worship crept down from Mesopotamia into the Middle-East, sub-Saharan Africans independently developed their own cattle domestication program during this same time period. African beliefs and strategies may have evolved into a unique brand of bovine worship with attendant rituals, and the antiquity of African cattle domestication may rival that of the recent Iranian *Bos* site dating.

It has long been thought that cattle domestication arrived down from the Middle East into Africa. However on-going genetic research suggests cattle domestication also may have occurred in southern Algeria on the Tassili-n-Ajjir Plateau in a time frame that may pre-date Mesopotamian efforts. Today, the plateau resembles a moonscape, a labyrinth of badlands and escarpments, but in ancient times, this region of the Sahara was verdant and significantly wetter. Perfect for cattle. Predictably, we also find evidence of psychedelic mushroom use by humans:

> In the Tassili-n-Ajiir, rock paintings date from the Late Neolithic to as recently as 2,000 years ago. Here are the earliest known depictions of shamans with large numbers of grazing cattle. The shamans are dancing with fists full of mushrooms and also have mushrooms sprouting out of their bodies. In one instance they are shown running joyfully, surrounded by the geometric structures of their hallucinations! The pictorial evidence seems incontrovertible.[16] (figure 13)

Researchers are attempting to prove conclusively that the first evidence of cattle domestication will be found in the Egyptain Napta Playa basin at Tushka

(c. 11,000 BC) and later on the site of Dibeira (c. 7,400 BC). Perhaps these herds were slowly imported up into the Nile Valley from the southwest along with the shamanic view of cattle as sacred animals. Stone-covered *tumuli* burial sites for *Bos* cattle—sometimes in conjunction with human remains—have been dated in Egypt to 5,400 BC, and evidence of emerging proto-Egyptian cattle cults are thought to have inspired similar burials later during Badarian (4400 to 4,000 BC) times. In pre-Dynastic Egypt, impaled cattle heads have been unearthed in Hierakonpolis, and bas reliefs of cattle heads (which are identical to the famous "Hathor bowl" artifact) have also been discovered.

The Egyptian's complex belief system anthropomorphized gods into animals and humans into hybrid animal forms, and there are countless examples. Many of these beliefs were imparted and/or influenced by the older Mesopotamian, and later by Minoan, belief systems, and there are parallels with Harappan (Indus Valley culture) and emerging Indian belief as well.

Ancient Egyptians at times represented the goddess Hathor as the celestial cow. Some of these images show her transformed completely into her bovine aspect; other depictions portray her with a human body and cow's head. She is also depicted with the solar disc of the sun hovering between her horns as she was thought to have dominion over the sun. To the ancient Egyptians, Hathor represented the great celestial cow that created the world and all it contained and her milk nourished creation. (figure 14)

The symbolic/religious use of the "bull" archetype in ancient Egypt *is more complex.*

> [T]he Egyptians worshiped bulls in general, for they seem to have commonly killed and eaten them. But a good many circumstances point to the conclusion that originally all cattle, bulls as well as cows, were held sacred by the Egyptians. For not only were all cows esteemed holy by them and never sacrificed, but even bulls might not be sacrificed unless they had certain natural marks; a priest examined every bull before it was sacrificed; if it had the proper marks, he put his seal on the animal in token that it might be sacrificed; and if a man sacrificed a bull which had not been sealed, he was put to death.[17]

Red colored bulls were associated with the corn spirit and crop fertility by the Egyptians since "these animals above all others had helped the discoverers of corn in sowing the seed and procuring the universal benefits of agriculture." The Egyptians also revered a special black-colored bull thought to be sacred to the god Ptah of Memphis. This bull, called the Apis bull, was a single, specially-selected animal that was pampered and worshipped throughout its life. It was housed in royal splendor and watched carefully for signs that were thought to be direct signals from the Gods. The Apis bull was also utilized as a divination intermediary for oracular prophecies. Questions were asked and the attending priests carefully interpreted the bull's physical reactions. When the Apis bull died, it was mummified and given funereal attention rivaling that of royalty. The bull's sarcophagus was then displayed alongside all of its predecessors at the Serapeum at Memphis. Immediately after its death, the Apis priests would scour the Egyptian countryside looking for its divine replacement.

Buddhist priests embark on a similar quest where they seek out and find the reincarnation of a saint or rimpoche after a particular avatar's passing. These replacements are sought far and wide, and special conditions must be met for the replacement/reincarnation to be acknowledged.

The Apis bull was probably the most important of all the black bulls on the land, but the Egyptians revered bulls in general and they played an important religious function as a divine protector/talisman for communities. (figure 15) Their bones were interred at an important burial site:

> [W]orship of the black bulls Apis and Mnevis, especially the former, played an important part in Egyptian religion; all bulls that died a natural death were carefully buried in the suburbs of the cities, and their bones were afterwards collected from all parts of Egypt and interred in a single spot; and at the sacrifice of a bull in the great rites of Isis all the wor-shippers beat their breasts and mourned…Osiris was regularly identified with the bull Apis of Memphis and the bull Mnevis of Heliopolis. But it is hard to say whether these bulls were embodiments of him as the corn-spirit, as the red oxen appear to have been, or whether they were not in origin entirely distinct deities who came to be fused with Osiris at a later time. The universality of the worship of these two bulls seems to put them on a different footing from the ordinary sacred animals whose worships were purely local. But whatever the original relation of Apis to Osiris may have been, there is one fact about the former which ought not to be passed over in a disquisition on the custom of killing a god.[18]

The Minoans and the Greeks

For a thousand or more years, sub-cultural and religious dogma in Persia morphed divergent Earth/nature-based and solar-based beliefs attributed to cattle into religious belief systems that may have resulted in the Bronze-Age Minoan culture on the island of Crete. That culture arose around 2,700 BC and flourished for over 1,200 years. Named after a mythical king named Minos, the Minoans were admired by the Greeks, who adopted many of their architectural and artistic innovations.

The "Bull" appears to have been a key symbol in the Minoan civilization, as carefully preserved bull heads and bull-horns unearthed in the Knossos royal palace complex would suggest. A sampling of ritual objects unearthed during excavations around Crete include: bull masks, the double axe (or lavrys), and elaborate bull-horn art. Surviving Minoan frescos and decorations also depict what may have been the first rodeo clowns performing an amazing bull-leaping ritual called the *taurokatharpsi*. This involved participants running directly at charging bulls and vaulting over them by grasping their horns and somersaulting over their backs. Bull leaping has become a controversial subject with anthropologists who in recent years have questioned whether this type of athletic feat was actually possible. Perhaps this was some form of voluntary sacrifice and the bull-leapers were actually impaled? We may never know for sure, but if the depictions are accurate, those were some fearless acrobats—as are the athletes who perform some of these feats every year in Pamplona.

As in all ancient civilizations, the structure of religious belief played an important, even a key, role on Minoan Crete, where they deified the female aspect of the natural world and devised a logical order that allowed them to live in harmony with the environment and each other. And the Minoans were ingenious engineers and builders. They may have invented the first flush toilets, constructed complicated water diversion systems and cisterns, and adorned their buildings with intricate tile and terra cotta. These were only a few of their many cultural and artistic innovations.

The sacrifice of the "Bull," and games that revolved around bovines, like the *taurokatharpsia*, were a central aspect of Minoan religious festivals, perhaps symbolizing man's triumph over these dangerous animals through extreme skill and luck. The statues of priestesses in Minoan culture and frescoes showing both men and women participating in bull-leaping indicates an unusual sense of gender equality not normally associated with other Bronze Age cultures. (figure 16) Minoan inheritance in society may have been matrilineal based, and Minoan religion was probably centered around the practice of goddess worship. Artistic renditions of religious life often depicted women officiating at sacred ceremonies and ritual celebrations that most often took place in sacred caves, on mountain peaks, and at sacred sites. Animal sacrifices, along with processions, were an integral part of ritualized ceremonies held in honor of the divine female, and during these festivities, worshipers used music, dance, and prayer to achieve a state of religious ecstasy that put them in touch with the supernatural.

One of the most enduring myths associated with the Minoans was the half-man/half bull, the Minotaur. The Minotaur's form was depicted in religious ceremonies where priests wore masks in the shape of a bull's head. (figure 17) One of the most famous stories involved the Minotaur and his home inside a maze known as the *labyrinth*, which may have been a maze-like cave system south of the city of Heraklion. In the ancient Greek language, the word labyrinth comes from the term for "the house of lavrys" and the following is the Greek legend of the Minotaur and the Labyrinth:

Zeus, in the form of a bull, brought Europe from the Phoenician seashore to Gortys in Crete where he made love with her under a plane tree (or on the plane tree after assuming the form of another sacred animal, the eagle), and since then the plane tree has been blessed to never lose its leaves (evergreen). From their union three sons were born—triplets. Next, Zeus arranged the marriage of Europe to the Cretan King Asterion (or Asterio), who appointed Europe's and Zeus's sons as his successors.

> As promised, the three sons of Europe and Zeus (Minos or Minoas, Radamanthis, Sarpidon) succeeded King Asterion to the throne of Crete. Initially they seemed satisfied to co-govern, but Minos, who wanted the reign to be his exclusively, ended up banishing his brothers…The gods loved Minos because his father, Zeus, honored him above all. They presented him with a wife, Pasiphae, daughter of Helios (Sun) and Persida, and sister of Circe, the sorceress Kalypso…
>
> Once, wanting to offer a sacrifice in honor of his uncle Poseidon, Minos asked Poseidon to send the best bull he could find from the sea. The bull was so beautiful that Minos didn't sacrifice him, but instead kept him with his flock (or in the palace gardens). To revenge Minos for not keeping his promise, Poseidon made the bull so ferocious and dangerous that his eventual capture in Crete became one of the twelve feats of Hercules (Cretan Bull).
>
> When Pasiphae, his immortal wife, saw the bull she fell in love and coupled with him. She was able to couple with him with the help of Daedalus, who constructed a wooden likeness of a cow, in which Pasiphae hid. From this union the monster Minotaur was born, a humanoid being with a bull's head, which Minos promptly jailed in the Labyrinth.[19]

To the Greeks, who adopted much of their iconography from the Minoans, the bull represented Zeus, who was able to transform himself into a shining white bull. It was said that he hid himself in the herd outshining the other cattle in an effort to attract the attention of Phoenician princess Europa. In eagle form he succeeded in wooing Europa, who is often depicted in Greek art as astride a white bull.

There are other examples: a feature found in the mythical character of Dionysus appears inconsistent with his supposed nature as a deity of vegetation, for he was often represented with the bestial horns of a bull—possibly the inspiration for the term, "horny?"

> [Dionysus] is referred to as "cow-born," "bull," "bull-shaped," "bull-faced," "bull-browed," "bull-horned," "horn-bearing," "two-horned," or "horned." He was believed to occasionally appear to mortals as a bull.

His images were often... made in bull shape, or with bull horns; and he was painted with horns. Types of the horned Dionysus are found amongst the surviving monuments of antiquity...At Aegira in Achaia the priestess of Earth drank the fresh blood of a bull before she descended into the cave to prophesy.[20]

The Greek goddess Hera's popular nickname was *Bo-opis* or the look of a cow that is "ox-eyed." This attribution may have more ancient roots and has parallels within the cow cults that emerged in India and Egypt. Selene, like the Egyptian Hathor, was often equated with the celestial cow. The daughter of the Titans, she was the personification of the moon. It was thought that great white bulls pulled her moon chariot across the sky. (figure 18) The Greeks did borrow some aspects of their bovine worship from the Minoans, but these beliefs were a subset that did not appear to attain the prominence found in the cow cults in India and Persia or the Apis Bull cults in Egypt.

The Golden Calf

In Jack Joseph Conrad's excellent 1957 book, *The Horn and the Sword*, we are reminded that the ancient Hebrews also had a spiritual relationship with cattle that has been morphed, and changed since ancient times with many cattle references lost in translations of the Old Testament.

Originally a nomadic people, they had long observed and stood in awe of the giant wild bull, the aurochs. The Hebrews called this creature *re'em* and, in the Septuagint version of the Old Testament, describe it as savage, swift, and merciless. Awed by its fierce strength, they, like most of the peoples of the Near East, worshipped the bull with hymns, poetry, and ritual...The earliest known bull-god of the Hebrews was called the "Bull of Jacob," Jacob being a prominent Hebrew hero and cult leader. For centuries this expression was used interchangeably with "god." However, many references to the bull cults and gods of the ancient Hebrews that were originally a part of the Old Testament have been distorted or deleted by latter-day translators, either through ignorance, or in an attempt to deny or minimize the importance of bull worship in the life of these people. Thus we find that in translation "mighty one" was substituted time and again for the original Hebrew word for "bull." Again, in certain passages of the King James Version reference is made to the "unicorn." This has been shown to be a mistaken translation of *re'em* which, as we have seen, was none other than the wild aurochs. In other passages what was once meant to be "fertile bull" has become "fruitful bough." [21]

In the Bible, we also have an interesting amalgamation of Eastern and Persian religious practices that involved animal sacrifice. A complex set of religious practices and protocols were supposedly given to Moses from God, and upon his return from the summit of "Mount Sinai," Moses gave these instructions to his brother Aaron, who then imparted them to the Israelites. But, when Moses came to his meeting with Aaron what did he find? The people had fashioned a "golden calf" and were worshipping the effigy, having lost faith in Moses who had been away for 40 days communing with Yahweh and receiving the "Ten Commandments." I remember the scene vividly from the Cecil B. de Mille movie. As a kid, *The Ten Commandments* starring Charlton Heston, had a huge impact on my Biblical education. As the story supposedly goes, Moses was not happy when he discovered that Aaron had acquiesced to the people who had fallen away from God. Aaron gathered all the available gold and fashioned a golden calf, and when Moses returned, the Israelites were fornicating and worshipping the idol in an act called in the Bible "the sin of the calf." (Exodus 32:4) Perhaps this ad hoc ritualized behavior was a vestige of their recent departure from Egypt where the Apis bull was venerated or perhaps the story has been changed?

> The fact, however, that these wanderers were bull cultists, as had been their ancestors for centuries, is not generally known. But of this there is no scholarly doubt. Indeed there is complete agreement that the construction of the golden bull by Aaron at the foot of Mount Sinai was not the act of a heretic, but the legitimate function of the high priest of the bull-god. In thus making the bull idol Aaron was simply following a long tradition of Israelite bull worship and had the full approval of his people. Called a "calf" because of its costly nature dictated a relatively small image, this idol was worshipped as the representation of the god who had brought the people out of the bondage of Egypt…There is the additional possibility that Moses himself was considered by his people to be a manifestation of their bull-god…The reader will recall that Michelangelo's famous statue of Moses, located in the Church of San Pietro in Vincoli in Rome, plainly depicts him as horned. (figure 19) The Vulgate or Latin translation of the Bible likewise speaks of Moses as "horned" rather than "shining." Thus it may be that Moses' estrangement from Aaron as described in Exodus was the result of the clash between two rival Israelite bull cults, or perhaps between two leaders vying for control of one such cult.[22]

At the very least Moses must have incorporated livestock worship into their rituals. He gave the people a complex set of instructions concerning the sacrifice of animals to "God." From Book of Leviticus:

1 The Lord called Moses and spoke to him from the tent of meeting, saying,

2 "Speak to the people of Israel and say to them, when any one of you brings an offering to the Lord, you shall bring your offering of livestock from the herd or from the flock.

3 "If his offering is a burnt offering from the herd, he shall offer a male without blemish. He shall bring it to the entrance of the tent of meeting, that he may be accepted before the Lord.

4 He shall lay his hand on the head of the burnt offering, and it shall be accepted for him to make atonement for him.

5 Then he shall kill the bull before the Lord, and Aaron's sons the priests shall bring the blood and throw the blood against the sides of the altar that is at the entrance of the tent of meeting…

19 Flesh that touches any unclean thing shall not be eaten. It shall be burned up with fire. All who are clean may eat flesh,

20 But the person who eats of the flesh of the sacrifice of the Lord's peace offerings while an uncleanness is on him, that person shall be cut off from his people…

21 And if anyone touches an unclean thing, whether human uncleanness or an unclean beast or any unclean detestable creature, and then eats some flesh from the sacrifice of the Lord's peace offerings, that person shall be cut off from his people."□

22 The Lord spoke to Moses, saying,

23 "Speak to the people of Israel, saying, you shall eat no fat, of ox or sheep or goat.

24 The fat of an animal that dies of itself and the fat of one that is torn by beasts may be put to any other use, but on no account shall you eat it.

25 For every person who eats of the fat of an animal of which a food offering may be made to the Lord shall be cut off from his people.

26 Moreover, you shall eat no blood whatever, whether of fowl or of animal, in any of your dwelling places.

27 Whoever eats any blood, that person shall be cut off from his people.

This strict admonishment set out a framework within which the ritual of animal sacrifice was to be conducted in the Judeo-Christian tradition and might be an important key with which to unlock the mystery of modern livestock mutilation—*which* that *occurs exclusively in Judeo-Christian countries*. There are underlying cultural developments that now provide a ritual bridge between effigies and true sacrificial victims. Could animal sacrifice be a substitute or replacement, for human sacrifice and a form of agreed-upon "collective murder?"

In verse three of the book of Isaiah, the prophet wryly observes: "The ox knoweth his owner, and the ass his master's crib." (Isaiah 1:3) In today's world, this adage bears disturbing connotations given the core deviance of "horse slashers." We will investigate these and other pathological types later.

"Cows are everything, they are our happiness."

As we have seen, in ancient North Africa we find some of the earliest depictions of cattle in prehistoric art that go back at least 12,000 years ago. The enigmatic Tassili frescos found in the mountains of Sefir and Tissili show realistic scenes of ancient Tuareg People interacting with herds of cattle. (figure 20) Notice the ghost-like figure with a tool at the head of the downed cow, and the figure working on the rear end of the animal. And notice the childlike figure at the lower right appears to be holding back a young warrior figure. (figure 21) There are so many artistic images of cattle at Tassili and other sites that archaeologists call this entire time in their history the "Bovidian Period,"

In present day Africa, pastoral Nuer tribesmen, the Dinka, and the Maasai people of Kenya and northern Tanzania still maintain a society that is deeply intertwined with cattle. These ethnic groups rely almost exclusively on cattle for sustenance and status. According to their oral tradition, the Maasai originally developed their belief system in the Lower Nile Valley before migrating south. The traditional Maasai diet includes milk, raw beef, and raw blood from cattle, and as a snack, while on journeys driving their cattle, Maasai herdsmen will make a small cut on a cow's neck and drink the living blood from the animal. The Nuer and Dinka are similar in that they base the relative worth of value within their culture on cattle for many aspects of their day-to-day life. They still keep alive ancient traditions that venerate and acknowledge the importance of bovines to their culture.

The Nuer tribesmen of the Sudan say that "cows are everything, they are our happiness." Every Nuer marriage involves a dowry of cows from the herd, and with this bride wealth close ties are created between generations and clans. Cows are a bond between brothers and a symbol of strength and goodness between all men. The bride wealth movements of cattle from kraal to kraal are equivalent to lines on a genealogical chart, each generation of cows being linked up with various agnate groups and harking back to ancestral cows as ancient as any human forebears. Nuer cows are never slaughtered for meat but are killed only for religious sacrifice. It is through cows that the Nuer establish contact with the ghosts of their ancestors and other spirits in the supernatural world, and the history of their cows can reveal a history of mystical connections. Those who have lived with them say that "He who would know the Nuer must first master a vocabulary referring to cattle and to the life of the herds." Indeed, men and boys are addressed by names that refer to the form and color of their favorite ox. A young boy, at the time of his initiation into manhood, is given a bull whose name he takes as his own. The Nuer social idiom, like that of many pastoralists, is basically a bovine one.[23]

Modern day Dinka also sacrifice cattle on important occasions. Some of their sacrificial ceremonies are revealing for they provide an ancient example of how cattle, exalted in their culture, are intentionally victimized and, through ritual transference, made to replace potential human victims that may be in conflict with other members of the tribe. This is a form of agreed-upon pressure relief, a valve to release emotional tension, a collective control mechanism that substitutes animal sacrifice for mutual human sacrifice. It may provide a clue to help us understand underlying compulsive inclinations toward war that have been acted out historically in western culture.

> [A]mong the Dinkas…[in] sacrificial ceremonies…participants begin to brandish weapons in mock warfare…From time to time somebody detaches himself from the group to beat the cow or calf that has been tied to a nearby stake, or hurl insults at it. There is nothing static or stilted about the performance; it succeeds in giving shape to a collective impulse that gradually triumphs over the forces of dispersion and discord by bringing corporate violence to bear on a ritual victim. In this rite the metamorphosis of reciprocal violence into unilateral violence is explicably and dramatically reenacted….[24]

Sacrificial rites strive to reproduce the mechanism of violent unanimity and the surrogate victim is a key to these rites. Considerable new light could be shed on the matter of animal sacrifice and how it may directly relate to the cattle mutilation phenomenon.

Whether we recognize it or not, animal sacrifice continues around the world, but in the West it is usually enacted privately, behind closed doors or apparently above certain darkened pastures. Millions of animals are sacrificed and 'honored' every day on the planet, and in the United States alone there are over one million adherents to Santaria who legally use chickens, ducks, goats, and other animals in their sacrificial rituals. Occasionally, newspapers carry stories of practitioners harming animals for "religious" purposes. Here is one account from Atlantic City, New Jersey in 1985.

> [P]olice arrested 19 people of Cuban descent in an apartment strewn with the remains of chickens, ducks and lambs, buckets of blood, and ritualistic altars. Hundreds of chicken, duck and lamb parts were discovered, along with three lamb carcasses minus legs and a number of live

fowl. The practitioners were in various stages of butchering and blood-smeared reverie. A similar scene had been discovered in a house in Pleasantville, [NJ] near Atlantic City, a week earlier.[25]

Human's ancient almost incestuous relationship with livestock must be considered as we continue to stalk the herd. We will more fully examine the subject of animal sacrifice and its possible connection to the livestock mutilation mystery later as we attempt to unravel the mystery.

Mithraism Arrives in Rome

As we have established, there was a melding of Mithraic belief with the invasion of northern India by marauding Aryan tribes on horseback. The bull cults also had Egyptian counterparts who had developed cattle worship. Around 500 BC, Zoroster (or Zarathustra) was born in Eastern Iran and the story of his life became what we now know as "The Zorostrian Texts." His wisdom and knowledge has, in some part, endured into the present day. Pliny the Elder in the first century called him the "inventor of magic.[26]

According to historian Jerome Clark, (who is decidedly skeptical about the subject of unexplained livestock deaths), influential journalist/author/curmudgeon John Keel told him about his earliest known livestock mutilation data. Keel, who had spent considerable time in the Near East, told Clark that these unexplained animal deaths had evidently been occurring for millennia. Clark wrote:

> [John] Keel…claimed that a "wave of mysterious mutilations occurred 2,500 years ago…[and] led Zoroster into his pioneering studies of demons and angels" (Keel 1984).[27]

I have never encountered anything concrete that would bolster Keel's claim, but it wouldn't surprise me in the least if and when I do discover texts that make mention of these and other claims by ancient peoples.

Zoroster codified Mythrism, and a formidable amalgamation of Sun Worship and Cattle Worship, combined with his strict moral code, swept into the Roman Empire and almost supplanted emerging Christian belief. Both of these radical monotheistic belief systems competed for followers in common Roman society during the turbulent first century AD. Ultimately, with the conversion of Roman Emperor Constantine in the mid-third century, the emerging Christian cult became a full-blown religion and overcame the influence of the Mithra cults along with pantheism, nature religions, the Gnostics, the Hermeticists, and other systems of ontological and spiritual thought.

Early Christianity showed a willingness to adapt to formerly influential ideas and practices, changing important feast days and replacing the "blood of the bull" with the "blood of the lamb." Christmas and Easter replaced the spring equinox and absorbed other "pagan" practices of the Mythraic, and other cults vying for converts. The quickest way to convert believers is to adopt already agreed-upon symbols and established feast days that are familiar. The early Christians were pragmatic in this regard, and this pragmatism also included symbolic changes within the practice of animal sacrifice. Replacing the Mithraic "blood of the bull," Christians changed to the less costly "blood of the lamb." It stands to reason that if you could get away with sacrificing less expensive animals, there would also be a financial incentive to switch from Mithraic rituals and belief to the emerging Christian belief in "the lamb of god." It should also be recognized that the sacrifice of the "Lamb of God" raised the meaning of the sacrifice to a higher conceptual and spiritual level as expressed in the language of the ancient hymn: "Lamb of God, who taketh away the sins of the World."

In the mid first-century, the spread of Mithraism through the Roman world was likely accelerated by the conquest of the Mythraic city of Cilicia by Pompey in 67 BC. According to the historian Plutarch, Pompey was evidently converted to Mithraism for he "performed strange sacrifices on Olympus…and practiced occult rites, among others those of Mithra." And some of these rituals combined the blood of the bull with the rite of baptism—literally a bloody shower:

> In the [Mithric] baptism the devotee, crowned with gold and wreathed with fillets, descended into a pit, the mouth of which was covered with a wooden grating. A bull, adorned with garlands of flowers, its forehead glittering with gold leaf, was then driven on to the grating and there stabbed to death with a consecrated spear. Its hot reeking blood poured in torrents through the apertures, and was received with devout eagerness by the worshipper on every part of his person and garments, till he emerged from the pit, drenched, dripping, and scarlet from head to foot, to receive the homage, nay the adoration, of his fellows as one who had been born again to eternal life and had washed away his sins in the blood of the bull.[28] (figure 22)

Perhaps nature inadvertently factored into the downfall of the Mythraic cults when, in 79 AD, converts living in Pompeii (Pompey's namesake city) and nearby Herculaneum were consumed by fire, searing heat, and blankets of ashes from the eruption of Mount Vesuvius—a horrific cataclysm that took the lives of an estimated 16,000 citizens. The utter destruction of these newly established, and beautiful, Mythraic strongholds could well have undermined the influence of the emerging Mithra cult in Rome. Nature might also play a major part in our bovine drama, as we will see later when we discuss "mad-cow" disease and the possible linking of outbreaks with natural events.

Perhaps fervid "blood of the bull" worship had finally run its high-profile course in Western/Greco-Roman culture—but remained latent within our cultural psyche for thousands of years expressed again today in the form of a $300 bil-lion-per-year beef industry. Today, in only one super-sized rendering plant in the United States, up to 400 head of cattle are unceremoniously slain, rendered, and processed every hour in a gross form of ritualized, industrial slaughter. There are no burnt offerings here in the bloody recesses of our cultural closet—only cold steel and colder temperatures for hundreds of tons of beef and inedible offal—"waste." Out of sight, out of mind, right? And that's just cattle. Sheep, swine, horses, chickens, farmed fish, etc.—that's for another book.

As we have seen, our relationship with cattle is thousands of years old, multi-faceted in its expressions, highly complex, and more deeply involved in our psyches than the simplified notion of 'ancient sacred cows' fast food hamburgers and newspaper accounts of modern cattle mutilations would suggest. For exam-ple, timeless, ritualized human behavior involving cattle today still draws millions of spectators every year to the spectacle and pageantry of the bullfight and the rodeo.

Olé!

In ancient Rome, the fighting and killing of bulls for sport constituted popular spectacles occasionally performed in the Coliseum, but that version of killing bulls for entertainment had a rather unceremonious, brutish quality that was prob-ably devoid of much ceremony. On the Iberian Peninsula in Spain, by contrast, an exalted and increasingly glamorized version of the ritualized bullfight, or *corrida,* evolved.

After the Visogoth conquest of the Roman Empire in the late third century, and during the early fourth-century ad conquest of what is now Spain and Portugal, the Vandals introduced a version of the bullfight more akin to a controlled display of hunting prowess than to ritual. North African Moors (who overran and conquered most of the Iberian Peninsula later in the early 700s) later converted bullfighting into a more stylized, ritualistic events held during impor-tant feast days. Mounted Moorish warriors skillfully darted around the charging Iberian bulls with grace and speed, ultimately killing them with spears to the roar of the assembled crowds. The practice of bullfighting continued to evolve.

Possibly the first historic bullfight was organized and held in honor of the coronation of King Alphonso VIII in 1113 AD. The event was wildly popular, and organized *corridas* became a staple celebration to commemorate important royal events. This bloody pagan practice became so popular by the reign of King Phillip II that an alarmed Pope Pius V issued the papal bull [sic] *De Sulte Gregis* in 1567, forbidding the practice as being "removed from Christian piety and charity."[29]

Spanish bullfighting fans completely ignored Rome and the practice contin-ued—gaining even more popularity for its forbidden nature. In 1575 Pope Gregory VIII, realizing the decree was ineffective, sought the advice of Spanish writer and mystic Fray Luis de Leon who observed, "bullfights are *in the blood of the Spanish people, and they cannot be stopped* without facing grave consequences," and thus the *Papal Bull* against bullfighting was lifted. [my emphasis] (figure 23)

Spanish fighting bulls have been selectively bred for aggressiveness for more than 700 years, and are thought by some geneticists to have originally been imported from African Maghreb strains by Moorish conquerors. They are among the purest cattle breeds on the planet. There are four acknowledged "foundational" breeds: Vistahermosa, Vázquez, Gallardo, and Cabrera, which are still selectively bred on ancient Iberian and French breeding ranches for their nasty temperament. Fighting bulls are noted for their sleek athletic build—well-developed shoulders and necks that give the bulls their distinctive, muscled look. They've also been selectively bred to develop over-sized horns that most often point forward rather than skyward, making them even more dangerous in the ring. During the selective breeding process, the cows are most rigorously tested for aggressiveness, for it has long been thought that male bulls get their "courage" from their mothers. Spanish law stipulates strict regulations for fighting bulls: "[T]hey must be at least four years old and reach the weight of 460 kg to fight in a first-rank bullring, 435 kg for a second-rank one, and 410 kg for third-rank rings."[30]

Needless to say, the 'sport' of bullfighting is reviled by animal rights organizations and it was actually banned in the Spanish province of Catalonia in 2012. As a result, a widely supported "motion to declare bullfighting a protected national pursuit—*bien de interés* cultural—was placed before Spain's parliament after the Catalan Bullfighting Federation gathered over 500,000 signatures across the country." Opponents of the "sport" were dismayed when the Spanish parliament declared bullfighting a protected national pastime in February 2013.

> Today the bullfight is much the same as it has been since about 1726, when Francisco Romero of Ronda, Spain, introduced the *estoque* (the sword) and the *muleta* (the small, more easily wielded worsted cape used in the last part of the fight). The amount of applause the matador receives is based on his proximity to the horns of the bull, his tranquility in the face of danger, and his grace in swinging the cape in front of an infuriated animal weighing more than 1,000 pounds. The bull instinctively goes for the cloth because it is a large, moving target, not because of its color; bulls are color-blind and charge just as readily at the inside of the cape, which is yellow.[31]

Because of their natural instinct and centuries of special breeding, fighting bulls will charge at anything that moves. Bulls selected for the *corrida* live a year longer than those bred to the slaughtered. Bulls used as opponents for *novilleros* (or novices) are legally required to be at least three years old and those fought by full matadors are to be at least four years old.

There has always been opposition to bullfighting, and those who have organized against the practice have presented a horrific picture of torture, maiming, pain, and death inflicted on the animals. For such people, bullfighting is a bloodthirsty and atavistic practice, an abomination, an outrageous engineered scene of torture and cruelty for the purpose of public entertainment and private profit. Here is an extract from a statement by the political action group "Stop Bullfighting":

> The bull is not an aggressive animal, and the reason he is angry and attempts to charge at the matador whilst in the bullring is mainly because he has been horrendously abused for the previous two days. In fact, what spectators see is not a normal, healthy bull, but a weakened, half-blinded and mentally destroyed version, whose chances of harming his tormentors is virtually nil. The bull has wet newspapers stuffed into his ears; vaseline is rubbed into his eyes to blur his vision; cotton is stuffed up his nostrils to cut off his respiration and a needle is stuck into his genitals. Also, a strong caustic solution is rubbed onto his legs which throws him off balance. This also keeps him from lying down on the ground. In addition to this, drugs are administered to pep him up or slow him down, and strong laxatives are added to his feed to further incapacitate him. He is kept in a dark box for a couple of days before he faces the ring: the purpose of this is to disorientate him. When he is let out of the box, he runs desperately towards the light at the end of the tunnel. He thinks that at last his suffering is over and he is being set free—instead, he runs into the bullring to face his killers and a jeering mob.
>
> The matador is supposed to sever the artery near the heart with one thrust of the sword—in fact, this never happens. It often takes 2-3 times before the creature is mercifully released by death. By this time, the bull's lungs and heart will be punctured and he always vomits blood. Miraculously, he sometimes attempts to rise again, and gets up on his knees, only to receive further mutilation at the hands of his tormentors. He finally gives up, goes to his knees and lies down. Even then, he is not allowed a little dignity to leave this world in peace, his ears and tail are cut off (often when he is fully conscious), and his broken, bleeding body is dragged around the ring by mules, to which he is attached by an apparatus made of wood and chains. Not content with his suffering, which must be too horrible to describe by words, the crowds boo and jeer him. They even throw empty beer cans at him. His body is then taken away to be skinned, and even then he may not be dead when this happens[32]

For obvious reasons, the activist group People for the Ethical Treatment of Animals (PETA) have also long been vocal critics of the ancient 'sport' of bullfighting. On their website they provide several sobering statistics and note that although the practice has spread over the centuries, it appears to be slowly falling out of favor amongst its fan base:

> Each year, approximately 250,000 bulls die in bullfights, an inaccurate term for events in which there is very little competition between a nimble, sword-wielding matador (Spanish for "killer") and a confused, maimed, psychologically tormented, and physically debilitated animal… According to a 2006 Gallup survey, 72 percent of Spaniards show no interest in bullfights, up from 31 percent in the 1990s. Interest in bull-fighting has also declined in Mexico and Portugal, and according to one report, officials in Beijing, China, decided not to build a bullring at a popular tourist destination for "fears of the country's image." Unfor-tunately, there are still more than 1,200 government-funded bull ranches and dozens of state-sponsored bullfighting schools in Spain. In France, bullfights are held in the cities of Nîmes, Arles, Dax, Toulouse, and Bayonne.[33]

Another form of bull torture dubbed "bull-baiting" was popular in England in the mid 1600s and into the early 1700s. The game may have developed during the court of James I of England who kept an impressive royal menagerie. James loved the bloody sport of "baiting" and had a spectator's platform built above pits where lions, bears and later bulls would be set upon by dogs for fights to the death. As we will see, James plays an interesting role in our process of stalking the herd. According to The Tower of London website:

> In later years, the variety of animals at the Tower increased and the Menagerie became a popular attraction. At the Royal Menagerie, visitors could see strange and rare beasts that they would never have seen before; The Menagerie finally closed after several incidents where the animals had escaped and attacked each other, visitors and Tower staff. The Duke of Wellington, who was Constable of the Tower, ordered the animals to leave and in 1822 they arrived at their new home in the London Zoo.[34]

After James I during Queen Anne's time, the sporting events became popular around the realm. Regularly scheduled events would feature bulls that would be staked out in the particular town's common tethered to a 25- to 30-foot rope. Dogs would be held back barking, straining on the leash waiting to attempt to immobilize the bull and as an added bonus just prior to the event, pepper would be blown into the bull's nose and eyes to enrage it further. The dogs would then be let loose to attack the bull and the blood would flow and money would change hands. (figure 24)

Another specialty type of bull-baiting was called "pinning the bull," which was where selectively bred and trained single dogs would set upon the bull, attempting to fastening its teeth firmly on the bull's broad nose. These fierce encounters year after year resulted in several breeds of highly specialized dogs such as the Old English bulldog, and ultimately spawned the American bull terrier breeds of today.

Running With The Bulls

The history of the running in front of bulls is lost to history, but most scholars agree that this organized practice probably began around the same time that bull-fighting became popular. Undoubtedly, countless times countless numbers of men had the unfortunate happenstance to find themselves running for their lives with an enraged bull snorting on their tail. Similar events may have been held in Minoan times and ancient depictions of Africans running amidst herds of Auroch would indicate this is an ancient activity.

Bullrings were built throughout Spain, and the only way to get the bulls from the corral on the edge of town to the bullring was by running them through the streets to the venue. Eventually people started running alongside the bulls. This event became more and more popular, and soon young men would dash in front of the bulls as a demonstration of machismo and fearlessness. This practice, referred to as *encierro* in Spanish*,* has grown into an important week-long event in Pamplona, Spain—the San Fermin Festival, held every year from July 6–14. The first bull running is on July 7 and is repeated on each of the subsequent mornings of the festival, starting promptly at 8 am when a rocket is lit and sent skyward. The Pamplona encierro is the most well known and has been broadcast live by RTVE, the PBS channel, for over 30 years. Ernest Hemingway attempted to romanticize the Pamplona run in his important 1926 novel *The Sun Also Rises*, though it's been recognized that the problems of the novel's two protagonists present an ironic comment on—and potentially a very deep psychological insight into—the reasons for that attempted romanticization.

There are few rules for those who take part in the run, but to participate one must be at least 18 years old, run in the same direction as the bulls, and not attempt to incite the anger of the bulls; there is also a prohibition on participation for anyone who has been drinking. The herd to be run is composed of 12 Spanish fighting bulls and three more steers that leave the corral two minutes later.| The average speed of the herd as they gallop through the streets is 15 mph and the length of the run is just under 100 yards. The course turns down four different streets before the herd is funneled into the entrance to the bullring. Here, acrobats mimic ancient Minoan acrobats in performing for the assembled crowd.

Spanish tradition says the true origin of the run began in northeastern Spain during the early 14th century. While transporting cattle in order to sell them at the market, men would try to speed the process by hurrying their cattle using tactics of fear and excitement. After years of this practice, the transportation and hurrying began to turn into a competition, as young adults would attempt to race in front of the bulls and make it safely to their pens without being overtaken. When the popularity of this practice increased and was noticed more and more by the expanding population of Spanish cities, a tradition was created and stands to this day. Not everyone can run the encierro. It requires cool nerves, quick reflexes and a good level of physical fitness. Anyone who does not have these three should not take part; it is a highly risky enterprise.[35]

Since record keeping began in 1910, 15 people have died during the run and thousands have been injured. In 2013, fifty people were taken to the local hospital, six of them gored by the bulls. (figure 25) It now appears that savvy promoters are planning bull runs for the United States. Recently seen on the NBC *Today* show, promoters explained how their idea would work, summarized here:

If you've always wanted to run with the bulls in Pamplona, Spain, but couldn't afford to take the trip, you may now get a chance. Two Americans have arranged to have similar bull runs in ten cities around the U.S. The idea seems to have caught on. Already 20,000 Americans have plunked down their $35 for the adrenaline rush that comes with running in front of a group of angry bulls that can reach speeds of 35 miles [per] hour.

Brad Scudder and Rob Dickens, the U.S. promoters, understand the appeal. "It's that thrill, the adrenaline rush that you get from putting yourself in mortal danger and then coming out the other side victorious and unscathed, " Dickens told Kerry Sanders on *Today*. "It's the real deal, and that's why I think it's getting people excited and that's why we're getting so much national attention." The bulls that will run in the U.S. won't be herded to a bullfighting ring like they are in Spain. They'll be coming from the professional rodeo circuit—and will return there once the "fun" is over.[36]

The Longest Eight Seconds in Sports

Today in the American West, rodeos continue some traditions that also echo back to ancient Minoan festivals and events held at the Coliseum in Rome. The main event is bull riding. Hands down, it is the most dangerous and potentially catastrophic sport, and bull riders are a tough breed. The sport evolved from a form of macho Mexican judging of cowboy skills known as *charreada*.

A variation of these contests was first held in Texas and California. The Rodeo Cowboy Association was created in 1936 and professional bull riding gradually became what today is a multi-billion dollar sport with the Professional Bull Riders, Inc. (PBR) drawing over 100 million total television viewers during the 2008 season. The premise is simple: stay on the back of the bucking bull for eight-seconds. Easier said than done. Bull rider Justin McBride, during the final round of the Alphatrade Nationals, rode the previously un-ridden powerhouse bull "Scene of the Crash." This eight-second ride earned him a cool $200,000, the highest amount ever awarded for riding a bull in a sport with prize purses in the hundred thousand dollar range at top events. McBride was on his way to a rodeo career that earned him over $5 million in prize money before he was forced to retire on account of injuries. He then went on to become a Country & Western singer. It's not a matter of if you'll be injured as a bull rider, it's how many times, how badly, and whether you are killed or survive with life and limbs intact.

> Bull riding has the highest rate of injury of any rodeo sport. It accounts for approximately 50% of all traumatic injuries to rodeo contestants, and the bullfighters [rodeo clowns] have the highest injury rate of any non-contestant group.[37]

As with selective breeding practices in Spain, to produce the fiercest bull for the arena, rodeo bull breeding has embraced advanced genetic breeding techniques to produce what are known in the trade as "rank" bulls. Like the cowboys attempting to ride them, the bulls are placed in competition earning points during the season. Every year there are bulls that remain un-ridden, and to draw one of these brutes strikes fear into all but the most courageous riders. There are several strains of bulls that most often produce champions, but two types stand out from the herd:

> [The] American Bucking Bull is widely considered among the best bucking bull breeds, as this line of genetics has dominated the Professional Bull Riding championship rankings as of late. Actually, Professional Bull Riding's top ten rankings are filled with this bloodline. Other highly regarded strains are Brangus Cross and *Brahman Cross*. [my emphasis]
> The Brangus Cross has a mixture of genes from both Angus and Brahman cattle. This engineered combination of genetics unites valuable traits from both parents to create one of the best bucking bull breeds. The Brangus Cross DNA recipe is favored slightly over the Angus, and the mixture creates a respectable breed that exhibits hardiness under stressful conditions…
> The parent genes of the Brahman Cross originate from India, and were introduced to the United States in the 19th century. This bloodline was the first to be developed in the U.S. as a result of crossing four different

gene strains: Gyr, Gujarat, Nelore and Krishna Valley. This DNA cocktail has evolved a string of fierce competitors in modern rodeo tournaments. Subsequent generations have improved beyond their older kin, creating a bovine that has established itself as a frontrunner in Professional Bull Riding championship discussions.[38]

Brangus bulls, a recent genetic strain started in the 1940s, are a cross between Brahman and Angus cattle. The breed was established and exploited for its aggressive hardiness. According to American Bucking Bull, Inc., with its Facebook page featuring almost 18,000 "likes," the company has been created in an effort to monitor the very best bucking bulls that livestock owners contribute every year to the sport of professional bull riding. They are integrating high-tech data and genetic manipulation into the business of producing ever-more nasty rank bulls that generate sizable potential income for the breeders:

> Originally started as the Rodeo Stock Registry by Bob Tallman in 1994, American Bucking Bull, Inc. is the official DNA registry for the bucking cattle industry. Formed in 2004, ABBI has since realized one of its key objectives of documenting the bloodlines of the most well-known and influential bucking bulls in the world. By preserving the genetic lineages of these elite bucking bovines through future generations, each year ABBI continues to register the descendants of the most famous bucking bulls of all time.[39]

And there have been some memorable bucking bulls including the infamous "Tornado" who devastated cowboys in the 1970s, and the incomparable "Bodacious," inducted into the Pro Rodeo Hall of Fame in 1999. Bodacious's bad-ass nature was the inspiration for a song by the funk-rap band "Primus":

> Perhaps no bucking bull in Pro Rodeo history was as feared as "Bodacious," a 1,900-pound cross-bred Charbray that burst upon the scene in 1992. In four years, "Bodacious" was virtually un-rideable. All muscle, the bull with the distinctive yellow coloring bucked off 127 of his 135 riders and became known for a bone-crushing style that sent many riders to the hospital, including world champions Tuff Hedeman and Terry Don West. "Bodacious" was known for his explosive exit out of the chute. He started out with such force it was not uncommon to see his belly from the top of the back of the chute. He was first ridden in 1993, and it took two years before another bull rider stayed on for eight seconds. His ability to buck riders off before they could nod their heads did not endear him to the cowboys. For his efforts, "Bodacious" was named PRCA Bull of the Year in 1994-95 and top bull of the National Finals Rodeo in 1992 and 1994-95.[40]

Professional Tricksters

There is another interesting parallel in the sport of bull riding and Spanish bullfighting—the tricksterish rodeo clown functions in a similar way to the Spanish bullfighter's assistants, the *torenos picadors* and *bandelleros*, in distracting the bull. The difference is that the assistants' job in Spanish bullfighting ultimately leads to the death of the bull, and this is not the case in rodeo. Extremely courageous and daring, rodeo clowns are without a doubt a bull rider's best friend. If the cowboy is tossed by the bull, the clown/bullfighters dart in front of the bull in an effort to draw the enraged animal's attention, in an effort to protect the vulnerable cowboy splayed on the ground.

Since this is every bit as dangerous as actually riding the bulls, rodeo clowns are the unsung heroes that have saved countless riders from devastating injury and harm. Occasionally they get too close, or are not quick enough, with disastrous results to themselves. Rodeo clowns are divided into two types, bullfighters to distract the bull and clowns who entertain the crowd, heckle the bulls. and sometimes rag on the rodeo announcers. Highly skilled, these brave athletes are trained to be able to ascertain a bull's quickness and agility and they possess lightning fast reflexes and nerves of steel. (figure 26) A number of rodeo clowns have been fatally gored or stomped to death over the years. I'd hate to be a rodeo clown's insurance agent.

> Rodeo clowns date to the beginnings of competitive rodeo in the early 1900s, when promoters hired cowboys to entertain the crowd between events or if the competition was delayed. These individuals began wearing oversized, baggy clothing and eventually developed more outlandish gear. When bull riding competition began to use ill-tempered Brahma bulls in the 1920s, the need for a person to distract the bull from fallen riders fell to the rodeo clown. The use of a barrel for protection began during the 1930s when a rodeo clown named Jasbo Fulkerson began to use a wooden barrel with a solid bottom…
>
> When not working to protect bull riders, rodeo clowns also have their own performances. Bulls are turned into the arena and the clown works with the animal, evaluated based upon the aptitude he displays in controlling and maneuvering the bull, precision in jumping the bull, contact with the bull, and handling of the barrel. Similar skills are sometimes displayed at traditional rodeos in intermission acts. A typical format is a 60- or 70-second encounter between bull and bullfighter, in which the bullfighter scores points for various maneuvers. In contrast to the older sport of bullfighting, no harm is done to the bull in rodeo bullfighting.[41]

The clown archetype is an ancient symbol that relates to the trickster in world mythology. As discussed at length in my last book, *Stalking the Tricksters,* tricksters can take many forms in many cultures, but the iconic rodeo clown may be the most fearless and athletic of all mundane modern versions of the trickster. This trick-sterish connection between premeditated human behavior and cattle may provide us with a clue to aid in our process of unraveling the cattle mutilation mystery.

With the popularity of bull riding and the continuing popularity of Spanish-style bullfighting, it appears that our bovines are exploited, bred, trained, and somewhat admired today in the early 21st century. But the deeply symbolic role of cattle in western, predominantly Christian, cultures has divided in two diver-gent directions. Humans have patiently worked with bovine genetics to create almost a thousand distinct cattle breeds bred as food sources, now accounting for over 1.3 billion head of livestock. Most of these breeds are used as simple sources of protein and dispensers of dairy products. Genetic enhancement of bulls, by contrast, has been geared toward developing an adversarial and often dangerous animal for use in bull rings and rodeos, an adaptation of these animals to fulfill the purposes of cultural symbols Bullfighting and bull riding may represent a subconscious recollection of a time when bulls were admired for their strength and virility, but the cow's religious and archetypical signifi-cance has for the most part, become lost in the modern western world. What else has been lost, and when and how, in terms of natural human regard and respect for other life forms with whom we share the earth?

Having revisited our species' ancient spiritual relationship and emotional bonds with cattle, and having seen how this relationship has devolved in modern times, we are in a better position to appreciate the potential emotional significance of this change, no doubt carried in the collective unconscious. The ancient, sacred traditions related to cattle have become blurred and forgotten in the conscious mind of the modern western world. For the most part, cattle are still considered sacred in India, but they have become a mere commodity in the West, a line item on a balance sheet of big agro-business, a source of protein and dairy products for a growing population, but nothing more than that (except for those individuals who live close to them on dairy farms and cattle ranches). Is this breakdown of the long-established spiritual tradition relating to cattle somehow related to the unexplained livestock death mystery? When and where did cattle mutilations begin, and why have these gruesome atrocities been reported *only in Christianized countries*? In Chapter Two, we will examine little-known examples of documented unexplained livestock death reports including genuine cattle mutilations that have been noted over the past 400 years. (figure 1)

Chapter One: Sources and References

1. Rifkin, Jeremy, *Beyond Beef,* Dutton Books NYC, NY 1992
2. *Rimas & Fraser Beef,* Harper Books, NYC, NY, 2008

3. McKenna, Terence, *Food of the Gods,* 1992, Bantam, NY NY
4. ibid
5. 3-27-12, Press Release, Journal Molecular Biology and Evolution, University College, London,
6. ibid
7. ibid
8. ibid
9. Cis Van Vuure, *Retracing the Aurochs.* Sofia, Bulgaria, Pensoft Publishing, 2005
10. Lhote, Henri R.U, *The Search for the Tassili Frescoes,* Hutchinson, London, 1960
11. Metropolitan Museum, New York, NY, metmuseum.org/toah/ hd/chav/hd_chav.htm
12. Rokosz', M. "History of the Aurochs in Poland," journals.cambridge.org/ 1995
13. Cooper, DJ., *Mithras,* 1996 Samuel Weiser, Inc., York Beach, Maine
14. "The Symbol Articles," Raghavan N. Iyer, M.A., D.Phil., Theosophy Trust Library
15. New York Times, 5-27-13
16. McKenna, op. cit., *Tracing the Origins of the Ancient Egyptian Cattle-Cults,* Michael Brass, 2003
17. Frazer, Sir James, T. Gaster, *New Golden Bough,* Criterion Books, NY, NY 1959
18. Paragamian/Vasilakis, *The Labyrinth of Messara,* Heraklion, Athens, 2002
19. Frazer/T. Gaster, op sit, Criterion Books, NY, NY 1959
20. Conrad, Jack Joseph, *The Horn and the Sword,* 1957, EP Dutton, NY NY
21. ibid
22. Girard, Rene *Violence and the Sacred,* John Hopkins Press, NYC NY 1972
23. ibid
24. Wisconsin State Journal, Madison, WI, 7-23-85; R. Heiden; Project Stigma
25. Beck, Roger, "Zoroaster, as perceived by the Greeks," *Encyclopedia Iranica,* NY 2003
26. Clark, Jerome, *The UFO Enclodedia Vol 3,* 1979, Omnigraphics, Detroit, MI, 1996
27. op. sit., Frazer/T. Gaster, *New Golden Bough,* Sir James, Criterion Books, NY, NY 1959
28. Pope Pius V, Bullarum Romanorum Pontificum, Vol. 4, 2nd Part, 1567
29. Miles Johnson, Financial Times, 2-11-13
30. spanish-fiestas.com
31. stopbullfighting.org
32. PETA homepage
33. Historic Royal Palaces, /hrp.org.ok/toweroflondon...menageriehistory
34. Government of Navarre, turismo website
35. Today Show. com, NBC, 8-8-13
36. Mullen, F. "Rodeo injuries: Mess w/ the Bull, get the horns," Reno Gazette-Journal, 6-21-05
37. exclusivegenetics.com
38. American Bucking Bull, Inc.
39. Pro Rodeo Hall of Fame
40. Hollman, H, "Clowning around in arena..." Decatur Daily, Decatur, IL, 3-26-07
41. stopbullfighting.org
42. PETA homepage
43, Government of Navarre, turismo website
44. todayshow.com, NBC, 8-8-13
45. Mullen, F. "Rodeo injuries: Mess w/ the Bull, get the horns," Reno Gazette-Journal, 6-21-05
46. exclusivegenetics.com
47. American Bucking Bull, Inc.
48. Pro Rodeo Hall of Fame
49. Hollman, H, "Clowning around in arena..." Decatur Daily, Decatur, IL, 3-26-07

Figure 1
(credit: Asya Pereltsvaig/geocurrents.info)

Figure 2
Bos Primegenius, or aurochs, a now extinct type of wild ox.
(credit: Charles Hamilton Smith, 16th Century)

Figure 3
Undulate dung-loving psychotropic cubensis mushrooms.
(credit: Mara & Alexey/travelphotoreport.com)

Figure 4
Çatalhöyük, a 9,500-year-old prehistoric village with a fascination for cattle.
(credit: James Mellart/McGraw-Hill)

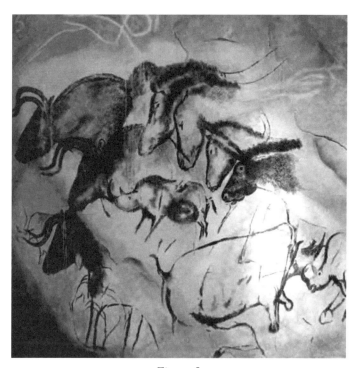

Figure 5
30,000 year-old depictions of cattle discovered in the Chauvet Caves, France in 1994.
(credit: artisanhistory.com)

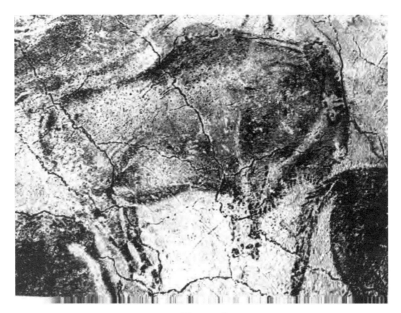

Figure 6
Extinct bison beautifully rendered in the Altimira Caves may be
older than Chauvet images. (credit: greenguidespain.com)

Figure 7
Laas Gaal paintings also show cattle in ceremonial robes and ceremonial beaded collars.
(credit: megalithic.co.uk)

Figure 8
Detail of decorated bull with ceremonial collar at Laas Gaal cave in Somaliland.
(circa. 18,000 B.C.) (credit: archive.cyark.org)

Figure 9
Summarian depiction of Gilgmesh and Enkidu killing the "Bull of Heaven,"
(circ. 2,000 B.C.). (credit: Conrad, Jack/Horn and the Sword)

Figure 10
Orphaned calves are sometimes wet-nursed in India.
(credit: LukesCorner.net)

Figure 11
Nandi bull shrine and the Shiva temple at Mahabalipuram, India.
(credit: quickiwiki.com circa 1872)

Figure 12
Shiva (as Rudra) is considered to be the Indian God of cattle.
(credit: blogheykrishna.blogspot.com)

Figure 13
Late Neolithic Tassili-n-Ajiir, Algeria, rock painting of a Shamanic "mushroom man."
(credit: Kat McKenna/ Food of the Gods)

Figure 14
Bas relief of the Egyptian goddess Hathor from Deir el Bahri, Egypt.
(credit: Vicky Metafora)

Figure 15
Statue of the Egyptian "Apis Bull." (credit: Louvre Museum, Paris France)

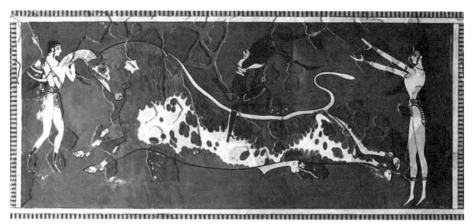

Figure 16
Minoan athletes performing the bull-leaping ritual called the taurokatharpsi fresco.
From palace of Knossos. (circa. 1,500 B.C.) (credit: Wikipedia)

Figure 17
The Minoan Minotaur (credit: British Museum, London UK)

Figure 18
The Egyptian goddess Hathor, the "celestial cow."
(credit: Jack Conrad/*Horn and the Sword,* 1957)

Figure 19
Michaelangelo's horned statue of Moses, Church of San Pietro, Rome.
(credit: Church of San Pietro, Rome)

Figure 20
Could this be a depiction of an ancient "cattle mutilation" at Tassili-n-Ajiir, Algeria?
(credit: Henri Lhote)

Figure 21
Could this be the earliest ever artistic depiction of a cattle mutilation? Note strange
being at the head of the fallen cow and the figure at the back-end of the animal.
(credit: Henri Lhote)

Chapter 2
Before That
Horse Was Snipped

For years I have had my feelers out for media stories and other potential documentation of so-called high-strange mutilation reports that predate the acknowledged 'Typhoid Mary' of all publicized mutilation cases—that of Snippy the Horse—September 1967, in the San Luis Valley of south-central Colorado. Widely acknowledged as the first publicized "cattle mutilation," even though the case featured a horse, named Lady, the "Snippy" case has become legendary among unexplained livestock death researchers. But Snippy was not the first. Even the most ardent followers of the mutilation subject are hard-pressed to come up with reports that predate 1967. If you research diligently, however, you will discover that a number of cases have been documented and publicized since as long ago as the early 1600s.

There was no mention of any animal mutilation report or case prior to the early 1970s in "Operation Animal Mutilation: Report of the District Attorney, First Judicial District State of New Mexico," released by ex-FBI agent Kenneth Rommel in June 1980. The former fed's report, an apparent effort to debunk the mystery, focused primarily on 1979 New Mexico mutilation cases that were equivocal. The lack of historical precedence and thorough background research by Rommel on the subject of pre-Snippy-era reports is not surprising given the research required to uncover the precedents. But the entire phenomenon would have been taken far more seriously

had its long history been recognized in 1980. The numerous historical examples that follow in this chapter illustrate that this mystery has been with us for decades, probably hundreds, and perhaps thousands, of years.

As we saw in Chapter One, cattle were venerated for their strength, adaptability, and vital role in supplying meat and dairy products for humans for millennia. Cattle were raised up, exalted, held in reverence and their blood was thought to be a magical elixir and employed for a variety of ritualistic purposes around the world adapted as cultures changed and developed. As an example, Christianity replaced the Mithraic "Blood of the Bull" with the more practical, "Blood of the Lamb." With the passing of time, this sacred, spiritual relationship gradually gave way to more practical, worldly, viewpoints related to physical human sustenance and material wealth and status. The Hindis of India are the only modern culture that has managed to hold on to the ancient view of cattle as sacred animals, but, as we have seen, this present-day Indian view of cattle is changing. By comparison in the West, we have "Exploding Cow" card games— "There's something magical about blowing up cows"—and cattle abduction desk lamps showing a UFO sucking up an unfortunate bovine.

"It tendeth toward some fireworks"

In what could possibly be the very first documented reference to livestock mutilations on record we have the following excerpt from a letter sent to mutilation researcher Tom Adams/Project Stigma by a reader of his *Stigmata* publication, Elizabeth Hilts from Regina, Saskatchewan:

> The sheep incident[s] I mentioned in my private book of "Oddities" appears to derive from a diary (or other personal papers) from the court of James I of England. The quotation is:

>> "10 February 1606: The minds of men are much troubled with a strange accident lately fallen out, which yet by no means can be discovered, about the City of London and some of the shires adjoining. Whole slaughters of sheep have been made, in some places to number 100, in others less, where nothing is taken from the sheep but their tallow and some inward parts, the whole carcasses and fleece remaining still behind. Of this sundry conjectures, but most agree that it tendeth towards some fireworks."

The above quote appears in: *A Jacobean Journal, being a record of Those Things Most Talked About...1603–1606*, by G.G. Harrison, London, Routledge, rev. 1946, page 279. The original source was: *The Court and Times of James I*, edited from the Collections of Thomas Birch, by the author of the Memoirs of

Sophia Dorothea, in two volumes, London, England 1848 (vol.1, page 44–45).

To help put these events into a cultural context, what was happening around London during this time period in early 1606? James the First had put into motion the third Church of England's translation of the Bible in 1604 and the fallout might have inspired a zealous plot to kill the king. An attempt to blow up the House of Lords while James visited was squashed on November 5th, 1605, when Guy Fawkes and seven conspirators were arrested and subsequently tortured before the bomb could be detonated. Fawkes was a conspirator in what has become known as 'The Gunpowder Plot' of 1605 to assassinate James I and place nine-year-old Elizabeth on the throne as Catholic head-of-state. This was an effort to gain more religious tolerance from the Crown. After his apprehension, Fawkes confessed, and on January 31st, 1606, he leapt from the stage upon which he was to be hung, breaking his neck to avoid the agony of hanging and to defy the mutilation planned for his drawn and quartered corpse. (figure 1) The principle Jesuit in England was also convicted and executed for his role in the affair.

Back then, getting caught trying to kill the king had serious repercussions. First the convicted were hung almost to the point of death while they were being emasculated and disemboweled. Then they were beheaded and chopped into four pieces. These quartered body parts were then sent around the country by the court as a public warning.

The accepted form of justice and punishment in the 15th century could be seen as an example of unceremonious death and mutilation. It's OK for the king to do it, but if something unknown and mysterious starts a bloody rampage out in the countryside, perhaps something more sinister is operative. Perhaps rather than dismiss the phenomenon, we should pay close attention to waves of live-stock deaths that are occurring in our modern culture. It's noteworthy that today the enigmatic, mustachioed smile frozen on the iconic Fawkes "Occupy Movement" mask is emblematic of some deep undercurrents in the West. I'm not surprised that Guy Fawkes Day is still observed in England, where traditionally his effigy is burned on a bonfire to the accompaniment of a fireworks display. "…it tendeth towards some fireworks," indeed! Kind of reminds me of the Burning Man gathering each summer in Nevada. (figure 2)

And what else was going on down the cobbled streets of London that cold winter of 1606? Shakespeare was putting the finishing touches on a short play called "Macbeth." The play is a sordid tale of arrogance, madness, and death that illustrates the corrosive, psychological and political effects of violence and murder chosen as a way to fulfill ambition and thirst for power. Lady Macbeth, in a waking dream, can't seem to get the spot of the King's blood off her hand; she rubs and rubs and says, "Here's the smell of blood still: All the perfumes of Arabia will not sweeten this little hand." Shakespeare's maudlin insight could be applied to the mysterious livestock deaths that were occurring during the time-period when he was writing Macbeth: "And thy blade and gouts of blood, which were not so before. There is no such thing: It is the bloody business that informs thus to mine eyes…It will have blood; they say, blood will have blood."

The controversy over Macbeth still exists today for it probably has more superstitions surrounding the work than any other western theatrical work. Allegedly there is a curse on the play:

> Rumor has it that Shakespeare used genuine rituals to create the first scene of [Macbeth] act IV, in which the audience observes the weird sisters dancing, chanting and mixing a peculiar concoction in their cauldron. Some people believe that the real witches of Shakespeare's time were displeased with the theatrical representation of their rituals and, subsequently, placed a curse on the play…In fact, it is rumored to have struck the premiere performance of the play. It is believed that Shakespeare had to take to the stage as Lady Macbeth, because the young man who had been cast in the role suddenly became very ill and, subsequently, died.[1]

Another version of the story of the premier performance mentions that an actor was accidentally knifed when a real blade was used instead of as prop knife. Orson Welles, Charlton Heston and others experienced catastrophes in their lives during or just after performing in Macbeth. In 1849, rioting broke out during a performance of the play and 20 New Yorkers were killed during the violence.

Abraham Lincoln allegedly read the play the night before he was assassinated at Ford's Theater. Whether this curse is real or not doesn't appear to matter as the superstitions surrounding the play endure. Today it is still considered bad luck to read lines from the play or utter the very words "Macbeth" while inside a theater.

King James I was an interesting fellow. (figure 3) He ruled during turbulent times in Europe and upon the death of his mother, Mary Queen of Scots, he ascended the throne of Scotland in 1567 when he was only 13 months old. Upon the death of Elizabeth I, in 1603, being the next in line of royal succession, he became King of England and united England, Scotland and Ireland. At that time England's debt was a staggering £400,000.

One of his first tasks upon taking the throne was prompted by the puritanical revolution that was sweeping post-Protestant reformation Europe when he commissioned a new translation of the Bible in 1603 to "resolve issues with different translations then being used." Completed in 1611, the "King James version" is still in wide used today. But he oversaw several important translation changes that may be worthy of note for our stalking of the herd. It would appear that the James Version has literally taken or changed most references to cattle as sacred animals.

There is some debate among scholars as to James' sexual persuasion as he appeared to enjoy the company of men over women. Although he did marry Anne, the daughter of Fredrick II of Denmark, it was not a union made out of love but one of political stability. On Anne's tomb she referred to as his "consort." His views on women and the weakness of their spiritual character is reflected in his writings and decrees:

> James I of England expressed the view, in his numerous texts on this subject, that females were intrinsically frailer than men, making it easier for them to be trapped by the Devil into doing his work. The Serpent's deceiving of Eve at the beginning, he asserted, had given Satan ready access to women ever since…To the satisfaction of the ruling classes, women had apparently graduated to the embodiment of depravity in the eyes of the public. Furthermore, women having allegedly entered into a pact, an agreement with Satan, and receiving intimate pleasure amongst other things as their reward, would not the Devil require certain subversive acts to be undertaken in return?
>
> This consideration allowed the authorities to increasingly supply this 'manufactured intolerance' of women, which they had fed the remainder of the populace. They pointed to the new scourge of syphilis, which had arisen. This linked female sensuality to an act of great evil against mankind. Here was an illness, painful and often fatal, caught through the agency of a woman. There was also, at this time, a startling increase everywhere in the amount of 'sexually deviant' crimes against morality, which were firmly placed by most establishments at the door of the female sex. The Parliament of Rouen, for example, began to hear frequent cases of adultery, buggery, sodomy and incest. This type of crime increased from less than 1% of the court's business in 1548-9 to *10% in 1604-6.* [my emphasis][2]

Daemonologie

It is interesting to note that during the wave of livestock mutilations around London, there was a marked upsurge in reports of sexual perversion as it was defined during the times. The courts must have wondered what in the hell was going on. Speaking of "hell," it should be noted that James was keenly interested in the black arts and those who practiced them, and he is known to have had a fascination with the practice of witchcraft. In 1597, he wrote a dialogue divided into three books titled: *Daemonologie* and begins Book One with the following observation that the works and workers of Satan must be hunted down and stamped out, thus giving royal sanction to the practice of witch hunting. (figure 4) He was undoubtedly influenced by the sensational North Berwick witch trials he attended in 1590 while still in Scotland:

"The fearful abounding at this time in this country, of these detestable slaves of the Devil, the Witches or enchanters, hath moved me (beloved reader) to dispatch in post, this following treatise of mine… to resolve the doubting…both that such assaults of Satan are most certainly practiced, and that the instrument thereof merits most severely to be punished."[3]

He continues on in this Jacobin vein laying out what to look for while witch hunting with an emphasis on the role that "daft wives" may play and the activities they might perform when practicing the darker arts:

I mean by such kind of charms as commonly daft wives use, for healing of forspoken [bewitched] goods, for preserving them from evil eyes, by knitting…sundry kinds of herbs to the hair or tails of the goods; by curing the worm, by stemming of blood, by healing of horse-crooks… or doing of such like innumerable things by words, without applying anything meet to the part offended, as mediciners do.[4]

James institutionalized witch hunting with a decree issued in 1604, just prior to the outbreak of sheep mutilations in southern England. He wrested control for the legal process of trying witches from the church to the court and he personally "supervised the torture of women accused of being witches."

James' 1604 Witchcraft Act transferred trials of suspected witches from the church to the royal courts. The "Witchcraft Act of 1604" ordered execution for the first offense of "raising evil spirits," was never used during the reign of James. In fact, the records show that it was only used once in 1645 and abolished in 1951. It was clear that while James feared a nightmarish death and evil, he recognized that it was better to recognize a witch and stay away from them rather than to commit murder.[5]

During the same month he penned the enigmatic descriptions of mysterious sheep mutilations, February, 1606, the sensational Pepwell witch trial was winding up. The trial absolved the accused three witches (one male and two sisters) and placed the blame for fabricating the charges on her accusers who were found guilty of false accusations against the Pepwells…

[P]rosecution of the Gunters finally commenced in February 1606, when Sir Edward Coke exhibited an information against Brian and Anne Gunter in the Court of Star Chamber. The charge was that the two had conspired "by false and wicked devices to bring [Gregory and the two Pepwells] into infamy and cause them to be reputed and taken for witches and there upon also to cause them to be indicted and arraigned for witchcraft." …Unfortunately, we do not have a formal record of the court's decision because most decrees of the court have been lost.' It is likely, however, that Brian Gunter was convicted and fined (although not mutilated) [sic], while Anne, having confessed to the king and the court, apparently received a royal pardon and a dowry. Much more important than any sentence, however, was the discrediting of a counterfeit possession and the demonstrable proof, so often lacking even in mere acquittals for witchcraft, that an alleged practice of witchcraft had never taken place. The trial of the Gunters in Star Chamber did much more to support the arguments of the witchcraft skeptics such as Reginald Scot than had the acquittal of Elizabeth Gregory and Agnes Pepwell at the Berkshire assizes. It also strengthened the emerging skepticism of the new king of England. Once the scourge of Scottish witches, he took particular delight during the rest of his reign in England in *exposing culprits who brought fraudulent charges against witches.* [my emphasis][6]

It is also interesting to note that the entire scare surrounding identifying potential witches in the community may have been a device intended for societal control. Were these waves of witch trials part of a premeditated effort of "manufactured myth"?

> …[T]he 'witch' was both created and killed off by the English, Scottish and the majority of the European authorities, when they considered it efficacious for their own aims, emphasizes that this figure was simply a 'manufactured myth'. Furthermore, the view that the witch was the product of the labeling and scapegoating perspective undertaken by the regimes at this time, can clearly be consistently supported.[7]

James I of England is credited with many accomplishments but the accomplishments with the most influence are less well known. His 22-year reign lasted from 1603 to 1625, when he suffered a stroke and succumbed to dysentery and the effects of arthritis, gout, kidney stones and probable alcohol abuse.[8]

For the next 250 to 300 years, there is little or no evidence that mysterious livestock deaths were noted in the historical record of the west or east. Aside from some good old fashioned "bull baiting," life was fairly quiet on the cattle front until the 1860s when *rinderpest* decimated European cattle herds. We'll cover cattle diseases in Chapter 12.

I've seen references to possible outbreaks of livestock mutilations in the 17th century, but nothing concrete with references, and we need to jump all the way forward in time to the late 18th and into the early 20th century, before we begin to see some form of documentation of unexplained livestock deaths. And not all blood-based mysterious phenomena feature dead bodies. The following strange events were documented in California:

The land of "fruits and nuts" has had its share of bizarre events reported over the years, but the following claims fall into my beyond the 'head-scratcher' category. A strange, truly inexplicable, story was published in the July 24, 1851 edition of the *San Francisco Herald* that covered an alleged event that was said to have occurred at a U.S. Army Base near Vallejo, California—located on the Sacramento River. (figure 5) It was reported that while the base's personnel were mustered on the parade ground, "blood and thin slices of fresh meat showered down on the parade ground. The post surgeon was quoted...to the effect that the meat was neatly sliced into pieces about one-eighth-inch thick"[9]

Sometime in early June 1869 a second fall of meat was reported in Santa Clara County and reported in the San Francisco newspapers. And yet another deluge of meat fell from the sky eight year later in Los Nietos, California, on August 1, 1869. These weird events can't be equated with any known livestock mutilations, but I feel they are worthy of note. Where exactly did the hundreds of pounds of shredded, bloody flesh that fell from the sky covering the J. Hudson Ranch and the other two locations originate? All three reports feature practically identical descriptions of the meat. The third event was well-documented and was a sensation at the time:

In three minutes time, two acres were covered with wafer-thin flakes up to four inches in width. The flesh was bloody and apparently fresh when it fell, but seemed to become putrid very quickly. The pieces had fine black bristles on one edge. The sky was clear and the sun shining. No buzzards are mentioned by witnesses (explainers usually suggest "buzzard puke" in falls of this nature.) The editor of the Los Angeles News observed in his issue of August 3rd, 1869: "That the meat fell, we cannot doubt. Even the parsons of the neighborhood are willing to vouch for that. Where it comes from we cannot even conjecture."[10]

Blood falls are a little known but prevalent phenomenon that has been reported since ancient times. The earliest record comes from Homer's *Iliad,* in which Zeus makes it rain blood "as a portent of slaughter." Pliny and Plutarch also mention rains of blood and flesh. In 1870, a few months after the second California meat fall, a rain of blood was reported in Sulphur Springs, Texas, where the first mutilations of 1975 were a January prelude to the slaughter that would ensue around the west that year.

Charles Fort Coins the Term

No stranger to weird falls of unexplained objects from the heavens, protoparanormal investigator Charles Fort was born 1874 in Albany, New York, and during the first half of the Twentieth Century he combed obsessively through newspaper morgues for strange and inexplicable accounts, including the meat falls. Fort spent years haunting the New York Public Library's extensive newspaper and book collections, and uncovered thousands of odd stories and fantastic claims from journalistic sources around the world. Few examples of the bizarre and inexplicable escaped his attention; fish and object falls from the sky (such as the California "meat falls,"), bizarre disappearances, crypto-creatures, spontaneous combustion cases, synchronistic events, weird aerial object sightings, etc. The amazing list of anomalies he compiled is bewildering—even to this day. Fort was able to amass an impressive compilation of strangeness that he presented in an eclectic writing style that still fascinates and puzzles readers. (figure 6) The "Fortean" events, as these types of unexplainable events have now been dubbed, were featured in his four groundbreaking books: *The Book of the Damned* published in 1919, *New Land*s (1923), *Lo!* (1931) and *Wild Talents* (1932). Re-reading *Wild Talents* and *Lo!* I found quite a number of unsolved mutilation cases that are as strange-sounding today as they must have been back in the 18th, 19th and early 20th centuries when the events allegedly occurred. There is a 200-year gap in mutilation accounts through the late 15th, 16th, and 17th centuries, and one must wonder if these types of occurrences were documented at the time but have been lost. Perhaps evidence of these events still lies in journals, dusty diaries, and obscure official reports. The following alleged accounts were published in *Lo!* and *Wild Talents*:

> In the month of May, 1810, something appeared at Ennerdale, near the border of England and Scotland, and killed sheep, not devouring them, sometimes seven or eight of them a night, but biting into their jugular veins and sucking the blood…and the losses by sheep farmers were so serious that the whole region was aroused. It became a religious duty to hunt this marauder [my italics]…Milking, cutting of hay, feeding of stock were neglected. For more details, see Chambers Journal, 81-4370…[11]
>
> …For almost four months, in the year 1874, beginning upon January 8th, a killer was abroad, in Ireland. In *Land and Water*, March 7, 1874, a correspondent writes that he had heard of depredations by a wolf, in Ireland, where the last native wolf had been killed in the year 1712. According to him, a killer was running wild, in Cavan, slaying as many as 30 sheep in one night. There is another account in *Land and Water*, March 28 [1874]. Here a correspondent writes that in Cavan, sheep had been killed in a way that led to the belief that the marauder was not a dog. This correspondent knew of 42 instances, in three town lands [sic], in which sheep had been similarly killed—throats cut and blood sucked, but no flesh eaten…[12]
>
> Then, in the issue of April 11th [1874]…came the news that we had

been expecting. The killer had been shot. It had been shot by Archdeacon Magennis, at Lismoreville, and was only a large dog. [Then] the shooting of [another] large dog shot, and the relief of the farmers, who believed that this one was the killer—still another dog shot, and supposed to be the killer—the killing of sheep continuing. The depredations were so great as to be described as 'terrible losses for poor people.' It was not definitely said that something was killing sheep vampirishly, but that 'only a piece was bitten off, and no flesh sufficient for a dog ever eaten.' (my emphasis) [13] (figure 7)

Fort goes on in this descriptive manner for several long pages in *Wild Talents*, listing example after example of strange, unsolved livestock deaths of mostly sheep, but also rabbits and chickens—all reported mutilated in the UK. Then he notes the "sheep slaying mystery of Badminton" in 1905 that was covered in the *Gloucester Jo*urnal, November 4th, and yet another outbreak of sheep slayings was reported in the *Bristol Mercury* of November 25, and still other outbreaks of mysteriously slain sheep—reported near Gravesend—*London Daily Mail*, December 19th, 1905. In all cases the perpetrator(s) were never caught, nor suspects identified.

Journalist/author John Keel was taken to task by researcher Jerome Clark in Clark's *UFO Encyclopedia*, where Clark attempted to refute Keel's assertions that Fort had been writing about true mutilations. Clark argues that the 1905 cases Fort reported were not true mutilations:

> "[Keel] characterized a 1905 British episode as a 'wave of mysterious mutilations' when all available evidence suggests the depredations of wild animals; the principle victims, sheep, "were devoured, all but fleece and bones" (Fort 1941)—not mutilated.[14]

Evidently, Clark missed the earlier 19th-century cases where it was clearly stated that the victimized animals were not eaten. Fort is very specific in his accounts, and in many cases the animals were not devoured as Clark implies they were by citing only the later 1905 wave of sheep deaths. One has to wonder why an esteemed UFO historian such as Clark would argue against all of Fort's reports when it is clear there are more than a number of cases that counter his assertion.

The UK animal mutilation cases continued and in the following account chickens were the chosen victims of wanton mischief, coincident with some interesting almost paranormal elements. In January 1906, this very bizarre sequence of events was reported in the British *Louth and North Lincolnshire News*. It was claimed that a servant girl working for the White family of Binbrook was rushed to the local hospital after her clothes inexplicably caught fire while she was sweeping the kitchen floor. Then the farmer's chickens were attacked, killed, and mutilated over the course of the next several nights. Fort describes the carnage in *Wild Talents*:

> Something was killing chickens, in the farm-yard, and in the hen-house. All were killed in the same way. A vampirish way? Their throats were torn. 'Out of 250 fowls, Mr. White says that he has only 24 left. They have all been killed in the same weird way. The skin around the neck, from head to breast, has been pulled off, and the windpipe drawn from its place and snapped. The fowl house has been watched night and day, and whenever examined, four or five birds would be found dead.[15]

Strange reports of 19th- and early 20th-century mutilations are not found exclusively in the British Isles; other countries experienced outbreaks of unsolved mutilations of livestock—including cattle. The following newspaper account was published in the February 8, 1909 *Ontario Daily Record*. Re-discovered by Canadian researcher Dwight Whalen, the article was titled: "Cattle Killed in a Cruel Manner—Elgin Farmer Suffers by a Malignant Enemy."

> St. Thomas, Ontario, February 7, [1909] — Tom Gilbert, a well-known farmer residing near Fingal, has lost several of his cattle since Christmas, and 11 were affected in the same way. Several became affected this week and a couple died. Examination by veterinaries from St. Thomas found that a sharp instrument had been forced down their throats, terribly lacerating them, and had almost severed their windpipes. The remainder of the cattle injured will all die, six having already gone. Mr. Gilbert has no idea who the offending parties are. The authorities are working on the case and have found a broken pick-handle sharpened to a point and covered with blood which may have been one of the instruments of torture used.[16]

One has to wonder how many events of this type have occurred that have been lost to history. Charles Fort's contribution to our understanding of these mysterious occurrences (as they were perceived and dealt with in the late 19th and early 20th centuries) provides a fascinating journey back into a time where these events were mostly ignored and hidden from the public, invisible to the culture-at-large. Likely the subject of "blood" and "mutilations" accounts for this repression of information, and it's not surprising that Fort pondered whether some kind of "vampiric" forces might be at loose in the world. Citing an unsolved mutilation outbreak in Africa in *Wild Talents*, Fort wondered if there might be "vampires other than vampire bats" haunting the pastures, fields, and forests of the planet.

If blood be desired, why not the blood of cattle and sheep? According to many stories there have been unexplained attacks upon human beings, also there have been countless outrages upon other animals…[I]n the Kenya Colony, Africa, baboons sometimes mutilate cattle. I'd not say that the case against them has been made out. London, *Daily Mail*, May 18, 1925—that for some years, an alarming epidemic of sheep-slashing and cattle ripping has been breaking out, in the month of April, on Kenya stock ranches. Natives are blamed, but then it was learned that their cattle, too, had been attacked…The wounds were long deep cuts, as if vicious slashes with a knife; but it was explained that baboons kill by ripping with their thumbnails…[17]

No baboons were ever observed perpetrating these attacks, nor were baboon tracks ever found at the crime scenes. The killings in Kenya continued unabated for the entire month before ceasing suddenly, for no reason. In his usual laconic manner, Fort doesn't seem to care one way or another and moves on to the next page.

Hindi Horse-Slasher Convicted: 1903

Another interesting case Fort cites features what may be *the first (and possibly only known) arrest and conviction of an alleged perpetrator of a livestock mutilation.* I find it especially intriguing that the alleged attacker was of Indian Hindi descent. In this case the victims were horses. In India cattle are considered sacred and not slaughtered as a food source, and the alleged perpetrator was an educated lawyer and a Christian clergyman. It's interesting that Fort calls the case a "cattle mutilation," yet the initial animals victimized were officially cited as horses. This curious misapplication of the designation 'cattle' to horse mutilation is also found in the pivotal "first publicized…cattle mutilation" of modern time, that of Snippy the Horse, and this interesting juxtaposition of terms might provide a clue to the process of the meme's dissemination out into the culture-at-large. In *Wild Tal*ents, Fort wrote:

> The most widely known case of *cattle-mutilation* [my italics] is that which involved a young lawyer, George Edalji, son of a Hindu, who was a clergyman in the village of Wyrley, Staffordshire, England. The first of a series of outrages occurred upon the night of February 2, 1903. A valuable *horse* [my italics] was ripped. Then, at intervals, up to August 27th, there were mutilations of horses, cows and sheep. Suspicion was directed to Edalji, because of anonymous letters, accusing him. After the mutilation of a horse, August 27th, Edalji was arrested. The police searched his house, and, according to them, found an old coat, upon which were bloodstains. In the presence of Edalji's parents and his sister, the police said that there were horse hairs [19 in total] found upon this

coat…The police said that shoes worn by Edalji exactly fitted tracks in the field, where the horse had been mutilated…The case against Edalji convinced a jury, which found him guilty, and he was sentenced to seven years, penal servitude.[18]

Edalji's parents steadfastly maintained their son's innocence and none other than Sir Arthur Conan Doyle (the creator of the detective Sherlock Holmes) championed his innocence. (figure 8) In his book *Great Stories of Real Life* (George Newnes, London, UK, 1935), Doyle points out that the parents never saw the alleged horse hairs said by police to have been on their son's coat and that by the time police investigated the mutilation crime scene, dozens of people had left footprints at the site. It is probable that the convicted Hindi horse slasher may have been innocent after all. Doyle's publicity in the media had a definite impact as Edalji's case became reviewed by the authorities. According to Fort:

> …[B]ecause of Doyle's disclosures, the government appointed a committee to investigate, and the report of this committee was that Edalji had been wrongfully convicted…According to a reconsideration…the slasher of *cattle*, [my italics] of Wyrley, remained uncaught. In the summer of 1907, in the same region, again there was a slashing…Aug.22, 1907—a *horse* mutilated, near Wyrley…Five nights later, two horses, in another field, were slashed so that they died. September 8—*horse* slashed, at Brentwood, Staffordshire… For about a month injuries to horses continued to be reported.[19] [my emphasis]

I am convinced this juxtaposition of horse for cow is important. I sense that there is some sort of collective trigger that is impacted by this confusion of livestock descriptions, and I will address this subject later in Chapter Three.

Fortean investigator and author Nick Redfern grew up in the Wyrley area and remembers hearing stories about the Edalji affair while growing up. Taking an interest in the case, he wrote an extensive article about the strange events, and he points out several intriguing crypto-zoological theories about the Edalji case that were proposed by Staffordshire locals and even Edalji himself:

> From time to time, despite its age, and the fact that as time passes it becomes more and more forgotten, the story of George Edalji still surfaces within the pages of books and magazines; however, there is one particularly intriguing, yet very seldom discussed, aspect of the controversy—namely, its deep and undeniable links to cryptozoology and exotic animals.
>
> When the Great Wyrley horse-maiming was at its height, a number of very odd animal-based theories for the attacks began to surface

amongst superstitious local folk, one being that the attacker was a man disguised as a cow or a horse! Another suggested that the culprit was a great bird of prey, and a third mused upon the idea that the killer was some form of 'malicious aviator'—animal-based or otherwise.

Then there were the strange revelations of George Edalji himself, who claimed to have been told by a confidante that the horse-killings were the result of someone releasing into the area late at night a number of highly aggressive wild boar. Supposedly, the notoriously bad-tempered beasts would seek out the horses, commit their atrocious and bloodthirsty acts, and then, under cover of darkness, return to the safety of their hidden lair. Edalji admitted to not being particularly impressed by such a tale, but related it for what it was worth—or not. And, of course, one has to wonder how on Earth someone would have the ability to train such wild animals, have them attack specific targets, and finally convince them to repeatedly return home afterwards, rather than enjoying their freedom in the wilds of Staffordshire!

Regardless of whether or not this particular story has any merit, it is a fact that wild boar do roam the depths of the very nearby Cannock Chase woods.[20]

Murder Down Under: 1902

Here are more examples of other historical reports publicized by the media around the world prior to the Snippy case. Australian researcher Michael Smith has spent considerable time researching newspapers for odd bits of mutilation-related arcana, and he has uncovered a number of intriguing early and unexplained livestock death reports worthy of consideration. One article, from the October 18, 1902 edition of the *Brisbane Courier*, may be the oldest documented Australian cattle mutilation case on record:

> Reports have been received from the country at various times of cattle having been found with their tongues cut out, and the supposition has been that this mutilation has been inflicted by swagsmen and travelers who have come across the beasts dying from thirst and starvation, and have brutally cut out the tongues to secure a meal.
>
> The Chief Inspector of Police has, however, received a report from a mounted police patrol, which gives a much happier solution. This man, it appears, had been called in by a station-owner who had found quite a number of his cattle lying about dead with the tongues cut out. It was noticed in each case that there were no marks of the animals having been shot or otherwise killed, though dead when found. Several had perished in creeks and gully holes.
>
> An examination of the heads showed that the tongues had not been

removed in the ordinary way, through the gullet, but had been drawn through the jaws. It was also noticed that the lips and nose had in most cases been gnawed. One beast, apparently only just dead, was found with the tongue protruding through the teeth, and one-half of the member gone. Returning, the next day the police officer saw that the whole tongue had disappeared, and from his observations he came to the conclusion that in this and the other cases, which had come under his notice, either iguanas or bush rats were responsible for the mutilation of the bodies. Consultation with an experienced stockman in the same locality confirmed this.[21]

More modern Australia cases will be scrutinized later on, but a few of our best-referenced pre-Snippy mutilation reports occurred "down under." Another series of unexplained mutilation reports visited the sheep stations two decades later in the 1920s. A thorough examination of obscure Australian newspaper archives will undoubtedly uncover possible cases from the early 20th century. (figure 9) The mutilation phenomenon appears to be a widespread mystery, and I sense that the role of the media may supply clues to key cases that may be worth noting. Here's a good example: The following story is from ranching operations near Lismore, Victoria. Titled "Cattle Slasher." It describes a 1953 outbreak that appears to feature many familiar descriptions of the disfigurements reported in thousands of North American cases 20 years later:

> Police expect the early arrest of a "full moon maniac," who, for three years, has mutilated cattle at Koonorigan, near Lismore. The maniac has cost farmers thousands of pounds by slashing the udders, hindquarters, and tails of cows. Cutting out their tongues. Carving flesh from their sides. Poisoning them. One farmer has lost 11 cows worth more than £250 in the last three years.
>
> Farmers believe that the maniac may work at the time of time of full moon because his madness is then at its peak. Most of the slashed cattle were found dead in outlying paddocks at the full moon."[22]

David Rees of the British Manchester Aerial Phenomena Investigative Team sent researcher Tom Adams/Project Stigma the following excerpt from *Starburst Magazine*, Volume 1 No. 2 (Jadwin House, London, England).

> I've done a bit of research on the history of Australian SF [Science-fiction] movies and discovered what must be the first SF movie ever made anywhere. It was called "Haunted Billabong" and appears to have been about the strange mutilation of sheep on a station [ranch] in Connabarabran. It was made in 1911 and was actually shot in the old

Padstow Studios in Sydney, which have long since been demolished.

From what I can gather, the sheep were mutilated by visitors from outer space, and this is only revealed at the end of the movie. Before that, it was assumed that it was the work of rabid dingoes, but at the end you learn that a flying saucer had landed in the billabong and was using it as a base.

Needless to say, all surviving prints of the film have vanished, but I got this info from an old paper which reviewed the movie. I dug around a bit and found in the Archive a shot of the director, Tom Jackson. I think it's all that survives of the movie.

Bruce G. Kennedy

Yagoona, Australia[23]

Both David Perkins and I have conducted an extensive search of the Australian film archives and film history lists and can find absolutely no mention of "Haunted Billabong" or the alleged director, "Tom Jackson." A search for a Padstow Studios in Sydney also came up blank. During the emerging phase of Australian movie making, during the first ten years of the 20th Century, it seems as if Melbourne was where the early Aussie films were shot and produced. Considered the world's first full-length feature film ever made, "The Story of the Kelly Gang," featured the saga of Australian renegade Ned Kelly and was released in 1906. You would think that there would be some indication that a sensational film such as the alleged "Haunted Billabong" would warrant at least some kind of mention in the history of film—let alone the history of Australian films.

We have discovered other interesting claims that suggest pre-Snippy/1967 cases were experienced by farmers, ranchers, and others. In the November 1985 edition of *Fate* magazine, there is an intriguing article titled: "Cattle-killing UFO of 1896." The story was recounted by Shannon Graham, who claimed her grandmother Pearl Chenowith had told her of an event that she had experienced as a nine-year-old girl growing up on a farm in Howell County, Missouri. The event she experienced allegedly occurred in August 1896 when Pearl and her family witnessed what she described as a "large saucer-like shape" adorned with brilliant lights. The object evidently hovered above the farm in the evening for a significant period of time. The following day, Pearl's family made a horrific discovery:

'[I]n a large patch of burned grass were three of our steers lying dead on the ground…[T]hey had been completely drained of blood. The only marks on them were some dried blood on their throats from two puncture holes in their jugular vein; these looked as if they had been made by a two-tined fork…Later that week, when the newspapers came from St. Louis…there were several stories of just such incidents all over Missouri that night."[24]

Jerome Clark stated that he conducted a thorough search of St. Louis newspapers from around this time period and mentions in his *UFO Encyclopedia* Volume 3 that he was unable to verify the Chenowith's claim. He suggests that perhaps she "had the date wrong," or that perhaps "her memory played a trick on her and fused the Hamilton yarn (see below) with modern reports." I find Clark's suggestion hard to understand as the Chenowith account bears little resemblance to the Alexander Hamilton account that was alleged to have occurred the following April, in 1897.[25]

Alexander Hamilton, Lies and a Liars Club

One of the first and possibly most sensational UFO flaps in American history began in California in 1896 when California citizens began reporting a light slowly traveling over Sacramento on the night of November 17th. Two nights later, witness Colonel H. G. Shaw, while riding in his buggy near Stockton reported a landed "150-foot long" craft with three tall, slender humanoid beings that came out of the craft and approached Shaw. In what may be the first-ever publicized claim of an attempted alien "abduction," Shaw was able to fight them off, and the beings retreated to their metallic-looking craft that quickly lifted off and "sped away."

Thus began the Great Airship Mystery. (figure 10) News of the unexplained flying craft circulated around the country like wildfire, as the airships then were reported in a wave of sightings that slowly made their way East, across the midwest. A number of alleged sightings garnered major newspaper headlines and the whole country was abuzz with rumors and reports that might have produced hoaxed tall tales and spurious newspaper articles. There are correlations and consistencies with many witnesses' descriptions, but there are many differing descriptive details of the mystery craft, report-to-report, enough to make one wonder what was actually going on. By the end of 1897, the airship sightings had reached the East Coast—stalling out in New England where they faded from public view.

One story stands out as a curious claim that may be one of the first descriptions of an alleged abduction and subsequent mutilation of a calf. The still-controversial story first appeared in print on April 23, 1897, in an obscure Kansas weekly called the *Yates Center Farmer's Advocate.*

The airship was first spotted in Kansas on March 26, [1897] and reports came in through April and early May. The most amazing account out of Kansas came from a farmer named Alexander Hamilton, in the little town of Le Roy. According to Hamilton, the airship had dropped down on his farm on the night of April 20th. The pilots lassoed a heifer from Hamilton's herd and carried it off into the air. Mr. Hamilton even produced a notarized statement from twelve prominent men of Le Roy, attesting to his honesty and truthfulness.

Le Roy, Kansas, 1897: "Last Monday night, about 10:30" wrote Mr. Hamilton, "we were awakened by a noise among the cattle. I arose, thinking that perhaps my bulldog was performing some of his pranks, but upon going to the door saw to my utter astonishment an airship slowly descending upon my cow lot, about forty rods from the house.

"Calling my tenant, Gid Heslip, and my son Wall, we seized some axes and ran to the corral. Meanwhile the ship had been gently descending until it was not more than thirty feet above the ground and we came within fifty yards of it. "It consisted of a great cigar-shaped portion, possibly three hundred feet long, with a carriage underneath. The carriage was made of glass or some other transparent substance alternating with a narrow strip of some material…It was brightly lighted within and everything was plainly visible—it was occupied by six of the strangest beings I ever saw. They were jabbering together but we could not understand a word they said…

"Every part of the vessel which was not transparent was of a dark reddish color. We stood *mute* with wonder and fright. [my italics] Then some noise attracted their attention and they turned a light directly upon us. Immediately on catching sight of us they turned on some unknown power, and a great turbine wheel, about thirty feet in diameter, which was revolving slowly below the craft, began to buzz and the vessel rose lightly as a bird. When about three hundred feet above us it seemed to pause and to hover directly above a two-year-old heifer which was bawling and jumping, apparently fast in the fence. Going to her, we found some material fastened in a slipknot around her neck and going up to the vessel from the heifer tangled in the wire fence. We tried to get it off but could not, so we cut the wire loose to see the ship, heifer and all, rise slowly, disappearing in the northwest.

"We went home but I was so frightened I could not sleep. Rising early Tuesday I started out on my horse, hoping to find some trace of my cow. This I failed to do, but coming back in the evening found that Link Thomas, about three or four miles west of LeRoy, had found the hide, legs and head in his field that day. He, thinking that someone had butchered a stolen beast, had brought the hide to town for identification, but was greatly mystified in not being able to find any tracks in the soft ground. After identifying the hide by my brand, I went home. But every time I would drop to sleep I would see the cursed thing, with its big lights and hideous people. I don't know whether they are devils or angels or what; but we all saw them, and my whole family saw the ship, and I don't want any more to do with them."

This amazing story was sworn in front of a notary that accompanied an impressive-looking affidavit:

State of Kansas
Woodson County
As there are now, always have been and always will be skeptics and unbelievers whenever the truth or anything bordering on the improbable is presented, and knowing that some ignorant or suspicious people will doubt the truthfulness of the above statement, now, Therefore we, the undersigned, do hereby make the following affidavit That we have known to 30 years and that for truth and veracity we have never heard his word questioned and that we do verily believe his statement to be true and correct.

Signed,

E. V. Wharton, State Oil Inspector
M. E. Hunt, Sheriff
H. H. Winter, Banker
E. K. Kellenberger, M.D.
H. S. Johnson, Pharmacist
J. H. Sticher, Attorney
Alexander Stewart, Justice of the Peace
H. Waymire, Druggist
F. W. Butler, Druggist
James L. Martin, Register of Deeds
H. D. Rollins, Postmaster
W. Lauber, Deputy Sheriff
Subscribed and sworn to before me this 21st day of April 1897. W. C. Wille Notary Public.[26]

According to history professor David Jacob's book *The UFO Controversy in America*, eight days after the affidavit was filed, on April 29 1987, the Burlington (Kansas) Daily *News* published the affidavit that attested to Hamilton's honesty and veracity. Alexander Hamilton's tail of a cow-knapping by strange beings aboard an airship quickly became a sensation. A number of U.S. and foreign newspapers covered the story, but after a few weeks the claim disappeared from view on the national stage.[27]

Over the years, locals kept the memory of this strange claim alive, and it wasn't until Frank Edwards re-visited the story in the mid-60s that the story regained popular attention. Jacques Vallee also mentioned the Hamilton case in his 1965 book *Anatomy of a Phenomenon: Unidentified Objects in Space.* One of the best accounts is from *The Great Airship Mystery* by Daniel Cohen who spent a considerable amount of time tracking down and documenting the Hamilton account:

"The first thing the researchers wished to establish was whether there really was an Alexander Hamilton. Indeed there was. He was a very substantial citizen of Kansas in the 1890s. A local history, published in 1901, described Hamilton's career in detail. He was, according to this history, "one of the most extensive stock dealers and leading business-men of southeastern Kansas, and is one of the honored pioneers of the commonwealth having come to the state in its territorial days."

Alexander Hamilton had been born in Kentucky in 1832 and had come to Kansas in the 1850s, already having established a career as a lawyer and teacher. The area he moved to was still a frontier and Hamilton served in the local militia, rising to the rank of captain. During the Civil War he was a member of the home guards; after the war he became a representative in the state legislature and helped to establish the county in which he lived. By that time Hamilton had turned from teaching and law to stock raising and trading. His business prospered. So did his family. His wife Jane had fourteen children, twelve of whom survived. Hamilton was sixty-five when the cow napping took place, hardly a teen-aged prankster or hysteric.

According to the local history, Hamilton's 'popularity in the community is unmistakable not only on account of his fidelity to duty in public office, but also because of his honorable business career, his fidelity to manly principles and his reliability in private life. During the long years of his residence in Kansas he has left the impress of his individuality for good upon the communities with which he has been connected and he feels just pride in the splendid advancement made by his adopted state.'

A little exaggeration in such biographies is pardonable, but it made one thing clear. Not only did Alexander Hamilton exist, he was a splendid representative of the type that in popular belief formed the backbone of America. A more reliable witness can hardly be imagined. The same 1901 local history contained biographical sketches of most of the signers of the affidavit attesting to Hamilton's honesty.

In 1976, *Fortean Times* magazine writer Robert Schadewald revisited the original story and asked ufologist Jerome Clark if he knew anything about Hamilton's claim. Intrigued, Clark also started digging. Naturally he began by writing to the *Yates Center News,* which supposedly put him in touch with one Ethel Shaw, then 93 years old, who allegedly was able to recall the incident as described to her by Hamilton himself. If her age was correct, she would have only been four years old at the time, not 14.

"How well I remember that beautiful afternoon, almost as though it were yesterday. I, as a young girl about 14 years old, was visiting in the Hamilton home with Mrs. Hamilton and their daughter Nell when Mr. Hamilton came home from town, put up his team and came into the sitting room where we were visiting. He pulled up a chair and almost immediately began relating this story by saying, 'Ma, I fixed up quite a story and told the boys in town and it will come out in the Advocate this weekend.'"[28]

Clark revealed this debunking of the case in an article published in *Fate* magazine in February 1977. He claimed that the whole incident was a joke perpetrated by Hamilton as a professed member of a local "Liar's Club," and he cites an affidavit filed to that effect published in the May 7, 1897 Kansas City *Times*. An article was supposedly published re-visiting the Hamilton case in the Buffalo *Enterprise* January 1943. Ed F. Hudson, who claimed he had been the editor of the Yates Center paper that printed the original claim, came forward and saying he remembered the incident well. He was quoted as saying, "I always considered Alexander Hamilton was the real inventor of human flight," because the story flew around the world and gained worldwide attention. His son Ben Hudson added the detail that his father and others had a weekly pow-wow where they put the yarn together. These second hand accounts and stand-alone versions are cited but where are they written down?

One would think that this would have put this particular over-the-top claim to rest once and for all, but as we all know sometimes the truth is stranger than fiction and Perkins and I began to dig further into the story. I can find no published corroboration of Clark's various versions that the Hamilton claim was a "joke," nor can I find any corroboration of the existence of a "Liar's Club" in or near Le Roy, Kansas. And I can find no sworn affidavit admitting his claim was a lie. The sworn and notarized affidavit above signed by Hamilton's friends—all pillars of the community—legally suggests that a "Liar's Club" scenario was not the case. To further ratchet up the intrigue surrounding Clark's assertion, it seems that the May 7th Kansas City *Times* article that Clark claims contained a sworn affidavit from Hamilton attesting to his lie, is nothing more than a tongue-in-cheek description of Hamilton's supposed misidentification of a ludicrously-mundane scenario—as told to the editor of the Kansas City *Times* newspaper who published his so-called *mea culpa*:

Yours of the [May] 27th came in due time, but I had so many of the same kind to answer that I have just reached your letter. And in answer to your inquiry about the air ship, will freely confess to you (as you are an editor) that I lied about it. I am sure, now, that it was *a lightning bug with a cow hair in one foot and an ant crawling up the hair. I must have taken the lightning bug for the air ship, the hair for the cable and the ant for the cow.* [my emphasis]. The whole thing must have been an *optical illusion*. Now, my dear sir, please do not say anything about this letter, for you are the only person that I have confessed the truth to, and I only do this because you are an editor, and I will not lie to the editor of a county newspaper intentionally. Yours with respect, A. Hamilton.[29]

In a postscript to his letter to the editor, Hamilton gave a thumbnail sketch of his personal history and mentioned he had been a supporter of the Kansas territory to be created as a slave state. To further complicate this confusing scenario, David Perkins has unearthed more intrigue. In a small public notice in the Kansas City *Journal,*[30] three days after the April 19th event, it was noted that one Alexander Hamilton had resigned as Woodson County Justice of the Peace. One could make the argument that Hamilton resigned as a result being publicly embarrassed by reporting his experience. Having cast at least some doubt upon the Clark debunking, and illustrating that the Hamilton story is more complicated than previously thought, this airship kidnapping of a calf scenario is still open in my mind.

Other researchers and revisionist historians have also noted that man's ingenuity suggests the possibility of unacknowledged aeronautical advancements and pilot shenanigans may have contributed to the Great Airship mystery and possibly earlier high jinks.

> "[S]ome of the aeronauts, even those who had serious intentions, behaved like irresponsible superior beings. On a dark November night in 1836, the English balloonist Charles Green, accompanied by an Irish musician and a member of the British Parliament, was floating invisibly over 'the unearthly glare of the fiery foundries' of Belgium, close enough to hear the coughing and swearing of the foundry workers. He lowered a Bengal light on a rope until its dazzling flare was skimming over the workers' heads. Then he urged one of his companions to shout out in French and German through a speaker trumpet 'as if some supernatural power was visiting them from on high.' He amazed the 'honest artisans' trembling like a primitive tribe, 'looking up at the object of their terrors.'[31]

We also have the following intriguing claim of powered human flight right in the middle of the Midwest airship wave in the spring of 1897, where it was claimed in the Kansas City *Star* that "A Nashville man ascends from the exposition and rides 26 miles" *against the wind!*

Arthur Barnard, the physical instructor of the Nashville [TN] YMCA, promised to ascend in an air ship of his own manufacture, from the exposition grounds, and to sail against the wind.

In the presence of exposition officials and visitors yesterday the ship moved off in perfect order and going against the wind. It soon passed out of sight and Mr. Barnard said he went as far west as Watkins, a village 15 miles from here. While returning the gas gave out when he was four and a half miles from Nashville, and he was compelled to alight. A sudden gust broke one of the spans of the ship

Mr. Barnard said that his machine could not be perfectly controlled in its present condition, but he hopes to perfect it. "A Real Air Ship At Last."[32]

Rare Cases From the 19th And Early 20th Century

Linda Moulton Howe, a staunch extraterrestrial hypothesis (ETH) believer as the sole perpetrators behind the mutilation mystery, testified at the "Citizen's Hearing on Disclosure" in May 2013. She noted that animal mutilation cases have been occurring "at least since the early 1900s."

Howe said there were many more similar cases of animal mutilations around the world, including across South America, North America, parts of Europe, and Australia. The earliest incident, she noted, was in the early 1900s in Australia, where it was reported that over 100 sheep were found mutilated.[33]

Verification of claims from the late 19th and early 20th Centuries is extremely difficult—even today with the Internet. But if you look hard enough, you can find them. One alleged account of a mutilation, prior to the first widely publicized Snippy the Horse case in 1967, includes an account I received in the late 1990s. The witness described a close proximity sighting of an unusual disc-shaped object in 1949 while hunting elk in Washington State. The hunter, then a teenager, along with several adult hunters, found a mutilated elk the morning of the craft sighting, right where the disc had seemed to descend and land in a clearing in the forest.

Project Stigma received the following account from Leon J. Sale of Oklahoma City, Oklahoma. His 1978 letter was published in *Stigmata* magazine that year

I don't remember the exact year, but it was either 1934 or '35 soon after I went to Missouri to live with my grandparents. We found a hog slaughtered in a mysterious way in a pasture after we had seen a shiny object flying over the farm at about tree-top level, and we thought it went down in the pasture across the creek from the house. By the time my grandfather and I walked over there it was gone, but there was a ring about 25 feet in radius burned in the grass and the hog was laying in the middle of it. At that time we had never heard of UFOs and I don't think my grandfather ever said anything to anyone about it.[34]

Another report featuring elk and also deer was told to David Perkins after he was contacted by a retired San Isabelle National Forest Service worker who claimed he had stumbled upon a pile of 15, or so, mutilated deer and elk west of Buena Vista, Colorado. The alleged find was located in the San Isabelle National Forest— just south of the Collegiate Peaks, where the highest mountains in Colorado are located. This allegedly occurred in the early to mid 1950s.

Reports and rumors of unexplained livestock death outbreaks rarely made the news prior to the sensationalism surrounding the Snippy case, which we will cover in the next chapter. Paris, Texas researcher Thomas Adams was able to collect a number of these stories from his home state, and the following was referred to in the 1984 MUFON International Symposium proceedings:

> In the middle of 1963, [a] series of attacks on livestock occurred in Haskell County in West Central Texas. In a typical case, an Angus bull was found with its throat slashed and a saucer-shaped wound in its stomach. It was reported that blood appeared to have been drawn from the stomach wound in a "vampire-like" manner. The citizenry attributed the attacks to a wild beast of some sort, though one was never caught. As it continued its furtive forays through the Haskell County outback, the blood luster assumed somewhat more mythical proportions and a new name destined to endure, "The Haskell Rascal."[35]

This naming of an unseen predator would be echoed again in the 1970s as wave upon wave of mutilations appeared to unfold across the Midwest and locals began to suspect high-strange perpetrators.

Claims of Canadian mutilations that allegedly occurred in the fall of 1967 and the summer of 1968 have been made over the years, but corroborated evidence is extremely scant and difficult to verify.

According to noted author John Keel, (figure 11) animal mutilations were reported in Gallipolis, Ohio in the upper Ohio River Valley. Keel mentioned in his book *A Complete Guide to Mysterious Beings*, that he heard accounts from locals of unexplained animal deaths that occurred in 1966 while investigating a particularly intense wave of unexplained light and craft sightings in central-southwestern Pennsylvania, West Virginia, and eastern Ohio. Keel went on to popularize the infamous "Mothman" sightings that occurred in 1966-67 around Pt. Pleasant, West Virginia.

Ivan Sanderson and I were investigating animal mutilations throughout the northeast in the 1960s. In 1966, I looked into 30 mutilations in the Scranton, Pennsylvania area alone. A year or so later, the frustrated farmers of Pennsylvania tried to form an association to halt the growing number of mutes. They failed to get any real government support and the effort eventually died out. When I first started examining the UFO literature of the 1940s and 50s, I was struck by the number of animal mutilation cases that had filtered into them. These phenomena are consistent over a long period of time and I doubt very much if any simple-minded government project is the culprit.[36]

Keel also mentions an intriguing 1962 case from Brazil that appears to have some credibility, and involves both UFO sightings and unexplained animal and human vanishings:

Officials investigating extensive flying saucer reports in Barcelos, Brazil, in September 1962, learned that 17 chickens, six pigs, and two cows had all vanished during the UFO wave. A man also disappeared during that "flap." His name was Telemaco Xavier, and he vanished near the village of Villa Conceiao late on the night of September 1, 1962. Three plantation workers testified that they had seen a lone man walking down a deserted road that night, when an illuminated circular object spraying sparks swept down from the sky. Three men leaped out, grabbed the lone stroller, and dragged him off. Whether or not Xavier was that man remains unproven. But he was never seen again.[37]

Mutilation investigators and researchers have heard rumors over the years that late-1960s unexplained livestock death cases had occurred on Western Canadian ranches and farms in North America. These stories are equivocal, at best, but they appear to show a direct UFO connection to mutilations. I find it interesting that these claims, if real, indicate a connection that might already have been made before the Snippy case, where I will show the link was indelibly forged. The earliest of these cases also feature horses, and the first of these alleged events, if real and accurately reported, predates Snippy by at least a week or so.

Nick Redfern wrote an interesting article on astronomer Frank Drake and an odd experience he had while at the Arecibo Telescope complex in Puerto Rico in the mid-1960s:

However, in the same way that NASA has been linked to SETI [Search for Extraterrestrial Intelligence], so have sightings of dark cloaked entities and reports of animal mutilations. When Frank Drake elected to make it his life's work to search for alien intelligences, he went down a road that eventually led him to the Arecibo Radio Telescope, which is located on the island of Puerto Rico, and where he, Drake, eventually rose to the position of Director. It was at some point early in his tenure as Director—in the mid 1960s—that a guard at the observatory claimed to have seen a sinister-looking man dressed in a black cloak "walking the narrow trail around the perimeter of the bowl"[38] The guard was of the opinion that the dark figure was nothing less than a blood draining—and blood drinking—vampire. Despite his skepticism, Drake politely accepted the guard's report and agreed to at least take a look at it. Forty-eight hours later, said Drake, "I really was forced to look into it…because a cow was found dead on a nearby farm, with all the blood drained from its body. The vampire rumor spread had already spread through the observatory staff, and now the cow incident whipped the fears of many people into a frenzy."

Although I don't consider this to be directly related to livestock mutilations, the following claim is worthy of mention. John Keel recounts a curious March 5th 1967 claim by the driver and passenger of a Red Cross Bloodmobile that was evidently filled with freshly collected human blood. They were traveling late that night to Red Cross Headquarters in Huntington, West Virginia, when they had a strange encounter:

"The driver was Beau Shertzer and he was accompanied by a young nurse. As they hit a completely deserted stretch of road, a large glowing object lifted from a nearby hill and swooped over the vehicle. Shertzer rolled down his side window and looked up.

"Not unlike the Viking apparatus which collects Martian soil samples, the driver was horrified to see some kind of arm or extension coming down toward them from a craft which hovered just above the blood mobile.

"The nurse saw another arm reaching down on her side of the truck. It looked as if the flying object was trying to wrap a pincer-like device around the vehicle. The nurse went into hysterics, understandably, and Shewtzer floored the accelerator, trying desperately to outrun the thing.

"Apparently they were saved by the sudden appearance of headlights from approaching traffic. As the other cars neared, the object retracted the arms and hastily flew off.[39]

Nick Redfern also reminded me that Col. Philip Corso, mentions in his book, *Day After Roswell,* that he had allegedly seen field reports concerning cattle mutilations in the late 1950s and early 1960s:

According to the late Lieutenant-Colonel Philip J. Corso (who served on President Eisenhower's National Security Council staff, the Operations Coordination Board, and claimed he was Chief of the U.S. Army Staff's foreign technology division):

> 'In the Pentagon from 1961 to 1963, I reviewed field reports from local and state police agencies about the discoveries of dead cattle whose carcasses looked as though they had been systematically mutilated...
> 'Local police reported that when veterinarians were called to the scene to examine the dead cattle left in fields, they often found evidence not just that the animal's blood had been drained but that entire organs were removed with such surgical skill that it couldn't have been the work of predators or vandals removing the organs for some depraved ritual.'

Corso continued that the first thought on the part of the U.S. military was that this was the work of the Soviets. However...

> '[I]t wasn't the Soviets who were going after our cattle...It was the EBE's [Author's note: EBE is an abbreviation of Extra-terrestrial Biological Entity—a term reportedly used within U.S. Intelligence circles to describe alien beings] who were experimenting with organ harvesting, possibly for transplant into other species or for processing into some sort of nutrient package or even to create some sort of hybrid biological entity.'[40]

Corso goes on to explain his impression of Cold Warrior thinking during the 1950 and 60s, when it came to unexplained livestock mutilations:

> We didn't know their reasons back in the 50s and 60s...but back then we were driven by a terror that unless we found ways to defend ourselves against the EBEs we'd corralled by them and used for replacement tissue or as a source of nutrition...this may sound like a nightmare out of a flying saucer horror movie, but in 1957 this was our thinking both in the White House and in the military. We didn't know, but we had irrefutable evidence that the EBEs were landing on farms, harvesting vital organs from livestock and then just leaving the carcasses on the ground because they knew we couldn't do anything about it...
> The mutilations that interested the National Security personnel seemed to have the same kind of modus operandi. Whoever went after the animals seemed most interested in the mammary, digestive, and reproductive organs, especially the uteruses from cows. In many cases the eyes or throats were removed in a type of surgery in which the demarcations line was almost microscopically thin and the surrounding tissue showed that the incision had superheated and then blackened as it cooled. But the crime scene and forensic specialists noted that in any

type of cut by a predatory animal or a human even a skilled surgeon—one would find evidence of some trauma in the surrounding tissue such as swelling, contusions, or inflammation…so if we couldn't protect our livestock or react intelligently to the stories of human abductions except to debunk them and make the abductees themselves think they were delusional we had to find weapons that would put us on a more equal footing with the EBEs.

Corso goes on to suggest that these laser-like wounds and the recovery of a laser-like device from the Roswell crash may have resulted in secret military funding for the development of the laser by Bell Labs and Hughes Aircraft. The term laser-like incision will crop up throughout the rest of *Stalking the Herd*. I do find Corso's assertion, that human abductions and unexplained livestock death stories needed to be debunked in the 1950s and early 1960s, interesting, to say the least, but without slam-dunk documentation (which his book lacks)—it's only another titillating claim.

Mutilation investigators and researchers have heard rumors over the years that late-1960s unexplained livestock death cases had occurred on Western Canadian ranches and farms in North America. These stories are equivocal, at best, but they appear to show a direct UFO connection to mutilations. I find it interesting that these claims, if real, indicate a connection may have already been made *before* the Snippy case where I will show the link was indelibly forged. Many of these cases also feature *horses* and the first of these alleged events, if real and accurate, predates Snippy by at least a week or so.

In Alberta in August of 1967, a dead horse was seen near an area over which a domed saucer-craft was allegedly observed earlier that same day. The horse's hair appeared singed and no rigor mortis had set in. When the witness returned to the remote site the next day (on the Sarcee Reserve, near Twin Bridges), the horse was gone, leaving the imprint of the carcass where it had lain.

Then on August 19, 1968, near Ashville, Manitoba, the carcass of a three-day-old calf was found, missing its genitals, right front leg and an ear. The cuts were clean and no blood was in evidence. The carcass turned up missing the next day but was then found a few days later—scarcely decomposed at another location.

Later that same week (August 1967) in nearby Sowerby, Ontario, two horses belonging to Lorne Wolgemuth suffered strange cuts. A favorite riding horse "Fury" came to the barn one morning with a long clean cut on its neck. When a mare, Susie, failed to turn up for breakfast, its owner went searching and found the animal dead in a field with its jugular vein deftly cut. That night, another horse owned by R. Boyer in Thessalon 'went wild…'[42]

Another tantalizing case from the Fall of 1967 was noted in a UFO database called thecid.com. It refers to a brief mention of a Kingman [Texas] *Leader-*

Courier article in George Eberhart's book *A Geo-Bibliographey of Anomalies*. The story mentions one Gene Walker who witnessed and/or encountered what were described as 'monstrous beings' on October 23, 1967. This encounter somehow was related to the mutilation of a head of cattle that was subsequently reported and mentioned in the article.[43] If this is indeed a bonafide case it could well be the first "official" cattle mutilation!

The Red Sun That Takes Away the Cattle

Claims of African cases are very rare, to my knowledge, yet stories have circulated for years among the Zulus, Masai, Xhosa and Dinka peoples. I found this interesting rustling reference online:

The Zulus have talked for at least two centuries of "the Red Sun that comes at night and takes away the tribe's cattle." Helicopters being unknown in the 19th century and Zulus being excellent herders (so able to tell at once if their cattle has been taken away by a leopard or a common cattle lifter), there has to be another explanation… (figure 12)

Two curious facts of this tradition: first usually only one or two beasts are missing from the herd and they are never found again. There are no traces of struggle and the remaining beasts do not seem scared in the least. Second, a faint red light has been associated with cattle mutilations and disappearances all over the world. Nobody seems to has ever tried to investigate these lights up close and, to be honest with you, I cannot blame the startled herders and ranchers for not rushing in armed with rifles and pitchforks and waiting for the sun to be well up.

The man who brought the "Red Sun" tradition to mainstream knowledge is a professional commercial pilot named Anton Fitzgerald. He became acquainted with this phenomenon while flying over the Veld, but later became really interested in it after observing it from "close range" near his homestead in Natal in 1964. Mr Fitzgerald had a large homestead, with a landing strip, an hangar and cattle.

One evening, before departing for Durban with an Aero Commander 500 (who was parked on the strip, ready for the customary preflight checks), he was standing on a small hill about 300 feet from the hangar with his farm manager, talking about some business matter. All of a sudden they saw this "red glow" enveloping part of the landing strip, and some sheep who were grazing nearby, before being rounded up by the farm hands for the night. A few minutes later the "Red Sun" shoot upwards without noise or any rush of displaced air. Only a single sheep was missing.

A Zulu farm hand named Ndolwana later told him that he had seen the "the Red Sun that rises straight up into the sky after devouring some of the tribe's cattle." According to Ndolwana the tradition was "very old." Given that Zulus, as well as other people of the area like the Xhosa, have been known to keep their cattle in stone kraals, often topped with branches from thorny bushes, to keep leopards and hyenas at bay, and given the facts that kraals are so solid that have been used as forts, there's little doubt that anyone getting in there to steal a single head of cattle while many armed men sleep nearby, it must be a pretty extraordinary occurrence.[44]

As we have seen in Chapter Two, there are quite a number of tantalizing alleged mutilation reports that extend back through time all the way into the Middle Ages. People were mostly uneducated and more prone to superstitious interpretations of the occasional unexplained events that had an impact on their daily lives.

One common theory that debunkers of the cattle mutilation mystery often tout is the theory that the mutilation mystery (as it unfolded with much fanfare in the mid 1970s) was simply due to media-induced hysteria—collective delusion generated by the misidentification of mundane scavenger action. If this is so, *why didn't these older, historic cases create the same conditions of fear and outright panic*—especially during the waves of mysterious animal deaths I have noted. The power of the media has become watered down through time. One would think that centuries ago these events would be far more likely to generate hysterical misinterpretations and outbreaks of mass-delusion and sensational press coverage, but evidently, based on the news reports, these deaths did not have that this affect on the culture. This may be our first real clue that today, in the 21st century, we may be dealing with a truly anomalous, blood-based mystery.

Now that we have studied humankind's ancient relationship to bovines and uncovered historic cases of mysterious, unexplained animal deaths, let's look at the most notorious mutilation case of all time: The "Snippy the Horse" case from 1967.

Chapter Two — Sources and References:

1   Markum, Samantha, "Superstition and Macbeth," 7-28-09, suite101.com

2   Dawson , Danny, "The Witch: Subversive, Heretic or Scapegoat?" 1999, University of Kent, UK

3   King James I, *Daemonologie*, 1597

4   *ibid*

5   Keys, J., *Collins Encyclopedia,* 1994, Harper Collins, NY NY

6   Kiser, M.L.,"Witchcraft in the Rein of James I," 5-26-11, Humanities 360, Andover, MA

7   Levack , Brian, "Possession, Witchcraft, and the Law in Jacobean England," 1-1-96, Washington and Lee Law Review, Lexington, VA

8   Dawson , Danny, "The Witch: Subversive, Heretic or Scapegoat?" 1999 U of Kent, UK

1   Brandon, Jim, *Weird America,* 1979, Dutton NY NY

1   *Los Angeles News,* 8-9-1869; *Weird America;* Jim Brandon, Dutton NY NY 1979

2   Fort, Charles, *Wild Talents,* Kendall Publishing, NY, NY, 1932

3   *ibid*

4   *ibid*

5   Clark, Jerome, *The UFO Enclodedia Vol 3 1979,* Omnigraphics, Detroit, MI, 1996

6   Fort, Charles, *Wild Talents,* Kendall Publishing, NY, NY, 1932

7   Ontario *Daily Record*, 2- 8-1909

8   Fort, Charles, *Wild Talents,* Kendall Publishing, NY, NY, 1932

9   *ibid*

10 *ibid*

11 "Flogging a Dead Horse," Nick Redfern, Center for Fortean Zoology 2011 Yearbook, CFZ Press

12 Brisbane *Courier,* 10-18-1902

13 *The Argus*, Melbourne, Victoria, Australia, 7-13-53

14 *Starburst Magazine,* Volume 1 No. 2

15 Shannon Graham *Fate,* 38 #11; Jerome Clark, *The UFO Enclodedia Vol 3* 1979

16 Clark, Jerome, *The UFO Enclodedia Vol 3* 1979, Omnigraphics, Detroit, MI, 1996

17 *Yates Farmer's Advocate 4-23-1897; The Great Airship Mystery, D. Cohen.* 1981, Dodd, Mead

18 Jacobs, David, *The UFO Controversy in America,* 1976, New American Library, Pennsylvania State University, College, PA

19 Clark, Jerome, *Fate* Magazine, 2-1977, Lakeville, MN

20 Kansas City *Times,* Letter to the Editor, 3-7-1897;

21 Kansas City *Journal*, "An Aerial Pirate," 4-30-1897

22 *Falling Upwards: How We Took to the Air*, Holmes, Richard, 2013 Pantheon, NY NY

23 Kansas City *Star,* "A Real Airship at Last," *5-7-1897*

24 *Epochtimes*, Shar Adams, 5-1-3 "Citizen's Hearing on Disclosure, "4-13, Nat Press Club, Wash DC.

25 Leon Sale, Letter to Project Stigma, *The Mysterious Valley,* St Martins Press, 1996, NY NY

26 1984 MUFON International Symposium proceedings

27 *Mysterious Beings, John* Keel, 1970, Faucett Publications, NYC

28 *ibid*

29 Drake, Frank & Sobel, Dava, *Is Anyone Out There?* Delta, McHenry, IL.,1994

30 *The Mothman Prophesy,* John Keel, 1975, Saturday Review Press, NY NY

31 Corso, Phillip/Birnes, Willaim, *Day After Roswell,* 1998, Pocket Books, NY NY; e-mail from Nick Redfern,

32 *The Saucer Phenomenon,* Kurt Glemser, Kitchner Ontario, 1970; Letter to Project Stigma

33 *ibid*

34 Kingman *Leader-Courier,*10-23-67; Eberhart, George, *A Geo-Bibliographey of Anomalies,* 1980, Greenwood Press, Westport, CT; thecid.com

35 mysteriousbritain.co.uk

Figure 1
In the 1600s, if you were declared an enemy of the state and executed, you were hung, disemboweled, drawn and quartered and your parts were sent to the ends of the realm. (credit: old English woodcut from the 1600s)

Figure 2
Burning Man Celebration, Nevada, 2013 Modern version of an ancient practice.
(credit: baltimoresun.com)

Figure 3
King James 1st: He re-wrote the Bible, funded Shakespeare and noted the first documented outbreak of unexplained livestock deaths in 1606. (credit: wikipedia)

Figure 4
Osculum infame—"the obscene kiss." One way to garner favor with the dark lord.
(credit: wikipedia)

Figure 5
Birds-eye view of Sacramento, California, circa: 1857. (credit: wikipedia)

Figure 6
Charles Fort, (1874-1932) The first paranormal investigator.
(credit: Fortean Picture Library)

Figure 7
Sheep grazing blissfully in the Scottish Highlands. (credit:
methowconservancy.blogspot.com)

Figure 8
The "Great Wyrley Outrages" horse-slasher George Edalji (1876-1953) Found guilty
of horse mutilation in 1903.

Figure 9
Some of the first known waves of sheep mutilations in the southern hemisphere
occurred on sheep station in Australia in the early 20th century.
(credit: mountmorrisstation.com)

Figure 10
The Great Airships of 1866–1897 were covered by newspapers across the United
States. (credit: old newspaper illustration, Chicago, IL, 1897)

Figure 11
John A. Keel (1930-2009) Early paranormal 'gonzo' investigator and thoughtful
author/theorist. (credit: algorythmic.com)

Figure 12
African 'Red Sun' legendary rustler of East African cattle. (credit: author digiart)

Chapter 3
"Oh Lord defend us from our defenders"

By far the most celebrated unexplained livestock death—the so-called "Snippy the Horse" case—is often acknowledged as the first publicized unexplained livestock death, and Snippy has become almost legendary. The horse probably died (or was killed) and disfigured on the night of September 7, 1967. Peripheral to the case were the dozens of UFO sightings that were also reported during that eventful autumn that have inexorably linked Snippy's mysterious death with the UFO phenomenon. This link, whether accurate or not, has existed ever since and will be addressed in-depth later in the book.

Also peripheral to the case was the first known outbreak of Chronic Wasting Disease (CWD), which was documented further north in Colorado during this mid-to-late 1967 time period. We will look at CWD, "mad cow" disease, and Cruetzfeld-Jacobs disease (CJD) and its variants vCJD and nvCJD, or mad-human disease, later in Chapter 12. This synchronistic time and regional correlation may be tremendously important, as we will see.

The "Snippy Case," has become a thing of legend among paranormal enthusiasts and in the two months following the horse's unfortunately horrific demise, the news item was picked up by the wire services and became a sensational international news story. Reporters from as far away as England, France, and Germany joined North American journalists at the site in the San Luis Valley that autumn. The site also

attracted the curious, who flocked to the remote King Ranch by the hundreds. Today, 45 years later, if you gaze down on Google Earth at the meadow where the horse lay that autumn of 1967, you can still see the hardened dirt path that led out to the location, a quarter-mile west of county road 150.

Setting the Stage

First a little history and some background on the location and the principles involved. The case occurred in south-central Colorado's San Luis Valley. I spent 13 years there, much of my time spent investigating current reports and researching the regions' colorful history. The SLV is the world's largest alpine valley and the valley floor sits at over 7,000 in elevation. Completely surrounded by mountains—some that rise to over 14,000-feet—this remote, majestic region is a perfect cultural petrié dish for sociological study. Isolated physically and culturally from the culture at large, the SLV is the subject of my first three books, *The Mysterious Valley, Enter the Valley,* and *Secrets of the Mysterious Valley.*[1]

The Mormon Urraca pioneers settled the western slope of the 14,000-foot Blanca Massif (which dominates the mid-eastern part of the SLV) in the late 1870s. One of those hardy families was the Kings, who homesteaded a 2,000-acre cattle ranch that extended down from the foot of the mountains out onto the valley floor. The upper ranch had a small cabin on the original homestead site and the main ranch house was located five miles away out in the valley, ten miles southeast of the Great Sand Dunes. A windswept area, the King Ranch sat on some of *the earliest meadows known to have been visited by humans in the lower 48 states.* Smithsonian archaeologists have been digging up artifacts near the dunes for decades.

The Kings were a hard-working cattle family, putting in long hours sun-up to sundown in one of the valley's most picturesque areas. Eighty-five-year-old widow Agnes King was the King Family matriarch and lived with her two sons, Harry and Ben, and a daughter named Nellie. Ben King was a self-styled mountain man who could identify every animal and plant in the San Luis Valley and name every creek that flowed down the western slope of the Sangres mountain chain. Harry was the King Ranch boss, running cattle and tending to the ranch's daily affairs. Nellie, married to Iowa native Berle Lewis, lived with her husband in the cabin on the upper ranch.

The Kings and Lewis were truly salt-of-the-earth ranchers with a documented family history of witnessing unusual celestial events, for example, a sighting by C.M. Lewis, Agnes's deceased husband, of the Alamosa Aereolite in the fall of 1898 on the Baca Ranch—about 20 miles north of the Snippy site.[2]

Prior to the Snippy case, UFO sightings had began in the SLV in late 1966 and all through the spring and summer of 1967. Residents near the King ranch began reporting sightings of strange small mini jets—described around 10 to 12 feet long—that were reported zipping around the region in early '67. Several reports mentioned these unknown objects dive-bombing cars on the dunes road, and still others mentioned seeing these objects disappearing *directly into* Middle Creek Hill, which sits just north of Blanca Peak. In one instance, a search party was formed to find the entrance. The whole hillside was carefully searched and no entrance was found. Navajo legends mention that this region of the range around Blanca is where "all though thought originates" and that doorways could be found on the western-facing slopes of the Blanca Massif.

In 2003, a pair of hikers observed a 15 to 20 foot-high doorway that was located high up on the cliffs located just south of the Great Sand Dunes. After an arduous climb to the site, no doorway could be found. There have been other similar reports through the years.

Where Did Snippy Go?

Here is what we know about the demise of the horse dubbed by the press as "Snippy." It was a blustery morning, September 8, 1967, and Harry King noticed that only two of their three horses were outside waiting for grain and water. Thinking this unusual, he headed out to feed them. He claimed later that he had sensed something was wrong and he was right: Lady, Nellie's three-year-old young mare, was nowhere to be found.

After waiting until the following morning for her to show up, Harry went searching for the missing horse. After an hour, he spotted something laying in a meadow a quarter-mile north of the main ranch house and it raised the hair on his neck. Lady's corpse was missing all the tissue from her shoulders to the tip of her nose, the exposed bones glistening, bleached white, as if they had been in the desert sun for years. The flesh, muscles, tendons, meat, and hide were missing from the tip of the nose to a wide circular cut just above the horses' shoulders. *No other case to my knowledge before, or since, has featured this description of complete cranial and neck disfigurement.* According to Berle Lewis, the skull and neck bones were "as white a sheet of paper…as if they'd laid out in the desert sun 30-years." The animal lay on its left side, facing east in a damp meadow located about one-quarter-mile west of Road 150, a two-lane, heavily traveled dirt road that went north another six or so miles to the Great Sand Dunes National Monument. There were no scavenger or predator tracks, bird-droppings, or evidence of how the horse had died or was subsequently disfigured. Over the next month or so the bones began to turn a rosy pink color and the bleached white appearance faded. This is the time frame when the most famous photographs of Snippy were taken.

It had rained off and on during the first week of September and the ground was still soft and muddy in places. This made ascertaining track evidence relatively easy. Harry King determined that the three horses had been running full speed headed southeast toward the ranch house and Lady had been "cut from the herd," then veered away from the other two, who continued on toward the house.

Lady's tracks continued galloping for several hundred yards, by King's estimate, where they then inexplicably *stopped in full gallop.*

It is interesting to note that the "official" story diverges at this point into two distinct versions. Version one is supported by several newspaper articles; Coral Lorenzen's *Fate* article, and Berle Lewis's account. These state that the carcass was found more than 100 feet farther along the meadow. Version two, supported by several articles and Don Richmond's original investigation, stated that the tracks went in a tight circle several times, like something was circling around the horse, and that the corpse was found only 20 feet away from Lady's circling tracks. This discrepancy has never been resolved one way or another to my knowledge.

A careful examination of the area a week later by Nellie, Harry, Berle, and friends, found what appeared to be four burned areas in the ground at four, nine, 13 and 21-feet away from the carcass to the northwest. Shaped like an upside-down question mark, the burn marks in the ground were found to the southeast ranging 40 to 50 feet from the body. Five 18-inch-wide by 8-inch-deep "giant horse tracks" were punched into the ground and were found among some flattened appearing chico bushes located near the body.

Nellie called Alamosa County Sheriff Ben Phillips to report the strange death of her horse. Phillips, immediately upon hearing the description, branded the horse's death a "lightning strike" and didn't bother to drive out to the scene to investigate. He later admitted that it was odd that the horse had no evidence of burn-marks usually associated with a lightning strike.

Nellie and the rest of the family, however, were convinced that something highly irregular had happened to her horse. She was well aware of the several UFO sightings in the weeks prior to her horse's demise, and she and Berle and close friends had experienced sightings that previous spring. The day before the horse disappeared, Agnes King had reported seeing a large bright object flying over the King Ranch corrals that allegedly sheared off the top of one fence post before flying off. Elderly Agnes had been doing the dishes in the kitchen during the day when she glanced out the window and saw the silvery object. She didn't have her glasses on so she wasn't able to get a clear, focused look at whatever-it-was. One would think that Nellie would have been impressed by her mother's claim.

On September 23, 1967, two weeks after the horse was discovered, US Forest Service employee Duane Martin, having heard about the case, visited Nellie. Martin borrowed a Geiger counter from a local civil-defense unit, and checked the area for increased levels of radiation. He received, in his determination, heightened radiation readings near the flattened chico bushes and burn marks. The readings decreased as he approached the carcass. Increased levels of radiation were also detected on Berle's boots.

Later, questions were raised of Martin's proficiency with the Geiger counter, and he admitted that he had only operated the equipment in indoor training sessions. He had never operated the detection equipment out in the field. I have never found reference, in any of the numerous articles about the "Snippy" incident, of Martin taking any control readings at the site. Without a control reading, determining true radiation levels is virtually impossible.

The Story Gets Out

The Lewis's were initially reluctant to go public with the story. But word about the case spread like wildfire locally during the first three weeks after the horse's discovery, and curious locals began showing up at the site. Initially, Harry tried to confine the visitors to a small area near the body to maintain the integrity of the scene, but this proved impossible as first dozens and then hundreds of onlookers made the trek out to the meadow to see the horse.

Nellie's nephew Don Hard, a high-school student at the time, was one of the first family members to hear of the strange death of Nellies' horse and he went out to see for himself what all the fuss was about. He is still impressed at what he saw:

> It looked like the horse had been picked up or something because tracks were quite a ways from where it was lying. It was found in a meadow under real strange circumstances. The flesh was missing from its head up. Its spinal cord was missing; its brains were missing. Organs were missing; the bones were white like they'd been layin' a long time. The meat was totally cleaned off the bones. Anybody that's ever butchered something, you can't scrape the meat off clean out in a field… I guess what impressed me was the esophagus was cut clean also and that's kind of a hard, bony type thing. We've butchered cattle before and it didn't look like something just anybody could do. The bones were still clean and white as if they'd been on the desert or in the sun for quite a while.
>
> Later on I returned to look at it. We'd looked at it several times, but later on it kind of grew a black growth around the ground. We didn't see any other incisions on the horse, yet they say the blood was missing and the organs were missing. I didn't see any scavengers or birds or anything on it. On our ranch we have cattle and if a cow dies pretty quick the coyotes dig a hole in it and eat it
>
> It seemed to [Nellie] like some kind of high technology had done it, rather than something someone could pull off as a prank. I didn't think it was a prank. I don't see how something could be done that precisely, to use precision to cut the flesh and the esophagus; take the spinal cord without damaging the bones. It just seems like something out of this world.

I've had a theory that maybe the government has such technology. It could be the government experimenting with new weapons because they did fly around the Valley at low altitude trying to evade radar. It was just practice flying, but you could imagine the pilot with a new weapon sayin' 'let's try this out and see what happens.'[3]

Nellie was positive the strange lights and objects that she and others had seen, and reported, were somehow involved. I have noted many of these 5 reports in my earlier books that didn't garner the same attention as the horse's death. At the end of the first week of October 1967, Nellie's longtime friend Pearl Mellon Nicholas, society editor for the Valley Courier, let the strange death of the horse out of the barn. During the next four weeks, the "Snippy" the horse story emerged quickly from the local to the regional, national, and international newspaper press.

Guilt By Association

A curious element of the modern ufological mythos was created (or miss-created) as the facts subtly twisted in the wind of dissemination. The "Snippy" case and the San Luis Valley's apparent corresponding UFO activity provided a "guilt by association" scenario that led to the inexorable linking of unexplained livestock mutilations with UFOs, and this link between UFOs and mutilations has endured as a cultural meme ever since. The press, by their very nature, can be careless. Even Coral Lorenzen of the well-respected Aerial Phenomenon Research Organization (APRO) got several important facts mixed up in her May 1968 *Fate* article.

Crucial elements, like the horse's gender and name got mixed up, jumbled up, and turned around. I wondered how basic facts could become so scrambled. The process of discerning reality from any subtle form of chaos is daunting. At the time, I checked and cross-checked each article against the others. As the discrepancies piled up, I wondered if anyone could eventually discern the facts from the various data provided. That the Snippy case was the first widely publicized "cattle mutilation" case has likely obscured rather than clarified the thousands of similar cases that were to follow.

So inconsistent were the details in the Snippy case that I hypothesized back in 1993 that they might have been altered by design in some instances. It appeared to me that a blatant process of creating misinformation might have been at work that October that continues today, almost 50 years later. "Snippy," whether we like it or not, is now a part of our cultural mythos, and I wonder if the case could be providing us with an insight into this particular meme and the myth creation process itself. Maybe the stranger cattle-related events that have occurred through time, and subsequently become a part of the mythic tradition, are somehow distorted by a veil of unconscious cultural uncertainty? The development of a myth can likely become exaggerated or overly dramatized through either an intentional or an inadvertent addition of disinformation.

The case certainly had an effect on me at the time when the press began to propagate the story. The following is from my book *Secrets of the Mysterious Valley*:

> Imagine the excitement of a bright-eyed, inquisitive ten-year-old—fidgeting while standing in line with his mom at Safeway—when his eyes behold something fantastically beyond belief staring out from a magazine rack, something beyond mundane human understanding. I remember thinking back then in the fall of 1967, as that kid, I have to somehow convince my mom to buy this news world paper with the headline, "Flying saucers Killed My Horse"! The headline adorned a cover photograph of three people inspecting the remains of the horribly mutilated corpse of a horse named "Snippy," located somewhere in the high-mountain wilds of south-central Colorado. Sometimes, even a motivated ten-year-old can move mountains and I was able to convince my mom to buy the paper trumpeting the sensational claim. Even as a kid, I recognized that in the after-glow of the summer of love, the events of the Snippy case potentially cast a foreboding shadow over the cultural glow and boy, was I ready to read all about it! The article was fairly well researched and I remember thinking, it must be true, only aliens could possibly have done something so horrific to that poor animal.

This was my introduction to the mysterious San Luis Valley in October 1967 and the death of Snippy, forty-years later, remains one of the most enigmatic and controversial so-called paranormal events in modern history.[4]

Back when I originally began investigating the Snippy case in 1993 I wanted to verify as many facts as I could about the event. I found newspaper accounts somewhat unreliable, but thought that the primary data—interviews with the principles (Nellie, Berle, and other family members), notes by the original investigator, Don Richmond, and accounts by Nellie's friend, Valley *Courier* editor Pearl Nicholas might fill in the blanks. By comparing the primary data against the press accounts, I hoped to discover the true story behind the death of "Snippy" the horse and possibly gain some insight into the thousands of livestock death cases that have been alleged to occur since that blustery September in 1967. I also hoped to discover how these mysterious deaths have created the "cattle mutilation" meme widespread in the culture. After over 20 years, I'm still struggling with the inconsistencies of the data about this pivotal case.

"Flying Saucers Killed My Horse"

With the gracious help of researchers Tom Adams, David Perkins, Dr. Lynn Weldon (Adams State College) and others, I have located insightful interviews and accounts from the principles. One of the first full-length interviews with Nellie Lewis was recorded five-weeks after Snippy's death and was sent to me by Tom Adams. On October 18, 1967, East Texas State University sociology teacher Ross Henderson and student Lonnie Furbay spoke with Nellie at length. Tom attended ETSU and sent me a copy of the interview. Here are some pertinent excerpts:

After some initial confusion as to who was calling, Furbay asked Nellie, "The horse that was involved in the incident is named Snippy, is that correct?"

"That is correct," she replied. [This was *not* correct according to Berle, as we will see later.] Furbay asked Nellie to describe the scene.

"We were in the mountains. We came by the ranch on September 10 and my mother told us about it and we went out and it was just as my brother described it. All the meat was gone from the neck and head. The bones were white, as if it had been sun bleached a long time. There was no muscle, no meat, no ears, no mane, not one hair of the mane stuck in the mud, and this was a real muddy meadow. There were no tracks except my brothers and he'd sunk down 2 to 2 and 1/2 inches in the mud. He had been stuck [in his truck] about a block from the horse and he said it took him two hours to get out. And his tracks still remained, even though it was suggested that there could've been tracks and they were rained out. Now, I checked with the weather bureau. There was no rain between September 7 and September 9 [1967]."

Nellie described a strange smell around the corpse. "A strong medicine odor. And I have a feeling it might be embalming fluid. I've been going to try to find time to smell some. Why there would be embalming fluid, I don't know. But it was a very strong odor." Nellie called Alamosa county Sheriff, Ben Phillips.

"What was his reaction?"

"I explained the condition of the horse and I said that my brother thought it was lightning but it was impossible because of the odor. There was no burn on the horse, no singed hair. The meat was just as fresh and pretty as you'd fry."

Sheriff Phillips decided the horse's death must have been caused by lightning and did not immediately pursue an investigation. Nellie then called numerous farmers, a game warden, a health department officer, Dr. Leary, a local veterinarian. "And to each one I explained the condition of the horse, and most all the farmers said they didn't believe lightning could do something like this."

"Okay. Would you describe exactly what the horse looked like as he lay on the ground," Furbay continued,

"His [sic] back body, up to his shoulders, was perfect, not a scratch or not a mark on him whatsoever. He [sic] had not struggled in the mud. He [sic] had fallen and never made a move because this is real muddy and you could have told. There was no blood whatsoever. Cuts absolutely smooth, all the way around, like you would mount a deer head, for instance, straight into the bone. And the meat was not running blood—there was no blood on the ground. And there were no tracks."

"What else was strange about the general area where Snippy was found?"

"Well, all that week, I refused to believe my husband [who said], 'Well, it has to be lightning. How could it be anything else?' So, Ernest Wellington, who died a week later, incidentally, and his wife Leona and their daughter, and a teacher from Creede [Colorado] Wayne Trapouski came out and after they looked the horse over and Ernest said, 'No, this couldn't have been lightning.'

"So, he started searching the area. He called us over—he was a block-and-a-half to the north. And there was a bush busted down close to the ground. Most of the top of the bush was gone, and it was in an open spot all by itself, and here the ground was all riled up. Now the rest of the ground, it was rain-pebbled and, you know, but this was freshly riled, and in this I found a glob-like sac of substance which I didn't touch with my hands; but there was some mane stuck to this sac, and it was the color of the inside of a chicken gizzard, and tough like that. But it was shaped sort of like a chicken liver, with pyramidish points on it. I jerked this mane (hair) loose from it, and took two sticks and busted it open, and a green paste oozed out of it."

Nellie wanted to take the sample for testing but Berle said, "You're not putting any of the horse in the car or I'll walk home." He did reluctantly allow Nellie to take some of the strange black soot-like material, as long as it was placed in the trunk. Furbay asked if Nellie had touched any of the material.

"I did touch that mane (hair) which I jerked loose. Now, there was no mane around the horse, not even stuck in the mud. And my hand started burning. It turned bright red with streaks across it, and it burned until, oh, about 30 minutes later. We got up to the cabin and I washed and washed and within an hour it had quit burning. But I knew then that something definitely had been done to the horse."

"And what became of the material?

"The NICAP (National Investigations Committee for Aerial Phenomena) team was hired by Dr. Condon, who heads our government office that's financed by the Air Force for the investigation of flying saucers; and they hired them to come down… one of the gentlemen from there did find it in the top of a bush and they took it back with them for testing."

"I see, and have you had any other ill effects other than the burning of your hand from this piece of material?"

"No, not that I know of. The night we found the horse I was sick all night and went to the doctor the next day for a prescription, and I hadn't been in his office for eight months, and I was dizzy and sick, and I feel it had something to do with the horse."

"Has anything, or had anything unusual happened around Alamosa before Snippy was found?"

"Well, there [are the] saucer sightings which have been quite frequent the last six weeks. Other than that, there was another horse found dead three miles SE of my horse, Snippy. It was a good pinto stud and it belonged to Walter Alsbaugh, who takes rodeo stock around, and it had a big gash on its head about four inches in diameter; but what they decided about it, I don't know."

"According to a newspaper article, ma'am, we also understand your husband made the statement that you all see something almost every night, or now and then. Is this true?"

"I haven't looked for ten days because I don't want to see anything. But there are a number of my friends and relatives and people here in town that have been out looking since the incident and a number of them have seen things. There's called a 'flap' going on here now. They're just getting all kinds of sightings, and it certainly isn't us. I mean, many highly respected people are seeing them and they know they exist. But maybe our government knows what this is, you see, and they came in to discredit this and call us liars because they do know what it is. I don't know the answer but I'm highly disgusted and I will take a lie-detector test, and so will my husband, on the condition of the horse, and they ignore it. I said 'there was no blood on him'. He said, 'Oh, your untrained eye didn't see it.' This was a rain-soaked meadow. People squished down three inches, at the time, walking in it. And there was no stain there, or anything, sir."

"Have any pictures been taken of these UFOs?"

"There was one on the front page of the Pueblo *Chieftain* today and it's taken of this ship or vehicle or whatever, airborne right near the horse's body, and it was taken last Friday night. I don't know the boys. They go to college. But the story and the pictures are in the Pueblo *Chieftain* today. Mark Conrad, who has a program in Colorado Springs, was here. He was making some television pictures and an object that's littler than a Piper Cub and has little short stubby wings dived right over the top of the ground by him. Now, this is the same thing that has been seen here in the daytime by quite a number of people. [Including this author, 26 years later!] And as yet, we haven't found out what it is but we assume it's a jet, something of our government's, but we don't know what it is."

It took Air Force investigators three weeks to respond to these unusual reports. Nellie recalled another incident that took place the day before the horse vanished. "Something flew over the ranch house. It was airborne but my mother doesn't have very good eyesight; she's 87-years-old, but very alert, and she went to the door, she has arthritis and walks very slowly. It was still right at the house. It couldn't have been a jet or a plane or anything; it was right at treetop level. It was bright aluminum, she could not see wings on it but she says she's not sure of the shape because of her eyesight. I'm sure this has some connection with the horse."

"How did the NICAP people treat you personally with their questions?"

"They were personally very nice but I could not get an official opinion from them, but each one gave me their personal opinion that it was 'very strange and very unexplainable.'"

"Has any organization or authority tried to censor you in any way?"

Nellie said a Dr. Adams, from Colorado State University, and Dr. Fred Ayers, who assisted with the Condon investigation visited her ranch. They claimed the horse must have been killed by passing hunters—perhaps a mercy killing. Nellie vehemently disagreed. "A mercy killing doesn't make any sense at all because you would cut under the throat. This animal was cut all the way around, absolutely smooth, in a manner, which you could not have done with a knife because I was raised on a farm and I know what it looks like when you butcher. You gotta make a jag when you pull that knife back. And who would carry this type of equipment anyway? And who would not go to the ranch house and say, 'You have a sick horse.' They can see it's got spots, it's a good [Appaloosa] horse. They wouldn't be about to cut its throat.

"I was going to tell you, when this veterinarian came in that night with Dr. Fred Ayers, to give me his report, my older sister was there... I heard him on a TV program where they were interviewing him, and they asked him, 'What was the smell?' He said, 'They smelled thistle and didn't know the difference.' Well, this is a distinct lie. There was a definite strong odor. The government, I read in last night's *Courier*, our local paper, they said there were no black spots. That is a damn lie. They are all out there for anybody to see and hundreds of people have seen them. Now, why is our government lying?"

Furbay ignores her and says, "Yes, ma'am. Would you answer this question, please? Has Snippy been moved from where he was?"

"No sir, He [sic] lays right where he was. They slit his [sic] stomach all down the middle next to the ground, and his [sic] head's been cut off when they were doing the autopsy but he is still there and I don't want to bury the horse because the government will say there was no horse. Now, why is our government... I thought they came in to investigate. Instead, they came in to discredit and call people liars when they were giving them the truth."

"We understand that a pathologist examined Snippy. This probably is the one who cut into the horse. What did he find?"

"There were 20 witnesses, highly-respected people who were witnesses. They just happened to be spectators at the time. He [Dr. John Altshuler] told us he found the brain cavity empty. He said that's very unusual. He said it should have had water in it, and there were no brains or nothing in there. He opened the abdomen with a knife and he said, 'They're [the organs] all gone.' Now we had 20 adult witnesses there to this but I understand they put [pressure?] on him and he retracted, but we have all the witnesses here who know the horse, that this was the condition of the horse. Will you tell me why, why does the government come in and try to make liars out of us when we in good faith gave them our evidence and our proof and then they ignored it and pretended we were lying? Will you tell me, sir? You should know. Why is the government doing this? Why are they calling us liars when they were true facts, ignoring them?"

"Well, this is what… very precisely the point we're trying to make by talking to you, Mrs. Lewis. We're kind of upset at the fact that they would do this."

"Well, I am not going to let the government intimidate me. I am going to tell the truth. I told the truth in the beginning and I will continue to tell the truth no matter how much they try to intimidate."[5]

The UFO Connection

"Flying saucers killed my horse!" The publicity generated by the horse's death brought the UFO watchers and the generally curious into the San Luis Valley in droves. A group of Adams State College students even repainted a billboard outside of Alamosa to read, "The Flying Saucer Capital of the World."

Nocturnal lights proved extremely elusive but more photographs were captured during the fall of '67. In October, two college students from Pueblo, Colorado, Bill McPhedries and a friend, with the help of APRO investigator Don Richmond, photographed mysterious lights over the Great Sand Dunes as they stood on the porch of the Lewis cabin, high above the valley floor. They had first noticed them in the Dry Lakes area, five miles due west of their vantage point. They seemed to hover close to the ground before flying off toward the dunes—passing just to the west of the Snippy site. Brilliant white and red, they seemed to the three observers to be under intelligent control. The photographs appeared in the Pueblo *Chieftain* along with a story by Pearl Nicholas

When I first became involved in researching the Snippy case in 1993, Tom Adams graciously sent me several dozen *Valley Courier* articles he had saved reporting the "Snippy" case and the ensuing UFO flap. Wyoming UFO researcher Tom Rouse added dozens of additional articles from the *Denver Post, Rocky Mountain News,* and *Valley Courier.* David Perkins contributed further information and first generation 35mm photographs.

The colorful cast of characters in the articles were perfect media fodder, and the press had a field day with the story. I decided back in 1993 that I needed to examine not only the alleged events but also concurrent cultural events and the process of dissemination that unfolded to see if there were any parallels with the cattle mutilation activity in later years. Berle Lewis, who died in 2005, was the closest principle involved in the Snippy case, so naturally he was top of my list of interviews.

From the Horse's Mouth

March 12, 1993, Great Sand Dunes Country Club:

I was finally able to sit down with Berle Lewis, Nellie's husband, for a video tape interview when he agreed to meet with me at the Great Sand Dunes Country Club maintenance shop where he worked. This was my first full-length video interview conducted for my first book, *The Mysterious Valley*. I was struck by Berle's colorful, casually humorous demeanor, which was offset by the honest and matter-of-fact way he described many unusual and some downright unbelievable stories from the late 1960s. I found him to be highly credible —a straight shooter.

"Berle, when did you first start hearing about UFOs and strange lights being seen around here?" I began.

"After '67, in August."

"So all the sightings started just before the whole Snippy episode?"

"It all started right there. I never paid no attention to it 'till after the horse was killed."

"Until it happened right in your back yard?"

"You might say the backyard, it happened right out back of the house." Berle laughed.

"Ok, let's get in a little bit and talk about Snippy, or Lady, I mean. The press changed the horse's name, I guess Snippy was a more colorful name?"

"I never corrected them when it came out. I kinda smiled and said hell, Snippy's all right with me, Snippy was the horse I rode on, Lady was her colt [sic], so it's kinda funny the way it turned out. They called the colt "Snippy," and the horse I had Lady, so I never corrected them."

"What did you, Nellie, and Harry think when you found the horse?"

"We had no idea what caused it because I know nobody with a knife could cut that meat so smooth and nobody could ever take the meat off the bones where it was as white as that piece of paper over there. Now I don't give a darn who you are, there's not a butcher of any kind that can make that bone look like it's sat there for years! The eyeballs were gone, the tongue was gone, the esophagus was gone, and the windpipe was gone. All the hair, the mane hair and hide on the neck, clear down to where the collar fit. But that cut, completely around, was smooth! It's just impossible to cut it that way!" I inquired about the medicinal smell.

"Well, it just hung over the horse really, it seemed to be floating in the area."

"Nellie was quoted as saying it smelled like embalming fluid."

"Naw, I wouldn't say it was embalming fluid, I've smelled plenty of that. It was like medicine. That's the way I'd put it but I don't know what kind of medicine."

"Do you have any idea how they removed the brain out of the skull?"

"Hell, I know how the skull got cut open, I was there and I held the light for the guy that cut it open."

"And there was no brain in there?"

"It was dry!"

"So there was no opening in the cranial cavity?"

"The was no opening of any kind."

"How about the green glob that looked like a chicken liver that Nellie found?"

"Well, I don't know what that was, I'll be darned if I do. It was like an acid burn, but there was no smell of acid or burnt hair."

"When you look back at the Snippy incident, and understand that Snippy was the first [publicized] livestock mutilation from all over the world, what do you think about that?"

"Well, I never thought nothing about it." Berle lifted his hat and scratched his head quizzically. "I guess, with the whole deal, I thought sooner or later I would learn what happened but hell, it's been 30 years."

"I read somewhere that Harry found a bull and calf he owned blinded right around the time of Snippy."

"He had a bull that was blind all right, it happened about a month or so before."

"A month before Snippy?"

"Yes, it just went blind. It was never tied to anything… but this one calf, his head looked like a basketball. His nose, off the end of a basketball, if you can figure out what that looked like. His hooves were about that long (he extended his hands about a foot apart) and they looked like sled runners. He had an awful time walking. The ears looked like they'd been frosted off, and his body didn't look like it had developed like it should have. We never tied the calf in with anything else."

"Did he ever have a vet look at it?

"I don't think he ever did."

"Was it born that way?"

"Well, not really, I don't think so, nobody ever said anything about it. But as he got older, why he just got worse. So, that one time, he just shot the thing and I drug it off into the bushes."

I was impressed by Berle's amazing recall of the events that had taken place over 25 years before. I asked him why his wife Nellie told reporters she was convinced that flying saucers had killed her horse.

"I don't think she was convinced it was UFOs or anything like that, but she knew it was something that we don't know about killed the horse. Now, I know it was something we, I don't know about, killed the horse. I figured after all these years I'd have the answers to it, but I don't have any answers. As far as I'm concerned, an unidentified object killed the horse! It wasn't anything natural. Couldn't be natural."[6]

Nellie's Diary?

I had moved to the San Luis Valley's Baca Grande Development, nestled at the base of the majestic Sangre de Cristo Mountains in 1989. In 1992, one of my neighbors, Pam LaBorde, mentioned a "diary" that her husband Roger and a group of friends had found while cleaning a cabin in the foothills of Blanca Peak—40 miles south of the Baca Grande development where I lived. At the time, I remembered the Snippy case, when she said the diary had been found in an out building of a King house that sat on the upper portion of the King Ranch. Evidently, the diary had belonged to *the* Nellie Lewis, Snippy the Horse's owner, so I called Roger to inquire about the discovery. The 'diary' turned out to be a handful of loose-leaf pages that Roger said had contained descriptions and drawings of UFO-type craft, dates, and accounts of visitations—even sketches of "strange beings in robes." He said there was a "drawing of a triangle and snake emblem [that] the beings had on their robes." Roger was sure that the pages belonged to Nellie Lewis. "It had her name right on it." I was somewhat intrigued, but thought anything having to do with Nellie Lewis was ancient history.

The LaBordes had been on a work party in 1988, with ten members of the Universal Education Foundation (UEF) who had just bought the old King Ranch from Berle Lewis, by then a widower. They were cleaning up the yard and out-buildings when Roger found the curious pages discarded in some garbage and he had called the rest of the work party crew to see them. Hosca Harrison, who had organized the clean up party, put them inside on the kitchen counter of the cabin for safekeeping, and everyone went back to their cleanup work.

Roger remembered, "A few minutes later, two men in the work party that I didn't know, left. I thought they were friends of someone else and didn't think much of it… Later we discovered that the pages were gone—somebody had taken them!" The UEF work crew had a real mystery on their hands. "Everyone there swore they hadn't taken the notes, and no one seemed to know who the two men were. I remember thinking they looked out of place—one of them was dressed in an undershirt but had on dress shoes and slacks." Neither of them had been dressed in work clothes.

Roger is a world-famous coma specialist. He has been instrumental in healing some very high-profile coma cases and is a spiritual, down-to-earth individual. Even so, this particular story was hard for me to swallow. Later, I checked with four others who were in the work party that day. All four told me the exact same story Roger had related. What would two strangers want with a handful of pages describing UFO sightings and alien visitations?

SLV UFO sightings were a fairly regular occurrence in the late '60s and at one point during my 1993 interview with Berle Lewis, I asked him to describe some of the various unexplained lights he'd personally seen back around the time of the strange horse death. He mentioned quite a few incidents. The first account is reminiscent of anomalous light sightings that I myself and others have witnessed on that part of the Sangre de Cristos where the King Ranch was located.

Berle thought back to some of the more peculiar events he had witnessed at the time. "One time we saw, from the cabin porch down to the corner of mile eight, in that field back that way, it just looked like a switchboard! The old-time switchboard, you know, with the lights flipping on and off? Well that's what that whole field looked like. If it had been back in Missouri or Iowa, I would've swore it was fireflies. Ain't no lightning bugs around here, though."

"Did the lights move?"

"It was just like that (he jabs all over in the air quickly with his finger) the whole field was lit up!"

"They chose to watch the lights from the porch through field glasses rather than go down to investigate. The phenomenon lasted around three hours. Berle related another sighting that occurred soon after.

"I come out of a town meeting in Blanca. They were getting ready to put water in the town of Blanca and they had a town meeting. Nellie covered it for the [Pueblo] *Chieftain* and I went with her. So when we come out and walked across the street, where the cafe is now, and over on the mountainside, we saw this light. I knew it couldn't be a house, and it was stationary. So I went back to tell them, and they all came out, I interrupted the meeting, and this one guy said he'd seen it there just before."

"How far away was it?"

"Oh, it looked like probably two or three miles. This one light, we left the meeting after they went back inside, we started back to Alamosa, and when we pulled in on 150 [the Sand Dunes road] … We parked there, and this light we had been watching back at Blanca, sitting on the hillside; it moved across and went clear back over to the Creede or Del Norte area. It went over the mountain, clear out of sight. We were sitting there talking, wondering what it could be and here it come! It got about 11:00 o'clock, and then it exploded! One light went into five, or three, then it closed and went into five, then went into six and seven, then it floated down over the Brown [San Luis] Hills.

"Berle contacted an Air Force investigator staying at the Alamosa Sands Motel to report the incident. "He never did go down to the Brown Hills to look, he just sat there in the bar a-drink'in. He wasn't even interested. I can't remember his name, I wished I could.

"How about the sounds everybody was hearing around here for awhile?"

"Motors, deep motors, it seemed like a big diesel engine running an air compressor and sounded like they was drillin'." This mirrors numerous contemporary reports from the Taos, New Mexico, area, 100 miles south, which have been dubbed 'The Taos Hum.'

Berle remembered one night when he and friends heard the sound. "Ken Wilson and Genevee, and Pearl Nicholas and Nellie and I, we sat down there, Ken had the car. And Ken always smoked a little cigar, about that long [he measured three-inches with his thumb and forefinger] like a torpedo, small at both ends. Ya never seen him without it. He was always chewing on that, and he had it in his mouth all the time, with only that much sticking out of his mouth. Odd way of smoking a cigar but that's the way he done it."

"So anyhow, we were sitting there looking and that motor started up on the hillside, about two miles or three miles away, and boy, I mean it was loud." Ken, excited, dashed around the car and, "All at once, he couldn't find his cigar." (We both break into laughter.) "So, we sat there and I had a flashlight and I looked around that whole area, I mean I really looked for it. We never did find that cigar."

"He swallowed it?" I guessed.

"That's right."

Berle mentioned that he, Nellie, and a friend had skywatched almost every night for six to eight months after the horse was killed. I asked who the friends were.

"That was Pearl Nicholas. And Father [Robert] Whiting used to come up. He had an experience through Del Norte and Monte Vista. He used to come up to the cabin quite often, he's the one that Leo Sprinkle, he hypnotized Father Whitting up there one night."

"One time, [we were] a mile west of the intersection [of the Mosca and Sand Dunes Roads]. There's a dirt road there and a gate. I looked out in the field and there was a pinpoint of light. Hell, it wasn't even as big as a light bulb. It was just a pinpoint about two blocks off the highway." They knew there were no houses, nor even roads, in that area. "Then all at once, why, I could see an outline of what I call, a Quonset hut. Probably 35-feet-high; 100-feet long. I was standing there looking at it, and all at once it come to me that something was moving toward us. Black. I described it as about six-feet-wide and about eight-or-nine-feet high. It was coming and, of course, Nellie got to feeling bad and got hysterical, so I came around and got in the car and we left. We got over to Harmony Lane and went north about a mile and a half and with a pair of field glasses. I could see this metallic building setting off the road in the pitch-black dark! You could still see that object!"

Just before dawn Berle took a co-worker back out to the site. "We walked that over and we didn't find nothin'! Not one mark, nothin' had sat down, but I know that building had to have been there!"

I had heard from Tom Adams that Berle and Nellie were missing a few hours that night.

"We don't know where we spent two-hours-and-a-half. We just drove back and it was 3:00 [a.m.] when we got in the house."

"And that's, what, about a 20 minute drive to your trailer?"

"It couldn't have been over 20 minutes," he assured me.[7]

Inexplicably, in 1976, Nellie committed suicide by carbon monoxide poisoning at the Urracca cemetery the day she buried Agnes, her mother. Several rumors were heard at the time by researchers concerning statements the mother and daughter had made to friends about passing on to the other side together. Nellie's friends claimed she had allegedly confided to them that, "Beings would come for her and her mother on the same day."

Ken and Ginny Wilson remembered changes in her behavior after Snippy died.

"Nellie became obsessed with the occult. She started using an Ouija-board and reading all kinds of books about UFOs."

Nellie's nephew Don Hard remembers that Nellie had what at the time were considered "far out" ideas and theories about who or what had killed her horse:

> Aunt Nellie was excited about it being a UFO that got hold of it… The family really got into this because of what happened. We used to watch for strange things; we'd go out and look for them. [But] this topped everything. There hasn't been anything like that since. Aunt Nellie was kind of into scary things. She kinda liked it, I think. She had seen strange lights in the Valley, so right away she wanted to say it was extraterrestrial or something from outer space that did this, maybe with a laser beam, or some kind of technology we don't know about because it seemed to distinguish between flesh and bone.[8]

The Snippy Skeleton Auction

Even today, the controversial Snippy endures. In the fall of 2006, Debra Goodman, head of the Alamosa Chamber of Commerce, contacted me. She asked if I could help with a fund drive to obtain the articulated and mounted bones of Lady. She mentioned that the owners of the skeleton wanted to auction off the bones. I was surprised to hear that the long lost skeleton had resurfaced.

Years before, I had conducted research to find out what had happened to the bones. I was able to track down that a local Alamosa vet had boiled the bones and had them mounted for display. Several fairly well known photographs were published. The bones were displayed for a few years at the vet's office and then were moved to Adams State College where they were on display for some time into the mid-70s. One story has it that the bones were thrown away; another claimed they had been put in storage at the ASC. But, at some point they disappeared. From what I can ascertain, the former janitor may have taken them home and put them into a railroad boxcar that he used to put his assortment of collectables he had no room to display. Upon his death, his estate re-discovered the bones and the family hired a representative to put them up for sale in 2005—hence Debra Goodman's call requesting my help.

I was hired by the Chamber of Commerce to produce a fund raising video and traveled to the SLV in December 2006 to shoot interviews, find out more about the sale, and, if possible, view the mounted bones. I was successful in landing a visit and headed to the location in Alamosa where the bones were on private display. Upon inspection of the skeleton, I was surprised to find small bits of connective tissue between a couple of vertebrae which runs contrary to claims *that all the tissue* was gone from the horse's remains. The bones had been boiled before they were mounted and one would think that no tissue would remain, but as I discovered, this wasn't the case. I suppose that sometimes appearances and descriptions can be deceiving.

The eBay sale went forward (with a reserve of $30,000) and it flopped. The highest bid was $1,800 and the bones were withdrawn from the action. If you have a spare $30K lying around and are interested in obtaining the infamous skeleton, I can put you in touch with the owners. I bet they would come down on their price, if you were serious.

All kidding aside, one thing is certain in my mind, the "Snippy Case" is ground zero for the establishment of public perception concerning the "cattle mutilation" myth and this case deserves the extra attention I have paid to it in this (and other) books. Even though Snippy was a horse rather than a cow, this first modern *cattle* mutilation case was an important unexplained livestock death and this case might hold important details and clues that could have tremendous significance in our attempt to unravel the mutilation mystery. Say what you will, but it appears that Nellie Lewis' Appaloosa, Lady a.k.a. "Snippy," has joined the ranks of notable horses in history; Pegasus, Traveler, Comanche, Man O' War, or perhaps the 'Trojan Horse.'

As was mentioned in the Nellie Lewis interview, the infamous Condon committee had sent down a team to investigate the Snippy case. Their findings made the final Condon report (case #32), and here is the excerpt that states their conclusions:

Condon Report:
Case 32 [Snippy the Horse Case] Fall 1967
Investigators: Ayer, Wadsworth

Abstract:
The death of a horse was popularly believed to be related to UFO sightings, but professional investigation disclosed nothing unusual in the condition of the carcass. No significant conclusions could be derived from numerous reports of UFO sightings.

Background:
During the early fall, 1967, news of a series of events that were popularly held to be related filtered in to the Colorado project. One such event had been the death of a horse under allegedly mysterious circumstances a month before. This death had become associated in the public mind with recent UFO sightings in the area.

The horse, owned by a woman and pastured on her brother's ranch, had not come in for water one day and had been found dead two days later. It was reported that all the flesh and skin had been removed from his head and neck down to a straight cut just ahead of the shoulder, and that crushed vegetation, strange depressions in the ground, and dark "exhaust marks" had been found nearby. The owner of the horse was a correspondent for a local newspaper, and a spate of releases had rapidly inflated public interest in the case.

When, a few days later, word came through that a second dead horse had been found, amid persistent rumors of unreported UFOs, it was decided that project investigators should go to the area.

Investigation

The area about the carcass had been trampled by several hundred visitors. The investigators therefore considered it was not worthwhile to try to investigate anything at the site except the carcass. When they learned that no veterinarian had examined it, they called in a veterinarian, who examined the carcasses of both of the horses. His essential findings were:

The horse's carcass was extremely old for an autopsy, but there was evidence suggesting a severe infection in a hind leg that could have disabled or killed the animal. There was evidence also of a knife cut in the neck, possibly made by someone who found the horse hopelessly sick. Absence of nerve tissues and viscera was normal for a carcass dead several weeks.

Magpies and other birds ordinarily cannot peck through the skin of a horse, but will eat the flesh and skin if they can get into it. In this case, they evidently had taken advantage of the cut and removed all accessible skin and flesh from the neck and head before the carcass had been found.

The second horse carcass showed evidence that death had resulted from encephalitis.

It had been reported that a forest ranger with civil defense training had found a high level of radioactivity near the "exhaust marks." When questioned by an investigator, he said that his meter had indicated only "slight" activity two weeks after the carcass had been found. The investigators concluded that the activity he had measured on his simple survey instrument had been no greater than the normal background radiation they measured three weeks later.

Conclusions:

There was no evidence to support the assertion that the horse's death was associated in any way with abnormal causes.

Other Sightings:

The investigators then turned their attention to the numerous reports of UFO sightings in the same area. Many were vague or involved direct lights at night. Only the more interesting cases are reported here.

1) A service-station attendant and former aircraft gunner reported three sightings in ten years. The second, about 1962, occurred while he, with three companions, was driving west at 65 mph., about 3:30 a.m. They noticed on the slope of a nearby mountain a point of blue light that moved toward the highway and then turned parallel to it, pacing the car a few feet from the ground. It soon pulled ahead and vanished over the valley. Suddenly, the witness saw what he assumed was the same light appear in the middle of the road some distance ahead and approach at high speed, so that he ran the car off into the graded ditch to avoid collision. As the light approached, it grew to at least the size of his car. As it passed, it shot upward a few feet, turned south, and disappeared.

In the spring of 1967, the same witness, with his wife, was driving west when he saw an object that resembled a box kite crossing the highway from the left. He associated it with a helicopter, although he was familiar with them and the apparition was silent. Thinking that it was some kind of aircraft that might land at the airport, he drove directly there. During this part of the trip, the object disappeared behind some buildings. When they arrived at the airport, it was nowhere in sight.

2) About 5:15 a.m., late summer, 1967, a couple were driving south when they saw two extended objects outlined with a dull glow, at an altitude of about 15°. One was directly south over the road, and the second was south-southwest. The objects moved northwesterly until they were apparently "directly over [the mountain]." There the second moved up beside the first and they hovered for several minutes before descending rapidly to the ground, where they merged with the vegetation and disappeared. The witnesses estimated that the minimum distance to the objects was one mile, and presumably was never very much greater; however, they hovered "directly over [the mountain]," which was at least 8 mi. away.

3) On an unrecalled date, late in the summer, 1966, about 5:30 a.m., two boys, ages 13 and 17, were traveling north when they saw an extended bright light in the road. The UFO kept ahead of them for about 20 mi., then [it] disappeared.

4) At 10:15 p.m., early fall, 1967, the owner of the horse mentioned above, with her husband, was driving west. They saw three pulsating red-and-green lights pass over, moving generally southwest.

After five to ten minutes, the third object seemed to explode, emitting a yellow flash, then a second flash nearer the ground, and a puff of smoke that the witnesses observed for ten minutes. Several fragments were seen to fall to the ground after the second explosion.

The husband and wife disagreed as to the location. He said the wreckage should lie somewhere between the second and fifth hill south of a nearby town, but she said she saw the explosion over a brown hill ten miles east of the same town. The explosion was also seen by a farmer, and his times and bearings supported the husband's account. Ayer drove between the second and third and the third and fourth hills, and he flew over the region south of the fifth hill, but he saw nothing of interest.

The data on this sighting were sent to Major Quintanilla, who reported that no satellite re-entries had been seen or predicted at the reported time. This finding, however, did not preclude the unobserved re-entry of a minor fragment that had not been tracked.

5) Another couple reported several sightings, one of these, between 9:00 and 10:00 p.m., fall, 1967, considered by them to be a "meteor." Its location was not given. This sighting was also reported to Major Quintanilla, but no satellite had been observed to re-enter on that day.

6) In the fall, 1967, "ten minutes before dark," two ranchers driving west saw a small cigar-shaped cloud, vertically oriented in a sky that had only one other cloud in it. The cigar was about the size of a thumb at arms length, 200 above the "horizon" and 45° south of the road, that is, southwest of the point of first sighting. It was slightly boat-tailed at the bottom and its outlines were not sharp. The second cloud was obviously a cloud, at a slightly greater altitude in the south. The two men drove about three miles while the "cigar" tilted slightly toward the other cloud and moved slowly toward it. They stopped the car to observe more closely. Pointing toward the larger cloud, the "cigar" continued to approach it. After a few minutes the witnesses drove on, and a few minutes later the "cigar" melted into the cloud.

Summary:
None of these sighting reports were considered to be current or strange enough to warrant detailed investigation. END OF REPORT[9]

Space does not allow another rehashing of the questionable agenda and credibility of the Condon Report. Needless to say, it has been fairly well established the Colorado State University professor Edward Condon went into the investigation with his mind already made up about UFOs. Some have asserted that he was tasked with debunking the whole thing partially as a cover for the discontinuing of the Air Force's Project Blue Book.

What Else Was Happening in the Fall of 1967?

So many nuances surround the unexplained events that swirled around the San Luis Valley and the King Ranch during the mid-to-late 1960s. I often wonder about the timing of these events and whether the strange death of Lady is somehow significant. One noteworthy element surrounding this exact time period within the culture, concerns the flowering of perception sweeping the USA during the late summer of 1967. Hundreds-of-thousands of "flower children" across the United States were becoming psycho-tropically aware through the use of mind-altering substances and this first week of September 1967 could be called the height of the "summer of love." For years I've wondered if this immense wave of expanded psychedelic "hippie" awareness could somehow be linked to the upsurge of unexplained North American UFO activity in '66-'67, and the subsequent birth of the publicized phase of the "cattle mutilation" phenomenon at the close of the "summer of love." The timing is there, but am I simply the wrong fence post?

To many this what-if idea I am proposing is a stretch, at best, and I agree, but my intuition has always been tweaked by this correlation. Or the correlation that psychedelic mushrooms prefer to grow in ungulate (cattle) dung. Is it possible we witnessed the opening of a collective psychic doorway with an inadvertent 'key' dubbed 'psychedelics?' Perhaps a game-changing wave of cultural impetuousness swept the culture and perhaps mutilations are somehow involved in this expanded awareness, or cultural growth process? As you will see, what is happening in the culture may somehow be directly involved with the waves of unexplained livestock deaths that ebb and flow through the years.

Here is a "what-if." However remote the possibility, if this is connection is somehow real, then perhaps some sort of preternatural predator (that has lurked around hypothetically for millennia) saw an opportunity to re-visit this reality and slipped through this opened door at that pivotal point in our history to enact an as-yet undefined agenda? We have (and still do) sacrifice animals to the gods. Perhaps this too is connected? If these perceived correlations are correct, I wonder why this predatory force (or mechanism) would select the SLV and choose to perpetrate the Snippy incident? As a warning perhaps? Even if this speculation is wildly wrong, the timing of the event may be highly revealing and important when you factor in the outbreak of chronic wasting disease in northern Colorado and southern Wyoming deer and elk herds that same fall of 1967.[10]

Looking at synchronistic correlations, I find the possibilities endlessly fascinating and a bit perturbing. So is the timing of the outbreak of foot-and-mouth disease in Britain a month after Snippy in October 1967 that is thought to be due to the importation of infected sheep from Argentina and Chile. We'll address F&M disease later at length in Chapter Twelve.

And what about this next event that occurred less than 100 miles away, to the southwest —just over the San Juan Mountains? Perhaps Snippy really was some kind of warning. Chronic Wasting disease is bad enough but consider what happened on December 10, 1967, exactly three months, three days after "Snippy the Horse" was discovered. On that day, the United States Atomic Energy Commission, with the help of the Laurence Radiation Laboratory, detonated a huge underground *29-kiloton nuclear bomb* in an attempt to free up untapped natural gas deposits over 4,000 feet down. The local Ute Indians peppered the top of a nearby butte top to watch the show and the earth moved. Dubbed Project Gasbuggy, this was a part of the U.S. Government's Operation Plowshare (the development of peaceful uses for nuclear explosions) and this explosion was the first of three proposed underground detonations. Ground-zero was located 21 miles SW of the town of Dulce, New Mexico—directly south of the Gomez Ranch where an intense mutilation wave would commence fewer than ten years later. Unfortunately for the investors behind the selection of the Gasbuggy site, the detonations *heavily irradiated the released gas deposits* and as a result the freed up gas could not be commercially exploited by El Paso Natural Gas, a partner of the project. And they may have inadvertently released a nasty genie into the environment.

In the intervening 45-years, increased rates of environmental cancers in the area are thought by some to be a result of this Gasbuggy experiment-gone-wrong. Dr. Howard Eliason has spent years conducting a survey of above ground radiation levels in the Dulce region and is working on an on-going scientific study to establish a link between local cancer rates and types and the radiation known to be present in and around the Dulce area.

Radiation may be another important clue we have to unravel the mutilation mystery. In 1979 David Perkins proposed a theory that areas of high-incidence of mutilation reports seemed to be downwind and downstream from where we mine, enrich, weaponize, and utilize radioactive materials. Perkins' Environmental Monitoring Theory has withstood the test of time. We'll discuss it and various other theories that have been proposed to explain the "mutilation" mystery later on. Various theories that have been proposed since the late 1970s have centered around the Dulce area. Conspiracy theorists in the know suggest that perhaps the "underground base" (said to be located inside Archuleta Mesa, which straddles the Colorado-New Mexico border and is on the Jicarilla Apache reservation) is where nuclear waste or discarded nuclear materials are being buried. And perhaps the underground "alien base" below Archuleta Mesa (or Archuleta Mountain) is a cover story to deflect serious attention away from the area.

One thing is certain: Snippy is truly a departure point for our unraveling process. The extent of the "flap" of 1967-1969 UFO, military, and mute activity in the San Luis Valley and elsewhere has become blurred through time. I tried for years to gain access to *Valley Courier* editor Pearl Nicholas' extensive listing of UFO reports from the 1967-1970 time periods when hundreds of sightings occurred, but surviving family members have resisted my requests for access. As a result, a vast majority of these strange events have become lost effectively beyond our reach, surviving within word-of-mouth tales and family legends. Facts have been mixed-up, added upon, deleted, forgotten, and inexorably altered. Even the primary eyewitnesses, who should be able to effectively clarify the events they witnessed, may have contributed inadvertently to creation of future mythos, folklore, or a cultural meme by their fuzzy recollection of these unusual events.

Again, I would argue that the Snippy the Horse case is our ground zero— located at the beginning of the cultural meme called "the cattle mutilation phenomenon"—the initial ingredient fueling the fodder of a new myth and legend. Is this a classic example of a primary meme, or building block in an aspect of culture? A keystone in the building of the edifice of religious and/or mythological belief, or a "memeplex" (a combination of memes) as Perkins likes to say?

As the Snippy case faded in cultural memory by late October of 1967, it was replaced by a bucolic glow brought on by a rapidly changing culture tuning in turning on and dropping acid. The baby boomers were being awakened to new possibilities, the Beatles were recording Magical Mystery Tour, and the contentious US presidential election of 1968 was heating up as a meat-grinder war was being escalated across the ocean in SE Asia. And cattle and other animals began to be reported as "mutilated."

Little Known Cases From the Late 1960s

I have discovered other references to possible fall 1967 mutilation cases in the United States in other countries. The San Luis Valley may have also experienced two *bison* mutilations on the nearby Medano Ranch, and possibly some "classic" cattle mutes during the 1966 to 1968 time period, but I have been unable to fully corroborate these claims.

In the mid-1960s, well-known investigator/author John Keel traveled to the Ohio River Valley/Tri-state area numerous times documenting strange aerial object activity and attendant animal attacks that included mutilation claims that seemed to be associated with these object and light sightings. Keel recounts a couple of instances where UFOs were seen and dogs that attempted to approach the objects were attacked or, in a couple of accounts, never seen again.

> In December 1967 [a] cow was found near Gallipolis, Ohio, with the unkindest cut of all—it had been neatly severed in two 'as if it had been chopped in half by a giant pair of scissors.' The organs and blood in the lower half had all been removed…
>
> A nurse who lives on a farm with her two teen-aged children outside of Gallipolis, sought [Keel] out and told [him] a long and involved story about her experiences with the objects and their occupants. She keeps cows on her farm and she claimed that someone was butchering them in

her fields. She had seen the "rustlers" on several occasions and had gone after them with a shotgun. "They're tall men in white coveralls," she explained. "And they certainly can run and jump. I've seen them leap over high fences from a standing start..."

[The nurse's] troubles with cattle "rustlers" had started around 1963-64... The cattle "rustlers," she explained, had ruthlessly butchered a number of her animals very expertly. But they didn't seem to want the choice steak cuts. Instead they rather pointlessly removed the brains and other organs of little commercial value. And there was never any blood in evidence. She had complained repeatedly to both the police and the FBI... She claimed that an elderly couple who had lived on her property for years had often told her about strange lights in the area. Sightings went back 30 years...

A year earlier we would have put [her] down as paranoid. Her story smacked of a persecution complex gone amok. But we have heard too many similar tales in our travels to take hers lightly...

Farmers in central Pennsylvania were so upset by their losses to the phantom animal mutilators that in 1968 they formed a local organization to try and catch the culprits.[11]

Over the years, South America has contributed its fair share of strange reports of unexplained livestock deaths. Some of these stories are beyond bizarre and feature what appear to be non-humans aided by high technology victimizing cattle, sheep, and other animals. The following case was mentioned by Jerome Clark in his *UFO Encyclopedia, Volume 3,* and is one of those real "head-scratchers." Researched by Oscar Galindez and recounted in *Flying Saucer Review,* it tells the tale of a "Violent Humanoid Encountered." I'm not sure what to make of this case that allegedly occurred several short months after the Snippy case. I'll let you decide what to think:

Otoco, Brazil, early 1968: A Bolivian newspaper reported that in the early evening a woman discovered a strange net over the corral where she kept her sheep. Inside the corral a humanlike figure, about four feet tall and clad in what looked like a bulky spacesuit, was killing sheep with a hooked tubular instrument and dumping the entrails into a bag. In a frantic effort to stop him, she pelted him with stones. The figure walked over to a boxlike instrument and turned a wheel at the top. The netting was then absorbed into the box. By now the woman had collected a club and was marching menacingly toward the intruder, who threw his weapon at her. Each time it would return to his hands in boomerang fashion. Each throw resulted in small cuts on the woman's arms. The humanoid gathered up both box and bag and rose into the air, "making a most extraordinary noise" and disappeared from sight. Local authorities, led by police Col. Rogelio Ayala, launched an investigation. They counted 34 dead sheep, each missing a portion of its digestive organs. (Galindez, 1970)[12]

Another intriguing story comes from UK researcher Tim Mathews, investigated for an article on UK mutilation cases:

> At a very successful meeting in Warrington, Cheshire, last night the British UFO Studies Centre received several intriguing UFO reports from members of the public. I was lucky to speak with a former RAF [officer]... who had served near RAF Upper Heyford in the late 1960s.
> In 1968, he (and several friends) were called to visit the site of a strange animal death by two US MPs stationed at Heyford, whom they knew. A sheep had been "cut in two" by what the witness described as "a laser." Moreover, there were no signs of blood around the animal, no footprints or tracks, and other animals in the field were very agitated. Both halves of the animal were particularly smooth and the blood inside the remains appeared to have congealed.
> This strange animal death may be the result of entirely explainable causes even if the farmer and local military personnel were at a loss to understand it. I have no idea at this stage whether the local vet or other government agencies were involved in subsequent investigations.
> There is a problem with such reports; skeptics always cite [sic] the work of sadistic cultists, satanic groups, and predators and so on whilst certain ufologists offer evidence of alien-human-animal experiments. There must be a better solution![13]

Back when I first began actively investigating and researching San Luis Valley region cattle mutilations in 1993, I heard several SLV old-timers mention two buffalo mutilations that were rumored to have occurred in the spring of 1968 on the Medano ranch, located about ten miles directly north of the lower King Ranch, where Snippy was found. I combed through the *Valley Courier* archives and was unable to verify the exact date of this case, but according to two ranchers, Berle Lewis at the King Ranch and Verl Holmes in Mosca, this had occurred in the early spring of 1968, and both ranchers claimed to have gone and checked out the crime scene. For obvious reasons, I have stayed away from mentioning rumored cases as much as possible, but I feel that this particular case has enough credibility to be worthy of mention because of the character and quality of the witnesses Bison/buffalo cases are extremely rare, the most notable case being the bison found inexplicably mutilated *inside* the Cheyenne Mountain Zoo on October 21, 1975, covered in the next chapter.

The Snippy case, as I noted, occurred three months before Project Gasbuggy, and the only known buffalo mutilation cases in the sixties occurred around the time of another government program that inadvertently released deadly toxins into the environment: the Dugway Proving Grounds fiasco of March 1968.

The Dugway event occurred on March 13th and 17, 1968, at the location where the U.S. military tests newly developed chemical and biological weapons. Located southwest of Salt Lake City, Utah, the proving grounds accident of March 1968 gained international news coverage after the U.S. Army Chemical Corp apparently let some nasty VX nerve agent get away from them during an aerial test when the shutoff valve on the plane failed to close. The gas drifted off the proving grounds into nearby Skull Valley, Utah, where herds of sheep grazed, and more than 6300 sheep perished in agony. The public was outraged when the Pentagon initially denied responsibility, and it was only after the ensuing news coverage and outcry focused attention on military chemical/biological weapons programs that they admitted their involvement. The military ended up paying out $1 million to impacted Skull Valley sheep ranchers.

Biological and chemical weapons development was "officially" banned by the United Nations under the Biological and Toxic Weapons Convention Treaty in 1972, which the U.S. Senate ratified. President Gerald Ford signed the treaty into law almost three years later, on January 2, 1975. By this time the Army had officially standardized and weaponized several biological agents including *bovine anthrax, foot-and-mouth disease, and Venezuela equine encephalitis* – all afflicting cattle and horses.[14]

A parallel proximity correlation appeared again in 2001 when a particularly nasty outbreak of UK foot-and-mouth disease occurred which "resulted in the destruction of over six million animals at the cost of $9.51 billion dollars…Tests on the virus strain involved was one which did not occur in nature and was held only *at the nearby Pirbright Research Complex…* In August 2007… British investigators were announcing that the new foot-and-mouth outbreak there had probably originated [again] at one of Pirbright's high containment research facilities… defend us oh Lord from our defenders."[15] Indeed.

U.S. congressional hearings in 1977 revealed that the Army acknowledged that "239 populated areas from coast to coast had been blanketed with bacteria between 1949 and 1969.[16] This little-known fact should give us an indication of the military's mindset of disdain concerning public health and the wellbeing of the population and its farming livelihoods. Never mind the lowly people that make up the 'great unwashed masses' obliviously munching our Big-Macs in front of their big-screen TVs.[17]

Whether our military and intelligence agencies have honored this ban on bio-chemical weapons development in the intervening years is questionable. There have been indications in subsequent years that development and testing of biological and chemical weapons projects still continue in secret at locations such as Fort Detrick, Maryland; Plum Island, Massachusetts; Long Island, New York;

the Rocky Mountain Laboratory, Ft. Collins, Colorado; Pine Bluff Arsenal, Arkansas, and probably at other less publicly-known and/or secret facilities here and abroad.[18]

All appeared somewhat quiet on the mutilation front in 1969, and I have been unable to find any noteworthy cases that were mentioned in the various databases or in searches of media archives. This would change as the new decade commenced, and it appears to have re-started in the upper Midwest.

Sources and References

1. O'Brien, Christopher, *The Mysterious Valley,* St Martins Press, NY NY 1996
2. O'Brien, Christopher, *Enter the Valley,* St Martins Press, NY NY 1999
3. O'Brien, Christopher, *Secrets of the Mysterious Valley,* Adventures Unlimited Press, Kempton, IL, 2007
4. O'Brien, Christopher, *Secrets of the Mysterious Valley,* Adventures Unlimited Press, Kempton, IL, 2007
5. Don Hard Interview w/ author, 12-20-05
6. O'Brien, Christopher, *Secret of the Mysterious Valley*, Adventures Unlimited Press, Kempton, IL, 2007]
7. Nellie Lewis Interview with Lonnie Furbay, 10-18-67; Tom Adams, *The Mysterious Valley*
8. O'Brien, Christopher, *Secrets of the Mysterious Valley,* Adventures Unlimited Press, Kempton, IL, 2007
9. *ibid*
10. Don Hard Interview w/ author, 12-20-05
11. "Scientific Study of Flying Saucers," Dr. Edward U. Condon, Director/CSU/USAF, 1968
12. Kelleher, Colm, *Brain Trust,* Paraview, NY, NY, 2004
13. Keel, John, *Strange Creatures From Time and Space,* Fawcett, Inc, NY, NY 1970
14. Oscar Galindez, *Flying Saucer Review 16,4;* Clark, Jerome, *UFO Encyclopedia Vol 3*: Omnigraphics, Inc, Detroit, MI, 1996
15. "Cattle Mutilations in 1968" Tim Mathews
16. Cole, Leonard, *Clouds of Secrecy,* , Rowman and Littlefield, Totowa, NJ, 1988
17. Ring Kenneth, *Germs Gone Wild*, Pegasus Books, NY, 2010
18. Cole, Leonard, *Clouds of Secrecy,* Rowman and Littlefield, 1988

Figure 1
The SLV's Great Sand Dunes—world's highest and most mysterious sand dune desert.
This is the view looking over the Folsom Man archaeological sites.
(credit: greatsanddunesnationalpark.gov)

Figure 2
Landed 'UFO' that flew over the Snippy site, 1967.
(credit: Bill McPhedries/David Perkins/AMP)

Figure 3
The King Ranch—located just southeast of where the Snippy case occurred.
(credit: Don Hard)

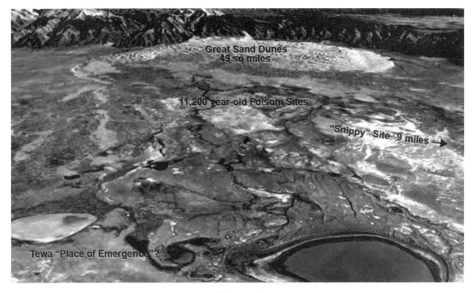

Figure 4
The San Luis Lakes. Alleged location of the Tewa Indians 'place of emergence.'
(credit: google Earth)

Figure 5
Nellie Lewis—owner of Lady a.k.a. 'Snippy.' (credit: Don Hard)

Figure 6
Berle and Nellie Lewis. (credit: Don Hard)

Figure 7
The most famous photograph of Snippy the Horse.
(credit: David Perkins/AMP archive)

Figure 8
from l to r: APRO investigator Don and Alice Richmond, Nellie
and Berle Lewis. (credit: David Perkins/AMP archive)

Figure 9
'Giant horse track' found near the carcass of Snippy the Horse.
(credit: David Perkins/AMP archive)

Figure 10
Examining Snippy the Horse. Who or what did this to this poor animal?
(credit: David Perkins/AMP archive)

SIGHTINGS REPORTED

Dead Horse Riddle Sparks UFO Buffs

Figure 11
Pueblo Chieftain headline, October 1967. After the article was published, word of the Snippy case spread around the world like a wildfire. (credit: Pueblo Chieftain)

Nellie Lewis Is Found Dead

Nellie Lewis, 55, a resident of the Great Sand Dunes National Monument and of Alamosa, was pronounced dead on arrival at the Alamosa Community Hospital at about 6:47 p.m. Thursday, Feb. 12.

Alamosa County Coroner Kenneth Butler said as nearly as can be determined, Mrs. Lewis attached a hose to the exhaust of her car and death was from asphixiation.

Figure 12
Nellie Lewis committed suicide the day of her mother's burial. (credit: Valley Courier)

Figure 13
Dr. Wallace Leary cleaned and mounted the articulated bones of Snippy.
The skeleton went missing in the 1970s. (credit: UPI October 6, 1968)

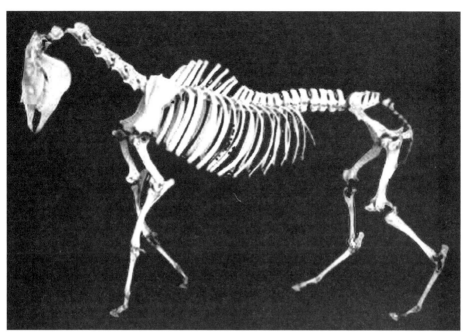

Figure 14

The skeleton resurfaced in 2005 and were put up for auction on ebay. Nobody met the reserve. The bones are still for sale. (credit: Frank Duran/snippy.com)

Students eating 'magic mushrooms'

Figure 15

Headline warns the public concerning student magic mushroom use. Magic 'shrooms prefer to grew in cow pies. (credit: unknown headline on Google.com)

Figure 16
Project Gasbuggy, December 10, 1967 occurred a month after Snippy—less than 93 miles away in Dulce, New Mexico. (credit: retronaut.com)

Figure 17
Dugway Proving Grounds. 6000 sheep were killed in nearby Skull Valley from escaped weaponized gas released by the Army Chemical Corp. (credit: wikipedia.org)

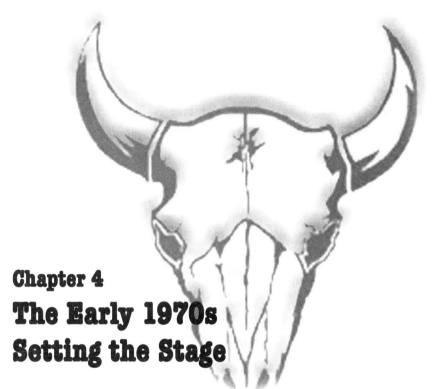

Chapter 4
The Early 1970s
Setting the Stage

In the three-year time period following the Snippy case and the documented but little-known mid-to-late '60s reports in the Ohio River Valley region, the mutilators appeared to move northeast into the Great Lakes region and the upper Midwest. Farmers in Minnesota, Iowa, Kansas, Wisconsin, South Dakota, and Nebraska, began reporting cases to authorities and the national media began to slowly take notice of local and regional claims.

In "Meet the Mutilators," Perkins observes that: "In 1970 the livestock rustling in Iowa had drawn national attention after a *New York Times* article (June 6th 1970) stated that the rustling epidemic in that state was costing Iowa farmers three to five million dollars per year."

Coincidentally, a worldwide UFO flap erupted in 1973, which was the year of the Judy Doraty abduction claim from Texas that we'll detail later in the chapter. But let's first set the cultural stage.

Since the beginning of my serious interest and research into the unexplained livestock death mystery in 1993, I have always had an intuitive feeling that there is something important lurking in these late-60s and early 70s reports. There seemed to be a melting pot of different memes churning out various possible scenarios as to who or what is behind the unexplained livestock death mystery, and possible telltale clues in the patterning may provide deeper insight into the true nature of the

127

phenomenon. These early rustling and mutilation cases are not well known—even though they did receive some national notoriety—and these cases have proven to be particularly difficult for me to uncover. (figure 1)

I could not have presented the following research into the early 1970s without the invaluable help, guidance and hard work of David Perkins. "Izzy," as he is known to his investigator friends, spent several weeks and countless hours combing through old newspaper archives, books, magazine articles and other potential source material in an effort to help me obtain a complete picture of how the early 1970s waves unfolded. The Iz and I were on the lookout for anything that could possibly be relevant— regions of high incidence that had concentrations of; UFOs, hairy hominid and other cryptid sightings, mystery helicopter reports, livestock rustling and mutilation cases. David kept reminding me that these potential correlations could somehow be highly significant and I readily agreed and helped him dig. We backtracked media reports in each category to ascertain when and where each particular theory to explain the mute mystery emerged. It was our thinking that when, how and where these memes were initially propagated, would provide us with invaluable clues to unravel the mystery behind what David calls: this "mutilation supermeme-plex."

Here is a possible example from the *The Daily Ardmoreite,* (Ardmore, Oklahoma) 3-3-71 (figure 2) that noted a series of events reported by residents of an apartment complex in Lawton, Oklahoma, witnessing a "tall, hairy 'Wolfman' creature with a distorted face and pants several sizes too small." Unexplained animal deaths had been reported in the previous months in the Lawton area. The fashion-challenged Wildman was described as wearing tight-fitting, dark-colored pants and a plaid jacket. The witnesses noted a slouching posture like that of an ape-man, and it had a "glazed expression, as if he didn't quite understand where he was." And, reminiscent of the "Spring-heeled Jack" from 19th century England, the "monkeyman" seen in India in the early 2000s, and the "dogman" witnessed in 2009 in Ft. Duschene, Utah—near the infamous "Skinwalker Ranch"—the humanoid creature was able to make impossible 25- to 30-foot leaps—roof to roof—from house to house.

C. Edward Green, 24, one of those who saw it, said Tuesday (3-2-71) it was no hoax as far as he is concerned. Green said he and his wife spotted the creature on a lake drive last Friday night. He said that after calling the police he went to his second-floor apartment to see what was going on—and there was the 'thing' staring back at him. Green said the creature leaped to a railing on the walkway outside the apartment and jumped to the ground below.

This coincided with other reports about the creatures amazing jumping abilities. Donald Childs, 35, reported that he saw the creature leap 15 feet over a small homemade fishpond, when he spotted the 'thing' Saturday night. The sighting caused Childs to suffer muscle seizures…Childs entered the hospital and was released Sunday.

Three other persons at an apartment complex reported seeing a "monkey-like" creature. Police officer Harry Ezell said one of the apartment residents thought it was a joke "until it turned its head and looked at him, then jumped off its perch on the second floor railing onto the ground 17 feet below." The creature had previously been spotted dodging cars and running wildly through the neighborhood near the apartments.[1]

David N. Brown sums up the possible perceived link between hairy ape-men cryptids and outbreaks of unexplained livestock deaths:

> This story presents a case of entities bearing a fair resemblance to "phantom clowns" [tricksters] being blamed for cattle mutilation and other supposedly mysterious animal deaths and disappearances, an association already widely reported with other Fortean phenomena such as UFOs and cryptids.[2]

The Lawton, Oklahoma area would be visited by the mutilators during the mid to late 1970s, but none of the perpetrators were seen—let alone hairy ape-men adorned in tight trousers and "plaid" ill-fitting jackets. Nearby are Shepard Air Force Base and Ft. Sill, where the Apache chief Geronimo was buried and later it was rumored that Prescott Bush—father of George H. Bush—dug him up and returned his skull and leg bones back to Yale's Skull & Bones fraternity in the early 1900s.

One intriguing Minnesota mutilation report from the early 1970s was investigated and subsequently publicized by Minnesota UFO investigator Terrance Mitchell. At the time, Mitchell was a lecturer under contract with the University of Minnesota and was actively investigating claims of the unusual in Minnesota. There had been a number of UFO sightings in the region that fall and this guilt-by-association scenario tying mutilations cases with UFOs was promoted by Mitchell. In an article in the [Brainard] *Daily Dispatch,* the paper notes:

> The mutilation killings began back in 1970 in Lyon County [Minnesota] with a number of incidents that year and in 1971. There was a lull until July and October of this year [1974] in that county when three incidents were reported. A rash this year occurred in other counties… [The] most recent [case]—a 400-pound heifer found on Dec. 1 in the field of farmer Frank Schifelbien near Kimball about four miles southwest of Kimball in Meeker County…The eye, left ear, tongue and part of the lip were taken from the animal and there were no external signs of [the cause of] death…Just as strange was a small pond Mitchell discovered about a half mile from the heifer. There was a perfect circle of melted snow and in the center a jagged hole gouged out of the ice that was then filled with water.[3]

"Large footprints went up to the circle and ended right there… And there are no springs in the pond." Probably the most baffling aspect of his visit was provided by Mitchell's friend, who was taking photographs from a light plane… the picture…shows a mysterious pattern of perfect circles in a pasture about a quarter-mile south of where the heifer was found… (figure 3) "Strange thing— the cow, the circles and the pond are in a straight line."[4]

An investigator from the Bureau of Alcohol Tobacco and Firearms, Donald Flickinger (figure 4) traveled to the farm to interview Schifelbien and quickly discovered that the scene and the attendant circumstantial evidence had possible mundane explanations to explain what Mitchell thought were unusual:

Flickinger demolished the UFO hypothesis. The saucer-landing divots in the pond turned out to be watering holes chopped in the ice; the tree branches had been broken by the wind and by Schifelbien himself; the saucer circles were actually snow-covered silage piles.[5]

We will cover Flickinger's involvement in investigating the early 1970's mutilations in a minute, but first here is an interesting stand-alone precursor proto-helicopter case that occurred near Leadville, Colorado in August 1971. It was reported that a Basque sheepherder had reported to authorities that he had witnessed a military-type helicopter buzzing around the ranch where he worked. He went out to check on the herd of 2000 sheep and was dismayed to discover that 40 of them were "clumped under bushes in a meadow, blistered…" The sheepherder's boss, Irving Beard, had originally told authorities that his sheep had been "shot," but this was later corrected as a misinterpretation (the Basque sheepherder didn't speak English). Evidently, the animals did not have any bullet holes, but when the Ft. Carson veterinarian Dr. Bernard Smith was called in to conduct necropsies, he was surmised the "blistered" sheep had been hit by a lightning strike. Ft. Carson spokesperson Lt. Col. G.D. Barrante denied that any army helicopters were flying near the ranch at the time.

The report was published on UPI and in a number of newspapers, including the Provo *Herald* and the Corpus Christi *Caller-Times,* and the articles debunked the deaths as due to a mundane lightning strike. Normally, multiple livestock killed by lightning have assembled under a tree that was struck, but in this instance, there were no trees located nearby, no thunderstorms in the area or further evidence to support a lightning strike scenario.[6]

It is important to note that this is may be the first known (publicized) case where *a mystery helicopter was witnessed and reported at an unexplained livestock death site.* It would not be the last. By the end of the 1970s, more than 150 reports of unusual helicopter activity near mute sites would be filed by U.S. ranchers with local authorities. As we will see, mystery chopper sightings would be documented by ranchers and law enforcement in the 1980s, 1990s and on into the 2000s. (figure 5)

Levitating Calves of Brazil

North America was not the exclusive playground for cattle abductions. A Brazilian account of interest appeared in issue number 29 (1980) of the French journal *Ouranos* (Bohain, France). In an article by editor Pierre Delval and Enrique Banchs, (the date may be in question—investigator Luiz do Rosario Real told Bob Pratt it had occurred in 1963), but here's the version from *Ouranos* as translated by George Andrews of Drury, Missouri. This incident allegedly occurred sometime between the 25th and 27th of October 1970, toward the end of the afternoon (around 4:00) under a rather cloudy sky. This one is one of those truly mystifying head-scratcher cases. Eerily reminiscent of the Alexander Hamilton case 73 years prior, perhaps this particular "Great Airship" had a cloaking device?

Pedro Trajano Machado, who at 66 years of age does not know how to read or write, and his 23-year-old son Euripides de Jesus Trindade were on their farm about 15 miles from Palma (in the Alegrete area, again in the state of Rio Grande do Sul) taking care of some cattle. They had shut up 18 head in a corral. They separated a red Jersey [dairy] cow from her month-old calf, which weighed about 60 pounds. The cow was led off to be worked on and the calf was not tied up but left loose in the corral about 15 feet from where they were working.

They noticed that the other cattle had suddenly become quite nervous and upset, and particularly the red cow. At first they didn't pay any attention, as these cattle were used to being out in the fields at liberty. But the cattle were getting more and more jumpy and panicking. The red cow was bellowing as if something was wrong and kept trying to turn her head to look in the direction of the calf. Pedro Machado decided to see if something was wrong with the calf, and turned his head in that direction. The calf was also bawling at this point, but it was no longer on the ground. It was suspended about three feet high in the air, in its normal position, not tipped over one-way or the other. Pedro called his son Euripides, and they both watched what happened: the calf was being moved along parallel to the ground at this same height of about three feet in the direction of the fields. The other animals bellowed and gave every sign of panic. The two witnesses remained rooted on the spot, incapable of taking effective action. After having continued to float about three feet above the ground for about 60 feet, the calf began to rise vertically, so slowly that it took three or four minutes before it was so high in the sky as to look about a quarter of its size, at which point it suddenly disappeared as if behind a curtain, though at a height well below the level of the clouds. When the calf started to rise vertically, it stopped bawling.

No other phenomena were noticed, such as noises, heat, wind, suspension ropes, etc. When this extraordinary event had ended with the disappearance of the calf, the two witnesses carried on with their work.[7] (figure 6)

I'm sure that if someone is looking for a research project and could afford a staff of researchers combing through newspaper archives from around the world, this effort would undoubtedly uncover additional, inexplicable accounts of all types. But for our purposes here, we have space constraints that won't allow for a more thorough examination of worldwide reports from the 1970 through 1974 time period. We have a lot of ground to uncover, but first—what happened in 1972?

When the Meme Goes Dormant?

Back in North America, after the brief flurry of publicized Minnesota reports from '70 through '71, 1972 (a leap year) was inexplicably quiet on the mutilation front. Soon-to-be mutilation investigators and law enforcement officials had not yet picked up on these early cases as the prelude to the hell years that would close out the decade of the 1970s. It was assumed later by researchers that cases probably had occurred, but according to long-time mutilation researcher and weirdness archivist David Perkins, officially reported mutilation activity *completely ceased that entire year*. I quoted him during a visit to his home in Santa Fe in August 2013, when he discussed this 1972 lull period:

> "It's like the mutilation meme went dormant in 1972. It had enough to build on initially because of Snippy, which entrenched the meme worldwide, and then it briefly re-animated itself in 1970. It had to maintain its hold within the culture so it could easily be revived and continue propagating. There was a lull for a couple of more years before it again began regenerating in the upper midwest in '71. However, a meme is not effective if it's not getting propagated through conversations, media, and the means of communication of the time.
>
> "So, in 1972, we find the culture being deconstructed, turned upside down and re-shuffled, and this was not fertile ground to nourish the meme to re-emerge because of the overriding cultural anxiety—and even natural disaster issues that occurred. In 1973, the mutilation meme returned on the back of a massive UFO wave which gave it a lot of juice for a running start."[8]

Momo the Hairy Giant

In 1972 there were other inexplicable events being reported in a few specific areas that would later be targeted by the mutilators in the next three-year period. In *Cryptozoology A to Z,* by Loren Coleman & Jerome Clark, the authors mention an interesting flap of "hairy giant" sightings in northeast Missouri near the Illinois border. The seven-foot-tall creature (later nicknamed "Momo" for "Missouri Monster") was described as having an over-sized head and a terrible stench. This region will figure prominently later in the mid-to-late 1970s mutilation waves.

The first official Momo sighting was apparently an encounter by two women picnickers near Louisiana, Missouri, on the verdant banks of the Mississippi River—July 1971. They evidently first spotted the creature lurking nearby their picnic site and were frightened enough to run and hide in their car which was parked nearby. They then observed the humanoid as it approached their picnic site, and noted later to investigators that they heard the creature make "gurgling sounds. The creature had evidently decided to join their picnic, and stopped to eat an abandoned peanut butter sandwich the startled women had left behind in their haste to escape to the car. The two witnesses were rattled enough by their experience they reported it to the Missouri State Patrol. (figure 7)

A year later, in July 11, 1972, a young woman in the Marbolf Hills, again near Louisiana, Missouri, reported seeing Momo standing beside a tree, and it appeared to be "flecked w/ blood with dead dog under its arm." It appeared to be around seven feet tall, had no apparent neck, and gave off a "horrible smell." Coincidentally, neighbors in the area said dogs had been disappearing during this time period. The "horrible smell," was reported sporadically over the next couple of weeks.

W. Haden Blackman, in his *Field Guide to NA Monsters* (1998), mentions witnesses reporting Momo carrying sheep and other animals, July 14th thru 28th 1972. Blackman's research mentions early 1940 reports of a similar creature, and then almost 30 years later in 1968, when the creature apparently returned. Blackman also adds interesting details about the July 11, 1972 encounter. He names the primary witness—eight-year old Terry Hanson—as the witness that saw Momo with a dead dog under its arm. There may have possible kidnapping attempt during the encounter, but her older sister evidently intervened by scream-ing loudly at it and the monster fled. In the Blackman version, it was six to seven feet tall, had no apparent neck and left three-toed tracks. Momo sightings continued for two more weeks, and Terry Hanson's father combed the woods for "21 consecutive nights" hunting for the creature. This outbreak of monster sightings evidently was mentioned on the national news. Ill-tempered, Momo reportedly roared at boys, tried to tip over cars, and generally scared people in this hilly area on the western side of the Mississippi River, where it had appar-ently decided to lurk.

In Jerome Clark's book, *Unexplained,* additional strange events that occurred in the area three days later. On July 14th 1972, witnesses reportedly observed two fireballs that appeared to descend behind a nearby school. They went to investigate and said they heard a "growling sound." Police were called in to investigate and found nothing. Later, the witnesses reportedly smelled the pungent odor now associated with Momo when they claimed to have seen a small glowing light that exploded and left behind that familiar fetid stench in its wake.

UFO and Momo sightings, and other weird reports, continued over the next two weeks, and some locals also reported hearing disembodied voices. One instance warned a group, "you boys stay out of these woods," another reportedly asked a startled passerby to bring them "a cup of coffee!" Go figure.

Fireballs and other unusual objects were also noted by other Louisiana, Missouri area witnesses. One was described as a UFO with lighted windows that landed for "five hours on a hilltop." That sounds impressive, but where were their cameras? Another sighting event mentions a glowing golden cross on the moon that lit up the roadway like day—a rather front-loaded observation from the buckle of the moonlit Bible belt.

According to George Eberhart in his excellent (but largely overlooked) 1980 classic: *Geo-Bibilography of Anomalies,* at the end of the sighting wave, on July 24th 1972, an unidentified encounter with a craft and its occupants was experienced by a group of Louisiana women—one of them "an experienced observer." The night after the previous event on the 25th, there were three additional reports of the same (or a similar) object that was reported by one witness to have "performed maneuvers beyond the capabilities of any known earthly aircraft."

Occasional sightings of Momo continued on through the late summer and into the early fall of 1972. Several incidents of the rank-smelling beast carrying dead animals away were reported, including one report where it escaped with a sheep under its arm. If real, this report is an escalation from the killing and abducting of smaller-sized pets by Momo to *abducting livestock*. Momo sightings in the region apparently stopped cold in the late fall of 1972, and it appeared to Eberhart that the creature(s) must have "migrated away."[9]

Six years later, Momo evidently returned, but this time a bit south along the mighty river in Ellsbury, Missouri, where according to a witness interviewed by David Perkins, in 1978, a hairy beast was seen picking through refuse in a local dump. Incidentally, this hominid sighting occurred during an intense wave of UFO and mutilation reports in the area that we will cover in the next chapter.

When I research a particular locale or region, I always have my eyes open for any other types of correlative synchronicities to be found. I had a suspicion that there might be archaeological finds that would round out this region's activity. The first possible correlation I potentially uncovered was west of the Louisiana/Ellsbury region of Missouri where an ancient "ritual" mask was allegedly discovered in the 19th century. I found this interesting reference to the strange artifact in the book *Weird America*:

In 1879, the *American Antiquarian* reported that a farmer had plowed up an ancient ritual mask in a field. At least, that's the label that was stuck on it, although I've noticed that, whereas a filing clerk gets dirty looks for stuffing too many papers into the "miscellaneous" file, antiquarians for years have been tucking away discoveries they don't understand under "ritual" or "ceremonial." The artifact was examined by one Hannibal Fox of Milan, who said it seemed to be an alloy of silver and iron that had been poured into a mold of a human face. It is doubtful that the Indians knew or cared about such technology. I do not know where the object is now, but I've made some inquiries, and am waiting for answers.[10]

1972: The Year the Mutilators Took a Sabbatical

To be honest, unraveling the unexplained livestock death phenomenon could be described as being upside down in a hall of carnival mirrors with a quicksand ceiling. But the more you dig, the more dirt you uncover. In the early 1970s, there are many divergent elements that enter and leave—all seemingly unrelated attendant phenomena. We have livestock mutilations and rustling, choppers, UFOs, weird hairy beasts, disembodied voices and rumors of satanic cultists and probably more. A kaleidoscopic array of phenomenal events and memes that seem to ebb and flow during waves of high activity in specific regions for no apparent reason. But there is a very telling anomaly within this five-year time period: The Lull of 72—when *no apparent unexplained livestock deaths were reported and/or covered by the United States media*. David Perkins and I have scoured every source, every database, multiple newspaper archive services and have come up empty. We cannot find a *single* documented mutilation case and I think this is highly significant. We found one tantalizing rumor of a 1972 mutilation case in Winlock, Washington, located just west of Mt. St. Helens ,but were unable to confirm it.

To somehow begin to put the puzzling 1972 North American time period into context, I suggested to Perkins we re-visit what was happening in a U.S. culture that had managed to survive the tumultuous sixties. We sat around David's dining room table late into the night on August 4-5th, 2013 and pondered why there appeared to be a complete cessation of unexplained animal death reports in 72.

After a final, thorough search earlier that entire day, Perkins produced from his files a single unexplained animal death report from that year, and we sat around that evening and wondered about this cases' possible significance. I was sure that the silent years have something about them that has the potential to educate us about the phenomenon and I made the analogy that the "silence between notes to a musician can be as important as the actual notes being played." A longtime musician, Perkins readily agreed. We both agreed that we not only look at what the culture had to offer that turbulent year, but bounce this year of incredible cultural change off the single report that David had uncovered.

David dove right in and began researching 1972 starting in January and later he dug into the location and players involved in our single, stand alone case. We both knew that many head of livestock (roughly 2% per year) died and were scavenged by predators, birds, coyotes, foxes, dogs and insects, but none (to our knowledge) were reported as being found with "surgical cuts" or "mutilated." We are talking about tens of thousands of livestock that died, were scavenged and not reported as strangely slain and disfigured. Helicopters continued to fly in the night skies, but no mutes were officially reported in the United States. Sweden, however, seems to have been visited by the mutilators:

> Police investigators in the Stockholm area are puzzled by reports of "shocking cruelty to animals"—calves have been slaughtered in a brutish way, their hearts ripped out and stolen. Other calves have had their throats cut, and bullocks and pigs have disappeared under mysterious circumstances. In recent years, increasing theft slaughtering has been reported to police. Agent Arne Thorsson of the Farm Producers Association has received many reports, as have the police.[11]

An interesting aside that should be mentioned is the apparent precursor aspect of the Swedish mutilation reports. When David located this obscure factoid about calves being slaughtered in Sweden, I immediately remembered the apparent precursor "ghost rocket" reports from 1946 and how they seemed to presage the first wave of "modern" UFO sightings in North America beginning with the infamous Kenneth Arnold sighting in 1947 near Washington State's Mount Rainer.

Working with David on this question of the preoccupation of the culture during 1972, we wondered if perhaps the culture was too "heated" up for these types of incidents to make their mark on the collective psyche of the time. So, what was happening in the world in 1972 that might preoccupy the culture? Helped by David's insightful research, I wrote the following summation loosely modeled after a mock news broadcast:

DATELINE Washington D.C.: January 5th, Nixon ordered development of the NASA space shuttle program, while Pakistan started their own nuclear weapons program.

On January 15th a confidential source, perspiring profusely, told a major UFO investigative organization that Malmstrom Air Force Base supposedly attracted strange intruders who were observed "checking out a ballistic missile's electronics." The "crew" of intruders never tripped any security sensors, and they were able to leap the high concertina wire with ease. Upon their discovery by base personnel, they boarded their "craft and flew away at speeds in excess of 50,000 mph" according to radar operators, who must have watched with awe and consternation. Hastily scrambled Air Force jets had a real tough time keeping up with the UFO crew. Was this the latest example of strange intruders invading some of our most secure missile sites, or simply the product of a febrile imagination?

On the political side, it was a particularly contentious U.S. election year, with a record Nixon Republican landslide; meanwhile other elephants, crazed by draught and heat, rampaged in India killing 24 in separate incidents; Nixon opened up China and won two giant pandas—a traditional Chinese gift; Nixon reciprocated by sending the Chinese two rare, long-haired *musk oxen*, one of the world's most ancient bovine-like species—noted for their strong musky odor and well-coordinated defensive posturing.

In 1972, Henry the K was wooing the North Vietnamese at secret peace talks that allowed for a dignified (?) U.S. disengagement, while seventeen-year-olds breathed a sigh of relief as the last draft lottery was held—ending U.S. military conscriptions.

The Apollo 16 astronauts were setting overland speed records on Luna and Pioneer 10 was launched. Pioneer is the first man-made object to leave our solar system, and has now officially left our star system. 1972 also saw the launch of LandSat 1—the first earth-resources satellite—and later that year, geologist Harrison Schmidt, who became a major proponent of the reality of cattle mutilations, rocked the moon with his hammer. Speaking of rock, we were all bummed because the Beatles had just broken up, but Pink Floyd was recording "Money" for the Dark Side of the Moon.

Dat gangsta film *The Godfather* won three Academy Awards that year and, later, Marlon Brando sent a beautiful Native woman to decline his Oscar. She adlibbed a pointed statement about the treatment of Native Americans in Hollywood and mentioned the Wounded Knee standoff.

Unfortunately, on June 9th near the Lakota Pine Ridge Reservation; the "Rapid City" flood killed 238 people. A few days later Hurricane Agnes killed another 117 people on the East Coast, but the Watergate affair really broke open June 17th and a political tsunami swept the nation. The bungled burglary eventually brought down the leader of the free world in true Shakespearian fashion. The day after the Watergate story broke, the "worst flooding and landslides in [Hong Kong] recorded history" devastated the city, and another 150 or so poor souls were added to the pile.

Independence Day ushered in the first "Rainbow Gathering" in the mountains of Colorado where thousands of psychedelically-fueled hippies communed with nature and one another. A couple of weeks later, George Carlin was arrested for public obscenity for uttering his famous "seven dirty words."

On August 12th, the last U.S. ground troops were withdrawn from Vietnam, while in September 'Black September' Palestinian tourists magnified the terror meme at the Munich Olympics. Unfortunately, 11 Israeli athletes died in a zealous effort by the terrorists to remind the world of their important cause.

In 1972, Atari introduced Pong—arguably the first digital video game. A primitive form of slow-moving tennis, it was the first widely played video game in the world. Some nerds might argue and insist that the 1947 missile war game simulator, the "CATHODE RAY TUBE AMUSEMENT DEVICE" (undoubtedly sold in Roswell) was the first. But we do know the world's first scientific pocket calculator, the Hewlett Packard HP-35, priced at $395, was bought by proto-yuppie-nerds beginning that year.

And, scientists announced the first successful manipulated recombinant DNA experiments and established the science of biotechnology. Humans now had short-circuited natural selection and substituted an ability to control and direct our own evolution. We have opened the door to unlimited variations of genetically modified organisms (GMOs) and the other "marvels."

Caribou, Nerve Gas and You

But now, back to stalking that herd…

DATELINE: Fairbanks, Alaska.

The only notable unexplained animal death case in 1972 occurred in the land of the bovine deficient, Alaska, where 53 caribou were discovered dead in "a peculiar circular arrangement…" near the Fort Greely military reservation. (figure 8) The base was powered by its own nuclear reactor, and had been the site of U.S. Army biological and chemical weapons projects since 1966.

Ken Neiland, a wildlife disease specialist with the Alaska fish and game department, said, "they were all drawn up in a circle, like Custer's last stand." The site was located 100 miles south of Fairbanks. Most of the carcasses were within 10 feet of each other in an elongated circle 50 to 75- yards in diameter. They had been fed upon by eagles and bears, but, apparently, there was more than enough evidence to go to the lab. But "Neiland was doubtful that forensic testing would ever determine why this had happened."

At the time, just down the road from Ft. Greely, was the Gerstle River Test Area. In 1962, one of its chemical warfare programs was masquerading as The Arctic Environmental Surveillance Program, which was used for testing mustard and VX nerve gas. "The gas was packed into artillery shells and fired from HE-155 howitzers," into nearby blue spruce forests and primordial marsh lands. The mock World War I war games ended in 1967 (the year of Snippy), but not every shell had detonated as expected. They didn't know what to do, the shells that did go off were starting toxic fires and local firemen refused to put themselves in peril, and the military found itself in a bind. They couldn't restore the toxic land nor exploit it further. They just left it and designated it a "contaminated sector." Outta sight. Out of mind.

So, here we go. They placed the *still live shells of lethal nerve and chemical agents* out on the pristine ice covering Blueberry Lake. When the spring thaw hit the shells descended unceremoniously to the bottom, and four years later the new base commander inquired as to their disposition and was horrified that they had been forgotten. Talk about your Environmental Surveillance Program! He immediately ordered the lake drained and the shells to be removed, post haste, and the caribou continued to dodge the other lost ordinance as they traveled on their ancient migration route. This standalone 1972 scenario was only the latest in a series of interesting animal death reports around other nefarious weapons facilities, as we have seen and will see again later.

Ken Neiland facetiously (?) responded, when asked by reporters for theories to explain what had happened to the caribou: "The theory that it might have been beings from a different planet testing weapons is as good as anything we have yet…[But] [w]hatever it was, I think it was something that happened rapidly… I think it's something right here on good old earth.[12] " Maybe he should have asked those guys up the road at the Arctic Surveillance Program; they're always on alert—surveillance is their middle name.

Rustling Pigs By Chopper in Iowa

The debunkers would argue that the media and rumors within the ranching and law enforcement communities fanned the waves of "hysteria" that would follow in the mid-to-late '70s. They would remind us that in '72 word had yet to spread about the Minnesota and Pennsylvania cases. However, I would argue that there have been several lulls in reports in the intervening 30 years that indicate this phenomenon is real—not simple misidentified scavenger action or hysteria. If you subscribe to the mass delusion theory of mutilations, you must wonder why in one year, countless ranchers are totally deluded, and in the next year none of them are. I've never heard anyone simply attempt to explain how mass delusion can be instantaneously turned on and then turned off. And then back on again, and off and so on.

As we will see later in chapters eight and nine, there have been several high-profile cases in Colorado since the 1990s that received major international media coverage, yet *no other reports were apparently generated by the publicity*, as the debunker's "media induced hysteria" theory would suggest they should.

In 1971, Sarpy County, in Eastern Nebraska, began to see reports of mystery helicopters and claims of rustled livestock—mostly hogs—but in some isolated cases cattle were also reported missing. Many of these reports were in and around Offit Air Force Base. This close proximately to Air Force Bases and missile fields would be echoed around Malmstrom, Warren and Offit all through the mid-70s. The Washington *Post* noted in a September 8, 1974 article "Ranchers Enraged by Weird Deaths, "Devil Cult' Sought in Nebraska:"

> Last March, as beef prices soared, in Sarpy County in more popu-
> lated eastern Nebraska there was [another] wave of cattle
> rustling—accompanied by a rash of helicopter sightings. The coinci-

dence was enough to induce [Sarpy County] Sheriff Thomas Paton to call out additional patrols and to check with aviation officials for authorized flights. There were supposed to be no helicopters in the area.

Meanwhile, ranchland mutilations of livestock began to be reported in Iowa, Illinois, and Missouri. These early reports are interesting in that they feature rustling, firearms, and intense targeting of specific farms and ranches. In this early precursor wave, cattle were targeted, but so were swine. Shortly after a sighting of a strange helicopter by law enforcement, someone paid Iowa hog farmer Craig Owen a visit. Much to his consternation, rustlers stole 59 of his "best" pigs. As David Perkins pointed out in "Meet the Mutilators," his extensive look at the 1970s mutilation wave: "This complaint came to be voiced time and time again…'they got my best animal!'"[13]

By the spring of 1973, there had been so many reports of dead or missing cattle and pigs in Iowa that U.S. Attorney Allen Donielson asked the FBI to make an "intense investigation." Helicopter sightings and missing livestock began to be reported in Illinois and Missouri during the summer of 1973, and reports began to be filed that fall by ranchers in Wisconsin and Pennsylvania.

> Attorney Allen Donielson said Wednesday the FBI has launched an intensive investigation into a rash of hog and cattle rustling and livestock frauds in Iowa.
>
> The federal attorney said he asked the FBI to probe the growing losses of livestock in the state. He said the thefts have occurred in 17 counties with losses of amounting to more than $300,000.
>
> FBI spokesperson said the federal law agency will join the Iowa Bureau of Criminal Investigation and county sheriff offices in probing all areas of livestock thefts, including the alleged use of helicopters and airplanes to aid the rustling schemes…
>
> Donielson said livestock fraud and rustling are increasing so rapidly that FBI intervention became necessary. He said some of the large losses indicate interstate rustling and fraud schemes are involved. He said the current high value of livestock makes them worthwhile to steal. He said the largest losses have been in a ten county area in southwest and south central Iowa.[14]

A farmer in Jersey County, Illinois associated a missing cow with the sighting of a "white unmarked cargo-type helicopter." In St. Francois County, Missouri, another farmer spotted an "Army-type helicopter" hovering over his cattle. The craft was unmarked except for a "large white spot" neat the tail. Near Pond, Missouri, James Hagler had five pigs stolen during a period in the fall when a helicopter was seen in the area. On one occasion, the occupants of the helicopter fired at Hagler. The outraged farmer shot back. *Someone on the ground then fired at Hagler*. [my emphasis] An investigation by law officials revealed no clues as to the nature of the shootout and the identity of the airborne pig rustlers."[15]

The mutilators apparently decided the pastures of Minnesota were greener than rangeland further south and returned up to Lincoln County later that summer. Documentation of "official" reports is scant and we don't know for sure if these cattle deaths were indeed "real" mutilations, but evidently the perception that something strange was afoot made the rounds of the state's ranching community and cases were being talked about. Again, in November 1973, we see the mystery helicopter being associated with a classic mutilation. On November 5th, in Canby, Minnesota, "low-flying helicopters" were observed flying low over cattle herds and at least one head of livestock was reported mutilated. That winter an impressive south-to-north wave of cases began that appeared to mirror State Highway 81. The Highway 81 cases were only a part of the wave that between November 30th and January 8th, 1974, accounted for 44 Kansas cows being reported in a mutilated condition.

> The cattle (both sexes) were found with sexual organs removed, blood drained and missing some combination of ear, tongue, rectum or patch of skin. Many of the cows were black (Hereford of Angus) prompting some authorities to view the killings as the work of "cultists." According to this school of thought, well-financed Satan worshippers needed the animal parts and blood for their exotic rituals. Panicky rumors began to spread though the rangeland. It was feared that the mutilators might soon turn their attentions to human victims. (figure 9)
>
> In response to the perceived threat, Kansas's agriculturalists armed themselves to the teeth. They patrolled the back roads in continuous shifts through the long winter nights. The National Guard directed their pilots to fly at higher altitudes. Authorities grew concerned that someone might get killed in the craziness...
>
> In Pottawattamie County [Iowa] another spectacular gun battle was reported. This time some 20 shots were fired at Robert Smith from a black, twin-engine plane and a white helicopter; both unmarked.[16]

The chopper teams evidently were not finished. In August, northwestern Nebraska was the focus when seven mutilations were reported amid a flurry of attendant chopper sightings. By this time word began to spread, and regional news outlets were seriously covering the story. It was inevitable that the national media would take notice of the claims of unexplained livestock thefts and mutilations.

Judy Doraty Case

The Judy Doraty "abduction" case from May 1973 is a UFO sighting event that has received some notoriety over the years, not because of what was reported to have happened at the time, but because of the retrieved "hypnotic regression" information that surfaced several years later. Here is a brief summery of the case which is then followed by a statement Doraty issued to the press in 2003.

The story is a rather simple and is reminiscent of hundreds of other UFO sighting events. Apparently, Judy, her mother, her 14-year-old daughter Cindy, and her sister-in-law, had been to the local bingo parlor and were driving back to there home in Texas City. They were about to drop off her mother and sister-in-law in Alta Loma when they spotted what appeared to be a UFO hovering in the night sky. They stopped and watched for an indeterminate amount of time before the object disappeared and they recommenced their trip home.

After the event, Judy began to experience intense headaches and heightened levels of anxiety. She tried to get relief from local doctors, but nothing seemed to help. It was suggested that she see noted abduction researcher Dr. Leo Sprinkle, who conducted a hypnotic regression on Doraty. Details then emerged about her sighting experience that seemed to be blocked memories.

Under hypnosis, it was revealed that Judy had apparently been abducted aboard an extraterrestrial spacecraft. Judy went on in detail, describing how a cow was taken up into the craft and methodically mutilated by two "small entities." During the hypnotic regression, Judy described the unusual sensation of being in two places at once. She said that she was still standing beside her car after they stopped to watch the strange light in the sky. However, Judy also said that at the same time, she was in a strange chamber watching the gruesome experiment unfolding before her eyes. She then stated…

> "[The two beings) were about three and a half to four feet tall; grey creatures with large egg-shaped heads…(figure 10) It's like a spotlight shining down on the back of my car. And it's like it has substance to it. I can see an animal being taken up in this. I can see it squirming and trying to get free. And it's like it's being sucked up."[17]

Press statement issued by Judy Doraty on February 1st 2003 as published on B.J. Booth's UFOCasebook.com:

> First I must say there is no doubt that abductions exist. My abduction took place in 1973. There were 16 eyewitnesses to the craft, though not all remember an abduction. My daughter who was 14 at the time and myself. This was first reported to Ellington Air Force Base in Texas, who denied anything was on radar at the time. Our abduction was also returning from a bingo game in Houston, to our home in Texas City, first going by Alta Loma to drop off sister and brother in law.
>
> There was another sighting of three people coming from a bingo

game in Houston that got burned by the effects of the sighting. Our sighting was almost a year before theirs. So much happened that night I would not attempt to go in detail, we were all changed and have never been the same since. We were first ridiculed so much by others who were not present (family mostly) I did not talk about it for a few years.

Then my husband returned home from Viet Nam and we were stationed in Yuma, AZ. I somehow heard about APRO. I called them and told them about my sighting and the very next day, a Mr. Daugherty and his wife and a doctor who had experience in hypnosis named Rose Tennant came to my house and spent the entire day going over what happened.

Dr. Tenant regressed me and a few details came out or shall I say surfaced. I had been having terrible migraines, and just the amount of surfacing relieved much. I know I remembered a formula that was given to me by the small gray alien. I think that is what caused a lot of problems. I did not say anything to anyone else as I was still gun-shy and afraid of ridicule.

A few years later I got a call from a lady named Linda Howe. We talked a long time her trying to convince me I needed to be regressed again for a TV documentary she was doing called the *Strange Harvest*. For some reason I began to trust her as she convinced me she believed what I was saying.

And as all abductees know this is one of the most important things to help one get on with their life. In my abduction I witnessed a small calf being transported in a LARGE CRAFT. At that time I somehow was teleported or astro-projected [sic] or something, as I was in the craft seeing what was going on as well as standing by my car I had gotten out of to see what the huge light was that had been pacing our car for about twenty miles or so. Anyway I allowed a Dr. Leo Sprinkle from the University of Wyoming to do his regression.

It was about a three-hour regression, I fulfilled Ms. Howe's agenda [and] she got an Emmy for her documentary, but I was left with all the information in my head that still needed siphoning. I asked her to help me write a book to be able to tell the amazing things that I was told and shown. She agreed and then kept putting it off... [The book was never written]

My main concern was I always wanted my abduction to be presented in a way that it would not be construed as a crazy woman venting her boredom...

Then about ten years ago I was told by someone in the UFO community who was familiar with my case that Ms. Howe had gone to Kirkland Air Force Base [and] was warned to keep my mouth shut but

Ms. Howe never told this to me. She told a ufologist who [then] called me. In other words the government did not want me to say anything about a formula I was given.

I became frightened and this is the first time I have shared anything. I hope someone reads this that will contact me and give me advice or help as the abduction is 30 years old, I am 63 and before I die I would love to know what many already know, and why they do not want my story told...thanks for listening.[18]

The Doraty case is interesting to me because of the details of a calf allegedly being taken aboard the UFO and experimented on before the cattle mutilation subject became a widespread mainstream news story. Another interesting point to mention is that David Perkins told Sprinkle about a possible link with "nuclear contamination," and he explained his "environmental monitoring" theory for the mutilations that impressed Sprinkle. Interestingly, Sprinkle then uncovered similar information from Doraty during her March 13th 1980 hypnotic regression—just weeks after speaking with Perkins—the details of which were included in Howe's book, *An Alien Harvest*:

> Sprinkle: Do they say why they are conducting tests? [on cattle]
> Doraty: They are concerned about man for themselves. [sic]...that men are going to kill themselves through polluting the earth...Something is going to get in the water. It's going to be in vegetation...plutonium or something. They've been here for quite some time...it has to do with somehow nuclear waste or testing or...causing change in the chemical composition of something.

Is this an example of one of the main criticisms of information gained through the use of hypnotic regression? That there is a transference or feedback loop established between the therapist and subject? Or, are nonhuman entities truly concerned with environmental contamination and humans' misuse of nuclear materials, and they are testing cattle parts to ascertain the extent of this contamination? This illustrates to me the need for critical evaluation of hypnotic regression as a viable investigative tool.

Here Come the Choppers

More helicopter sightings and missing livestock were being reported in Illinois and Missouri during the summer of 1973, and reports began to be filed that fall by ranchers in Wisconsin and Pennsylvania as well. The advent of the mystery helicopters in 1973 put a high-tech twist on the age-old saga of livestock rustling. David Perkins noted, "it doesn't seem terribly cost-effective considering the weight limitations of helicopters and the high cost of operating them." Perkins also notes the following claim that seems to indicate that the possibility of a range war loomed as farmers and ranchers began to arm themselves, create vigilante posses, and they proceeded to actively protect their herds.

The mystery rustlers are still haunting America's feedlots today. An October 24th, 2011 *Associated Press* article noted that, "6000 lambs were stolen from a feedlot in Texas, and nearly 1,000 hogs have been stolen in recent weeks from farms in Iowa and Minnesota." Almost 45 years later, livestock rustling is still a major problem, but how do you steal 6,000 lambs from a single feedlot? This claim, if true, almost seems paranormal in nature!

The mutilators returned up to Lincoln County, Minnesota later that summer of 1973. Documentation of "official" reports is scant and we don't know for sure if these cattle deaths were indeed "real" mutilations, but evidently, the perception that something strange was afoot made the rounds of the state's ranching community. The meme appeared to be branching out and spreading.

Bill Ellis notes, in his extremely well researched 2000 book *Raising the Devil,* that the satanic cult explanation began to be touted by local newspaper coverage:

> The nationwide wave of mutilation reports began in 1973, when rashes of animal deaths began to show up in newspapers. In parts of Pennsylvania, something killed a number of domestic pets and livestock including chickens and sheep; some had been dismembered, while others had had their throats 'expertly' slit. In November [1973], farmers in rural counties of Minnesota and Kansas found some of their cows dead with no sign of a fatal wound; yet their genitals, udder, or sometimes am eye, ear, or tongue had been cut off with no sign of blood or bleeding. A veterinarian in Canby, Minnesota, suggested that the culprit had paralyzed the cattle with a tranquilizer gun, immediately drained out their blood, and then returned about six hours later to cut of parts of the bodies…"[19]

This report from Canby, Minnesota also featured "low-flying helicopters" that were observed flying low over cattle herds, prompting the above observation by the local veterinarian.

Farmers and ranchers further west into Kansas and Iowa, began seeing and reporting mysterious unmarked helicopter activity in the spring and summer of 1973, before news of other cases further east became publicized outside of the impacted communities.

In one of the most dramatic incidents, a Baptist minister from Mark, a tiny settlement in southeastern Iowa, awoke one April morning when an intercom installed for security purposes picked up a two-way radio message in which "there was plenty of use of the Lord's name in vain." Suspicious after a strange car had been seen the night before, he and a friend decided to drive around and see if any mischief was going on. When they came to a local rancher's place, he told authorities [sic] "this helicopter started to rise out of the field right in front of us…" Highway patrol troopers received scattered reports of an aircraft in the area and attempted to follow it toward the Missouri border, but they found no traces of it: "It's like it vanished at the Iowa border," one said." When the occurrence was reported on the front page of the Des Moines *Register*, lawmen were soon "besieged" with similar reports across the state.[20]

1973 Chopper/UFO Wave

1973 has gone down in the annals of ufology as one of the most intense periods of UFO activity ever documented. Dr. J. Allen Hynek, founder and head of the Center for UFO Studies (CUFOS), was interviewed by Ian Ridpath about the 1973 UFO wave for the prestigious scientific magazine *Nature:*

> Hynek is impressed by the fact that the nature of the phenomenon itself is the one thing that has not changed. "The typical UFO report today is essentially the same as it was 10 years ago," he says. Yet he carefully points out that he does not support the idea that UFOs are nuts-and-bolts spacecraft from other worlds: "There are too many things against it. It seems ridiculous that any intelligence would come from such great distances to do reportedly stupid things like stopping cars and frightening people. And there are far, far too many reports."[21]

CUFOS alone logged over 1,500 reports from around the world, but for our purposes here, it is interesting to note that hundreds of sightings were logged in Indiana, Illinois, Missouri, Pennsylvania, Ohio, with other states such as Tennessee, Georgia, Texas, California, Idaho, etc., also reporting heightened activity. One state that is curiously absent from any UFO database report is Iowa. States located all around Iowa were being hit—sometimes nightly—however I can find no mention of any UFO reports in Iowa, or, for that matter Nebraska and Kansas. The sighting wave appeared to begin in the southeastern U.S. in May and reports appeared to travel up river valleys. By the fall, dozens of sightings were being reported every week, with a strange, mid-to-late month surge in October. October 17th 1973 may have been the most active single night for UFO sightings and attendant humanoid reports ever reported:

> The 1973 sighting wave was concentrated in the last half of the year, and featured the largest number of humanoid occupant sightings in many years. Several abductions were reported during this period. The sightings peaked in mid to late October, with October 17th [1973] representing perhaps one of the most extraordinary single days for "high-strangeness" cases in UFO history.[22]

Ohio, for some reason, managed to escape the attention of large-scale livestock rustlers and mutilation reports during the 1970s. Having said this, an interesting standalone report was filed from the Dayton area the week prior with the sensational headline: "UFO Blamed for Killing Cow."

A woman told police Sunday morning that an oblong object with blinking lights killed two cows when it landed in a field. Her report was one of 80 sightings of unidentified flying objects that residents of west central Ohio told police about that night. However, the sheriff's office said a three-hour search by several cruisers and an airplane in the area where the UFO supposedly landed uncovered nothing.

"Her directions were only half way reliable", said patrolman Charles Conklin. "The only directions were 'behind Boston, Ohio on Petersburg Pike', which runs about ten miles through farm country". The woman, "hysterical" and "screaming," said a couple of cows were killed when the object landed, Conklin said...

Along Interstate 75 in a three-county area, the UFOs were described as "grayish discs with red and bluish-green lights." Others were described as "orange-colored objects" and "blimp-shaped objects." Some had "red lights around the rims with a blue flame or flare coming out of the bottom..."

In Montgomery County, an officer reportedly took a black and white photograph of a red and green blinking UFO hovering over the village of Union for about five minutes.[23]

 Evidently, Iowa, Missouri, Minnesota and Illinois (figure 11) were having sightings of a more earthly, mundane sort: mystery helicopters that were linked to cattle rustling. The following collection of reports comes from Tom Adams' (figure 12) Project Stigma publication *The Choppers...and the Choppers*. In early April a Wayne County, Iowa farmer spotted and reported to authorities a helicopter hovering above a pasture, shining a spotlight to the ground. "Lawmen in 20 vehicles unsuccessfully gave chase" to find where the chopper was based.[27]

In the early morning hours of April 17th, 1973, a witness near Mark, Iowa reported watching a "non bubble-type helicopter" rise out of a pasture and head toward the Missouri state line. Another report, also from April, mentions a deputy spotting a helicopter "hovering over a farm." The deputy turned off the lights of his police cruiser and "the lights on the chopper went out." According to Adams, "hog rustlings" had occurred in the area.[25]

On May 3rd, a group of six witnesses witnessed a "dark green helicopter" flying low over pasture land near Rome, Iowa. A flurry of reports then surfaced across the river in Illinois. In Randolph County, near Percy, a farmer observed a green helicopter without markings. Three to four days later, 35 head of cattle turned up missing. Then, in Jersey County, Illinois a "white, unmarked, cargo-type helicopter" was observed by Mrs. Phyllis Beutell and her son. The craft was observed as it "lifted up from a field containing cattle." A neighbor's cow allegedly disappeared a day or two later.

During the early-to-mid-summer of 1973, in Ottawa and Cloud Counties in Kansas, numerous mystery helicopter reports were filed with authorities. In August a livestock mutilation wave broke out in the region. Cloud County sheriff Fred Modlin was quoted as mentioning that helicopters had been seen "over cattle loading pens."[26]

Farmers in Ste. Genevieve, Iron and Reynolds Counties in Missouri filed rustling complaints with officials in July, and there were also several mystery chopper sightings in the area.

The following month, on August 17th, Perry County, Missouri Deputy Louis Layton observed a large cargo-type chopper fly low over a ranch near St. Marys, and during this same time period two St. Francois County Deputies reported seeing a helicopter hovering over a heard of cattle on a ranch.[27]

Mystery chopper activity seemed to move east back into Illinois the third week of August 1973, when reports were filed in Randolph and Union Counties. In one incident, a "Mr. Peters fired two warning shots over a helicopter which he observed hovering low and shining a light on his cattle." The chopper, described as "quiet-running," turned out its lights and fled. In another event near the town of Red Bud, "a helicopter was observed that matched the description of one suspected of being used for rustling." In another sighting, "lights on a helicopter suddenly went out" as a Pike County deputy watched. "Radar picked up low-flying aircraft slowly circling in Pike and Adams Counties" that night.[28]

Then Missouri erupted with "41 reports" filed to local sheriffs in Lincoln and Pike Counties of "unmarked helicopters." One early Fall report was especially noteworthy, as it featured a gun battle between a farmer and a mutilation team:

Near Pond, Missouri, James Hagler had five pigs stolen during a period in the fall, when a helicopter was seen in the area. On one occasion, the occupants of the helicopter fired at Hagler. The outraged farmer shot back. *Someone on the ground then fired at Hagler*. [my emphasis] An investigation by law officials revealed no clues as to the nature of the shootout and the identity of the airborne pig rustlers."

Law officers searched but found nothing. After they left, Hagler was fired upon again. A second search was again fruitless.

A farmer in Jersey County, Illinois associated a missing cow with the sighting of a "white unmarked cargo-type helicopter." In St. Francois County, Missouri, another farmer spotted an "Army-type helicopter" hovering over his cattle. The craft was unmarked except for a "large white spot" neat the tail.[29] [my emphasis]

That winter, an impressive south-to-north wave of mutilation cases commenced that appeared to mirror both sides of State Highway 81. The Highway 81 cases were only a part of the overall wave that unfolded between November 30th 1973 and January 8th, 1974. These cases officially totaled 44 Kansas cows as being reported in a mutilated condition.[30]

The cattle (both sexes) were found with sexual organs removed, blood drained and missing some combination of ear, tongue, rectum or patch of skin. Many of the cows were black (Hereford of Angus), prompting some authorities to view the killings as the work of "cultists." According to this school of thought, well-financed Satan worshippers needed the animal parts and blood for their exotic rituals. Panicky rumors began to spread though the rangeland. It was feared that the mutilators might soon turn their attentions to human victims.

In response to the perceived threat, Kansas's agriculturalists armed themselves to the teeth. They patrolled the back roads in continuous shifts through the long winter nights. The National Guard directed their pilots to fly at higher altitudes. Authorities grew concerned that someone might get killed in the craziness...

In Pottawattamie County [Iowa], another spectacular gun battle was reported. This time some *20 shots were fired at Robert Smith from a black, twin-engine plane and a white helicopter; both unmarked.*[31] [my emphasis]

The chopper teams evidently were not finished with their agenda. In August 1973, northwestern Nebraska was the focus, when seven mutilations were reported amid a flurry of attendant chopper sightings. By this time word began to spread and regional news outlets were seriously covering the story. It was inevitable that the national media would take notice of the claims of unexplained livestock deaths and mutilation claims.

The Meme Expands

After midwest farmers complained to local authorities and politicians about the choppers, rampant rustling and the first wave of mutilations, the first major national news story appeared in the September 30, 1973 issue of *Newsweek* magazine: (figure 13)

Since last May [1973], more than 100 cattle have been found dead and gruesomely mutilated in Nebraska, Kansas and Iowa... A few residents report sighting strange creatures resembling bears and gorillas, and at least one farmer claims that a shiny UFO landed in a field where a slaughtered animal was later found...A helicopter often has been seen hovering over the range around the time of a mutilation, and some ranchers swear they have been chased down lonely roads by helicopters. Helicopters are also said to have been used in cattle rustling, and some stockmen think the rustlers may be collecting blood and organs as lures for cattle grazing on the open range this fall...

"The predators are not wolves," insists Senator Burbach. "They are a semi-domesticated, two-legged animal called man."...Some officials are beginning to worry that the real danger is not some ghostly butcher, but keyed-up vigilantes themselves. After two slugs pierced the canopy of a utility-company helicopter checking power lines, the Nebraska National Guard ordered its helicopter pilots to cruise cross-country at higher altitudes than usual…to avoid being fired upon by frightened ranch hands…' [Folklorist Richard Thill was quoted as saying] 'It could be someone setting up a fertility cult of some kind…or it could be someone putting you on. If they [sic] are putting you on, they are pretty sick.'[32]

As noted, reporter William Schmidt presented several interesting asides in his *Newsweek* article. One of the most curious was the claim that, in a few cases witnesses reported, "strange creatures resembling bears and gorillas," and in one report a farmer allegedly reported that a "shiny UFO landed in a field where a slaughtered animal was later found." This may have been a subtle attempt by Schmidt to place the veneer of ridicule onto rancher's claims of high-strange mutilations and rustling activity—word of which had spread across the midwest during the spring and early summer of 1973.

Folklorist Richard Thill was further quoted in a later in an article published in the November 25th 1973 edition of the magazine *Midnight*: "The mutilations may have a ritualistic significance. The only speculation that makes sense is some kind of pagan motivation. There is a strong worldwide belief in the practice of magic. It wouldn't surprise me if what we are seeing is the result of some devil cult's rituals."

One of the Kansas Highway 81 cases occurred on the ranch of Kansas State Senator Ross Doyen (figure 14), who was convinced cults were responsible for the death and disfigurement of his cow. An autopsy was performed at Kansas State University and the pathologists determined that the animal had died of natural causes, and that coyotes had then scavenged the carcass. Doyen was unconvinced by this finding, "If that ear hadn't appeared cut, I wouldn't have thought anything about it. Whoever's cutting on them always cuts an ear off, that's their trademark."[33]

Some local Kansas law enforcement officials also disagreed with the KSU post-mortem test results and echoed Senator Doyen's suspicions that these deaths and disfigurements were unnatural:

[Kansas] Deputy Sheriff Gary Dir said: 'I've spent all my life except the last eight months on a farm and I know when a critter's been cut.' He confirmed the deaths as suspicious and suggested the animals had been drugged with an untraceable tranquilizer and then drained of their blood. In other places [Montana], autopsies turned up traces of chemicals like nicotine sulfate, suggesting that the animals had been drugged before the mutilation, In some cases, investigators claimed to have seen puncture mark's on the animal's jugular vein, suggesting that its blood had been sucked or pumped out. One theory that spread among law agents was that witches or hippies tranquilized cattle with PCP, a common veterinarian drug, but also a hallucinogen known as 'angel dust' by drug users. The blood was then drained and drunk by the witches, 'which caused them to trip out.'[34]

Probably as a result of the high profile Doyen case and the rest of the Highway 81 wave of reports, the Kansas Farm Bureau offered a $500 reward for information leading to the arrest and conviction of the parties responsible, but the cases continued and eventually the Kansas FBI office became involved after a sensational Kansas City *Times* article was published on December 22, 1973. In the article, suggestive terms and descriptions such as "…knife marks… butchering of the sexual organs," and "satanic cultists" were used.[35]

"The Killer Cult Terrorizing Mid-America"

Enter "Dugan & Bankston," two inmates who came forward to UFO investigators and the FBI, with alleged inside information on who was responsible for the growing wave of livestock mutilations. In hindsight, it was determined that they had come forward in an effort to get their sentences reduced and/or be moved out of a maximum-security prison into a less stringent medium security facility. The two claimed that a group called, 'The Sons of Satan,' were behind the mutilations, but it appeared that their revelations were spurious. Authorities were unable to use their assertions to further law enforcement investigations and no arrests were made.

This story came out of an odd collaboration between the U.S. government and UFO researchers. In January 1974, A. Kenneth Bankston, an inmate of the Federal Penitentiary at Leavenworth, Kansas, contacted Jerome Clark, whose investigation of the 1973 mutilations had been published in the magazine *Fate* the longest, continuously published periodical that covers paranormal subjects.[36]

Two months after the *Fate* article appeared, a second national article was published in *Saga* magazine. The article, "The Killer Cult Terrorizing Mid-America" penned by Kevin Randle under a pseudonym, also proposed the occult theory that a group of devil worshippers were responsible for the livestock mutilations. A mysterious leader named in the article as "Howard," was intent on creating "Hell on Earth," but, again, the evidence presented was highly tenuous and probably furthered the perception in the media and law enforcement that occultists were mutilating cattle.

Meanwhile, as the mutilation panic began to spread through the Great Plains late in 1974, UFO networks became more involved in trying to explain away the phenomenon. Dr. J. Allen Hynek, director of the Astronomy Department at Northwestern University and head of the Center for UFO Studies, was one person who felt that the cattle mutilation link detracted from responsible study of verifiable "close encounters" with UFOs.

He contacted Donald E. Flickinger, an agent for the Federal Bureaus of Alcohol, Tobacco, and Firearms (BATF), who had for some time investigated UFO incidents for him on a private basis. Hynek asked Flickinger to look into the Meeker County cattle mutilation being promoted by [Terence] Mitchell to see if any extraterrestrial connection could be verified. Flickinger found no basis for the UFO theories, but he concluded that "a certain pattern existed…the animal would be found in the middle of an open field, various parts of the body had been surgically removed, such as the sex organs, eyes, ears, lips, tongue, teats, etc. In many of the cases the blood had been drained from the animal and in several cases, veterinarians were unable to determine cause of death…most concurred that the removal of the various organs was surgical with some sort of sharp instrument."

[Jerome] Clark learned of Flickinger's investigation and passed on Bankston's letters to the agent. Flickinger contacted the Minneapolis US Attorney, who agreed that the case should be pursued officially. Bankston was transferred to a Minnesota jail along with another Leavenworth inmate, Dan Dugan, who claimed to have been a member of "the occult" for some years…

Bankston's story was taken seriously enough that, in 1975, the federal government apparently did initiate a nationwide investigation of satanic organizations, contacting and questioning well-known occultists. One of the first contacted was Anton LaVey, (figure 15) who, in his own defense, began compiling a "complete, centralized file…on the cattle mutilation hoax."[37]

Also of note that November was an interesting observation by Dr. J. Allen Hynek who issued a statement on November 15th; [1974] "The press has speculated that UFOs are in some way responsible for cattle mutilations…not one documented report exists in which a UFO sighting is directly connected to a cattle mutilation. Research has been done on the problem, and a confidential government report has found that a satanic cult is responsible." Hynek adds that the report must remain confidential "as arrests have not been made in all cases, and sources need to be protected…"

The UFO community, which was beginning to get nervous about possible links between UFOs and mutilations, breathed a sigh of relief. APRO [Aerial Phenomena Research Organization] released a statement in March 1975 to vindicate the ufonauts and clear away 'the suspicion of UFO involvement in the grisly mutilations: "Our study has provided a glimpse into a satanic organization with national political overtones which has grandiose plans of bringing about a 1,000 year reign of terror and darkness." The public could sleep more soundly knowing they were up against blood-thirsty Satanists rather than blood-thirsty extraterrestrials or cold-blooded U.S. government commando surgeons.[38]

Hynek & The Flickinger Report

David Perkins notes that, by the end of 1974, it was estimated that "22 head of cattle had been mutilated in Minnesota between 1970 and 1974," and this perception gave rise to the first official assessment of the phenomenon. Written by an U.S. Treasury, Bureau of Alcohol, Tobacco and Firearms agent Don Flickinger, the "Flickinger Report," had been the idea of J. Allen Hynek and it had been compiled confidentially for the U.S. Attorney in Minneapolis and wasn't originally meant for publication. But, somehow the report was leaked, and it contained speculation that the mutilations may have been due to a national "religious cult." The cult meme is an interesting undercurrent that persists to this day, and it appears to have been initially fueled by leading figures in the UFO community!

The so-called Flickinger Report, which summarized Bankston's and Dugan's confessions, traveled far beyond the BATF and Minnesota police channels that commissioned it. The report was distributed to police departments throughout the affected states. The Aerial Phenomena Research Organization, a major UFO network based in Tucson, Arizona, summarized it in a public statement, and, in other cases, details from the report were published in local newspapers. It caused several local panics, one in Mayflower, Texas, after a sheriff's deputy told townspeople that cult members planned to murder and mutilate two humans.

On May 25, [1975], John Makeig summarized the report in the *Star-Telegram,* blaming a "super, super wealthy group of amateur Satanists" for the mutilations. To the cast of suspects, Makeig added 'The Process,' already notorious from Sanders's work, and a local gang called 'The Flaming Stars.' He implied a link with a series of allegedly satanic murders committed in Florida and New Mexico during the past three years. Flickinger, who had by now appeared on several radio talk shows, reported that he had received death threats and that blood had been smeared on the front of his door.[39]

1974 burbled on and cases began to be reported in newly targeted states: Wyoming, Montana and North and South Dakota, where ranchers began finding their livestock in a mutilated-appearing condition. A targeted wave of cases blistered South Dakota in September and October. Wildlife was now being reported as mutilated and a deer was found with the unusual-appearing incisions in South Dakota on October 6th 1974.

Also reported in October 1974, was a mutilated cow whose jawbones had been "cut out and crossed," that was discovered within sight of the rancher's house near Chester, South Dakota—in Lake County. "Ten feet from the carcass were three pairs of indentations in the shape of a triangle (with each pair at a 'point'). Each impression was approximately four inches deep."[40]

A Conspiracy?

The reaction by law enforcement officials to the growing mutilation problem was predictable. Little green men from Mars didn't seem like a viable explanation and so, naturally, because the cases had the veneer of ritual blood sacrifice, they tended toward a "Satanists" or "cultists as the most plausible explanation to explain these strange cases of livestock death and disfigurement. Bill Ellis sums up police officials' thinking at the end of 1974:

> The mutilation mythologies cut deeply through American culture, revealing some of its priorities and anxieties. The idea that the mutilators were following some sort of religious rite or scientific agenda, provided structure and motivation for apparently random acts. Thus, the implied cult members were mirror images of the investigators. Paranormal investigator R. Martin Wolf was the first to observe that law enforcement agents favored the cult mythology because it linked the mutilations to a group bound together with strict rules of conduct and procedure like their own. A cult committing crimes was, in this mythology, the exact inverse of a police force preventing crimes. And in fact, the cult scenario continues to be the dominant police explanation for animal mutilations, as the data collected by Jeffrey Victor on more recent rumor panics shows. References to animal deaths appear in 75 percent of newspaper reports of such cult scares, more than any other single motif.[41]

The conspiracy-minded researchers also had ammunition to support a government-as-perpetrator scenario, a direct result of the mystery helicopter sightings that had now become associated with the mutilation mystery. (figure 16) Ellis also notes that the mystery further supported the minority view of the time that these deaths were due to UFOs. Again, Ellis does a good job summing up this rationale:

Similarly, the government conspiracy mythology was initially attractive to both the far left and the far right, because it reflected an impersonal central government absolutely insensitive to the needs of individuals and bent on scientific and military success at any cost. Others maintaining the UFO link, could provide no more detailed theory than this and sought comfort in what he called the "reflective factor" of paranormal events—namely, that unexplained phenomena "appear to transform themselves to reflect the beliefs and expectations of witnesses." The "dark side" UFO mythology incorporated this and the government conspiracy mythology into a single coherent one: the aliens, like fairies and vampires in earlier mythologies, harm cattle and steal children, so they are in some form diabolical in nature. The US government's collusion is a kind of Faustian bargain, making military and scientific personnel into technologically enhanced witches and Satanists. This was yet another inversion: it explained ambiguous scientific data by turning to a power beyond science, or using the unknown one more time to comprehend the unexplained.[42]

October 1974 ended with a heavy silence. Apparently ranchers filed no additional reports to law enforcement officials and the rangelands of the western United States went eerily quiet the rest of the cold months of late fall and winter months. Then in January 1975, the mutilators returned with a vengeance and all hell broke loose on the range…

Chapter Four: Sources and References

1. *The Daily Ardmoreite,* (Ardmore, Oklahoma) 3-3-71
2. Brown, David N., *Exotroopers!* Create Space Pub, 2010
3. *The* [Brainard] *Daily Dispatch,* Brainard, MI,12-27-74
4. *Associated Press,* 8-71; "Meet the Mutilators,' David Perkins, 1979
5. Sanders, Ed, "The Mutilators," *Oui* magazine, September 1976
6. *The Daily Herald,* Provo, UT, 8-16-71; Corpus Christi *Caller-Times,* 8-15-71
7. *Stigmata,* Tom Adams, *1980*
8. Interview with David Perkins, Sante Fe, NM, 8-13
9. Blackman, W.H., *Field Guide to NA Monsters,* 1998, Three Rivers Press, NY NY; Clark, Jerome, *Unexplained,* 1993, Visible Ink Press, Detroit, MI; Eberhart, George, *Geo-Bibilography of Anomalies,* 1980, Greenwood, Westport, CT
10. *Weird America,* Jim Brandon, 1978, Dutton, NY NY
11. "The Mystery of the Invisible Butchers," *Norrkopings Tidninger,* 11-11-72
12. Fairbanks *News Miner;* Vancouver *Sun,* 7-26-72; Ken Neiland AFWS
13. "Meet the Mutilators,' David Perkins, 1979
14. Ames *Daily Tribune,* Ames, IW,4-19-73 "FBI Probes Iowa Rustling & Livestock Fraud "
15. "Meet the Mutilators," Perkins, David, 1979
16. *ibid*
17. UFOCasebook.com; Booth, BJ; Howe, Linda, *An Alien Harvest,*1989, self-published
18. UFOCasebook.com; Booth, BJ
19. Ellis, Bill, *Raising the Devil,* 2000, University Press of KY
20. *ibid*
21. Ridpath, Ian, "The Great UFO Wave," *Nature,* Vol. 251, 10-4-75
22. Ridge, Francis, NICAP Site Coordinator, NICAP.org
23. *Huron Daily Tribune* (Bad Axe, MI) 10-16-73
24. Des Moines *Register* (Iowa), 4-18-73, Adams, Tom, 1993, *Chopper and the Choppers*
25. *ibid*
26. Chicago *Sun-Times,* 8-19-73; *ibid*
27. *ibid*
28. *Southern Illinoisian,* 8-22-73, *Arkansas Gazette* (Little Rock), 8-23-73
29. FBI, St. Louis; report, 9-9-73 and memo, 10-4-73
30. Ames *Daily Tribune,* 4-19-73 "FBI Probes Iowa Rustling and Livestock Fraud "
31. *Newsweek,* 8-30-73
32. Ellis, Bill, *Raising the Devil,* 2000, University Press of KY
33. Ellis, Bill, *Raising the Devil,* 2000, U Press of KY; *Mystery Stalks the Prairie,* Wolverton/Donovan, THAR Institute, MT

34. Kansas City *Times,* 12-22-73
35. Ellis, Bill, *Raising the Devil,* 2000, University Press of KY
36. Randle, Kevin, "The Killer Cult Terrorizing Mid-America," *Saga,* 11-75;
37. "Meet the Mutilators," David Perkins, Animal Mutilation Probe (AMP), 1979
38. Ellis, Bill, *Raising the Devil,* 2000, University Press of KY
39. Meet the Mutilators," David Perkins, Animal Mutilation Probe (AMP), 1979
40. Ellis, Bill, *Raising the Devil,* 2000, University Press of KY
41. *ibid*
42. *ibid*

Figure 1
Chopper sightings around cattle herds and cattle rustling plagued the Midwest in the early 1970s. (credit: loughfield/youtube.com)

THE DAILY ARDMOREITE, Ardmore, Okla., Wednesday, March 3, 1971

SOME DON'T THINK SO

Lawton's 'Wolfman' a Hoax?

Figure 2
The Lawton Wolfman: Who was this fashion-challenged wildman who could leap from tall buildings with a single bound? (credit: *Daily Ardmoreite*)

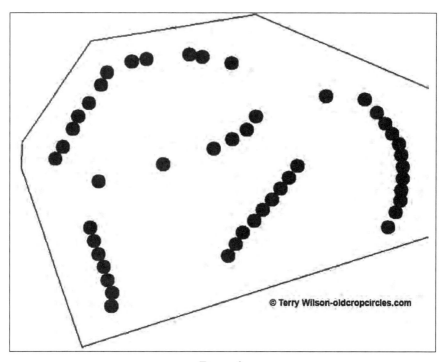

Figure 3
Diagram of the Schifelbien snow circles. (credit: Terry Wilson oldcropcircles.com)

Figure 4
ATF official Donald Flickinger. (credit: Bob Zeller/Billings Gazette, MT)

Figure 5
Mystery chopper sightings around mutilation sites increased all through the 1970s.
(credit: US Army.gov)

Figure 6
A ranch dog takes a leap—calves in Brazil don't leap. (credit: crazymranch.com)

Figure 7
Witness drawings of Momo—figure on the left allegedly stole the sandwich.
(credit: frontiersofzoology.blogspot.com)

Figure 8
Entrance to Colorado's Ft. Greely. (credit: usarmy.com)

Figure 9
Ritual occult scene. (credit: cvltnation.com)

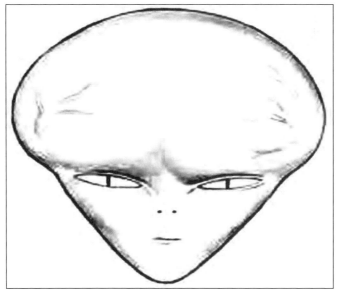

Figure 10
Drawing of Judy Doraty alien. (credit: projectufoskywatch.com)

Hovering helicopter 'eyes' cattle in Southern Illinois

Figure 11
Hundreds of chopper reports have been filed around mute sites.
(credit: Southern Illinoisan, 8-22-73)

Figure 12
Mute investigator Tom Adams. (credit David Perkins/AMP archive)

162

Figure 13
Newsweek headline 9-30-73. (credit: moremagazines.net)

Figure 14
KS senator Ross Doyen was victimized by the mystery cattle mutilators.
(credit: usd333.com)

Figure 15
Anton LaVey, started the Church of Satan and was forced to research
cattle mutilations to establish his group's innocence. (credit: wikipedia.org)

Figure 16
Who is flying all the mystery helicopters seen near mutilation sites?
(credit: Craig Gifford/heliaustralia.com

Chapter 5
The Hell Years
1975–1978

W
hen it comes to 1975 through 1979, there is no way that anyone could possibly illustrate the nervous tension, consternation and intensity experienced by ranchers and law enforcement affected by countless mutilation reports during this whirlwind time period in the western United States. Researching the mid to late '70s, I knew going in there was no way I would be able to cover every case and every outbreak of reports and still have room for the rest of the information in this book. 1975 was the peak year for mutilation reports and these waves of cases truly deserve an entire book on their own. For *Stalking the Herd,* I have elected to focus on what I feel are the most representative cases during this time period. As with earlier chapters, I show time correlations (and the presence of other elements: UFOs, choppers, crypto-creatures and synchronistic world events) and note the dozens of other cases not covered in state totals compiled by law enforcement and researchers. As you are surely aware by now, I can't over emphasize the potential importance of the perception of attendant phenomena lurking around the "mutilation" phenomenon.

This time period was insightfully summed up by David Perkins in his article "Meet the Mutilators*"* his overview of the 1970s cattle mutilation phenomenon and the attendant weirdness reports that blistered regions that experienced these perplexing livestock deaths. Mutes, mystery choppers, UFOs, military base incursions, plane

and helicopter chases, Bigfoot sightings, hooded figures lurking about, apparent occult activity, maniacal ranchers trying to drive out neighboring ranchers, posses attempting to shoot down choppers—as we are about to see, the mid to late '70s had it all and then some.

> It would be tempting to dub [1975] "all around strangest" in the recorded history of the West. Indeed, many folks felt that the world had gone mad as they were deluged with a steady stream of events that bedazzled and befuddled even the most down-to-earth westerners.
> What could have been a triumphant year for the cattlemen turned into a massive bummer for many ranch families. Besides being the peak of the mutilations, 1975 was also the highpoint for the cattle industry. In that year some 165 million beef cattle were grazing in American pastures—more than ever before or since.[1]

Perkins wrote the above in 1979 and since 1975 the beef cattle population has steadily declined in the U.S. to numbers today well below 100 million head. Funny how 1975 represented the height of the beef cattle population and number of ranching operations in North America, and at the same time, it was the height of the cattle mutilation phenomenon at the apex of the mystery's dissemination out into the culture. Is this a simple coincidence or does this potential correlation provide us with something important to ponder as we attempt to unravel the mystery? Is this a perfect illustration of meme propagation and if so, why?

Kagan & Summers in their well-researched, but largely forgotten book *Mute Evidence* based their findings on facts obtained from investigators, researchers, media coverage and law enforcement officials. They summed up the time period in Kagan's "Jack Webb"-like fashion: "Between 1973 and 1980, between 8,000 and 12,000 cattle and horses had apparently been killed and surgically mutilated. This had happened in between 21 and 40 states…"

As we will see, an important companion to the hundreds of mutilation reports from the fall of 1975 were the dozens and dozens of mystery helicopter reports. This subject alone is worthy of an in-depth research project and book. UFO sightings were also an important element, but during the 1975 wave, reports of choppers sighted in and around mute sites poured into local sheriffs' offices in the Western United States. As we saw in the previous chapter, the mystery helicopter reports (often described as "black," but not always) appeared to begin in Iowa but were associated with *livestock rustling*. Then, after these initial reports, the helicopters began to be seen around cattle mutilation sites in Iowa, Kansas and Minnesota. By 1975, attendant chopper sightings became a common theme in areas where mutilations were being reported, but this was not well known to the general public. UFOs were also being sighted, but compared with the number of chopper reports at the time, UFOs almost become an afterthought as many reports of lights may have actually been choppers seen in the night sky. In some reports, literally fleets of choppers were reported flying in formation! I've often wondered where a chopper sighting ends and a UFO sighting begins, or vice-versa?

Meet the Databases

Tom Adams compiled an impressive listing of all this unexplained helicopter activity in a self-published book called *The Choppers...and The Choppers* (1980) that documented over 200 sightings around mutilation sites, including some highly noteworthy reports from the secure airspace around U.S. Air Force Bases including Malmstrom and Offitt AFB—the nerve center of our anti-ballistic missile fields in the upper midwest. I have utilized Adams' research to help compile the following reports and also have relied on Robert Hastings' *UFOs and Nukes* and David Perkins' meticulous documentation in "Meet the Mutilators." I have also used the remaining databases of Tommy Blann (most of his case files and documentation were stolen from a storage unit in the early 1990s). These and other source material have helped me present standout mutilation case reports—sometimes with other attendant phenomena—in an attempt to put the time period in perspective within a larger worldview. I have included some interesting synchronistic world events and pertinent regional UFO information for correlative context and perspective, even though in 1975, perspective was in short supply when it came to what were perceived as "cattle mutilations."

I would argue that the mutilation mystery suggests a relentless scourge and psychical hit to the independent, small ranching communities around the western United States. Eighty percent of these small ranching operations have disappeared since 1975. At the time, dozens of counties became perceived cattle killing grounds and the constant drone of persistent helicopter sightings suggested government involvement. But that lingering underlying sense of something occult and sinister also burbled underneath the press coverage and this "satanic" element would be seriously considered throughout the decade by law enforcement and the national media. One thing stands out: helicopters were being seen in and around areas where livestock were being reported as "mutilated" and the whole mystery reverberated with a sense of a diabolical, clinical expertise.

The Early Cases in 1975

The initial reports from early January 1975 are a perfect illustration of this choppers chopping "guilt-by-association" meme. These first "official" cattle mutilation reports of 1975 were filed quietly east of Dallas near Sulphur Springs, Texas on January 7th, where a black cow was discovered mutilated, missing its sexual organs. The same day, another bull was reported mutilated to the west in Brackenridge, Texas. On the 17th a cow was reported mutilated just to the southwest in Comanche County. Then reports were filed from the Texas panhandle area—in Corchran County. On February 5, 1975 Cochran County sheriff C. G. Richards received a call from a rancher reporting that his cow had apparently been targeted and then mutilated. Within a day or so, the mutilator crews apparently jumped back to the northeast corner of the state in Greg County. Unidentified helicopters had been seen shortly before the discovery of the mutilated cow and the prior week, residents of neighboring Smith County has also seen helicopters that were described as having "constant white lights underneath." One witness described an "awfully loud" chopper the night prior to a cow being discovered mutilated on his northeastern Texas ranch.

Then things really became strange back west in Cochran when on March 10, 1975, sheriff Richards was contacted by rancher Darwood Marshall who reported that a heifer and a steer had been mutilated, and that the sheriff should come out and see the two crime scenes. Richards made the trip out to the ranch, and according to his sheriff's report, he found the heifer dead "with its head twisted straight up and laying inside a 30 foot diameter circle of grass that had pressed downwards and rotated."[2] All of this was inside what was described as a "perfectly round circle" apparently burnt into the grass. Then the rancher took him to where the steer lay about a quarter mile away. Again, the second mutilated animal was laying inside a burned circle of grass about 30 feet in diameter. The fields were covered with winter wheat about four inches tall and the circles were "burned clear." Richards was intrigued enough with the crime scene evidence to return to the sites with a Geiger counter where he discovered that "radiation was present." The sheriff contacted Reese Air Force Base which sent out a team to investigate. The AF investigators also detected radiation, but according to their interpretation of the results there was only about "one half of one percent radiation" above background levels. They told Richards not to worry about it, and they left.

Evidently, UFOs had been seen in the general area where the mutes were discovered on the Marshall ranch and Richards noted this in his report:

> I have had reports of UFOs in this area but have not seen any myself… [the witnesses] all tell the same story. It is about as wide as a two-lane highway, round [shaped] and looks the color of the sun when it is going down and has got a blue glow around it.[3]

Another noteworthy early 1975 incident was a spectacular chase featuring Dundy County, Nebraska law enforcement and one of our mystery helicopters. The incident featured a chopper that apparently was tracked by radar and witnessed hovering over a missile silo near Haigler, Nebraska. A large black bull was reportedly mutilated during the same time period.

Texas was particularly hard hit in 1975 and Paris, Texas researcher Tom Adams was on alert—some of these cases occurred mid-state close to where he lived.

Apparently, in 1975, no part of the Lone Star state escaped attention from the mutilators and/or the resulting press coverage that accompanied each new wave of local claims. By the end of the year, even the extreme southern portion of the state around the Brownsville area military installations—not previously targeted in the early 70s—had reported cases.

In early 1975 the mutilators are reported to have also targeted Colorado's Garfield County and other areas on the Colorado Front range, although I could find no official documentation of these reports. There were unsubstantiated rumors that mutilations had occurred in Elbert County in May, along with claims of helicopters being heard in the areas where cattle were later discovered mutilated. The Elbert County-based *Ranchland News* began covering the mutilations in earnest. Today, looking back at the time frame, it seems that the ranching community-at-large was unaware of what was about to unfold across the west, and there seems to have been a lid of self-imposed non-disclosure on rumors of these spring cases. Toward the end of March all appeared quiet on the western front, but not for long.

For a bit of context, during the third week of March 1975, the Alaska Pipeline project broke ground; King Faisal of Saudi Arabia was shot to death by his nephew; the Black Eyed Peas's Fergie was born in California; and the mutilators appeared to move north into Montana's Chouteau County where the first of over a hundred 1975 cases reported in Montana was investigated. A sizeable number of the 1975-1976 Montana mutilation reports were reported in close proximity to major U.S. military installations, as we will see later in the chapter.

On March 24th, Chouteau deputy sheriff Robert Blades was called out to a ranch on the Missouri River where a cow (that had just given birth two days prior) was found in the center of a trampled-down circle. This case was a bit unusual, as it appeared to be "sloppy" to investigators. There was some blood in evidence on the ground and some blood was dripping from the carcass, which is not your normal mutilation feature. The udder had been removed with a "very smooth incision" and the animal's intestines and internal organs (favorite scavenger delicacies) "hung out from the rectal area" but remained untouched. No tracks were found in the partially snow-covered ground around the carcass, however tracks either from a dog or coyote were found circling the site about 50 to 60 feet away. These tracks did not appear to approach the carcass. Investigating officers did a thorough search of the crime scene and discovered a newborn calf that had been attacked and mutilated. It was missing its tongue and one lip, but *the newborn calf was still alive.* The rancher determined that this was not the calf that had born from the mutilated cow and four days later, the mutilated cow's calf was discovered laying on a snowbank alive, but barely.

The rancher later reported that the next four calves born on his ranch were inexplicably delivered dead on arrival. I have been unable to locate any other "official" Montana reports until the following August, but there were a series of reports filed in Idaho, which until the summer of 1975 had escaped the mutilators attention. This changed on June 15th 1975 when three cows were found mutilated on a ranch in the beautiful Snake River Basin area on the rim of the aptly-named "Hell's Canyon"—located in Adams County. (figure 1) Over the next week and a half, three more head of cattle were reported mutilated in a similar condition as the previous three—sexual organs, tongues and udders cleanly removed with no blood or other evidence at the crime scenes. Predators appeared to be leery of the carcasses and refused to approach these easily-obtained potential meals.

Adams County officials were not taking any chances and organized range patrol units to monitor the region where the reports were occurring. Sheriff Jim Hileman was understandably confused as to what the mutilators' motivations could be. When he was asked if Satanists were responsible, he told the *Idaho Statesman:*

> I'm told they [Satanists] look for things for their fertility rites that symbolize virginity. A young white-faced cow could be construed as a symbol of virginity and its sexual organs used in such rites. [He suggested that the killer is]… a bi-sexual individual… some sort of weirdo who is very involved in the occult.[4]

As word circulated around the remote Idaho ranching communities in Adams County, unusual police reports began to be filed by nervous folks where media coverage had alerted them to the mysterious mute cases. In one report a stranger was seen and reported lurking in a machine shop and in Bear, Idaho there were reports by residents who told authorities they had been "hearing people" quietly walking around in their homes.[5] The Idaho mutilation reports abruptly ended around the Fourth of July, the media coverage ceased, and the initial reaction and uneasiness in the community apparently subsided. Life returned to normal in the Snake River Basin, but not for long—those cattle surgeons that targeted "Hell's Canyon" would return to the region in three short months.

May 1975 seems to have been a curious lull period in North American mutilation reports. As I noted earlier, these brief bits of downtime are somehow important. Is there a pause for big picture events to take center stage? Or are these downtimes simply planning and positioning periods before the next phase of the operation(s)? There is something indicative in the silence, some sort of clue waiting to be discovered, perhaps.

What was going on in the world that month? On May 7, 1975 President Gerald Ford declared an end to the "Vietnam Era." On May 11th, a crowd of about 75,000 people in New York City's Central Park celebrated the end of the Vietnam War. On May 14 the U.S. performed yet another nuclear test at the Nevada Test Site. On May 24 the last naturally occurring case of the smallpox virus *variola* major was reported: a woman named Saiban Bibi, was found ill at a railway station in

Karimganj in the Assam state of India. And life went on.

The Cheyenne Mountain Cases

Daniel Kagan insightfully pointed out in *Mute Evidence* (figure 2) that by June 1975, Colorado Front Range small town local newspapers had begun covering rumors, reports and stories of cattle mutilations in the ranching communities. This may have helped stoke the fire of cultural dissemination that may have helped bolster the mysterious nature of the meme, and it was during this time period that the regional papers began to take notice.

> The larger newspapers in Colorado began to carry articles about the mutilations, because responses to them had begun to assume a solid shape. The Elbert County Livestock Association, in answer to the rumbling concern of its members, had posted a $1,000 reward for information leading to the arrest and conviction of anyone stealing, mutilating, or illegally killing cattle.[6]

A month or so later the Colorado State Grange organization offered an additional $500 reward. I find it curious that Kagan & Summers for some reason made the decision omit the July case that occurred on the boundary between NORAD and Ft. Carson. It was actually the first of two intriguing 1975 cases reported just outside the NORAD facility inside Cheyenne Mountain.

On July 6, 1975 as the Argentine government fell and the rapper "50 Cent" was born, *a very important mutilation case* occurred to the southwest of Colorado Springs. This particular act of bloodless, bloody deviltry was perpetrated literally on *NORAD's front doorstep*—on the road outside the entrance to the huge underground secure facility located inside Cheyenne Mountain. (figure 3) It is very apparent to me that someone or something must be confident, talented and brazenly tricksterish to be able to pull off a stunt such as this on the thin strip of land that separates Cheyenne Mountain from the huge, well-secured Army facility at Fort Carson. Or maybe it was a clever "red flag" experiment. I've always suspected that parties as yet unknown were sending some sort of blatant message to the world that July 4th weekend. But who is watching whom?

Before we detail the case, here is NORAD's description of its underground facility and the various programs that are housed 1,500 feet deep inside "our" huge mountain complex:

> The Cheyenne Mountain Complex is located at Cheyenne Mountain Air Force Station (CMAFS), a short distance from NORAD and USNORTHCOM headquarters at Peterson Air Force Base in Colorado Springs, Colorado. Cheyenne Mountain Air Force Station falls under Air Force Space Command and hosts the activities of several tenant units.

At the height of the Cold War in the late 1950s, the idea of a hardened command and control center was conceptualized as a defense against long-range Soviet bombers. The Army Corps of Engineers supervised the excavation of Cheyenne Mountain and the construction of an operational center within the granite mountain. The Cheyenne Mountain facility became fully operational as the NORAD Combat Operations Center on April 20, 1966.

Over the years, the installation came to house elements of the North American Aerospace Defense Command (NORAD), U.S. Strategic Command, U.S. Air Force Space Command and U.S. Northern Command (USNORTHCOM). Under what became known as the Cheyenne Mountain Operations Center (CMOC), several centers supported the NORAD missions of aerospace warning and aerospace control and provided warning of ballistic missile or air attacks against North America.[7]

Fredrick Smith, author of the little-known, self-published 1979 examination of the 1970s mutilation wave in North America, *Cattle Mutilation—The Unthinkable Truth* highlights the two Cheyenne Mountain reports that (in my opinion), defy debunking. These reports received some regional attention, but because of the wave of cases that were being reported all around the west, to my knowledge, they were not featured in the national press. I can find no reference to these cases in the mainstream national media, but I can't underscore enough the potential importance of these NORAD cases. Here is what we know from Smith:

> Highway 115 is a busy divided expressway serving Ft. Carson and NORAD just beyond the city limits. A huge area there, thousands of acres, is military reservation, artillery ranges and so on. Near NORAD's super secret Cheyenne Mountain bastion, of course, the area is under the strictest possible surveillance. Immediately opposite the main entrance to Ft. Carson is the unmarked NORAD Road, an excellent, wide three-mile long highway that twists up the steep mountainside to the heavily guarded installation. NORAD Road isn't even on ordinary road maps…
>
> The steep hillside up to the electrically controlled high entrance gate to the huge tunnel into this worldwide intelligence nerve center is covered with rock and brush. Surprisingly, a few cattle are also grazed there, no doubt to lower any possible fire hazard. So, right there, immediately overlooking thousands of military buildings, the protective covering of hundreds of planes and helicopters and 20,000 soldiers, and immediately in front of the electronic brain and senses that survey the entire North American continent so that even a needle couldn't get in undetected, plus monitoring all of space from here to the moon so as to detect even an 8-foot length of fine wire orbiting the earth, someone thought this would

be a neat place to have a cattle mutilation.

It was a standard mutilation of a cow due to calve in two months, and Deputy Sheriff Sgt. Robert Stone "ruled out the possibility that the animal's sex organs were removed by a coyote." Sgt. Stone said in his opinion, "the animal did not struggle when it went down, but was possibly induced with a tranquilizer."[8]

The second NORAD area case occurred sometime during on a cold, crisp October 21st, when a 1,500-pound captive bison was found mutilated *inside the Cheyenne Mountain Zoo*—located just outside of the Cheyenne Mountain complex. The temperatures had been hovering around freezing that week; these were perfect conditions to maintain the carcass in pristine condition and two expert scientific analyses were conducted on-site within 24 hours of the bison's discovery.

The Cheyenne Mountain Zoo, located on the northeast flank of Cheyenne Mountain, contains a number of wild, exotic animals and the mutilated bison cow was housed in the North American Panorama section. (figure 4) The zoo is within sight of luxury homes located just beyond the famous Broadmore Hotel, and again, these are some of the most guarded and secure sections of real estate in the world.

It was documented that the animal's udder, an ear and a 24 x 24 inch square section of hide looked as if they had been expertly excised. The female reproductive organs were cut out and very little blood was apparent around the wounds except for a small amount of blood in the mouth where the tongue had evidently been bitten by the bison. Upon further professional examination, it was discovered that there was excessive bleeding into the internal organs that may have been an indication of the presence of an anticoagulant. Unauthorized access into the North American Panorama display is not difficult, but bison are wild animals, aggressively dangerous and unpredictable and the official examination of the carcass established that *a predator had not killed or scavenged the animal.*

Dr. Rodney C. Walker, the zoo's veterinarian, performed a gross autopsy, and soon after, the El Paso County Coroner Dr. Raoul W. Urich was called in to examine the carcass. Fluid samples were obtained and sent for analysis to the Colorado State University animal pathology lab at Ft. Collins. Zoo director, Dan Davis was understandably bewildered according to the Colorado Springs *Sun:*

It looked as though the animal was lying down sleeping in a dusty area where the animals sleep. There are about 50 bison and 10 American elk in the pen and only their tracks were visible. *There's no doubt the animal was mutilated with some sort of sharp instrument handled by man.* [my emphasis]

According to Dr. Walker, the zoo's veterinarian who performed the gross autopsy, "It was very, very strange…there was an excessive amount of sero-sanguineous (blood-tinged) fluid in the abdominal and thoracic cavities and the fluid had seeped into the body tissue and even into the eyeballs." Walker said he had spent hours trying to find a disease that might account for this condition, but to no avail. He said that because of the freshness of the carcass, authorities might have a better chance to determine a definite cause of death…[9]

Dr. Urich, the county coroner, said: "The cutting was done neatly, cleanly, obviously with a very sharp instrument. The dissection was of the type that would eliminate any type of predator." He said *the hide was removed by someone who did not puncture the tissue layer directly under the hide. "It was better than I could do if I were trying. It was really an expert job…"* Dr. Urich estimated it had been dead "up to 24 hours, but no more."[10] [my emphasis]

Fredrick Smith observed that the location of the animal (and importantly—exactly where it was found mutilated) absolutely negates debunkers' assertion that *all* mutilations are the work of predators and scavenging:

> What less than a full grown grizzly or a large pack of hungry timber wolves could bring down a 1500-pound bison anyway? And predators, except for taking a few birds, have never been a problem in the zoo's entire history.
>
> The carcass was in the best possible condition. And the nights were very cold. How could such a thing have been done in that completely exposed public place so near to houses in the daytime? Or how could it have been done at night without a good light plus a certain amount of time, noise and equipment?[11]

To the east of Cheyenne Mountain, out on the Front Range, mutilations began to be reported by ranchers in Lincoln, El Paso and Logan Counties, and the alleged discovery of physical evidence that suggested government complicity in the mutilations is especially noteworthy. The items were not discovered at a mutilation site, but nearby. Was some sort of message being left for the ranching community along the banks of the Big Sandy River? Tommy Blann mentions this curious claim in chapter 9 of his privately published book *Unmasking the Enemy*:

> [I]n July 1975, a prominent farmer in Lincoln County, Colorado found a blue plastic satchel near his driveway on his property that was stamped with a government seal. The satchel contained a cow's ear, part of a cow's tongue, a government-issued scalpel and a pair of gloves. It was

evidently placed in an area where it would be found, as if to suggest to the public that the government was involved in the cattle mutilations.[12]

The Scourge Begins to Spread

In late July 1975, a couple of weeks after the first NORAD case near Ft. Carson, strange, atypical cases began to crop up back in Cascade County Montana. A rancher located outside Fort Shaw found a heifer dead *inside an 18-foot "trampled" circle* missing its individual teats. There were no other apparent wounds or disfigurements. The rancher also reported that he had witnessed "red blinking lights" flying through his pastures and a short time later *two additional head of livestock disappeared and/or were stolen* from his ranch—never to be seen again. Here is another example of rustling activity ushering in a mutilation wave, as in 1972-73 in Iowa.

Early August is when we see a dramatic upsurge into the fall 1975 wave in the western United States. Cases were first reported northwest of the San Luis Valley during the first two weeks of the month and a week later back up in Montana. Over the next two weeks almost a dozen states' law enforcement agencies and cattle inspectors would log reported mutilation claims by dismayed ranchers.

The San Luis Valley (SLV), in south central Colorado/north central New Mexico, apparently escaped the attention of the mutilators that spring and into the summer, but this abruptly changed in early August. First came rumors of mutilations and then the 1975 unexplained livestock death wave descended on the SLV—down from Cochetopa Pass on the Continental Divide. These early, unpublicized reports in August 1975 occurred during a two-week period concurrent with rumors of Gunnison County cases on the western slope. The eastern slope cases appeared to have begun in extreme northwestern Saguache County—at the foot of Cochetopa Pass—along the western edge of northern Saguache Park. These were the first known mutes since the rumors of SLV cases surfaced, unverified, in 1970. In August, 2012 cases reported from the same area alongside Highway 114.

Back in 1975, investigating Saguache County deputy Gene Gray was convinced there was "something unnatural" about the condition of the "half dozen" cows, calves, and one horse reported as "mutilated." He took a few dozen photographs and interviewed the puzzled ranchers but no one had noticed anything else.[13]

The Loman family had a secluded ranch just west of the small town of La Garita Colorado on the western side of the northern SLV. The night of August 7, 1975 Mr. Loman remembered hearing his dogs barking around 3:00 AM. The following morning he went out early to feed his horses and noticed his daughter's palomino show horse lying in the pasture several hundred yards from the house. (figure 5) The rear end appeared to have been "burned-off," the horse's lips and eyes had been removed and a thick, black, tar-like substance ringed the upper body incision areas.

Photographs of the horse appear to show a horse dead for many days, although Loman had seen it alive the night before. Gray investigated and took photographs that morning. "I knew after that one, that something really weird was going on," he told me in 1993. "There's just no way that animal should have looked like that."[14]

The following week, helicopters were spotted and reported flying around back to the west near the earlier "mutilation" sites in Gunnison County. A rancher saw an unmarked helicopter hovering over a hog in Gunnison County that he "chased off." *A hog allegedly turned up missing* from a neighboring ranch. This is reminiscent of the 1973 hog rustlers in Iowa.

On August 21, 1975, Tom Adams (who, at the time, happened to be visiting the San Luis Valley with research associate Gary Massey) noted the following chopper sighting in his book *The Choppers...and the Choppers*:

> Leaving the (Gunnison County) sheriff's office after discussing mutilation investigations with Deputy David Ellis, Project Stigma investigators Tom Adams and Gary Massey drove south toward Saguache County [*not knowing that between six or seven cases had been reported two weeks before on this exact stretch on*] State Highway 114. Nearing the [Saguache] county line, they observed a small helicopter— of the Hughes Cayuse type—flying west-southwest across the highway toward the Powderhorn/Los Pinos area, where a cattle mutilation had occurred earlier in the week. The helicopter was filmed on Super-8 movie film as it passed out of sight over a ridge. The distance was too great to discern details."[15]

Another noteworthy case from the Cochetopa region featured a calf mutilation with a rare *downside mandible incision.* This detail again is one that defies debunker's assertions that only upward facing organs on the head are found excised. (figure 7) The udder is completely missing with a clean cut with no break into the body cavity. (figure 8)

I couldn't help but wonder if rumors of "mutilations" in neighboring south central Colorado counties contributed to perceptions of possible misidentified scavenger action in the SLV. It's as if the ensuing mayhem in the SLV was being set up on some level that didn't rely on media coverage. And so, apparently was the chopper activity that burbled up out on the Front Range.

During this same August 1975 time period, a helicopter was seen and reported spotlighting a herd of cattle in Logan County, Colorado, as eastern Colorado ranchers reported new claims of mute cases. We also saw the beginning of local Colorado law enforcement attempts to follow and track down where these chopper flights were being staged to conduct their nefarious operations. Tommy Blann pointed out:

> Several sightings of helicopters, including one hovering over a herd of cattle with a spotlight on near Cedar Creek, were reported and investigated by the Logan County Sheriff's Office [LCSO] on a Friday in August 1975. While LCSO officers attempted to locate the helicopter, another sighting was reported near Padroni [CO]. Then, about 30 minutes later, a LCSO officer patrolling Highway 6, near the Hall Ranch, approximately halfway between Sterling and Fleming, sighted a low flying helicopter, when it was suddenly illuminated by a flash of lightning. The LCSO officer said the helicopter did not have any lights on. The sightings of these helicopters came two nights after several law enforcement agencies were involved in a chase of one, possibly two, helicopters which lasted the better part of five hours. Animal mutilations were being reported during this time period in Logan County.[16]

By early August, County Sheriff's departments and local ranching groups were beginning to put political pressure on the state to investigate the growing reports of mutilated livestock. The Colorado Bureau of Investigation (CBI) contacted the Diagnostic Laboratory at the Colorado State College of Veterinarian Medicine at Colorado State University (CSU) and the two organizations put the word out that they would conduct post-mortem forensic examinations of alleged mute cases. They instructed local vets and law enforcement to send in samples of the incisional areas on the cattle, or even better, if the case was fresh enough, to bring the carcass in for examination at the CSU lab.

On August 14th, 1975—exactly one year to the day after the first Cascade County Montana mutilation report—another atypical case was reported to Captain Keith Wolverton, who would soon be placed in charge of investigating the state's growing number of livestock mutilation reports:

> [Wolverton] a native of Great Falls, was a member of the Cascade County Sheriff's Office from 1965 until 1990 when he retired after 25 years in law enforcement. He was one of two men responsible for establishing the Cascade County K-9 Academy where lawmen and their dogs are trained in a unique school. It was the only resident K-9 training academy in the United States. Captain Wolverton taught at the academy until 1975 when he was transferred to duty with the sheriff's office in Great Falls.[17]

Wolverton would co-author an important but little-known book titled *Mystery Stalks the Prairie* that chronicled the three years he coordinated livestock mutilation investigations in and around the Malmstrom missile fields of Cascade

County, plus a bewildering array of other weirdness. (figure 9) A rancher in the Belt, Montana area reported a mutilated cow, and her calf was missing. Both had been inside a locked pasture and the momma cow's left ear, tongue and some hide were discovered excised and gone. The reproductive organs and bag were untouched and according to Wolverton, "There was an attempt to skin the jaw. Examination showed that the gland behind the left ear had been removed." They never found the calf.

The time period between August 1975 and May 1976 was extremely busy for Montana law enforcement officials in Cascade County. They logged an impressive official log of 130 reports of helicopters and/or UFOs. During this same time period they investigated over 100 mutilation claims by Montana ranchers.[18]

Let's Chase Down Them Choppers!

Back in Colorado on the evening of August 21, 1975, Logan County Sheriff Tex Graves and several other lawmen took part in a spectacular aerial "chase" worthy of Hollywood. The elusive object being chased was one of our mystery choppers—flying around the heart of our county's largest missile field array. (figure 10)

At 10:00 PM the chopper was seen entering the area from the east. Undersheriff Jerry Wolever led one group—flying a fixed wing aircraft. Sheriff Graves coordinated the 17 ground units involved in the chase. For several hours the lawmen pursued the helicopter through the missile/silo-infested rural areas of Logan County, Colorado and adjacent Kimball County, Nebraska. At one point, the Sheriff's car was stopped by two armed "Air Force" men in an "official" truck. After identifying himself and explaining the situation, the Sheriff enlisted the aid of the Air Force men. The two men offered to coordinate the pursuit efforts with radar operators at Warren AFB in Cheyenne. The Sheriff roared off. Until 3:00AM the Air Force men "directed" the wild goose chase—mostly relaying conflicting and confusing information.

The madness ended at 4:30 AM, when the spotter plane closed in on the chopper as it was hovering over a missile silo near Bushnell, Nebraska. Suddenly, the helicopter "turned off its lights." Thinking the craft had landed and capture was near, the airborne officers buzzed the area repeatedly at an altitude of 100-150 feet. Nothing—the mystery helicopter had "disappeared." The next morning Undersheriff Wolever called Warren AFB "to find out a little more about the radar tracking." The operations officer at Warren told Wolever that the base didn't have a radar unit to cover that area and denied any participation in the event. The identity of the helpful "Air Force men" was never determined...[19]

During the chase, which spilled over into southern Nebraska, the putative Air Force men in the pickup truck kept announcing that "radar" indicated that there was another aircraft flying near the chase plane rented by the Logan County Sheriff's Department. Sheriff Graves told the Greeley, Colorado *Tribune,* "[R]eported radar showed this other aircraft around our plane at various times, but the officers and pilot, three men with glasses, never saw a thing, (and it was a moonlit night)."

The chase ended around 4:30 in the morning near a missile site in southwestern Nebraska, when the spotter plane lost sight of the phantom copter. The plane, reporter Bill Jackson of the Sterling, Colorado, *Journal-Advocate*, told us, "saw the lights of the thing below them, and you know, it was a clear night. And when the light went out, that's what everybody thought, that they'd landed, but when the plane came down to 100-150 feet, he couldn't see anything...the only thing that was there was a missile silo."

Several questions remain after this incident:

Were the two officers from the Air Force merely practical jokers having fun with local law enforcement? (It must be remembered that, in addition to Logan County officers, the Nebraska State Police and the Kimball County, Nebraska Sheriff's office were also involved.)

Were the two men merely masquerading as Air Force personnel and were they actually part of the mutilation network? (This network must have spent millions of dollars on copter fuel, maintenance, security and man-hours in the 22 or so states that have suffered mutilations.)

Sad to ask is this: is the United States Air Force involved in supplying cover for the mutilators?[20]

Senator Floyd K. Haskell [CO] wrote a letter to the FBI requesting assistance from them due to mutilations in Colorado. He indicated that a helicopter was reported as having been used in the mutilations, and that several persons in Morgan County had reported being chased by a similar helicopter. Senator Haskell repeated his requests that the FBI enter the investigation because he felt it was too big for local authorities. The FBI declined, however, claiming that it was not within their jurisdiction.[21]

The Greatest Outrage in Ranching History?

By September 1975, the uproar in the Colorado press and in the Front Range ranching communities had reached a crescendo. According to Kagan & Summers, by the end of the summer there had been around 70 official mutilation reports in Colorado. As we have seen, the unpublicized SLV/Gunnison County reports appeared to have been underreported in late July and August, so this number may have been as high as 80 cases.

Bowing to pressure, Governor Richard Lamm finally came out and made a formal statement to the press that would become the most memorable quote from his entire tenure as governor of Colorado. Addressing the Colorado Cattleman's Association meeting in Pueblo, he was quoted as saying that the mutilations were "one of the greatest outrages in the history of the western cattle industry,"[21] and helped the group announce a $5,000 reward for the arrest and conviction of a cattle mutilator. Lamm also stated, when asked by reporters, that the widely held theory that some kind of cult may be responsible for the mutes was being considered and that there appeared to be a correlation with unexplained helicopter activity being reported by ranchers and lawmen. Colorado law enforcement welcomed the public statements and understanding of the governor:

> Undersheriff Gary Gibbs, of the El Paso County Sheriff's Office welcomed Lamm's support, then [Gibbs] went on to say, "Ever since the mutilations began we have been fighting the skeptics who have claimed that lightning or predators were responsible for everything." He then voiced a rather oblique complaint about the way that the CBI was going:
>
> "We have always tried to cooperate with the Colorado Bureau of Investigation, and will in the future, but that cooperation has to be reciprocated. So far we still haven't received any written reports from Ft. Collins [the CSU pathology laboratory] about the carcasses we have sent up there, and we haven't been advised about any meeting the CBI has held regarding the mutilations. We want to cooperate and end these things, but we do feel that all law enforcement agencies must work together to get the job done."[22]

The public focus had been on Colorado, but unfortunately, Wyoming and other states were not able to escape the late summer scourge unscathed. Although some details never made the media or researcher's databases, Teton County Sheriff John Howard stated that by the end of August 1975 he estimated that 60 head of livestock had been "sexually mutilated in Wyoming during the last year." He also expressed surprise that predators were unwilling to scavenge many of the mutilated carcasses.

In the last week of August 1975, mutilators apparently didn't care what governors or law enforcement-types thought, for they descended back onto the San Luis Valley with impunity. Or so the headlines wanted you to believe. The Friday, August 29, 1975 edition of the Alamosa, Colorado *Valley Courier* screamed "Five More [SLV] Cattle Are Mutilated." I could find no reference to earlier cases but this much is known: two cows were discovered mutilated in the mountains west of Antonito and an additional three animals were discovered near Fox Creek. All five animals were discovered on August 26th.

A bull belonging to Max Brady from Manassa, Colorado *had been shot* and the tail and an ear had been removed. Another bull owned by rancher Farron Layton *had been shot* and the tongue reportedly removed with a "sharp instrument." A third animal *"had been shot but was not mutilated."* According to the *Valley Courier*, "vandals" were blamed. Correct me if I'm wrong, but you've never heard of "aliens" using firearms that propel small lethal lead projectiles, have you? For me, researching these 1975 cases back when I began in 1993, this was the first instance of hearing about "mutilations" involving firearms, but as we have seen, this detail had been reported in cases in the upper midwest in the early 70s.

The fourth and fifth SLV mutes were discovered west of La Jara, Colorado on the west side of the valley. A steer owned by Jim Braiden was "missing the tail, tongue, penis, and right ear," and the animal had reportedly been drained of blood before being "mutilated with a sharp instrument." I should note the words "sharp instrument" constantly appeared in Miles Porter's *Valley Courier* articles during the rest of 1975.

On August 31, 1975, the first "official" New Mexico unexplained livestock death report—that summer—was filed by Abiquiu, New Mexico rancher Alva Simpson. He reported his prize Hereford seed-bull mutilated and missing its rear end and valuable sexual organs. This was the first report from "The Land of Enchantment," but quickly another claim was filed with the State Livestock Board of a calf mutilation on the Texas border, near Portales, New Mexico.

Two days later the deaths jumped back to the San Luis Valley when a calf was reported "mutilated" to Conejos County officials. They concluded that it occurred Tuesday night, September 2, 1975. The white-faced 400 lb. calf owned by Ed Shawcroft was found missing its "tongue, ear, genitals and tail."

To the east, at the base of the Sangre de Cristo Mountains in Costilla County, Deputy John Lobato and Sheriff Ernest Sandoval were quoted as confirming reports of helicopters flying in the area where a mutilated cow was later found. Dr. Joseph Vigil reported a mute on his ranch south of San Luis, Colorado on September 3rd. Helicopters were seen by Costilla County officers over the next thee nights. Sandoval said that early Thursday morning he saw what he believed to be a "helicopter with a red light fly south into New Mexico."

On Friday, September 5th, rancher John Catalano reported to the Alamosa County Sheriff the discovery of a dead calf on his ranch south of Alamosa. News sleuth Miles Porter was dispatched to the scene. To his untrained eye, "The black heifer calf had definitely been cut in the removal of its left ear, and some internal sexual organs. The calf had been dead about two weeks." It is important to note that without veterinarian pathology training no one could ascertain that the rotting animal "had definitely been cut" two weeks after the animal's death. But the story ran and the local fear was notched up a bit more through the local SLV media coverage. None of these stories were picked up by the national news wires to my knowledge.

Later that same Friday, Ted Carpenter, foreman of the Medano Ranch (located just west of the Great Sand Dunes and north of the Snippy site), found a yearling steer laying on its left side, missing its *downside ear* and tongue and *a suspicious heel print was found near the carcass*. Unlike most of reports from the fall of 1975 where only upside organs were removed, this report and the early Cochetopa calf case differed. These downside-excised cases indicate something other than predation or scavenging was at work.

These were the first official mutilation reports in Alamosa County since the rumored 1968 mutilation of two steers on the Zapata Ranch.

On Saturday, September 6, 1975, unknown helicopters were reported near three mutilations that were reported in the South Park portion of Park County, 45 miles north of the SLV.

During the next three weeks, the San Luis Valley got a break as reports suddenly hopped to the extreme northeast corner of Colorado, back in Logan County. Reports were also filed in Texas, Idaho and Wyoming during the second and third weeks of September; apparently the cattle surgeons are able to target an immense amount of geographic territory in a short amount of time. This is when all hell appeared to break loose for real—across most of the Western United States.

On September 15, 1975, the mutilators paid a quick return visit to Idaho. This time they had horses targeted for their acquisition of excised body parts. Murtaugh, Idaho rancher Keith Perkins reported finding two of his mares mutilated on his ranch in picturesque Snake River Canyon. One was missing its sexual organs, the other only the left eye and a section of the lower lip.

> [Rancher] Perkins was impressed with the precision with which the cervix was cut away from the bladder without puncturing it. The *Twin Falls Times* ran a story on September 19th "Slain Horses Radioactive" stating that Mr. Perkins' son, Calvin, had tested the site with a Geiger counter on September 17th and found "unusually high" readings near the carcasses.[23]

It was during this same time period that Wyoming ranchers also "officially" began witnessing unexplained aerial activity in Albany County. The first event occurred the night of September 16th. The Casper *Star Tribune* ran a story later in October that covered a report by two ranch hands, Todd Sermon and Nathan Vance, who claimed to have come upon a "helicopter sitting on Howell Mountain behind the Sermon Ranch." They quickly dimmed their vehicle lights and observed the landed craft. Vance grabbed his rifle to get a better look through his scope; the helicopter it flipped on "red, green and white" lights when it reached about 300-feet in altitude. Sermon told the *Star Tribune*:

It's a hell of a pilot that can land a helicopter on top of a mountain in the middle of the night. We interrupted some sort of operation… I think they tranquilize them (the cows) and then do their thing."[24]

A close friend of mine who, at the time, lived near Jackson Hole, Wyoming, recalled hearing about the cattle mutilations back in 1975: "When I was starting high school my oldest sister befriended a lot of ranchers, and it was common knowledge that cattle mutilations happened around here on a regular basis. Stories were passed down from father to son and it seemed that the mutilations had been going on for years, perhaps as far back as the 1800s."

The mutilators were not done with their Idaho foray, for on September 18, 1975 they turned their attention to Fremont County which would go on to become the hardest hit Idaho county in 1975. According to a flurry of reports too numerous to fully describe here, something apparently targeted 13 head of livestock in the next three and a-half weeks in the picturesque region west of Yellowstone National Park. As word of these cases blistered Fremont County they created a stir in the isolated ranching communities.

Idaho ranchers and law enforcement were at a loss to explain what was happening and people began to notice little out-of-the-ordinary things in their reality.

> A farmer living near the site of the first mutilation in Wilford, [Idaho] Tom Robinson, discovered a strange plaque on a telephone pole near the scene of the crime. Robinson remembered seeing the plaque *before* the mutilation, but never stopped to examine it, figuring it was "a religious organization's sign." The white plaque portrayed a "black temple-shaped object" and some illegible black lettering. A similar plaque was found near a mutilation zone in Chester. [emphasis retained][25]

The list of reported unexplained helicopter sightings mounted as sightings continued all up and down the Front-Range of Colorado. Rumors of new cases also bounced around the region and by the end of September, press reports began to differ in their listings of how many mutilations had occurred in the state. One version said 136; another put the number of cases at 175.[26]

> In the weeks of September 1975, the toll of reports mounted. Some unmarked helicopters were chased by night-flying sheriff's deputies. A sheriff in one county insisted that two mutilated animals he investigated had been picked up from one locked pasture, mutilated, and then dropped from the air into another pasture two miles away.[27]

Elbert County Sheriff George Yarnell and his deputies were being run ragged by the beginning of October. The county had sent sample after sample to CSU for analysis and Yarnell became frustrated with the consistent results that indicated predators and scavengers. He suspected that something was amiss. In one report the techs reported that the incisions on the sample were made by a "fox." A fox hadn't been seen in the county for a 100 years. In another attempt to ascertain the accuracy of lab testing, he purposefully indicated his knife cut on the sample was the side from the mutilation incision area. He personally drove the sample to the CSU lab and waited for the results. Predictably, and much to his chagrin, the test results indicated once again it was "predators." He went back and confronted Carl Whiteside who headed up the mutilation probe and complained to him. Whiteside offhandedly told him "we're only human, we all make mistakes." David Perkins recounted the story to me and I thought, "oh great, so how about all the mundane findings from all the other samples submitted by sheriffs from all over the state of Colorado? Were they all mistakes, or only some of them?" In *Messengers of Deception,* Jacques Vallee mentions additional observations by the puzzled sheriff:

> [Yarnell] was quoted by Fredrick F. Smith as saying that his "most memorable case," was one in which an udder was "neatly cleaned out, leaving only the skin, which was then tightly packed with several gallons of sand." In other cases, organs were cut out and left on top of the carcass. Perfect squares or circles were taken from the hide. In one incident a scalpel had been left behind; it was an ordinary article of military surplus neatly cleaned out, leaving only the skin, which was then packed with several gallons of sand."

Sheriff Yarnell and rancher Rueben Olson were quoted in an article in the Washington *Post* on October 27, October 1975:

> The mutilation reports in this county of 9,000 persons began trickling [into] June and swelled to almost one a night in September, dropping off slightly this month. "It's the biggest challenge of my career," said Yarnell. "We've exhausted everything we have on this thing and so far we've come up with absolutely nothing." …Just this week, said Yarnell, "I got a call from a sheriff down in Arizona who says they've had about 17 more that turned up down there. And some guy even called me from western Pennsylvania last week and said it happened to one of his dairy cows."
>
> "It's downright eerie," said Reuben Olson, a rancher who lost two calves, one of them only a few hundred yards from his little white ranch house about 15 miles east of Kiowa…Oh, I've heard 'em out behind my corral, " said Olson. "I've seen lights come down out of the sky out there but never seen one of them. Myself, I think it's one of those devil cults

that's doing it… I've been here for 79 years and I guess I know the work of a coyote when I see one," said Olson, whose hundred head of cattle are just small dots on the landscape of his 1,280 acre ranch…" One of my neighbors had a steer picked up right out of his corral and dropped five miles away before it was cut up. I've never heard of any coyote that could do something like that."

Those must be some talented, pesky trickster coyotes and foxes out there on the range where the deer and antelope play and the cattle are nervous. Maybe they had a flock of buzzards help them carry the cow?

On the night of Monday, September 22nd, Arizona finally entered the list of states targeted by the mutilators in the fall of 1975; the Apache County sheriff received a mutilation report from the J & J Cattle Company the following day. The Phoenix-based operation ran cattle up on the Mogollon Rim in northeastern Arizona and they reported to Sheriff Art Lee that five heifers had been either *"wounded or killed."* The sheriff's office determined that one animal had been mutilated as it was discovered missing its tongue, rectum and udder. "The other cattle exhibited strange *identical burn marks on the inside of their right rear legs.* One of the burnt cows died shortly thereafter." [my emphasis].[28] Coincidentally, this is the same region on the Mogollon Rim where the infamous Travis Walton abduction would occur just over a month later in early November 1975.

That same September 22nd night, our busy mutilators were re-engaged over 1,000-miles away back up in Cascade County, Montana. The following day a rancher near Belt called the sheriff's office and reported two mutilated cows. One animal's udder, rear end and reproductive organs had been taken out. The cut on the udder was the first of a few, rare, "cookie-cutter" incisions found on mutilations. The cut left precise serrations like what you would imagine pinking shears would leave behind and photos are featured in Linda Howe's Book *An Alien Harvest.* There was a slight discoloration on the tips of serrations on cuts from a subsequent case, similar to what would happen if a hide were heated up by a hot cutting tool. Documented examples of this cookie-cutter incision are very rare.

A week prior to this "serrated" cut case, we also have the beginning of an intense wave of Montana chopper and unknown aerial light sightings. The first report featured a description by Cascade County deputy Arne Sand, who had the chopper fly right over his car. He was able to hear "a 'quiet whirr,' but although it was a clear night, he was unable to see the craft. The same evening a couple in nearby Ft. Shaw saw a helicopter turn off its lights while flying south."[29]

Two days later on September 24, 1975, a rancher all the way down in Robles Junction, Arizona, located in Pima County just above the Mexican border, discovered a mutilated cow. He reported it to the state livestock inspector Mack Matlock who noted that, "the animal's tongue, udder and rectum had been cut away cleanly with little sign of blood."

Ranchers and a state patrol officer reported helicopters in Pueblo County, Colorado. One interesting incident from *The Choppers, and The Choppers* notes:

> A man in a pickup truck was run off the road by a helicopter. He called for help on his CB radio and two auxiliary policemen responded to find the victim 'frantic.' One policeman fired a shot from a 30-30 rifle at the still-hovering helicopter and heard a ricochet. Deputies from three counties, guards from the Pueblo Army Depot and Colorado state patrolmen chased the helicopter west to the Pueblo airport before it turned to the north and disappeared. The chopper made a noise 'like the whistling of air coming from a tire.' Other area residents reported being chased by helicopters during this time period.[30]

Here is where we see a clue. That same afternoon as the Colorado chopper incident, September 23, 1975, a two-year-old San Luis Valley heifer was found mutilated on *rented pasture several hundred yards from a house on the Taylor Ranch* in Costilla County. The Taylor ranch was suspected by local law enforcement of being involved in and/or aiding and abetting chopper-born mutilation teams targeting Costilla County. This admonishment by law enforcement is unparalleled in mute-ology and we will examine this alleged link later on.

"No tracks or blood was found around the calf," undersheriff Levi Gallegos told *Valley Courier* reporter Miles Porter. "The heart, right eye and sexual organs had been removed through skillful incisions. The eye was removed in a 'two-inch diameter hole around the eye, clean to the bone and then they pulled the eye out.'" Porter states a continually valid point: "The number of the cattle mutilations here in the valley is not known, due to the lack of reports and also the lack of any central clearinghouse recording of the incidents." Two days later another cow was found near Hoehn, Colorado, in Los Animas County. An autopsy determined that "a toxic substance was present in the spleen, liver, and kidneys, all were badly decomposed. Other organs including the heart appeared to be healthy."

The following day, on September 26th, a six-month-old calf belonging to Verl Holmes was discovered six miles north of Alamosa, Colorado—missing its tongue and the entire section of hide from its right mandible. Holmes said that he had seen the animal alive hours before. He was alerted to the dead calf by his herd of cows pressed against the opposite fence line, "baw'lin." According to the *Courier* sub-headline, "Predators were ruled out by authorities." CBI was sent tissue samples that later revealed evidence of tooth marks they attributed to "kangaroo rats." I wondered how many of these reports were actually true, high-strange mutilations with extraordinary explanations, and how many were fear-induced misidentified scavenger action.

Then, *six mutilation reports were filed in Costilla County on Sunday, September 28, 1975* by area ranchers. Costilla County Sheriff Sandoval stated, "It is getting out of hand. There are no clues. This is what's really bugging me!" Five of the reports came from Chama Canyon on the Ernest Maes Ranch. All of the animals were missing sexual organs and various other parts. A sixth was discovered six miles to the west. Locals had seen a bright light in the sky on the night of the 25th near the Sanchez Reservoir—southwest of the town of San Luis—but officers were unable to get close enough to identify the craft before it flew away into the gloomy night.

The following day, September 29, 1975, a potentially important case occurred: the "Manzanares bull" was discovered "on top of a table" in an abandoned adobe shack. The bull was a huge animal that weighed well over 1,500 pounds. In his article covering the report, Miles Porter does not mention the table and the picture in the *Valley Courier* showed the bull on the ground outside of the shack. But I have interviewed two former county sheriffs who investigated the case and they told me the *huge bull was found inside a shack on a stout, low table*, and that even "if the bull had tried to walk through the door, it wouldn't have fit." I wonder why this sensational detail was left out of Miles Porter's article. Wouldn't this crucial fact prove, without any doubt, that this animal's death not natural attrition as the skeptics continually insist—that all mutilations have mundane, natural explanations? Says Thomas Blann of this case:

> At several mutilation sites, evidence was found on the ground that reinforced the theory of the use of helicopters in cattle mutilations… Sheriff Ernest Sandoval, in Costilla County, Colorado, found helicopter landing skid marks near a barn in high grass where a mutilated bull had been discovered. Sheriff Sandoval said… "It looked like a wheel barrel had come from the chopper to the barn [later called an "adobe shack"] where the mutilated bull was found." The tracks led back to the chopper. They had been dusted inside the barn to make it appear as if no tracks were around the animal. The bull had an eight-inch perfect circle cut out of its rib cage without disturbing the subcutaneous tissue.[31]

On September 30th, "a large black Angus steer," owned by rancher Bonnie Lobato, was found three-quarters of a mile away from the five Chama Canyon dead cattle, and was tied to the other reports by investigating officers.

The following week was quiet in the San Luis Valley, except for several mystery helicopter sightings—including one report of a landing "on the mountain, southeast of San Luis." (The Taylor Ranch?) Locals were asked to keep a vigilant eye skyward and report any unusual aerial activity over the valley and surrounding foothills. But, as we have seen, the phenomena like to keep everyone guessing and move around—playing the trickster. Is this by design?

During the end of September 1975, no helicopter reports were filed by Idaho ranchers in Fremont and Blaine Counties were the mutilations were being reported—instead UFO reports were being called in to authorities. Some of them are noteworthy because of the descriptions of what appeared to be strange behavior and odd flight characteristics.

Blaine County authorities received several UFO reports during September. The Fremont County Sheriff's office logged at least three separate UFO reports during late September and early October [1975]. Many people reported seeing low-flying, "high-winged planes" during this time. A spectacular aerial display was mounted by several strange lights in the skies of Cassia County on September 29th. Several residents of Albion [Idaho] watched as two "multi-colored lights" circled the town. After about 45 minutes, the larger of the two lights appeared to "split." Chris Cagle told the *Times-News* in Twin Falls [Idaho]: 'Over the airport the two smaller objects split from under the large one and went in opposite directions, but soon returned to be engulfed in the larger one.'

The next morning at 7:00 a.m. Mrs. Wally Sears saw a "round silvery object" in the same area. Silent, colorful lights were seen again on Thursday October 2nd. The "lights" returned [the next night]. Residents of Elba watched the show. According to an *Associated Press* release (October 6th), the big light looked like a "diamond in a woman's ring." One person (using binoculars) observed "three smaller, disc-shaped objects near the large light." Cattle bawled and dogs ran for cover when the lights were in the area.[32]

As the helicopters buzzed around the southern SLV, unusual chopper activity was also being reported in Uinta County, Wyoming. Most of these reports were centered on areas where the mutes were occurring. (figure 11) In one sensational encounter, a law officer claimed he was "chased by a helicopter at 90 mph." Evidently the officer was so spooked that he fired on the craft with his shotgun. The helicopter allegedly took off and flew away. Helicopter sightings were not the only correlation associated with the mutes in Wyoming. As in the Idaho wave, David Perkins noted that the mutilation activity was centered in areas around where uranium is located—this time it was the extensive uranium-mining district in Fremont and Natrona Counties.

This end of September/beginning of October 1975 time period also featured Wyoming mutilation cases being reported to authorities. Ten counties were apparently hit in short succession, and by the end of October, around "35 cows" were reported mutilated to local authorities.[33]

Who are Those People in Them Hoodies?

Fremont, Clark, Madison, Teton, Bonneville, Bingham, Caribou, Power, Custer, Blaine, Lincoln, Minidoka—virtually every Idaho county surrounding the National Reactor Testing Station (commissioned in 1949—the largest and most varied collection of nuclear reactors on the planet)—reported mutilations the fall of 1975. (figure 12) And there were other reports of weirdness along the Upper Snake River Drainage.

On October 6, 1975, at around midnight, a rancher near the town of Parker, Idaho reported two people lurking in his pasture. He told the sheriff that the two figures were wearing "dark, army-type ponchos." The hooded figures must have beat a hasty retreat before law enforcement officers arrived on the scene. Then, a real head-scratching report was filed two days later on the other side of the state near Lewiston, Idaho. Who were these people? (figure 13)

> Ralph Paul called Lewis County Sheriff Rex Farris to report a frightening encounter. Paul, driving his Jeep along Highway 95 at 3:30 in the morning, suddenly came upon about 15 people with "masks over their faces" who attempted to stop his forward progress by linking arms to form a "human chain" across the road.
>
> Two hooded figures were seen again—this time in Blaine County. During the first week in October (after a number of mutilations in the area), a Forest Service employee saw a suspicious couple just at dusk. They were dressed in "body length, black, hooded robes." The taller of the two was carrying a bag. The hoods were "pointed." The figures moved quickly—never turning their heads. The forest ranger noted that the area became "very quiet" just before he spotted the duo. The ranger had been expecting an elk to appear…
>
> By the first of November, when activity tapered off drastically [in Idaho] more than 90 mutilated animals had been reported in 22 Idaho counties. Fremont County counted the losses of 21 cattle and one horse. Sheriff Tom Stegelmeier later confirmed that mutilated dogs had been found in Fremont County—missing sex organs, and eyes. Some had been skinned.[34]

The strange hooded figures were reported in Idaho on October 6, 1975. That same night, the mutilators visited Devil's Tower in Wyoming. Newcastle, Wyoming rancher Spud Jones called and reported to Weston County authorities that he had found one of his cows disfigured and laying next to a two-foot in diameter "strange yellow circle of grass." Sheriff Willis Larson noted that "the whole udder area [was] cut away, except for one nipple." He also thought that the tongue and lower lip had been excised and that the lower lip "displayed two definite cut marks."[35]

Weston County also had a mini UFO flap erupt during this time. Starting on October 7th a string of UFO sighting were reported and investigated by local law enforcement in and around mutilation sites. The sheriff and his men responded to a call from a woman who lived in the vicinity of a mutilation who said that a strange flying 'object' was in the sky.

> The sheriff, along with Airport Manager John Bockman and deputy sheriff Gregg Kayl, arrived on the scene just in time to catch a glimpse of the thing before it "vanished straight up." Sheriff Larson said the craft was silent and about the size of an airplane. "It looked like an orange colored light. It was big in front and tapered down." Apparently the Sheriff's sighting convinced others to come forward with their own reports. Sgt. Stephen Doughty, of the Newcastle Police Department recalled that during mid-September he observed a "bright object" hovering about 300 feet above the Weston County Hospital."[36]

The mutilators were apparently busy that October 6th evening, as the pasture surgeons also returned to the Mogollon Rim and then perpetrated the largest Arizona mutilation wave of 1975. The first report was of a cow mutilated near Nutrioso in Apache County. Two days later, on October 8, 1975 another report was filed, by a rancher in the St. Johns area. Another report was also filed from nearby Hunt Valley. This was the same night as the second Newcastle, Wyoming UFO sighting. Two days after these reports another case was reported near Big Lake, Arizona and the following day another one near Greens Peak.

The Apache County undersheriff was seeing these strange animal deaths for the first time and he noted what appeared to him to be an apparent correlation: "that's the really strange thing—it's always the left ear and left eye." Investigators thought that some Apache County cases appeared more expertly perpetrated than others, and undersheriff Gilchrist was pretty sure that more than one person was involved in the apparent field excision exercises: "You can see which cows were killed by the better surgeons." Then, the Arizona cases moved south toward the Mexican border near the town of Oracle in Pinal County. There a hunter discovered a mutilated cow with "its heart and other organs cut away," and the headline from the *Arizona Daily Star* (Tucson) stated: "Hooded Figures Seen Near Site of Mutilated Cow."

> Pinal sheriff's deputies were investigating a report yesterday that two persons wearing black hoods and jackets were spotted within a few hours and a few miles of the discovery this weekend of a mutilated cow near Oracle... Charles Touchstone, a security guard at the Arizona College of Technology investigated the original reports. He noted: "It wasn't all that cold about then for someone to be wearing hoods and jackets."[37]

The San Luis Valley Gets Hammered

While the mutilators were busy in Arizona, helicopters were also seen nightly in the SLV during the first week of October 1975, where they seemed to have focused their interest exclusively on Alamosa and Costilla Counties. On the night of October 7th (the same night as the first UFO sighting in Newcastle, Wyoming), Chama, Colorado rancher Emilio Lobato reported one of his cows dead. It could not be determined if this initial animal had actually been mutilated because scavengers had already begun tearing up the carcass. But two additional calf mutilations were discovered in Lobato's pasture by Sandoval and his deputies while investigating the first report. "Sandoval said the one calf had probably been dead only one-half hour and the other for about an hour."[38] I wonder how this time frame was estimated. These two animals were evidently the first of *49 head of livestock that Lobato would lose over the next two weeks.* Some were *shot and killed,* others were mutilated and *some animals simply vanished.* A number of Lobato's cows were found in an area out near the Rio Grande River about 20 miles from Chama Canyon where Lobato's ranch is located.

Now we must immediately leapfrog our way back up to Judith Basin County, Montana, for a bull calf mutilation near Utica, Montana that same night. It was apparent to investigators that the unfortunate calf was dead and its testicles had been removed. After the initial investigation, the rancher called the sheriff's office and asked him to come out and see something strange. Undersheriff Jerry Skelton "returned to the original site ten days later. *The carcass and surrounding dirt were covered with a filmy white substance 'like cobwebs.'* Laboratory analysis revealed it to be some sort of 'petroleum distillate.'"[39]

On October 10, 1975 San Luis, Colorado rancher Pat Sanchez reported to the sheriff's office two fresh mutilations at his ranch, located two miles west of the town.

During the next two weeks of October 11th through the 25th there were no reports of mutilations or mystery choppers covered in the local SLV press, but according to Espinoza, Sandoval and Lobato, it was during this two-week period that Lobato lost *49 head of livestock.* Why was this amazing crime spree never publicized in the press? This should have been the ranching story of the decade in the entire country, let alone the SLV, and I can find no evidence that the media ever caught wind of this alleged fury. I believe Lobato, Sandoval, and Espinoza were telling me the truth when I interviewed them separately in 1993, but I wonder how this could have been kept quiet back in 1975? Was the rapid targeting of Lobato's herd simply too disturbing to divulge to the public by law enforcement? Were these crimes covered up because of the well-founded suspicion that the influential Taylor Ranch (Lobato's neighbor) may have helped perpetrate these crimes?

Ex-sheriffs Sandoval and Espinoza and rancher Lobato all three have gone public, on-the-record, and suggested that John Taylor was "aiding and abetting" teams of helicopter crews operating out of the Taylor Ranch. It appears that this was an attempt by Taylor to drive Lobato to sell off his ranch, or was there some other agenda at work?

During this same two-week period, reports of mutilation activity moved northeast into El Paso County, where the Cheyenne Mountain Zoo bison case occurred on October 21st, and the phenomenon moved out east into Baca and Routt Counties. And then it bloomed into Oklahoma, Wyoming, Montana and New Mexico. This extremely active time period is when attention was thrust upon the region of Montana around Malmstrom Air Force Base while other cases around the west were filed without much notice. (figure 14)

A Wyoming report from Weston County during the last two weeks of October was made by three different law officials who observed a white light "similar in shape to a light bulb with red and green flashing lights" that was observed by all three from different vantage points. This lighting description was similar to the landed chopper seen taking off from Howell Mountain on September 16, 1975.

The Surgeons with the Pinking Shears

To the north in Cascade County, Montana, on October 16, 1975, Captain Wolverton and a local vet investigated another case from the Belt area. The cow's tongue was gone, and the mandible flesh and hide appeared to have been skinned out in classic fashion, but the vet ascertained that the missing eye "had been removed 'not from the socket, but through the bone above the eye.'" He also found what appeared to be a "needle mark" on the upper left leg and noted that there were burned-appearing serrated cuts on the flesh around the eye and jaw cuts.[40]

> The burned cuts tended to confirm Captain Wolverton's suspicions— that the cutting was being done with lasers. Many other lawmen and investigators have speculated that laser surgery (or intense heat) was involved. According to some theories, this would account for the neat, bloodless "cauterized" appearance of the incisions.[41]

Linda Howe published detailed photographs of these serrated cuts in her book *An Alien Harvest.*

Montana was heating up. Malmstrom AFB experienced a bewildering night on October 18, 1975 when *nine separate sightings of unknown aerial objects* were detected in the region south of Great Falls. This kicked off an extensive wave of unusual aerial craft and helicopter sightings around some of the most secure air space in North America.

Robert Hastings has spent years compiling event logs of these cases in his exhaustive look at sightings of unknown craft around nuclear bases and missile silo fields, *UFOs and Nukes.* They are much too numerous and too involved to detail fully, but according to Hastings, "at least 80 mutilation cases" occurred in or around Malmstrom AFB and other missile silo sites in northern Colorado and South Dakota:

> [I]mmediately after some of the sightings, ranchers began finding strangely slain cattle in their fields, surgically-sliced apart and sometimes devoid of blood. In short, for much of 1975, Malmstrom AFB seemed to be the focal point for some kind of high weirdness.
>
> In mid-October, well into the sighting and mutilation wave, Captain Keith Wolverton...requested a meeting with...USAF Lt. Col. Robert Peisher [commander of Detachment #5 of the 37th Air Rescue—the only helicopter wing at Malmstrom] to discuss the worrisome reports of helicopters being sighted in the vicinity of some of the strangely slaughtered cattle. Wolverton told Peisher and other commanders at Malmstrom that there was an urgent need for such a meeting because several irate ranchers had publicly vowed to shoot at any helicopter seen flying low over their livestock. Some of them apparently suspected, without any proof, that the helicopter unit at Malmstrom was somehow involved in the bizarre animal deaths.
>
> Peisher told [Hastings] that he and Wolverton met at his office on base, where they first compared notes. "[Peisher] had a map with all the missile launch facilities... and a map of the unknown sightings and cattle mutilations. Most of the mutilation sites marked on [the] map were located within the missile [field] complex." According to Peisher, over 80 UFO sightings and mutilation sites fell within those boundaries, many of them quite near the missile sites themselves. Despite this striking pattern, Peisher remained composed. "Even though we were alert that something unexplainable was happening, it was hard to get excited about it, especially since there was no apparent threat to the missiles. It might have been a big hoax."[42]

The fall 1975 wave in Montana was a bewildering array of weirdness that included crypto-creature sightings. The follow summation was published by Keith Wolverton in his little-known book co-written with Roberta Donovan, *Mystery Stalks the Prairie:*

> Law officers have been unable so far to find an explanation for the sequence in which the strange events have occurred. First, there was the rash of cattle mutilations, then the many sightings of unidentified helicopters, followed by numerous UFO sightings and more recently, the reports of people who saw one or more strange hairy creatures that

walked upright like a man. There were overlapping events. One type of activity seemed to decline as another started. Was it a piece of the puzzle or coincidence? Speculation seemed futile.

The first report officers received of the hairy creatures came December 26, 1975, from two very badly frightened junior high age girls. One girl, who lives in Great Falls, was spending the Christmas holidays with another girl in the Vaughn area and it was here the incident occurred. The girls told the deputies that in the late afternoon, they noticed the horses were acting very strangely, pawing the ground and rearing on their hind legs. They went outside to see what was the matter and it was then that they saw a strange creature about 200 yards from their mobile home and 25 yards or so away from a thicket.

The Great Falls girl found a .22 rifle belonging to her friend's father and looked through the scope at the creature. She described its face as "dark and awful looking and not like a human's." The girls said the creature was 7 to 7.5 feet tall and twice as wide as a man.

To see if she could frighten the creature, the girl with the rifle fired it into the air. When nothing happened, she waited a short time and fired into the air again. The second time, the creature dropped to the ground and pulled itself along with its arms for a short distance before standing erect once more…

When officers questioned the Vaughn girl's father later, he told of a hair-raising experience he had had shortly after midnight Christmas morning. He said he had awakened to a sound that he could only describe, as like a human dying an agonizing death. He said he took his flashlight and rifle and went outside to check, but his dog refused to go with him… Reports from some areas where the biped creatures have been seen say that they emit an unpleasant odor compared to rotten eggs.

Over the next several months residents in the area reported hearing weird human-like screams in the woods, finding tracks in the snow and smelling that awful smell. Then, according to *Mystery Stalks the Prairie*, another Bigfoot sighting was reported to authorities—this time there were two of them:

> By far the most startling report so far and the one that produced the most evidence was one from a 16-year-old Helena boy. When Captain Wolverton learned of the incident, he and Deputy Ken Anderson went to Helena to interview the boy and his family. The youth told the officers that he had awakened about 4:30 a.m. the morning of April 4, 1976, and stood looking out his bedroom window for a time. The second story window provides a grand view of the pasture to the east of the house.
>
> At about 5 a.m., the boy told the officers he saw a tall, hairy creature walking in the pasture, coming from the south, or to his right. He said the creature was taking long strides and his arms moved back and forth

as a person's would. The creature did not appear to have a neck, but it was capable of turning its head and it appeared to be looking around. Except for its face, it was covered entirely with brown or black hair about an inch to an inch and a half long.

The youth was unable to describe the face, but said the forehead protruded out and then upward to a rounded head. The nose looked pushed in. He did not notice any ears… When the creature moved, the boy said it walked very smoothly without stooping and did not appear to bend its knees much. When the creature's arms were at its side, the arms were as thick through from front to back as its body. The creature's back seemed to go straight down to below the buttocks, without any curve at the small of the back. The youth estimated the creature's height at eight feet…

As the boy watched, the creature kept walking until it was directly east of the house, at which time it was joined by a second hairy creature. The second one was abut a head shorter than the first, but just as wide and the color was the same. At this point, the boy related, the larger creature reached down and picked up something dark colored, "about the size of a bale of hay." Something was flapping from the ends of the object which looked similar to a piece of dark plastic. The larger creature handed the object to the smaller creature who carried it. The larger hairy creature then started walking straight toward the house. When it was within about 100 feet of the house, it looked directly toward the window where the boy was watching. The boy vaulted downstairs to wake his father and the two returned to the window in not more than two minutes. But when they looked out, the strange creatures were gone…

The boy appeared badly shaken by the ordeal. Later in the day, the boy's sister found a track in the pasture. She and the boy covered it with wood until the next day when they made a plaster cast of it. Captain Wolverton and Deputy Anderson made their own cast from the one the youth had. The track measures 17.5 inches long and 7 inches wide and appears to have three toes. The boy drew three sketches of the creature for officers…

The boy said he had taken a lot of kidding about seeing the creatures, but he wasn't kidded by the officers. They did not doubt him and Captain Wolverton added to his official report, "After talking to [the boy] and his family, I believe that [the boy] did see what he reported."

David Perkins has reminded me over the years that mainstream science often wears blinders and decides arbitrarily to factor out potential data when researching so-called paranormal mysteries—like unexplained animal deaths and UFOs. A perfect example of this would be the paper published by Robert Bigelow's now defunct National Institute for Discovery Sciences (NIDS) that attempted to analyze the 1974-1979 Montana wave of anomalous activity. NIDS went defunct soon after the 2001 paper, and Bigelow now concentrates on his module space station he has contracted with NASA to build for the U.S. Government. (figure 16)

[NIDS] Summary Report on A Wave of UFO/Helicopters and Animal Mutilations in Cascade County, Montana 1974-1977
Captain Wolverton allowed NIDS full access to his original papers and files detailing the investigations that he carried out on behalf of the Cascade County sheriff's department in 1975-1977. NIDS was able to analyze the data in these files and they comprise an interesting picture of a wave of anomalous activity within a 40-mile radius of Great Falls and Malmstrom AFB. Captain Wolverton's files comprised the original police blotters, original memoranda and original photo negatives detailing the department's investigations into 192 UFO and unknown helicopter sightings, and 67 reports of animal mutilations, the vast majority happening within a forty miles radius of [Malmstrom]AFB. *The files also contain references to over 60 other anomalies that are not presented in this report.* Further, detailed investigations of local cult activity and surveillance of unusual vehicles and people in the area was routine for the department. [my emphasis]

In their paper the NIDS team also ignored evidence of possible "cult" activity in the region. David Perkins contributed the following observations in his foreword to my book *Secrets of the Mysterious Valley*:

One of the primary reasons the UFO community has been so spectacularly unsuccessful in solving the UFO enigma is its propensity for self-censorship and intellectual dishonesty. "High strange" cases are treated as statistical anomalies. Data that doesn't fit the ETH [extraterrestrial hypothesis] is suppressed and neatly swept under the rug. With its emphasis on preserving the True Faith and stamping out heretical insurgencies, ufology is more akin to religion than science.
A group that briefly threatened to break this mold was the National Institute for Discovery Sciences (NIDS). This secretive and well-financed group boasted a roster of world-class scientific hired guns. In 2001, NIDS published a professional and thorough report on the wave of UFO/helicopters and animal mutilations, which occurred in the Great Falls, Montana area between 1974 and 1977. The report carefully listed the correlations between 192 UFO and helicopter sightings and 67 [official] reports of animal mutilations. As a brief aside, the report mentions that NIDS files contained "over 60 other anomalies that are not presented

in this report…"

Malmstrom was not the only northern tier Air Force base to be swamped with reports of all kinds. Government documents obtained through the Freedom of Information Act (FOIA) reveal that between October 27 and November 19, 1975, sightings of unexplained objects over classified "nuclear, military installations occurred in Montana, South Dakota, Michigan, Maine and Ontario, Canada." These craft (or objects) were described as "helicopters, aircraft, unknown entities and brightly lighted, fast-moving vehicles." All reports were filed in and/or around extremely secure flight areas above missile arrays.[43]

On October 11, 1975, another mute team evidently branched off from the SLV crew and headed east—over the Sangre de Cristo Mountains into northeastern New Mexico along the Colorado border. The *Denver Post* noted in an October 24, 1975 article that two other head of cattle had been mutilated near the gate to the Rocky Flats hydrogen bomb manufacturing plant located just west of Denver. These are the only known official mutilation reports from the county. (figure 17)

On October 27, 1975—a week after the Cheyenne Mountain Zoo case on October 21st—the surgical team evidently returned to the SLV when rancher Pat Sanchez discovered another mutilated cow on his ranch west of San Luis. Later that afternoon, after searching for a missing cow, he found a second animal mutilated. Josephine Maestas of nearby San Pablo also reported a mute that same day.

Then, if the press coverage is accurate, the SLV flap temporarily ended for over 15 months. Either the mutilators left for bloodier pastures, or people developed a temporary cure for their "mass hysteria." This complete cessation of reports appears to negate debunkers' assertions that the media is responsible for creating or prompting misidentified cases. Cattle must have died natural deaths during this 15-month time period and yet these animal deaths were not reported as "mutilated."

The activity appeared to move out of south central Colorado at the end of October and immediately, during the first week of November 1975, reports began to be filed in northeastern New Mexico. Along with the mute reports were perplexing sightings of mystery helicopters and unidentified lights—all observed in and around mutilation sites. Some of these reports are real head scratchers. In one instance as many as *seven helicopters* were seen flying in formation. To those following the mystery, this whole bewildering mess appeared to be getting severely out of hand!

The *Tucumcari News* on November 7, 1975, contained a statement from James Gordon, Federal Aviation Administration local area coordinator, who said that the FAA had officially entered into the investigation of unknown aircraft over northeastern New Mexico. Gordon was quoted as saying, "At the present time, the FAA investigators are in the field taking depositions from individuals who have seen these aircraft."

Texas law enforcement investigators maintained files on cattle mutilations throughout the state. These files showed many instances where a helicopter with no markings was seen by farmers and law enforcement personnel in areas where mutilations were later discovered.

> In Young County Texas, five miles south of Olney, a 500 to 600 pound bull was discovered in November 1975 with its sex organs removed. In a four-inch radius around the wound the hair slipped from the skin as if it had been burned or scalded. The next day, the owner and a report went back to investigate and *found that the bull had disappeared from the pasture.* No tracks other than those noted in the previous investigation of the incident were found. The mutilated bull was taken from a fenced pasture with no way on or out except through the locked gate. This clearly indicates that the bull was lifted out of the area by a helicopter. [my emphasis][44]

California was relatively untouched by the mutilators that entire year and apparently the only known activity was in Butte County that reported mutilations and UFOs during October of 1975, and seven clustered cases in Mendocino County around Covelo that occurred between November 1975 and January 1976.

How Do You Explain When the Cases Stop Cold?

Debunkers have propounded the theory of "misidentification of scavenger action" to explain all unexplained livestock deaths. If these skeptics are right, and these reports are simply "media-induced hysteria," then why do waves of reports stop cold after a furious flurry of apparent activity? The sudden, complete cessation of reports seems to belie the simplistic explanation of hysteria. I think a better question should be asked: did predators and scavengers suddenly decide to stop eating for a year? Or did the mutilators decide to target other regions, for whatever reason? Many of the investigators out in the field who examined the bodies refused to believe predators were involved, and this had a profound effect on the small ranching communities affected by the "unexplained" livestock death mystery. By now ranchers understood that nothing good could come from reporting the deaths—besides unwanted publicity and social stigma. Could the sudden cessation of reports have been due to ranchers' growing reluctance to report unexplained cattle deaths to officials?

After examining the publicized SLV mutilation reports from the fall of 1975, I uncovered numerous examples of other verified unpublicized, unreported accounts. Adding up the Southern Colorado/Cochetopa cases from August and the additional Lobato animals, the reported figure of 23 "mutilations" in the SLV doubles. Adding the Lobato animals "shot or stolen," the number is almost tripled. If the total number in the SLV alone was much higher than the publicized 39, and if this holds true around the west, we may be missing hundreds—if not thousands-upon-thousands—of undisclosed cattle mutilation events!

During the entire month of December 1975, almost nightly, mystery helicopters were reported to Alamosa and Costilla authorities, and at the same time, the mystery cattle surgeons diverted their attention to northern New Mexico, Kansas, Texas, Wyoming, Idaho, Nebraska and Montana. Government officials claimed no knowledge of nocturnal chopper flights in the SLV during this time period and this was echoed around the west.

Another potentially important aspect of the SLV fall flap of 1975 was the abundance of unpublicized UFO sightings. The only aerial craft reported in Miles Porter's *Valley Courier* articles were described as "helicopters" but other objects were evidently flitting through the skies over the SLV that fall. According to former Costilla County sheriffs Lobato and Sandoval, there were sightings of objects that appeared to defy the laws of physics. In addition, I uncovered several claims of "classic" UFO sightings during September and October 1975 and none of these accounts ever made the papers. Witnesses have come forward independently regarding an incident in the late fall of 1975 when a large cordoned-off area was set up by "troops," just north of the Taylor Ranch, and rumors circulated of a possible "UFO crash" retrieval operation. One account mentions a "UFO dogfight" with one combatant ship evidently being shot down by another.[45]

There may have been a press blackout regarding this alleged UFO crash and/or dogfight event and many other anomalous aerial craft and light sightings all up and down the Rocky Mountains. The late fall of 1975, in particular, had many sightings of unexplained, non-ballistic craft but these may have been downplayed as being "helicopters."

These high-strange claims were perfect media fodder so, again, why did these sightings by Costilla County locals and law enforcement in the SLV go unpublicized? Was it possible that reporters had a reason for not reporting the full extent of the SLV and other regions' aerial activity?

Down through the years, mute investigators and researchers have attempted to find patterns and correlations within the bewildering lists of documented reports. David Perkins was the first researcher who noticed that areas hardest hit by waves of mutilations were often located downwind and downstream from facilities where nuclear materials were located, mined and/or utilized. Missile silos, uranium mines, weapons enrichment facilities and nuclear power plants are often located at the epicenter of regions garnering the mutilator's apparent attention. Perkins insightfully observed that this correlation held true in hard-hit Idaho:

The upper Snake River Valley greatly attracted the mutilators. Besides Fremont County, many of the incidents occurred in the areas adjacent to the huge National Reactor Testing Station. Established by the Atomic Energy Commission in 1949, the area holds over 50 experimental nuclear reactors—the largest and most varied collection in the world.

The Testing Station also claims the most varied collection of nuclear accidents in the world—some, fatal to workers. Confirmed leaks of radioactive gas into the atmosphere have occurred…

The motiveless mutilators "circled" the sprawling nuclear facility, striking with a vengeance in five of the six adjoining counties. Apparently they got all the udders, rectums and sex organs they needed just in time. In early 1976, the Teton Dam broke inundating much of the area and killing thousands of animals.[46]

1976: The Cases Return with a Vengeance

1976 had barely commenced when the first mutilation report of the year was filed. David Perkins kept an accurate record of the mid to late '70s activity and the following reports were compiled mainly from the files of Perkins' Animal Mutilation Probe (AMP). (figure 18) My work is elucidated by Tom Adams/Project Stigma, (figure 19) and supplemented by Tommy Blann, Keith Wolverton's book *Mystery Stalks the Prairie,* the *UFO Newsclipping Service* as well as other databases and compiled media sources.

On January 3, 1976, the inaugural case of the year award went to Cameron County, Texas—home of Harlingen AFB. A mutilated three-month-old calf was discovered, missing one eye and its tongue. Uncharacteristically, there was *an oval cut, six to eight inches long on the back of the calf's neck.* Cameron County Deputy Sheriff Larry Molano was quoted as observing that the unexplained death and disfigurement "appeared to be the work of humans."

I suspect that there were possibly other noteworthy reports during the early part of 1976 but I have no "official" documentation or media accounts. The "mutilation" story had faded from regional and national news replaced by more pressing issues of the day. Following is a sampling of the news stories from the start of 1976.

The Cray-1, the first commercially developed "supercomputer," was released on New Year's Day by Cray Research. On January 19th Jimmy Carter won the Iowa Democratic Caucus and two days later the first commercial Concorde flight took off. On January 27th the United States vetoed a United Nations resolution that called for an independent Palestinian state, and two days later the First Battle of Amgala broke out between Morocco and Algeria in the Spanish Sahara. On January 29th twelve Provisional Irish Republican Army bombs exploded in London's West End. The February 4th opening ceremonies of the 1976 Winter Olympics began in Innsbruck, Austria. That same day, in Guatemala and Honduras, an earthquake killed more than 22,000 people.

This early 1976 time period is another of those inexplicable down periods when the "official" databases are bereft of solid reports or media accounts. I am chasing rumors of southern U.S. cases below the winter freeze line and other possible lower midwest cases during this time. David Perkins noticed early on that the vast majority of mutilation reports occur after the last frost and before the first frost—spring through fall—when livestock are grazing on fresh vegetation. I have investigated a number of cases where the temperature has been at or below freezing: they are rare but they are often simply not reported.

In a classic, tricksterish example, here is a rare wintertime report from Colorado's hard hit Logan County. In February, Sheriff Tex Graves responded to a mutilation report filed north of Sterling. It probably appeared to Graves (who had seen over a dozen of these cases by then) that this was your standard-issue classic case, but this particular case had an interesting twist. It was a Hereford cow missing an eye, an ear, udder, rectum and sex organs *with "a wad of finely shredded aluminum stuffed in [it]s mouth;"* however, it was discovered with its tongue cut out. Other rare crime scene evidence consists of an "empty cardboard container [found] 20 yards away." The aluminum material was "later identified" as your standard U.S. Government issue radar chaff used as a counter measure by military aircraft. During aerial combat missions, pilots expel chaff in an effort to confuse heat-seeking air or ground-to-air missiles. This atypical chaff evidence found at a cattle mutilation site would be duplicated later on the Dulce, New Mexico ranch of Manuel Gomez.[47]

The rest of February was quiet on the mute front, but a weird discovery was made in early March at San Francisco's Mission Dolores Park when park attendants found two plastic bags containing "the butchered parts of a lamb, two chickens, a calf and a duck." The animals' heads had been cut off with a "sharp weapon" and the blood had apparently been drained.[48]

The *Berkeley Barb* published "Fear, Mutilation on the Range" authored by investigative journalist, Michael Reynolds who claimed while on a visit to Washington County, Colorado, Sheriff Bill McDonald and Deputy Bob Jones told him "they had been visited by an agent from the Colorado Bureau of Investigation. The CBI man informed the law officers that *'the Army had over 400 helicopters stolen off bases in the United States last year [1975].'"* Perkins and I combed through the databases and media sources but were unable to find any other corroborating statements that would back up this incredible claim. Four hundred is a lot of helicopters to turn up missing, and this claim appears to be wildly improbable, but Reynolds wrote this as a stated fact in his article. At the time, Perkins made an FOIA request to the Army, Air Force and FBI. He included a copy of Reynolds' article claiming the stolen helicopters. A month or so later Perkins received confirmation of his request from the Air Force. He never received any files from the Army or FBI. Months later he received two reports of near-incursions of restricted air space around Loring AFB in Maine, *one of the only states never to report an official livestock mutilation.* The first chopper was described as a cargo type owned by a local charter company that accidentally flew too close, and the other was a helicopter that belonged to one Howard Hughes, from Las Vegas, Nevada. Talk about a "red herring!"

Five months had passed in the SLV since the last (publicized) mute on the Pat Sanchez ranch in Costilla County. After an exhaustive search, I found no articles reporting suspected cases during this apparently quiet period but several interesting cases did make the papers concerning the killing of livestock—this time by "vandals." On April 12, 1976, a single "mutilation" case was reported to the Costilla County sheriff's office. Investigating deputy Levi Gallegos was at a predictable loss trying to explain the unexplained livestock death.

A strange calm appears to have descended on the SLV through the rest of 1976. To my knowledge, no additional mutilations, UFO sightings, or mystery helicopter reports were filed or publicized in the SLV that entire year.

Not so the rest of Colorado: on April 19, 1976, El Paso County officials were informed of a bull calf mutilation. A "mystery helicopter" had been reported in the same area the previous day. After a month-long period of silence, on May 29th and 30th, Neillsville, Wisconsin rancher Kenneth Karnitz reported two of his "brood" cows were found mutilated on his ranch in Clark County. One of the cows had just calved and the other was ready to calf. A vet was called to the scene and veterinarian E.H. Brekke noted both cows had had their udders removed with "a very sharp knife." One animal was missing the left ear and a 10-inch by six-inch patch of skin on underbelly. On the second animal, it appeared that the hair in this same underbelly area was "brown," possibly "singed."

Rancher Frank Krozinski of Humbird, Wisconsin also reported three mutilated cows during May. According to Dr. Brekke: "It appeared as though the animals had been running half wild and just dropped over." Clark County Sheriff's Department Sgt. Harlan Sundermeyer said: "UFOs have been reported in the area in the past month, by reliable people whose descriptions coincide."[49]

We then have a brief one-week lull until Dr. LaVerne Fox, a Henderson County, Illinois rancher, reported a mutilation on June 8, 1976. The sex organs and the udder of the cow had been "removed with such skill that the membrane behind the bag was not even punctured." There was no blood on or around the carcass, but Dr. Fox noticed something strange. When *flies landed on the exposed membrane they died*. Although a veterinarian never determined the cause of death, it was suggested that somehow the flies may have died from some kind of radiation poisoning.

Grant Callison, a field investigator for the Mutual UFO Network (MUFON) out of Galesburg, Illinois, contacted the Henderson County Sheriff (Mr. Daryl Thompson) and asked his opinion:

Among many law officers the cult theory seems to be the most predominant. The irony of it is that these same law officers are very reluctant to conduct an extensive investigation to support their theory and bring the culprits to justice. For example: In the case of the LaVerne Fox mutilation in Henderson County, Illinois, [Thompson] immediately said it was the work of a religious cult, whereupon I remarked that since he was so sure he should be able to make an arrest soon. He responded by saying he had no idea who they were. Dr. Fox later told me that since the first day that Mr. Thompson was there to view the carcass, he had not seen or heard from him since. Apparently no extensive investigation was ever made.

In the most recent rash of mutilations around Des Moines, Iowa, the Chief of the Iowa Division of Criminal Investigation, Gerald Shanahan, and his assistant, Mr. Motsinger, seem to have considerable evidence that witchcraft and/or cultists are responsible. Mr. Shanahan did not hesitate to release this evidence to the press, which gave me the impression he was using "scare tactics" in the hope those responsible would go elsewhere (out of his jurisdiction) to continue their operations. In my opinion, an extensive investigation should have been conducted undercover if he really wanted to catch the criminals involved.[50]

The first of a disturbing series of cattle mutes that took place over three years was reported June 14, 1976 on Manuel Gomez's ranch, located southwest of Dulce, New Mexico, in Rio Arriba County. A three-year-old animal was discovered dead and missing its udder, rectum, ear, eye, tongue and tail. New Mexico State Policeman Gabe Valdez (figure 20) investigated the report. In another example of rare trace evidence left behind at the crime scene, Valdez and Gomez found a "tripod mark" about 50 yards from the cow, "as if something heavy" had landed on three legs. The triangle formed by the three indentations measured roughly six feet on each side. Smaller tripod marks (28 inches each side) were left in the vicinity of the large triangle and moved to within 50 feet of the cow. The path of the smaller triangles toward the cow looked "scorched" and "greasy."

After the first mutilation at the Gomez ranch, Officer Valdez handled twenty-three cattle mutilations in approximately sixteen months. They discovered a high dosage of atropine in one mutilated cow. A large number of animals also tested positive for blackleg, most commonly caused by *clostridium chauvoei*. Los Alamos labs provided a lab report from one of the Gomez mutilations to Gabe that indicated the animal had an unidentified strain of clostridium in the heart chamber, leading many skeptics to claim the mutilations were simply explained as blackleg.

Some investigators, like Kenneth Rommel, later suggested that blackleg was the cause of the mutilations. Ranchers in the area routinely vaccinated for blackleg and were familiar with evidence of blackleg in deceased cattle, and blackleg doesn't leave evidence that an aircraft landed or cause the animal to have broken bones after being dropped from an aircraft. What is important to remember is that anthrax is structurally similar to blackleg, and blackleg is an environmental disease that animals obtain from eating contaminated grass that is transferred through the soil.[51]

On July 8, 1976 forty wild horses were found dead on the Dugway Proving Grounds, Utah. No apparent cause of death could be determined, but with the types of weapons testing conducted at Dugway, there was press speculation of another accidental discharge of gas. This was addressed by Dugway base commander who "categorically ruled out" Army experimentation. Hundreds of sheep had been killed near Dugway in 1968.

During the first week of August 1976, Logan County, Colorado was fiendishly revisited by the mysterious prairie surgeons. On three successive nights, *cows were mutilated in a feedlot* near Sterling. These mutilations are extremely noteworthy because *mutilations in feedlots are practically nonexistent, and these cases represent a statistical anomaly*. Two personnel began a "stakeout" the following evening to watch the well-lighted cattle pens, and on the second evening of their vigil, at about 4:00 A.M., the cowboys reported seeing three "human-like figures" going over the feedlot fence. According to the eyewitnesses, the figures didn't move like humans, "they seemed to glide." The watchmen notified the sheriff's office. Two cars were on the scene within six minutes. The figures had disappeared leaving no tracks in the muddy ground. It's important to re-emphasize that feedlot mutilation reports are extremely rare. As I mentioned previously, a vast majority of cattle mutilation claims arc filed by small ranchers with less than 200 head of cattle. This case perpetrated on a feedlot and the descriptions of the intruders may somewhat bolster alien-as-perpetrators theorists' views that the mutes are the result of "alien" interest in the planet's cattle herds.

Oui magazine published an article by investigative journalist Ed Sanders, "The Mutilation Mystery," in the September 1976 issue. Sanders speculated in the piece that government agents (specifically chemical/biological warfare researchers) were responsible for the mutilations. David Perkins spoke at length with Saunders and offered the following analysis:

In his well-researched article "The Mutilation Mystery" (*Oui* Magazine, Sept. 1976), investigative journalist Ed Sanders puts little credence in the alien hypothesis. He chooses instead to focus on the biological warfare testing theory and the evidence suggesting cult involvement in the mute mystery. Sanders calls this the "copter-cruising satanists hypothesis."

Sanders had authored the best-selling book *The Family* which detailed his investigation of the Manson clan in 1970-71. He was hoping for a respite from years of having his mind bombarded by "gore data... and snuff buffery," when in July, 1975 his literary agent received a large cow's tongue in the mail. Sanders surmised that it was a "message" from Manson gals Squeaky Fromm and Sandra Good in Sacramento, California. With much trepidation, Sanders entered the fray of mutilation research: "I mean, who really wants to have a rumble with airborne surgical professionals? And the ugly headlines: "Beatnik Investigator Mailed to Friends."

In the course of his travels and investigations, Sanders interviewed veterinarians and read several vet autopsy reports which indicated that the cattle in question had died from natural causes and had the been set upon by predators. These 'natural causes' were frequently listed as diseases attributed to the Clostridium bacteria family. Sanders, who was well-versed in biological warfare issues, perceptively noted that the presence of super-toxic *clostridium* in an animal's body did not necessarily mean that it had died a "natural" death.

As of 2014, more than 120 species of the clostridium bacteria have been identified. They are ubiquitous in soil, dust and water. Some of these varieties are recognized as the world's most toxic substances. The Centers for Disease Control lists the clostridium botulinum as one of the top six highest threat risk agents for bioterrorism. A mere one gram of its aerosolized toxin has the potential to kill 1.5 million people.

It is now known that at the end of WWII, the U.S. military was the sole beneficiary of the results of the nefarious biological warfare tests done on prisoners by "Unit 731" of the Japanese Imperial Army. Several thousand hapless prisoners died gruesome deaths as a result of these tests of weaponized diseases, including a variety of Clostridium strains. It is also now known that the Chemical Corps of the U.S. Army was hard at work in the 1950s perfecting "aerosol-generating bomblets" to disperse Clostridium *botulinum* and other death-dealing biological agents over enemy populations. Clearly humans have come a long way since the Middle Ages when soldiers used catapults to fling the bodies of plague victims over castle walls to sicken and kill the inhabitants.

In 1972, President Nixon signed the Biological and Toxin Weapons Convention which ended all U.S. biotoxin weapons research. Sanders wonders whether the development of such weapons may have continued on after 1972. The mutes might be a clandestine and authorized part of that program. If the Russians questioned U.S. compliance with the treaty, the military could say, "Hey, we're not doing it. It's those space aliens messing around with our cattle." Plausible (?) deniability. According to Sanders, another possibility was that "a rouge band of researchers" took it upon themselves to continue the Clostridium-related research.

It does seem suspicious that the treaty was signed in 1972 and in 1973 the first mute wave engulfed the Midwest. In Kansas, where at least 12 counties were affected, Dr. Harry Anthony, director of the Kansas State University veterinarian lab, stated that his lab had examined nine of the supposedly mutilated cattle. According to the lab, four of them had apparently died of blackleg (*clostridium chauveoi*) The so-called mutilations were the result of routine predation.

In neighboring Oklahoma, Governor David Boren ordered a full investigation under the aegis of the Department of Public Safety. A panel of "experts" investigated 26 possibly mutilated animals and issued a report dated March 3, 1975. It was the opinion of the task force that the mutilations "can be attributed to individuals getting in on a fad or young people dissecting dead carcasses for biological or experimental purposes." Sanders comments: "A fad! You know like Hula Hoops, phone booth packing, the twist ...and now recectomy and teenagers with secret dried udder sacs hidden in their closets."

In his investigations, Sanders was able to find only one U.S. Government official who stated publicly that a mutilated animal had been injected with a toxin of bacteria. Dr. Robert Hedelius, a Utah veterinary medical officer for the U.S. Dept. of Agriculture, told a local TV reporter that the mutilated animal he had examined had been killed by " a disease of the Clostridium family ...it was extremely localized ... I believe the bacteria were injected into the heifer." After the interview Hedelius claimed he was "muzzled, both by state and Federal people and told I was not to talk to any of the news media."

Sanders tracked down one further case of a mutilated cow death by clostridium bacteria. He states that "well-informed investigators" in Colorado were apparently the first to suggest a link between biowarfare experiments and mutilations. One such investigator he spoke with was Lou Girodo, Sheriff of Colorado's Las Animas County. Girodo told Sanders that both the Colorado Bureau of Investigation and the lab at Colorado State University had "clamped down" on test results from mutilated cattle. "They didn't let a word out," said Sheriff Girodo. Frustrated by the lack of official cooperation, Girodo arranged to have his own testing done. He didn't have to wait long for a fresh mute, found near Trinidad, Colorado in the fall of 1975. The animal had been dead less than 12 hours.

As arranged, Dr. Susan Colter, director of The Trinidad Animal Clinic, conducted an autopsy on the animal. Samples were sent to a private lab for analysis. Results showed that the cow had been infected with a culture of *clostridium sordellii*. Its larger organs had "turned to mush" which is a characteristic of clostridium infections and a not uncommon description of mutilated cow organs. The animal had been in excellent health at the time of its demise. According to The Merck Veterinary Manual, sordellii causes malignant edema and can attack both cattle and humans. It is "generally rapidly fatal." Girodo also asked Dr. Colter to try to duplicate the heart extractions on two mutilations near Walsenburg, Colorado. Dr. Colter tried and failed. "There is no way you can do it," she told Girodo.

As Sanders summarizes the Colorado investigators: "The mutilators, the theory went, were deliberately trying to put the blame on UFOs or satanists or predators as a cover for what was really going on." This is yet one more variation of the endless mutilation blame game we have become familiar with.

In a 1978 interview with [me] Sheriff Girodo said that he had been leaning toward the biowarfare in the mid-1970s. As time went on and he encountered more examples of the mutilators' handiwork, he became more skeptical of the theory. He doubted that even the U.S. government had the sophistication and wherewithal to pull off such a massive program so flawlessly. As Sheriff Girodo told [me], "It may sound crazy, But I think we have to at least consider the possibility that the mutilations are being done by creatures from outer space. I just can't figure out what else it could possibly be."

But what about the weird reports of cloaked and/or hooded figures? Who are these lurking figures in alchemist lab coat? Cass County, North Dakota became the targeted region for those spooky types dressed in hoodies—seen around an area where a mute site was located. On September 6, 1976 a bull was reported mutilated near Kindred. Two nights prior, on September 4th, a 15-year-old boy fishing in the nearby Cheyenne River observed a single figure "dressed in a long white robe." He was so frightened of the sight that he quickly fled. During early September law officials also received a report of a group of *persons dressed in long black robes and masks, carrying candles* along Highway 46. Perhaps a magical war was underway in the area? Police in Valley City were told of *"persons in long white robes—some carrying candles."* I'm not sure what we are to make of reports such as this. It kind of sounds like an archetypical clash between the forces of good and evil. Go figure.

Paranormal writer and researcher Tommy R. Blann of Lewisville, Texas supplied the following account of a case that occurred near Teulon, Manitoba on August 14, 1976:

> A farmer was taking count of cattle when he noticed that two cattle were missing. He indicated that he takes a count of his cattle daily and keeps a pretty close watch on them. He went in search of them and found both cows looking "like they were dead for years, and charred to the bone." Nearby were some willow trees with a few branches that were facing the cattle that had also been burned and charred. The RCMP investigated, but were unable to arrive at an explanation for the animals death. The farmer did indicate that the RCMP took flesh samples that had been charred, along with some of the charred vegetation.[52]

On September 26, 1976 a suspicious helicopter was reported flying low over pastures in Pawnee County, Kansas, near where mutilated cows would later be found on September 27th and 28th. There were a number of other Kansas reports of mutilations during the fall of 1976.

On November 6, 1976, a 1,000-pound cow was found mutilated near Canby, Yellow Medicine County, Minnesota. The cow was missing its tongue, udder, both ears, part of its jaw. In a stand- alone, atypical description of a mutilated cow carcass, veterinarian John Snyder noted *unusually loose joints in the carcass* possibly due to the introduction of a powerful muscle relaxant.

On November 9, 1976, the mutilators turned their attention back to Montana where an Angus bull was reported as mutilated near Raynesford, in Cascade County. The bull's left ear was missing and the jaw was "skinned out" in classic mute fashion. Investigators discovered *five unidentified "indentations," 74 inches apart*, in nearby brush.

A November 5, 1975 article referring to a bizarre claim from Wisconsin made the local evening news. Evidently, "A UFO dropped an albino turkey on a guy's house in Grant County that broke his antenna." Those aliens must have interesting early Thanksgiving turkey dinners and it's nice of them to share their bounty. Two cows had also been rumored to have been found mutilated in the area, and by November 12th there was a rumor of the mutilation of two hunters. Again, as we will see later, rumors of this kind are nearly impossible to verify. One of the cows had a bad lung, and the vet stated that "something had run it until it died." Teenagers were blamed. Of course they were, who else runs cattle around until they die?

November and December 1976 were busy in Colorado's Logan County. There were four confirmed mutilations reported between November 1st and December 17th, and during this time several lawmen report seeing strange lights in the skies. Sheriff Graves reported seeing a large bright object later dubbed 'Big Mama' by the press that appeared to disgorge three smaller fast, brightly lighted objects. On one occasion, officers chased 'Big Mama' in a small aircraft. The object would "disappear" then reappear looking more "pear-shaped" while changing colors from white to red to green to white. Sheriff Graves discovered strange indentations near a mutilated cow and "a tripod formation, five feet on a side."

The ensuing coverage of livestock mutilations during 1977 and 1978 were relegated to small, non-sensational articles in a number of local papers. If the local press coverage in the SLV, for instance, determined the extent of the flap, I would be led to believe the "problem" had subsided or ceased altogether in south central Colorado. Some reports were evidently still being filed with local authorities but were not covered in-depth by the media. I continued to ponder how Miles Porter's style of coverage, during the fall of 1975, dictated the public's perception of mutilation claims in the SLV. After his departure from the *Valley Courier*, the tone and substance of the coverage dramatically changed, but had local perceptions changed as well?

Ernest Sandoval brought home numerous mutilation reports and files after leaving as Sheriff. The reports currently in his possession are only from the 1976 through 1978 period, leaving him confused because much of the material he thought he had is now "missing." He was able to provide me with 12 complete reports and accompanying photographs, but Sandoval claims these were a mere portion of the overall official documentation he actually brought home. Fortunately, these surviving reports cover the period when press coverage was scant.

1977: Shotguns, Bioweapons, Choppers and Horse Slashers

Kentucky led off 1977 with a multiple mute case reported by Grayson County rancher Clifford Large. Five of his cattle were found dead and two of them had been mutilated. Local vet Dr. William Payne declared that "humans were involved." In another Grayson County case, a single mutilated cow was found on the Don White farm:

> The cow was reportedly *killed by a shotgun blast though it was also classically mutilated*. Don White's son, Allen, told Indiana investigator Don Worley that he and his brother observed a high-intensity light illuminating the farm a few nights *before* the mutilation. The victim calf was found at the bottom of a cliff *with a 600 or 700-pound rock laying on the carcass*, from which the rectum and sexual organs had been removed.[53] [my emphasis]

Researcher and author Nick Redfern sent me the following description of a curious, unexplained case from Devonshire, England that occurred in the spring of 1977. Perhaps the mutilators became bored with the dry, dusty pastures of the western U.S. and decided to visit the greener pastures of the UK.

> The British affair, I learned from carefully studying old newspaper articles on the affair, essentially began on April 11, 1977, when no less than fifteen wild ponies were found dead at Cherry Brook Valley, Dartmoor, Devonshire, England, by a Tavistock storekeeper named Alan Hicks, who had been crossing the moors with his children. It was not until mid-July, however, that the media began reporting on the incident indepth. Newspaper articles in my possession showed that the story traveled as far as South Africa; however, consider the following story, extracted from Britain's *Western Morning News* of July 13 [1977]:

Fears that the mystery deaths of fifteen ponies near a Dartmoor beauty spot were caused by visitors from space were being probed by a Torbay team yesterday. Armed with a Geiger counter, metal detectors and face masks, four men are investigating what leading animal authorities admit seems a 'totally abnormal happening,' and are hoping their equipment will throw a new light on the three-month-old mystery. While other investigators have looked for signs of malnutrition, disease or poisoning—or even gunshot wounds—the four men are seeking proof that extra-terrestrials were responsible for the deaths.

"If a spacecraft has been in the vicinity, there may still be detectable evidence," says the Team Leader, Mr. John Wyse, founder of the Devon UFO Center. His team is investigating the Postbridge mystery because the ponies' deaths have similarities with unsolved cases in the United States. Many of the Dartmoor ponies—all found within a few hundred yards of each other in the Cherry Brook Valley below Lower White Tor—had broken bones.

"Horses and cattle have been found in the United States in strange circumstances with the bones smashed or the bodies drained of blood," said Mr. Wyse. "Our members have already made a preliminary investigation and we know the bodies are now decomposed, but there may still be some evidence of an extra-terrestrial visit."

> The *Western Morning News* also quoted the secretary of the Livestock Protection Society as saying: "I still suspect that something dramatic happened—something very strange indeed. No one can give any logical explanation. One theory is that the ponies died of red worm—but that does not explain the broken necks and legs." [54]

The mutilators appear to have then returned across the big pond that spring with the SLV firmly back in their sights. According to a small three-paragraph article in the *Valley Courier*, May 27, 1977, a 14-month-old bull belonging to San Pablo rancher Alfonso Manzanares was reported to Costilla County authorities as "mutilated." The article stated, "The bull had been cut in a manner similar to mutilations in the area two years ago."

Law enforcement officials' cattle have also been targeted by our fatal surgeons. On June 17, 1977, former Alamosa Sheriff Jim Cockrum reported to the Costilla sheriff's office he found a 600 pound white-face steer that belonged to him "mutilated" on rented pasture at the "Lobato property at Ventero." He estimated the time of death as being three or four days earlier. Ernest Sandoval's official report stated:

> Jim Cockrum reported to the sheriff that one of his white-faced steers was mutilated in the same fashion as prior mutilations done before. Tail was cut off, testicles were cut off. The right ear and tongue. Went to area described and verified the fact that this job was done by the same professionals as before. No tracks, no blood and no nothing.[55]

My observation? Steers don't have testicles: they are steers, so of course they are missing testicles. And how in the world could Sandoval possibly tell that the animal was killed by the same professionals who were thought responsible for prior cases?

Here is a perfect illustration of how potential explanations of mysterious animal deaths can be misinterpreted by law enforcement and the public in general. Without the services of a qualified veterinarian pathologist, no one could accurately ascertain the cause of death or establish what caused the damage to the carcass. It may look like a mutilated cow, it may smell like a mutilated cow but that doesn't necessarily make it a mutilated cow.

Over the years, my skepticism has grown immeasurably concerning the pervasiveness and validity of many mutilation claims. Ideally, all claims should to be backed up with irrefutable, substantiated data obtained by trained forensic professionals. *Otherwise these "mutilations" are just claims based solely on appearance.* Specific cases might appear to be mysterious to the untrained eye but they might be commonplace to a veterinarian pathologist, or diagnostic crime lab scientist.

This realization, that it was impossible to accurately study the historical mutilation phenomenon based only on anecdotal research, photographs and hindsight, was a bit disheartening. I did not, however, let this important fact dampen my enthusiasm while investigating and researching cases in the early to mid 1990s. The very fact that ranchers and law enforcement officials viewed these animal deaths as "mysterious" is compelling from a sociological perspective. But, the "garbage in, garbage out" scenario is hard to avoid and almost impossible to overcome when attempting to unravel the mutilation mystery.

In the spring of 1977 an interesting skeptical analysis of the cattle mutilation phenomenon was published in *The Zetetic* magazine (now known as *The Skeptical Inquirer*). The author discounted and debunked the so-called "mystery" with a rather off-hand dismissive paper that equated the phenomenon to an outbreak of perceived "windshield pitting" in Washington State and elsewhere. This rather uninformed paper has been touted over the years by debunkers as being an adequate explanation as to why these unexplained animal deaths are simple mass hysteria. If this is so, then why do we see a complete cessation of reports for months—even years—at a time? And why has no sociologist bothered to look closely at this massive wave of societal "delusion" and offer up an in-depth dissertation looking at the sociological implications of an entire segment of the population descending into the unhealthy realms of mass hysteria? A synopsis of the dismissive paper, "Cattle Mutilations: An Episode of Collective Delusion," by James Stewart from *The Zetetic*, Spring/Summer 1977 edition follows:

Cattle Mutilations Called Episode of Collective Delusion

During the past several years, farmers in the western states have been reporting dead cattle that seemed strangely mutilated. Soft, exposed parts, such as the ears and genitals, were apparently removed with surgical precision. Some corpses seemed bloodless. Local papers blamed Satan worshippers and UFO occupants.

This paper analyzes the 1974 mutilation "flaps" in South Dakota and Nebraska, with special attention to the rapid rise and equally rapid decline of public interest as measured by newspaper coverage. In the opinion of the author, these two episodes are classic cases of mild mass hysteria, similar to the occasional crazes of automobile window-pitting [suddenly people started looking *at* their windows instead of *through* them]. *In all cases where university veterinarians examined the corpses, the mutilations were ascribed to small predatory animals.* [my emphasis—this is absolutely NOT true] The veterinarians also pointed out that blood coagulates in a couple days after death, accounting for the frequent "bloodless" condition. With such expert reassurances, the "mass delusions" subsided quickly. Cattle mutilation flaps are thus seen by the author as episodes when people interpret the mundane in bizarre new ways, due perhaps to cultural tensions.

It is noted, however, that expert veterinarians examined only a few of the dozens of mutilations, and that some people rejected the above commonplace explanations.

Contrary to the skeptic's assertions to the contrary, more than a few scientists have become intrigued by the mutilation phenomenon. Occasionally they uncover atypical cases. Dr. Nancy Johnson Smith of Calgary, Alberta informed Project Stigma that in June 1977 a bull was discovered with its scrotum and penis removed west of Cochrane, Alberta; and she reported that in July 1977 a cow was discovered missing its udder. This case also occurred west of Cochrane. "According to RCMP Corporal Lyn Lauber, the cutting was 'less refined' than on some of the 1979 mutes, and the RCMP says that *both animals were "shot"* with firearms. No tracks or additional evidence was found near either animal. [my emphasis][56]

JFK, Jr. and the Wind River Mutes

The following account comes from a 1996 *George* magazine editorial written by publisher John F. Kennedy, Jr. (figure 21) In the piece, he recalled the aftermath of a strange incident that he witnessed in early September 1977. The remembered experience occurred while he was working as a ranch hand for the summer on a cattle ranch in the Wind River Range in western Wyoming. He claimed to have accompanied the foreman of the ranch to a remote area of the spread where they stumbled upon what appeared to be a mutilated cow:

> When I was 17, I witnessed something so diabolical it could only have come from outer space or Washington, D.C.... The cow had been completely drained of blood. Its udder and reproductive organs had all been removed and the wounds cauterized. An incision had been made along the snout, removing the upper lip, tongue and one eye with an instrument so sharp that the hair along the cut had not been disturbed. These cuts too, were cauterized. There was no blood or footprints on the muddy

ground, nor any visible mortal wound, only a mysterious inch-long incision across the animal's windpipe.

I learned later that while no mutilations had been reported in that area in some years, mutilations had occurred in the three adjoining counties at about the same time our cow had met her end. The mystery was never solved, and the ranch never suffered another like it. Among the local folks familiar with this periodic phenomenon, the consensus held that it was either the work of UFOs or the government. "Who else," they said, "would do something this weird or this dumb?"[57]

Washington State (which had been quiet for the most part since 1976) briefly became the new killing ground zero during the fall of 1977. Seattle resident Jacob Davidson forwarded the following Snohomish County reports to Project Stigma, investigated by Jerry Phillips of Everett, Washington, who interviewed rancher Jack Henning regarding the mutilation of one of his colts.

On October 14, 1977, Henning went and checked on one of his mares and the two colts she had given birth to several months earlier—everything appeared normal. When he went back out to feed the horses a short time later, at 10:00 that morning, he was horrified to discover that one of the colts was dead and mutilated, with "a heart-shaped hole extending from the base of the tail and halfway down to the hip section. The rectum, genitals and about 40-pounds of flesh were missing." Henning's veterinarian was called to the scene and Dr. John Carr ascertained that the colt died from loss of blood after some "unknown procedure." There was no blood in evidence and only a small amount in the heart and chest cavity. There was no other apparent crime scene evidence and no tracks in the three-inch tall grass in the pasture. It looked "as though the colt had been dropped out of the air… In the same field, 30 to 40 feet of electric fence was down, with two fence posts snapped off at the base. There were no tracks around the fence."

On the second day a cobweb-like material developed over the open wound. Later the second day a large German shepherd dog was observed coming into the field. When he spotted the dead animal he stopped, smelled the air, made a circle around it and continued on its way. The third day, a coyote that had been seen in the area several times in previous months, came into the field, circled the animal several times, and then began eating on the head and neck. He would not go near the rear of the horse. Mr. Henning went out to have a look and found plenty of evidence on the ground and in the grass to show where the coyote had dug his paws in when pulling at the neck hide…Mr. Henning brought the mare and her other colt out and tried to get them near the dead colt. Neither one would come within 50 feet of it. He tried laying hay next to it and they still would not approach it. Mr. Henning has two Labrador dogs…he turned them loose to see what they would do. They circled the animal, but would not get within 20 feet of it.

Henning told Phillips that he had been working with the surviving colt before the killing and she was fairly gentle. After the mutilation she stood in the barn and quivered. Henning had difficulty even approaching her for a week. The mare was very possessive and protective of her colts, and she would become very upset if anyone even walked between them. There was no evidence that she tried to interfere when the victim colt was in danger that morning. Afterward, "she acted as if the colt had never existed."[58]

Reports continued to be filed with Cascade County, Montana authorities. David Perkins noted the following report and description in "Meet the Mutilators" that sounds eerily like the West Virginia "bloodmobile" encounter in 1967 with the unknown craft with two arm-like appendages:

On December 23rd [1977] at 6:00 in the morning, a woman driving to work at the Great Falls International Airport saw an "egg-shaped object" which paced her car for a short distance. The shaken woman told authorities the object was "as large as a two-story building." The craft had three red lights on the top and "windows" on the bottom.

An egg-shaped craft had been observed earlier in December. A ranch couple in Teton County called Sheriff Howard to report a rather unusual occurrence. At 4:30 in the afternoon, the couple noticed a large egg-shaped object on the ground about five-eighths of a mile from their house. They watched the craft for five minutes with binoculars. One light on the egg varied in intensity—a yellowish-gold or light orange color.

The most unique feature of the craft was two "appendages" which stuck out—one on each side. The two "arms" moved in a continual motion "like a breast-stroke." After five minutes the arms retracted into the craft. The athletic egg then shot straight up and out of sight.

Meanwhile, Mrs. Gloria Dow (not her real name) kept her colt in a pasture owned by a radio station that was located next to her spread near Salt Lake City, Utah. On December 27, 1977, a neighbor happened to see that the horse was down and not moving. The unfortunate animal had been killed and was terribly disfigured. The sheriff's office was called and Salt Lake County Sheriff's Deputy Franson investigated the case. An autopsy was conducted by Dr. Craig White, a veterinarian with the Utah State Department of Agriculture, who found that "the horse had been severely mutilated with both blunt and sharp instruments." White's report stated:

The skin and superficial muscles were removed from the face from the caudal [toward the tail] portion of the left occipital bone [at the rear of the skull] to two-centimeters interior the left nostril; from the midline of the skull to the left facial crest. The incision included complete removal of the left eye and pinna [the external part of the ear]. There was a small slab fracture two-centimeters in diameter midway between the eye and nostril in the left facial bone. The damage on the face was done with a sharp instrument.

The genital organs were mutilated severely. The penis had been removed. The anus was completely removed. The colon was intact. On the abdomen at the location where the penis had been removed there was a large opening into the abdomen, which had been gouged with a blunt instrument. There were also several areas of skin where small areas of tissue had been gouged out…the anal sphincter had been removed with near surgical precision.

The animal had been definitely alive while being mutilated, that the cut marks on the face of the animal, where the left side of the face had been skinned off, including the eye, muscles and the ear—that the animal was definitely alive after that point due to the fact that the head had been swinging back and forth and blood had been deposited on the ground…[59]

1978: Investigators Scratching Their Collective Heads

A series of "odd reports" were made to Arapahoe County, Colorado sheriff's deputies in early 1978. The *Denver Post* noted these reports in an article dated April 9, 1978.

In addition to five reports of UFOs, the sheriff's department has received reports of men in sheets, bodies by the road and mysterious fires. Detective Harry Vohl said most of the reported sightings have been in the general area of the old Lowry bombing range, southeast of Denver. "The strange thing about these UFO sightings, like most others, is that it's not drunks and weirdos who are reporting them," Volhl said. "They're being reported by respectable people who have nothing to gain by making false reports."…other reports were made in mid-March about men in sheets. As in most of the other cases, deputies found nothing to substantiate them. Vohl said similar reports were made in 1975, during a period of cattle mutilations, some of them unexplained, in many parts of the state.

I can picture those tricksterish aliens now, sitting astride unexploded ordinance—roasting Rocky Mountain oysters—shouting. "Toga, Toga, Toga," in some indecipherable language.

Another strange report was filed from a ranch near the remote British Columbia town of Prince George in April 1978. The case was reported after a beam of light allegedly descended on a barn containing six horses.

Three horses on one side of the barn were apparently unaffected, but the other three were badly frightened. One was struck momentarily unconscious; one kicked both hind legs through the side of its stall and one horse charged wildly around the barn 'as though scared to death.' One of the animals exhibited two bare patches of hide as though the hair had been burned out or torn out. Thirteen people observed a UFO (in addition to the "beam") from two different areas of Prince George that same night.[60]

In the late spring of 1978, the mutilators again paid a visit to Snohomish County Washington where one of 30 Herefords owned by Williams Hordyk was found dead and mutilated on May 16th. The pregnant, three-year-old, 900-pound cow had probably been dead for several days. The Hordyk's two dogs would not go within 25 feet of the carcass and Hordyk told Everett, Washington investigator Jerry Phillips that a perfect three-by-five-inch cut had been made where the left ear had been. The left eyeball was missing completely, but there were no cuts around the eye. Hordyk also told Phillips that he got quite a shock when he lifted the leg up:

> [He] discovered a perfect cut from the tail to the middle of the belly. The rectum, sexual organs and the complete udder had been neatly taken out. On closer examination, a hole about 11-inches in diameter was discovered right in the center of the area where the udder had been. This hole went straight into the unborn calf. You could see the calf's hair at the bottom of the hole. Mr. Hordyk describes the cut as very professional (he has butchered a lot of animals). It was cut in a perfectly straight line like with one continuous motion. The hide seemed to be beveled inward from the cut. There was no blood on the animal or on the ground... the cut around the udder was just skin-deep. Not once had the instrument used penetrated the stomach lining.[61]

When Jerry Phillips visited the site on May 19th, he noticed what appeared to be a magnetic anomaly around the gravesite of the cow. As he held a compass over the grave "it [the compass] would not settle down. Moving around the grave, the needle always wanted to go to the cow."[62]

On June 5, 1978 in Huerfano County, Colorado, three mutilations were reported to the sheriff's office and a "cowboy [witnessed] an unmarked green helicopter near one of the dead cows."

On June 8th the first of a furious wave of cases was reported from the Elsberry, Missouri region. A heifer calf was reported as mutilated and it was apparently missing its right ear, right eye, tongue and the udder had also been removed.

On June 12th and 15th 1978, two more reports were filed with the New Mexico State Patrol from the Dulce area. They were described as your standard-issue "classic" mutes.

Then on June 17th reports again began to surface in Elsberry. David Perkins, after he visited the region, noted in "Meet the Mutilators" that there were a bewildering number of inexplicable sighting reports:

[On] June 28th, Venus Durham arrived at the dump to find a "four-to-five foot tall hairy monkey" picking through the refuse… Other out-of-the-ordinary events recorded by Marshall Livengood include: 'Barrels' that rise up out of the [Mississippi] river and fly away, three '55-gallon drums' flying in formation, and 'dark-colored, unmarked helicopters.' One local merchant, who insists on anonymity due to fear of ridicule, claims he saw a 'child-sized figure wearing what looked to be a glowing suit.' The merchant was fishing at Taylor Lake (scene of a future mutilation) when he first saw the illuminated entity at the edge of the lake. The glowing kid disappeared into the woods taking unusually long, bouncing steps.

Five days later another unexplained livestock death report was filed with authorities by a rancher outside Las Vegas, New Mexico.

Around mid to late June, rumors surfaced from the deep south in Copiah County, Mississippi that mutilations were being found by area ranchers. After a brief respite, the reports again returned to northern New Mexico when a mute was reported to officials from Tierra Amarilla. And another report was filed from a ranch south of Dulce near Lindrith on July 10th.

Do They Glow in the Dark?

On July 5, 1978, Gabe Valdez, Howard Burgess and Manuel Gomez conducted an ingenious experiment to test a theory that Burgess had proposed. He surmised that victim cattle were somehow being marked for mutilation in advance and that this marking process would be geared for aerial identification. Burgess proposed that this marking would be in the form of ultraviolet paint that would be invisible to the naked eye. (figure 22) So, the three men ran 100 mixed head of Gomez cattle through a cattle shoot at night and subjected the animals to five different ultraviolet lamps that ranged through the light spectrum. Burgess noted the effort in an article he and his wife Lovola wrote in 1979 titled "Close Encounter at the Old Corral:"

Officer Gabe Valdez of the New Mexico State Police summed it up, "All mutilations seem to happen at night, some in pretty wild country. In the present cycle nearly all are either four-year-old cows or very young heifers. How do they select them from the air?" Then he asked, "Are they marked in advance?"

This question had possibilities. But how? Most of the process including the marking on the animal would have to be invisible to the human eye. Invisible infrared rays can be used to locate animals at night, but selecting a certain animal could be difficult. However, ultraviolet rays are another story. An animals splashed with an "invisible ink" would glow when illuminated from the air with an invisible beam from an ultraviolet generator. An interesting test of the theory would be to try ultraviolet viewing of a herd of cattle that had already been hit with several mutilations. Perhaps there might still be marked cattle remaining in the herd.

The herd of Manuel Gomez near Dulce, New Mexico, met the requirements for such a test, and Manuel was willing to volunteer his herd, cowboys and a remote corral in the mountains away from all lights, vehicles and people. One hundred mixed cattle were put in the corral before sundown.

Five different types of ultraviolet lamps ranging through the spectrum were put in place over a narrow chute into which only one animal could pass at a time.

It was late before all was in readiness and the last light of a summer sun left the mountain peaks in total darkness. Sounding like a western rodeo, the cattle were started moving through the chute under the lamps.

Near midnight during the operation, Tribal Police Chief Raleigh Tafoya of the Apache Indian Police climbed up on the corral beside us to see how things were going. After a few questions he asked, "Did you see the orange light moving around in the sky a while ago? It was the kind that always shows up when there's a mutilation. Maybe they're watching you tonight." We had been too busy to see the light but, sure enough, later that night there were two mutilations a few miles away on a remote mountain slope.

The final results of our night's work? To our amazement, out of 100 mixed cattle and calves, three four-year-old cows and two young heifers had bright fluorescent splashes on their backs or topsides—fitting the pattern of animal types being mutilated in that area at that period. No markings were found on their sides, underneath, or lower parts.

Samples of the fluorescent hair and control samples of normal hair were removed for laboratory analysis. A spectrum analysis was done by the Schoenfeld Labs, a professional clinical laboratory in Albuquerque.

We were not able to find any liquid or solid in the corral or pasture that glowed with the same color or brilliance as the marks on the animals. The fluorescent marking was not from material picked up locally. If the animals were marked in advance, how was it done? When? By whom?

About four weeks after the fluorescent hair had been removed from the animals, the fluorescence suddenly "turned off." We don't have an explanation.

On July 7, 1978, a dead steer was discovered near Hereford, Texas and the animal was inspected by a deputy sheriff who stated: "The animal died of black-leg, but the incisions were inflicted after death." The steer evidently had not been drained of blood. That same day, a case was filed from Prairie Grove, Arkansas where a calf was reported mutilated. The tongue and other organs appeared to have been removed.

In August 1978, reports began to surface around Iberia, Missouri and in Lincoln County, Wisconsin. On August 4th a heifer calf was reported as mutilated; the left ear and sexual organs removed. The term "surgical incisions" was used to describe the animal's condition. That same day, another report was filed from Elsberry, Missouri, and again on the 7th when a six-month-old calf, weighing 350 lbs, was found mutilated in a thicket in a field one mile from the road. The right side of the calf was stripped, the right front leg missing. The following day yet another Ellsberry case was reported.

On August 15th, Cave Springs, Arkansas became the apparent target when a calf was discovered missing both eyes and its tongue; the sexual organs were also removed. The next day another calf was found with the same missing parts. Officials speculated that there appeared to be "evidence of cultism." The following day, in nearby Centerton, another cattle mutilation was reported. This time only the tongue removed from the animal.

The following SLV reports are from August 1978 and center around three ranches just east of the town of San Luis. The Pat Sanchez, Mike Maldanado and the Eban Smith Ranches appear to have been singled out and hit repeatedly throughout the next year and a half. Emilio Lobato, Jr. and these three ranchers may be the hardest hit in the entire documented "mute" phenomenon. The four together claim to have lost around 80 cattle. I looked for some common link between Maldanado, Smith, Sanchez and Lobato.

I called Mike Maldanado in 1993 and asked him about a possible connection between himself and the other ranchers. "Do you belong to the same organizations? Do you go to the same church? Are you politically active in the same party or…" He interrupted me. "Now that you mention it, we do share something in common, we're *all teachers."* (my emphasis)

> On Thursday, August 17, 1978, at 1:58 p.m., a Mr. Mike Maldanado called the sheriff's office to report that some of his cows had been mutilated *or so it appeared like they were.* On August 19, 1978, at 12:00 p.m., deputies Steve Benavidez and Arnold Valdez went out to the incident scene. This incident was the same as all the rest of the possible mutilations that have happened in this area. No evidence was found in the immediate area. Pending further investigation."[63] (my emphasis)

This report shows a change in perception. For the first time, we see indications that the rancher and investigating officers view these latest reports as "mutilations, *or so they appeared to be.*" The two animals, a cow and a bull, were not found for over a week and the photographs show bird droppings on the carcasses and what appear to be uneven incisions.

On August 28, 1978, Eban Smith called to report a "mutilation" of a cow the previous night on his ranch. Deputy Valdez was again dispatched to the crime-scene and noted at the end of his report, "My opinion is that it was unprofessional due to the fact that it was very sloppy compared to some of the previous mutilations." Again there is evidence of doubt, so were these cases true, high-strange mutilations or hyperbole?

On September 28, 1978 a mutilated steer was discovered and reported in Piermont, New Hampshire. *This is only the second case known to have ever been reported in the state.* The following day 12 sheep were found killed but not scavenged in Taos, New Mexico. Authorities surmised that this was due to supposed dog attacks, but this style of carnage is not normally associated with dogs.

A horse mutilation was reported in Logan County, Colorado on October 2nd and four days later four separate cases were reported on the Jicarilla Apache Reservation around Dulce, New Mexico.

Cases would also be reported in October and November 1978 in Mancos and Durango, Colorado; New Albany and Stockton, Kansas; Avoca, Brush Creek, Benton (on the Sam Walton of WalMart fame ranch) and again in Cave Springs, Arkansas. Also, reports surfaced in Rodarte, Dulce, Espanola, Chimayo and Lamy, New Mexico.

On Halloween, two "butchered" cows were reported near Westcliffe, Colorado. Authorities suspected poachers of being responsible, as choice meat cuts were taken.

A month after the first of a half dozen UFOs was reported over the Santa Clara Reservation, the mutilators showed up and commenced more of their handiwork. On November 13th two mutes were reported to Santa Clara tribal officials. Another report was then filed by a witness who claimed to have seen a mystery helicopter in the area. That same day another mute was reported just to the northeast in Santa Fe County, New Mexico.[64]

Over the next five weeks, UFOs were reported in Ojo Caliente, Dulce and again over the Santa Clara Pueblo. Then, on November 25, 1978 two more mutes were reported in Chimayo and Hernandez, New Mexico.

A rancher on a spread north of Spillimacheen, British Columbia reported a dead "bull with a half-inch hole penetrating six inches into the back of its head. Part of the bull's genitals had been removed, but there was little or no blood in evidence." The case occurred in November of 1978.[65]

Then our mute reports leapt across the country on December 6th, 1978 when allegedly "hogs were mutilated" and a UFO was spotted by the victimized farmer in Norway, South Carolina. Only a handful of South Carolina mutilations had ever been reported up until this point.

Around 8:00 p.m., on Wednesday, December 6th, 1978 hog farmer Richard Fanning, accompanied by his wife and another couple, drove out to feed Fanning's several hundred hogs. As they approached the hog pen, all four saw a circle of light along with four smaller lights (two red, two green) hovering over nearby treetops. The four were frightened by the noiseless apparitions and decided that the hogs could be fed later. As the witnesses drove from the scene, they were followed by the large white light and the red and green lights for about 300 yards. Suddenly all five lights returned to hover over the area of the hog pen. After three or four minutes, all of the lights went out.

Fanning did not return to feed the hogs until Friday morning, December 8th. He found one hog "standing up dead. I kicked him and he fell over." Fanning told reporter Roberta G. Boman of the *Times and Democrat* (Orangeburg, South Carolina) that a second dead hog lay nearby with its jawbone removed. He told Boman that "the body was sort of like sponge, with all the weight gone, kind of like jelly (Fanning said the hog, normally weighing 200 pounds, weighed no more than approximately 50 pounds). "In my opinion, no animal got that hog."

Fanning went on to exclaim, "I was scared, and I'm not scared of many things. I go hunting and fishing a lot. Never seen anything like it. It's the weirdest thing I've ever seen in my life. I'm an outdoorsman, and I wouldn't have said nothing unless the other three people saw it too."[66]

The following day on December 9, 1978, a mutilation was reported in Deaf Smith County, Texas. On December 15th Benton County, Arkansas experienced their "24th mute reported since April 8, 1978."

This flip-flopping from one side of the country to the other would not be as widespread in 1979 when intense waves of activity would appear to descend on specific regions with a fury. At least that's what it appears like on the surface looking back with 20/20 hindsight.

David Perkins, who visited Ellsberry, Missouri earlier that fall and, with partner Cari Sewell and journalist Bill McIntyre, bought "Mutilated Cow Country" tee-shirts (figure 23) noted in "Meet the Mutilators," that there were a bewildering array of sighting reports all the way into December 1978. And, on December 22, 1978 Chicago serial killer, "The Killer Clown," John Wayne Gacy was arrested and charged with the murder of 33 young men. (figure 24)

Thus ended the three hell years of 1975 through 1978 in the pastures and on the plains of America. By this time the national press had for the most part, ceased covering the livestock mutilation story, but hometown and regional media continued to publish articles detailing local claims.

Dr. Jacques Vallee investigated the cattle mutilation phenomenon in the mid to late 70s and insightfully summed up the mystery in his 1978 book *Messengers of Deception*:

> We are entering a new area where we must tread carefully. Some of the evidence may have been planted to mislead us into false conclusions. The connection with UFOs appears especially *tricky* and, if proven, would still not answer all our questions. [my emphasis] Someone could be simulating UFO events to turn the investigators' attention away from the real cause of the mutilation. Or it may be that the mutilations are in fact the "next step" in the unfolding process directly related to the UFOs.

As we will see, in 1979, while the mutilators, scavengers and tricksters continued stalking the herd, the UFO meme would receive a boost from a new crop of investigator/researchers who emerged on the scene in the 1980s.

Chapter Five: Sources and References

1. "Meet the Mutilators," David Perkins, 1979
2. *Unmasking the Enemy,* Tommy Blann, unpublished 1993
3. Corchran Sheriff's report, 3-11-75; "Meet the Mutilators," David Perkins, 1979
4. *Idaho Statesman,* 7-6-75; "Meet the Mutilators," David Perkins, 1979
5. *ibid*
6. *Mute Evidence,* Kagan & Summers, Bantam, NY NY, 1983
7. norad.mil/about NORAD/CheyenneMountainAirForceStation.aspx
8. *Cattle Mutilation:* Fredrick Smith, 1979; *Gazette Telegraph,* CoSprings, CO, 7-6-75
9. *Colorado Springs Sun,* 10-23-75
10. *Gazette Telegraph,* Colorado Springs, CO, 11-21-75
11. *Cattle Mutilation: The Unthinkable Truth,* Fredrick Smith, 1979
12. *Unmasking the Enemy,* Tommy Blann, 1993; "Meet the Mutilators," David Perkins, 1979
13. Interview w/ Gene Gray; *The Mysterious Valley,* St Martins Press, NY NY 1996
14. Loman Interview, The SLV Event Log, 1993
15. *The Choppers, and The Choppers,* Tom Adams/Project Stigma, Paris TX, 1993
16. *Unmasking the Enemy,* Tommy Blann, 1993
17. *Mystery Stalks the Prairie,* Donovan & Wolverton, THAR Institute, Raynesford, MT, 1976
18. "Meet the Mutilators," David Perkins, 1979
19. *ibid*
20. Project Stigma Interviews with Logan County Sheriff's Office, and with Bill Jackson, *Sterling Journal-Advocate;* AP dispatch from Kimball, Nebraska, printed in *Omaha World-Herald,* 8-22-75, *Greeley, Colorado Tribune,* 8-22-75; *Sterling Journal-Advocate,* 8-21-75
21. "Meet the Mutilators," David Perkins, 1979
22. *Mute Evidence,* Kagan & Summers, Bantam, NY NY, 1983
23. *Twin Falls Times,* 8-19-75; "Meet the Mutilators," David Perkins, 1979
24. *Casper Star-Tribune,* 10-27-75; "Meet the Mutilators," David Perkins, 1979
25. "Meet the Mutilators," David Perkins, 1979
26. *ibid*

27. *Mute Evidence,* Kagan & Summers, Bantam, NY NY, 1983
28. *ibid*
29. *ibid*
30. *The Choppers, and The Choppers,* Tom Adams/Project Stigma, 1993
31. *Unmasking the Enemy,* Thomas Blann, 1993
32. *ibid:* Associated Press, 9-6-75; *Times-News,* Twin Falls, ID, 9-5-75
33. "Meet the Mutilators", David Perkins, 1979
34. *ibid*
35. *ibid*
36. *ibid*
37. *ibid*
38. *ibid*
39. *ibid*
40. *ibid*
41. *ibid*
42. Hastings, Robert, *UFOs and Nukes,* 2008, Author House, Bloomington IL; The Paracast radio interview 5-18-13
43. "Meet the Mutilators," David Perkins, 1979
44. *Unmasking the Enemy,* Thomas Blann, 1993
45. *Secrets of the Mysterious Valley,* Christopher O'Brien, AUP, Kempton, IL, 2007
46. "Meet the Mutilators," David Perkins, 1979
47. *Project Stigma,* Gabe Valdez
48. *ibid*
49. *ibid*
50. *Stigmata #5,* 1978; Grant Callison
51. *Dulce Base,* Greg Valdez, Levi-Cash Publishing, Albuquerque, NM, 2013
52. Tommy Blann; *Stigmata #5*, 1978
53. Don Worley; *Stigmata #6,* 1978
54. *Western Morning News,* 7-13-77; "Slaughter on the Moor," Nick Redfern
55. *Valley Courier,* 5-27-77
56. Project Stigma, #6 1978
57. *George* magazine, editorial 12-96, Kennedy, JF Jr.,
58. Jerry Phillips; *Stigmata #6,* 1978
59. *ibid*
60. *Res Bureaux Bulletin* (No. 35, 6-15-78, Stigmata #5, 1978
61. Jerry Phillips; *Stigmata #6,* 1978
62. *ibid*
63. *The Mysterious Valley,* Christopher O'Brien, St Martins Press, NY NY, 1996
64. "Meet the Mutilators," David Perkins, 1979
65. John Magor via W.K. Allan of Kelowna, BC; Project Stigma
66. *Times and Democrat,* Orangeburg, SC; Leonard Stringfield; *Stigmata #6,* 1978

Figure 1
Hells Canyon, Upper Snake River Basin, Idaho. (credit: griffsfamilyoutdoors.com)

Figure 2
Mute Evidence. Kagan & Summers dismissal of the mutilation phenomenon.
(credit: Bantam Books)

Figure 3
Entrance to the NORAD facility inside Cheyenne Mountain, Colorado.
(credit: norad.mil)

Figure 4
American Bison. (credit: myzoo22.blogspot)

Figure 5
Loman horse mutilation, LaGarita, Colorado, 1975. Not burnt appearence
of rear end. (credit: Gene Gray, TMV archive)

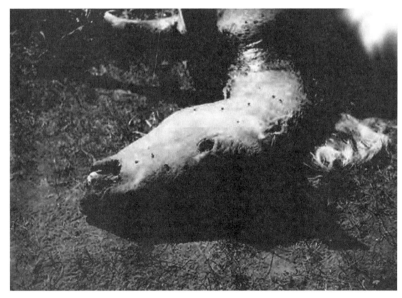

Figure 6
Loman horse mutilation, LaGarita, Colorado, 1975. Note tar-like substance
around neck. (credit: Gene Gray, TMV archive)

226

Figure 7
Cochetopa cow, Saguache County, Colorado, 1975. Note downside mandible excision.
(credit: Gene Gray, TMV archive)

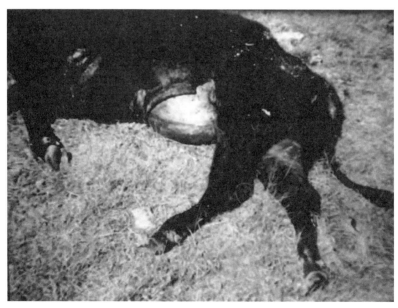

Figure 8
Cochetopa cow, Saguache County, Colorado, 1975. (credit: Gene Gray, TMV archive)

Figure 9
Captain Keith Wolverton documented Montana wave in his book,
Mystery Stalks the Prairie. (credit: Keith Wolverton/Roberta Donovan)

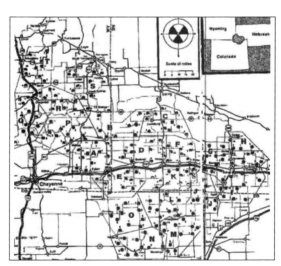

Figure 10
Montana/Colorado/Nebraska missile fields. (credit: angelfire.com/tx/missileaway)

Figure 11
Mystery Chopper. (credit: dhakatribune.com/photoshop by author)

Figure 12
The National Reactor Testing Station, Idaho. (credit: atomicpowereview.com)

Figure 13
Who are the hooded figures seen near mutilation sites? (credit: conanmovie.blogspot)

Figure 14
Malmstrom Air Force Base, Montana. (credit: mil.gov)

Figure 15
Wildman have been reported for millenia. (credit: stephenfowler.blogspot.com)

Figure 16
Bigelow Aerospace modular space station. (credit: space.com)

Figure 17
Rocky Flats Hydrogen Bomb Manufacturing facility, Near Arvada, Colorado.
(credit: commons.wikimedia.org)

Figure 18
Mutilation investigator/theorist David Perkins. (credit: AMP/David Perkins)

Figure 19
Mutilation investigators Tom Adams and Gary Massey. (credit: AMP/David Perkins)

Figure 20
New Mexico State patrolman Gabe Valdez.
(credit: Candyce Valario, AMP/David Perkins)

Figure 21
John F. Kennedy Jr. (credit: totakethetrain.wordpress.com)

Figure 22
Mutilation investigator Howard Burgess. (credit: AMP/David Perkins)

Figure 23
Investigators David Perkins Cari Seawell & Bill McIntyre in Elseberry, MO.
(credit: AMP/David Perkins)

Figure 24
The "Killer Clown" John Wayne Gacy. (credit: natgeo.com.uk)

Chapter 6
Hell Year
Return: 1979

1979 started off with a cold bang in Atchison County Nebraska where ranchers experienced three cases in January featuring one cow and two sows. Then later a calf was reported mutilated in March. According to an article in the Atchison *Globe:* "Officers said they are convinced that the mutilations are the work of humans and not done by animals." The Atchison County Sheriff's Office declined to provide further details concerning their on-going investigation.[1]

On January 12, 1979, the mute teams appeared to head back out west to northern New Mexico where a Taos County rancher reported a five-year-old heifer had been mutilated. This was in the dead of winter at almost 7,000 feet in elevation and this rare below freezing case was investigated by New Mexico State Patrolman Gabe Valdez:

> The animal was discovered near Ranchitos, less than a quarter-mile from the site of an earlier controversial UFO sighting and residue-dropping in July of 1978. One eye, the tongue, anus and reproductive organs were removed. It used to be thought that most or all mutilations occurred in warm or moderate weather, but this carcass was found *frozen in the grip of a Taos winter.* State Policeman Gabe Valdez stated that the animal had been "definitely tranquilized" and then the blood was pumped out and the parts removed.[2] [my emphasis]

Another New Mexico cow, which was expected to give birth in three weeks, was found dead with the udder neatly sliced off near Dilia, in Guadalupe County. A report was filed with the State Patrol. A similar mutilation had been rumored to have occurred in the same region in the fall of 1978, but was not reported. Around the time of the Dilia mutilation, and two-and-a-half miles away, barbed wire fences around several tracks of grazing land were 'cut and torn down.'

> Four expensive show horses, all mares and all in foal, died under odd circumstances in an area south of Carlsbad, New Mexico in Eddy County. The three apparently died on Friday, January 19, 1979, and two of them appeared to have been classically mutilated. In a strange twist, it was claimed by investigators "[a] foal was removed from one of the mares..."[3]

...[T]he deputy in charge of the investigation, John C. Neill, visited the scene on Monday, [January] 22nd, along with Sheriff Tom Granger. That night the owner of the ranch, Clarence McDonald, kept watch over the area until midnight. The next morning, Tuesday, the 23rd, a fourth horse was found dead and mutilated. One of the other three mares, which was found dead but not mutilated on Monday, was found mutilated on Tuesday. Carlsbad veterinarian M.C. Reynolds revealed that, in his opinion, the horses died of "acute toxic hepatitis" (an experienced mutilation investigator has pointed out that severe liver deterioration has been noted in other mutilated carcasses, the suggestion being that this could have occurred in the Eddy County horses and was mistaken for hepatitis). Beyond that, Dr. Reynolds did not offer an explanation for the mutilation of the horses.

A confidential source informs [Project Stigma] that at least one other mutilation occurred in Eddy County around the first of the year. Also, there have been sightings of unidentified helicopters in the areas of the mutilations. Then, in May, a "makeshift altar," containing deer and dog skulls, rocks, glass and cheap jewelry, was found along a street two miles north of Carlsbad.[4]

Then, in June 1979, the Artesia, New Mexico *Daily Press* reported that Sheriff Granger's office was investigating the discovery of three mutilated goats and a dozen dead hens in the general area of the January horse mutilations.

In August 1979, Project Stigma interviewed John Neill, who went back to ranching and is no longer associated with the Eddy County Sheriff's Office. Mr. Neill is a disgruntled and frustrated ex-mutilation investigator. Though he was unaware of the goat and hen deaths in June, he expressed no confidence in the outcome of any future investigations in Eddy County.

At the invitation of U.S. Senator Harrison Schmitt, (figure 1) Neill attended the Albuquerque mutilation conference in April, to his dismay and disappointment: "I've never been made a part of or exposed to such idiocy in my life. The whole reason for (the conference), and you can quote me on this, was to get a damn grant for a couple of ol' boys that needed a job and got themselves a fifty-thousand-dollar grant. Nobody asked to see the photographs that I had with me in my briefcase. They didn't as to see the mare that I've had veterinarians look at. Photographs (of the mare) had been taken consecutively for 130-140 days and *the mare hadn't decomposed*—they didn't ask to see anything regarding the January mutilations, Neill says, "It was something that defies my imagination."[5]

On January 24, 1975, a strange report was filed by security guard Bob Roberts at the Great Western Sugar Plant, located in Johnstown, Colorado. Roberts described the events that occurred just after 9:00 P.M. to a reporter for a February 2, 1979 article in the *Breeze* (Johnstown, Colorado):

> I was watching a television program... 'Chariots of the Gods.' After the program was over, I walked outside...I saw a large round pulsating white light. I said to myself Jesus Christ, what is that? I thought it was a spacecraft or a UFO. It came from the north or northwest. It was brighter than a vapor light. As I watched it, it moved toward the [Ft. St. Vrain— Colorado's only] nuclear plant, going southeast. There were two lights, red and orange... The diagonal lights went back into one. The light hesitated two or three minutes over Milliken [Colorado]. The lights headed southeast again, east of the nuclear plant.

Directly downstream from the nuclear and sugar plants was the Front River epicenter of the mute waves of 1975 and the late 70s in Logan County, Colorado.

On January 29, 1979, a six-month old, still-warm steer was found near Duran, New Mexico, in Torrance County. The penis had been removed and the "intestines were removed through a hole in the scrotum." Both ears appeared to have been "beveled out...with precision."

> Circular hairless patches were found on both sides of the animal; the hair appeared "rubbed off" rather than pulled out, and there were small lacerations within the patches. The jugular vein had been punctured in two places, the neck was broken (leading to the oft-repeated speculation in New Mexico that mutilated carcasses are dropped from the air), and there was no blood in the heart and little elsewhere in the body.[6]

Later in May, State Patrolman Gabe Valdez announced that two common drugs had been identified in samples taken from the carcass: Chlorpromazine (a "widely-distributed" tranquilizer) and a common blood-clotting agent. Valdez told the Santa Fe *New Mexican*: "We know this stuff is made here, and it is not from outer space. Whoever is doing it is highly sophisticated, and they have a lot of resources. They're well-organized."[7]

On February 9th an 850-pound heifer was reported mutilated northeast of Harper, Kansas. "One eye and hind portions were cut out. A large amount of blood was found in a nearby creek, and tracks from a four-wheel-drive vehicle were noted at the scene." The animal appeared to have been butchered for meat. A very similar case supposedly transpired near White City in Morris County in March.[8]

Then, on March 14, 1979, a 200-pound bull calf was reported mutilated near Atchison Kansas. These cases may have been the proverbial tip of the iceberg, as rumors swirled around the ranching communities of other unreported mutilations.

Meanwhile our mutilator tricksters apparently went on vacation to, of all places, the Canary Islands located off the coast of northwestern Africa. The following events were well documented by the local media and these alleged events deserve a mention as we continue stalking the proverbial herd.

Canary in a Coal Mine?

The following cases unfolded over the spring, summer and fall of 1979 and are sometimes referred to by researchers, but the actual details are little known outside of the mute investigator community.

The 13 islands collectively called the Canary Islands are Spanish possessions located off the northwest coast of Africa. The largest of the islands are Tenerife, (figure 2) Gran Canaria (Grand Canary) and Fuerteventura. The Canaries feature a mild climate and rugged, mountainous terrain. World attention was focused on the Canaries when a major airline crash occurred on the runway at Tenerife.

A spectacular sighting event had taken place on the night of June 22, 1976, when the Spanish Navy corvette *Atrevida* was anchored several miles off Punta Lantailla, Fuerteventura Island. Sailors observed a "bright yellow light traveling above the horizon." The object had no radar signature. The light became a "luminous" rotating beam and then a glowing halo grew around the object. The halo lasted for some time and its light could be seen by witnesses aboard ship, reflecting off the water and illuminating the shoreline. By the conclusion of the sighting event, the light had been observed by the entire ship's complement. The descriptions of the growing object are unique and few sighting claims have ever described this exaggerated growth effect. No known unexplained animal deaths were reported around the time of this sighting.

Meanwhile, Doctor Francisco Padron Leon was in a taxi outside of the town of Guia headed to see a patient in nearby Las Rosas, Gran Canaria. While traveling in the cab, he and the driver witnessed a glowing blue sphere that appeared to be hovering close to the ground in front of the vehicle. Leon described the spherical object as having a radius of approximately 100 feet and being "sufficiently transparent for him to make out the stars in the night sky beyond." He also testified to Spanish Air Force investigators that he could see two figures inside, working at consoles that were mounted on a metal platform occupying the lower third of the sphere. He said they dressed in red. The doctor and driver witnessed the sphere fill up with "bluish smoke," which appeared to expand the sphere to the size of approximately a 20-story building. The huge object then rose into the air and flew off in the direction of Tenerife. Several other less sensational sighting events were reported in the intervening two or so years, until 1979.

Most of the following incidents occurred on Tenerife, but 1979 also featured strange, perplexing events all over the Canaries. We are primarily concerned with the strange animal deaths that occurred, but as you will see, other possibly related events i.e., UFO and craft sightings may be connected with the unexplained animal deaths.

A spectacular UFO sighting kicked off the events of 1979 and the light was visible from at least three of the larger islands—Grand Canary, Tenerife and Gomera. It was observed by hundreds of witnesses on March 5, 1979 at about 8:00 P.M. Descriptions varied depending on the witness' vantage point, but observations included descriptions of the light/object "cylindrical," "pyramid-shaped" or "cup-shaped," plus some witnesses mentioned the light left a "definite, V-shaped wake." Motorists complained of headlights and engines failing as the object appeared. According to the *National Enquirer* of Lantana, Florida (July 24, 1979), the Spanish government launched a "top secret" investigation into the incident.

About seven weeks later the unexplained animal deaths began, on the nights of April 30-May 1 and May 2-3 on the island of Tenerife, near the town of Taco.

Six trained, ferocious German shepherd guard dogs were enclosed on the grounds of a factory. On two occasions, on the morning of [May] 1st and 3rd, one of the dogs was found dead outside their enclosure. There were no tracks, no evidence of struggle and no sign of bleeding. However, each dog had a hole in its chest, through which it was thought the heart and lungs had been removed. The Tenerife Department of Health Services was not interested in investigating, as the killings were considered to be the work of "human hands." The speculation was that a "religious cult" might have sought the heart and blood for use in rituals. Later in the first half of May, near Icod (still in the Taco area), the carcasses of two goats were discovered. According to the account in the newspaper *Diario De Avisos*, both goats were beheaded and exsanguinated. Then, during the same period of time, in the Guamasa area, a hog was discovered disfigured with its liver "seeming in very bad state" and the carcass was reportedly missing some "viscera." Police said that the hog was in a condition similar to the dogs at Taco. Again there was no sign of blood. Then, near Garachico, beheaded carcasses of rabbits and goats were discovered. A veterinarian at Los Silos thought dogs might have been responsible and he doubted that the beheadings were related to the Taco killings. Back on Tenerife, on a ranch at Puerto de la Cruz, a few banana trees were found broken, reportedly as though something had damaged them from the air.[9]

The staff of *Diario De Avisos* ascertained that the Guardia Civil (police) conducted "intensive investigations" into the animal killings, but downplayed the reports to reassure the public and "diminish the importance of the incidents." And the newspaper *La Provincia* summarized these first reports by stating: "the circumstances which surround these strange happenings (extraction of organs from the bodies, removal of blood, lack of signs of violence) could indicate that the deaths were caused by something well prepared and with scientific interest." *La Provincia* also reported that in early to mid May reports came in of a purple rainfall on the town of Estrasburgo (on Grand Canary Island), and in February a blue rain had been reported in Lyon. How colorful!

Wallabies, Cookie Cutters and More Mutes

Shooting to mid March in our unfolding 1979 timeline, a very unusual report was filed on March 13, 1979 from the Cornwall, England town of Newquay. According to media reports, local zookeepers reported discovering a series of unexplained animal deaths when three ducks, a goose, a swan and *two baby wallabies* (figure 3) were discovered dead at the zoo—apparently in a mutilated condition. According to the report, "radiation was present" and the deaths "[were] linked with recent sightings of UFOs in the area" One month later, another rare and decidedly weird wallaby attack would be reported in the Jackson, Mississippi zoo. (see below)[10]

On March 16, 1979 on the Pine Ridge Reservation near Kyle, South Dakota, a female cow was discovered mutilated and investigators claimed to have discovered helicopter "skid marks" near the carcass.[11]

Then, the reports jumped back to the west when on March 26, 1979 Huerfano County, Colorado rancher Sergio Abila reported a bloodless mutilation on his ranch near Red Wing. Abila's wife, Dora, told Animal Mutilation Probe Director David Perkins that the udder had been removed "as if by a cookie cutter." The cow had just given birth to a male calf three days prior and the calf was found near the dead mother, but evidently none of the other 150 head on the ranch were harmed.[12]

Several cattle died in the weeks that followed the disabling accident at the Three Mile Island nuclear plant in Pennsylvania in March of 1979. Nineteen cattle died on a farm four-and-a-half miles from the plant and two cows died on a farm three miles away. The state Agriculture Department reported that laboratory autopsies and tests indicated that "most died of complications in calving and two suffered infections of the uterus."

There are rumors making the rounds to the effect that the federal government brought psychics to the plant to see if they could pick up indications of sabotage, and that some of the cattle in the area that died were in fact mutilated. Interesting, but unsubstantiated.[13]

The following spring 1979 reports were documented by David Perkins, Tom Adams/Project Stigma network, and Tommy Blann.

First one, then a second Torrance County, New Mexico mutilation of a five-year-old cow was reported around March 28th. Investigating sheriff Bobby Chavez reported that clamp marks had been found on the hind legs suggesting that the animal may have been dropped back in the corner of the corral where it was found. Inside the corral, 25 feet away, were "tripod tracks or markings." Orange lights had been reportedly seen in the area around the ranch.

On April 5th UFO reports descended back onto Rio Arriba County at Santa Clara Pueblo, New Mexico when a "large triangular UFO was spotted by two tribal policemen." Three nights later, a "silent aircraft" was seen and reported "spotlighting" cows near Dulce.

On April 11, 1979, *fourteen wallabies* were killed in the Jackson, Mississippi zoo. The cause of death was thought to be "wild dog" attacks, but in light of the previous UK case, I can't help but wonder. Is there a correlation between these wallaby cases?

A Clark County, Kansas rancher reported a cow mutilated, and the next day, April 12, 1979, two jets out of White Sands, New Mexico disappeared while on training mission. Reports were filed in Walters, Oklahoma of "wild dogs attacking area cattle."

April 14th or 15th a bovine, sex unknown, was discovered mutilated on the Pine Ridge Indian Reservation in southwest South Dakota. An earlier case on the reservation had evidently occurred in mid March, near Kyle, but the latest report featured a cow that was found with its udder and genitals removed. A few days later a similar case occurred in the same area, but in addition, the tongue was discovered excised. "A helicopter had been heard but not seen and a series of skid-like tracks were found in the snow near one mute site. The third mute then occurred on that mid-April weekend near the town of Pine Ridge." This was the fifth mutilation on the Pine Ridge Indian Reservation.

On April 16, 1979 at 9:30 P.M., Air Force security guard Lt. Stone "disappeared from Kirtland AFB in Albuquerque, New Mexico." Coincidentally, a few hours later at 1 A.M., amateur astronomer Dave Darling sighted a large cigar-shaped object close to the crater Isidorus, near the Sea of Nectar, while observing the moon with a 12.5-inch reflector telescope. He reported that the object was "...about ten miles in length, and 1-1/2 miles in diameter. [S]ilvery metallic, casting a distinct shadow onto the lunar surface.. [It] landed about fifty miles from the sunset terminator..."

On April 20, 1979, U.S. Senator Harrison Schmitt, hosted the first Multi-State Mutilation Conference in Albuquerque, New Mexico and a Regina, New Mexico rancher reported to Rio Arriba officials that his cow had been discovered mutilated. Let the fun begin!

The Albuquerque/Harrison Schmitt Conference

Texas mutilation investigator Tommy Blann and Ft. Worth *Star* reporter/investigative author Jim Marrs flew west from Texas to attend the conference in Albuquerque. Blann and Marrs took notes, networked and paid special attention to the proceedings, as did presenters David Perkins and Tom Adams. First let's hear Blann's analysis:

> The conference was held to gather as much significant data as possible from lawmen and investigators throughout the U.S., and to try and develop a systematic approach to this phenomenon, with the FBI acting as a centralized database. It was attended by a broad set of participants, including federal, state and local law enforcement officials. Also in attendance were a gamut of other interests ranging from scientists to corporate executives, state representatives, private investigators, motion picture producers, brand stock inspectors, ranchers, ufologists and others.
>
> It was the hope of all that this conference would bring forth a concentrated effort by all those concerned, so that the long sought-after answers to this mystery would be forthcoming. Many veteran lawmen who attended had become frustrated and disillusioned with the way things were being handled by state agencies in their home states, and the fact that some of therm were being made to look like a bunch of fools. One of the main problems suffered by these dedicated lawmen was the lack of a national coordinated effort with the proper funding so that samples could be procured and submitted to laboratories. They were literally left on their own, struggling to obtain data with whatever resources were available, and sometimes spending many off-duty hours investigating it. Statements being made by UFO researchers and the press didn't help matters, and caused some investigators to keep a low profile in their investigations. Politics also reared its ugly head in the mutilation phenomenon, thus making the problem that much more difficult to solve. In his opening statements, Senator Schmitt said:
>
> There are few activities more dangerous than an unsolved pattern of crime. There is always the potential for such crimes to escalate in frequency and severity if allowed to go unsolved and unpunished. Such a dangerous pattern of crime is the mutilation killing of thousands of cattle,

horses, and other animals over the past several years throughout many states. These crimes are obviously continuing despite the excellent efforts of state and local law enforcement officials and the growing publicity the mutilation killings have received. In the past five years, and probably longer, in at least fifteen states animals have been killed and systematically mutilated for no apparent purpose, by persons unknown… One of the most extraordinary facts of this problem is that the group or groups responsible for the mutilation killings have shown almost unprecedented discipline. There have been no leaks or informants to assist the state and local law enforcement officials in their investigative efforts… now the economic losses suffered by individuals probably have reached two-and-a-half million dollars or more nationally."

After his statements, the Senator presented the forum of speakers. Topics ranged from types of predators and scavengers that could create what may look like mutilations, to environmental testing by an unknown agency, to mystery helicopters and UFOs. Unfortunately, very little hard data was presented. Some law enforcement officials felt that the conference had become a circus of UFO believers, and backed out from giving a presentation. After the conference, a special meeting was held between law enforcement officials and investigators. There was still hope that something beneficial would come out of the conference, but these hopes would later be dashed when a special LEAA-funded probe directed by former FBI agent would take center stage.[14]

Tommy Blann goes on to describe Schmitt's thinking about the mutilation conference he organized in an article and interview that was conducted with Schmitt three years later by the *Rio Grande Sun* newspaper:

In the summer of 1982, U.S. Senator Harrison "Jack" Schmitt of New Mexico, who co-sponsored the 1979 mutilation conference in Albuquerque, was interviewed *by the Rio Grande Sun* of Espanola, New Mexico, the principal newspaper of mute-plagued Rio Arriba County. The Senator reiterated his concern over the mutilation problem, his belief that "individuals" (humans, that is, not predatory animals) were responsible for at least some mutilations, and he discussed the "mystery helicopters" as a relevant aspect of the problem. Schmitt had been criticized for holding the 1979 conference at public expense. But the SUN cites Schmitt aide Wayne Ciddio as pointing out that the conference was held in a public building and "cost no money to speak of" while Kenneth Rommel received LEAA grant on the order of $50,000 for his "investigation."

When questioned about the few mutilations that had been reported in Northern New Mexico in the spring and summer of 1982 and whether this renewed activity might justify another conference, Schmitt replied:

> I think that depends upon whether a pattern of mutilations starts to develop again. Clearly right after that (1979) conference we found that there was almost no mutilation activity in the state of New Mexico. So that if nothing else, it appears that the conference had the purpose of protecting the property of many small ranchers and farmers for that period of time. Now if these individuals have returned to New Mexico and are continuing to violate federal law and state law, then clearly it would warrant…

Schmitt at that point was cut off and interrupted by the reporters, Tom and Lester Kinsolving, but he later returned to the subject of the 1979 conference:

> …As a consequence of that conference, or seemingly as a consequence of it, the mutilations stopped for a number of years [This is not the case, as we will see]. And I see nothing wrong with that cost-benefit analysis. Every one of those cows was worth several hundred dollars, and there were many, may reported instances of the loss of cows.

Schmitt was asked how he managed to "keep a straight face" at the 1979 conference:

> I always keep a straight face when the property and potentially the lives of New Mexicans are involved. Clearly, whatever the explanation of the cattle mutilations has been or is—or explanations, plural, it has involved the loss of property by individual ranchers and farmers. [They are] small ranchers and farmers for the most part and they had asked me to try to do something about this. The first step was to get the Justice Department to admit that there was a federal jurisdiction which they didn't want to admit under the Carter administration, but finally did, and then agree to have a joint hearing conference on this subject to air the issues publicly, and then to see where we would proceed from there.
>
> The federal authorities have been very reluctant to step forward and exercise their jurisdiction in this matter. I don't know why, unless they just didn't want to be dragged into something they don't think they can explain. But clearly the rustling of cattle and the killing of cattle represents a crime in the state of New Mexico and if committed on federal property represents a federal crime. And the law is very clear on that, no matter what the Justice Department may have originally said.

The article ends with Schmitt remarking that he knows of "no definitive evidence" leading to whatever forces are behind the mutilations, and, to Schmitt's mind, there has simply been "no full explanation."

Ex-astronaut and moon-walker Schmitt clearly had something else to worry about—his reelection campaign to retain his U.S. Senate seat. His opponent was New Mexico Attorney General Jeff Bingaman—one of his campaign slogans was "What on earth has Jack Schmitt done for New Mexico?" or something to that effect. In a campaign that got a little nasty toward the end, Bingaman won.[15]

Less than a week after the Schmitt conference, the mutilators reminded investigators that they were still interested in New Mexico, when on April 29th a pregnant cow was discovered dead and mutilated near Dilia, and reported to Guadalupe County law enforcement.

Latin America, Fools Gold and the King Ranch

Early May 1979 found rarely reported Central American livestock deaths being claimed in Panama. On May 10th livestock were reported "missing" in Colombia, South America after UFO sightings were reported in the area where the cattle were apparently stolen. Also that May 10th, a cow was reported mutilated in El Paso County, New Mexico.

AMP Director David Perkins visited the office of the Santa Clara Pueblo Tribal Police on Friday, May 11th. The pueblo is located on the east border of the Los Alamos National Laboratory. He had been monitoring UFO and mutilation reports in the region and wanted to find out more about these reports. Tom Adams noted this trip in *Stigmata #7*:

> He inspected their log-book which cited numerous reports of "unidentified aircraft" in November and December, 1978. That night, a mutilation occurred on Santa Clara land and though tribal authorities tried to keep the matter quiet, Gail Olson of the *Rio Grande Sun* was tipped off about it. Even then, Tribal Police Chief Roger Naranjo said the cow in question died giving birth, and he asked that no one come out to look at it. But investigators did "boldly go" to the site on May 13th and again on the 14th. The rectum and genitals were neatly excised from the pregnant cow and a one-inch hole had been cut in the side of the still-attached udder. The calf was visible inside the mother. The cow lay on its left side, with its face in a running creek. (figure 4) The carcass was scratched and branches of a tree just above the site were broken. Hair from the cow's tail marked a trail from the tree to the creek.
>
> David Perkins reports that a light meter belonging to a photographer would not work at the site, but functioned perfectly a mile away. The brakes went out on the investigators' car as they drove from the scene.

At that time an unmarked, twin-engine airplane circled low over the departing car three times.[16]

Perhaps some ironic trickster decided to have fun at Perkins' expense. On the day after Perkins left, May 12, 1979 another mute was reported—again near the Santa Clara Pueblo where he had just visited.

The mutilation reports moved northeast, back into Huerfano County, Colorado, when on May 19th a *high-dollar, prize rodeo seed bull* named *Fool's Gold* was discovered missing his valuable jewels. The 1,300-pound bovine was Mr. and Mrs. John King's prize bull. The ol' fool had been fighting with other the bulls, so the big boy had been moved on May 10th to a remote pasture out on his own. A couple of days later he was apparently attacked and mutilated. It is important to note that *registered seed bulls and papered breeding stock are seldom targeted by the mutilators*. The vast majority of cattle are simple hybrids—not top dollar investments of professional cattle breeders.

This particular report is highly intriguing as are the Kings' claim of *over 50 head of cattle being stolen* back in 1973 and another 50 cattle *stolen* in 1975. Included was another valuable seed bull. I wonder if these Huerfano ranching "Kings" were related to the Alamosa "Kings" of Snippy fame, or were friends with Emilio Lobata from Chama Canyon, Colorado? I doubt these Kings are still in business.

Thanks to David Perkins and Tom Adams for this following "King" ranch report:

> A ranch hand discovered the mutilated carcass on Saturday, May 19, [1979]. Mr. King estimated that the animal had been dead for five to seven days when found. There were no tracks, nor any signs that predators had touched the carcass. AMP Director David Perkins, who lives in western Huerfano County, investigated. At the time of his report to us, he had not been able to travel to the very remote pasture where the carcass lay (due to rainy weather). From viewing photos of the animal and from interviews conducted with sheriff's investigators and with Mrs. King (Mr. King was [out] on the rodeo circuit), Perkins reports that the condition of the carcass included the following details:
>
> (1) The rectum had been "cored" with a perfectly round cut with no blood in evidence.
> (2) One testicle had been removed. A grapefruit-size hole in the groin was evident.
> (3) There was a burned circle 1.5-inches in diameter on the thigh of the right hind leg.
> (4) The left ear had been removed with an incision that extended into

the head.

(5) Splattered blood was on the bull's neck and chest – no other blood was present.

(6) The carcass attracted no predators – including flies.

(7) The left eye was intact; the right eye appeared either "popped" or missing.

Sheriff Harold Martinez said he also noted a small amount of blood coming from a corner of the mouth and he assumed that the tongue was probably missing, though the mouth was not opened for examination.

This was the third mutilation in John King's herd, the other two coming during the siege of 1975. They've had problems with missing cattle as well. In the fall of 1973, 50 head disappeared from a ranch they leased in Wyoming. Another 50 head turned up missing from the Colorado ranch in the fall of 1975. Then, in the spring of 1978, "Mr. Charlie," another prize rodeo bull, vanished from his pasture. Rustlers? Perhaps, though the Kings have no evidence.

On May 24, 1979, an AMP investigative team drove to the King Ranch to interview Mrs. King. Near the ranch entrance they observed a dark green or black helicopter (with no markings that could be discerned through field glasses) which flew from the south and passed over the King house, flying northeast. The craft was flying at roughly 1,500 feet and, as it passed within one-half mile to one mile of the AMP team, they could hear no sound from the chopper. Mrs. King, at the house, did not hear or see the craft as it passed directly overhead.[17]

On May 24, 1979, another mutilation was reported by a local livestock removal worker in El Paso County, Colorado. He told David Perkins (and later Linda Howe who interviewed him for her film *A Strange Harvest*) (figure 5) that he had picked up many dead cows that appeared to have been disfigured unnaturally. If these are real but unreported mutilation cases, the total number of possible mutes may be much higher than the quoted figures in media reports:

> Drexel Lawson, who runs such a service in Colorado Springs, reports seeing "dozens" of mutilated carcasses, but few are reported to authorities. At least half a dozen cases have occurred in El Paso County since May 1, 1979, according to Animal Mutilation Probe investigator David Perkins. Lawson told Perkins that he had picked up 20 mutilated carcasses in the last two years—in El Paso and Lincoln Counties. Other livestock removal services have reportedly picked up mutilated carcasses. For instance, in the Roswell, New Mexico area, several mutes were picked up but, to our knowledge, these were officially unreported

or at least unpublicized.[18]

The mystery choppers were still being reported that spring of 1979. A mystery chopper was reported flying east out of Huerfano County on May 24th and also the following morning. On the morning May 25, 1979, Calhan, Colorado rancher Wendel Hertel witnessed at least two, possibly more helicopters hovering over rangeland near his ranch. Thinking this that flight activity was suspicious he became extra vigilant, and later that afternoon he went back out to check on his cattle. Everything appeared to be normal. Early the next morning, May 26th, much to his consternation, he found the mutilated carcass of his prize cow. Said the AMP report quoting Tom Adams:

> "$1,000 Geldzieh cow (a rare crossbreed of German and English strains). The udder had been cleanly removed. There were no tracks or anything else on the undisturbed ground, and there was reportedly no blood nor body fluids in the carcass." Tom Adams pointed out that during a "several-week period in late spring, there were numerous accounts of dark helicopters flying around ranches in El Paso County."[19]

Ground Zero in Arkansas and New Mexico

In 1979, Arkansas may have earned the dubious distinction of being the hardest-hit state. Mutilation reports were filed in at least 15 Arkansas counties: Conway, Cleburne, Franklin, Crawford, Lonoke, Jackson, Little River, Prairie, Faulkner, White, Newton, Marion, Stone, Van Buren and Washington. These many reports are too numerous to recount here, but Tom Adams carefully documented the '79 Arkansas wave for Project Stigma—paying special attention to appraisals by veterinarians and professional law enforcement officials:

> [T]hese incidents included a 10-day-old pig seemingly-classically mutilated in Marion County, at least five horse-slashing incidents in Stone County (likely not classic mutilations) and at least three helicopter/mute cases. There is not complete unanimity among Arkansans concerning the authenticity of their mutilations. State Police Sgt. Doug Fogley, specifically assigned to investigate mutilations, told Project Stigma that he doubts that any classic mutilations have occurred in Arkansas in 1979. He does feel, however, that authentic cases occurred in 1978, especially in Benton County.
>
> As far as the 1979 events are concerned, we have little to go on at this point beyond the fact that most of the recent cases, as reported in the press, sound "classic." From these accounts come such comments as:
>
> "…surgical, perhaps super-surgical precision." (Little River County mute report)

"…Veterinarian Gary White said the missing parts were professionally removed with what appeared to be surgical instruments." (*The Spectator*, Ozark, AR, 6-7-79)

"…surgical precision." (Crawford County Sheriff Trellon Ball)

"…surgically." (Franklin County Sheriff Bob Pritchard)

"The best we can tell, this is the same quality work as in the northwest part of the state. This may not be the same people, but it's the same kind of job as in Benton County." (State Police Investigator J.R. Howard, regarding a Cleburne County mutilation.)

"There's no way anybody just like us could do this with a knife. It might have been a cult or something. But they used something like a surgical knife and knew how to do it." (Mrs. Bobby King, Crawford County)

An Arkansas source questioned by Project Stigma feels that publicity following the Albuquerque conference (an *Arkansas Gazette* article and a four-part TV news report by a Little Rock station) prompted hoaxers and sleazo-warpos to perpetrate pseudo-mutes throughout much of Arkansas. Indeed, although many cases appeared "classic" on the surface, others were reported as "sloppy," cruel and decidedly and contrastingly unprofessional.[20]

Hazen, Arkansas rancher Reverend Charlie Perry discovered a mutilated calf on May 28, 1979, and this case, like many others, was simply noted by law enforcement who were being swamped by reports from all over the state. May 30, 31st and June 1st, three "slashed" horses were reported by Onia, Arkansas rancher, Alan Nixon. These were unusual, atypical mutilations *as the animals were discovered still alive.* Two days later a bull calf was reported mutilated in nearby Cleburne County, near Greers Ferry.

On May 30, 1979, the mutilators were extremely busy. Three different cases around North America were reported almost simultaneously. One targeted a six-year-old cow near Calhan, Colorado, in El Paso County. The unfortunate cow had just given birth three days prior. A bull calf was discovered that same day mutilated southwest of Hanna, Alberta, Canada missing its tail, rectum, penis, scrotum, lips and an ear.

The following day, Stacy Fuchs reported three dark, unmarked helicopters "playing around and doing figure 8's at low levels," and that same day, 17 dairy cows were "struck by lightning" and killed near Piedmont, South Dakota.

On June 2, 1979 a cow was reported mutilated in Crawford County, near Mulberry, Arkansas, and two days later they hit a ranch near Alix, Arkansas in Franklin County.

On June 6, 1979, a three-month-old female pig was discovered "cut in half around the mid-section with a neat bloodless cut." All the internal organs were missing and there appeared to be no blood. Pork was evidently on the menu that day, for another pig was discovered mutilated back in Arkansas in the Rhea Valley. This was a ten-day-old piglet with its right eye, tongue and rectum "neatly cut out." The other piglets were unharmed.

The mutilators ratcheted up their fiendish work in Arkansas through the rest of June. On June 7th a female calf was reported mutilated near Searcy in White County. Three days later a Hereford bull was targeted near Hazen in Prairie County, Arkansas and the same day they hit a Calhan, Colorado ranch again. Then they set up shop for several weeks. On June 14th, in the Washington County town of Farmington, Arkansas, a 100-pound calf was hit and two days later Norfolk, Arkansas farmer Harry Miller heard a "commotion" in his pasture around 5:30 A.M. Miller went out and discovered his cows scattered, frightened and upset. Evidently, a three-month-old heifer had been killed and was missing one ear and the intestines were "neatly cut out" and left at the site. Also on June 14th a local news report stated that a cow had been reported mutilated in Jackson County, Arkansas

Eddy County, New Mexico then became a target on June 18, 1979. A Carlsbad rancher reported to authorities that three goats and 12 chickens were mutilated near the site where four horse mutilations had occurred in January. Two of the goats were pregnant and one was a kid goat. Puncture wounds were found in the throats of the goats and their udders had been removed. The dead chickens were evidently found in the pen "stacked up with a lot of care." That same day back in Lonoke County, Arkansas, two head of cattle, sex unspecified, were reported dead and disfigured.

We see an apparent three-day lull before the next flurry of cases commenced on June 21st in Rio Arriba County, New Mexico. A Coyote, New Mexico farmer reported that he had discovered a mutilated cow on his ranch. Three days later, between 2:00 A.M. and 5:00 A.M., witnesses in Santa Fe, New Mexico reported three UFOs flying around the area. The following morning, a bull was found mutilated 15 miles northwest of Walsenburg in Huerfano County, Colorado 100 miles to the north. David Perkins heard that two more suspected mutilations (a cow and a calf) were reportedly found near Gardner on the 29th and another mute was reported near Tres Piedras, New Mexico. The night of June 27th, three days after the prior UFO report, six UFOs were seen around Santa Fe. The objects were reported to authorities. Officials said the lights seemed to head north toward Colorado.

It was during this late June time period that a rare eastern Canadian mutilation case was reported to authorities. The case occurred on Ile d'Orleans (or Island of Orleans, in St. Lawrence River, near Quebec City) and featured a young bull found with its rectum and the genitals missing. In an interesting atypical twist, burns were found on the carcass that some investigators thought may have been caused by "naptha."[21]

Controversy over claims by Nova Scotia farmer Werner Boch still continues to this day. Boch estimates that he has lost well over 50 head of cattle from 1975 through 2012. Space does not permit a full recounting of his claims, but he has amassed a sizeable body of suggestive evidence to indicate his farm has been targeted by two-legged varmints intent on driving him out of business. He has a pending Canadian court case as I write this.

Back to the herd: On the night of July 2, 1979, Santa Fe, New Mexico experienced an odd 15-hour long power blackout. That same day Animal Mutilations Probe Director David Perkins investigated cases northwest of Santa Fe, where he found:

> …two reported mutes in the Regina area [around the Sandoval and Rio Arriba County border. Perkins] also learned that perhaps 12 other [mutilations] had occurred nearby in the last year or so. The two mutilations were uncovered by campers Bob Moench and Frank Murphy. They took photos which Perkins later described as appearing "classic." One of the animals was apparently killed on April 20th, the date of the Albuquerque mutilation conference. Then, on Tuesday, July 3rd, rancher Charlie Schmitz found one of his cows mutilated north of Regina. The anus, udder and genitals were missing.[22]

On July 6th a 16-month-old heifer was reported mutilated back in Conway County, Arkansas and another was reported the following day in Franklin County, Arkansas right near Interstate 40. These regions would be hard hit later that fall.

Then our phantom prairie surgeons evidently decided they needed to visit Dewey, Oklahoma. A mutilated carcass of a cow was discovered on the Oscar King ranch and reported to officials. The female, "not the first in Washington County," was found missing both eyes and the udder had been removed "in an almost perfect circle." No blood was in evidence at the mute site. I cannot find references to other Washington County cases.

On July 9th Bert Withelm, a District Wildlife Manager based in Saguache, Colorado, found a mutilated bull elk near Saguache. He immediately wrote a letter to David Perkins and described the horrific find:

> A bull elk was found on Sargents Mesa July 9, 1979. On investigation I found what appeared to be a definite mutilation. The elk was killed approximately two days before I found it. It apparently had been *shot in the right eye with a varmint type rifle.* [my emphasis] The rectum was removed, both testicles removed and parts of the antlers which were still in velvet. All cuts were made with a sharp implement.

It is interesting to note that just up and over the Continental Divide from Sargents Mesa is Blue Mesa Reservoir where two separate piles of dead elk were found, drowned, 50 yards apart on May 10, 1979. Sixty-two animals in total were discovered and 29 of them had been pregnant. The elk apparently fell through the ice sometime during the prior December, but two mass drownings next to each other is highly improbable.

The final wave of unexplained animal deaths in the Canary Islands would commence later in October, but on July 10th, the newspaper *El Dia* (Santa Cruz de Tenerife) reported a weird event that was experienced by pilots of a commercial flight into the Canaries. It may or may not be important or relevant to the wave of mutilations:

> The crew of an aircraft on a flight from a European city to Tenerife registered a surprising and seemingly unexplainable action of the aircraft's radar, which, in mid-flight, gave strange signals in regard to something occurring in the vicinity of the aircraft. Although the causes of the astonishment of the crew have not yet been determined, the possibility that the occurrence might have been due to the presence of a fleet of "UFOs" has not been completely rejected. There are also theories regarding the actions as possibly being the result of some very peculiar climatological conditions.[23]

We'll revisit the Canaries in a minute. Meanwhile, the mute teams back in Arkansas were unfinished with their mayhem as the state's case totals mounted. On July 10th a two-week-old calf was reported mutilated in Faulkner County, Arkansas after another mystery chopper sighting by the rancher. The farmer told investigators he had heard about another mute/chopper case in nearby Martinsville, Arkansas that had occurred "a few weeks ago." This additional case had not been reported to County authorities.

On July 14th the first official July 1979 Nebraska case was filed when a mutilated calf was reported in Madison County. The following day brought the first "official" summer 1979 Texas case when a strange report was filed in Bexar County. Rancher Roy Martinez reported finding a young bull mutilated. But there's a devilish possible twist with this one:

> A young bull was killed and mutilated south of San Antonio on July 15th. The genitals and anus were intact—except that the tail had been cleanly cut off. Both eyes were gone, and there was a puncture wound in the jugular vein. Cowboys in a line shack *25 yards away heard nothing that night.* [my emphasis] Bull owner, Roy Martinez, and his family have seen cultists meeting and dancing around bonfires in nearby river bottoms. Remember the film, "Race With The Devil?" Filmed in the same area, ironically enough.[24]

Two days later in Pierce County, Nebraska, two mutilated calves were found with identical wounds. Both were missing the genitals, one ear, both eyes and an oval patch of hide from the hip. Sheriff Bill House observed, "…this is probably related to the one in Madison County. These animals have the same identical marks and clean cuts. It has to be a bunch of weirdos."

Over the course of four days, there was a flurry of activity in Arkansas. Cases were reported on July 18th, 19th, 20th and 21st in Van Buren County near the towns of Scotland and Cleveland and also in Conway County. All these end-of-summer Arkansas cases were reported from locales in or near areas that had already been targeted earlier that spring and summer.

New Mexico UFO sightings continued to be reported that summer as well. On July 22nd witnesses in Lordsburg, New Mexico reported three UFOs flying overhead at 9:20 P.M., and coincidentally, the following day (July 23rd) another Huerfano County, Colorado mutilation case was reported up north near Walsenburg. David Perkins investigated and noted in his field log:

> [I] found Brubaker's cow muted. Tire tracks in field one mile away. Note: On [July] 21, blue pick-up truck with camper seen "cruising" mute area. That evening, three machine shops in Walsenburg "ransacked." Owners couldn't determine what (if anything) was stolen. On [July] 22nd, vehicle carrying several figures wearing white robes seen near Walsenburg.[25]

About this time in late July, David Perkins noticed that travelers headed south out of the San Luis Valley on State Highway 285 were greeted by two fresh deer heads unceremoniously mounted on the "Welcome to New Mexico" sign (deer are out of season in July). Yellow cattle crossing signs would be adorned with stenciled UFOs over the top of the cow image later in the 1980s and '90s. (figure 6)

A weird news report was filed on July 30th in England when a farm family claimed they saw UFOs and encountered silver-suited aliens. Shortly after they alleged that, several of their cattle disappeared from their farm. I have yet to find corroboration of this "news story" but it supports some who think that aliens are stalking cattle herds in the UK and elsewhere.

But the reports continued to pour in from all over Arkansas. On July 31st a 1,200-pound bull was discovered mutilated in Little River County. This latest case was found near the site of where another mute that had been reported "two years ago."

That end of July 1979 found rumors of mutilations beginning in western Canada. Outside of Saskatoon a quarter horse had allegedly been attacked and was reportedly found with its tail and ear hacked off. Fortunately, in another rare case of equine luck, this horse managed to escape its attackers and was found alive and kicking by its owner. Then it happened again in early August when two horses were attacked and discovered each with its tail, manes and one ear cut off. They didn't survive. There were also rumors of other similar horse attacks in the Saskatoon area, but those remain unconfirmed. This early activity appeared to be a prelude to an extensive wave of classic cattle mutilation cases that would sweep with a fury across Alberta and Saskatchewan in the fall of 1979.

But the mutilators were still unsatisfied with the results from Arkansas, as they appeared to be focused on Faulkner County through the remainder of August. Nine cases were reported in Faulkner County between August 4th and August 11, 1979 with another on the 26th. An additional mutilation was reported from Van Buren County, which was allegedly the sixth case reported from this county located just north of hard-hit Faulkner County. A silver helicopter and a chopper with "an orange tail" were also reported flying around near the Faulkner County mutilation sites.

In a seemingly inexplicable coincidence, once again 17 cows were killed by a "lightning bolt" near Piedmont, South Dakota on August 11, 1979. This happened three and-a-half-miles away from where the 17 cattle were struck in May. What are the odds?[26]

A prize Simmental bull was found mutilated on August 12, 1979, near Calgary, Alberta. A mystery chopper had also been sighted previously. The *Calgary Herald* made mention of other mutes in the area on August 10th, 11th and 13th. A six-year-old bull named Blackie, valued at upwards of $45,000, was discovered missing its rectum, most of the penis, testicles, left ear and tip of the tongue. There was no sign of a struggle. How many men would it take to tackle one of these huge animals? (figure 7) Former Calgary policeman Don Seney investigated the case and told reporters, "At first I thought of a coyote, but all the cuts were clean, exactly like a knife cut... the nature of the cuts show signs both of a surgical instrument and knowledge by whoever did this." [27]

On August 14th, in Little Rock, Arkansas, The Arkansas Mutilation Conference commenced and Tom Adams filed the following report:

> The mutilation furor in Arkansas led to a meeting in Little Rock on August 14, [1979]. Attending were humane society members (who have asked Governor Clinton to appoint an investigative task force) and representatives of various state agencies, including State Policeman Doug Fogley—plus Kenneth Rommel, head of the mute probe in New Mexico's First Judicial District. Rommel told the assemblage that "professionals" should investigate the Arkansas mutilations in the manner used to investigate homicides. He declined to discuss the specifics of any case with reporters. Fogley asked for news media cooperation, fearing the sensational headlines about mutes could bring "every kook

out of the woodwork."

Between August 11th and the time of the Little Rock meeting on the 14th, at least nine potential cow mutilations were reported in Faulkner and Conway Counties, immediately north and northwest of Little Rock. A silver helicopter was spotted in Faulkner County on the 10th and a blue unmarked chopper was seen near a Conway County mute site on the 12th. It was suggested that the former was a military craft headed to a nearby Titan II missile silo, but there has been no further word on whether that was substantiated. As with the reports of unmarked helicopters seen over missile fields during the mutilation outbreak in Montana in 1975 and 1976, the craft and their pilots were never identified.

On August 13th, two Conway County veterinarians, Drs. Norman Gray (President of the Arkansas Veterinary Medical Association) and Tom Brown, held a press conference in which they stated their opinion that the mutes in Conway County and elsewhere in Arkansas were the work of natural scavengers, primarily buzzards. They felt that the reason for the abundance of recent mutilation reports was simply that such reports were "fashionable right now…"

At a meeting in August, Arkansas Humane Association official B.J. Kready and others asked Arkansas Governor Bill Clinton to appoint a task force to study the mutilation problem. The governor provided meeting space for an informal group but refused to appoint the task force. By the time another meeting was held in October, the task force idea had "crumpled" and interest appeared to have long-since-peaked.[28]

Law enforcement officials were deeply divided as to the cause of the deaths and disfigurements of Arkansas livestock. Some thought that these cases were real strange, while others were convinced that this was all misidentified scavenger action. To prove their point, the following experiment was conducted by the Washington County Sheriff's Department:

In a controversial experiment in [Fayetteville, Arkansas] Washington County, sheriff's officers periodically photographed the carcass of a sick cow that had intentionally been "put to sleep" and left in a field. The officials involved claimed that the carcass had been attacked during the period by predators and the results looked like what had previously been thought of as a "classic" mutilation. After that September experiment, most officials and agencies wrote off the majority of the Arkansas mutes as predator-caused following natural deaths.

But the official experiment was not without its detractors. Dr. Gary White, an Ozark vet, said two carcasses he autopsied were *"done by someone skilled, someone with sharp instruments.*" [my emphasis] Former Benton County Deputy Don Rystrom (who investigated many northwest Arkansas mute cases and had one of his own animals victimized, and witnessed a helicopter-like UFO) called the experiment "a bunch of bullshit." …The concerted mute attack began to cease by Labor Day… there were numerous reports of unidentified helicopters near the time and location of mutilations in north central Arkansas, an area in which 18 missile sites are located, serviced by three helicopters which operate out of Little Rock Air Force Base.[29]

Aliens Shootin' and Mute'in

In an eerily similar detail that mirrors the early 1974 cases in Iowa and the early August 1975 San Luis Valley cases, the beginning of the fall 1979 wave in Canada featured cases where animals were discovered *shot to death by firearms and then mutilated*. During the end of the first week of August in the Brooks-Tilley area of Alberta, two cows and a steer were shot by a high-powered rifle and found with the "genitals mutilated."[30] Bestiality had been confirmed in a similar incident in this area in October 1978 and was also suspected in these cases. This extremely odd, sick motivation is also suspected in UK horse slasher cases from the 1990s. If true, there are some extremely perverse individuals walking around out there in the world that could use some serious help.

Marshall County, Minnesota probably experienced the UFO case of the year when on August 27th at approximately 2:00 A.M., law officer Val Johnson was allegedly "attacked" by a UFO that flew into his windshield, cracking it. Johnson claimed he experienced an episode of missing time. The damaged patrol car—left untouched—is currently on display in a local museum. The case has been featured in numerous television programs.

August 27, 1979 also found the mutilation reports returning to Perkins County, Nebraska when a cow was found dead and mutilated. Shortly before the animal was discovered, two unknown aircraft sightings were noted. Two choppers and a white plane were also seen and reported to authorities. Two mutes were reported in the Madrid area in late August-early September. Rancher Earl Nutt found a cow on August 27th and ascertained it had been dead for about 10-12 hours. "Although coyotes frequent the area, no predators [would] touch the carcass, from which was removed all of the meat from the shoulder blade to within eight-10 inches of the ear, plus the tongue."[31]

On August 28th Alberta, Canada became ground zero when an 800-pound steer was found with its penis and anus removed. This occurred on a ranch about five miles west of Disbury. During this same time period, two horse mutes were reported in neighboring Saskatchewan Province.

In a strange stand-alone report filed on September 3rd, a White House, Tennessee resident reported that a "Bigfoot creature" had killed dogs, sheep and pigs in the area. None of the animals were eaten.[32]

On September 7th the Nevada Test Site detonated a nuclear device, which in turn detonated a second bomb that had failed to explode in an earlier "test."

On September 9th, two mutilated cows were found and reported in Saskatchewan, Canada and on the following day a mute calf was discovered in Seward County, Nebraska. An interesting detail was the claim the animal was found with its "teeth clipped." It was a 300-pound, four-month-old Angus/Hereford cross heifer on the Clarence Ihde farm near Beaver Crossing.

> Ihde reported that the animal's top jaw was skinned back to the eyes, its tongue and several lower teeth had apparently been cut out and the lower jaw was skinned back to the throat: "Just the jawbones remained to the seen." State Patrol Investigator George Fauver said there was evidence of "man-made incisions," despite a University of Nebraska-Lincoln report which suggested that predators could be responsible. He added that the autopsy report showed that the animal's skull had been fractured and he said his other animals seemed "more scared for a few days."[33]

On September 11, 1979, a two-year-old heifer was reported mutilated near Truchas, New Mexico, and two days later a six-year-old Hereford cow was found with its tongue and udder missing. There was a suspicious large hole in rear that was probably due to scavengers. Another report was filed from the area on September 16, 1979.[34]

The following day, September 17th, a Danville, Iowa rancher reported a mutilated steer and a news report warned that recently a 'rustled' steer contains high levels of DES, a synthetic non-steroidal estrogen that is a controversial livestock supplement.

Alberta, Feedlot Demons and Canaries

Between September 21st and September 30, 1979 seven cattle mutilations were reported in Alberta, Canada. On the 23rd, a mutilated five-month-old female filly was found missing its mammary glands, groin skin, right eye, an ear and parts of the muzzle.

A *rare feedlot case* was reported on September 26th when a bull was discovered in a mutilated condition next to a feedlot, five miles northwest of Fort Macleod, Alberta. The heifer reportedly died of blackleg and was then dragged by feedlot staff into a nearby field. It was discovered the next day missing its vagina and a piece of one ear. It appeared "similar" to other Alberta mutes but was described as "fairly crude." The case was later designated by the RCMP as a "copy cat" mutilation performed by someone imitating the other "classic mutilations" that had occurred in the region.

Three Alberta bull mutilations were reported on October 1, 1979. The first was discovered about five miles from Elk Island National Park. The three-year-old bull had its genitals removed and was found with its "head folded under the carcass." The second case was reported from Rocky Mountain House.

The third case occurred near Tofield. The six-month-old Charolais-cross bull was found with its rectum, testicles and part of penis "neatly removed." The bladder was also removed. Investigators noted "no blood had been spilled" and the carcass was apparently bruised on the neck and shoulder, leading officials to surmise that the animal had suffered a broken neck. Constable Jim Warren told the press, "It was hard to believe at first, but you can't doubt it when you see one."[35]

The following day, October 2nd, the Neudorf area of Saskatchewan was targeted. A yearling Charolais was reported mutilated and a veterinarian was called out to examine the animal.

> The autopsy was performed by a Melville, Saskatchewan veterinarian, Dr. Cochrane [and] editor Dennis Corneau of the *Melville Advocate* obtained the following details about the autopsy from Staff Sergeant Don Buchanan of the Melville RCMP… The autopsy revealed the cow had suffered a rear attack of some nature in which its body had a large hole in the skin just ventral to the vagina. The vulvar lips of the cow's vagina were absent. The hole in the skin was heart-shaped and about nine centimeters by eight centimeters in size. The area bordering the wound was slightly irregular and rough in appearance. A small number of "v-shaped" cuts varying in length from three millimeters to nine millimeters with their base located toward the opening were present at the periphery of the wound. Certain organs were missing and examination revealed irregular lacerations in the tissue edges. A number of smooth-edged areas around the wound and inside were also found. After performing the autopsy, Dr. Cochrane determined that the wounds had been caused perhaps by a coyote or other carnivorous animal.
>
> Editor Cornea writes that the police and other observers at the site were not satisfied with the autopsy findings, so samples were sent to the Saskatchewan Provincial Veterinary Laboratory in Regina for analysis. There, Dr. M.S. Swendrowski concurred with Dr. Cochrane's opinion.[36]

Three separate mutilation reports were filed on October 4, 1979 in Alberta. (figure 8) The first, about 20 miles west of Claresholm was a five-year-old cow with an ear, genitals, udder and part of the tongue removed. The heart appeared to have been removed through a 20-cm hole in the chest. The hole was on left side and no blood was found at the site. The second October 4th was filed from Nanton—a yearling steer was discovered missing its anus, penis, sheath and scrotum. The third report came from the aptly named, Blood Reserve, about 20 miles west of Lethbridge. This report featured an interesting claim of a flotilla of UFOs seen by 14-year-old Newton Long Time Squirrel. The boy reported watching "nine bright lights in a circle on or near the ground a quarter-mile from his house." The lights took off apparently, though Newton did not actually see them rise. The next thing he knew, the lights were airborne and they suddenly zipped one by one over his head, without a sound. Newton's elders found a cow "with a hole where its heart had been" where the lights had first been spotted.[37]

Starting at the beginning of October 1979, strange animal deaths began to be reported around towns on Tenerife Island—located in the Canary Islands. These reports were investigated by *Diario De Avisos* reporter Jorge Bethencourt, and here is the first of several translated excerpts from his articles. The first story was published on October 4, 1979:

Eight Sheep with Their Blood Drained in Barranco Grande

In a small corral, a plastic bag covers the bodies of three sheep. The bodies present the same symptoms that the other victims (there have been a total of eight) did: circular holes in the sides, no blood inside the bodies and no signs of violence around. The account of Antonio Hernandez Cubias: "My father was alerted by the sheep bellowing and the dog barking. He went to the door but didn't go out because the dog quit barking as soon as he saw a familiar person. Mr. Hernandez went back to sleep. The next morning he went to the corral to find his three sheep were dead. The bodies were on the ground in a symmetric line, two of them with their feet against the right wall of the corral, the other one with her feet in the opposite direction. Blood spots were all over. The corral's door was open and three-and-a-half feet high from the floor was a bloody hand print, like somebody held himself against the door before going out. The hair around the holes [on the sheep] seems like it was cut with scissors or some very sharp instrument. Sheep's hair was all over.

"The murderers—and I will explain why I think there were more than one—used a box that was in the corral for sitting in and they put into it the instruments they used for the surgery, plus the animal parts and blood. On a sidewalk near the corral, I could see blood spots and also a bloody hand mark on a stone. I think the murderer was carrying the box in one hand while using the other one to steady himself to keep from falling.

"Last Sunday six sheep were killed beside the Himalaya Cookie Factory. They did a good job in there. Now let me tell you why I think there is more than one murderer and why I think they are persons. First of all, to steal a box, probably in which to put the instruments, viscera and blood, as I said; well, the act of stealing is a human action. To operate those fine instruments, the mark of the bloody hand on the door and stone—all are human traces. To subdue the animal and operate on him at the same time is a very hard job for only one person. But why they do it—I have no explanation.

"...One hundred meters away from our corral is Raymundo's corral. Five sheep were found dead there [this makes a total of 14 so far]. Their backs were shaved, showing the dry, flesh-colored skin. One of the sheep had a little hole, still bleeding, in her neck under the throat. Blood spots were all over the corral and, on the door, the same bloody handprint. On the path from the corral to the backyard fence were five-toed footprints, like a dog or a tiger's footprint. The marks were all along the path, showing an undecided course, and I found many more near the corral. Just to compare, I printed my feet into the ground and I think that an animal, to print those tracks, has to weigh around 40 or 50 kilos (approximately 90 to 110 pounds). Now that I've seen the dead bodies and the perfect work of the murderers, I'm sure they were persons and not animals. No animal can open doors or use a box for sitting or like a container—and also, no animal can cut perfect circles. It's possible the murderers had dogs with them to lend mystery to the act."

No one in the neighborhood heard any noise or bellowing that night, but all are afraid because "anyone who kills sheep in such a horrible way can also kill people." The police told the people that the murderers are rats; but people do not listen to the police anymore, unless the rats weighed 40 or 50 kilos, which is impossible.[38]

Then, another article was written by Bethencourt and published by *Diario De Avisos* in its October 7, 1979 edition:

The Taco & Barranco Grande Killers are People— Autopsies Kept Secret by Police

We had come to the Regional Agrarian Laboratory seeking information on the autopsies performed on the bodies of a goat and rabbit found under strange circumstances Thursday night. The bodies had been kept under refrigeration. Veterinarian Joaquin Quilos is director of the laboratory. Although he received us in a friendly way, he refused to provide us with any data until three police inspectors arrived.

Later the inspector in charge of the case told us personally that the results of the autopsies were to be kept secret and that *Diario De Avisos*-—although a public servant—should not hinder the police investigation. That evening *Diario De Avisos* already had some information on the results of the autopsies. Usually well-informed sources confirmed what had been rumored that morning: the goats were strangled, probably with some metal instrument having several sharp points, shoved down the throat, which was perforated. The wounds on the animals' sides, the autopsy revealed, were not made by an animal but by a cutting instrument. The doctor doing the dissection told the police that these wounds pierced the carcass in an attempt to reach the chest cavity.

Who would do this and why? In numerous African tribes—if our memory serves us, among the Masai—it is customary to drink the blood of animals; they think of it as a religious rite, to strengthen body and soul. Certain religious sects connected with devil worship appreciate the physical and spiritual qualities of blood. Someone connected with Africa could have brought with him the paw of a panther or wolf or jackal to make tracks where the killings took place, thus misleading the investigators. We know that one or several human beings are the killers; we know what methods they employed. The forensic examination by the police will reveal more details, such as if drugs were used in the killing or if the animals were first poisoned (which we doubt if the killers intended to drink the blood).[39]

Then another article appeared in *Diario De Avisos* two days later, on October 9, 1979:

Superior Police Headquarters have begun an in-depth investigation to determine the cause of the recent deaths of animals in the area of Barranco Grande. *Diario De Avisos* is informed that three departments are participating in the investigation: the department of city security, the department of identification and the department of criminal investigation, with its second chief in charge. The first indications following examination of the carcasses of the goats by a veterinarian revealed that almost all exhibited bites in the throat, evidently done to drain the blood from the animal. Only carnivores like panthers, wolves or wild dogs act in this way. In regard to the holes in the carcasses, the veterinarian thinks they are caused by bites made in order to tear out the internal organs. It is supposed that the non-visceral meat of the victims is rejected by the killers. Even though the police do not discard any hypothesis, at this point they do not seem to be considering the possibility of the killers being people.[40]

In the same October 9, 1979 edition of *Diario De Avisos* the following article by Jorge Bethencourt reports on additional mutilation investigations by police:

The carcasses of two goats have been added to the long list of victims of the "vampires of Taco" that struck yesterday in the Tincer area. The animals found in a gully, had had their throats torn open with the usual lack of blood. The police conducted an investigation on the spot and made a thorough examination of the slaughtered animals. According to a reliable source, the instrument used by the vampires was "metal and extremely sharp," possibly a scalpel. More than 15 police are assigned to the investigation which considering the mobility of the unknown butchers and the large area involved, presents great difficulties. It appears that the blood of the animals was carried away in containers, traces of which have been found. It seems certain that the "vampires"—as we pointed out the other day—are accompanied by a dog. This—as we indicated elsewhere—would serve two purposes: the dog tracks would mislead the investigators; the smell of the dog, familiar to the goats, would keep them quiet.[41]

Then, in another follow-up article, Bethencourt reported on Senora Barbara Guanche Otazo, who reported she witnessed two enormous wolf-like dogs killing three of her goats by biting them on the neck. This occurred in the Taco area, and in the area of Vistabella, two huge dogs were again reported attacking a goat, tearing out virtually all of the viscera:

At the same time, in certain districts of the area of La Torre de San Matias were found the carcasses of three goats. They resembled the victims of what used to be called "the vampires of Taco." Are animals alone causing these deaths? We believe Senora Guanche's story. We also think that the wounds of a dead goat that we observed in Taco could have been caused by an animal. We are not experts in this kind of thing but we have listened to the advice of those who are more experienced. But we are thoroughly convinced that in certain deaths, such as some which took place on Wednesday, October 3rd in the Taco area, the hand of man, using extremely sharp instruments, was responsible for the wounds on the carcasses of eight animals. We cannot deny that dogs are the cause of some of the deaths. But we would not be honest with ourselves, nor faithful to our observations, if we did not hold the firm opinion that a group of people were the perpetrators of "the exploits of Taco." The motive is obscure; it defies logic. The deeds are always done in the same area, and repeated frequently. It would be a real work of detection to find the killers.[42]

The last press reports covering this strange outbreak of animal attacks appeared in the October 16, 1979 *Diario De Avisos*. Authors Bethencourt and B. Morales reported that the "Taco vampires had struck at least 14 animals within a month." Two separate corrals had suffered an attack on Sunday, October 14th. One sheep was found dead in each corral. A distance of 100 meters separated the corrals, with a third unaffected corral in between. The victimized sheep were left with "circular holes in their bodies and necks, and no blood" and were apparently missing their kidneys. The article does not state whether any autopsies were conducted.[43]

North of the Border

All the way back thousands of miles to the west in Alberta, Canada, ranchers experienced a whirlwind of cases that entire month of October 1979. On October 6th, an Enoch Band Reserve rancher had a three-year-old Charolais bull mutilated. The animal was missing its anus, penis and scrotum. Two days later on October 8, 1979 another bull and a cow were reported mutilated. That same day a bull calf was discovered mutilated south of Oyen, Saskatchewan. On October 12th, a Charolais steer was reported mutilated north of Oyen and a Hereford steer was discovered with its anus and tongue gone—but its genitalia intact—west of Ft. Macleod, Alberta.

On October 14th a three-year-old heifer was found with the udder, genitals, one eye and the end of the tongue removed. Also on the 14th, this time west of Markerville, Alberta, a three-year-old Hereford heifer was found and reported as mutilated. According to RCMP investigation coordinator Corporal Lyn Lauber: "the cuts were definitely made with a knife." Corporal Lauber also told the press he thought introverts were responsible for Canadian mutes—we will explore that comment later.[44]

On October 16th there were two Alberta mutes. The first was a calf and later that day a seven-year-old Hereford cow was found minus teats, anus and vulva. These reports were filed from the Rocky Mountain House area of western Alberta.

October 17, 1979, we return back to Saskatchewan, Canada to the Goodeve area where a steer mute was reported. Editor Dennis Corneau of the *Melville Advance* asked the farmer who owned the steer for a description of the mutilation site as he found it:

> It was just lying there in the ditch and I couldn't figure out how it got there. I checked and all my fences were okay. But, the animal was just lying there in the ditch, with a leg broken off…no blood anywhere, either on the animal, or in the ditch. I thought then that it had been hit by either a truck or a car. I noticed an odd semi-circular track going down into the ditch, where the steer had been dumped. But I also noticed that the track did not show any tire imprint. It was strange, really strange. We hauled the steer out of the ditch and back to the farmyard and it was then that I noticed something else about the animal. The tongue was missing and one ear had been cut off, the ear in which had been implanted an ear tag for identification purposes. Then, I noticed that the animal's throat had been cut…very neatly with something that had to be extremely sharp.

The thing is, there was no blood anywhere, either on the animal (where the cuts had been made) or in the ditch. On the steer's abdomen, there was a small white circular impression, as if it had been injected with something.

The funny thing is, that steer had been in the pasture before and, when we found it, it was in the ditch alongside the road. Yet there were no tracks leading to or from the pasture— just that odd semicircular track in the ditch and really just one of those, with no imprint of a tire. Whatever made that track had to be pretty heavy and there was something else funny about it. In the dirt by the side of the road, the track made an indentation, but when you project where the track went into the ditch through some weeds, the weeds are not broken or damaged in any way. It's just as if whatever dropped the steer there was hanging low above the ground.

I just don't know what to make of it… I noticed that our family dog just wouldn't go near the dead animal and no birds such as crows or magpies would go near it, either. Usually, our dog will at least sniff around something like that and the birds will feed on it. But they seemed to want nothing to do with it. And, you gotta [sic] remember that the animal had been lying there dead in the ditch for several days.

Mr. Corneau's informant told him that a number of observers on the nearby Little Black Bear Reserve saw three or four large, silver objects hovering low nearby. When the witnesses flashed their headlights at the objects, the objects quickly took off and left the area. This occurred on Saturday night, during the weekend on which it was suspected that the steer died.[45]

About 25 miles south of Glentworth, Saskatchewan, near the U.S. border, a cow was reported dead and disfigured on October 26, 1979 with its rectum, genitals, udder and tongue missing. There was no blood at the scene nor blood present in the ventricles leading to the animal's heart. It appeared as if the ventricles had been washed clean. The meat was pink, resembling "chicken meat."

Another report was filed that same day, this time on a ranch nine miles east of Esther, Alberta. A 12-or 13-year-old Hereford cow was found with its udder, anus and at least one ear gone. According to the Oyen, Alberta *Echo* (November 2, 1979), "rigor mortis had apparently set in the front legs but the rear legs were very flexible and 'crossed in an unusual way.'" Later, a nearby bull mutilation was reported.

Two days later on October 28, 1979, north of Fort Macleod, a Hereford cow was found with its tongue, rectum and a patch of skin near its udder removed with a "sharp instrument," according to RCMP Corporal Emil Smetaniuk. Then, two more reports were filed on November 3rd from a ranch northeast of Airdrie, Alberta. The two heifers had identical wounds: the skin had been cut away around the jaw and cuts were made to the vulva and anus. According to RCMP Corporal Randy McKenzie, the first was "carried out in an amateurish fashion" but the other was quite "professional." McKenzie was of the opinion, however, that the same mutilator(s) did both and may have been "just practicing or whatever" on the first one. Genitals were not removed from either animal.

The RCMP had a brief nine-day respite from cases, and then reports again began to be filed by panicky ranchers. On November 11th in Nanton, Alberta, on the on Chester Crozier's dairy farm, a mutilated Hereford heifer was discovered with its right ear cut off, and the hide around its right eye taken. The work was described as "precise cuts" with a "sharp instrument." That same day, this time near Namao, Alberta, a young heifer turned up after a search missing its genitals and bladder.

The next day a second case was reported from the Crozier Dairy Ranch. This one was especially bizarre. The pregnant cow was dead and missing the genitals, two teats and a piece of the tongue. The cow was about to give birth and an *ear on the unborn calf had been cut off as it lay in the mother's womb*. If true, explain that one!

The next day, November 13th, a mute cow was discovered near Airdrie in Alberta. This one was a white-faced heifer. The genitals had not been removed but "attempts had been made to take them"—veterinarian and RCMP consultant Dr. David Green of Airdrie confirmed it as a "classic mutilation."

An Iowa rancher found his six-month-old calf mutilated with a "tooth broken out" on December 8, 1979 and two miles away another calf was found in a similar condition. Eight cattle mutes occurred in five Iowa counties in the last half of 1979 (Polk, Black Hawk, Hardin, Washington and Boone Counties) and more cases would be filed in 1980.

Despite the relatively small number of known UFO accounts during the Alberta/Saskatchewan mute siege, the ufonauts, even in Canada, remain a favorite target for finger pointing. Cult expert and University of Alberta professor Bill Meilen was questioned about mutilations by the *Edmonton Sun* (11-13-79). Though he "would like to avoid" the term "UFO," Meilen feels that all the evidence extant regarding mutilations "points to biopsies being performed by beings using a means of flight 'beyond our comprehension.' Meilen told reporter Lance Beswick that among the Canadian mute items of pertinence to be addressed are:

—The discovery of fractures in many of the animals consistent with injuries caused by being dropped from a height of at least 10 feet;

—A seven-year-old heifer whose unborn calf had been removed and, mutilated WITHOUT (*Sun's* emphasis) the placental bag being broken.[46]

The *Edmonton Sun* asked RCMP Corporal Lyn Lauber (figure 9) for his reaction to Meilen's statements and Lauber told the *Sun* in their November 26, 1979 article: "We're looking for humans doing these things, not UFOs or little green men." Lauber discounted Mailen's contention that some of the mute carcasses suffered crushed bones as though dropped from the air. "We haven't experienced anything like that in Alberta," said Lauber. He also said it was not true that the unborn calf was mutilated without the placenta having been broken. Lauber added, "We haven't figured out what's killing them, but we are looking at a cult. There are cults here in Alberta. There's no doubt about that, and we assume that these mutilations are being done for cult practices—either for voodoo, witchcraft or Satanism."

A Canadian wire service story in the *Vancouver Sun* on October 16, 1979 had Lauber and the RCMP speculating that the mutes might be attributed to introverted, outwardly respectable persons "bored with their dull lives." Lauber speculated "outwardly they may appear to have high moral standards and be family-oriented, but they crave some sort of excitement." So, could an insidious, crafty, quietly desperate band of crazed introverts be grimly taking out their frustrations on helpless bovines? The speculation has it that, operating "during the dark hours, perhaps just before dawn," they would not need light. With a "good hunting knife and a sharpener," they "could do it by feel."

The *Toronto Star* on December 17, 1979 quoted Corporal Lauber, succinctly summing up his assessment of the possibility of UFO involvement in the mutilations, as saying, "I can't see what the attraction of a bull's ass would be to a UFO."

The controversy continued—which should come as no surprise. In late 1979, in Alberta and Saskatchewan, winter took its time setting in (a climatological anomaly in which some might find or seek significance), but finally winter arrived and the mutilations—or at least reports of them—ceased by mid-December. But numerous cases had occurred that fall, and that fact cannot be erased from ranchers' memories nor from history. The noble and justifiably reputable RCMP may, privately at least, be a bit humbled by it all. In that, of course, they are not alone. But, on this occasion, the Mounties did not get their, er…culprit.[47]

Black Hawk Cow Down

In Black Hawk County, Iowa, the first mutilation of 1980 was reported on or about January 18th. The Iowa Division of Criminal Investigation looked into the possibility of cultist involvement. …the DCI drew criticism when they tried to subpoena records of the Des Moines public library to check out the identities of individuals checking out books on the occult. DCI Chief Gerald Shanahan, who had seen *Stigmata* #5, noted that the photos of mutilated animals in that issue (from Natrona County, WY and Van Zandt County, TX) were "carbon copies" of the Iowa cases. Mutilations in general at last became "legitimate" news when *Newsweek* briefly reported on the recent Iowa cases in its edition of January 21, 1980. The cover read: 'America's Get-Tough Strategy'.[48] (figure 10)

Thus ended the great mutilation waves of the 1970s. No one will ever truly know the actual extent of the scourge that swept across the midwest and western pastureland of North America. In hindsight there is no possible way to differentiate between genuine high strange cases and mundane examples of unusual-appearing scavenger action generated by news reports. However, after studying these hundreds of reports, several things are obvious to me: not all of these cases can be simply explained away. Without question, in my opinion, a sizeable, noteworthy percentage of cases were perpetrated by parties as yet unknown, for purposes that still remain undefined. Was it aliens? The government? Sicko "introverts" out on a lark? Bloodthirsty "cultists?" What about all the hundreds of chopper sightings? The jury will be forever out on these questions, but perhaps our mystery livestock predators left behind some form of evidence to help identify who they are and what their possible agenda could be in the next decades?

Jacques Vallee observed at the end of his chapter on cattle mutilations, "A Cow for NORAD," in his 1979 book *Messengers of Deception*:

The stage was set for new attempts to explain the facts. The "delusionary spiral" theory clearly did not hold up, and something had to be found. As each new hypothesis became more complex and more incredible, a specter began to rise. It gave the whole idea of "contact" with friendly space brothers another deadly blow. It froze the blood of the believers, and it gave the skeptics some interesting new items to think about. But more than anything else, it challenged the law-enforcement community.

As you'll see, we'll have plenty of cases to ponder along with law enforcement all through the 1980s, 1990s and into the 2010s. All the way to the month when this book was completed—January 2014—when mutilated cattle washed ashore on the ocean beaches of Sweden and Denmark.

Chapter Six: Sources and References

1. Atchison *Globe*, 3-15-79; Project Stigma
2. Gabe Valdez *Stigmata #5*; AMP/David Perkins
3. New Mexico *Daily Press* Project Stigma; Eddy County Sheriff's Office
4. *ibid*
5. *ibid*
6. Gabe Valdez; Santa Fe *New Mexican*; AMP/Perkins; Project Stigma
7. *ibid*
8. Project Stigma
9. APRO *Bulletin,* 1979

10. Project Stigma
11. *ibid*
12. AMP/Perkins; Project Stigma
13. *ibid*
14. *Unmasking the Enemy*, Tommy Blann, 1993
15. *Stigmata;* Project Stigma, 1982
16. AMP/Perkins; *Stigmata #7*
17. AMP/Perkins; Project Stigma
18. *ibid*
19. *ibid*
20. Project Stigma
21. *ibid*
22. AMP/Perkins
23. *El Dia,* Santa Cruz, 7-10-79; Project Stigma
24. AMP/Perkins
25. *ibid*
26. Project Stigma
27. *Calgary Herald,* 8-16-79; AMP
28. Project Stigma; Lucius Farish/*UFO Newsclipping Service*; Dr. Nancy H. Owen, U of AR
29. *ibid*
30. Project Stigma
31. George Gengenbach; Earl Nutt; Project Stigma
32. Project Stigma
33. *Omaha World-Herald*, 9-11-79 and 9-20-79; Carol Werkmeister; Project Stigma
34. AMP/Perkins
35. *Alberta Report*, 10-12-79; Project Stigma
36. Melville *Advocate* 10-24-79; Project Stigma
37. Lethbridge *Herald*, 10-6-79; Project Stigma
38. *Diario De Avisos,* 10-4-79; Project Stigma
39. *ibid*
40. *ibid*
41. *Diario De Avisos* 10-9-79; Project Stigma
42. *Diario De Avisos* 10-11-79; Project Stigma
43. *Diario De Avisos,* 10-16-79; Project Stigma
44. Red Deer, Alberta *Advocate,* 10-16-79,;Project Stigma
45. Melville *Advocate,* 10-24-79; Project Stigma
46. Edmonton *Sun,* 11-13-79; Project Stigma
47. Tim Tokaryk, Bill Allan, Bob Pratt, Don Worley, Walter Andrus, Dr. Nancy Smith, Tommy Blann, Kenneth Pawson, Dwight Whalen, Jenny Jackson, Richard Houghton,
48. Helen E. Ball, Link Byfield, Denis C. Corneau, Ralph Thompson, Paul Rockley, Randy Burton, Bernice Duguay, John Jacksom; Project Stigma
49. Peter Jordan; Grant Callison; Nancy Raffensperger; Gerald Shanahan; Project Stigma

Figure 1
Apollo Astronaut, geologist and ex-New Mexico Senator Harrison Schmitt.
(credit: nasa.gov/AMP/David Perkins)

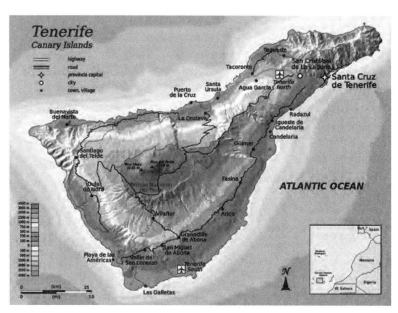

Figure 2
Canary Island Tenerife. (credit: wikipedia.org)

271

Figure 3
Wallaby. Who mutilated wallabies in UK and USA zoos? (credit: wikipedia.org)

Figure 4
Cari Seawell and David Perkins investigate mutilation just downstream from the
Los Alamos National Lab in New Mexico. (credit: AMP/David Perkins)

Figure 5
Linda Moulton Howe directing her award-winning documentary, *A Strange Harvest.*
(credit: AMP/David Perkins)

Figure 6
New Mexico road sign. The locals at least have a sense of humor.
(credit: TMV Archives)

Figure 7
Simmental bull. You and what army could mutilated this big guy?
(credit: wikipedia.org)

Figure 8
Canadian Cattle Herd in Alberta. (credit: fao.org)

Figure 9
Royal Canadian Mounted Police officials investigated hundreds of cases in the 1970s through the 1990s. (credit: rcmp-grc.gc.ca)

Figure 10
Newsweek magazine cover 1-21-80. This issue had an article on the mutilation mystery. (credit: ebay.com)

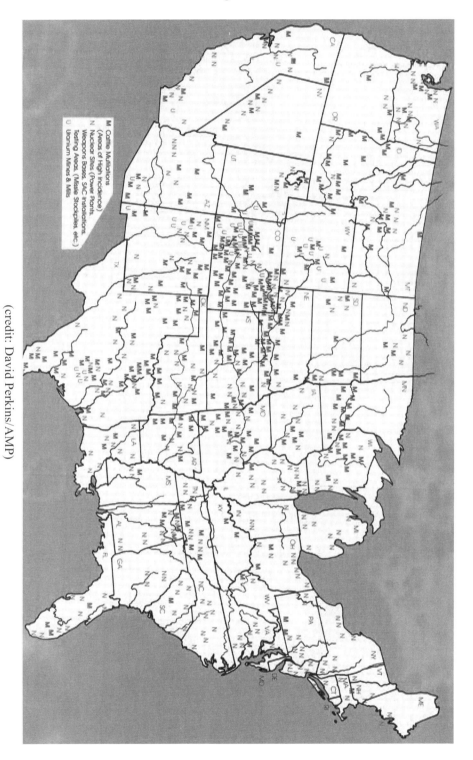

(credit: David Perkins/AMP)

Chapter 7
The 1980s

The arrival of 1980 closed out the five plus years of whirlwind mayhem (and the resulting media hyperbole) of the mid to late '70s. As we've seen, 1979 featured the mutilation conference organized by New Mexico Senator Harrison Schmitt which brought together for the first time the loose network of independent "mute" investigators, law enforcement officials, livestock board inspectors, UFO buffs and media types who had been covering the mystery since the hell year of 1975. But this high tide of interest did little good, for evidently, the mutilators weren't finished with their diabolical work out on the range.

The new decade began with an active spring of new mutilation reports and although a number of them were undoubtedly misidentified scavenging, the apparent high strange cases we'll cover in this chapter are noteworthy. The mute investigation community kicked itself into high gear with the enthusiasm, help and dedication of Linda Moulton Howe, who covered the mutes as Director of Special Projects at Denver's KMGH-TV. All through the 1980s, 1990s and into the 2000s, she has continued her personal field investigation of mute cases and as a journalist, tirelessly covered unexplained livestock death reports through the entire eastern half of Colorado and to the east—out into the plains of the midwest. A crack, award-winning investigative journalist specializing in environmental stories, in 1979 Linda rapidly brought herself up to speed so she could properly look into these perplexing animal death cases. Of

course, the first thing she did was contact the handful of dedicated mute investigators working on the scene, most notably Tom Adams, Gary Massey and David Perkins. They took her under their wing and she began her ongoing (now 35-year) investigation into the unexplained livestock death mystery. (figure 1)

As 1980 commenced, Tom Adams continued to publish *Stigmata* and provided investigators, law enforcement and the media with a central clearinghouse for mutilation-related news and updates. David Perkins started the Animal Mutilation Probe (AMP) in 1978; E. Austin started his Animal Mutilation Data Center in October 1980; Tommy Blann and law enforcement officials continued to investigate cases and compile data. During those early months of 1980, the mute investigation community waited somewhat nervously for the June publication of ex-FBI investigator Kenneth Rommel's *Operation Animal Mutilation* (OAM) report.

With the June 1980 release of the controversial Rommel report, hackles were raised in the investigator community. Most hard-boiled mute investigators and knowledgeable law enforcement officials considered Rommel's report to be a whitewash and a deliberate attempt to debunk the entire "cattle mutilation" phenomenon and the principles involved were not happy.

Longtime mutilation researcher Tommy Blann was one of the first to dissect the Rommel report when it was released and he pointed out its obvious deficiencies. In his book *Unmasking the Enemy,* he first provides some background and then an insightful critique:

Operation Animal Mutilation

Senator Schmitt had fought hard to get the LEAA-funded probe into the mutilations. It was the understanding of some that the New Mexico law enforcement community would be directing this effort. The District Attorney's office in the First Judicial District in Santa Fe, New Mexico, however, gave the job to Kenneth Rommel, who retired early from the FBI to head the mutilation probe. In May 1979, Rommel became the director of the $50,000 LEAA-funded probe into mutilations in the State of New Mexico. Some lawmen and other investigators felt uncomfortable about this appointment, since the FBI had been dragging their feet on this matter for some time. They had previously refused to get involved due to jurisdictional matters, even when evidence pointed to the possibility of interstate criminal activity. There were some who predicted what the outcome of this probe would be before it ever started, and the answers that would be given—predators! They had heard it too many times before.

Rommel, nicknamed the "Desert Fox" after the famous German World War II general, had spent 28 years in the FBI. He had been an FBI agent for five years in Santa Fe, with previous assignments in New York City and San Juan, Puerto Rico where he specialized in investigations of bank robberies and counter-espionage. He said he had been drawn to his new job partly because of "the intrigue that has gone with it." He further related that his new assignment would be a nice way to end his 28-year career with the FBI, which he truly loved.

Initially, Rommel's FBI background and training began to show in the methodology of his investigations. He began building a database by researching past articles on mutilations from magazines and newspapers, and critically examined written law enforcement reports and photos. After reviewing this information, he contacted officials in other states to determine what evidence they may have gathered. During this time, he kept his comments to the press brief while conducting his investigations. He was quick to point out, however, some of the problems that he felt were the primary cause of the mutilation phenomenon. He felt that much of what had been said about the mutilations was due to too many irresponsible statements by the press and others who were not forensic pathologists. He then enlisted the help of some individuals with impressive credentials, knowing that one must have factual information in order to stand up in a court of law.

Rommel tore apart much of the false evidence that supposedly supported the reality of the mutilations with one natural explanation after another. Unfortunately, in his determination to get to the bottom of the mystery, he would soon find himself doing exactly the same thing that he had pointed out others had done—not looking at all the facts. It was clear that Rommel wanted to conclusively discredit the entire mutilation phenomenon. In his investigations he determined that the majority of these cases were due to predators, and the others had more mundane explanations. Rommel pointed out that the parts of the carcass that were allegedly removed in classic mutilations were the same ones normally consumed by predators and scavengers. He also explained that the appearance of the cuts was not sufficient evidence to indicate that it was done with a knife, and the only way to determine this was through microscopic inspection. Rommel, however, failed to include any photos of such microscopic inspections in his final report.

During the course of his year-long probe, Rommel investigated only 15 of the 27 mutilations reported to him. Some complained that Rommel was not conducting his investigations properly, while others felt that he was "brusque" or "too flippant" and that he didn't take their ideas or their reports seriously. The mutilations dropped off considerably when the probe began, as if whoever was doing it knew not to make waves in Rommel's territory.

The final report, a 297-page document, entitled *Operation Animal Mutilation*, (figure 2) consisted of Rommel's 15 personal investigations in the

State of New Mexico, along with correspondence from various state and federal agencies that were investigating the mutilation phenomenon. The report was an excellent example of taking a certain set of facts, while interjecting disparaging statements from time to time, to form a conclusion that was not based upon the overall evidence.

There were a number of cases mentioned in this report in which not all of the facts were presented. In some instances, when Rommel could not find a satisfactory answer to a certain finding, he resorted to more ludicrous explanations. For example, he explained puncture marks found in the jugular vein of a cow as a rattlesnake bite. He explained precision cuts of the sexual organs of a horse as having been made due to the castration of the horse by the farmer. Since when did the castration process require cutting off part of the male sexual organ? Peyote cactus was used to explain one occurrence of a drug when this type of cactus is not found in the state.

The finding of *succinylcholine* in the bloodstream of a horse was explained as an overdose of the drug given by the farmer. Another drug found in a horse was said to have come from "hippies" possibly camping on the property. What was interesting about this final report was that there was no mention of the subject of satanic cults.

Rommel's final conclusion was that the so-called mutilations were being done by predators and scavengers. In the few cases where human involvement was determined, these could be attributed to pranksters and publicity seekers. Several state diagnostic labs that did postmortem examinations on a few of the mutilated carcasses supported his conclusion. However, other diagnostic labs and agencies found evidence of human involvement and drugs in the mutilated animal. This included the Royal Canadian Mounted Police (RCMP), who had been investigating Canadian sites where mutilated cattle and horses had been found.

When the Rommel report was finally made public, there was a tremendous uproar among those who had spent many years investigating this phenomenon. Many felt that it was a cover-up of the real facts, and had been a waste of the taxpayers' money. Some had predicted what Rommel's conclusions would be from the very beginning. Senator Schmitt had also said that the report was not a definitive study of the phenomenon.

[Blann's] Critique of the Rommel Probe

Let us now look at some of Rommel's statements in the final report as compared to other findings. On page 175 of the final report, Rommel states the following:

The phenomenon seemed to peak in 1975, for between the months of April and December of that year, 203 reports were investigated by the

Colorado Bureau of Investigation (CBI). Thirty-five suspected mutilations were examined by Colorado State University, 19 of which were found suitable for tests. Of these 19 animals, the university determined that 11 died of natural causes. In the remaining eight cases, the cause of death could not be determined. Five cases were confirmed as predator attacks and nine as willful mutilations. Three incidents were thought to involve a possible combination of the two. The university also determined that in all mutilations involving the use of sharp instruments, the cuts were made following the animal's death.

In a letter to the New Mexico State Police dated July 10, 1978, the CBI describes their investigations more explicitly: "During our investigation of the cattle mutilation problem in Colorado, the CBI laboratory examined approximately 40 hide samples. Of these, two were found to have been cut with a sharp instrument. In a six-month period, our agents spent 2,557 man-hours on this investigation, which included undercover operations. We were never able to identify any person or persons as being responsible for these, so-called mutilations. The scientifically based evidence obtained points to cattle which died of natural causes being attacked by predators."

Rommel chose to adhere to the last sentence as indicative of supporting his conclusions; however, let's look at what was stated earlier by Carl Whiteside, deputy director of the CBI, at Senator Schmitt's conference. On page 108 of the transcript of the proceedings, Whiteside states that, "Nine of the 19, almost one-half, were willful mutilation with a sharp instrument." On page 111, he further states that, "CSU (Colorado State University), in their examination, as I previously said, found nine that they considered to be the result of a mutilation with a sharp instrument."

Rommel devoted very few paragraphs to the Montana mutilations. He stated that the book, *Mystery Stalks The Prairie*, written by Capt. Keith Wolverton of the Cascade County Sheriffs Department and Roberta Donovan in 1976, was a sensationalized account of these cases. He further stated that no lab reports were offered to substantiate their claims that the animals had been cut with a sharp instrument. [This assertion was untrue]

This was an extremely interesting statement, considering that the very state diagnostic lab at Fort Collins, Colorado that he mentioned in his report had a report done for Capt. Wolverton. The necropsy report (diagnostic lab number 5570) from the Diagnostic Laboratory, College of Veterinary Medicine, Colorado State University at Fort Collins, which was done for Capt. Wolverton by Dr. A.E. McChesney, states: "This strip of skin has a long, straight cut edge with regular serrations (approximately 3/16 of an inch in width). Hair in one area had knowingly been clipped but in untouched areas the hair had been cut at the laceration edge. Changes on the skin edge resembled neither tooth marks of predator nor those of wire lacerations. The changes were similar to those that could be made with a knife except for the regular striations."

Color photo documentation done by Capt. Wolverton showed that this could not possibly have been done by predators or scavengers. Capt. Wolverton had also been informed by another law enforcement officer in the state that he had information that the mutilations involved a cult of witches who were drinking cow's blood mixed with PCP, but was reluctant to talk about it.

Unknown to Rommel at the time, I [Blann] had been in touch with the royal Canadian Mounted Police. The RCMP had been following the mutilation mystery from the very beginning in the provinces of Alberta and Saskatchewan in the latter part of 1979. They had been conducting their investigations with a six-man investigative team assisted by a veterinary pathologist. The Canadian findings revealed that there were two types of mutilations: those that had been done with a sharp instrument, and those which were sloppy in comparison, which were labeled "copycat" killings. A number of other reported mutilations were the results of predator and scavenger activity.

Corporal Lyn Lauber of the Calgary detachment had been put in charge to head the mutilation probe. Lauber spent numerous hours compiling data and reading voluminous material on occult literature in hopes that it might furnish him with some clues since he felt that there might be some type of cult involvement. The UFO connection came up as usual, but Lauber stated he "didn't believe that any little green men were involved in these mutilations." During his investigations, he found evidence of a possible cult connection with the cattle mutilations.

When Rommel's final report was released to the public, [Blann] contacted Lauber and asked him what he thought about the report. Lauber responded with a letter to the author dated May 27, 1980, which stated: "Your information regarding the New Mexico press release is quite interesting. I find it difficult to understand how Rommel could make a statement such as this, without ever having personally witnessed a mutilation firsthand." He was referring to a newspaper clipping that [Blann] had sent to him earlier stating Rommel's conclusion as to the cause of mutilations—predators.

When [Blann] asked Rommel what he thought of the Canadian mutilations, his reply was somewhat shocking. Rommel said, "they have a different problem," and then he further stated that he had sent them a copy of his final report. Rommel went on to say that, "we have agreed that they are not going to talk about my findings and I am not going to talk about theirs." He then said that if anybody wanted to spend money investigating this mutilation phenomenon, "that was fine and dandy, but not one more cent of the taxpayers' money is going to be spent on it." He further added, "I have done my job and I am through with it."

To show how conflicting statements were being made, [Blann] wrote a letter to the RCMP in Edmonton, Alberta in March 1985 requesting further information on the investigations. The reply came back from the RCMP that: "I have received advice from the Attorney General's Department indicating that they will not release copies of the requested necropsy reports to outside agencies. It is our opinion, from the investigation conducted, that any occurrences of alleged mutilations are the result of nature and the normal course of events and that there is absolutely no evidence which would support any conclusion to the contrary."

This is contradictory to the [later] findings of two journalists (Kagan and Summers), who wrote the book *Mute Evidence* in 1983. They indicated that the RCMP and Dr. Green, veterinarian pathologist, admitted that there was human involvement in cattle mutilations. They alluded to puncture marks and drugs that had been found in the mutilated animals. Their book also discussed the satanic cult connection with these animal mutilations.

As previously stated, Corporal Lauber had told [Blann] in 1980 that he couldn't understand how Rommel could make such a statement about predators being responsible for the mutilations. A few years later, Kagan also asked Lauber about the Rommel Report. On page 257 of *Mute Evidence*, Lauber said that he had only one comment about the Rommel Report. He said that he would like to see him (Rommel) write off our confirmed cases as predators. He further added that Rommel's report was influenced by local politics and that there appeared to be an ulterior motive behind it. Wonder what Lauber meant by an "ulterior motive?"[1]

After publication of *Operation Animal Mutilation*, reported cases around the country appeared to subside somewhat, but not entirely. As we will see, there were quite a number of noteworthy reports throughout the 1980s that deserve close examination. And, as in the seventies, there were further efforts by diagnostic laboratories to *scientifically* establish if there was evidence validating the potential high strange nature of the mute phenomenon. The results of some of these testing procedures have been ignored over the years by the skeptics who have already made up their minds that there is no mystery.

For some in the media and law enforcement who tended to be on the skeptical side of accepting the true nature of the mutilation mystery, Rommel's report gave them plausible deniability. In this chapter we will see how the cases continued to be reported and taken seriously by law enforcement, the media and (in a select few cases) scientists in diagnostic labs. Some of the "post Rommel" cases I've highlighted from the early 1980s are fascinating and in my estimation, deserve your attention.

New Mexico State Patrolman Gabe Valdez and hard-hit Dulce rancher Manuel Gomez were dismayed by Rommel's report. Gabe told me back in the 1990s that during the six to eight months when Rommel was actively investigating the mutilations in New Mexico, the state (especially the northern tier) became suddenly quiet with very few (if any) true mutilations being reported to officials. Gabe was convinced that Rommel never was able to investigate a single high-strange case, because the mutilators moved their operations to other parts of the west.

The Mutilations Recommence

As public awareness of the mutilation mystery began to fade in the months leading up to the June 1980 publication of Rommel's now infamous *OAM* report, several early spring 1980 cases occurred that never made the papers—real head-scratchers in my opinion. They include expert forensic testing, strange apparent occult activity, antique choppers, alleged UFO/ET involvement and a leapfrog-ging of reports around North America. Early spring cases were reported in Alberta, Colorado, New Mexico, Iowa and elsewhere.

April 24, 1980, El Paso County—south of the town of Simla, Colorado rancher Robert Blake reported to El Paso County authorities that his wife had discovered their 16-year-old registered quarter horse "Skip Easy Cash" mutilated about a mile from the ranch house. The horse had been seen alive and well on the 21st when the herd was checked. The following night a neighbor living a mile east and a little north of the Blake ranch told them she had heard the sound of heli-copter or perhaps "loud farm machinery" around 2 a.m., but she didn't hear anything fly over. Then, about an hour later, the Blakes heard what they thought was an expected feed truck gearing down to cross over the cattle guard near their ranch, but although the sound subsided no truck showed up to deliver feed. Then, at around 4 a.m. the Blakes heard the engine noise a second time, but no truck went by or pulled in to their ranch. After speaking with the neighbor, the Blakes wondered if they too had heard a chopper nearby.

The animal lay on its left side in a grove of trees. The right ear had been cut off at the scalp. The right side of the lower lip had been cut away "in a kind of beveled shape," sliced off from the center of the mouth back to the jaw hinge. Strips of skin were cut from the area of the genitals. The strip furthest to the right was about two inches long and ¾" wide, the next was somewhat shorter, the next even shorter, and the next still shorter and the next shorter still. Most notable of all, the right eyeball was intact, but a circle of tissue completely surrounding the eyeball had been cut out in some fashion, leaving the orb to languish like an island in the socket...The official investigation was performed by El Paso deputies Donna Cunningham, David Smith and detective Robert Demetry. Cunningham's report indicated the investigators thought natural causes and scavenging animals were to blame. But Blake...[said] that he traps every winter and uses dead calves and sheep as bait. He stated: "We used a horse for bait once, and the coyotes ate everything but the head. That's the last thing they'll touch, unless it's the tongue, and our horses tongue wasn't even touched. On top of that, no predator would eat around the eyeball for two inches deep to the bone and leave the eyeball in, as was done on our horse."[2]

Several noteworthy elements were found at the scene. The grove of trees where the horse was found appeared normal, however, the tree under which the horse lay appeared to be "both bent and severely twisted. The damage mostly occurring about four feet off the ground." About 25 feet away to the east another tree appeared blackened, as if burnt on one side, starting "about four feet from the ground and extending four feet up the trunk." Linda Howe (who investigated the scene on May 23rd with David Perkins) also noted that the tops of this tree appeared blackened and scorched. None of the other 50 or so trees nearby appeared to have been impacted in this manner. Howe had visited the scene after being alerted to the case by Dorothy Aldridge from the *Gazette-Telegraph*. She filmed the scene, interviewed the rancher and the footage was later featured in her documentary *A Strange Harvest*.

On May 30, 1980, Howe and investigator Richard Sigismond took radiation readings with a Geiger counter and they claimed to have found no unusual reading directly at the horse, but detected higher than normal radiation levels on the blackened, scorched-appearing tree some eight feet from the horse. Detectives also picked up elevated levels at the tree and noted that a branch, similar to a dowser's rod, was found near the horse stripped of bark, and smaller branches lay strewn around the stripped branch.

Another interesting point that deserves mention: Like many mutilations, the horse appeared to exhibit a "remarkable lack of [necrotic] deterioration." Two weeks after the horse's unfortunate demise, Blake noted that "the carcass 'hasn't bloated and there's no odor around him.' Blake directed the deputies to a downed cow that died around the same time and it was about a quarter-mile away. 'That cow carcass really stinks. You can smell it an eighth of a mile away.' In fact it wasn't until a month or so after death that the horse had noticeably begun to deteriorate. 'No flies or ants have touched him and no predators have been at him," Blake noted to investigators.

On Monday the 21st, when Skip Easy Cash was last seen alive, in nearby

Ramah, Colorado another horse was discovered apparently mutilated. "Rebel" was missing his right eyelid; part of his right ear and the rear end had been neatly "reamed out." This was the third horse discovered mutilated in Colorado that spring. Another case featured a nine-month old Arabian colt in Cripple Creek, CO, that was discovered mutilated and allegedly dropped in the snow "25 feet from the owner's back door."

Those Damnable Devil Worshippers!

On May 11, 1980, Washington County, Iowa rancher James Waterhouse found the remains of his 125-pound Charolais bull calf near the community of Keota. The story never hit the press but was immediately reported to authorities by the rancher. It seems, while checking his cattle Waterhouse noticed a mother cow near a small creek that ran through the hard dry pasture. A calf was down and disfigured about 75 feet from the stream and the calf's mother was standing nearby bellowing. There was no obvious sign of how the calf died, there were no signs of a struggle, no apparent tracks and no significant blood was present around the animal. No evidence was ascertained that would have suggested a predator kill. The tongue had been deftly removed far down into the throat; *both eyes* and eyelids—upper and lower—were missing, with some blood left pooled in the sockets. It also appeared that a small amount of blood had spilled onto the calf's face. The scrotum had been deftly sliced off and there was what appeared to be a needle mark on the jugular vein and an unusual bruise on the belly. County officials were on the scene by 4:30 p.m. that same day. The animal was beginning to bloat but it was still fresh and worthy of laboratory examination by pathologists.

> Because of its timely discovery, it was decided the remains of the Waterhouse calf were fresh enough to justify an attempt at a thorough investigation. Under the auspices of Special Agent Joe Motsinger of the Iowa Department of Public Safety, the Division of Criminal Investigation [DCI]… [t]he calf was transported to the Iowa State University Veterinarian Diagnostic Laboratory in Ames, Iowa. There, a necropsy examination was conducted by John J. Andrews, D.V.M, professor of Pathology and G.W. Stevenson, D.V.M, Post-doctoral consultant…[3]

We'll get to the necropsy results in a minute, but first a bit of background: Special Agent Joe Motsinger, an ex-Marine, was familiar with the mutilation mystery having seen a unreported muted cow on his brother-in-law's ranch back in 1975. He was hired by the Iowa DCI the following year and because of his interest in the phenomenon, and having seen another mutilated cow, volunteered to investigate the rash of cases that began the fall of 1979 and extended into the spring of 1980. The late 1979 Iowa cases were mentioned in *Newsweek* in a January 1980 issue. Motsinger seemed forthcoming and agreed to speak with inquiring investigators, journalists and the media.

He mentioned to *Mute Evidence* authors Kagan & Summers that upon taking charge of the investigation into Iowa cattle mute cases one of the first calls he made was to Idaho DCI investigator Steve Watt, who had successfully linked some of his cases to a "local cult group." As mentioned in the *Newsweek* article, Motsinger's investigation had uncovered intriguing circumstantial evidence of an apparent "occult" presence near the site of several Iowa mutilations.

According to Motsinger, two abandoned houses in the area where the November and December 1979 cases had occurred contained what appeared to be occult paraphernalia and symbols written on the walls. The first house featured a circle and pentagram drawn on the floor and the walls had what appeared to be written incantations in some sort of ritual language. There were drawn inverted crucifixes and other symbols as well. These sound to me like your garden variety, wannabe ceremonial magic/witchcraft symbols and accoutrements. A dog skull had been placed inside the pentagram on the floor. The second house was similar—there were symbols written about the place, inverted crucifixes and also words and phrases in English: "Devil Son was Here," "Death," "The Devil is You and I," "Evil Lives," etc. According to Kagan, who saw photographs of the scene, there was a "makeshift altar on a wooden box," and the altar featured two skulls—one of them from a calf with a "blood-red" candle placed on the top and burnt.[4]

In their rather skeptical examination of the cattle mutilation phenomenon, Kagan and Summers note that *Newsweek* highlighted this apparent "occult" angle and mentioned law enforcement's thinking that there was a link between the discovery of witchcraft/ceremonial magic activity and the recent outbreak of mutes in Iowa. Although an informant came forward and provided investigators with some leads, no direct cultist link was ever established by law enforcement to the extent that someone was actually charged of any crimes linking ritualized activity to the Iowa mute cases. Nor has anyone ever been charged for anything related to perpetrating unexplained livestock deaths in North America—ever.

> [T]he reaction to the local media coverage given the reports had caused an upsurge of the same pattern that always developed in places where the mute phenomenon made itself felt. But in this instance the DCI had had cult leads right from the start, and they had some real evidence to back up that approach. Houses had been found in the area where the mutilations had been reported, covered with occult and Satanic symbols. There were informants. Unfortunately, until May of 1980 none of the reportedly mutilated animals had been examined and confirmed by a veterinarian pathologist, so there was a good deal of doubt about whether all the reported mutilations were real or mistaken predator damage…[T]he DCI was fairly sure they were investigating a real occurrence, not the phantom results of a wave of hysteria…

DCI investigators had gone to the public library in Des Moines to do some research on occult practices involving animal sacrifice. When they got there, they found that almost all the books on occult practice and witchcraft, especially those books that had information on animal sacrifice, had been checked out...

[T]he DCI had asked the library to supply them with the names of the people who had taken out the books...The library director refused to give out the information. [Motsinger said] "We got a court order for their records, and the Library Association went to the [American Civil Liberties Union] ACLU, and they filed suits against us. The press really jumped on this, and that was how we ended up in *Newsweek*...I think we may be due for a couple of more mutes around Halloween, if you know what I mean."[5]

The Waterhouse case and post-mortem investigation was extremely well documented and is crucial in our process of noting that there are cases that *scientifically establish* that at least some mutilation cases have unusual evidence and are not the result of natural attrition and scavenging. The Keota case establishes the probability of extraordinary involvement that runs contrary to Rommel's assertion that all mutilations can be dismissed with prosaic explanations. This case (like many others) was different and you can argue with me, but not the evidence obtained by veterinarian pathologists and the results of accepted forensic science.

Here is a brief recap of the post-mortem process: Dr. John J. Andrews had the Keota calf brought from the Waterhouse ranch to ISU diagnostic laboratory. Motsinger attended the work-up and watched the scientists conduct the rigorous process of establishing scientific data from the carcass, now in the beginning stages of decomposition. Later, after the team of veterinarian experts had presented their findings, Gerald W. Shanahan, Chief of the Iowa DCI told Tom Adams:

[B]oth doctors stated that the animal had been cut with a very sharp instrument and that it was definitely not the work of predators. Dr. Stevenson stated that he was especially interested in the removal of the eyes in that it was a very neat job. Dr. Stevenson further stated that it would have been hard for him to duplicate the same removal.[6]

According to their necropsy summary, the team "used a blacklight to examine the external surface of the animal for fluorescent material. There was approximately 10 to 15-and-a-half one-centimeter foci of fluorescent material on the left hip and shoulder...only on the tips of the hair...in very small amounts." There appeared to be a normal amount of blood in the carcass.

Kagan and Summers admit that it is hard to argue with the results of good science performed by professionals. They describe Kagan's meeting with Dr. Andrews and later quote a letter in which Dr. Andrews provided them with further candid assessments of the test results:

[Andrews] was a professor of pathology as well as a board certified vet pathologist. It was good to be in the presence of an expert…"The tongue was the most suggestive evidence of human intervention of all the wounds," said Andrews. "It was removed much too far back in the mouth to have been done by a predator. In fact, we were able to reproduce the tongue wound on another dead calf we had in the lab. The wound on that mutilated calf is perfectly consistent with what we did to the other one in the lab; pull the tongue way out, reach in, and cut it off. The cut we made that way on the other calf fell in almost exactly the same place as the one on the mutilated animal…

There was possible human action on the eyes. The birds could have done it; they will pluck out the eye and clean out the musculature, too, so, it's possible that the [top side] eye could have been taken out by predators. But also by humans…because *both* eyes were taken. The up *and* the down side eye. [my emphasis] I'd absolutely stand by the idea of predators if only the upside eye had been taken. But with both gone, it's hard to tell.

We tried to duplicate the eye surgery on another calf, using a knife. It was extremely difficult to do it that way without cutting the lids…"

Kagan then asked Andrews what he thought about the leads Motsinger had turned up pointing toward local cults being responsible for this animal and possibly others.

"Well," said the doctor, "I'm a Catholic, and that kind of thing gives me cause for concern. I have children, and I worry about what kinds of things they might be exposed to. If you believe in God, then you've got to believe in the devil, and if there are people running around who have taken allegiance to evil, the odds are they will do something to back up their beliefs."[7]

Mother Nature Coughed and Bellowed

On May 18, 1980, Mount St. Helens in southwestern Washington State erupted, leveling seven square miles of the north-facing slope of the peak. The series of eruptions sent ash clouds into the upper atmosphere, and blanketed the land downwind to the east. There was a corresponding lull in mute reports in this entire region. This changed ten days later when a strange multiple death case was reported by Wyoming resident Ross Younglund and Ross' brother Walter (a Colorado State Representative).

On May 28th, the Younglund brothers and Walter's son Monty were riding on

Ross' ranch located on the Colorado-Wyoming border north of New Raymer, when they happened upon five dead cows laid out in a perfectly straight line—east to west—over a distance of a mile and a half. The five animals were aged between five and six years old and all five were facing north.

> To Younglund, the cow laying furthest east "had clearly died of lark-spur poisoning," had become bloated, and coyotes or other scavengers had obviously been feasting on the bovine corporeality. [sic] However, proceeding along the section line to the west, it was noted that the other four carcasses had not bloated nor been touched by scavengers. Instead, each of the four had a "perfect square cut out of the belly where the udder had been." The cuts appeared "straight" to Younglund, not torn. The rectums of all four were "cored out," leaving a hole six inches wide and four to 6 inches deep. On two of the cows, one half of the face was gone to the bone and the ear on that side had been "cut down to the skull." The heads of the other cows were untouched… all four animals had their legs drawn up funny "as if they were set down after death and sort of crumpled on their legs." There were no tracks, signs of a struggle, nor blood evidence around the four. The ground around the larkspur-poisoned cow, however, indicated she had kicked and flailed before death… "On the one cow to the east where the coyotes had been at her, her rectum was torn out about a foot to a foot and a half wide—pretty jagged and clear down to the bone. On the other four, the rectums were smaller holes that were pretty much perfectly round as if cored out by something."[8]

On June 3, 1980 a series of deadly tornados slashed through Grand Island, Nebraska killing five people and causing $300 million in damage. Then, two days later on the night of June 5th, a 1,700-pound bull was mutilated in Moffat, Colorado. We'll return to this case in a moment.

Near Oyen, Alberta, near the Saskatchewan border, about 12 miles north of town, rancher Marilyn Flaht reported a mutilation to officials that also probably occurred the night of June 5th. Her registered three-year-old female quarter horse was discovered missing its female genitals; the left ear and eye and the tongue was removed. There was a fist-sized hole in the chest through the brisket. In a *Medicine Hat News* article from June 11, 1980 it was noted:

> [T]he parts of the horse appeared to be surgically removed "and the person who did it had to be trained or must have very sharp instruments." [Flaht] said the prairie was still damp at the time and there were no tracks made by a car or truck coming into the area, but it would have been possible for someone on horseback to get to the animals undetected. The

animal, which she valued at between $900 and $1000 was one of five on the pasture and the hardest one to catch, she said. When she was examining the dead horse her four-year-old gelding came up and sniffed it "then sneezed and snorted and ran away from the animal as if to tell me to get back." She said the horse was left in the field for a week and the coyotes didn't touch it. The incident was reported to the RCMP and the horse was examined by a veterinarian. Flaht said she was told they preferred her not to be present when the examination took place. She was later told the horse died of something other than natural causes.[9]

It was later reported that three separate witnesses in different nearby locations had seen "a weird light" on the night of the mutilation. Then the following Sunday (June 12, 1980), a second horse was discovered mutilated in a separate pasture from the first horse. The carcass lay in long grass that was about one foot high. No weeds around the animal appeared to have been disturbed and "it appeared as though the horse had been dropped from above." The Mounties were called in, as was a veterinarian, who performed a field autopsy. The second victimized Flaht horse was missing half of its udder and there was a strip of hide missing from the flank. The vet attempted to duplicate the cuts but "he was simply unable to do so." The rear end was missing and a small piece of bleached white intestine was found on the ground. It was "snowy white, as though it had been washed, and there was no manure." The vet was puzzled when he discovered there was only a syringe full of blood in the heart. The blood was taken to a lab, but Flaht was never told the results of testing.[10]

[Veterinary pathologist] Dr. Carroll (a pseudonym) revealed that an apparent mute case had occurred on June 10, 1980 near a town in Manitoba. Dr. Carroll's examination (the carcass had been transported to his lab) had found that the left ear, scrotum, testicles, tail and anus had been cut and removed. There were also two cuts on the left flank. Dr. Carroll related that the cause of death was determined to be peritonitis, and the mutilation was done after the death of the animal. [A] local veterinarian indicated that the male calf was found in an alfalfa pasture amongst the rest of the herd. There were no marks to be found on the ground to indicate how the perpetrators affected the mutilation. He also remarked that the parts removed presented an "unusual collection of coincidences," and that predators seemed an unlikely, although possible, explanation. He also said that the calf was found in a not easily accessible location. There had not been any publicity about mutilations in this area to encourage pranksters. The RCMP investigated the incident, taking photos, etc., but did not make any public statements.[11]

Trickster Rides the Chopper

The June 5, 1980 bull mutilation in Mofatt, Colorado, happened to be the first mutilation case that I personally investigated, but I became involved with the case 13 years later in 1993. *This head-scratching case had a profound affect on me* for it jump-started my ongoing 20-plus-year process of investigating and pondering the conundrum called the "cattle mutilation" mystery. I've often joked publicly that on that January 1993 day at the Sutherland ranch, I was kissed by a mutilation trickster or "tarbaby."

First, a quick background on my involvement in this particular case. In late November 1992, a riveting two-object UFO sighting had been observed by over a dozen people who lived in the little town of Crestone, Colorado (in the San Luis Valley), where I called home. I missed the sighting event, as I was out of town playing a gig with my band Pyramid, but later, on New Year's Eve, I was told about the sighting. I was also told that *the same night a cattle mutilation had occurred on the Manuel Sanchez ranch* about 60 miles south in Costilla County. I thought that these synchronistic events were interesting and would make for a fun *Crestone Eagle* newspaper article, so I began an investigation into the history of mute and UFO cases in Saguache County where I lived.

According to Tom Adams, Linda Howe, David Perkins and others, no official Saguache County mutilation reports had ever been documented. Didn't matter, I contacted the local sheriff who (much to my surprise) provided me with 24 Polaroid photographs of obscenely-disfigured cattle and horses that had been taken in the county from 1975 to the early 1980s. I was able to locate the deputy, Gene Gray, who had taken the photographs and over the course of a couple of days, we were able to identify the ranches where these cases had occurred.

One of the photos was of a mutilated bull found on the Sutherland ranch located 13 miles away in Moffat, Colorado. Since this was the next town over, I called and spoke with Virginia Sutherland and made an appointment to interview the family about their mutilated bull from June 1980. This was to be my very first on-site investigation and interview. If I had known beforehand what would transpire, I might have thought twice about going there and kissing that mute tarbaby, starting an investigative process into what may be *the greatest unsolved serial crime spree of the twentieth century*.

Here's the Cliff Notes version of my first foray into the mystery: Their seed bull had been kept in a separate pasture about 500 yards south of the Sutherland ranch house which is located a mile or so west of the town of Moffat, Colorado. At dusk that early June night in 1980, the Sutherland family had sat down to dinner when they heard what appeared to be a helicopter fly slowly over the house, from the north headed south. They had seen utility company choppers checking the power lines three miles west of the house many times and found it unusual that a helicopter should be flying so low over the ranch at dusk, so far from the power lines. Fifteen to twenty minutes later, they heard the sound of what seemed to be the same chopper, but this time it seemed to be hovering close by, so they went outside to get a look at the low-flying craft. The chopper, "was an old-fashioned, two-man, whirly-bird-type of helicopter, mustard-yellow in color." It rose from the pasture where their bull was located and flew directly over them, headed north in the direction from which they thought it had arrived. "It didn't seem to have any markings what-soever" Virginia told me, still puzzled after all those years.

"I thought that strange," commented Mrs. Sutherland. "I also thought it was peculiar that it had evidently landed in our field." The chopper flew back to the north, right over their house. "We all got a real good look at it. It was one of those, like-you-see-on-*M.A.S.H*-type helicopters. It was only 30 or 40 feet over our heads."

The next morning, they discovered the dead bull, its penis and eyes gone, its rear end "deeply cored-out," and a "one-inch plug missing from the brisket."

The Sutherlands, understandably angry at the loss of their prize seed-bull, immediately called all around southern and central Colorado and northern New Mexico, trying to determine where the old-fashioned yel-low helicopter was based. They came up empty. No airport had ever seen a mustard-yellow, whirlybird-type helicopter and they were told that this type of craft was extremely rare and astronomically expensive to keep in the air because of its age. It had very limited range, [90 miles] due to limited fuel capacity.

"It was the strangest thing. That bull was never touched by scavengers. Flies that would land on one side of it died and it took years for the car-cass to melt into the field," Virginia remembered. We went out to the site and much to my surprise, there was the bull's skeleton, laid out on its back. I asked her if she would mind if I brought the skull home. She said I could have it, so I took it home and later painted it and hung it on my wall. My first (and only) mutilated cow trophy." (figure 4)

After examining the mute site we returned to the ranch house, I thanked them for their time and for a second photo of their unfortunate bull Virginia gave me. I promised I would give them a call if I unearthed anything that might shed some light on the untimely demise of their ani-mal. Much to my surprise, I would make that call the very next day.

The following morning, as I sat over a cup of coffee in the dining room and reviewed the Sutherland interview notes, I heard the faint sound of a helicopter coming down the Sangre de Cristo Range from the north. I glanced out the window and saw a mustard-yellow, old-fashioned, "like you see on M.A.S.H-type helicopter [UH-47]…" [My girlfriend] Isadora [Story], her eight year-old daughter Brisa and several neighbors also saw the chopper as it flew by. I was floored. Almost 13 years after the fact, the antique helicopter had apparently returned, flying over the house of the investigator, me… I had been so startled I forgot to grab my camera.[12]

The above example is a textbook illustration of what could be interpreted as a manifestation of a synchronistic, tricksterish force (or mechanism). This mechanism appears to be interjected into or triggered by, manifestations of seemingly unrelated paranormal events. I cover this subject extensively in *Stalking the Tricksters*. It appears that there is apparent patterning within these seemingly bizarre coincidences that adorn the logs of investigators and experiencers of the inexplicable and sublime. This mechanism may be a crucial clue to consider while unraveling the mutilation mystery. Meanwhile, back at the ranch…

Hoeppner's Samples and More Cases

Northern Colorado seemed to be ground zero that late summer, early fall of 1980. On September 2nd, just north of Briggsdale at the Eagle Rock Ranch, ranch hand Jessie Frazier discovered the eye-less body of a six-year-old bull lying flat on its back near the ranch road that snaked through the property. The reproductive organs had been removed and where the testicles had been removed, there was a "real smooth cut-out circle about four inches across." The tongue had been removed and there were no apparent signs of scavenging.

> The head was "straight" with the horns on the ground. There was no sign of tracks or a struggle in the soft sand. Frazier said: "Usually we see signs of [a] death struggle. He should have thrown that head of his and those horns would have dug up the ground. But there was no sign of anything. It's as if he was laid out down there like that, dead…I never found any animal like that before." …There were little trickles of blood running from both eyes…[that was] the only blood in evidence…with what appeared to be a straight cut, the tongue had been removed "as if you had pulled it out as far as you could and cut it off."[13]

This description of the tongue removal echoes Dr. Andrews' description of the Keota, Iowa case where veterinarian pathologists had possibly determined how the tongue on the Waterford cow had been expertly removed. According to Adams, "a week after Frazier found the bull, he found a cow that had died an apparently natural death." Unlike the bull, which the scavengers wouldn't touch, this cow was torn apart "down to the bones" by coyotes and other scavengers in a single day.

Frazier and the owner of the Eagle Rock ranch, Virgil Prewett, reported the unexplained livestock death to the local authorities and were "disturbed not only by the mutilation, but by the cool reception they received at the sheriff's office when they visited there…"

"They don't die that way..." Prewett feels the killing and mutilation of the bull was not done where it was found: "All the evidence was that it was done away from there and brought back and set down." Prewett thinks the possibility of cult involvement should be looked into more closely. He suspects a helicopter might have been used to transport the bull, but the sighting of a helicopter in that area would not be at all uncommon due to the ranch's proximity to Warren Air Force Base, [figure 5] across the border in Wyoming.[14]

On September 16, 1980, two 350-to-400-pound steer calves were discovered dead near Briggsdale, Colorado, located north of Greeley. Weld County Rancher Roland Ball estimated that one of them had been dead four to five days, the other less than 48 hours. The animals appeared not to have become bloated after death. On one animal, the ear had been neatly removed with the cut going into the skull and the tail had been cut off into the tailbone. The skin of a rear ankle had been removed but the tendons had been left intact.

The other calf was discovered about a mile and a half away and it was missing the tongue. The rear end had been cored out and some of the tail hair had been pulled out and scattered around on the ground. Ball found the calves' mother lying next to her offspring as if protecting the site from scavengers. Besides the tracks of the mother cow, no other tracks, footprints or evidence of the perpetrators, animal or otherwise, was noted.

Mr. Ball immediately called Weld County Sheriff Harold Andrews who came out to the ranch to investigate the scene and obtain forensic samples from the most recently killed calf. Andrews sent his samples to the Colorado State University (CSU) diagnostic laboratory in Ft. Collins. Mrs. Ball called her friend Iona Hoeppner, the local science teacher, to help investigate the case of the fresh calf. Hoeppner had B.S. degrees in physics, biology and chemistry from the University of Southern Colorado, Fresno State and Memphis State. She obtained forensic samples, blood and some unusual-looking reddish fluid that had pooled on the ground next to the calf for testing at the school's science lab.

According to Tom Adams' *Project Stigma* report #13, at this point, the story became rather unusual. Hoeppner claimed she had prepared slides and did a preliminary microscopic analysis of tissue samples obtained from the belly area of the calf and set up cultures in the incubator. She then carefully wrapped and tagged the samples, taped them up securely and placed them in a freezer along with other samples.

Around midnight Mrs. Hoeppner's husband and a friend, a school coach, arrived at the lab and assisted in closing all the windows and locking the lab as they departed for home. Around six and a half hours later, around 6:30 am, the maintenance crew arrived to prepare the school for the day's activities (Friday, September 19, 1980). An hour or so later, around 7:30 am, a school employee called Mrs. Hoeppner to ask "Did you leave the doors (to the lab) open and stuff all over the floor?" She rushed to the lab to find [it] in disarray. The lab door, with its old lock, was not all that secure, as one could "jimmy" it open without too much difficulty, especially by someone who knew what they were doing. After entering the lab, apparently through the door, the intruder(s) took all the fluid samples that had been gathered at the mutilation site plus all of the cultures that had been prepared, placed in the incubator and stored in one of the many cabinets in the room… Mrs. Hoeppner's chemical cabinet had been gone through. A container of formaldehyde had been set aside but not taken. A newly acquired container of methyl alcohol was still on the shelf, but all the alcohol was gone. Hoeppner speculated that, though the intruders may have initially planned to preserve the specimens in the formaldehyde, they may have opted for the alcohol instead.[15]

Hoeppner was perplexed by the break in, but (for some reason) did not report it to the sheriff. She did immediately call the CSU lab to inquire about the samples the sheriff had procured from the mute site and sent along to CSU. CSU claimed the samples "never arrived." Iona Hoeppner fortunately had a friend who worked at CSU and they discreetly asked pathology lab personnel about the specimens. He was told that they had arrived but "they were misplaced." Puzzled, Iona immediately went back out to the site and gathered two additional sets of samples, being careful, using sterile gloves. She gathered additional samples of the unusual fluid on the ground that looked exactly as it had two days prior. It had not absorbed into the ground and appeared not to have evaporated at all. Something strange and misleading appeared to be going on and she set up a sting to try to bait whoever was responsible for stealing the first set of samples from the Ball calf.

Returning to her laboratory, she carefully hid the real samples she had just acquired and took pains to put out "dummy" specimens in the same racks and cabinets as before. The next morning the doors and windows were still closed and locked—but all the dummy samples were gone… The only people (as far as can be ascertained) with direct knowledge of Hoeppner's sample gathering and of the first break-in had been the Hoeppner family, the Ball family, the school superintendent and a close woman friend of Mrs. Hoeppner's. Judging by what occurred, it would seem someone else knew, too… The reddish fluid which had pooled on the ground: Thinner than blood, it was not organic. There was no detectable bacteria in the liquid at all… "It was as sterile as anything

I've ever looked at, and I looked at it both before and after filtering through filter paper to get any soil and dirt out. I don't have any equipment powerful enough to see viruses, but there was absolutely no bacteria." Under a microscope the uniformly clear liquid contained two constituents of interest. First, there were "some strange looking rectangles 10 microns by 3 microns (estimated) with striations on them running crosswise. They didn't look like anything I had seen before…" And secondly, "One other thing in the fluid were small crystals one by two microns… throughout the liquid sample." The liquid itself remained on the ground at the mutilation site for at least two weeks. It finally left a maroon-brownish spot of discoloration on the ground, and the grass in the immediate area was dead.[16]

Hoeppner experimented with other liquids at the site and poured out amounts of water, carbon tetrachloride, a potassium chloride solution and mineral oil to see how long it would take for these materials to either evaporate off or soak into the ground. "All penetrated the ground easily, though the mineral oil was absorbed more slowly." Hoeppner then turned her attention on the cut hide. There were three sets of cuts on her sample. Her cut, the sheriff's cut and the mutilator's cut. The results of her examination were noteworthy and she outlined her findings in an interview with KMGH-TV reporter Linda Moulton Howe:

> "I did careful microscopic exams on the tissue cut from the belly. It was not a cut, not a laser burn. No cell was destroyed. It (the incision) was separated between the cells, cell for cell. No cell was disrupted in the mutilator's cut. There is nothing that I know of that could do such a thing." She explained that there is a natural cohesion among these tissue cells, and that an incision would normally cut through the cells, such as was evident in the sheriff's and Hoeppner's incisions. Incredibly, then, the cells along what was the mutilator's "incision" were separated along their boundaries—not really an ordinary "incision" at all—and according to Iona Hoeppner: "I don't think mankind has the ability to do what was done."[17]

Later in a November 2, 1980 article, penned by Harold Jackson for the *Greeley Tribune*. Jackson reported that Weld County Sheriff Andrews told him that they had used the department's lab to examine the samples from the Ball's calf: "We clipped a piece of the hide out and under examination we found a very definite, smooth cut. We could even tell the difference between that cut and the one we made removing the piece of hide." He claimed that the mutilator's cut was straight up and down while his was jagged and uneven. CSU never released any further information about the whereabouts of the missing samples, nor indicated that the samples had been found and tested.

Adams veers off the mutilations with the following *Stigmata* report from Linda Howe of an incident that reportedly occurred on September 23, 1980. At around 7:00 p.m. Littleton, Colorado resident John Crumby was on the phone looking out his western-facing window when he noticed what appeared to be a silent helicopter flying toward his house. It seemed to be about 100 feet up and was traveling toward him about a mile away. It was silhouetted by the glow of the sun, which had just set behind it and he was unable to discern the spinning rotor blades. The craft stopped in mid-air:

> [It] began to rise slowly. It had been merely a dark color; but suddenly there was a silver tint and the "chopper" turned into a ball-shaped object, somewhat smaller than the "original" craft. It ascended out of John Crumby's view… [He] called to his mother-in-law…[who] had run into the back yard. After it had passed from Crumby's view, she saw the "ball" assume a "square shape" at perhaps an altitude of 4,000-feet above the ground. There then appeared a sort of slightly elongated appendage which hung down from one side of the craft… the object vanished—but then a second or two later, it re-appeared at perhaps several hundred feet to the (viewer's) right. The fluttering appendage was still there. The object then shot straight up, to be lost from sight in about a second.[18]

Normally, I wouldn't include an apparently unassociated claim like this, but since we're talking synchronicity and correlations, I thought this interesting account had elements worthy of note. On September 29, 2009, at 11:24 a.m., the San Luis Valley Camera Project captured some intriguing video footage of what appears to be a small, two-man helicopter traveling just east of Alamosa, Colorado. The apparent chopper was flying south to north and as it caught the late afternoon sun in the west, the canopy seemed to catch the light at a perfect angle and it bloomed into what appeared to be a brilliant silver ball that kept traveling—leaving apparent light blobs to fade in its wake. To see this footage go to: **youtube.com/watch?v=P3cwcIlWK6w** Light can be a marvelous trickster—at the proper angle—and perhaps we can explain Cumby's sighting as simple light reflections and honest misinterpretation, but where was the engine and prop noise? How could it have appeared to move so quickly? Could light bloom off conventional craft explain many misidentified UFO sightings? Or, can UFOs masquerade themselves as helicopters? We can't factor anything in or out, or speak in absolutes about anything involving the mutilation phenomenon.

Although no nearby mutilation reports had been filed in Littleton, suburb of Denver, as we have seen, helicopters are obviously linked somehow to the mutilation mystery. There are far too many good quality reports to ignore. In 1980, Tom Adams published a list of 250 documented chopper sightings seen in and around mutilation sites. Since 1991's revised edition there have been dozens and dozens of additional chopper sightings in and around regions where mutes have been reported. Not only in North America, but in the British Isles as well. This is not, in my estimation, merely a coincidence, but could suggest that some clandestine group or groups are utilizing helicopters to (at the very least) monitor outbreaks of mutilation reports, and/or they may be directly involved in perpetrating these animal deaths and disfigurements.

As for UFOs, there have been many unexplained craft sightings around mute regions: "Big Mama," the Missouri lights, the Malmstrom wave and other sightings of orange globes/spheres. But these cases are relatively few compared to the constant detail of eyewitnesses hearing and witnessing helicopters—mostly before and after mutilations have occurred. As we have seen, there are tantalizingly few claims of witnesses sighting helicopters *during* a mutilation, but hundreds of choppers have been sighted before and/or after a case is discovered. Conversely, there are only a handful of alleged UFO sightings witnessed while a mutilation is in progress and at least some of these reports may have been misidentified conventional craft.

Less than a week after the Ball mutilation case, on October 1, 1980 Orvil Harms reported to Weld County Sheriff Harold Andrews that he had discovered his five-month-old steer dead out in his pasture missing its genitalia, ears and rear-end.

> "It was definitely cut with a knife because it was sort of jagged, like they had stopped and started over at places trying to cut…" *Both* ears were cut off "like they'd did it with a scalpel." [my emphasis] Six inches up the nose and between the eyes, a six-inch by six-inch oval of hide was missing. There were no tracks or sign of a death struggle. There was some kind of liquid on the ground…[19]

According to Tom Adams, Harms informed Howe who interviewed him, that there were no bird droppings at the site, however coyotes had apparently torn off pieces of hide, but dropped them without dragging them off and eating them, even though according to Harms, "we got a lot of coyotes out here and they're starving all the time." Harms mentioned to Howe that an antelope [pronghorn] had been struck and killed by a vehicle on September 30th by the highway that ran near Harms' ranch. About 12 hours later the coyotes had "eaten everything but bones and a little patch of skin"… On October 9th, one of Harms' calves died, apparently overcome from pneumonia. "To confirm the diagnosis, he had a veterinarian cut into the animal. It was left in the pasture. By the next day, coyotes hadn't touched it. Harms speculated this was because of a 'human smell' associated with it."

The rest of the fall appeared to be a lull period on the mute front however, in late December 1980 two of the most spectacular UFO close-encounter cases on record occurred. The December 26 and 28th encounters by RAF Bentwaters personnel in southern England of a strange landed craft is widely considered to be one of the most well documented cases on record. The following night, December 29, 1980, the puzzling "Cash-Landrum" close encounter event occurred northeast of Houston, Texas.

Betty Cash and Vickie Landrum and Vickie's son Cody allegedly observed a diamond-shaped object shooting out flames from the bottom as it hovered at tree-top level over the road they were traveling. All three suffered what were reminiscent of radiation burns. A short time later two squadrons of what appeared to be dual rotor Chinook helicopters were sighted in the vicinity of the UFO. The events are too complicated to go into detail here, but I note them because of the curious time frame correlation. I have not uncovered any mutilation reports from this final week of 1980, but consider these two historic UFO encounter cases noteworthy nonetheless.

1981 Starts With a Bang

Unlike some past years with inclement cold weather, January of 1981 started out with a warm weather bang. On January 3, 1981, a rare mid-winter heat wave had enveloped the Front Range of Colorado and conditions were perfect for the cattle surgeons. The following report was published January 8th in the *Ranchland Farm News*: (figure 6)

> El Paso County—near Ramah—3-year-old Hereford heifer—missing hide and flesh on right side of jaw; also, right eye and rectal area removed—*a blue nylon rope was tied around the right rear leg* [and] *the throat had been cut.* [The] investigating deputy theorized that someone intended to butcher the cow, then they were scared off and coyotes removed the parts.[20] [my emphasis]

On January 14, 1981 a mutilation was reported from Washington County, Arkansas, near the town of Prairie Grove. A rancher reported that his "600-pound 18-month-old red white-face calf was discovered missing its tail and rectum." The rear end appeared to show "'searing' on the rectal incision." There was no indication of bleeding. *Hair, apparently taken from the calf's tail, appeared to have been "arranged in a neat cone-shaped pile."* (The calf went missing on the 14th, and then discovered by the rancher two days later on the 16th —"100 yards from [the] house.")[21]

What? Does this mean we have closet hairdressing coyotes mutilating cattle? This is an interesting recurring observation that occasionally tail hair has been removed and laid out with intent. And in this case, arranged into a cone-shaped pile. This makes absolutely no sense, if this is the act of animals. If you are simply looking at these cases as misidentified scavenger action, you have to entertain *all* the evidence. If this was done on purpose, with intelligence, perhaps there is an agenda-driven rationale for this type of evidence to be left behind?

This report is reminiscent of another southern Colorado report I investigated in 1995. I was alerted that there had been a mute case reported on Colorado's Front Range where the tail hair had been carefully cut and laid out behind the body, neatly combed out, and it appeared (to the rancher and this investigator) that this act had been done carefully—possibly in a ritualistic manner. Unlike your garden-variety "classic" mute, the stump of the tail had sprayed some blood on the ground, as photographs of the crime scene indicate. (figure 7) Does this prove that at least some human perpetrators of these mutilations have a ritualized agenda? No, but it should give one pause.

Some mute investigators discount out of hand that any true mutilations are the result of ritual acts. I don't think it is by accident that over the years, the media and some law enforcement officials have been led to this conclusion. I intuit that this aspect of theatricality (in some cases) may suggest that the ancient practice of animal sacrifice is somehow tied to at least some of the mutilations. (figure 8) I'd be very surprised if this was not the case, and we'll revisit this theory later.

I have a hunch that there may be another clue or two in this particular case with ritualistic overtones. It is interesting to note that there are only a few solid unexplained livestock death reports from Alabama in the early 1980s. A few cases made the papers in the 1970s, but it wasn't until the early 1990s that the mutes became headline news with the cases around Fyffe. As we'll see, 13 years later, the mutilators returned in force to Alabama when several dozen alleged mutilations were investigated by local and state law enforcement. These cases may have indicated a different agenda, as we'll soon see.

From the *Daily Olympian* February 3, 1981: It was reported that in the Hills area of Pierce County, near Olympia, Washington—on an "unidentified ranch," a nine-year-old registered Hereford bull, valued around $2,000, was allegedly discovered missing "part of lower jaw, left ear and testicles." The animal was last seen January 30th and found three days later on February 2nd. (Another Hills Area rancher claimed that he discovered a mutilated cow on his ranch later in February.) Julius Scammon Rodman read the article about the rare Washington State case, and the article was forwarded to Adams via Denver investigator/researcher Kalani Hanohano.

For a quick breather let's go to completely unrelated synchronistic news from around the world. That same week, on February 6th, Queen Frederika of Greece died and later that night, Prince Charles proposed marriage to Lady Diana Spencer. Tragically, two days later on the 8th, Greece experienced the Karaiskakis Stadium disaster when 21 people were killed and 54 seriously injured at a hotly contested soccer match. Also on the 8th, an unexplained human decapitation case was reported to have occurred in San Francisco's Golden Gate Park. According to a local paper, a "man's body was found in a sleeping bag near Alvord Lake." The head (which was not found despite an extensive search) was removed 'with precision' and authorities suspected a 'ritualistic murder.'[22]

On February 15, 1981 in Meigs County, Tennessee a Fairview rancher named Jessie Templeton located his missing 700-to 800-pound, black angus female cow. Much to his dismay, it was found with its eyes "gouged out," the teats cut out, and the genitals cut out leaving "just a big circle where they should have been." The discovery of "vehicle tracks and footprints in the pasture led some observers to suspect 'cultists.'" Templeton also claimed that another cow was missing; it had not been found as of late February.[23]

That same February 15th, four dogs were discovered dead at an intersection in the Carter Lakes area of suburban Omaha, Nebraska. On April 14th "one dog was found…with burns, stab wounds and a metal rod imbedded in [one] carcass. All of the dogs were large breeds and some had been reported by their owners as missing. The last week of April 1981 "a cat was found with its head apparently twisted off and three legs torn off." [24]

Ongoing media coverage that spring of Washington State reports gave rise to several interesting rumors were disseminated into the community. In one story, a lady "reports that she fed her two prize horses around 6:00 p.m. one day, then found them on the ground, mutilated (no specifics), around 9:00 p.m. the same evening—she found her guard dogs (which had not made a sound) cowering near the horses." A few mutilations had been reported in Pierce County "over the past several years, with most of the victim animals being horses."[25]

And back in the real world, on April 9, 1981, the first confirmed diagnosis of AIDS, the sexually transmitted disease that causes Karposi's sarcoma, was made by Dr. John Guillett in San Francisco. And Eric Harris, one of the Columbine high-school shooters was born. Then, the following day two strange mutilation reports were filed from Sequoyah County, Oklahoma.

The *Saturday Oklahoman* reported that on April 11, 1981 in Sequoyah County, south of Muldrow, the O'Bryans discovered the first of two unusual cattle deaths. The first report was of a pregnant cow that was found with its "genitals removed [and the] blood apparently drained." The perplexed rancher noted that there was "no trace of [the] fetus." The local sheriff *says the cow was shot 4 or 5 times with a .357 revolver or high-powered rifle.* " No tracks were found at the site and "the carcass remained undisturbed by predators." On the 13th, another head of livestock was discovered mutilated on the O'Bryan ranch. This time it was a bull that was "partially castrated" and there was "no evidence of bleeding; the blood was thought to be drained. There were no tracks, no disturbance[s] by dogs or predators. As with the first report, the sheriff says the bull was *shot nine times.*"[26] [my emphasis]

This rare detail of the animal being shot is somewhat unusual, but reminiscent of fall 1975 San Luis Valley/Costilla County cases that occurred on the Emilio Lobato ranch south of San Luis (and cases in Iowa and elsewhere). The Lobato case featured 49 head of cattle either shot, stolen or mutilated during two weeks in October 1975.

On April 15, 1981 Linda Howe was notified that a rancher had reported a mutilation in Larimer County, Colorado, near the town of Masonville. A four-month-old heifer calf was allegedly found with its right eye, rectum and tongue missing. The rear end incision left a "large circular hole." The calf was last seen on April 13, 1981.

Shannon County, South Dakota authorities estimate that sometime between the 15th and the 18th, a white-faced female bovine was mutilated on the Pine Ridge Indian Reservation. It was discovered with its udder cut out and its rectum "reamed out." The report came from the Kyle area, near Montieleaux. The disfigured carcass was found on April 22nd and it was estimated to have died the previous week. It is intriguing to note the synchronicity that *a cattle mutilation had been reported on the reservation on the same date in 1979, 1980 and 1981.* According to the source of this report David Brewer, of the Bureau of Indian Affairs, unidentified lights had also been reported on the reservation during these April time periods.

B.C. or Bust

On May 16, 1981 the mutilators evidently turned their attention to British Columbia, Canada where a 3-year-old female Hereford was reported dead with "half of tongue missing, anus removed [and] a portion of right side of face cut away—hide and hair." The incision was "in half-moon segment removed above right eye." There was also "a hole in upper right chest cavity" and a lateral cut on the neck.

The mutilation occurred in southeastern BC, five miles from Fernie, and Lloyd Phillips covered the story for the *Edmonton Journal*. Phillips was also the owner of the White Spruce Ranch who reported the case. Evidently there was "a considerable difference of opinion between the RCMP (police) and rancher/newspaper editor Phillips" as to what was discovered and when.

It seems the night of the 16th, around 8:00 p.m., a motorist passing the White Spruce Ranch witnessed what appeared to be "a cow down on the ground near Highway 3." The next morning another motorist saw the same animal. The motorist notified the owner, Lloyd Phillips, who immediately called the Royal Canadian Mounted Police. "When the first motorist, Lewis Cloutier, saw the animal Saturday evening, he was fairly certain that the head and face area was not damaged or mutilated (although apparently and admittedly he did not take a close-up look). Plus, *the animal was found by Phillips lying in a different position from that on Saturday evening.*"

> Upon examination of the 3-year-old female Hereford, it was noted that half the tongue was missing, the anus had been removed and a portion of the right side of the face had been cut away. Hide and hair in a half-moon segment (which included the eyelid) was cleanly removed

from above the right eye. There was not the slightest nick or cut in the underlying flesh. There was a hole in the upper right chest cavity near the shoulder. Although apparently made with a sharp instrument, it looked as though dogs or coyotes might have chewed on that area, as well. And, there was a "lateral cut" on the neck.[27]

It was thought by investigators that the mutilation must have occurred on the night of May 15-16 as the cow was seen alive and well on the 15th. Veterinarian Dr. David Lawson of Fernie examined the carcass in the field, and the RCMP also arrived and conducted an investigation. The following is another excerpt from the *Fernie Free Press* article of May 27, 1981, authored by Bruce Ramsey, like Lloyd Phillips, also an editor of the *Free Press*:

> Conflicting statements from the two constables from the RCMP's live-stock investigation section in Kamloops and Fernie veterinarian Dr. David Lawson, who conducted the autopsy on the mutilated cow, confuse even more an already confusing situation. The full RCMP report has not yet been received. The RCMP believe the animal died from natural causes, but they admitted to rancher Lloyd Phillips that they had no explanation for an eight or nine inch cut in the neck which runs, not across, but in a lateral direction, cutting squarely the large tendon in the neck. It was not frayed or chewed, as would be the case if a predator had felled the animal.

Dr. Lawson said he was unable to determine the cause of death "on the basis of my examination." In his official report, Dr. Lawson noted "the wounds on the head definitely appeared to have been made sometime after the animal's death, and quite possibly the other wounds as well. The external wounds appeared to fall into two categories. The wounds on the rear end and the neck and shoulder appeared to be characteristic of damage inflicted by carnivorous animals, with irregular edges, shredding of the tissues, and what appeared to be tooth marks."

Then Dr. Lawson concludes with this significant remark: "The wounds on the head appeared to have been made much more cleanly except for the irregular part on the muzzle. I find it difficult to imagine how an animal could have made the skin wounds or cut off the tongue so deeply inside the mouth. Therefore, it appeared more likely that *wounds on the head were made by a person using a sharp instrument*." [my emphasis]

Phillips does not rule out the possibility that the animal died from eating a poisonous plant, but he is critical of the authorities who did not send the vital organs to a pathological laboratory in Lethbridge to determine scientifically the cause of death.

I am critical of the fact that no examination of the stomach contents was made, no examination of the liver and no examination of the glands in the flank or shoulder areas was made," Phillips said, adding that when government inspectors check animals at an abattoir, the first thing they examine is the glands and if they are not up to scratch the animal is consigned to dog food.

The question of the animal dying of natural causes is questioned by Phillips and other area ranchers who examined the mutilated corpse. Phillips maintains the animal was not bloated, no symptoms of blackleg, nor symptoms of hemorrhagic septicemia which affects the bloodstream, nor were there symptoms of grass tetany which occurs in the spring when the animals are turned out into the green grass. [Phillips said:]

> I am at a loss to know what the police mean when they attributed death came from natural causes, except the possibility the animal could have eaten a poisonous plant, such as larkspur or wild parsnip, the presence of which could have been determined by blood samples or any examination of the stomach contents. No blood or tissue samples were taken.

Phillips said that in some statements attributed to the RCMP, they said predators go for the softer parts of an animal, which I [author Ramsey] agree with, "but in the light of that," he questioned, "why would the predators go for the bony area above the eye, take only the hide and hair, leaving the flesh untouched? Also, in the area above the eye, *you could see where hairs had been cut* as if by a knife or scissors. [my emphasis] To me that indicates it was no predator that mutilated the cow," he stated.

With regards to the tongue, the police said it was normal for a dead animal to have its tongue protruding, and Mr. Phillips agrees with that. The police, he said, stated that if the tongue was protruding a coyote or other predator would bite it off. That, they say, is the reason why half the tongue is missing. [Phillips said:]

> The police told me that anyone cutting the tongue from the side of the mouth would be cutting it at an angle. It was not cut at an angle. In actual fact, there were signs which indicated to me that the tongue had been cut half way from one side to half way from the other, because in the center of the tongue there were two notches that did not jibe. It was cut at a right angle, a square cut.'

Further, he stated the eyes were untouched, and he pointed out that, normally, animals go after the eyes. Also predators go into the flesh of the haunch, but in this case the flesh of the haunch was untouched. All that was taken was approximately four inches of the large intestine.

When the RCMP team came from Kamloops, Constable M. J. Chorney and Constable. R. J. Convey gave Phillips a copy of an article from *Penthouse* magon cattle mutilations which was subtitled "The Truth At Last." Phillips has no quarrel with the article… although he wonders what the qualifications of the writer, David Rorvik, are. He wonders, too, about something else.

> "I think," he said, "the RCMP investigation was geared to fit what was said in this article. They had a preconceived idea that there were no mutilations. There had to be a natural explanation."
>
> They argue, Phillips said, that blowflies eat the hide so it looks as if it were cut with a knife. "I say there were no blowflies anywhere around," he said, and the enlargements of pictures he took of the dead animal show no trace of them.
>
> "I will give $10 to the Tom Uphill Memorial Home for every blowfly that shows up in those photos," he said.
>
> As Dr. Lawson pointed out in his report, "the wounds on the head were made by a person using a sharp instrument." That is the real mystery, and one that causes no end of concern to everybody involved in the cattle industry.
>
> Phillips has a theory—that the cut on the neck might have resulted from somebody shooting the animal with a dart gun and then, using a sharp knife, cut the dart out in a lateral direction, removing the telltale evidence.
>
> He reports that a man told him that about the time the incident is believed to have occurred, he spotted a small-sized bluish car, similar to a 1971 Valiant, parked beside the road, and two men were standing beside the car. And, Phillips does not believe the animal was mutilated to observe some weird occult rite.[28]

Later, sometime during the last week of May in Washington County, Nebraska—outside the town of Herman—rancher George Tyson reported to authorities that his six-year-old female Hereford was discovered with its "udder and teats missing." This appeared to have been done with a "sharp instrument," taking a "perfect square cut" 8" X 8" out of the hide. There was no evidence of bleeding. The report was further investigated by Carol Werkmeister for the Study on Animal Mutilations, Madison, Nebraska.

Reports in several Iowa papers suggest that the mutilators' attention (or media-induced hysteria) descended on eastern Iowa from the end of May into June 1981. The articles mention an unspecified number of cattle and sheep deaths as having been reported mutilated but they go on to state that officials blame "critters" (rodents, crows, etc.).[29]

I find it interesting that a number of cases are lumped together by newspaper editors who provide no real facts, but they discount any possible validity to the ranchers' claims. How many animals were found in the condition? Where were they found? What were the dates that the animals died? So many questions nei-ther asked nor answered by regional newspapers, but are influenced by the slant of their disingenuous editorial staff.

Oregon had largely escaped unnoticed by the mutilators all through the 1970s. However, something attracted their attention because on Saturday, May 30, 1981, 25 miles from Paulina in Crook County, Earl McConnell on the Grindstone Ranch reported that his 600-pound female Hereford was discovered dead and mutilated. He found the animal lying in a shallow creek. The poor thing was missing its udder, genitals, rectum and a patch of hide from the right hip where the brand had been inscribed. Investigating deputies described the wounds as having been made with a knife, though crudely. Samples were obtained and sent to the State Crime Lab for testing. Forensic analysis allegedly found traces of a "tranquilizing drug" in the carcass that was not identified in the newspaper story that ran later the following week.[30]

During a three-week period in May and June 1981, four animals were found dead under unexplained circumstances on four separate ranches near Vilna, Alberta. These ranches are located north of Edmonton in northern Alberta. One case, on the Kucher farm, appeared to have burns on the ears. Although no light-ening had been observed in the area for at least a week, "authorities suspected lightening" had made the burns.[31]

Alberta rancher Steve Popowich also reported a cow that was found dead miss-ing an ear, part of the tongue, rear end and lips. Scavengers appeared to be hesitant to approach the carcass and, as with many unexplained cases, the wounds appeared to have been performed with the flair of a sharp instrument.

Popowich was interviewed by Tom Adams, and he said, "I've seen dead ani-mals. I've been around animals all my life. This isn't [due] to natural causes." A "bright light" was seen in a field near Smokey Lake, west of Vilna, and investi-gating officers apparently found that the "ground was burned to a depth of six-to-7 inches in a cigar-shaped area about 30 feet across." Also, mounds of cold ashes and a "weird sulfur smell, were left at the scene. Maybe it was a visiting devil who is a hotshot pilot of a flying saucer? (figure 9) Although this light was not thought to be connected to the three mute reports, it is obviously worth men-tioning.[32]

New Mexico, Oregon, and Back to Canada

Sometime on either June 10 or 11, 1981 on the Gomez ranch near Dulce, New Mexico, Manuel Gomez reported finding one horse and one cow that had been victimized. According to the *Rio Grande Sun* (on June 25, 1981), the two-year-old cow was missing its rectum and genitals; the 14-month-old horse was also missing its rectum and genitals—plus an eye and part of the face. The neck and jawbone appeared to have been broken. This brought to eight the number of apparent mutilations that had occurred up to this point on the Gomez Ranch located on the Jicarilla Apache Indian Reservation. State Policeman Gabe Valdez investigated these new reports. (figure 10) His son Greg was now coming along on some of his father's investigations. He was especially intrigued by finding "marks and broken skin" where it appeared clamps of some sort had been applied to the horse, plus "spike marks in the ground where the grass had been uprooted near the scene." Strange airborne lights had allegedly been seen during those same June time periods since 1976.

On June 18 or 19, 1981, a little over two weeks after the Grindstone Ranch report, another Oregon claim surfaced from Eagle Creek, north of Estacada, in Clackamas County. The Ward Ranch reported a mutilated female bovine found missing *both* eyes, its heart, udder and vagina. Investigating deputies seemed to suspect cultist involvement—similar mutilations had occurred in the Clackamas County area three years prior.[33]

Also during early to mid June time, other Oregon cases were evidently being reported. Terri Lowry of the Grindstone Ranch claimed to have been told about a Deschutes County mutilation case near Sisters. As with the other cases, the genitals had been removed from the victim.

In mid June it appears the mutilators changed tactics and targets for several nights. The following case occurred in Jefferson County, near the town of Lakewood, Colorado. The small animal owners, the Bylons, reported a series of "night-caller attacks" with a particularly head-scratching, Fortean twist. It seems that seven rabbits were somehow decapitated and drained of blood over a several night time period. The perpetrators left behind the headless carcasses and, oddly enough, also left the ears. The culprit(s) were never seen or heard despite the efforts of homeowner Bylon to catch the intruder(s). In an eerily familiar case, a similar rabbit decapitation was reported in Fort Collins, Colorado that prior Easter and another multiple rabbit mutilation case would be reported on a ranch south of Eugene, Oregon.[34]

On June 22, 1981, Bob and Denny Wilkins couldn't find their five-month-old shorthorn bull calf. Their ranch is located east of Arlington, in Washington County, Nebraska. When the animal was located, the couple was horrified to discover that a large area of the lower abdomen had been "cut away" and the heart and genitals were gone. The back legs of the carcass appeared to have been forcibly spread apart until the "legs popped out of the sockets" and there was very little blood found at the scene. In another strange twist, the young bull's intestines were discovered "in a neat pile" about 25 feet away. Tom Adams noted at the time that in a few cases over the past several years, intestines or other internal parts had been left in a similar pile or in a neat row near the carcass.[35]

On July 3, 1981 the mutilation reports returned to British Columbia. On the TLR Ranch, near Armstrong, British Columbia, the Ternier family discovered their purebred five-year-old female Hereford missing the right upper lip and part of the nostril, all of the udder and external genitalia; all organs appeared excised by a "sharp instrument." This was the seventh case near Fernie since the prior May and there was a wide difference of opinion between the RCMP and other observers, veterinarian Dr. Maidment, and the rancher:

> [RCMP Constable Mike] Chorney was one individual who appeared to hold fast to the theory that predators were responsible, going so far as to say that he "doesn't believe in cattle mutilations." Chorney also pointed out that the night of July 2, the Ternier's dog was outside only a short distance from where the dead animal was discovered. The dog, which according to Chorney is rather excitable by nature, made no noise the night the cow died, something that would be expected if there were strangers nearby. On the other hand, there were reports of two strange vehicles being seen in the vicinity of the incident the evening before and again in the early hours of the morning the cow was discovered by Ternier. To add strength to his predator theory, Constable Chorney told *Country Life* that in the past two years with over 550 dead animal complaints received in Alberta, all with the exception of seven possible mutilations, had been eliminated as being caused by natural causes or predators.
>
> The mysterious circumstances surrounding the manner by which the Ternier cow died led [veterinarian] Dr. Mailment to advance with conviction the mutilation theory. He emphasized that in his opinion the removal of the tissue from the animal was performed with precise surgical skill and could not possibly have been the work of predators. Death by natural causes was virtually ruled out when Dr. Mailment reported that all the vital organs were perfectly normal. The mutilation theory was supported by Keith Miller who confirmed the "clean" surgery statement and added that there was not a drop of blood in evidence on the ground or around the animal.[36]

After a brief lull, the reports recommenced when on August 20, 1981, we saw the return of officially reported mutilation cases in Rio Arriba County, New Mexico. On his ranch near Tierra Amarilla, Victor Salazar discovered a female bovine with its tongue missing and the rectal area removed. There were no footprints at the site except those of the calf that came to stand by its mother's carcass. Two days later, on the 22nd, another cow was discovered mutilated, again with its calf standing nearby. In the second case, the mother's udder was missing, and it appeared as if the "anal area was cut." In an interesting twist, the dewclaws on one leg were neatly snipped off. Salazar's herd also suffered mutilations around this time of year in 1970 and 1980.[37]

On August 23, 1981, in Howard County, Iowa, near the community of Cresco, rancher Merlin Christiansen discovered three of his cows "*shot to death*—one wounded, had to be destroyed." [my emphasis] One cow had a loin carved out and although reported as "mutilations," the motive was suspected by law enforcement to be cattle rustlers butchering for meat.[38]

Another Huerfano County case surfaced three days later on August 26th, this time seven miles west of Walsenburg, Colorado. The victim animal was a three-year-old heifer; its tongue had been removed and the rectum removed as if a "stovepipe" had been shoved up the rear of the animal and the "core" removed. At least some additional damage on this carcass is thought to have been "caused by predators."[39]

Three days later, on August 29, 1981, yet another Huerfano County report was filed with authorities. This time the Corsentino Dairy Farm was apparently targeted—about four miles east of Walsenburg. The animal was a two-year-old Holstein heifer with the left side of its face cut away; its left eye and the tip of its left ear were gone. A teat was possibly removed and like the previous case on the Gomez ranch, the vaginal area was cut out in "stovepipe" fashion leaving the rectal area intact. A possible helicopter flying nearby was heard the morning of the 29th. The Huerfano County sheriff reported the hide "sounded like a drum" when hit, and that the hide on the upper half (lengthwise) of the carcass was stiff and brittle like a dry chamois cloth while the hide on the bottom half was still soft. A vet called out to the site thought the carcass was struck by lightning (cause of death) but confirmed that some cutting was also done.[40]

Evidently, our phantom mutilators had unfinished Rio Arriba County business to attend to, for they decided to return to gather more cow parts. On September 11, 1981, five miles from Salazar, New Mexico the Casale Ranch reported that a five-year-old Charolais was found dead and missing its tongue, udder and anus. State Patrolman Gabe Valdez investigated the report and noted finding "bruises all over back of carcass."[41] Valdez would notice these types of bruises in later cases from northern New Mexico in the '80s and '90s.

The following day, in Auburn, Washington (near where I went to high school in King County) the mutilation mystery visited rancher Edna Mock. Upon going outside that morning, she found a steer missing a front leg, shoulder, lips, nose, ear, larynx, tail and genitals. Horrified that the site was located a mere 300 feet from her house, she noted that no blood was in evidence, and she claimed no one heard a thing the night the animal had been killed and disfigured. A King County Animal Control spokesman said the wounds were "too neat to have been caused by predators."[42]

Two days later and about 2,000 miles to the northeast, on September 14, 1981 in Falun, Alberta—located between Edmonton and Red Deer—rancher John Cummings discovered his bull calf missing its penis, testicles, anus and half of its tail. All parts appeared to be "cut out with surgical precision." The animal was found one quarter mile north of the house and there were no apparent tracks. Cummings claimed that the herd was checked on September 11th and all was well; there was nothing on the site where the calf was found. However *a human corpse (killed by shotgun) had been found on an adjoining ranch on 9-14-81.* Evidently no connection between the two coincidental unexplained events was suspected by the RCMP. [my emphasis] A murdered human and a mutilated bull calf discovered the same day on two adjoining ranches? And no one thought to look into a possible connection? OK.

> Mrs. Cummings told Project Stigma: "The police came and looked— and immediately they said it was predators. We disagreed with that, very much so. Our neighbors looked at (the calf). Also my father-in-law, who has had a lot to do with animals all his life. And our neighbors are older people that have lived with animals all their lives, and they had never seen an animal like that."[43]

But what about the human found shot to death? How could law enforcement officials not link the two discoveries that occurred in the middle of bumf**k nowhere, Alberta? Someone—anyone— should have investigated these two coincidental events and been all over them like a bad case of sun poisoning.

As we shall see, 1981 saw an active fall with mutilation reports jumping around the western U.S. and Canada. A week after the Alberta case, on September 23rd, near Norris, South Dakota, the Graff Ranch reported that a two-year-old Hereford steer *was found in a neighbor's pasture*. It was missing its genitals and the surgery left a perfectly circular six-inch-diameter patch. *Both ears* were missing as was the left eye; the right eye was popped out of its socket but was still lying at the site. Part of its tail was missing; *the hair from the end of its tail was left in a circle around the carcass,* as in the 1980 Iowa and 1995 Colorado cases where the tail hair appeared to have been ritualistically arranged at the site. There was a hole in the ribcage from which the heart appeared to have been taken out, leaving no blood in evidence at the site. The rectum was "cored out," leaving "a clean hole" as though made with an "ice cream scoop." One-half of one of the missing ears was found under the carcass, and the steer was not found on the Graff's property where it should have been, but on a neighbor's place. The neighbor's dogs had "raised hell" the night of the 22nd.

Laboratory analysis indicated that the hair from the tail may have been severed by something "hot." Adams noted that several other mutes had occurred in this area in the last two years, all of them found *"on their backs with their legs straight up into the air."* [my emphasis] As you can tell, I sense that these types of recurrent synchronicities are extremely important.

There had been reports of UFOs and "weird lights" from the Norris and Kadoka areas that fall, and five nights before steer was found, Mrs. Graff, while driving home from Gordon, Nebraska saw a farmhouse that she thought was on fire. As she approached to within a half mile the "fire" rose into the sky and flew off to the west like a "burning full moon" until it vanished in a "bright flash."

Driving the short distance home, she arrived and found her four dogs whimpering and whining.[44]

On September 28, 1981, in Grant County, Minnesota, a 500-pound, seven-month-old registered Hereford bull calf was discovered dead and disfigured on the Werk family farm near Macsville Township, east of Herman. The bull was missing its genitals, right ear and eye, part of its left ear and a two-inch by three-inch piece of hide from the right front shoulder. A hole in the left side of the neck appeared as though made by a tranquilizer dart or awl and there was little blood in evidence anywhere at the site. The Werks estimated the bull's value at about $1,000. University diagnostic lab analysis of samples found no drugs and no disease and could not ascertain the cause of death.[45]

That same night in Balzac, just north of Calgary, Alberta, Stan Jones reported that his 600-kg. purebred Hereford bull, one-and-a-half-years old, was mutilated by someone or something. There was a circular hole, 30 centimeters in diameter, in the abdomen where the testicles had been removed; missing also were the tongue, nose and some "entrails." There was some evidence of dripping blood from a puncture mark in the neck. No tracks were discovered but "three triangular patches were worn down into the nearby grass—a helicopter had been heard the night before, and a helicopter was seen nearby as the Jones family examined the bull at the site."[46]

Betty Hill: Mute Investigator

Leapfrogging on October 1, 1981 all the way to New Hampshire's Center Tuftonboro area of Carroll County, farmer Charles Whitten found his seven-year-old female Hereford with half of its face cut away, an eye, ear and part of its nose missing. Half of the tongue was removed and the jugular vein appeared severed, but there was no evidence of bleeding. It is interesting to note that this is only the second known "classic" mutilation case in New Hampshire—the other was a 1978 incident near the Vermont border. The animal appeared unnaturally bloated, considering the cool weather the area was experiencing. Normally when it's cool it takes longer for the animal to bloat.[47]

Here is the newspaper article from the *New Hampshire Sunday News*, dated October 4, 1981 and headlined "Local Officials Remain Puzzled By Strange Death of Hereford:"

> Tuftonboro, October 3, 1981, Charles Whitten has a dead cow on his hands and no explanation to how it met its demise. Whitten, who raises beef cows, found the disfigured body of a seven-year-old polled Hereford dead in his pasture at 9:00 a.m. Thursday morning. The cow was missing an ear, an eye had been ripped from its socket, half its nose was missing, its cheek and lower jaw were laid open to the bone and half its tongue was gone. Whitten said, "There was no sign of any struggle. It was just like

somebody laid her there." Not only was there no sign of any struggle, but there was absolutely no blood at the site according to Conservation Officer Lt. Peter Lyons. "I don't think the cow was shot or that an animal killed it," Lyons said. "There were no tracks, no other marks on the body, or any signs of a struggle; the strangest phenomenon was there was absolutely no blood." A search of the area by Whitten failed to turn up the missing ear. Whitten said he was also amazed at how fast and how completely the animal bloated. "I have never seen one bloat up so quick in cool weather," said Whitten. He went on to say that he never saw an animal feed that way. "An animal will usually go for the soft parts first...The way it was disfigured with no signs of any tracks or struggle, and with no blood around it just doesn't add up. It's mysterious," said Whitten. Matt Craigue, a Western cattleman from Tuftonboro, said after viewing the cow that he had never seen anything like it and that perhaps the disfigurement could have been with a knife. But he had no explanation as to how the cow died.[48]

On October 12, 1981, the *Portsmouth Herald*, also published a short article about the Whitten report:

> The mysterious mutilation of a seven-year-old cow last week was blamed on everything from aliens to cults, but investigators say the cow probably died of a heart attack. Charles Whitten, a farmer, found the cow in his pasture. An eye, ear and part of the Hereford's tongue and nose were missing, authorities said. People from all over the country have barraged Whitten, police and the Fish and Game Department with dozens of theories. "They range from flying saucers to witchcraft," said Fish and Game Lt. Peter Lyon [who was not a veterinarian pathologist]. [He] said the cow died of natural causes, probably a blood clot in the heart, and was mutilated by other animals and birds.[49]

For a third interesting perspective, the famous abductee, Mrs. Betty Hill (who, along with her husband, Barney, was involved in the infamous New Hampshire UFO abduction in 1961), read the article about the Whitten case and started her own investigation into the unexplained cattle death. In the ensuing years after the abduction Betty (figure 11) became an enthusiastic UFO and paranormal investigator and she owned property in the mountains of Carroll County, not far from the Center Tuftonboro/Wolfeboro-area farm of Charles Whitten. Betty, who died in 2004, visited the farm shortly after the 1981 article was published and she sent the following report to Project Stigma's Tom Adams:

> On October 12, 1981, our local newspaper carried a small item about the mutilation of a cow, so I called the family and visited them on Octo-

ber 15th. Jean and Charles Whitten live in Center Tuftonboro, New Hampshire. He is a farmer— mostly beef cattle— and she works the midnight shift at the local hospital in Wolfeboro as a nurses' aide. He owns 600 acres of land, apparently inherited from his family as he has been living in the same house since he was two years old. The land includes acres of trees, as well as cleared land. This family is the only one in this area who grows beef cattle. Most are Herefords. The cow that died was seven years old and was used as a breeder. A next-door neighbor has milking cows, and as of October 2, he is putting them in the barn at night…

On the morning of October 1st, about 9:00 a.m., the Whittens were leaving the house when Jean looked toward the pasture where they keep their cattle, and made a comment about one cow, which looked different. Mr. Whitten picked up his binoculars to get a better look, and could see the cow was lying on her back with all four legs straight up in the air. As he walked across the pasture, all the other cows were a distance away from this cow; but when he approached they all came toward him and began circling around the dead cow. He has a herd of twenty cows and had one bull, which he had borrowed from a friend. He looked at the dead cow and could not believe what he was seeing. One half of her face had been cut away, clean down to the bones. The cutting ran between the nostrils, circled one eye and one ear and down into the neck. The mouth was closed but half the tongue had been removed from the cutaway side. The jugular vein had been cut across, without any blood showing. All the cutting was very smooth, with no rough spots.

Mr. Whitten returned to the house and called Lawrence Toms, a veterinarian who lives in Wolfeboro. He came out and checked the cow to see if he could find the cause of death. It is believed the cow died instantly for no traces of a struggle were found. He has had cows die before and they do struggle during the process. No cause of death was found. It was decided to leave the cow for a day to see what would happen. Incidentally, the cow was badly bloated when it was found, although the weather was very cool. All day the other cows stayed around the dead cow, circling it.

At the suggestion of the vet, Mr. Whitten called the authorities and reported this. The Police Chief is Bill Keyes, who has been overwhelmed with calls from all over the country since the publicity started. The next day the vet, Lawrence Toms, did a complete autopsy on the cow. The "effects of a needle" were found in the jugular vein, to quote Mr. Whitten. There was no blood in the body and no apparent cause of death. The newspaper had reported a blood clot in the heart was the cause, but Mr. Whitten said this was not true; no clot was found. Also, Fish and Game

Commission members told him that it must be animals or birds, but no teeth marks or other signs of animals were found. He has seen animals killed by other animals so he knows the traces left—there were none in this situation.

The Whittens are puzzled and upset by this event. They checked all the fences around the pasture and did not find any traces of anyone going over a fence—no grass trampled down. The entrance gate to the pasture is behind their home and the dog would bark if anyone tried to enter—he is chained and sleeps outdoors. If he did any barking, it was not unusual— nothing to attract attention, as he would have done if a stranger tried to enter the yard. They did not hear any sounds that night, but the next day they heard a helicopter but they could not see it. Then a low-flying plane circled the pasture (Bill Jackson of the *Greeley Tribune* talked to a New Hampshire reporter who said there were unconfirmed rumors and "talk" of "black helicopters" around one of the nearby towns).

Since then, the Whittens learned that three men visited the Libby Museum in Wolfeboro and asked if there were any sheep in the area, as they were looking for some for religious purposes. A few are in the area, but the men apparently did not go to the owners, and the sheep are all right—nothing has happened to them. A check was made with the local library, and it was found that a great interest in witchcraft has developed since the cow was killed, for all the books were on loan but two.

At first Charles Whitten thought someone in the town had done this for revenge, but he was sure if a person had done this, he probably would have shot the cow. He is one of the three Selectmen of the town and prob- ably has made some enemies by some of his decisions. But the vet looked for signs of a bullet and there were none. Whoever did the cutting was very skilled.

I walked out in the pasture with Mr. Whitten to the spot where the cow was found. He said this spot, where the head lay, had been wet, and had something that looked like saliva on the ground. Now the grass is dead in that one spot. I would estimate the distance from the home to be about 500 yards. I looked around for any kind of marking on the ground and found nothing. The ground is hard, grass covered and eaten off at a close level by the cows. The pasture itself is tree-lined on two sides and par- tially tree-lined on the third side. Deep woods are on these two sides, but Mr. Whitten told me that power lines cut through the woods about a half-mile from the pasture. The family is completely baffled by this event, and they are afraid it might happen again. They do not have any outside lights, only one light on the porch. They may install yard lights or keep the porch light burning. The weather of September 30—October 1st was very cool, a very dark night with no moon or stars.

This area is one of rolling hills, rural and houses not very close together. About 15 miles away, via highways, are the Ossipee Mountains, which can be seen very clearly from the Whitten home. *I have received so many UFO reports from this general area that it would be impossible to count them all. People have told me that the mountains are "haunted" by UFOs.* [my emphasis] To the south is Wolfeboro, another area with a high number of sightings. I was sitting in my car on the night of July 4th, waiting for the fireworks to begin, and a group of children were sitting on a park bench in front of me. They were telling each other to watch a certain spot in the sky for that is the spot where the UFOs come in each time to watch the fireworks. So I watched and saw one come in, using all red lights, and now I realize it was in the direction of Center Tuftonboro.

One of the most interesting aspects of the Ossipee Mountains is that most of the area cannot be entered—no roads, miles of territory uninhabited. Sometimes hunters may go into the mountains a short distance, but they do not stay long—fearful of becoming lost. There are no trails.

Mrs. Whitten told me that the month of October is known in Wolfeboro as UFO month, for this is the time of the year when they reach a peak in numbers, and right now everyone is talking about UFOs all the time.[50]

Let's Play Leapfrog

Unlike New Hampshire, Huerfano County, Colorado, has been the site of dozens of mutilation reports. This is also the home of investigator David Perkins who lives in a house at 9,000 feet on the western slope of Greenhorn Mountain on the north side of the Huerfano Valley. The following case occurred near Red Wing, on October 20, 1981 directly across the valley from Perkins' Gardner home. The Hubert Aguirre Ranch reported a mutilation case on their spread located near Sheep Mountain and the (former) Atlantic Richfield Company (ARCO) CO2 drilling site. According to the veterinarian who was called out to examine the animal, it was a classic bovine mutilation. The victim was a pregnant cow, and the calf had been removed from a slit in the uterus.[51]

Two days later, back across the country in Minnesota, the Telkamp farm reported a four-week-old Holstein heifer missing one ear, part of an eye, the tail and rectum and one hock from each of three legs. William Moore, infamous in UFO research circles, sent Tom Adams the alert to this Grant County case. The county sheriff observed that the cuts were clean although he noted teeth marks in gristle where the ear and hocks were missing.[52]

As in the seventies, the mutilators must have been extremely hard-pressed to crisscross North America in a day or two. On October 23, 1981, in Rabbit Lake, Saskatchewan rancher Nick Kowerchuk found his two-and-a-half-year old Charolais bull missing its penis and testicles. No tracks were found even though there had been a light snowfall. It appeared that the rest of the herd would not return to the fall pasture after the bull was killed. In a report filed by Mr. Kowerchuk, he stated:

> "The cut made around the penis was a hide cut only. There were no scratches or marks on the meat at all. A strip of hide was taken off the brisket. The testicles were taken out one at a time. There was no sign of struggle and no blood had dripped on or around the animal. The bull did have a rubber ear tag #908 on it. It was taken out of the hole in the ear. The ear was not torn and the last I had seen him he had the tag. There was a dark coloring on the neck that could have been made by a rope or chain. Also a small scar that looked like a burn under the back leg [was present]. By the anus were small jabs into the hide. They were not deep enough to draw blood but were noticeable."

The carcass was found 10-23-81; checked by vet 10-24-81 and taken to Saskatoon that date for analysis at Western College of Veterinary Medicine at the University of Saskatchewan. Dr. G. Wobeser's pathologic diagnosis found (1) *Valvular endocarditis*, (2) *Septicemia*, (3) *Embolic pneumonia*, (4) *Embolic glomerulonephritis*, and the presence was noted of the bacterium *Pasteurella hemolytica*. Wobeser commented that "this is a very unusual type of infection for this bacterium which is usually associated with shipping fever; however, there is histologic evidence of generalized septicemia."[53]

After a three-plus-week lull in known mutilation reports, Washington County, Colorado rancher Richard Merrill had an unwelcome trick-or-treater. The Merrill Ranch—located near Woodrow, Colorado—experienced the second of three mutilations that happened on Halloween. The following morning, November 1, 1981 Merrill found his seven-year-old, 1,000-pound female cow dead and disfigured. It was missing its udder and genitals and there was no evidence of blood or bleeding at the site. The cow had given birth three weeks prior and the baby was left bawling but unhurt. Another cow, not mutilated, was found dead nearby—both animals died Halloween night. There were other mutes south and west of the Merrill spread, as we will see.[54]

In mid-November the Merrill ranch reported the third unexplained livestock death that allegedly occurred on their ranch. As in the case from Halloween night, this female bovine was found missing its udder and genitals; also missing from the animal was part of the hide and most of the tongue. There was no evidence of blood or bleeding and this latest case was found about 600 feet north of Halloween mute site. At the time, investigators heard rumors of at least a couple of other mutilations that occurred on ranches south and west of the Merrills, but were not reported to authorities.[55]

Glen Botsch's ranch is located in Colfax County north of Richland, near Leigh, Nebraska. On November 23, 1981 he found his 1,100-pound female Hereford dead and disfigured. Missing were the rectum, the udder, the tip of the tail and the right ear. The animal had been cut open "from rectum to navel" but there was "very little blood" in evidence at the site. On that previous night, a neighbor who lives just west of the mutilation site was awakened by a "fluctuating high-low sound" which lasted for about five minutes.[56]

Big Horn County, east and south of Manderson, Montana—near Highway 31—is the location of the Harrington Ranch. They reported two mutilations to officials on November 27th:

(1) Heifer, less than a year old; hide and flesh removed from right side of face, including nose; tongue cut off "just above throat"; right ear cut off close to skull; ear canal looked "cleaned out"; anus cut away; circle of hide removed from genital area; hint of singeing on hair around ear and anal cuts. (2) A calf, 200 yards away from the heifer; anus and genital wounds "identical" to those on other calf; head undamaged; a small amount of blood appeared to have dripped from the nose. Both animals were found on Friday, November 27th; they were estimated to have died two to three days earlier.[57]

Dulce Gas Mask, Radar Chaff and Ultraviolence

As noted in Chapter Six the area around Dulce on the Jicarilla Apache Reservation was particularly hard-hit by the mutilators in the mid to late 1970s. Many of the cases seemed to be centered around the Edmund and Manuel Gomez ranches—located about 13 miles from Dulce. These cases were investigated by New Mexico State Police officer Gabe Valdez.

Edmund claimed to "Branton" (author of the controversial *The Dulce Book*) that he had witnessed combat-ready troops on numerous occasions. He said they had been spotted in the area around Dulce and the Archuleta Mesa that dominates the town to the north where it straddles the Colorado/New Mexico border. In a 1983 interview conducted at their ranch, the ranchers told Branton: "Some of these troops were found in areas that are only gotten to through four-wheel drive trucks or on foot… The troops were also spotted in areas that only the Apache has permission to go…"

From 1975 through 1983 the Gomez family ranch operation appeared to be ground zero for much of the cattle mutilation activity that took place in the north central New Mexico area around the Jicarilla Apache and Southern Ute Indian Reservations. Directly east, along the border, the southern San Luis Valley area of south central Colorado appeared to be the epicenter for cases in southern Colorado during the mid to late '70s.

The Gomez family were not recent arrivals to the area. They first homesteaded the Dulce area over 100 years prior and as a result of the mutilations on the families' ranches, they claimed to have lost upwards of $100,000 in cattle over the eight-year period. At the height of the slaughter, one of these cases occurred only "200 yards behind [Edmund's] home…"

Many myths have grown up around Dulce and Archuleta Mesa (figure 12). At the height of the mute wave around the Jicarilla, and on the Gomez ranches, a meme arose that the U.S. government had established an underground presence north of Dulce using the Ute Indians as their plausible deniability. There is no unequivocal data (to my knowledge) that supports this theory, nor is there data to confirm the reality of an underground alien base under Archuleta Mesa. The enigmatic researcher known as "Branton" alleged the following in his controversial *The Dulce Book*:

> [I]n 1978 there was an agreement between the Ute Indians [Colorado] and the Federal Government. This agreement consisted of the Ute Nation receiving all the territory now occupied along the New Mexico/Colorado border with the explicit agreement that they would strictly enforce a 'NO TRESPASSING' regulation along the border of their territory. Therefore, it is not possible to even cross the Ute Reservation without special permission from the Tribal Headquarters. If caught without this permission you are liable for a fine and/or jail and expulsion. There is now a road leading to the Archuleta [Mesa] area through the reservation. It is patrolled by the Indian Forest Service.[58]

New Mexico State Patrolman Gabe Valdez spent over 30 years investigating a bewildering array of unexplained event reports from the Dulce/Rio Arriba County region where he was posted. Over the years, he dealt with it all (UFO reports, cattle mutilations, bigfoot sightings and abduction claims), but he never published a book. Unfortunately, Gabe died unexpectedly on August 6, 2011 just as he was publicly opening up concerning his theories to explain the Dulce region's activity. His son Greg, who followed his father into a career in law enforcement, was tasked by the Valdez family to be the custodian of his father's extensive files pertaining to his investigations since the mid 1970s. Greg, who accompanied his father on many investigations, distilled these files into long form. His book, *Dulce Base: The Truth and Evidence from the Case Files of Gabe Valdez,* (figure 13) is filled with interesting details pertaining to Gabe's 40-plus-year investigation of New Mexico's unexplained cattle mute and UFO cases. They include cases he officially investigated for the State of New Mexico, and those conducted on his own time. Later, in the '90s, Valdez was hired as a field investigator for the National Institute for Discovery Sciences (NIDS). We will revisit Gabe's NIDS work later.

Before I begin my accounting of 1982's mutilation reports, I should mention the fact that the popular conception that no introduced crime scene evidence is ever found is usually correct, but not always. There have been several interesting, albeit rare, discoveries of circumstantial evidence in the immediate vicinity, as we saw in the 1975 Weld County case with the satchel containing the scalpel and cow parts. Gabe's investigations of the Gomez ranch and the objects he found may be coincidental, but they are noteworthy nevertheless—regardless of what Kenneth Rommel said in his OAM report.

Gabe's son Greg has carefully combed through his father's files and notes the following in his book *Dulce Base,* that examines his father's work:

> On June 14, 1981, at one of the Gomez mutilations, investigators found a large amount of radar chaff near a mutilated cow. The aircraft that dispensed the chaff seemed to have malfunctioned and left whole packets of chaff in a flight line that traveled directly to the deceased animal. The chaff was found intact with the wrapping still around it. The specific chaff was later identified as RR-72B. When investigators began identifying the chaff and its origins, the Air Force indicated that they used this type of chaff on experimental aircraft and that it was considered top secret. They were very interested in where the chaff was found and how the investigators had obtained it…
>
> The chaff located at the Gomez mutilation site was tested, and it was determined that the radar frequency it was intended to distort was the same frequency used by the Longmont, Colorado, radar observatory. Because the town of Dulce is in close proximity to Colorado, the radar tracking station for the Dulce area is in Longmont, Colorado, and not Albuquerque as some people might assume. Investigators also found radar chaff at the site of another mutilation in Colorado. In this case it had actually been stuffed into the cow's mouth. Besides the obvious military implications of the chaff, investigators never ruled out the idea that it was intentionally placed at the site to distract them or throw them off the trail of what was really happening.[59]

Radar chaff was not the only unusual evidence Gabe Valdez allegedly discovered. As mentioned earlier, apparent fluorescent markings were discovered by Valdez and Howard Burgess on several head of Gomez's cattle, but they also found a gas mask (figure 14) and a scientific pressure sensor at a mutilation site. Again from Greg's book, *Dulce Base*:

> To further complicate the matter, a gas mask was also found at a Gomez mutilation site on June 12, 1982, and two weeks after the date the radar chaff was found, an electronic device that seemed to have been dropped from the air turned up at the Gomez ranch. Investigators traced

the device back to the manufacturer that provided the machine to the Air Force on contract and determined that the unit was a high-altitude temperature/pressure sensor. A transformer in the sensor's head transmitted in high frequency (X Band), and a receptacle located on the machine was used for *collecting air to include chemical and biological samples of the atmosphere*.[60] [my emphasis]

What's wrong with this picture? Since when do "aliens" need gas masks, paint splotches and U.S. government-issue scientific gear that could protect them from airborne particles?

Half-Cats, Dogs and Mutes

For years, I've been asked what I thought of the weird, unexplained "half-cat" mutilations that have been reported occurring in waves in urban and suburban areas of several western United States cities. (figure 15) I frankly don't know what to make of these strange animal deaths. I should stress that although cattle make up around 90% of mutilation cases, practically every species of warm-blooded animal found in North America has been reported "mutilated" at one time or another. Obviously, the first thing I think of is strange-appearing predator and scavenger action, but this simple explanation doesn't work for a sizable percentage of these weird feline cases. And these reports have quietly been going on for almost 40 years! Californians have reported these strange cat deaths since at least the early to mid 1970s. In a short article published on October 16, 1974, the *Associated Press* noted:

> A series of cat killings in the wealthy suburb of Brentwood—perhaps at the hands of devil worshippers—has stirred the anger of residents and puzzled police. Residents with $100,000 homes in the area near the UCLA campus have been plagued by the cat killings in which the bodies of pet felines are found either on the front porch or lawn of their owners. "There is absolutely no blood or fur left at the scene," police Lt. Roy Salls said in an interview. "This does away with the theory that coyotes from the nearby Santa Monica Mountains have been responsible for these weird deaths."
>
> Kenneth Williams, district supervisor for the West Los Angeles Animal Shelter, said some cats "have been mutilated, but we don't know whether it is ritualistic or some person is mad at the world." He said he knew of 12 such killings in the Brentwood area. Salls said ritualistic killings by some occult group were a possibility, "but it seems unlikely that they would advertise that they were in the area by leaving the carcasses."[61]

In the closing weeks of 1981, households in Laguna Hills reported that six cats were mutilated. A state game and fish officer told the *Saddleback Valley News* that he doubted the killer was a coyote, stating, "it sure doesn't sound like a coyote, they'll generally eat the entire animal or drag off the carcass." One of my thoughts was it could be a dog or great horned owl. He doesn't totally discount the possibility that the killer could be a dog or "weird coyote."[62]

The San Fernando Valley to the west of Los Angeles had also been experiencing strange pet mutilations since the mid-'70s. It would appear that the cat killers were still lurking around ten years or so later. In 1983, Adams had accumulated reports from west of LA that he summed up as follows:

> One count cites over 150 cats killed in the area of Agoura and West-lake Village. In 1982, 16 "cat mutilations" had been reported by mid-summer. In August 1982, noted paranormal authority/investigator D. Scott Rogo explained to [Project Stigma] that, although there had been a little television coverage of the 1982 cases, nothing had been published in the newspapers about it. Rogo told Project Stigma:
> I thought perhaps these mutilations might have something to do with the cattle (mutilation) mystery, so I met with animal control officials today on the incidents. It seems that the cats are surgically mutilated, with genitals and all internal organs removed. Usually the cats are cut in two. No blood is left at the site of the mutilation.[63]

On September 8, 1982, the half-cat reports finally wiggled out of the bag when the *Los Angeles Times* reported that since 1976 about "200 cats" had been killed and dismembered in Conejo Valley—west of Los Angeles in the San Fernando Valley. Sgt. Martin Broad of the Los Angeles County Animal Control Department told the *Times* that the cats were being disemboweled and cut into sections with "considerable surgical skill." The *Times* article stated:

> There is seldom any blood on the cats or signs of struggle, leading police to conclude that the killings are done elsewhere and the bodies are returned to the scene and left in plain view, presumably for maximum shock value. Usually, the victims have been family pets, rather than strays; often they have a record of never wandering far from home.[64]

All through the seventies into the 1980s, only a dozen or so official unexplained animal death reports had surfaced in Arizona. Although Arizona has more cattle than most of the western states, mutilation reports have been few and far between. Over the years rumors have circulated about potential cases, however actual documentation is scant. Perhaps this is because a sizable portion of the state contains Native American reservations. This fact may have dampened outside knowledge of any potential cases as the Navajo, Hopi and Apache reservations could be considered "closed societies." I heard rumors of a sizable wave of cattle cases from one Apache Reservation—the number of cases bantered around was "about sixty" in all—but unless there is an evidence and/or documentation chain, these claims remain in my rumor pile, set aside.

Sometimes I wonder if its scant record of official cases is perhaps why I moved to Arizona in 2004—to get away from this mute mystery. For years back in Colorado, it sucked having to drop everything and go out to investigate a regional case when invariably a fresh one was reported. Tom Adams notes in *Stigmata #20* that other animals appeared to have been targeted in Arizona. The following summation was sent to Tom Adams by E. Edwin Austin of the Animal Mutilation Data Center (Orange, California).

The Maricopa County Sheriff's office in Phoenix reports in excess of 150 coyotes, dogs, cats, a few possum, mutilated or skinned in urban, suburban and rural Maricopa County. Except for one unconfirmed report from Show Low, [AZ] the incidents were confined to Maricopa County.

Heads and legs were cut off; the animals were disemboweled, a few skinned, note: this description parallels a group of about 20 cats killed in Irvine, California about two-years ago. [Also is similar to half-cat reports from the 1990s in Denver and Salt Lake City.]

Inaccurate media coverage stresses cult connection. A sheriff's spokesman says there was only one such incident involving 11 greyhounds and one possum…the time frame for the incidents in Maricopa County was from January 1982 to mid-March 1982. During this time, the ASPCA was the investigative agency. When the sheriff's office took over in mid-March, the rate of occurrence dropped sharply. There was a heavy local media coverage and substantial public reaction, but unusually low level of panic, mob syndrome or vigilantism…[65]

The first cattle mutilation of 1982 was a January 8th report from Rio Arriba County. The ever-vigilant Gabe Valdez investigated the case two days later. The report came from a small ranch located eight miles north of Espanola, where a five-year-old Hereford cow was discovered missing its rear end and tongue; allegedly the heart had also been removed. According to Valdez, while conducting a careful examination of the carcass, two needle-like marks were discovered on the lower abdomen.[66]

Then we jump to Washington State where the 25th known horse mutilation report since 1975 was filed in Pierce County. The horses reported attacked on February 19, 1982, had been either stallions or geldings and unlike the cattle mutilations, many of these victimized horses actually survived their attack. Tom Adams noted in *Stigmata #20* that these horse slasher cases usually featured "ample blood and bleeding," as we will see in the outbreak of the 1990s UK cases.

> The events are most often characterized by the removal of the penis with a sharp instrument. The gelded quarterhorse found on February 19th was alive but bleeding profusely from the wound where the penis had been severed. The horse was found near the house but as in the other cases, there was no noise or disturbance—leading some investigators to theorize that some sort of pain-killer/sedative may have been applied with a tranquillizer dart gun—using a drug that dissipates soon after the mutilation. But in the Graham, Washington area case of the 19th, Puyallup veterinarian William J. Briskey was unable to locate any areas on the body that would indicate an entrance wound from a dart or needle…the horse looked normal except for the bleeding. I wish I knew how they were doing it."[67]

That spring the mutilators refused to leave northern New Mexico. After a two-month lull they returned with prejudice. Two bulls were reported mutilated between the communities of Cuba and Counselor—just over the Rio Arriba line—in northern Sandoval County, on the night of March 21st. Both animals were owned by the Jicarilla Apache and were thought to have been dead for five or six days. Although "it appeared that the reproductive organs had been removed with a sharp instrument," we know that scavenger action can fool the local vet and the deputy sheriff. What makes this case interesting is the alleged temperament of the bulls and the locations they were found.

Tribal caretaker Travis Chavez was the first to discover the bulls and he immediately made a report to the State Police. State Police Officer Michael Avilucea responded to the call, his very first mutilation investigation. He was later interviewed by Mary Frei of the *Albuquerque Journal:*

> Avilucea recalled that Chavez described the bulls as two of the healthiest in the herd, and although most of the bulls are docile, one of the mutilation victims would have been extremely difficult to catch. "Each one's got an individual temper and this particular bull, I guess you might say, he's the king of the roost." Avilucea said he believes that the bulls had "an unnatural death" and speculated that an airborne object must have picked them up and later dropped them to the ground. The backs of both bulls were broken, and they were found about a half-mile apart lying partially on their bellies, he said. One of the bulls was in an arroyo, and there were no animal tracks leading to the carcass. Adding to the mystery is that in order to get to the arroyo, the bull would have had to cross another arroyo with a vertical 12 to 15 foot embankment. Avilucea said he has received reports of low-flying aircraft in the area around the

time the bulls were mutilated.[68]

On the night of March 26, 1982, Raymond Skor claimed something attacked and killed a milk cow and her newborn calf. His ranch is located near Crosby, North Dakota—north of nowhere—just below the Saskatchewan border. Evidently, two other calves also died and *nine other cows required sutures to close up multiple wounds.* Evidently, it took a veterinarian "seven hours" to treat the impacted members of Skor's cattle herd. Yeah, either the aliens must be getting really sloppy, or we have some klutzy keystone cop coyotes on the loose in one of the most remote locales in North America. I'd hate to be the one who had to pay Skor's vet bill for that visit!

> Two federal government trackers visited the scene Monday, and decided the footprints available appeared to be canine. But the wounds did not appear to be what would be expected in an attack by a dog. Most of the cuts were single slashes, and very deep—appearing to have been caused by an animal with a single, very long and very sharp tooth. "They sliced just like a knife, shaving some of the hair next to the wound," Mrs. Skor explained in a telephone interview… The possibility of human vandalism seems even more unlikely, because there was severe blizzard conditions that evening.[69]

Raymond Skor claimed he had checked the barn around 10:30 that night before going to bed. At that time, there were about 100 head of cattle and a few pigs on his farm. When he went out the following morning at 6:30, he discovered the evidence that his animals had been attacked by something. One of the government trackers confided to the Skors that the animal appeared to be the size of a bear and perhaps it was a bear that had lost part of a claw in a trap, leaving a single claw. Sure, sounds plausible, but kind of unlikely. No other unexplained animal deaths occurred in the area, including cases featuring a single-clawed bear. An uneasy lull recommenced across the west through April 1982.

Manuel Gomez must have been one unlucky rancher with some strange beef-based karma. On May 9, 1982, his ninth mutilation was discovered. The rancher estimated that the cow had died about a day earlier. In a familiar-sounding description:

> The udder and tongue were missing, as was part of a lip; all removals appeared to be the result of 'clean-cutting.' The jaw cut was banana-shaped and 'cut clear to the bone,' and a two-inch diameter hole was noted on a back leg. There was no blood on the cuts or around the carcass. The rectum was cut into. The womb remained intact though part of the fetal calf could be seen inside.[70]

Prior to this ninth case, since 1976 Gomez had reported he had lost five cows, two bulls, one heifer and one horse. Gabe Valdez had spent the six years since the first reports amassing an impressive case log and database. In previous mutilation cases around Dulce, on several occasions in the weeks prior to this latest case, "'The Light' was seen in the sky over Dulce." This strange light had been reported by witnesses over the years as orange, orange-red, red and in one report it appeared to be "blue." Unexplained lights around the area are practically routine to area residents "and ['The Light'] frequently comes from the northeast and veers west." The local lore has it that sightings of these low-flying orbs is somehow a portent (or indication) that the mutilations will re-commence in the area.[71]

Mary Frei revisited the Gomez ranch and asked about his insurance policy and how these mutilations were impacting his ranching business:

Last year Gomez' insurance company canceled its policy after he reported the mutilated horse and his fourth mutilated cow, which were both discovered on June 14th. "That insurance company was supposed to be a helping hand to the farmer and rancher," Gomez remarked. He found insurance elsewhere but now pays a higher premium. And he's reluctant to report the latest mutilation. "It's getting to the point where I won't be able to get any insurance," he said. "It's getting serious."[72]

These are Some Sick Individuals
The horse slashers apparently were not done with their cruel antics around Pierce County, Washington. A six-year-old thoroughbred colt was discovered with a deep three-inch gash in its groin area with its intestines trailing out on May 12, 1982. The rancher noted that the neighbor's dog had been "barking wildly" at about 4:30 the night of the 11th when the attack probably occurred. Evidently (unlike most of the other 24 reported cases from the region) this animal put up a fight. Most of the other cases featured horses that apparently didn't try to fight off their attacker(s) as they were attempting to sexually mutilate them.

Tom Adams noted that by November 1982 the reward for the arrest and conviction of the mystery Western Washington slasher(s) had risen to almost $10,000. North of Seattle/King County, "a significant number of horses in Snohomish County had turned up missing—and presumably stolen. Of about 30,000 horses in the county approximately 30 disappear or are stolen each year." The early 1980s saw an increase in horse snatching, and a three county area (Pierce, King and Snohomish) being targeted by the mutilators. Washington State law enforcement and local Humane Society investigators were as "stumped" as they were in the western and northern Los Angeles area. And then, the mystery pet mutilators headed to eastern Washington. Across the Pacific Coast Mountains, around Yakima,

[U]p to 14 dogs had been skinned within a year [1982] and their carcasses tossed over the back fence at the Yakima County Humane Society animal shelter. Also, at least six cats had been 'partially skinned' (using 'very smooth razor cuts'). All survived, although at least some of them had to be put to sleep. As for the dogs, it was difficult to determine whether they had been alive when skinned.[73]

On May 25, 1982 the mutilators again returned to northern New Mexico, this time back to Sandoval County on the Verdelia Gutierrez Ranch (between Cuba and Counselor), near the site of the two mutilated bulls found in late March. A cow was discovered missing its reproductive organs and its right front leg was reported "broken and bruised." The mutilators would revisit the ranch the following month.

Three days later on May 28th, the cattle surgeons turned their attention to the Aztec-Bloomfield area of northwestern New Mexico. The rancher was out counting heads when he discovered a missing cow in a gully where it had apparently fallen into the nine-foot-deep wash. The animal was estimated to have died several days earlier, which puts the time of death near the same time as the Sandoval County case. The "healthy" animal had a four-month-old calf. The cow was missing its tongue from deep in the throat, all the hide and hair had been removed from the lower jaw and the rear end and genitals were left intact. The rancher noted that coyotes and dogs expressed interest in the carcass, but their tracks only came within six feet of the body. No other scavengers would touch it, including birds. Rancher Robert Truby noted: "There's a bunch of magpies in the area that always go to the dead stock, they didn't go to this one. I've been around cattle all my life, and I'm 66 years old. I've never seen anything like it. It was a real eerie thing. It's something we don't understand. Or else we do understand and don't want to come out with it."[74]

Sgt. Howard Donaldson and San Juan County Sheriff's Office and New Mexico livestock inspector Mel Miller investigated. They brought along two employees of the El Paso Natural Gas Company, with their Geiger counter. They noted *abnormally high radiation readings from just around the carcass and extending out to about 10 feet*. The highest reading, however, was detected at the cow's mutilated lower jaw. Plus, *prints of a large shoe or a very flat-heeled boot were found in the sand near the animal's head*, according to livestock inspector Miller…Sgt. Donaldson commented: "Something that we can't explain went on."[75] [my emphasis]

Nebraska researcher Ray Boeche sent along an early June 1982 report to Project Stigma. His account typifies researchers' frustrations in the early eighties. Two Nebraska Hereford heifers were evidently discovered mutilated and reported to the sheriff's office. The "udder, vulva and anus were missing from both carcasses." According to Boeche's report, "There were no tracks or blood in evidence at either site." Much to the rancher's annoyance, "The *sheriff would not respond, would not even come out to investigate, claiming he didn't 'want to get involved.'*" [my emphasis]

Perhaps other cases were being discovered in the midwest but because of growing apathy in the law enforcement community, these cases were also being ignored. Tommy Blann and Ray Boeche had their ears open that spring and they were hearing plenty. "In mid-autumn, a Texas truck-driver delivered a load of livestock to a facility in Lincoln, Nebraska. While unloading, he overheard a number of people discussing the livestock mutilations that had been going on in that area…These cases may have gone unreported, officially, which may [have] explained why no details have surfaced."

Other rumors heard in May and June 1982 were of a more chilling nature. Researchers were encountering "persistent rumors of human mutilations in and around Lincoln. Most commonly the story would claim that young boys had been genitally mutilated in public restrooms—but there was never any evidence whatsoever that the rumors were anything more than just that."[76] As with the overwhelming majority of these "human mutilation" rumors over the years, law enforcement would not acknowledge in any way that these cases were occurring.

Northern New Mexico appeared to be the center of North American reports that early summer of 1982. At the end of the first week of June, two cows were discovered dead near the mountain town of Chama, located at the base of La Magna Pass, but they were too decomposed to ascertain the cause of death and disfigurement.

Gabe Valdez noted "virtually every year around June 14th and 15th a mutilation is discovered in Rio Arriba or the surrounding counties." Manuel Gomez near Dulce had been the victim on this date several times since 1976. So, true to form, on June 15, 1982, the mutilators came back to visit this time at the Verdelia Gutierrez ranch. A three-year-old cow was missing its "uterus, tongue, and one eye. One or more ribs were broken." Valdez surmised that this was due to the animal being dropped from the air. The previous morning Verdelia's two sons had watched "a dark-green helicopter," that flew low over the ranch.

> A veterinarian from Farmington was called in to examine the animal. The vet found the heart very "mushy," much to his surprise. Although blood was present, the vet was puzzled over its *failure to clot properly*. But most puzzling to the veterinarian was the removal of the eyeball, as he was unable to understand how it was done in such a precise manner.[77]

Ten days later, the mutilators returned to the Gomez ranch. Sometime between the 25th and the 28th of June a tenth animal mutilation report was filed by Manuel Gomez. As is the usual description: "The tongue upper lip and half the udder were removed in the usual way." At this point Gomez was genuinely angry and confused. His cases from the late seventies had been singled out by Kenneth Rommel and debunked out of hand. Of course during Rommel's investigation, there had been no cases on the Gomez ranch to submit to the study for scientific testing. Gomez sat for an interview with Mary Frei from the *Albuquerque Journal* and expressed his frustration:

> The older Gomez is a soft-spoken man until the subject of former FBI agent Ken Rommel's 1980 mutilation investigation comes up. Rommel concluded that natural predators mutilated already-dead cows. "Mr. Rommel never did come out here to talk to me… of course, during the year that he was in, there were no mutilations in this part of the country. They were mutilating up in Canada. We've been in the ranching business for a long time, and we know the difference between a mutilation and a cow that has been killed by a predator. We know the difference, and any animal that we find dead and hasn't been touched by predators, we know that it was a mutilation. Because they sense something on the carcass and they won't eat it."[78]

There was almost a complete cessation of known unexplained livestock deaths in North America in late July that lasted until mid-August 1982. There were reports that animals had been found, and these stories circulated through ranching communities across the United States, but nothing definitive was logged by mutilation researchers. North Carolina may have had a couple of reports that summer, as it was noted later in a January 1983 *Salisbury Post* article. Officials at the local Rowan County Humane Society were told of cases between Greensboro and Charlotte, and Bonnie Smith, Humane Society spokesperson, said in a January 1983 interview:

> Two animals were mutilated within a one-mile area of Woodleaf in June and July and another injured on Old Concorde Road…Mrs. Smith said it's hard to tell how many other mutilations might have occurred, because people don't talk about it. She found out about some cases by talking to veterinarians. A couple of years ago she found six or eight white rabbits skinned, with carcasses and skins stacked in two piles, in woods behind her house… Don Barbee, the Woodleaf postmaster, said someone cut an ear and eye out of a bull he owned in June. "No, it definitely was not killed for the meat," Barbee said, "It didn't make any sense

at all. It was a clean cut, like with a sharp knife." Mrs. Truett Smith of Old Concorde Road, whose family owned the 1100 lb bull mutilated at their home in June, said the animal was definitely not killed for the meat. The Sheriff's Office thought it might be some cult, because of the organs that were removed.

…Bonnie Smith of the Humane Society told project Stigma that the Smith bull *was found near the house, tied between trees, and nearby were two cigarette butts—different brands. No one in the family smoked those brands.* [my emphasis] But the cuts on the bull were remarkably clean and bloodless—just no evidence of blood or bleeding. Mrs. Smith also informed us that in mid-July, 1982 and near the site of the Barbee mutilation, a week-old calf was found with one ear apparently having been cut off." [79]

The North Carolina cases are the only indication I can find that summertime cases occurred until mid August when the mutilators returned to northern New Mexico. Gabe Valdez was told by other State patrolmen that a there had been a mutilation near Quemodo in Catron County around August 10, 1982, but no official report was filed and the details of the case were never logged. Gabe didn't have to wait long to hear about a fresh case from his stomping grounds around Dulce and Rio Arriba County.

On August 15, 1982 "a rancher who had previously been struck in 1978 found a four-year-old female Charolais west of Dulce…" It appeared as if the animal had been dead for two days. As with most of the northern New Mexico cases, "the tongue and udder had been taken; the rectum had been 'cored out'" but this one had a strange twist, "two teeth were missing from the mouth."

Incidents were rumored to have taken place since the last official case on the Merrill Ranch in November 1981, but no official cases had been investigated on Colorado's Front Range in 1982. That changed on September 10, 1982 when dogs began barking at around 3:00 a.m. on Glenn Daniels' ranch, about 20 miles northeast of Castle Rock in Douglas County. No one bothered to get up to check, and the next morning a 1,000-pound, 15-year-old black Angus cow was found dead and disfigured. A 12-inch diameter hole about six to eight inches deep had been cut under the tail and the udder had been excised with "a clean, generally circular cut."

Daniels said it appeared that *the animal had been dragged downhill by its hind feet* as it struggled to get away. Although the tail was intact, an investigating Douglas County deputy noted the *hair had apparently been pulled out of the tail*. The animal's eyes and tongue were present. The tongue was protruding and it looked like magpies had pecked on it…the veterinarian [who was called to the scene] found that *the animal's back was broken*...Both the veterinarian and the deputy appeared to downplay the unusual elements of the case in favor of a natural-causes explanation. A newspaper reporter who visited the scene was spooked by it all and apparently became convinced that a cult was involved. *She refused to send any information on the case through the mail, fearing she might somehow incur the wrath of the cult.*[80] [my emphasis]

In Preston County, West Virginia in the Bruceton Mills region just below the Pennsylvania border, a series of strange goat deaths were reported in late August into early September 1982. Then the mutilators apparently decided to return to the Front Range of Colorado with a vengeance. Some of these unholy predators were evidently hungry for some prime parts, not the genitalia normally taken in your run-of-the-mill, classic mutilation case.

On September 13, 1982, three would-be-grill-masters were spotted by ranch foreman Bob Heath and his daughter while they were out repairing a windmill. They noticed a commotion in the adjoining pasture and spied a white Chevy pickup that didn't belong there, so they headed over to see what was going on. As they approached they witnessed "two people working on something in the pasture...At first we thought they'd killed an antelope [pronghorn] or something, but when we got closer to the gate, we saw a dead steer and two men lying on either side of it like they were trying to hide from us."

> ...Heath said his first reaction was to draw his rifle, but his daughter convinced him to go for help. At that point they went to the Pat Dawson residence, where Dawson notified authorities. Heath and his daughter then circled around back toward the suspects. Dawson described the ensuing action: 'When they saw me coming. They took off and headed toward me (westbound) on Sweet Road. They went by so fast I couldn't see the license plate number, so I wheeled around and took off after them. I really had my Subaru humpin' trying to catch up with them. In fact I didn't think I was going to, but they had to slow up quite a bit at the bend going into Peyton. I know the road a little better and could keep my foot in it more, so that's where I finally got close enough to get their license plate number.[81]

Heath and Dawson's quick action resulted in the El Paso County Sheriff's Department arresting three alleged perpetrators. They were apprehended with "the left hindquarter of the steer in the pickup... they were in the process of removing a front quarter. The cutting was done very adroitly and it was unclear just how the steer was killed..." According to the rancher, upon careful inspection of what remained of the steer, a bullet hole was discovered in the belly of the animal. The suspects arrested were: "Gerd D. Arnold, age 36; Michael Badial,

37; and Martha Ann Muel, 38." All three were released on bond.[82]

Three days after the botched butchers were apprehended, a broad daylight mutilation was reported *on the same road where the three rustlers had butchered the steer on the 13th*. The mutilators were back in force sporting various guises and multiple agendas.

Less than a week after the Daniels mutilation case, to the southeast in El Paso County, about 30 miles east of Colorado Springs, a noteworthy case was reported from the Dzuris ranch. Bill and Linda Dzuris had had two cows "mutilated" in 1979 that were found 100 feet apart with their rectums excised.

On the bright, sunny morning of September 16, 1982, the Dzuris' went out to check on the herd to see if any of their cows had calved. Seeing nothing amiss, they went inside to have lunch. At 5 p.m., Bill climbed up into his semi truck to go pick up a load of hay. He turned onto the road and about a half mile west of his driveway he saw a six-year-old Hereford-Angus crossbreed laying on its right side. The cow was down about 100 yards off the road. He kept going to his hay pickup, but called his wife to go out and check on the animal as he thought the animal may have been in trouble. Linda went out and was shocked at what she discovered: "parts had been cut off and blood was still dripping from some of the wounds." Later Linda Dzuris told reporter Linda Howe, "I was horrified at the thought of *what could do this in broad daylight when we had checked the cows only a few hours before.*"[83] [my emphasis]

> El Paso County Sheriff's Deputy D.R. Kelsey noted that some blood and fluid appeared to have dripped off the head area. Approximately half of the animal's udder had been removed with a clean vertical ("kind of a square shape, cut with a knife clean and smooth.") Two remaining teats had been cut cleanly across about an inch from the bag. The rectal area had been cut out in a vertical oval or egg-shaped wound about a foot wide and six to eight inches deep; the tail remained intact. Deputy Kelsey noted that 'it would seem that these areas were cut by some type of instrument rather than being torn away by some type of animal.' Mrs. Dzuris reported that the animal's hair appeared to have been rubbed off on the front of the back legs near the hooves. When Dzuris dragged the cow away from the site a few days later, all the hair came off on the underside of the animal as it was pulled along.[84]

According to Project Stigma, the following rather synchronistic-sounding account with an interesting helicopter twist comes from Linda Howe's files. It's another head-scratcher. Evidently, according to Linda, Bill Dzuris' sister, "Mrs. Kobilan," lived on a ranch near her brother's spread. "She was up late one night in mid-September when she heard the sound of a helicopter nearby." Evidently this sparked her curiosity and she went out onto her balcony to have a look. "She saw nothing but could still hear what seemed to be a helicopter, with *a sound so low that she could 'hear the wind through the props.'* Her *dog reacted to the invisible chopper by growling* and retreated into the house, she followed." [my emphasis] Feeling uneasy she called and reported the apparent "chopper without lights" to the sheriff's office. Kobilin claimed a similar event occurred on September 29th, but this time she was able to see the chopper. Out her window, "a clear yellow light" flew in low from the bluffs north of Peyton. Kobilan went outside in time to watch it fly away and disappear into the darkness. It was headed in the direction of the Larry Mikita ranch.

The following morning on the Mikita ranch, a six-year-old cow was discovered laying dead and mutilated in "an area of wheat stubble…Mikita said the straw around the head appeared trampled down." The right ear had been removed close to the skull in a "jagged circle." The right eye was missing with a circle of hide around the socket excised. There was blood both inside the ear cavity and the eye socket. The hide and the lips on the right-side mandible were peeled away and missing. Except for "just a tiny amount on the ground," there was little or no additional blood present at the scene. Mikita declined to officially report the disfigured animal to the local sheriff because, "it wouldn't have done any good."[85]

That same third week of September, in Daggett County, Utah, a Hereford cow was discovered mutilated. The animal was found missing its right ear—cut down to the bone—and half the left ear had been removed. *The cow's identifying ear tag had been removed and left on the cow's neck.* As in the Dzuris and Faulkner cases, *half of the udder* had been removed. The Daggett County sheriff reported that the Utah State Veterinarian who had examined the animal told him, "It was his opinion that the cow was dead before it had been mutilated. He also stated that the mutilation was done with a cutting instrument and not done by an animal." During that same week the rancher's brother allegedly experienced a mutilation on his ranch and it was thought that this animal probably was killed the night of September 23, 1982.

On September 26th yet another Utah report was filed in Daggett County. This time it was first of four mutilations—reported in quick succession—on the same ranch. The deaths probably occurred as follows: September 26th, a cow; September 30th, a four-year-old cow; October 10th, one of his cows was found muted on a neighbor's ranch; and October 19th, a two-year-old bull was found mutilated—left ear gone to the bone, penis removed with an oval-shaped clean cut. Some blood was noted on the bull's nose and its neck appeared "swollen." Because of the possibility of unwanted publicity, the rancher asked authorities to remain anonymous, but was willing to work with a private investigator wanting to document the details of the demise of his unfortunate animals.

In a rather strange report, on October 11, 1982 a Rush, Colorado rancher (who had been victimized in 1975 and 1978 by the mutilators) found his three-year-old cow as if "she had been running or trotting and been 'zapped' to the ground."

The cow was found in an unnatural "sitting up position." The ear and "a strip of flesh" were missing from across the jaw. A neighbor baling hay late at night had coincidentally observed a *"bright, mercury-vapor-like light moving at or near ground level through the pasture."* [my emphasis]

Texas became targeted in the fall of 1982. A report was made on October 20th when ranch workers discovered the remains of a six-year-old calf that was found in a mutilated condition. The cow was found about a mile from the ranch house, which is located near the town of San Diego, in Duval County. Cases had been reported in the seventies in Duval and Brooks counties, but the mutilations had officially subsided in this part of west Texas during the early eighties until this report. The animal had been seen on October 18th, so it was thought that the attack occurred later that night due to the horrific, slightly necrotic condition of the animal and the 80-degree weather. The crime scene showed a radical departure from your standard "classic mute" scenario.

> The *calf's head and tail* both appeared to have been cleanly severed from the body and both were missing. There was a cut or incision from where the tail had been cut away all the way up to the neck and, as far as could be discerned, all the internal viscera was also missing. There was no blood or evidence of bleeding. A *piece of 'tin' sheet metal lay on the ground just where the calf's head should have been and a white powder could be seen on portions of the carcass.* [my emphasis] An empty sardine can lay on the ground about 12 feet from the piece of 'tin' and a jawbone lay about four feet away.[86]

Evidently, no scavengers appeared interested in the cow and the unexplained livestock death was immediately reported to the local sheriff. Much to the annoyance of the rancher, the sheriff claimed he "couldn't care less," and the rancher was also told that the local livestock inspector "would be of no help." Maybe the sheriff knew something, but he wasn't saying? Adams notes in his recounting of the case that another possible explanation might be behind the strange demise and disfigurement of the doomed cow.

> On the [Duval County] ranch where the recent livestock-death occurred and in the surrounding area, an *unidentified "lion-like" animal had been spotted frequently*. It had a "big head" and the body was a reddish color. One witness, driving at night, saw what she thought were red reflectors, as illuminated in her headlights, by the side of the road. As she drove closer, she realized they were the eyes of a cat-like animal. A number of animals, which had been killed and/or mutilated and/or eaten in the area, were thought to have been *victims of the "mystery cat,"* and scratches on some horses were attributed to the same animal.[87] [my emphasis]

The reports leapfrog north to Sweetwater County, Wyoming, where a 400-pound Hereford steer calf was apparently killed and disfigured on October 19, 1982. The sexual organs were gone along with its left ear. The tongue appeared to have been excised and the lower mandible flesh was cleanly removed from the jaw.

Five days later the same Wyoming ranch allegedly had a second steer calf mutilated. This time only the left ear was taken and a Rock Springs vet said he felt that "the animal might have died of natural causes, as the lungs exhibited some infection." It appeared as if the calf had struggled some before dying, although no actual cause of death was ever determined.

Linda Howe covered these Wyoming cases and interviewed Sweetwater County Deputy Theron Wilde:

> "They tell me it's predators, which I do not believe, because I do not feel a predator can do these things. I don't feel a predator can come up and chew half a bag off a cow or the end of a penis off a bull and not touch any of the rest of the cow. [sic] I've been around predators and they'll go inside the abdominal cavity first and eat the insides, which is easy eating."[88]

As noted in the section covering 1977, this part of Utah and Wyoming featured a number of attendant helicopter sightings around the ranches where mutilations were being reported. The same holds true for the above reports where Deputy Wilde observed with binoculars a small two-seater chopper circling over ranches surrounding his ranch on October 10th. He described the helicopter as having "a glass bubble, silver tail with red at the end of the tail." He was unable to discern any other markings or identifying numbers. Then on November 7, 1982 he noted that the same chopper flew over the same area in a circling pattern, as before. Again, this sighting mirrored chopper activity reported over the area in the 1977 reports.[89]

Other late October cases were reported in several states, including a Huerfano Valley, Colorado case that was investigated by Animal Mutilation Probe investigator David Perkins. A rancher down the hill from Perkins' house near Gardner, Colorado suffered his third mute case since 1975. This latest one was a year-old steer that had its penis removed, leaving behind a 12-inch wound. "One ear was severed with a 'clean knife cut,' and the anal area had been cored out to a depth of 18 inches." It's interesting to note that the case occurred during a three-night time period when Gardner residents observed "bright lights hovering over the area of the victim's ranch." One night, Joyce Aguirre, the wife of a local law enforcement officer, was in her kitchen when she suddenly felt she was 'being watched.' She looked out the window and saw what she described as a *'saucer-shaped' object, with red, blue and green lights*, moving erratically over the area west and south of Greenhorn Peak—apparently right over David Perkins' house. According to Perkins, Joyce was "frightened" by the sight. [my emphasis]

At the time, mute investigators Tom Adams and Gary Massey happened to be visiting Perkins for a "mini" mute conference. As they sat there trying to figure out how they were going to catch the mutilators, they had visitors hanging out just overhead. Funny how that works, sometimes. A similar event occurred in the mid nineties when Adams, Massey and I were visiting Perkins and the following day, a strange, lighted object was again seen over the house filled with oblivious investigators. Are we tuned in, or what?[90]

After a brief respite from reports during the first two weeks of November, the phantom mute surgical team visited the Faulkner ranch, located in extreme northeastern Weld County, just below the Wyoming border. On November 22, 1982, a valuable nine-year-old Charolais cow was found missing half of the right side of its udder with the left side missing two teats. The rear end reproductive organs had been removed with a five-inch deep hole cored out of the animal. It was also missing an eye, cut in such an expert fashion that it astonished the veterinarian who was called to examine the animal. Says the Project Stigma report:

> [It] was the removal of this item [the eye] and the precise fashion in which it was done that amazed the [veterinarian] most of all, certifying—at least to our satisfaction—that this was an out-of-the-ordinary event. He [also] found evidence of some hemorrhage in the pia mater [the delicate innermost layer of the membranes surrounding the brain and spinal cord], as though, he felt *something was injected into the brain*. His best guess as a cause of death, in fact, was 'possible injection of material into the brain with [an] unknown object without causing cerebral trauma…' [Rancher Faulkner noted] 'As of December 15, [1982] no coyotes had touched the remains of the carcass.'[91]

On December 3rd, Norfolk, Nebraska rancher Jim Lehman was checking his herd when he discovered his prize seven-month-old Simmental heifer mutilated on the fence line that looks at U.S. Highway 81, a main regional thoroughfare. He was "kinda sick" at the loss of his purebred breeding stock and called the report in to the local authorities. Deputy Sheriff Darrell Grebe investigated the scene and noted "both ears were missing, *the ear tags had been removed, with one on the ground and one lying on the right hind leg*." [my emphasis] Lehman also reported that the right front leg had been "severed cleanly," plus all the hide between the missing leg and the face was gone. A nine-inch half-moon cut was present on the right flank. Grebe told the *Daily News* "'[I]t appeared the animal was cut with a very sharp knife and there was no indication that it had been shot.' Grebe called the whole event 'unusual, very unusual.'"[92]

Directly south about 370 miles, another case was reported on December 11,

1982. A seven-month-old bull calf was found missing an eyeball and ear, and the hide on the jaw was excised revealing that "a good portion" of the tongue had been removed. "It was suspected that the blood had been drained, but this was concluded as a result of the lack of blood or evidence of bleeding." No autopsy or professional examination was performed at the site. Investigating officer Cowley County Deputy Craig King tried to take pictures of the carcass, but interestingly, *his camera refused to operate*. Orville Bair, the victimized rancher mentioned later in an interview with Project Stigma that "normally coyotes would be expected to 'start in' on the carcass right away. The carcass was fed upon, but it did not begin until 'several days' later."[93]

1983 and 1984: And You Thought We Were Through

My files are rather lean when it comes to 1983 through 1985. It appears as if the mutilation reports in North America vanished from view. There were rumors of unreported cases, but very few "official" unexplained livestock death reports were investigated by U.S. County Sheriffs in the two years surrounding the publication of *Mute Evidence*—Kagan & Summers' dismissal of the mutilation mystery. Was it due to the increasing sense of futility? Or perhaps the mute program moved elsewhere. Where Kagan leaves off in "their" narrative, the mystery continues onward.

During the time period just after the publication of *Mute Evidence,* mutilation cases were being reported in the northwestern England and in Australia. One of the Australian reports apparently featured interesting attendant landing physical evidence allegedly discovered at the site—plus there's the claim of military interest and a hint of possible subterfuge. According to the lead media report in Sydney's *Telegraph* titled "UFO Death 'Cover-Up by Army:'"

> The Army is trying to cover up the bizarre killing of four cows on a farm, UFO researchers say. Reports said each cow had a hole drilled above the right eye, through which the brain apparently was removed. A director of the Australian International UFO Research Society, Mr. Colin Norris, said yesterday that egg-shaped pod-marks, suggesting the landing of a craft, were found near the property, in the Adelaide Hills. He said rocks in the pod-holes were crushed, *treetops burned*, and many birds found dead.[94] [my emphasis]

And some of the salacious details surrounding the event were repeated two days later in the Perth *Sunday Times*, but this time we have the added detail that burn marks were found on the ground. Is this another classic example of subtle media embellishment or did this second story correct the original media account?

Farmers in the Adelaide Hills have discovered mutilated animal corpses and *burn marks on the ground*. ...In one incident, researchers say a farmer discovered four cows with holes drilled into their skulls and the brains removed.[95] [my emphasis]

The inexplicable wave of identical sheep slayings (figure 16) in western Wales began in May 1984, and by October upwards of 120 lambs had been reported mysteriously killed. Law enforcement officials were genuinely baffled, especially when in the mid-fall, the wave of unexplained deaths ceased as mysteriously as it had begun. There were few if any leads and investigators must have drawn a sigh of relief that it was over before the first of November. The relieved Welsh sheepherder community probably thought it was over as well. I am not aware of any additional UK reports from October 1984 to May 1985.

In hindsight, the lull of "official" unexplained North American livestock death reports throughout most of 1984 was probably due to a complicated set of factors. First, the mutilators may have moved elsewhere to redder pastures; second, they may have ratcheted back their activities for some unknown reason. Add in a dash of media indifference and it appeared that ranchers and law enforcement may have 'thrown in the towel' and given up attempting to solve, or even report or *publicize* the countless numbers of mutilation reports from the prior ten years. No matter how much effort and energy had been expended by law enforcement, no matter how many reports had been filed, no one in the equation seemed to be any closer to figuring out what was happening, how it was being done or who was responsible. Sure, many cases may have been simple "misidentified scavenger action," but as we have seen: *not all cases can be explained away with this rationale.* It appeared to most investigators that something slick, high-tech and slippery was operating with impunity inside the darkened pastures of the world.

1985: Keeping the Livestock Alive

At the start of 1985, it was apparent to all concerned that there were no easy answers to the mystery—nor in hindsight were there any ready answers to the questions that *investigators didn't know to ask*. A burbling frustration grew in the mutilation research subculture, which fed the sense of fear, or trepidation. The fear helped breed paranoia that undoubtedly fueled ranchers' reluctance to report new mutilation cases.

Many naysayers used the publication of the dismissive Rommel report (June 1980) and the publication of Kagan and Summers book *Mute Evidence*—considered by the mutilation researcher crowd to be an offhand dismissal of the mystery—as further motivation to lock the door behind what were already closed minds. Rather than digging deeper into the mystery and examining the data that doesn't conform to the one-size fits all explanation of "misidentified scavenger action," skeptics had their out: Rommel and *Mute Evidence* rendered the mystery moot. Nothing to see here—move along people…

But many ranchers and sheriffs and other investigators who had dealt with reports on the ground knew in their gut that something far more involved and strange had been going on, that the core of the phenomenon wasn't simply mundane predation, misidentified scavenger action and small town paranoia. Something was still unexplained at the core of the phenomenon. In the culture at large, mutes were already old news—the subject had been moved out of sight/out of mind by the mainstream media and found itself placed firmly back in the closet. By the end of 1984 the ranching community realized that no good could come from filing a mutilation report, so why bother? This for the most part became the path of least resistance during the mid to late 1980s and into the Alabama wave of the early nineties. But mute cases continued to be reported through the nineties up until today. As we will see, some of these little-known reports are worth noting.

The first official mutilation reports of 1985 began the first week of January in south Texas when a Duval County rancher discovered one of his older breeding cows classically mutilated. The Corpus Christi *Caller* paper spoke with the investigating Deputy Adolio Briones who noted there was no blood at the site. Rancher Tomas Hinojosa mentioned that his brothers saw the animal during the day before, it was discovered that night.[96]

Then, later in mid-March, the remains of two horribly mutilated horses in central Texas near Leander were found. One was a 10-year-old mare, the other a seven-year-old gelding, and the two horses were laying 50 feet apart in a pasture just over the county line (in Travis County). The County Sheriff's Office declined to speak with the media about the case, but the attending veterinarian, Guy Rowland, spoke with Project Stigma and the *Williamson County Sun*, which later published an article about the case:

> …An autopsy was performed on the horses by a Round Rock [Texas] veterinarian, who said the horses had been mutilated. He said he was unable to determine the cause of death. The veterinarian, Guy Rowland, told the *Sun* that the animals were killed, the eyes removed, their tongues cut out, and their sex organs sliced off… he could find no signs of starvation or disease. He said the animals had been killed by people… Rowland speculated that the horses may have been drugged before they died…"This is the first time I've ever seen anything like this."[97]

A February 10, 1985 Pratt County case near Sawyer, Kansas was reported and checked by a local veterinarian who said he "couldn't figure out" how the animal died. And then the reports jumped down to southern Rio Arriba County, New Mexico on March 29th. It is interesting to note that the hard-hit northern Rio Arriba County region and *the rest of New Mexico* had registered no official mutilation reports in 1984. And, I should also note, the March 29th case on Tony

Martinez's ranch was the only New Mexico report for 1985 listed in Project Stigma's extensive database.

Two weeks later a strange series of occult-tinged events were covered by Ohio regional media that blossomed into a *New York Post* article published in June '85. In December 1984, after a series of unexplained animal deaths in the Union County area—located northwest of Columbus, Ohio—Sheriff John Overly appointed a deputy to investigate *"an outbreak of 'animal mutilations,' and ritual slaughters believed associated with at least 200 animal mutilations in Union County, involving the torturing of lambs, dogs and other animals, the eating of the animals' flesh and the drinking of their blood."* [my emphasis] The media zoomed in and the story grew legs. There is a lot of interesting circumstantial evidence in this saga. The investigating officer, John Lala, and his boss, Sheriff Overly, expressed concern that the crimes they were investigating could "escalate from animal mutilations to something even more serious." Investigators were able gain access to some suspects' homes and found rather pedestrian-sounding occult books, written for the casually curious. During the same time period, according to Project Stigma's media database, authorities to the north of Columbus, around Toledo and in parts of Lucas County, were allegedly looking into reports that *"cultists had ritually slaughtered up to 75 people, most of them children and newborn babies.* [my emphasis] Unidentified informants were making such claims anyway."[98]

This questionable story is too involved to go into here at length, but it seems that this was another textbook example of the ever-present interpretation of unexplained animal death outbreaks as somehow being related to (or being a result of) ritual occult activity. This slant appears to me to be a misinterpretation made by investigators that have no clue what actual "occult activity" is, let alone how it relates to the (ancient) practice of ritualized animal sacrifice. Possible occult involvement in the 1980s unexplained animal death phenomenon is a consistent theme that burbles underneath regional (and sometimes national) media coverage of the mutilation mystery. And, occult activity appeared to be the prevalent go-to assumption among law enforcement investigators of many *small animal death outbreaks*. However, within the mainstream cattle mutilation investigation community, occult activity seemed to be the least likely explanation.

As we saw in several head-scratching cases from Montana in the mid-seventies, and in some Idaho and Canadian cases from the mid to late seventies, occultists were supposedly identified by law enforcement investigators, but nothing solid ever seemed to be ascertained; to this day, no black magicians or dark, devil-worshipping adepts have ever been charged with or convicted of a single livestock mutilation. As we have seen, evil-worshipping-baby-blood-drinking, witchy stereotypes in the media have done little to bolster law enforcement's effort to get up to speed—rather this cliché appears to have muddied the waters and made the mystery even more impenetrable and potentially unsolvable.

Cases All Over the Map

As we have seen, cattle make up the vast majority of unexplained livestock death reports, but across the cold Atlantic in Wales, they have to keep their eyes on their flocks of sheep. The sheep surgeons had been busy in the hilly region south of Barmouth in 1984, and like clockwork, exactly a year later in May 1985 they were back supplying more mayhem for local "bobbies" to ponder. As we will see, unexplained sheep mutilations would be reported in the hill regions between Barmouth and Shrewsbury, on and off for the next two decades.

In the second week of May 1985, Welsh sheep farmer Major Norman Corbett discovered three of his snowy-white lambs dead—each from an apparent deep puncture wound "the size of a 10p piece" drilled into its side. There was no blood, and the puncture wound was the only evidence of trauma on the animals. As the sun arose the following morning, *21 lambs on two nearby farms* were discovered dead in the same condition as the Corbett sheep. All 21 had the same type of wound, and none were outwardly marked in any other way. The *Sunday Express* had covered the 1984 that bloomed on the Welsh coast, and the reporters were back to take stock of this latest deluge of springtime 1985 reports:

> Major Corbett has seen it all before. Last year, he and other farmers in the area became used to finding dead lambs with identical wounds and severe internal injuries.
>
> Although Police, vets and farmers mounted a major investigation, they could find no explanation for the mystery puncture-marks. Investigators considered many theories, but one by one, they ruled out attacks by crossbow, shotgun, and other animals, such as dogs.
>
> The killings have also concentrated almost exclusively on one type of lamb, pure-white Welsh ewes. Brown and oil-white lambs, and male lambs, have almost always been ignored. And most of the attacks have been directed at only two farms, Major Corbett's, and that of his neighbour Mr Richard Lewis at Tywyn, South Gwynedd.
>
> Major Corbett, who has more than 1,000 sheep, *has lost 35 lambs,* worth £1,000. Mr Lewis has *lost more than 70.* [my emphasis] Superintendent Elwyn Davies, of Dolgellau Police, South Gwynedd, said: "It is made worse because, in this area, sheep are people's livelihood."[99]

We now need to teleport our way back to the Pine Ridge Indian Reservation in South Dakota, near the town of Porcupine, during the same time period as the Wales reports. The following unexplained animal death report was forwarded to reporter Linda Howe by David Brewer from the Bureau of Indian Affairs. According to sources, on May 22, 1985 a cow was discovered about two to three miles away from the nearest road or homestead. The only way to easily get out to the pasture where the mutilation allegedly occurred was to "pass right by the owner's house." Over the past several years mutes had been reported from this part of the 'Rez,' and this 'classic' case was familiar: the jaw was stripped of flesh and hide: the tongue, rear end and udder were missing. White-colored flecks of an unknown material (probably bird droppings?) were observed on the carcass. "Some sort of 'skid mark' was said to be on the ground nearby." No veterinarian was apparently called and no necropsy was performed.[100]

There are countless reports like this scattered throughout researchers' databases: classic-appearing "incisions" on an animal in a rural community: maybe it was reported, maybe not. Then word of the strange-appearing animal death circulates by word of mouth throughout the community. Maybe a story appears in the local or regional newspaper, maybe not. Invariably it appears that people in the impacted area gravitate toward extremes. One side goes into a place of fear, the other into the realm of denial. Need I remind you—ranchers are not stupid. They are in business to raise and properly maintain their herds, however, when faced with the inexplicably improbable, they tend to become polarized into two ways of thinking. Either these deaths and apparent disfigurements are natural events—there's nothing to it—or what is being done to livestock is an unnatural event and something abnormal is being perpetrated by unknown agents. Law enforcement officials are caught smack in the middle. They have no recourse and are rendered impotent and frustrated. Besides documenting the scene, in most cases officials have no leads, no motives and no recourse.

Occasionally, a case is reported in a timely enough manner that forensic scientists become involved. The results of these rigorous reports and studies cannot be overlooked or glossed over. Many cases are probably (unusual appearing) scavenger action, but a sizeable percentage of cases show that "sharp implements" are involved in excising cattle parts in an *unnatural* manner.

The month of June 1985 was thankfully quiet in the western United States, but a farmer in Perryopolis, Pennsylvania reported losing 11 cows within a week "mutilated in various ways." A "tail was removed on some of them, one had both ears cut off, and all had a hole about eight-inches in diameter in the chest area." Pennsylvania Association for the Study of the Unexplained investigator Stan Gordon listed the case in the group's publication.[101]

On July 6, 1985, in a rather strange report filed by a helicopter pilot flying over a farm outside of Ft. Worth, Texas, (near Keller) he allegedly witnessed "approximately 50 cows of various sizes and ages, lying in a circle." Tarrant County law enforcement and North Texas Humane Society investigators were notified and conducted a quick search of the area, but turned up no dead animals. According to a Humane Society official, "*about 12 horses had been found dead and sexually mutilated in the Keller area in the preceding year.*"[102]

Evidently there were more unexplained animal deaths and attacks occurring than regional media was made aware of (or were willing to cover), for none of these reports, to my knowledge, made the Texas newspapers or TV newscasts.

Every day thousands of animals are ritualistically slaughtered for religious purposes. Most Americans are unaware of this ancient practice, and it would shock many to know that there are over a million people (mostly of Caribbean descent) who follow Santeria, Voodoo, Candomble and other blood-based belief systems that involve the routine practice of animal sacrifice. (figure 17) Mostly fowl (chickens and ducks), but with some goats and the occasional sheep, are ritualistically slaughtered at select rituals and festivals. These religious practitioners are protected under the Constitution, but occasionally law enforcement swoops in at the behest of horrified accidental witnesses and outraged animal rights groups to scenes of what appears to be wanton, bloody slaughter.

DATELINE: Atlantic City, New Jersey, July 1985:

[P]olice arrested 19 people of Cuban decent in an apartment strewn with the remains of chickens, ducks and lambs, buckets of blood, and ritualistic altars. Hundreds of chicken, duck and lamb parts were discovered, along with three lamb carcasses minus legs and a number of live fowl. The practitioners were in various stages of butchering and blood-smeared reverie. A similar scene had been discovered in a house in Pleasantville, [New Jersey] near Atlantic City, a week earlier.[103]

Texas continued to experience the occasional unexplained livestock death and Paris, Texas-based investigator Tom Adams continued to collect and file newspaper stories and track down additional unexplained animal death claims from the midwest. But he was beginning to realize that there were no easy answers to the cattle mutilation mystery. (figure 18)

Linda Howe continued her work combing the Rocky Mountain states for new reports and the incidents of unexplained animal deaths continued, but were generally not publicized outside of the local, rural communities where these deaths were discovered. These cases included a possible mutilation reported on July 18, 1985 by rancher Max Kelly to El Paso County law enforcement and a quick series of four cases in early to mid September 1985. All of these cases featured young calves as the target of the mutilators.

The following accounts are compiled from a variety of sources including Project Stigma, David Perkins, Linda M. Howe, Bill Jackson, Shirley Rickard, and articles published in the *Ranchland News,* Colorado Springs *Gazette, Rocky Mountain News,* and the *Greeley Tribune.*

On September 2, 1985, George Cvaniga discovered a nine-month-old heifer calf was mutilated on land he leased for grazing located near Ramah, Colorado. About a week later a "healthy" seven-month-old calf was discovered by rancher

Art Rasner, apparently mutilated, in the southeastern corner of El Paso County. The animal's rear end appeared cored out with a "smooth circular cut around the rectum." Also during early September, on the 6th, Ralph Rickey (who had lost another cow in a similar fashion in the mid '70s) found a five-month-old calf strangely slain and disfigured on his ranch about 32 miles southeast of Simla, Colorado. He told *Ranchland News* reporter Monty Gaddy: "Right behind the front leg was a perfect circle about 12-inches in diameter, just like somebody used a real sharp object to cut it." The calf also appeared to have an unusual incision around the mouth.

On September 14th, a fourth case was reported—this time in Elbert County. The latest case was an older cow, aged five. Caretakers on the Gertsch ranch (located about 20 miles south of Matheson, Colorado) discovered the animal with additional forensic evidence at the crime scene not usually associated with you garden-variety, "classic" mute. There was the standard circular cut on the rear end, the udder was apparently excised and there were no tracks, footprints or additional blood evidence at the scene. Ranch caretakers Jim and Billie Trembly, who oversaw operations on the ranch that consisted of 75 cattle, spoke with Gaddy, who noted in his article:

> Besides the classic clues pointing to a mutilation, the animal had several other unusual features. *There was a substance slowly oozing from the animal's nose.* "I've never heard anyone say anything about oozing from the nose in any of the mutilations I've read about," Mrs. Trembly said. Even more peculiar was an unexplainable spot on the cow's belly where the hair had been rubbed off. Additionally, there were marks directly in front of both the left and right rear legs. Judging from the marks, it appears some sort of claw device must have pinched the hide with such intensity as to break the skin and cause bruises… [The] Tremblys said they suspect the animal was airlifted and dropped at the point where they made the discovery.[104] [my emphasis]

In 1986 the *Rocky Mountain News* ran a short article on mid 1980s mutilation cases reported in Colorado where they quoted Mrs. Trembly about the Gertsch Ranch case, which had occurred the previous year:

> She's convinced the government is doing something "sleazy." The cuts are so precise she believes they could only have been made with a laser. "It's frightening," she said. "Our dog wouldn't go near the dead cow. The birds left the area for a long time."[105]

During the first week of December 1985, in the northern part of Summit County, Colorado, about a mile east of State Highway 9, three calves and an adult cow were discovered mutilated near Cow Creek Gulch. Investigating officers found that a male calf was missing its genitalia with "a clean edged incision," while a female calf had a strange oval shaped, 12-inch circle of hide missing from just in front of the udders. The third calf was discovered with "its hide completely cut from the underside and pulled over the ribcage so that the interior was exposed to the open air." The adult cow had a "clean edged vertical incision running the length of the hindquarter and leg and had a circular puncture behind the ear."[106]

Weld County—located at the northeastern corner of Colorado—has been a hotbed of mutilation claims by small ranching operations, as we saw in the seventies into the eighties. A welcomed respite in cases occurred in1985 with only one known "official" report being filed with Weld County authorities. Rumors of a prior September case circulated around the local ranching community but no official report had been filed.

Then, on October 7, 1985, a motorist driving by a ranch belonging to Robert Holsten noticed two animals down in the pasture. The ranch was located a couple of miles south of Roggen, Colorado. The rancher went out to investigate. Holsten and the investigating deputy sheriff noted, "it was pretty obvious it had been mutilated. Its penis was removed, the scrotum had been cut away and the anus area had been cut. There was no obvious cause of death that we could find."[107]

Logan County—probably the hardest hit county on the Front Range of Colorado in the 1970s— escaped without a publicly acknowledged "mutilation" problem throughout most of the eighties. Reports were investigated in November 1985, but for the most part "official" cases were few and far between in 1984 and 1985. This lack of publicized reports was good for business and besides; remote rural communities won't long abide controversies. The mutilations had become a bone of contention in many small communities and 'no cases' were the best cases. In November 1985, at the end of the prolonged lull, Tom Adams received a letter from "a Logan County law officer" who, at the time, sensed unease, fear and socio/political trepidation within the higher echelons of Front Range ranching culture. This unnamed law enforcement official summed up his feelings:

> "As a law enforcement officer in Logan County I have had the privilege to discuss the [mutilation] phenomenon with numerous individuals who were involved with the mutilations in varying aspects. Some of these individuals held, and still hold, high and respectable positions within their communities. When discussing the issues, I couldn't help but feel a strong paranoia pervading from these people, especially the ones who were active in the investigation of the mutilations. Some were evasive, angry and even hostile! This is very peculiar, considering the mutilations supposedly ceased in the late '70s! I have even been *warned* to proceed with caution upon examining the matter! [emphasis retained]

Unusual! I am not implying that the mutilations are still occurring as frequently and that a fantastic "cover-up" has been implemented, but I do believe that [the mutilations] are still happening on a limited basis [in Logan County] and that the ranchers and other involved citizens are no longer reporting the strange deaths to the proper authorities because doing so, of course, would be in vain.[108]

Was this unease among the influential locals due to simple paranoia? Were the prominent individuals he encountered that were "active in the investigations of mutilations" simply embarrassed by their apparent impotence and by their inability to solve the mystery? Or was everyone's fear justified? At the very least, there appears to be some presence and/or group exercising damage control over the principles involved in the areas of high incident. Someone is apparently behind the scenes 'a-movin' and a-shakin.' We have seen hints of damage control in Alberta, British Columbia, Iowa, Texas and Kansas, and possibly England. In November 1985, why the apparent reluctance by the Logan County socio/political structure to acknowledge new cases were occurring—or to allow themselves to be publicly associated to these mid to late 1980s reports?

As in Logan County, Colorado and northern New Mexico, the entire country of Canada was relatively mute-free in 1985. Again, we can't ascertain for certain whether this was due to an apparent cessation of the mutilators' activities, or whether this lack of reports was also due to a growing frustration and sense of futility within the Canadian ranching community—an apathy that resulted in a reluctance to report cases to authorities. Or, perhaps there was a combination of the two factors? No matter, Canada 'officially' escaped the wrath of the phantom cattle surgeons until the following strange report was filed in October.

On October 20, 1985, Wesley Cook, whose farm was located about 100 miles north of Winnipeg, Manitoba near the town of Ashern, realized one of his cows was missing. Cook (and his son Lyle) began scouring the land looking for the animal. They looked for two days and could not locate the cow anywhere on their property. Then, on Tuesday the 22nd, Mrs. Cook happened to look out her window with binoculars at her men out in the pasture when she noticed what appeared to be a dead cow lying on the ground in an adjoining pasture that had already been checked numerous times over the past two days. This pasture had roads on either side and was in plain view of the main road and the farmhouse. Rancher Cook had seen flickering lights out in the field that Saturday night/early Sunday morning—the night the animal was apparently killed.

Upon examining the dead cow, Cook noticed right off that the animal's throat had apparently been cut and it bled out. The udder had been removed and the tongue was gone. Cook immediately reported the slain head of livestock to the RCMP who came to his ranch and investigated the site.

On Wednesday morning an RCMP officer arrived with Dr. L. Milin, the Ashern area veterinarian. Dr. Milin inspected the animal and reports, "someone cut the throat of the animal and it bled out, then the tongue was removed and the udder cut off." …Dr. Milin, noting the lack of blood on the ground [besides where it bled out], decided to have a look at the animal's heart. He cut out the heart and cut it open. There was no blood in the heart.

When asked what he thought happened, Wesley Cook explained, "I believe that someone is doing demonic, ritual killing and taking the tongue, udder and blood for an occult ritual." Lyle Cook…agreed, "It's got to be something haywire like that because if they were rustling beef, they would have taken some choice cuts of beef…" When asked for a statement regarding the dead cow in Cook's pasture, the RCMP spokesperson stated, "We can't determine foul play but we can't rule it out either." [109]

Cascade County, Montana rancher Tom Denning apparently had a diabolical trick-or-treater on Halloween night, October 31, 1985. He discovered his horse laying in a "strange position" on a hilltop on his property. He noticed right off that the face had been stripped of hide on one side down to the bone leaving the jaw and skull denuded of tissue and hide. The poor horse was also missing its sexual organs, mammary glands, an ear and an eyeball. All of these cuts are your "classic" mute descriptions. He also noted that the throat had been peeled of hide and the neck muscles removed, exposing the animal's windpipe. Denning commented to the *Great Falls Tribune:* "The cuts were so precise, where it's cut off her face, it's an absolutely straight cut with nothing left at all except the bone structure."[110]

Denning was alarmed and a bit puzzled by the apparent lack of bleeding or blood at the site and called in Capt. Keith Wolverton to investigate. Wolverton had already investigated dozens of Cascade County mute cases in the mid to late seventies. The Cascade County sheriff, Glenn Osborne, told the *Tribune* that Wolverton "said it was nothing but predators." The *Tribune* contacted Wolverton to get a statement, but he refused to talk about the case. Denning was taken aback by Wolverton's analysis of the site:

"He tried to tell me it was predators on the back end. There's no way I'd agree with that because it was too precise a cut—it wasn't something that was chewed out, it was a perfectly circular pattern. If it was a predator it would have had jagged edges." While Wolverton said predators might have caused the cuts on the back [end] of the animal, Denning said Wolverton could not explain the cuts on the horse's face. He said "It was unusual and he had no answers."[111]

December is usually a slow month for unexplained animal death reports, but occasionally cold weather cases are reported. Sometime during the first couple of days of December 1985, El Paso County rancher Eldon Butler and his family heard the sound of a helicopter that was apparently hovering "about 300 yards" from his ranch house. Because of the nearby military bases, they often hear choppers over their ranch, but this one seemed to be hovering nearby. Butler wasn't alarmed enough to go out and see what the chopper was doing, but the next morning he wished he had. There, out in the pasture, he discovered one of his cows dead and apparently disfigured in an unnatural way. A call was immediately made to the sheriff, who came out to investigate the animal death. The official report stated that there appeared to be a "14-inch hole cut by 'some type of sharp instrument.'" The animal was also missing its genitals. The report then goes on to declare, "it's the work of predators."

Butler was not happy with this apparent discrepancy: "That makes you kind of sore when you can see with your own plain eyes a butcher couldn't leave such a clean hole."[112]

1986: Are These Guys Ever Gonna Stop?

The New Year started out quickly with a January 2, 1986 case of two unexplained dead horses discovered on a ranch near Yelm, Washington (located in Thurston County). The animals were discovered in a field *where the fence line had been cut*. The horses were found with their throats cut, and one of them, an Appaloosa, was missing its genitalia.[113]

In early February 1986, a mutilated bull was discovered about 30 miles southeast of Walsenburg, Colorado, in Huerfano County. The animal had been seen earlier in the day alive, but a few hours later it was discovered—*still warm*—missing its rear end with what was described as "a perfect circle—like a one motion cut." The testicles were missing, but the penis was intact. There were no apparent signs of any struggle.

This mutilation site is about ten miles away from what was then the U.S. Army's Piñon Canyon Training Area and helicopters were a daily sight to the locals. According to law enforcement (and the tireless work of David Perkins) stories were being told locally that "some very sensitive and exotic activities" were occurring on the training area. These were persistent rumors heard from several sources that prefer to remain anonymous—for obvious reasons. One story involved alleged "aliens" and not the illegal kind, either. Of course, having heard many stories from the rumor mill, nothing would surprise me.[114]

After a brief, uneasy lull in reports, the mutilators apparently struck the Houston, Texas area displaying a bizarre sense of grim, trickster-like humor. It was reported in the *Houston Chronicle* on March 7, 1986 that three carcasses of small Welsh ponies had been discovered mutilated *at a drive-in banking facility*. There was no mention of who owned the animals and no mention of how they were brought to this urban location.[115] Go figure. Texas bankers could be considered as suspect as anyone else.

David Brewer, a Bureau of Indian Affairs officer on the Pine Ridge Indian Reservation in South Dakota, reported to Project Stigma that there had been two, possibly three early spring 1986 mutilations on the eastern part of the reservation. Evidently, no official reports were filed and the owners' names, the dates of the alleged cases and other information was not relayed to Tom Adams.

Exactly one year to the day after the April 21, 1985 mutilation on the Tidwell Ranch, west of Guntersville, Alabama, Tidwell's neighbors, the Vandervoorts (whose ranch adjoins the Tidwell spread) experienced a mutilation. A cow was found the rear end and heart missing, plus one teat had been removed from the udder. There was "a little blood on the animal, but none on the ground," according to Sheriff's investigator Ed Teal. He noted that the parts missing were "not just ripped out. They're specifically cut out. It's very weird."

Both targeted ranches adjoin the local school principal Les Click's property. The night after the Vandervoort mutilation occurred, Click reported hearing a helicopter flying low over his farm.[116]

There was another apparent late spring lull until a mutilation was reported in June on the Strath Kay Ranch near Escalante, Utah. Then another case was reported to the southwest in hard-hit Rio Arriba County, New Mexico; Ojo Seco rancher Orlando Sanchez, Sr. found a six-year-old cow mutilated missing the udder, anus, left eyeball and lip—all removed with "neatly incised cuts." The rancher told a reporter that he couldn't understand why coyotes had not attacked the carcass.

Evidently, the mutilators were not finished with their Marshall County, Alabama visit either. In the third week of July 1986, in the Nixon Chapel area, Clyde Gilliland found his bull dead, missing its testicles. They appeared to have been cut off. Unlike many mutilations of bulls, no other wounds were found on the animal.[117]

In late August 1986, David Perkins and the Animal Mutilation Probe were alerted to a mutilation claim from a ranch 25 miles southeast of Trinidad, Colorado, in Los Animas County. There was a short (few hour) time window between when the 1,200-pound Angus bull was seen alive the night prior and early the next morning when it was discovered in a mutilated condition. The tongue was missing from deep in its throat, some teeth were missing, an eye was gone and the lips and nose had been cut away. Also, a large triangular section was taken from the underside, where the genitalia and the rectum had been removed. It should also be noted that claims of unidentified lights had been reported two miles away from the mute site three nights before the bull was killed.[118]

During the third weekend of September 1986 another strange horse mutilation was reported in urban Houston, Texas. This time, it was a full-sized horse discovered dead and *"slashed with a sharp instrument," lying on the tennis courts of Clear Lake High School,* near NASA's Johnson Space Center. The press jumped on this case and it was covered in a local TV news broadcast. NASA contractor (and future MUFON Director) John Schuessler alerted Project Stigma about the strange report.[119] Was a message being sent to the communities around (NASA's Johnson Space Center), or was this another one of those inexplicable coincidences?

Veteran Pennsylvania paranormal investigator Stan Gordon was contacted in early November 1986 concerning a 700-pound cow that was found mutilated in Fayette County, which has a long history of unexplained event reports. This one was merely the latest in a long line of reports of so-called "paranormal" activity. A rancher at his Uniontown ranch discovered his cow with its tail "sharply cut off." All the teats on the udder had been removed and there was an abnormal lack of blood on the cuts and at the scene.[120]

Other cases undoubtedly occurred that fall of 1986, but the aforementioned growing reluctance within the ranching and law enforcement communities apparently still had a dampening effect on the reportage of "officially filed" mutilation claims in the media. There were many rumors and whispered claims bereft of actual dates and times through the end of the eighties—there are exceptions to this, of course—but a pattern of denial and a growing sense of impotence permeated the local county sheriff's departments across the mid-west and Rocky Mountain states. This sense of law enforcement helplessness translated into a reluctance by the ranching community to acknowledge cases were occurring, but as we will see, this reluctance changed later in the early to mid 1990s, when again, the cases were perpetrated fast and furious across the west.

1987 through 1989: Is This an Alien Harvest?

According to hardworking investigative journalist Linda Howe, [On] August 13, 1989, The *New York Times* reported about 67 cats have been found mutilated in Tustin, California—an affluent suburb of Los Angeles near Santa Ana. The *NYT* observed:

> Some of them were cut in half with what some say is almost surgical precision, others disemboweled or skinned. One resident said, 'There is never any blood at the scene, the animals are often dismembered with surgical precision and paws and other body parts are often left on the ground in strikingly similar arrangements. No one ever seems to hear anything, nor do dogs bark during the killing.' It was believed the cats are captured, taken elsewhere, their blood drained and organs removed, then replaced on their owners' lawns.
>
> Cycles of cat mutilations have re-occurred in Tustin and in Plano, Texas—an affluent suburb north of Dallas. In 1991, 1993 and again these

these past couple of years, police received dozens of reports about cats found cut in half, usually with the front half near the owners' yards or sidewalks. Plano Police Detective Mike Box also had missing reports on more than 80 domestic house cats that wore collars and I. D. tags, but were never found. Detective Box investigated satanic cult activities, but could not find any evidence that connected them to the mutilated and missing cats and other animals such as dogs.[121]

The final two years of the 1980s featured sporadic cases being reported in Colorado, New Mexico, Kansas, Nebraska and elsewhere. In 1989 Linda Moulton Howe published her highly influential book *An Alien Harvest* (figure 19) that championed the extraterrestrial hypothesis to explain the mutilation mystery. As a result of her book, public perception within the mainstream "paranormal" crowd has been irrevocably swayed. By the early 1990s, most of those still interested in the mystery would've agreed that these unexplained livestock deaths had to be the handiwork of extraterrestrials. But does this knee-jerk answer *completely* explain the thousands of cases that have been reported over the decades? Personally, I don't think so. Sure, it might be aliens, but if so, something else appears to be operative in the darkened pastures of the world, piggybacking an agenda onto our mystery. Inquiring minds deserve to know…(figure 20)

Chapter Seven Sources and References:

1. Blann, Tommy, *Unmasking the Enemy,* 1993
2. *Stigmata* First Quarter 1982 # 16
3. *Stigmata* Second Quarter 1981, Number 13
4. Kagan & Summers, *Mute Evidence,* Bantam, NY NY 1984
5. *ibid*
6. *Stigmata* Second Quarter 1981, Number 13
7. Kagan & Summers*, op.sit.*
8. *Stigmata* Second Quarter 1981, Number 13
9. Medicine Hat *News* June 11, 1980
10. *Stigmata #15* second quarter 1981
11. *ibid*
12. O'Brien, Christopher, *Secrets of the Mysterious Valley*, AUP, Kempton, IL 2007
13. *Stigmata* Second Quarter 1981, Number 13
14. *ibid*
15. *ibid*
16. *ibid*
17. *ibid*
18. *ibid*
19. *ibid*
20. *Ranchland Farm News* (Simla, CO), 1-8-81; El Paso CSO; Linda M. Howe, KMGH-TV
21. Project Stigma 1981 INTERVIEW w/Mrs. Betty Thomas; Dr. Nancy H. Owen U of AR
22. *Press-Democrat,* Santa Rosa, CA 2-9-81; Ted Schultz

23. *Meige County Statesman* (Decatur, TN), 2-25-81; *Chattanooga Times*, (TN) 2-28-81; *Tuscaloosa News*, (AL) 2-28-81, credit: Robert E. Morgan. [Second case] *Bigfoot Co-op*, June 1981 (letter); Constance Cameron
24. Lincoln *Journal*, NE 5-1-82; Ray Boeche; Project Stigma
25. *Bigfoot Co-op*, June 1981 (letter); Constance Cameron, Project Stigma
26. *Saturday Oklahoman*, Oklahoma City, 4-18-81
27. *Edmonton Journal*, 5-21-81; *Fernie Free Press*, L. Phillips, W. K. Allan, T. Tokaryk, J. Duncan
28. *Fernie Free Press* 5-28-81, Project Stigma
29. Cedar Rapids *Gazette*, Iowa, 7-26-81; Ottawa *Courier* 7-28-81
30. *Central Oregonian* 6-2-81; *UFO Newsclipping Service*
31. *National Examiner*, 9-1-81; Aerial Phenomenon Clipping & Information Service; Cleveland, OH CFRN radio; Edmonton, Alberta
32. Edmonton *Journal*, 8-29-81, Steve Popowich,Tom Adams
33. *Clackamas County News* (Estacada, OR), 7-22-81; P. Guttilla via *UFO Newsclipping Service*; Plumerville, AR
34. *Rocky Mountain News* (Denver, CO), 6-28-81; Linda M. Howe, KMGH-TV, Denver
35. Arlington *Citizen*, 6-25-81; Carol Werkmeister, Study on Animal Mutilations
36. *Country Life in British Columbia* (White Rock, BC), September 1981; Mrs. Jeanette McKay; W. K. Allan; Dr. R. C. Maidment; Robert Ternier
37. *Albuquerque Journal*, 9-2-81; F. Hudson via *UFO Newsclipping Service*
38. Waterloo *Courier*, 8-25-81
39. Sheriff Harold Martinez via Linda M. Howe, KMGH-TV, Denver, Project Stigma
40. *Denver Post*, 9-4-81; Sheriff Harold Martinez via Linda M. Howe, KMGH-TV, Denver
41. State Policemen Gabe Valdez; Dulce, NM
42. Mrs. Linda Williford, Project Stigma
43. Edmonton *Sun*, 9-17-81; Tim Tokaryk
44. David Brewer, B.I.A., Linda Howe, KMGH-TV, Denver, Project Stigma
45. Herman *Review*, 10-8-81
46. Calgary *Herald*, 9-29-81; Edmonton *Sun*, 9-30-81; Tim Tokaryk
47. *New Hampshire Sunday News*, Manchester, NH, 10-4-81; Portsmouth *Herald*, 10-12-81; Loren Coleman, Betty Hill, Chas. Whitten, Project Stigma
48. *ibid*
49. Portsmouth *Herald* 10-15-81
50. Betty Hill; Project Stigma
51. David Perkins, Animal Mutilation Probe; Farisita, CO
52. Herman *Review*,MN 10-15-81; Bill Moore; Project Stgma
53. Project Stigma, Nick Kowerchuk; Denis C. Corneau; Dr. G. Wobeser's
54. Wray *Gazette*, 11-12-81; Mrs. S. Rickard via Linda M. Howe; Richard Merrill; Project Stigma
55. *ibid*
56. Schuyler *Sun*, NE, 12-3-81; Omaha *World Herald*, 11-27-81; *UFO Newsclipping Service*
57. Roger W. Harringon; Project Stigma
58. Gomez interview, "Branton"
59. Valdez, Greg, *Dulce Base*, Levi-Cash Publishing LLC, NM, 2013
60. *ibid*
61. *Associated Press* 10-16-74; Project Stigma
62. Project Stigma, The Animal Mutilation Data Center, *Saddleback Valley News*, 12-23-81
63. July 5, 1982 Letter to Project Stigma; AMDC; Scott Rogo; Tom Adams

64. Los Angeles *Times*, 9-8-82; Project Stigma; Scott Rogo

65. Project Stigma, *Stigmata #20*; the Animal Mutilation Data Center; E.E Austin 1982-3

66. Project Stigma; NM State Patrolman Gabe Valdez

67. *Stigmata, #20* 1983; Dr. William Briskey

68. Albuquerque *Journal* 3-31-82; Project Stigma

69. Crosby *Journal* (ND) March 31, 1982; Sklor ; Project Stigma; *UFO Newsclipping Service*

70. *Stigmata, #20* 1983, Tom Adams

71. *ibid*

72. Albuquerque *Journal* 5-31-82; Manuel Gomez; Tom Adams

73. Tacoma *News Tribune* 2-24-82, 5-12-82; [Eatonville,WA] *Dispatch* 2-24-82; [Everett, WA] *Herald,* 2-5-82; *Nisqually Valley News*, Yelm, WA, 2-25-82; Seattle Post-Intelligencer, 10-17-92, 11-28-82; *Olympian* Olympia, WA, 11-28-82; *Stateman-Journal*, [Salem, OR,] 11-27-82; *Herald Republic,* [Yakima, WA,] 10-12-82; Linda Wiliford; Kalani Hanohano; Jacob Davidson; Toyo Yamamoto; Peter Guitilla to Lucius Farish/*UFO Newsclipping Service*

74. *Stigmata #20, 1983* Adams; Truby; Miller

75. *ibid*

76. Ray Boeche; Tommy Blann; Project Stigma

77. *ibid*

78. Albuquerque *Journal*, 5-31-82; Frei; Gomez; Project Stigma

79. Bonnie Smith; Project Stigma

80. Project Stigma #20 1983

81. *Ranchland Farm News,* Simla, CO, 9-16-82; Project Stigma

82. *ibid*

83. *ibid,* Linda M. Howe; Project Stigma

84. *ibid*

85. *Ranchland Farm News,* Simla, CO, date unspecified; Project Stigma; Mikita; Linda M. Howe

86. Project Stigma #20 1983

87. *ibid*

88. Linda M. Howe; Wilde; sheriff Jarvie of Daggett County; Project Stigma #20

89. *ibid*

90. AMP/David Perkins; Aguirre; Project Stigma

91. Linda Howe; David Perkins; Shirley Rickard; Martha Thompson, Project Stigma

92. *Daily News,* (Norfolk, NE); 12-15-82, Ray Boeche, Tommy Blann, Project Stigma

93. *Cowley County Reporter,* KS, 12-16-82; Guttilla/Farish/*UFO Newsclipping Service;* Blair; Linda M. Howe; Project Stigma

94. *The Telegraph*, Sydney, Australia 7-13-84, *Flying Saucer Review,* 1985

95. *Sunday Times*, Perth, Australia, 7-15-84; Linda Howe/Earthfiles.com

96. Corpus Christi *Caller,* TX, 12-31-85; Walt Andrus/MUFON; Project Stigma

97. *Williamson County Sun*, 4-17-85 TX; Walt Andrus/MUFON; Connie Grady; Guy Rowland;

98. *Daily Oklahoman,* 4-16-85; *The Montana Standard,* (Butte, MT), 4-9-85; *The Plain Dealer* (Cleveland, OH), 4-15-85; *National Examiner,* 4-9-85; New York *Post,* 6-21-85; Jack Gilluly; RW Anderson; Project Stigma

99. *Sunday Express*, London, 5-l2-85

100. BIA/David Brewer; Linda M. Howe; Project Stigma

101. *Pasu Data Exchange*, Issue #3; Gordon

102. Fort Worth *Star Telegram*, 7-7 & 8- 85, Philip White; Project Stigma

103. *Wisconsin State Journal,* Madison, WI, 7-23-85; Richard Heiden; Project Stigma

104. *Ranchland News,* 9-19-85; Gaddy; Project Stigma

105. *Rocky Mountain News,* Denver, CO, 4-21-86; Project Stigma

106. *Middle Park Times,* Kremmling, CO, 9-26-85; Project Stigma
107. Project Stigma, Number 23, 1986
108. *ibid*; letter to Tom Adams
109. Stonewall *Argus/Teulan Times*, Stonewall, Manitoba, 9-30-85; Denis Corneu; Project Stigma
110. Great Falls *Tribune*, 11-08-85; Leming; Wolverton; Osborne; Project Stigma
111. *ibid*
112. Project Stigma/*Crux #2* 1986
113. Seattle *Post-Intelligencer*, 1-4-86; Julius Rodman; Kalani Hanohano; Project Stigma
114. Huerfano County Sheriff's report, 2-6-86; David Perkins/AMP; Project Stigma
115. Houston *Chronicle*, 3-7-86; Project Stigma
116. Birmingham *Post Herald,* 4-22-86, 4-23-86, 4-30-86; *Advertiser-Gleam* (Guntersville, AL) 4-23-86; Huntsville *Times,* 4-22-86, 4-30-86; Lynn Phillips; Mark Hall; *UFO Newsclipping Service*; Project Stigma
117. *Advertiser-Gleam*, Guntersville, AL, 7-30-86; *UFO Newsclipping Serice,* Project Stigma
118. David Perkins, AMP; Project Stigma
119. Channel 11, CBS-TV Houston; John Schuessler; Project Stigma
120. *Pasu Data Exchange*, Issue #3; Stan Gordon; Project Stigma
121. Linda M. Howe/ Earthfiles.com

Figure 1
l to r Tom Adams, Linda Howe, Gary Massey. (credit: AMP/David Perkins)

Figure 2
Kenneth Rommel's Operation Animal Mutilation. (credit: AMP/David Perkins)

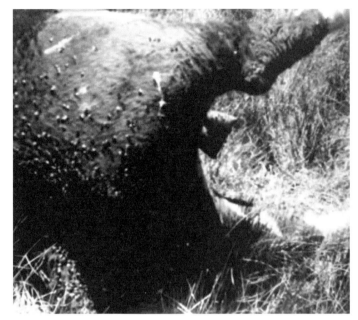

Figure 3
The Sutherland bull, 6-80, Moffat, CO. (credit: Virginia Sutherland)

Figure 4
Painted Sutherland bull skull. (credit: author/TMV Archive)

Figure 5
Warren AF Base. (credit: afgc.af.mil)

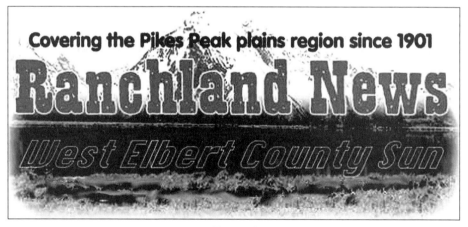

Figure 6
Farmland New masthead. (credit: Farmland News)

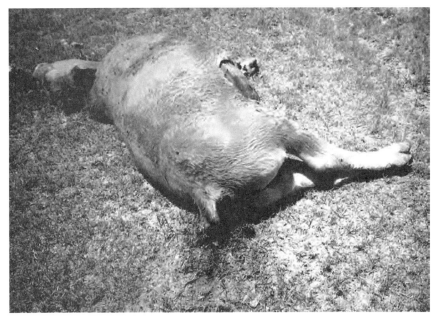

Figure 7
Tailless cow with tail hair neatly combed out. (credit: TMV Archive)

Figure 8
Cattle sacrifice. (credit: escapeartistes.com)

Figure 9
Iconic Devil image. (credit: *Secrets of the Mysterious Valley*)

Figure 10
Gabe Valdez on a NM investigation. Son Greg is at the squad car.
(credit: AMP/David Perkins; Greg Valdez)

Figure 11
Abductee and aspiring mute investigator, Betty Hill. (credit: fenomenum.com.br)

Figure 12
The notorious Archuleta Mesa, Dulce NM. (credit: Norio Hayakawa)

Figure 13
Dulce Base: The Truth and Evidence from the Case Files of Gabe Valdez.
(credit: Greg Valdez)

Figure 14
Gas mask like the one found by Gabe Valdez on the Gomez ranch. (credit: etsy.com)

Figure 15
Who is responsible for killing thousands of cats?
(credit: Zahib Arab/Channel 8/Las Vegas)

Figure 16
UK sheep have been mutilated since at least 1606. (credit: Philip Hoyle/APRU)

Figure 17
Over 1 million U.S. citizens belong to Santeria. (credit: latino.foxnews.com)

Figure 18
Tom Adams finally gave up the chase. (credit: AMP/David Perkins)

Figure 19
Linda Moulton Howe's influential book, *An Alien Harvest.* (credit: amazon.com)

Figure 20
l to r, Tom Adams, David Perkins, Christopher O'Brien—1993. (credit: TMV Archives)

Chapter 8
The 1990s

Many of the following reports were investigated by the author in the San Luis Valley (SLV), Colorado and further south in northern New Mexico. I've decided to retain the descriptions I provided of these cases in my first three books, *The Mysterious Valley, Enter the Valley* and *Secrets of the Mysterious Valley*. For those of you who are not familiar with my earlier work, this is an opportunity to share in my personal experience of investigating unexplained livestock death reports, in the field—firsthand. These cases document how I became swept up by this mystery into a bloody, bloodless conundrum of freaked out ranchers, perplexed cops, puzzled "mutologists" and came to the understanding that this subject is truly mysterious, and perhaps may never be solved.

The early nineties found the U.S. ranching community breathing a temporary sigh of relief. Few if any cases can be found in investigators' data logs, and it appears that 1990 was significantly quiet when compared with prior years. Not so in the UK. Police Officer Sgt. Tony Dodd (figure 1) had his first close encounter with a UFO in the North Yorkshire Dales in 1978 while on duty. As a result of this up close and personal encounter he became fascinated with UFOs and later the unexplained animal death cases. He investigated hundreds of mutilations over the next 25 years, and for many years he was head of investigations for Quest International, which became *UFO Magazine* (UK). Throughout the 1980s and '90s he investigated

mutilation reports all over the UK and Ireland. Dodd describes one such case:

> On Saturday 30 July 1990, the activity was centered on Wiltshire, and two crop circle researchers were out early, hoping to find a new circle. At 7:15 a.m. they were horrified to come across the body of a dead and mutilated horse near the famous White Horse earth monument.
>
> They described the horse as a large white male, lying on its left side. There was a wound where the sexual organs had been removed, but there was only one spot of blood on the ground, no bigger than a ten-pence piece, four feet away from the corpse. Its feet were caught up in a large chain link fence and there was foam at the corners of its mouth and its eyes were bulging…The horse had died within the previous two hours, as rigor mortis had not set in, and the foam on the mouth was still wet, so there should have been plenty of signs of wet coagulating blood. Another crop circle researcher, out even earlier, had heard cries, like those of a child, coming from the valley where the body was found about an hour before the horse was discovered. Within a short space of time, the body of the horse was gone.[1]

Dodd investigated another case in March 1991—this time it was a series of sheep slayings and disfigurements in and around the Scottish Highland village of Kinlochewe, Wester Ross. He was alerted to the outbreak from an article in the *Sunday Mail* newspaper with its headline: 'Vampire Beast on the Loose.' The 'beast' was visiting farms in the dead of night and killing sheep—nine by that point. It was leaving behind evidence in the form of a puncture wound under each ear, and the animals appeared to be drained of blood.

> The vets had been quoted in the newspaper as saying: 'We cannot suggest any animal which could have been responsible for the wounds of this nature, and the total loss of blood.' The researchers who alerted me questioned the vets at length, and again the vets confirmed that they were baffled by what could have caused such distinctive injuries, and how the blood could have been drained so expertly from the body without leaving any marks on the ground. There was no sign of struggle and no tracks in the fields…A few months after the mysterious sheep killings in Scotland, 45 sheep died in one night in a field in Kettewell, north Yorkshire. The animals were not mutilated, but their bodies were found in a pile next to a dry stone wall…The report did not make any sense to me.[2]

The following is taken from a July 1992 article published in *Fortean Times,* a UK magazine that chronicles strange occurrences that are reported from around the world. Evidently, as we've seen with the Scottish and Edmonton,

Alberta cases, the far northern latitudes are not immune to our mutilators' attention. This next outbreak, similar sounding to UK cases in the 1990s, was reported from Sweden:

> For two or three years, someone or something has been attacking and mutilating horses and cows in western Sweden. (figure 2) Around 200 horse attacks had been reported to the police when the mystery was brought to national attention by journalist Siewert Ohloms' TV program "Svar direkt" on 25 February 1992.
>
> In the summer of 1989, the number of reports increased. In 90% of the incidents, the victims were horses, almost always assaulted in the same way. They were cut with a sharp, scalpel-like instrument in or beside their sexual organs. The wounds were often 30 centimeters long, and five or six cm deep. About 50% of the animals were so severely maimed that they had to be put down...
>
> In August 1991, several horses were assaulted in the neighborhood of Fargelanda in Dalsland. It began when a mare, belonging to Marianne Gothberg, was cut around the vagina. Another of Mrs Gothbergs' horses was cut the following day, and a day after that a foal was found bleeding on a neighboring farm. More horses in the area succumbed, and some 40 farmers formed a sort of equine "home guard". Pairs of farmers policed the roads at night, armed with whatever weapons their farms could provide. They caught a suspicious individual one evening, and turned him over to the police; but he turned out to be a frightened bilberry picker who had lost his way...
>
> Several farmers and horse breeders appeared on the TV program. They stressed that several attacks had taken place almost in their presence, and couldn't understand why their horses had submitted without offering resistance. The perpetrator was like a phantom or a supernatural being. A vet said that the attacker had a good knowledge, not only of animal behaviour, but also of animal anatomy. Some of the wounds had been very professionally cut.
>
> When the horses were turned out to pasture again after the winter, the Fargelanda "home guard" were again mobilized, and others were organized all over western Sweden. The first mutilation of the year was reported in "Expressen" on 14 April [1992]. A mare was found at a place called Vitehall near Kyrkekvarn, bleeding from wounds in her vagina and hind legs. A "mysterious" red car driven by a young man sped away from the spot as the mare was found; but it was not clear at the time of the report how the wounds had been inflicted.[3]

Swedish investigator Jan-Ove Sundberg investigated many of the Swedish cases that had been reported since the 1977 outbreak. He contacted Tony Dodd and gave him this information on the cases he had researched:

> Throughout the 70s and 80s, more and more cases were reported, and vets again agreed that the mutilations, which as usual involved the removal of the rectum and sexual organs, had been carried out with unprecedented surgical skill. Jan-Ove has studied in depth more than 132 cases which took place between 1988 and 1991, including the killing and mutilation of a pet rabbit. Vandalism was ruled out, because the animals had been drained of blood.
>
> One of the cases he investigated involved 50 pigs out of a herd of 100. The dead pigs had been typically mutilated, but also had unusual triangular marks on their bodies (similar marks had been seen on mutilated horses in the 1970s). Remarkably, the pigs which were wounded and killed had apparently made no noise, and the rest of the animals, which squeal and panic at any intrusion into their yard, were calm and quiet.[4]

When people ask me if North America is the only place where mutilations are reported, or if any other animals have been reported in a "mutilated," high strange condition besides cattle, I tell them that this appears to be a worldwide phenomenon and most species of warm-blooded animals in western countries have been targeted. But the following aquatic seal cases are strange to say the least.

During the winter months of 1991-92, I heard reports of strange mutilations taking place in the Orkney Islands. The victims were seals. In a short space of time, the headless bodies of over 30 were found on the local beaches. (figure 3) Animal welfare officers, police and local vets were baffled. Mike Lynch, an inspector with the Scottish Society for the Prevention of Cruelty to Animals, said:

> We're at a loss. I've never seen anything like this before. A post-mortem examination of one of the dead animals revealed that the head had been removed almost surgically. Whoever did this must have used a very sharp knife…there is no sign of serrations, which rules out normal predators like sharks or killer whales.[5]

Tony Dodd mentions other parts of the UK that were being targeted. The Cornwall region had also been the location for a number of cases since the late 1980s:

> At that time, July 1992, there had been a spate of other animals in the area being killed or going missing; these included chickens, sheep and domestic pets. Again, foxes or dogs were blamed. In the same month, a horse was found dead and mutilated in Wiltshire, again near a crop circle.[6]

After a brief lull in U.S. cases from 1989 through 1991, a wave of cattle mutilation reports commenced around Fyffe, Alabama in late 1992. From October 1992 through May 1993 over 35 cases were reported to local authorities that included Fyffe police officer Ted Oliphant. Ted is credited as one of the first to recognize the possible link between real mutilation cases and the emerging disease of bovine *transmissible spongiform encephalopathy*, or "mad cow" disease that was sweeping through UK cattle herds in the 1990s. He also toyed with a theory that the Army (or some military group) may be testing bacteriological weapons in Alabama. Oliphant became officially involved in an attempt to track down the perpetrators of these alleged crimes and, as a result of his investigation, came up with an intriguing hypothesis in the following article.

The Alabama Wave

Hello, I'm Ted Oliphant. As a police officer in Fyffe, Alabama I investigated over 35 cases of cattle mutilations over a six-month period from October 1992 through May 1993.

Over the last ten years, law enforcement officers in dozens of States have been trying to track and identify unmarked helicopters sighted where area livestock have been discovered dead under suspicious circumstances. The helicopters are seen before and after these cows are found in pastures, missing certain organs. The same things are always taken. Bovine jaws are stripped to the bone, reproductive organs removed, digestive tracts and rectums "cored" out. There is little to no blood at the scene. Tissue samples taken by police investigators and analyzed at veterinary labs, all show signs of exposure to heat, three hundred degrees or more. The tissue is cooked and the incisions are cauterized by the heat. This prevents blood and other fluids from leeching onto the ground. Everything taken has to do with input, output and reproduction.

In recent mutilation cases, Alabama 1993 & 1994, California 1996 and Florida 1997; pharmaceuticals have been found in bovine blood. They are: Barbiturates, Anti-coagulants, Synthetic Amphetamines, Aluminum-Titanium-Oxygen-Silicon flakes, and Antimony [Antimony: A brittle lustrous white metallic element occurring in nature, free or combined, used chiefly in alloys and in compounds in medicine. Webster's]. The drugs found are NOT veterinary drugs, they are pharmaceuticals associated with humans. Among those law enforcement agents who have thoroughly investigated these bovine excision sites, there is a consensus that some kind of medical testing is going on. The additional presence of un-marked helicopters on scene, before and after cattle are found dead missing specific organs, leads both victimized farmers and investigating officers to conclude that there is a connection. But why use human drugs on cows? Use your imagination.

Every organ taken from affected livestock has to do with input, output and reproduction. Where entire jaws have been excised in large, oval excisions, the bone is exposed and is perfectly clean. The wounds have been cauterized and there is no presence of blood. The jaw is an important part because enzymes are produced there. Enzymes that can kill viruses and bacteria, it's an antibody factory. The digestive tract also acts as a filter that absorbs, collects and stores traces of any chemical or toxin introduced. The rectum is a similar filter as are ears. They store traces of toxins and chemicals like a library. Because many diseases (like CJD and BSE) can be inherited, the reproductive system may be a good place to look for clues on how it passed to the next generation.

In 1993, I got a call from a man who told me that if I went to a certain place on a certain evening, I would see several helicopters land and refuel. He was right. Well after dark, two Chinook helicopters [the large twin rotor type] landed in the field behind some trees and opened their doors revealing large black plastic fuel bladders. Minutes later several smaller scout helicopters landed nearby shut down and crews from the Chinooks walked over with large hoses and refueled each of a half dozen helicopters. The whole operation took less than 30 minutes and the helicopters took off and headed across the border where we tracked them to their home base, Fort Campbell, Kentucky. Now we knew who they were but we couldn't figure out why they refueled on Sand Mountain.

The next morning a reporter, Steven Smith from the *Rainsville Weekly Post*, called the Public Affairs Officer, William Gibbons of the 101st Airborne and asked if they might've been in our area the previous evening. "We have no aircraft in your area, it wasn't us" said the captain. It certainly was. So we knew then that some kind of secret operation was being conducted, but we didn't know what it was. We still don't, but when you look at each piece of evidence and try to use them as puzzle pieces, these so called "cattle mutilations" might be associated with government studies of epidemiology. With BSE & CJD being such devastating "new" diseases, is it possible than many alleged cases of "cattle mutilations" are actually evidence of our tax dollars at work?

The Evidence Suppression Team from Maxwell Air Force Base, Alabama; and the F.A.A. Investigation of Unmarked Helicopters Over Sand Mountain.

The 101st Airborne Division is not suspected of being directly involved in the cattle mutilations that occurred between October 1992 and May of 1993. But it seems possible they may have refueled the unmarked helicopters that we eventually traced to Maxwell Air Force Base. The 101st's inability to tell the truth about where they had been seems to be a constant in Federal Government employee behavior: You don't tell the truth unless somebody holds a gun to your head.

When unmarked helicopters were witnessed by local farmers and law enforcement officers, Albertville Police's Chief of Detectives Tommy Cole called in the Federal Aviation Administration to investigate. Detective Cole had lost a cow to the phantom surgeons and his wife had seen an unmarked helicopter over their pasture January 8, 1993; the day before they discovered one of their Black Angus steers mutilated.

An FAA investigator came to Albertville and Cole took him for a ride in his police car. The FAA investigator was skeptical until an unmarked helicopter flew near them. The FAA investigator couldn't believe his own eyes and pulled out a hand held radio and hailed the helicopter. The helicopter pilot didn't respond and ignored demands that he identify himself. This infuriated the FAA investigator who had now reversed his skepticism. He was able to trace the helicopter to Maxwell Air Force Base in Southern Alabama. When he launched an inquiry at the base, he was immediately told to drop it and never talk about it again. A week later Chief Detective Cole received a call after midnight, it was the FAA investigator. It seems that while out in a boat on nearby Lake Guntersville, he and his family had witnessed a large triangle shaped craft flying maneuvers above them. I wonder if he ever reported that to his superiors.[7]

On April 7, 1993 the Fyffe police department, along with Fyffe Mayor Boyd Graben, conducted a press conference to address rising concerns in the local ranching community after the 30th report had been filed with authorities that week. In a statement to the press they noted:

...Dr. Jim Armstrong, Auburn professor of zoology and wildlife science... states, "It would be obvious if a coyote had been tearing through. The wounds would not be similar to a smooth cut. Coyotes bite through and pull to tear away the flesh. It would have a 'chewed on look'. There are other scavenger animals such as vultures that will eat at the softer regions of a cow, but there's not going to be these clean, surgical-type cuts. There is no way a coyote or other predator inflicted those wounds." In the past week Dr. Armstrong has examined dozens of photographs of mutilated cows taken by the Fyffe Police Department. He states, "I went over the pictures with a USDA expert along with several wildlife biologists. With the exception of one individual, we all agreed that many of the cases were not typical predatory damage. The caution here is that we're dealing with photos, that there is no other physical evidence for us to look at. But the USDA agent and most others agreed with my conclusion that many of the pictures were not coyote or other predator damage."

DeKalb County Auburn Extension Agent Curtis O'Daniel also discounts the likelihood of predator animals removing circles of cowhide. "Predators are not bad about eating hide, they'll eat up the rest of it first. Along with the bones, the hide will be one of the last things to go."

These statements made by expert professionals agree with the statements made earlier this year by the Fyffe Police Department, that predators are not responsible for the mutilations. The conclusion, however, indicates a greater mystery: Who is doing this and why is there a lack (for the most part) of physical evidence at the scene?

Police Chief Junior Garmany and Mayor Boyd Graben, themselves involved in farming, believe the results of our investigation require further attention. It is incumbent on all of us military, state and federal government [officials] to assist farmers to find out who the phantom surgeons are. It seems basic to help the man who is responsible for ensuring there is food available for our dinner tables. The farmer is not interested in politically correct official explanations. He wants to know what has happened to his livestock. It should be the responsibility of all law-enforcement to join together to find an answer to this problem that is adversely affecting the cattle farmer, here in Alabama.[8]

I became directly involved in investigating mutilation reports during the fall 1992/spring 1993 time period. I kept copious notes and interviewed and videotaped targeted ranchers whenever possible. Most of these cases were included in my first two books. Throughout the 1990s the San Luis Valley was a hotbed of mutilation activity. Other counties in Colorado and elsewhere suffered a retargeting by the mystery mutilators.

One of the first calls I made when I began my own investigation in January 1993 was to Linda Moulton Howe. She graciously instructed me in the art of field investigation and proper interviewing techniques. I owe her a big thank you for taking the time to bring me up to speed in this regard and I still use many of her suggestions in the field today.

"There were no tracks, no blood, no nothin'!"

David Perkins noted a bizarre claim by a Canadian rancher in his May 1998 article titled "High Heat" for *Western Spirit* magazine. It would seem that not all animals that are found dead in an unusual manner are specifically targeted. Sometimes they may simply be at the wrong place at the wrong time:

In August, 1992, near Milestone, Saskatchewan, farmer Joe Rennick was surprised to discover a three circle crop formation in his wheat field.

He was even more astonished to find a dead porcupine in the center of one of the circles. The animal was "smashed flat as a pancake." The porcupine's quills appeared to follow the same swirl pattern as the wheat. At about the same time, another dead porcupine was found inside a crop formation near Kyle. Its remains were "very black as if covered in soot."

As we have seen, cattle are not the only animals found in a mutilated condition. The city of Vancouver, British Columbia has experienced waves of cats found cut in half, often times left in people's yards. A wave of these cat killings took place in British Columbia in 1992-1993, but these strange feline deaths have been reported all across the western United States and Canada since the early 1970s. The Supervisor of Animal Control for the Vancouver City Pound was quoted by the press saying: "The cats are clearly being butchered by someone. It's a real surgical job. And all I hope is that these cats were already dead when they were cut in half."

During this time period I befriended pathologist/ hematologist John Altshuler, MD, who lived in Denver, Colorado. Altshuler was the mystery pathologist who performed the postmortem examination on the infamous "Snippy the Horse" in 1967. I was introduced to Altshuler by Linda Howe, who had convinced him to 'go public' in 1989. She spent a considerable amount of time coaxing him into performing hematological testing on mutilation samples, and Altshuler performed a number of tests on some of my cases from 1993 to 1996. It was in 1993 that Linda had Dr. Altshuler conduct tests on one of the mysterious half-cats. "[He] confirmed that the entire excision had been cut with something hot enough to cook the collagen and hemoglobin."

Official southern Colorado reports began on October 31st when rancher John Torres' herd of cattle had a deadly Halloween visitor. His ranch is located 40 miles west of Trinidad. The following morning Torres discovered a deceased three-year-old cow in a remote area of his ranch. The animal's tongue, genitalia and eyes were missing. Torres had "never seen anything like it" in his years as a cattle rancher. "That was no predator. They were real, real sharp cuts with no ridges. There were no tracks, no blood, no nothin'!"

Later, when Greg Barman, an NPR reporter, asked him who he thought was responsible for the "mutilation" of his cow, Torres answered with a nervous laugh, "Well, as far as I'm concerned, it was aliens. Seriously, I really think it was something from out of this world, to do something like that without leaving any evidence whatsoever."

November 27, 1992, 2:30 A.M., 80 miles south in Costilla County: Manuel Sanchez couldn't sleep. He peered out the window of his modest ranch house across the pitch-black pasture, seeing and hearing nothing unusual. He finally fell into a fitful sleep until just before dawn. As he left the house the following morning to check on his herd, he stopped. Not 50 feet away from the house, one of his prize breeding cows lay motionless on her side, obviously dead. Its rear end, udder and tongue were cleanly removed with the mandible bleached a ghostly white.

He had seen this before. He had lost a cow in an identical fashion 18 years before. An angry, worried Sanchez immediately called Costilla County Sheriff Billy Maestas who investigated the scene with Deputy Roger Benson. "No predator could have done that," Maestas agreed. "I've seen a lot of dead livestock in my time and this really concerns me." Maestas immediately called Los Animas Sheriff Lou Girodo to ask the acknowledged mutilation expert for assistance, and found out John Torres had lost a cow in the same manner.

Sanchez also called the *Valley Courier* (figure 4) and spoke with reporter Ruth Heide. "I called the paper to warn everybody to keep their eyes open for lights or anything. I mean, if they could do this to my cow, maybe they could do it to humans. A lot of people disappear in the mountains around here and are never seen again!"

Girodo, a longtime law enforcement official had puzzled over unusual animal deaths for almost 20 years. He had been interviewed in Linda Moulton Howe's book, *An Alien Harvest* and in her documentary, *Strange Harvest*, about the cattle mutilation reports. He was convinced that the phenomenon was a true mystery, worthy of investigation.[9]

Careful What You Wish For!

December 31, 1992, Crestone-Baca Grande, Saguache County: My actual involvement in investigating and researching the unexplained livestock death mystery began innocently enough. My significant other, Isadora, and I were in the midst of hosting a New Year's Eve party at our home, and as the party wound down and folks eased toward the door, I overheard a friend recalling UFO sightings she had experienced recently with her boyfriend. She told a small, captivated group about unusual lights and "glowing" objects. I listened to every detail. The speaker appeared calm, yet excited, as she described the experience almost poetically. I started asking questions, trying to find out as much as I could about these occurrences. She named other witnesses who had apparently seen the unknown lights over three nights. Some of these witnesses, including her boyfriend, were at the party. As the conversation progressed, first one, then another "witness" walked in from the other room and joined the animated conversation describing sightings over the Baca Ranch on November 25 and December 9-12, 1992. I found it disconcerting to hear people talking so casually about glowing orbs and dancing lights.

Then came the clincher. Charlotte Heir, a local closet-UFO buff, mentioned she had seen a short article in the *Valley Courier*, reporting the Sanchez "mutilation" on a small ranch in Costilla County. The mutilation took place the same night that many Baca area witnesses had seen those unexplained lights. Unbeknownst to me, I was grabbing firmly hold of a tar baby! My full-time investigation literally began that night and I can't help but look back at that pivotal evening and view my naive excitement with a smile. If I had known what I was getting into, my excitement would have undoubtedly been tempered with the realization that years of frustrating and unrewarding hard work lay ahead with no promise of any firm answers.

One of the first full-length interviews that I conducted that spring of '93 was with ex-Costilla County Sheriff Ernest Sandoval and hard hit rancher Emilio Lobato. Lobato suffered the loss of 49 head of cattle in October 1975 and Sandoval headed the investigation. During my interview with Lobato, the trickster reared its leering head when his home phone rang. It was his nephew, Dale Vigil. Vigil had called ex-sheriff Sandoval to tell him he had just discovered a 'mutilated' cow that very morning, at his Chama Canyon ranch, two ranches from Emilio's! Sandoval told him about our investigation. Dale agreed to take us to his ranch to investigate the downed cow.

Synchronicity crackled. I couldn't believe it. This trip was, without question, right out of a movie script. We continued our conversation with Lobato as we waited for his nephew to show up and found out that there had been attempts on Lobato's life back in 1975! He claimed that on three different occasions, there had been shots fired at him on his Chama Canyon Ranch.

Vigil arrived in a pickup and we followed him at breakneck speed over the winding back country roads to his small ranch. We drove around the back of the ranch house to see a knot of men standing over a dead cow less than 150 feet from the Vigils' home. My first "fresh one." We hopped out and, as we walked over toward the cow, I hoped feverishly that I had enough juice left in the video battery to document the scene. Emilio introduced us to the seven or eight local ranchers and I set up the camera. The animal lay on its right side underneath a grove of scrub willow. The rear end was missing, the udder had been removed, the upside eye looked like it had been sucked out, and a patch of hide, just above the left knee, was missing. Vigil said the cow had given birth at "around 3:30 a.m., last night," and when he and his brother, Clarence, went out "at 5:30 a.m., they found the calf bawling over its mother, who was dead." He immediately called Sheriff Billy Maestas, who came out with Undersheriff Roger Benson to investigate the scene a couple of hours before we arrived.

They found *a small amount of oily, clear, yellowish matter on the animal's side,* which they collected to have tested. We also found a small amount of this strange material on the neck that we placed into a sealed film container. We carefully cut off tissue samples from the incision areas and collected about 20 ccs. of uncoagulated blood from the body cavity. These samples would be sent, overnight air, to Denver hematologist, Dr. John Altshuler, (figure 5) for testing.[10]

I asked Dale to show me where the calf had been born, and he took me 100 yards east by the small creek that flows through his ranch. "She was born right there," he said, pointing to a fairly large spot of dried blood. By this time, my battery had died, and I carried the now-useless camera in my hand. As we started back to the dead cow, I noticed that a large, red Limousin bull had been slowly edging over toward the carcass. The rest of the small herd was grazing obliviously 300 yards away, at the other end of the pasture. The bull cautiously walked up to the carcass, sniffed it, and let out the most heart-wrenching, mournful "MOOO-O-O-O!" Instantly, the other 30 to 40 head of cattle came thundering across the pasture to the dead cow. They gathered around, snorting and pawing at the carcass and the whole herd started slowly circling around it in a clockwise motion. Damn, I sure wished I had some battery power left so I could have video-taped this unusual spectacle. If only I could have panned the cow ritual, then zoomed in on the line of ten ranchers, watching with their mouths dropped open in amazement, I'd have captured a classic movie shot.

I asked the ranchers if they had ever seen cattle do this before. Several couldn't even answer—they just shook their heads NO! Lobato, said, "In all the years I've been a rancher, I've never seen cows do that before!"[11]

I had come down to Costilla County with ex-*Valley Courier* editor John Hill and a fellow investigator, Dave Clemens. After finishing up our on-site investigation, we left the Vigil Ranch, and headed south toward Mesita, to check on the three possibly mutilated cows we'd heard about that morning. I spotted the faint outline of a dirt road exactly where the woman in the coffee shop had described it would be. I noted fresh tire tracks heading off to the south. Sure enough there were three large carcasses about 200 yards down the road. We hurried toward the site.

Through our open windows came the powerful smell of cadaverine molecules. There are a lot of elements that are unsavory in unexplained livestock death cases, and this is the worst of them. We were downwind and it really stunk, bad! I am often asked how I can stand it. My trick is to put Vicks VapoRub under my nose and hold my breath if I need to be downwind. Unfortunately, at the time, I had not brought any with me but vowed I would never leave home without a jar of Vicks again.

I took a deep breath, and ran to the upwind side of the animals. A bull and a cow lay back to back in the dirt road. Twenty yards away to the east was a horse skeleton. The horse carcass had apparently been devoured by scavengers but the cattle remained intact. The bull was missing its rear end, genitalia and an upside eye, and upon closer examination (holding my breath, I might add) I found that several downside ribs and the downside horn had been snapped off! It looked as if the animal had been dropped from a great height.

We noted the location of the animals in the environment. We were standing in a remote, unfenced area of sparse prairie that obviously was not used as grazing land. There were no signs at all of any other grazing animals for miles. Could the carcasses have been dropped off there by a passing rancher? How about the snapped off ribs and horn? Something didn't make sense but I hesitated before jumping to conclusions. John and David took some pictures and we started back toward home. Here were three unreported apparent mutilations. How many others littered the countryside I wondered?

When Altshuler opened the film container we sent with the sample from the Vigil case, there was *no trace of the strange yellow material! Tests on the container revealed only plastic and traces of the film that had been in the container.* Tests on the blood revealed that the animal may have been hit with a dose of carbon monoxide. Later that year Dr. Altshuler was quoted as saying, "It seems enigmatic to even perceive in the wildest imaginations that animal mutilations, that are so pervasive and so common everywhere, continue to defy witnesses."[12]

"This is Getting Too Weird,"

A ranch near DeSmet, South Dakota reported three mutilations in October 1993. A Charolais bull and two cows had apparently been targeted for mutilation. The cows were found three miles apart and the bull was located about seven miles away from the cows. "These mutilations are unlike anything I've ever seen in my 50-plus years in the cattle business," rancher Art Geyer was quoted as saying. He was positive that his cattle had not died of natural causes. The testicles and penis of the bull and an ear and the tongue were missing. Geyer said the only noticeable blood was where the bull's tongue had been removed. The cows were similarly mutilated. Apparently no predators scavenged the cows while they lay in the field in the ensuing days.

November 23, 1993, five miles south of Eagle, Colorado: It's early. The morning chill permeates the air and rancher Lloyd Girard rubs his hands briskly together to warm up his cold fingers. He walks over from his truck and opens the door of his locked potato barn, enters and stops in his tracks. Lying several feet inside the door is a dead cow, the entire left side of its head and neck laid open, the exposed bones gleaming. (figure 6) He kneels down and carefully looks at the dead animal. The tongue, windpipe and all the tissue are gone.

He searches the barn for clues. There is no visible indication of struggle, footprints or blood. He angrily heads back to the house to call the sheriff, muttering to himself.

That same morning, neighboring rancher Bill Bradford is outside when he notices one of his cows missing from his herd, which is milling around, agitated. Bradford scans the pasture and there, several hundred feet away, he spots it. It's lying on its side motionless, upside legs stretching straight out. The animal's mandible is exposed, all the hide on the jaw and the tongue are gone, one eye is missing. The local newspaper, the *Eagle Valley Enterprise* noted in its article: "Bradford says the animal was found after a fresh snowfall, and there was no sign of blood on the carcass or the new snow beneath it. The only nearby tracks were those of the cow." The story also mentions a local veterinarian who was asked by the reporter about hypothetical extraterrestrial involvement: "[The veterinarian] waves aside the idea that scalpel-wielding visitors from outer space might beam to planet earth so they could nab beef parts, noting that a good, sharp hunting knife in the hands of an experienced skinner—or prankster—can appear to be quite surgical."

December 14, 1993, 6:30 a.m., The Bradford Ranch, Gypsum, Colorado: Bill Bradford was up early. He quickly set about his daily morning tasks on this frigid morning. Around 7:30 a.m. he headed out into the pasture to find another "mutilated" cow. He called the sheriff to report the unexplained death and disfigurement.

"This is getting too weird," he told me later. "When I dragged the second cow up to my bone pile, the first one I lost last month in November was laying there missing a perfect 10 X 10 X 10 (inch) triangle of hide off its side. Someone had to have cut that triangle out but who would go up there and do that? I put that in the bone pile where it's pretty remote, no one goes there."

Bradford described the condition of the second carcass: "She was missing an eight-inch plug out of the brisket. I didn't look but I'm pretty sure they took her heart … Do you know what in the heck's going on?" I assured him I really didn't.

That same night the Vigils in Costilla County had another visitation from the nocturnal butchers. 7:00 a.m., The Vigil Ranch, Costilla County: It had been a bitterly cold night. A sharp wind cut through Chama Canyon, gusting down from the tall mountains just a mile east of Clarence and Dale Vigil's secluded ranch. A snowstorm had dumped two inches two days earlier.

According to both brothers their prize Limousin seed bull (figure 7) had appeared healthy and normal the day before. As Dale went out for his routine check of the herd, he felt uneasy. He drove around the frozen pasture, looking for the bull where they had last seen him, off by himself. Nothing. Vigil climbed into his pickup and drove back to the house to get help to locate the bull. Clarence and his young son accompanied Dale back out to the snow-covered pasture to look.

"There he is," Clarence's son called out. They looked toward a row of scrub willow, and sure enough, there was their bull. The red-colored animal lay on his left side and they could see a faint trace of steam rising from the carcass in the frigid air. They climbed out of the truck to check him. He had been "mutilated." The animal's rear end had been cut out and his genitalia were removed. Both brothers were angry as they carefully examined the area around the animal looking for signs of predators. This was getting out of hand. They couldn't find a single track.

"Over here," Dale, who was examining the scrub willow bushes 20 feet to the east of the animal, called out to his brother. They looked at the branches carefully. Small clumps of red hair adorned the tips of branches that looked like they'd been bent over and snapped off. One clump of hair even had a small drop of blood on it.

I received a worried call from Dale that morning. "I had another one," he told me. "I can't take this! I'm going to sell my herd, I can't afford this!" He asked me to make the long trip down to his Costilla ranch to help investigate the animal death.

I arrived by early afternoon and headed out into the frozen pasture. The Vigils were gathered around the dead bull.

"Thanks for coming down, you just missed the vet," Dale told me as we unloaded the video camera. An Alamosa veterinarian had done a necropsy on the animal and found that the bull's lungs were riddled with pneumonia. It had been laid open during the necropsy, and his examination determined that the animal had died of pneumonia and scavengers had inflicted the suspicious wounds.

The Vigil brothers were pretty confused by the vet's findings. "The vet said he died of pneumonia but I don't know about that," Dale says. "He seemed to be perfectly healthy, he didn't appear sick at all. We looked everywhere for predator tracks but there aren't any." He then led me over to the scrub willow thicket, just to the east of the animal. "Look at this." He pointed to the broken branches with bits of red hair sticking to the tips. "It looks like they crashed him into the bushes here," he concluded.

I examined the six-foot high branches. There were clumps of red hair, the exact shade of the bull's hair. "I didn't know cattle could high jump," I said, trying to lighten up the distraught brothers who shook their heads.

We returned to the bull. I studied the immediate area. The animal lay under overhanging scrub willow branches, and about six feet above the carcass the tips of the branches had also been broken off. I bent one downward to snap it off. Freshly broken branch tips littered the ground below it. "These branches were broken off too, and it really looks like they were broken off from above, in a downwards motion," I told the Vigils. It looked to me as if the animal had been dropped. I suggested, "I'll bet they tried to sling him in under the branches and missed on their first try. They must have snapped off the branches when they initially tried to drop him."

We began taping. I noticed Vigil's dogs stayed 20 feet from the carcass. They seemed wary and hesitant to venture close.

I sent forensic samples to Dr. John Altshuler in Denver. He reported a couple of weeks later that, "Evidence of high-heat was found around the incision areas." Gee, those predators are getting clever!

The remainder of 1993 was officially quiet, as was the spring of 1994. However, several reliable sources told me of a rumor that a Maxiville-area farmer had two, possibly three, cows "mutilated" on Monday night, May 9, 1994. These sources also mentioned a landing by some sort of craft on the farmer's property. The landing traces allegedly consisted of "a 12-foot by 12-foot burn mark" in the farmer's freshly irrigated field. According to his neighbors, the farmer didn't want to officially report these cattle deaths and landing because "he doesn't want to scare folks." Evidently the farmer quickly disposed of the carcasses and possibly covered the evidence of a landing. Over-flights of the area by a local pilot revealed nothing.

This possible example of a witnesses' reluctance to acknowledge the high strange is probably the norm, not the exception. Again, it may be the fear of ridicule. The human mind has built-in mechanisms to help to deal with that which it cannot comprehend, and very often the result is denial. If they close their eyes, maybe it will go away…[13]

Tony Dodd was still getting UK reports that he and other officers investigated. He mentions quite a list of animal species that were being reported dead and mutilated:

> Throughout 1993 and 1994, my phone rang many times with reports of animals being found with strange mutilations in an area stretching from the southeast coast of Scotland down to Whitby, Scarborough, Bridllington and Grimsby, on the northeast coast of England. The animals involved included cattle, sheep, deer, foxes and badgers. In the case of the cattle, the rectums were cored out and various parts removed from their bodies, including the udder, tongue, brain and internal organs. In the case of the small animals, the rectum was again removed, and each animal had a neat hole bored in the forehead, through which the brain and spinal column were completely removed. In every case, there was no spillage of blood at the scene, and the removal of the brain and spinal column through a hole no bigger than a 10-pence piece again required a surgical skill far in advance of anything known to man.[14]

Adams and Perkins County

The field of "mutology" (as coined by long-time mutilation researcher David Perkins in 1979) seems to have a propensity for name-game synchronicity. The father of mutology, Tom Adams, observed that the three recent mutilation cases in Eagle, Colorado in November and December and the two new cases that occurred the following May in Eagle Nest, New Mexico, have that tantalizing name-game connection.

In the fall of '93 there were reported unexplained livestock death cases in Adams and Perkins Counties in North and South Dakota. Is someone (or something) sending blatantly subtle messages to Tom Adams and David Perkins? As I have previously stated: when investigating this unsolved serial crime spree of the century, one must scrutinize the evidence from as many angles as possible.

Two cows were found in a mutilated condition by rancher Eli Hronich on May 10, 1994, next to a lake, in Eagle Nest, New Mexico. The cows were found with "classic mutilation" incisions, rear ends cored out, mandibles excised, etc., and this case may represent an historic first. New Mexico paranormal investigator

Gail Staehlin, New Mexico cattle inspector Philip Cantu, veterinarian Tim Johnson, rancher Tom Reed and hematologist Dr. John Altshuler were all on the scene together within ten hours of discovery. (figure 8) To my knowledge, there has never been such expertise on-site so quickly in the history of the unexplained livestock death phenomenon. Test results derived from preliminary forensic testing indicated cooked hemoglobin and cauterization of the incisions.

Doctors Altshuler and Johnson also noticed that both animals' lungs were riddled with pneumonia. Altshuler remembered the Vigil bull, and the finding of pneumonia in that animal's lungs, and thinks the affliction may prove significant. Very few animals that appear to be true mutilations are examined as carefully as the two Hronich cows.

The area just beyond the southern end of the SLV (near Taos, New Mexico) has quietly undergone a wave of unusual cattle deaths since the fall of 1993. By this time, Hronich had lost (and reported) ten head since September. He was one of several ranchers in the area that had been plagued by the mysterious cattle surgeons of late.

These cases (and the cow found in March, 1993—right in Taos) were a prelude (publicity campaign?) to the "Animal Mutilation Conference" presented by Gail Staehlin on May 21st in Taos. The conference was publicized in the area for three weeks and "somebody" may have seen the ads and flyers. Proper forensic, postmortem photographic and general investigative techniques were presented to a dozen ranchers, two state cattle inspectors and a local veterinarian over the course of the five-hour gathering.

This type of networking with ranchers and local officials is crucial. Expediency is of paramount importance when investigating unexplained livestock deaths. In the words of Gail Staehlin, "Somebody's got to help these folks!"

May 30, early a.m., North of Questa, New Mexico: Ranch foreman Tom Reed found a three-month old heifer "mutilated," and reported it to cattle inspector Jerry Valario. Valario drove out to the ranch to investigate the death.

Cutting the animal open, Valario was startled to find that the meat looked like it had been boiled, or cooked in a microwave. It was gray and flaky. He probed inside the calf's mouth, inadvertently getting the animal's saliva on his hand. "My hand started getting irritated," he later told me. "It started itching and turning red. It was like an acid burn, or something." He had noticed the burning sensation several minutes after examining the calf, as Nellie Lewis had 27 years earlier.[15]

July 24, 1994, Moreno Valley, New Mexico: Eagle Nest, New Mexico rancher Eli Hronich found another steer "mutilated." He also reported that a gray unmarked helicopter hovered over him as he examined the animal. This happened five days after he was interviewed by the television program *Sightings*. The cases on the Hronich ranch continued with a vengeance through the summer. On August 17, 1994, Eli Hronich found another "mutilated" steer, and the following day three mutilations were found 20 miles south, near Truchas, New Mexico, on the Max Cordova ranch. Cordova was sure the cows were pregnant but no fetuses were found. According to Albuquerque investigator Gail Staehlin, who has spent a considerable amount of time investigating New Mexico cattle death cases, "These latest ones seem to decompose abnormally fast." They may have been killed and kept for a day or two before being dumped where they were discovered.

Two members of the Cordova family reported that they also received chemical-like burns after touching one of the animals and the entire family coincidentally suffered "flu-like symptoms" the following day. Hronich claims his hand "burnt like hell for two weeks" after touching one of his dead cows, just as Inspector Jerry Valario had a burn-type rash on his hand after touching Tom Reed's dead calf earlier in May. I'd never heard of this being reported anywhere since Nellie Lewis burnt her hand on the piece of Snippy's mane hair. Less than a week later, on August 23, a 13-month-old bull was found "mutilated" 50 miles northwest of Colorado Springs on the Ted Hasenbalg ranch.

On August 30th, Eli Hronich found yet another dead steer. "I wish I knew why they're picking on me," he wondered while informing me. It was grazing on rented pasture at the T.V. Gorman ranch south of Eagle Nest. Hronich had suffered a substantial financial loss at the hands of these mystery cattle slayers who seemed to have singled out his herd of 2,500. "This whole thing just doesn't make sense," he added. "We've got to get some help from somebody." Meanwhile, Eli moved his herd down to winter pasture and hoped for the best. Before they were done, the mutilators would decimate Eli's herd.[16]

A wave of mutilation cases were reported to the west, to the east, and southeast of Taos. The Raton, New Mexico area had filed several reports and Sandoval County rancher Ray Trujillo reported 20 of his cattle slain on his Jemez Mountain ranch since April 1993. One of the animals allegedly had "its spinal cord excised." David Perkins investigated the claim. An April 1994 case in Arroyo Secco, north of Taos, involved a nine-day-old bull found with its mandible exposed.[17]

September 5, El Paso County, Colorado: Pikes Peak Cattlemen's Association board member Clyde Chess found one of his cows missing its genitalia, tongue, lips, ear, and udder. The heart had been removed from an incision behind the leg. The cow's unborn fetus was also reported missing. The hide around the incisions was "curled, as if they were cut with something hot." Chess also noted that rigor mortis never set in, the bones were bleached clean of meat and all the hair fell off the face within days.

September 12, 1994, El Paso County: Rancher Mary Liss found a 1,200 pound cow mutilated on her ranch, northeast of Colorado Springs. The animal's reproductive organs had been removed with what she described as "a technology that's not readily available to just anybody. This was a cow that you don't just walk up to. We had a hard time getting her in for a vaccination." She had seen the cow alive the evening before. She also mentioned, in an article in the *Rocky Mountain News*, that a nearby rancher had found another "mutilation" about a month prior.

September 13, 1994, 4:30 p.m., Chacon, New Mexico: Linda Moulton Howe investigated this highly unusual case. Evidently, Larry Gardea was bear hunting on the ranch where he worked when he heard a loud humming sound. As it began, a group of cattle nearby were startled and ran from the noise. According to the Las Vegas, New Mexico *Daily Optic,* September 15, 1994, Gardea claimed that a cow was dragged by the sound backwards, up the hill, into the underbrush. He said it appeared to be struggling to get away but was unable to escape. Gardea said the animal sounded as if it was being tortured. Being understandably spooked, he fired several shots from his 30.06 towards the sound, and it stopped.

Gardea headed to the sheriff's office and returned to the site with a deputy. They found one cow had been "mutilated," a second cow crippled, and the third cow, which had been dragged uphill, was missing. Gardea also mentioned the humming sound ("like an arc-welder") being heard by locals several times before the incident he reported. My repeated calls to Gardea went unanswered.[18]

September 30, 1994, Salida, Colorado: Rancher James Neppl reported to the Saguache County sheriff's office finding a dead cow and (40 yards away) its dead calf. The site was rented SLV pasture on the former Triple L Boy's Ranch. Neppl thinks they were both killed the night of September 30th. This is the exact area where three women claimed to have seen a red pulsing light that night.

It was the first official mutilation report in Saguache County (to my knowledge) since June 1, 1980. Both animals were missing udders, rear end, and ears. Neppl said, "I do most of my own vet work. I've never seen anything like those two animals. The cuts were so clean and precise, there was no blood anywhere… the hair quickly fell off the faces." He also noticed that they were untouched by scavengers until human scent had been introduced to the crime scene. The calf had the entire left side of its skull "peeled and cleaned" of tissue, and all hoof material had been removed with the underneath foot bones bleached white. "The joints were cut as smooth as could be," he observed.

Neppl said that the animals had not been hit by lightning and the calf was cut from chin to rear end with what can only be described as pinking shears. A front foreleg had been completely excised of tissue and hide. I obtained video footage for the *Sightings* mutilation update segment. This case was reported by Michelle Le Blanc Hynden in the *Center Post Dispatch* on October 14th and in the November issue of the *Crestone Eagle*.

As per the norm, the entire crime scene was gone over with a "fine-tooth comb" by investigating officers and no tracks, footprints, or additional physical evidence was uncovered. Saguache County asked the Colorado Bureau of Investigation for help with the case. Commented then-Saguache county sheriff Dan Pacheco, "You hear about them [mutilations], but you don't think they'll ever happen in your county. Then when they do, you really don't know what to think.

There was something real strange about those cattle!"

October 7, 1994, Conejos County, Colorado: Rancher Mack Crowthers reported to the sheriff a mutilated steer had been found on his ranch in Sanford. The ears and testicles had been removed and a "leg had been boned-out" (all the tissue and hide excised from a leg bone). The steer was found in dense scrub-willow, suggesting it may have been dropped. The boned-out leg is very similar to the Jim Neppl case from the previous week.

A neighbor, Mrs. Warren Reed, claimed to have seen "weird green floodlights" in the Crowther's pasture the night this steer had apparently been killed. Investigating deputy Steven Gottlieb and undersheriff Joe Taylor Jr. found fresh tire tracks heading into the pasture near where the animal was found. These tracks stopped cold and there was no indication that the vehicle turned around nor that the tracks had been obscured. "It was like it had been picked up from the air and whisked away," Gottlieb said.

Crowthers reportedly lost three more cattle the following week. Two of the animals were found dead on their stomachs, with their legs splayed out to the sides. There was no evidence of bullet holes nor obvious signs of cause of death. The animals with "classic mutilation" wounds seemed to decompose unusually fast and "did not bloat," similar to the last five Hronich cows in Eagle Nest. Complete photographic evidence was obtained.

According to Gottlieb, another Conejos County rancher had "found a bunch of dead cows" on his ranch in a similar condition. This happened during the last week of September and the first week of October.

Alamosa County, having escaped any official mutilation reports for over a decade, may have experienced three unusual cattle deaths during October and two more in November. During a lecture I gave at Adams State College on November 4th 1994, I was approached by an Alamosa Wildlife Refuge worker named Donna Knowles (who had attended my first lecture at the college two years before). She said she'd been patrolling, late in the day during the first week of October, when she found three "mutilated" cattle in a remote part of the refuge. There were many locked gates and fence lines between the cattle and any nearby pastures.

She returned early the next morning with a 35-mm camera and a coworker and found only one cow. The other two had vanished without a trace. She told me emphatically, "There is no way cows could get in and out of there without being dropped and then picked back up!" As she and her co-worker examined the animal, according to Knowles, they both heard a "high-pitched whirring sound."

She took four pictures at the end of a roll and dropped the film later that afternoon at an Alamosa one-hour photo shop. She later picked up the pictures, slipped the negatives in her purse and put the packet of photos on the dashboard (including the four shots of the dead cow, which she looked at immediately to make sure they had come out) and went into a store.

When she returned to her vehicle, she discovered "the four pictures of the cow were gone!" Because she had separated the negatives from the prints she was able to provide me with reprints. The animal was missing the hide and tissue from the left side of its face and the rear end appeared to be cored out. Knowles says the animal's wounds appeared to be caused by a laser-type instrument.

The cattle surgeons returned to the eastern Colorado plains on the night of October 18, 1994. But this time they were playing a different game. A bison was discovered the following morning, mutilated, on the Denver Buffalo Company ranch near Simla, Colorado. Linda Moulton Howe happened to be in Colorado and investigated the case. A second bison was found in a similar condition later on the same ranch, November 8th. According to Howe, the necropsy of the first bison showed two holes between the ribs, and no break in the hide. Tissue around the incision areas on the cored-out rear end was hard and the spleen was an abnormal pinkish-white. Lab results revealed no virus or bacteria and the vet said the animal had "died of illness four days before."

This was impossible, for the bison was seen inside its pen with 20 other animals at 6:30 p.m. the previous night when the rancher was medicating his herd. The genital incision area had unusual characteristics. One side of the incised oval was hard, the other side soft. There were also holes in the muscle tissue.

Linda told me, "I couldn't believe that this buffalo death was not a few hours old." She noted that fresh, liquid feces were present and that the blood present was not congealed. The lab called her back two days later with the observation that the tissue was already rotten. Could this be yet another example of the Eagle Nest-style "advanced necrosis?"[19]

I finally confirmed rumors of an additional mutilation case south of Alamosa in October. My bass player's uncle-in-law, rancher John Harr, told him of a strange occurrence. Harr and his family were awakened the night of October 20th by what Harr described as a terrible noise. It sounded like a "huge helicopter hovering right over the top of the house." Harr, also the Del Norte Postmaster, said, "I went outside and all I could hear was the downdraft from the propeller, there were no engine sounds. I didn't hear anything mechanical!"

Who are the Chopper Pilots?

Two days later, on October 22, 1994 Harr's two sons discovered two cows and two calves a half mile away from the house to the east, dead for "no apparent reason." (figure 9) According to the rancher, the oldest cow, who "would've died soon anyway," was discovered missing the flesh off her jaw, and the tongue and rear end were "cut out." He also noticed that, "It looked like she'd floundered around a bit before she died."

The other cow and two calves "looked like they had just died in their sleep." These three animals displayed no incision-like marks and scavengers made short work of two of them. The second cow was untouched, even by birds. No additional clues were present at the scene. No tire tracks, footprints, scavenger tracks or blood was discovered at the scene. No vet examined these animals, and Harr never bothered to roll the "mutilated" cow over to ascertain if the downside had been butchered. Alamosa County K-9 deputy Jim McCloskey investigated the Harr report. For some reason, he left his animal partner in the car while at the site and no animal reactions were noted.

The Alamosa River snakes through a corner of the ranch where the animals were discovered. This river is officially polluted with heavy metals for 17 miles below the Summitville Mine Superfund site, located 40 miles upstream from the valley floor. It is one of the only known sources of pollution in the pristine Greater SLV. This appears to give more ammunition to the "mutilation as environmental monitoring" theorists.

Harr stewed for a couple of days and then started making phone calls. He called Senator Ben Nighthorse Campbell's office about the matter and was referred to the governor's office. The governor's office told him to talk with Colorado State Veterinarian, Dr. John Maulsby. The vet spoke knowledgeably about the phenomenon. "He [Maulsby] told me he was going to put an article in our local paper requesting ranchers provide him with fresh samples for testing," said Harr. "But if he ever put one in, I never saw it." Later, *Jane's Defence Weekly* aerospace investigator Nick Cook visited the SLV and interviewed Harr for the BBC documentary *Billion Dollar Secret.* (figure 10)

During this active fall in the SLV and on the Front Range of Colorado, the La Veta-Spanish Peaks region had also been experiencing strange aerial sightings and a multitude of interesting rumors had been circulating in the area. Unfortunately, confirmation of these stories proved difficult.

Then, I received a call from David Perkins concerning a new series of unexplained livestock death cases that had just come to his attention. It seems that rancher Ermenio Andreatta, five miles west of La Veta, Colorado had discovered a crippled cow on Sunday, October 23, 1994 in a remote rugged section of his ranch. Returning to the same area the following day, he found a mutilated cow; the rear end, reproductive tract and left-side teats were removed, and the animal was half submerged in a small creek. Nearby were several nine-foot wide circular discolorations in the grass. "It looked like giant tractor tires had been laying there," Andreatta said. Two more mutilated cows were found over the next three days.

A *La Veta Signature* article dated November 3rd stated, "a fist-sized dark spot was visible on the chest of each of the dead cows." District Wildlife Manager Lonnie Brown investigated the site, and according to the *Signature*, "Brown just shook his head in amazement and perplexity as he examined the cattle for bullet holes or other causes of death."

A carload of Huerfano residents told Perkins that they witnessed an unusual aerial craft hovering over the Yellowstone Road shortly after the Andreattas lost their livestock. The craft was silent and was seen shining a powerful spotlight down toward the ground. The witnesses were "pretty freaked out" by their sighting.

The Andreattas experienced a fourth case later that November. Linda Moulton Howe, who had arrived in the SLV at my invitation for a sheriff's mutilation training seminar, went to the Andreatta's Middle Creek Road Ranch and conducted a thorough investigation of these four cases. They were included in her Research Grant Report of Mutilation Cases in 1994.[20]

Howe also obtained plant samples from the scene for analysis. She had begun carefully collecting flora from the head and rear end of mutilations, along with a control sample taken some distance away from the carcass. Preliminary results from other mutilation cases have shown changes in the plants' respiratory process. According to Howe, this result is similar to findings from plants affected in crop circles.

Reports continued around the towns of La Veta, Blanca and the Forbes Trinchera ranches. They are all found within The La Veta Military Operations Area, previously associated with UFO activity. Locals are used to seeing military flights over their area on a daily basis. Some of the UFO reports could be misidentified conventional military flights but several reports remain unexplained. Helicopters were reported over La Veta Pass on October 27th, 28th, and 29th. On Friday the 28th, around 10:00 p.m., a large disc-shaped craft was spotted by a Forbes Trinchera resident that appeared to be shining a spotlight down at the ground. A short time later helicopters were seen "buzzing" the area where the disc had been seen.

On October 29, 1994 at around 10:00 a.m., two Crestone residents on their way to Gunnison spotted a military convoy on Highway 50, headed west out of Humvees; two of them were "large ones;" the other five were the standard smaller versions. What immediately impressed them was the fact that none of the vehicles had license plates or insignias. All vehicles had "desert-style camo." I was under the impression that any vehicles, private or otherwise, were required to have license plates and identifying markings.

Any relationship between this activity and the unusual aerial craft reports could be anybody's guess but my suspicion is that there is a link. These reports of government activity have a tendency to ebb and flow in concert with the reports of unusual craft.

On November 10, 1994, a group of investigators met between Taos and Eagle Nest to pool data and discuss the ongoing activity in the southern Colorado-northern New Mexico region. Gail Staehlin, Carolyn Duce-Ashe, Becky Minshall and Debbie Stark made the trip from Albuquerque. Tom Adams and Gary Massey arrived from Texas. David Perkins arrived on Friday. My brother Brendon and a friend, Richard Copeland, went with me. (figure 11)

At one point during the chaotic get-together, Gail brought up an alleged incident where an Eagle Nest rancher, John Mutz (no kidding!) in broad daylight, watched his cattle form into a group out in the pasture. When the cows moved apart, there was a mutilated calf lying there. All in attendance instantly agreed that the cattle mutilation phenomenon must be "a cow thing" and we should let the cattle work it out amongst themselves. Information was then exchanged in a more serious manner. Mutz would suffer more mutilations to his herd.

Close proximity to an actual mutilation in progress is exceedingly rare, according to my research, but these events are reported from time to time. The following case was noted by UK police Sgt. Tony Dodd:

> Determined to get to the bottom of what was going on—and protect their stock—the farmers arranged a vigil at one field between Scarborough and Whitby where a spate of mutilations had occurred. They hired infrared cameras, which would be triggered by movement in the field. The sensors were rigged so that they would record any movement above the height of the sheep, so that they would not be fired by the sheep moving around the field at night. Armed with shotguns, a group of farmers spent the night in the open, next to the field. The cameras flashed three times, but the farmers neither saw nor heard anything. The following morning, however, they found another mutilated lamb, only yards from their observation point, and two more at the other side of the field. There had been no sound of disturbance in the flock during the night, and again the mutilations were surgically precise and bloodless, each animal having a small, neat hole in the forehead and its rectum cored out.
>
> The farmer whose sheep had been killed arranged for a private autopsy of one of the bodies, which was carried out at a university department of veterinary studies. The report stated that a one-inch hole had been made in the lamb's skull, through which the brain and the spinal cord had been expertly removed. There was, according to the 40-page pathology report, a high level of radiation in the animal's body, and the DNA structure of the blood was abnormal...
>
> In October 1994, a dead and mutilated cow was found near a forest in Newry, Northern Ireland. The rectum of the animal had been cored out and the udder was removed in a precise and surgical way. The flesh of the jaw and face had been totally removed, leaving the exposed skull bones. There was no sign of struggle, or any tracks left by either an animal or a human predator.[21]

Cases in Ireland are rarely reported outside of the close-knit communities where they allegedly occur, but reports have been filed over the years—as noted above. Misidentified scavenger action is probably to blame for some cases but not all. There are supposedly no large predators in the UK or Ireland.

Back in North America, law enforcement officials and Livestock Board officials took steps to bring themselves up to speed as to how to properly investigate these puzzling unexplained livestock deaths.

Training the Investigators

On November 14, 1994, Linda Howe, Tom Adams, David Perkins, Gary Massey, Chip Knight and I, met with sheriffs and deputies from six Colorado counties. I had been asked by several law enforcement officials if I would consider conducting a mutilation training seminar, so I made arrangements to help conduct the training. With all the recent publicity surrounding the latest wave of animal deaths, the officers wanted some information and help.

The turnout was less than expected. Due to the murder of the Mineral County sheriff, adjoining counties were involved in an extensive manhunt and could not send anyone to the training. Brian Norton (Rio Grande), Steven Gottlieb (Conejos), Martin Dominguez and John Luther from the Alamosa County Sheriff's Office, Bill Mistretta, Tom Davis from the El Paso County Sheriff's Office, Kevin McClellan and Steve England from the New Mexico Livestock Board attended.

Tom Adams started the session by giving the attendees a quick overview of the history of the unexplained livestock death phenomenon. He also detailed the helicopter sightings he had documented around mutilation sites. David Perkins covered some of the most prevalent theories about who is conducting these experiments, and why. I covered some of our region's most recent cases. Then Linda began the training session.

Armed with videotape, Linda took the officials step by step through the mutilation investigative process. The burly lawmen sat politely and listened, seemingly a little bored. A couple of them seemed to be dozing. Then, while showing video of one of the recent bison mutilations, Linda pointed at the screen showing a veterinarian excising a bison penis. Someone coughed as I took a quick glance around the room. Everyone was suddenly wide awake.

The lawmen watched, riveted, as the vet expertly removed parts of the organ with a scalpel. Several eyes grew wide, postures stiffened, and a couple pairs of legs were crossed. Linda, with her back to the audience, described the process in detail. David Perkins and I had to stifle chuckles. Here was an attractive woman, surrounded by burly lawmen, innocently describing most males' darkest fear, oblivious to the subtle responses in the room. You could have cut the air with that scalpel.

The Del Norte Colorado Calf

On March 7, 1995, I received a call from Rio Grande undersheriff Brian Norton (figure 12). He had attended the unexplained livestock death training seminar in November, but up to now, he had never investigated a mutilation case. He told me of a report filed that morning by a rancher a mile south of Del Norte.

Bob Kernan had been driving past his pasture when he noticed his herd circling around something on the ground. At the time, he thought this unusual but didn't check. Later, he noticed the herd had drifted away from the area and saw a calf lying on the ground. Thinking the animal was sick, he went out and made a grisly find.

Of the hundreds of mutilation cases I had personally investigated or researched, this is the one that physically gave me the creeps. When I arrived on-site and viewed the unfortunate calf, the hair literally stood up on the back of my neck, and I got a severe case of goose bumps.

The month-old female was missing its spine from the hips to the skull and the brain was gone. (figure 13) Also missing were the right front leg, all but two ribs, both eyes plus a two-inch circle of hide around the upside socket, both ears, the intestines, reproductive tract, lungs, and a small two-inch diameter coring out of the rectum. The heart and liver, scavenger favorites, were left intact. The spine appeared to have been savagely torn out. (figure 14)

The rancher's dogs had never barked, there was no blood, no tracks or signs of scavengers, and a strange cloying smell emanated from the body cavity. Kernan had put the calf in his garage on a piece of plastic and after five days there wasn't even a hint of decay. The closest description I can think of to describe the unusual odor would be "a sweet, pungent, earthy smell." Not everyone agreed. Visiting Colorado Springs investigator Ed Burke said it smelled "just like a bathroom disinfectant."

Bob Kernan initially didn't want the animal death publicized. He told me, "I don't want to alarm people." This reaction made sense after seeing the carcass. Kernan was overwhelmed by the response to the death of his calf: "If I had it to do over again, I wouldn't even have called the sheriff." Because an official report was filed by Kernan, Sam Adams of the SLV Publishing Company caught wind of the case and called him. Kernan granted Adams an interview that resulted in a front-page article in the *South Fork Tines*, March 16, 1995.

Another rancher, half a mile away, reported to the sheriff's office that he had watched a strange beam of light shining straight up in the air, just north of his ranch, at 3:00 a.m., around the time the calf was killed. A motorist driving on highway 160, west of Del Norte, also reported a strange light coming out of the pasture, near where the calf was found.

Kernan also lost another calf during this time period. "It just plumb disappeared," he told me. "We never did find any trace of it."

In May 1995, a strange discovery was made by a group of hikers crossing through a series of fields in northeastern England. They "came across a scene of carnage, with the bodies of sheep, lambs and, curiously, badgers littered around the place." According to Sgt. Tony Dodd, "The farmer was called, and when he had finished sorting out the mess he counted 17 dead sheep and five dead badgers, each with a hole in its forehead and the rectum cored out."[22]

The summer of 1995 was blissfully quiet and I have not been able to identify any cases worth noting through the summer months. That changed in late September when the following was reported in the SLV.

United Parcel Service driver David Jaramillo and his family were spending quality time relaxing up at their Osier Park cabin directly west-by-southwest from Antonito, Colorado, just above the New Mexico border, when they discovered a "mutilated cow" near their cabin on September 22, 1995. The animal, lying on its left side, was missing its udder, rear end and tongue. There was a large circular portion around the right ear that was missing, and the tip of the animal's tail appeared to have boned-out. About one hundred feet away from the carcass, much to Jaramillo's surprise, he found three, four- foot swirled circles flattening the lush meadow grass. Each circle was about twelve feet from the others arrayed in a triangle pattern. Around each four-foot circle were three small four-inch holes in a triangle configuration, punched into the ground. In the middle of the triangle patterns of circles, Jaramillo's brother found long tail hairs that appeared to be the missing hair from the unfortunate cow.

Jaramillo happened to have his video camera with him and documented the entire scene. He tracked me down the following day while delivering in Crestone, and told me of his find. We watched his video tape, and I cringed to see Dave's brother standing in the middle of one of the four-foot circles—perfect physical evidence, now rendered not-so-perfect. The animal had no brand or ear tag, and Jaramillo was unable to ascertain who was the animal's owner. His remote cabin was occasionally visited by the local rancher's herds that meander around the La Magna Pass area during the summer and early fall, before they're herded together and taken down to winter pastures. As bad luck would have it, an early fall snowstorm that night made the site inaccessible to me, much to my annoyance. Yet another chance to conduct "good science" was thwarted by this remote, high-mountain environment.

Jaramillo's footage was broadcast in a *Strange Universe* television segment later that fall. I directed and field produced the segment produced by Scott Catamas.[23]

Approximately the same time in September, a rancher (later) reported to undersheriff Brian Norton at the Rio Grande Sheriff's Office that he had discovered a "mutilated cow" in the center of a 30-foot swirled circle in the grass. The area was about 15 to 20 miles north of the Jaramillo mute site. The rancher's horse would evidently not approach the grass circle, and upon examination, the rancher reported to Norton that there was a fine dusting of a substance that appeared similar to "baby powder" on the carcass and on the swirled circle. To my knowledge, there were no UFO sightings associated with this unofficial mute report, however, while the rancher examined the carcass, a "military helicopter" allegedly flew low over the site, obviously watching the rancher. The chopper swooped in, then left from treetop level. [24]

They Stole His Pet Bear!

Here is the story of an interesting character from the mid 1990s. Even with impressive documentation and physical evidence, I don't quite know what to think of the following events. Running in a straight northwest to southeast line for over 220 miles, the rugged Sangre de Cristo Mountains, the longest continuous mountain range in the United States, border the eastern side of the SLV. I have traveled the mountainous region stretching from Alaska to Mexico, and the Sangres are truly one of North America's most breathtaking scenic wonders. Seven peaks soar to over 14,000 feet and scrape the thin Colorado Plateau sky. A perfect natural barrier, the imposing rock wall soars over a dozen high-altitude lakes found nestled in vales located between the mountains. Most of SLV's population is located in the center of the Valley, and at the time I was blessed to be able to look out my window and see four "14'ers," less than three miles away.

In a high, remote area 25 miles north of Crestone, just over the Sangres and the Rio Grande National Forest and Wilderness area, a small trailer sits in a clearing surrounded by the quiet piñon forest. There are no houses, stores or residents, just miles of quiet dense forest in the area. The trailer belongs to Larry Williams (not his real name), a mountain man, Vietnam vet who prefers the company of his pet black bear over people.

A mutual friend called me about Williams and told me I should contact him because he claimed some very unusual events were occurring at his property. "Almost nightly" during June and July, 1995, Larry noticed strange lights buzzing low over the forest that clings to the steep eastern side of the Sangres. He couldn't help but wonder what the lights could be. During several days in late July, he noticed increased military helicopter activity over his high-mountain property. He began to notice odd things around his place. A stream that flowed down from the mountains through his land would inexplicably raise and lower its water level for no apparent reason. Then something happened that he was really not expecting.

Williams arrived home from town August 15th, at 8:45 p.m., and noticed a bright light off to the north. Checking to make sure he had his camera with him, he sat in his truck and watched the light carefully. It appeared to either get brighter, or to head south toward his location. The man took a series of sixteen still photos that show the light as it apparently flew toward him. The final photo was taken shooting straight up at an "enormous boomerang craft" as it hovered above him. Then, quite inexplicably, he found himself sitting in his truck looking out over a dark, quiet Wet Mountain Valley.

He checked his watch, and was startled to find out that 35 minutes had elapsed since he last remembered checking the time, right when the boomerang craft began to approach. Confused, he got out of his truck and looked around with a flashlight. He was amazed to find his truck sitting "six inches away from its tracks," like something had moved his truck up and over a half foot. He ran to the house to check on his pet black bear and was again startled to find whatever-it-was had moved his trailer "six inches off its foundation" and picked up his bulldozer and set it down, "six inches from where its tracks ended!" Fresh branches, up to sixty feet off the ground, appeared to have been sheared off nearby trees, and Williams' pet bear had vanished.

This was the last straw. A couple of days earlier, he had discovered quite a number of animal skeletons scattered around his property. He could not venture a guess concerning why so many unexplained animal carcasses littered his land. "I've found elk, deer, fox, raccoon, and a lot of cattle skeletons. They're just laying around. Nothing touched 'em and tore 'em up... I've seen at least 15 to 20 cattle carcasses and skeletons alone since last year. I don't know who they belonged to." Coincidentally, a rancher directly over the Sangres in the SLV reported losing several dozen cattle without a trace since 1992.

Williams told me, "I've been waking up at exactly 2:00 and seeing lights pretty near every night since June... We've found little tiny four-toed tracks walking around the perimeter of my place. I've seen some pretty odd things in my life, but nothing like I'm seeing in those Sangre de Cristos." Much to his dismay, he couldn't help but notice that he now had a thumb-sized wart located in an uncomfortable location after his 35 minutes of missing time. It required medical attention.

The same evening, at 10:00 p.m., a family of four was returning to Blanca, Colorado after watching a movie in Alamosa with a family friend. This is about an hour and 15 minutes after Williams claimed he returned. As the family headed east on State Highway 160, about five miles out of Alamosa, a large bright light caught their attention. Surrounding the brilliant light were "lots of helicopters" traveling in a southwest to northeast direction. The family pulled over to the side of the highway and got out. The huge light never varied in intensity, and at one point the adults got so excited that two little boys in the backseat became very scared and started to cry. One of the excited witnesses, guitar player George Oringdulph, called me the following day to make a report. "It was huge, whatever it was, and it was pretty strange the way all those other blinking lights seemed to be flying with it." George and I had a band named Laffing Buddha and we gigged up and down the Rocky Mountain States along with guitarist Chris Medina, bass player Lyman Bushkovski and drummer Jay Wegner. (figure 15)

The day after Williams' close-proximity sighting, on August 16, 1995 ten or twelve choppers were "buzzing all over his place." His house had also been broken into and all his photographic equipment rifled through. "Thank God, I had my camera with me. Whoever they were, I'm positive they were looking for those pictures I took the night before!"

Williams reported the strange events to the local sheriff who conducted a brief investigation. Williams was frustrated. "I showed 'em how my truck, trailer, and bulldozer had been moved, but what could they do?!" He was very protective of his property, and his privacy, and was not pleased when he found large boot tracks and cigarette butts at the edge of the clearing where his trailer sat. He was also perturbed when a large mirror outside his trailer was repeatedly moved from its secure position. Someone was snooping around his place, and with all the other weird events, Willliams was starting to get pretty paranoid about the whole situation. I called the local sheriff and found that investigating officers were skeptical of these alleged high-strange events, but they did acknowledge receiving reports of unidentified lights in the same vicinity.

Williams also mentioned to me that images of a "large post" kept appearing on freshly developed rolls of film. He could not identify the location in these photos, and doesn't recall taking the pictures. If something like this only happens once, not a big deal... but after a fourth time, one would REALLY start to wonder. Williams was not amused.

> Members of two investigative organizations visited Williams and "someone used my name publicly even after being asked not to." This incensed him to the point that he was absolutely unwilling to talk about his experiences with investigators, or the press. "I don't care if you weren't the one who used my name...you can all GO TO HELL!" he told me angrily during our final conversation.[25]

Floating Humanoids in the Huerfano

After almost an eight-month lull in cattle mutilations reports, our mystery perpetrators may have returned to the Huerfano and the Greater SLV. But, did they ever leave? Our intrepid Huerfano investigator David Perkins related to me the following report, and we both wondered if these were the tip of the iceberg.

On Tuesday, September 26, 1995, Gardner, Colorado rancher Larry Chacon found his old horse "Whiskey" dead with a six inch diameter, perfect circle rectum coring; half the tongue had been removed with a clean diagonal slice; the upper eye was "sucked out;" the hair and hide were "blackened and stiff" as if heat had been applied. As per the norm, no additional tracks, footprints, signs of predators, or signs of a struggle were noted. Just another one of those inexplicable animal deaths.

The Huerfano County sheriff's office investigated the report, which occurred about 15 miles north of where a 100-yard rectangle was seen by Huerfano residents earlier, on September 22nd. Incidentally, the horse was found in the same area where SLV reporter Barry Tobin and I happened to find an unclaimed dead and cut-up horse in March 1995.

Chacon had been renting grazing pasture from an old "hermit" who had told him of strange activities on the remote ranchland on the overlooked eastern slopes of the Sangre de Cristos. The old man told David Perkins he has also "seen ships in the sky" over the ranch, and even claimed one had landed near his cabin a couple of years ago. He said "two bearded human-looking" beings had appeared from the craft and "floated" toward his cabin shining a very bright spotlight. The man claims that when they pointed the light at his cabin, "the light went through the wall." Holding a gun, he says he was blinded and paralyzed as the light illuminated the inside of his cabin. The hermit noted that the two beings were "not from around here."[26]

To the northeast, during this same end of September time period, Douglas County officials investigated a two-year livestock killing spree on the Mike and Kandy Toll ranch. The Tolls claimed 30 sheep and a bull calf had been killed on their Franktown, Colorado champion sheep spread. "The animals have been brutalized, led astray and possibly poisoned."

According to a *Denver Post* article, Douglas County Sgt. Attila Denes said, "The Tolls hadn't reported the incidents in the past because they had hoped they would just go away, but it looks like she had several incidents this week that made her think it over… A seventy pound lamb that drowned Wednesday would have had to be lifted and placed in the three-foot tank with its head held down in only three-and-a-half inches of water." A neighbor claimed to have found all her turkeys locked in a hot enclosure with no food or water. She said, "I hope it's not people just killing for the shear meanness of it." Good point. Why on earth were these animals killed? I bring up these stories to illustrate the probable involvement of human vandals in some cases. I wonder where human culpability ends and non-human culpability begins? In these unrelated Douglas County cases, law enforcement (and the ranchers) suspected someone in the rapidly growing suburban community around the Toll's ranch.[27]

"… It was an Environmental Hazard."

The following fall 1995 possible mutilation deserves mention. I investigated this covered-up case that probably occurred October 8, 1995. Evidently, the rancher had discovered a cow "missing her rear end and bag" on his ranch the morning of the 8th and thought it had been killed the previous night. I learned of the case from rancher's sister on the 9th, and she arranged for us to go to the ranch that afternoon. I made the two-hour drive with my brother Brendan and a mutual friend of ours.

Upon arriving at the remote, idyllic ranch, it quickly became apparent that the rancher was a no-show. His sister introduced us to his wife, who claimed she hadn't gone out to see the animal since her first look at it that morning. I noticed a large beautiful horse across the driveway in a small pasture limping badly.

I asked her what had happened to the animal. She told me they weren't sure what was wrong, but it happened the same night the cow had been killed. The corral area where the cow was supposedly found was empty. No sign of a carcass. We found large tire tracks indicating a tractor had been used in the area recently. We decided to cover the front part of the ranch and look for a bone pile while waiting for the rancher to show up. The rancher inexplicably ducked our meeting. He never showed.

His wife was pretty puzzled by his absence, claiming, "If he told you he'd be here, he should be here." We easily found where the animal had lain, less than one hundred feet from the house; we found the drag marks and tractor tracks, but no dead cow. She described the condition of the vanished cow for us, but claimed she didn't know who had moved it, or what had happened to it. Another mystery. I found out that evening, when I called the rancher, that he claimed the government had told him to bury it. He was told, "'… it was an environmental hazard.'"

According to the rather brusque Hispanic man, officials had told him to keep the animal death quiet. He reluctantly admitted the animal's discovery, and mumbled an excuse for not showing up for our meeting. He had told me during our initial conversation, "We found her right behind the corral, just a few feet away from the house. My dogs never even barked." I could tell he was nervous even talking with me about his dead cow. It's interesting to note that it's a common practice in the SLV to leave your dead livestock on a bone pile, or simply right where it dies. Carcasses from the two to three percent of all grazing animals that routinely die every year can be found laying in repose in the vast pastures of the SLV. It can literally take years for some carcasses to finally melt into the ground.[28]

This perfect example of local authorities' secretive way of dealing with "mutes" illustrates the fear and uncertainty that's pervasive in many North American rural ranching communities where these types of unusual animal death cases occur routinely. I have found local officials, while in office, can be extremely reluctant to even acknowledge the existence of these reports.

This southeast Colorado corner of the Valley is a world unto itself. And, does it have a history. The quiet little ranch where this October 8th case allegedly occurred lay just below the Taylor Ranch; about two-miles to the west. Several ranches away to the east were rancher-neighbors Clarence and Dale Vigil. The Vigils lost two cows to the cattle hackers, one in April and another in December 1993.

This small isolated Chama Canyon area, in my estimation, is the epicenter of the cattle mutilation phenomenon. I can find nowhere else that can rival the ferocity this little picturesque region suffered through two wild and woolly months in the fall of 1975, when as many as 100 head of cattle may have been mutilated.

These cases may reflect the injection of a human element ignored by all but a few investigators. Evidence of possible Taylor Ranch involvement was made public in 1996 when ex-Costilla County Sheriffs went on the record claiming at least some of the helicopter crews responsible for many of the county's mutilations were "taking off and landing at the Taylor Ranch." This was the first time to my knowledge that *any* law enforcement official anywhere publicly stated names of parties suspected to be involved in conducting livestock mutilations.

They're Both Lumberjacks and They're OK

On May 13, 1996, at 8:00 a.m., two loggers were headed up State Highway 114 toward the Canero Pass Road that turns to the south eight miles west of Saguache, Colorado. As they traveled up the dirt road after making the turn, they noticed "a cow lying near the road." One of the loggers (who had been avidly following my mutilation investigation) blurted out, "That's a mute!" They stopped and climbed over the fence to investigate, immediately noticing that the rest of the herd seemed "trapped in the corner of the pasture." They appeared to be agitated. "There were about 30 to 40 head, maybe 20 cows with calves, milling around mooing like the dead one was blocking their path… There's a stream that runs through the pasture with only about 25 feet between the fence-line and the stream. The dead one was in the path and they wouldn't go around it."

The other logger took up the story. "I started to walk over to the dead one and the biggest cow in the herd charged over and stopped about 20 feet away and let out a moooo… You know how a herd moves like water, one goes and they all start to go? Well, when that cow mooed, and a momma and a baby ran past the dead cow, I mooed again and that momma cow and me kept mooing until the rest of 'em made it past… I used to ride bulls and it was pretty weird the way they were acting. I don't know, it was almost like us being there gave them courage to go around it." The two loggers described the "mute" as missing its rear end. "It was definitely cut in a circle," and "its udder and an upside eye and ear were gone… There was what looked like strap burns behind the front legs… We luckily had a camera with us and took a bunch of good pictures."

"Did you get any good close-ups of the incisions?" I asked. "Yes," came the reply. The jaw cut went up around the eye and a stain that discolored the ground spread out from its face. We didn't see it when we were there, but you can see it in the pictures." They had visited a one-hour photo shop and had the film developed. "It was really fresh. We could see that a little blood was still uncoagulated and oozing. It looked like it happened maybe two or three hours before, around dawn."

They quickly scoured the scene for clues. "There were no tracks or footprints that we could see. No bear or cat did that. We didn't spend much time because we had to get to work." Their untrained eyes revealed no additional clues. No drops of blood, cigarette butts or clues to what or who did the unfortunate animal in were found. "When we came back about four hours later to cut samples and check around again, it was gone! Somebody must have hauled it away; there was no sign of it." The two loggers were convinced that their discovery was no accident. "I couldn't help but think that this was done for us to find. Like, somebody knew we would be on that road that morning!"

I did some checking and found out the name of the owner of the pasture. He was not very helpful. In fact, he seemed nervous that the local busybody, me, had found out about it. "I rent out that pasture and I'll tell him to call you." He wouldn't tell me where the cow ended up, and I could tell it would take quite a bit of hounding to get anywhere with him. If they bury it in their mind it goes away. Permanently.

The area where the animal was found was within five miles of Hoagland Hill where the cops were supposedly chasing "lights" on the night of May 4th, and it's the western end of the area that had the first cases in the SLV back in the fall of 1975.[29]

Who is Playing Copycat?

During the late summer and early fall of 1996, *Taos News* reporter Phaedra Greenwood and long-time *Spirit Magazine* reporter/investigator David Perkins covered a half a dozen "mutilation" reports from the Taos, New Mexico region of the southern SLV. While researching one of several articles concerning ongoing "mutilation" wave, Greenwood contacted Dale Spall, an analytical chemist at the Life Sciences Division in the Los Alamos National Laboratories. Spall, who had conducted testing of animal mutilations to look for evidence of carcinogens and radiation back in 1978, at the behest of the infamous Rommel Investigation, was very interested in the phenomenon. He told Greenwood:

> "We looked at the liver, the spleen, did gross observation and a number of other studies. The problem with cattle mutilations is that a lot of information tends to be anecdotal in nature. There is a certain natural death rate among cattle."[2%] He said he thought most cattle mutilations were natural deaths and scavengers. "There is a distinct possibility some people are playing copy cat," he said. "Cattle mutilations follow a fifteen to twenty-year cycle," he added. "They've been reported in England, Brazil, Argentina, Venezuela." [Also in Puerto Rico, Mexico, Canada, Ireland, Scotland, Australia, New Zealand, Kenya, the Canary Islands and probably other countries as well].[30]

As I related in my 1999 book *Enter the Valley*:

> Spall said he experimented with one of his own animals; when he slaughtered it, he also did a mimic mutilation. "I cored the anus, took out the sexual organs, cut off an ear, cut out the tongue." He said he did the whole thing in about half an hour with a skinning knife. "If you leave it lying out for about six hours, it does the same thing. The edges of the wound curl and stretch as they dry and look like precision laser cuts," he said. He admitted he had never seen the 'cookie cutter' kind of edges mentioned by pathologists in Montana back in the mid-1970s. He also said he had never heard of a mutilation that took place in the winter and thought this was because ranchers kept a closer eye on their cows in the winter... He said he enjoyed his volunteer research and had actually brought a whole cow into the lab to do an autopsy that included an analysis of urine, blood and tissue. He also scanned the animal for radiation and took bacteriological samples. Unfortunately, *all his reports disappeared from the lab*, he said, and nobody knows where they are. [my emphasis]
>
> "The deeper you get into it, the more mysterious it gets," [Spall] told me during a phone call in early 1995. What Spall didn't mention to Greenwood is that, on a whim, he had pulled the files out and left them

on his desk one afternoon in 1994. He went to lunch, and when he returned, the files had vanished! I had spoken with him about cattle mutilations, back during the so-called New Mexico Wave of 1993-1996 and Spall had related the mysterious disappearance of the 1978-1979 mutilation files from his desk. He sounded genuinely puzzled. "I have no idea why someone would have just taken them."

Pure Hemoglobin and BLT

On January 17, 1997, ranchers Jean and Bill Barton were out checking their cattle on their ranch near Red Bluff, California when they discovered their 2,000-pound Angus bull mutilated. The young bull was lying on a hillside about one half mile from the only dirt road into the area. The field can only be reached on foot or horseback. Field investigator Jean Bilodeaux was alerted of the case and went out to investigate:

> [The] Bull was lying on its right side, positioned along a north/south axis, with his head pointing north. His right foreleg was drawn way up, almost under his chest; his right hind leg was up underneath his body, and he was lying on his tail which was curved upward with the end of the tail protruding out over its rump. His back towards the rear end seemed curved under his body in a very unnatural position as if he might have been dropped from a height. The right shoulder appeared crushed by the rock underneath the animal and the grass around him was standing undisturbed with no stems broken. There were no obvious signs of a struggle as his front legs were lying against some small rocks which had not been dislodged.[31]

Bilodeaux obtained tissue, grass, soil and samples of the unusual hardened dark particles from the bull's testicles and the chest near the excision. The particles would be found to be "pure hemoglobin." The samples were sent to biophysicist W.C. Levengood (who operated the Pinelandia Biophysics Laboratory) who analyzed the unusual evidence and later told Linda Howe, who publicized the case on her popular earthfiles.com website:

> The particles were non-magnetic. They were hard, resinous black particles rather easily broken into fragments when crushed with forceps. The matrix color of these fragments was a deep red with a fine grain amorphous structure. There were no cellular composites whatsoever. There was a slow dissolution in water. It was not highly soluble. In the early stages of hydration, two to three hours, an occasional cluster of blue colored tissue was found in isolated patches on the slide. After 24 hours, the slide had dehydrated and there was an excellent example of

uninterrupted mud crack-type patterns formed around the edge of the slide…This has to be an extremely sophisticated process. And remember, the molecules are completely dehydrated, but they are not destroyed and not injured. They are still active hemoglobin with all the other components removed… Further, the hypothesis that everyone has had, or the assumption, that the blood is removed, I don't think it's removed at all. I think this sample gives us a very good clue that the blood is disintegrated, maybe to its very elemental material. If that is the case, the only thing that would be left to look at is the iron that is left over from the center of the hemoglobin molecule.

I think if someone would examine the arterial wall with an EDS (energy dispersive spectroscopy) to get some idea of the amount of iron on the arterial wall of one of these bovine excision sites and then get one from a slaughterhouse, from a normal animal, then you might find a much higher iron level in the veins and arteries than ordinarily. And another thing I think is interesting is that we've got this information from a number of sites now—that when people take a compass with them, they find that when they are right over the animal, they get a very strong deviation from the normal north position. Then a couple of days later, the magnetic abnormality disappears…

It is quite apparent from the black particles that probably a non-oxidizing, maybe even chemically reducing, atmosphere was present at whatever process was carried out to break the blood down and remove everything but the hemoglobin. In that case of total blood disintegration, in a possible non-oxygen atmosphere, the iron would end up in the reduced state, which would be in the magnetite form. If it is a high deposit in the arteries and blood cells, that could cause the deflection of a magnet…

Conversely, over time all the oxidizing compounds and liquids inside the animal could, in a matter of hours, oxidize the concentrated iron residue to the non-magnetic form of hematite. So, it would not be surprising if that change could explain the disappearance of the magnetic effect after a day or so.[32]

In July 2000 chemist Phyllis A. Budinger analyzed two sets of the anomalous particles from Red Bluff, California. She noted in her report to Levengood and Howe:

Infrared spectra were obtained from both samples [from the bull's testicles and side] as well as references of hemoglobin and whole bloods using the Harrick SplitPea cell attached to a Nicolet Avatar 360 spectrometer. The ATR crystal used was silicon. Microscope photographs were obtained from the Leica GZ6 stereomicroscope interfaced to a Kodak Digital Science MDS 120 camera. Additional SEM/EDX elemental information from the bull testicle sample was procured by Levengood and is included in this report for the purpose of consolidating all the analytical data in one place.

Results:

Infrared spectroscopy identifies both residue samples from the excised bull as bovine hemoglobin, a component of blood. Pertinent bands in the infrared spectra of the samples compare to those in a reference of pure bovine hemoglobin purchased from Sigma Aldrich. Additionally, the spectrum of the bull (chest) side residue shows absorption in the C-H stretching region between 2,800-3,000 cm-1. This absorption plus additional bands are enhanced in a difference spectrum generated between the bull testicle and side spectra. The difference spectrum suggests a long chain glyceryl type ester. Following are the spectra of the two excised bull residues and a reference of hemoglobin for comparison.

Conclusions:

Both residues are identified as bovine hemoglobin, a component of blood. Its presence suggests a processing of the whole blood has occurred at the excision site. Additionally, the chest area sample has a very small amount of possibly a long chain glyceryl ester.

The usual procedure for isolating hemoglobin from whole blood is rather complex. It involves separating red blood corpuscles from the lighter plasma components by centrifugation. The plasma is siphoned off and ether is added to the corpuscle paste, causing the cells to burst. Another centrifugation removes the ruptured cell envelopes and leaves a clear red solution of hemoglobin. (Merck Index, 12th Ed., S. Budabari, Ed., p. 794, # 4682, 1996)

It is unlikely that a procedure such as this would be done on site (in the pasture field). It is unknown how or why this occurred.[33]

We Were in the Same Pasture When it Happened!

On March 10, 1997 one of the most sensational mutilation reports ever filed was logged at the National Institute for Discovery Sciences (NIDS) offices in Las Vegas, Nevada. Terry Sherman, the owner of a ranch just south of Ft. Duchesne, Utah was understandably spooked when he called. He had endured several years witnessing a variety of unexplained occurrences that sounds like a virtual laundry list of the bizarre—oversized wolves and other crypto-creatures; large and small UFO-like objects; strange poltergeist activity; disembodied voices; large yellow portals opening up in the air above his ranch with ships floating through from what seemed another dimension—the list of unexplained phenomena he and his family experienced is beyond bewildering. But that cold March afternoon when he and his wife Gwen went out to check on their newborn calves was positively frightening. They had driven out to the pasture and checked on a calf and the momma cow. Driving another three or so hundred yards, they checked on a second mother-calf pair. It was the middle of the day and they saw and heard nothing unusual. Imagine their horror, fear and revulsion when they returned to the first calf 30 to 40 minutes later and found it horribly mutilated *while they had been in the same pasture within sight of where the mutilation took place!*

In their popular and controversial book *Hunt for the Skinwalker,* George Knapp and Colm Kelleher described the scene they observed after racing by private jet to the Sherman Ranch along with other NIDS scientists and a veterinarian that same afternoon:

> We were looking at a scene of horror… This was something truly bizarre. My immediate impression was that an enormous force had ripped the [calf] apart. One of the leg bones was lying ten feet away, having been yanked free of the knee joint. Even with a young calf, the brute force necessary to rip a femur off a knee joint and snap a tendon suggested something very powerful. Yet there was a fastidious delicacy to the way the mutilated calf had been carefully laid out on the grass with all four legs spread neatly away from the body. There was no smell. The inside of the animal looked pink and tender, very healthy and very clean, almost unnaturally clean. All of the internal organs were gone and the broken ribs jutted forlornly toward the sky. The head lay sideways, its lifeless eyes staring toward the western sun now low in the sky. We estimated that it was an 84-pound calf, at least 40-pounds of which were gone, if you counted the three liters of blood.
>
> And this was the most chilling part of the scene—the complete lack of blood. It was as if a giant vacuum cleaner had gone through, in and around the calf's carcass and sucked up every drop of its blood. We looked for even a speck of blood on the grass or on the animal's hide. Nothing. Not a drop.[34]

Interesting to note that results of the necropsy and postmortem testing were never released by NIDS. One has to wonder when all the data gathered by NIDS at the Sherman Ranch will be released. I'm not holding your breath.

Up to the late 1990s, Florida had escaped the attention of the mutilators. Incidents from the Deep South were reported over the years, but they were few and far between. This changed when the early 1990s northeastern Alabama wave unfolded. In late summer 1996 and continuing into the early months of 1997, Florida ranchers began reporting mutilations to authorities; these cases represent the first official mute wave in Florida. The mystery mutilators would return to Florida ten years later. Billy Cox related the following in an April 1997 *Florida Today* article:

> According to Jack Hill, investigator with the Department of Agriculture and Law Enforcement, as many as 20 dead cattle in Brevard, Seminole, Lake and St. Lucie counties can be linked by at least some of the following wounds: missing tongues, eyes, ears, anuses, udders and genitalia. Furthermore, a number of the wounds—some involving the extraction of organs through circular holes—reportedly show little or no evidence of bleeding.
>
> "We're not really sure what's going on," said Hill, who heads the state's task force. "We don't even know what the cattle are dying from. Only one necropsy has come back so far, and that's probably inadequate for what we need."
>
> The [Florida Cattleman's Association] FCA is offering a $1,000 reward for the arrest and conviction of the killers, and the April issue of The Florida Cattleman magazine warns ranchers not to handle mutilated cattle because "unknown persons have been poisoning (them)." Hill, however, says poisoning is only a theory. But he discloses few details for fear of jeopardizing the investigation.
>
> Palm Bay Police Lt. Buck DeCoteau isn't in on the information loop, but he has investigated animal deaths related to satanic or alternative religious activity. Perhaps, he surmises, the killings coincide with milestones on the Satanic Ritual calendar requiring blood sacrifice.
>
> "They're constantly killing chickens, goats and pigs," DeCoteau says. "But cattle in the middle of a pasture—that's new to me. Cattle are hard to handle. They're big and bulky and they can't be easily transported."
>
> At last count, in February, five Brevard cattle were being tentatively linked to the mutilations, but local sheriff's investigators will not comment on the record.[35]

Springtime in Wales also featured another round of mutilation reports according to investigator and policeman Tony Dodd:

> From Wales I have also received several reports of the dead bodies of sheep being found, with their thyroid glands cut out. In April 1997, 40 pigs mysteriously died in one night on a farm near the coast of England. Every one had a neat hole on the forehead, but there were no other obvious signs of injury. The vet who was called ordered their immediate burial, although the farmer was not told that he had an infectious disease problem. The animals were buried that same day.[36]

On November 10, 1997, a mutilated six-year-old cow was discovered dead, but still warm, just outside of Wiber, Nebraska. The rancher was sure this was a genuine mutilation, and he called his local veterinarian to conduct a postmortem examination. There was no apparent cause of death. The udder and lip were neatly excised with apparent precision. The farmer had seen her the day before alive, and she appeared normal and healthy. She had a four- to six-week-old calf that was missing. A veterinarian was called in to conduct an autopsy. He mentioned that he had a case exactly like this one eight years ago. Local officials speculated that "because it is hunting season, the cow may have been shot and then mutilated to make it look like 'satanists' to cover up." This is a highly unlikely-sounding scenario, plus the mutilated cow's calf was never found.

On November 29, 1997, at 11:15 p.m., four witnesses reported seeing a large multi-colored ball of light bobbing slowly over the northern part of the SLV, and several hours earlier, a slowly disintegrating meteor was spotted in the same area. The prior day, a heavy snow had blanketed the Valley, with the foothills of the Sangres receiving a three-foot pasting.

Seven hours later, on early Sunday morning, a dense fog descended over the center of the Valley. At around 5:36 a.m., dogs began barking outside of a ranch house northwest of Hooper, right in the center of the northern SLV.

The following afternoon, a still-warm "mutilated" calf was discovered about five hundred yards from the house, lying in a pristine, untouched snow-covered field. (figure 16) The calf's right-side mandible had been exposed in an arc that went up over the eye socket. The rear end had been cored out in a ten-inch diameter circle, and the coring extended 18 inches into the animal's rear end. Magpies and crows showed an interest, but no coyote or other scavenger tracks were noted around the carcass. The Saguache County sheriff was called, and I visited the site to help investigate this latest peculiar animal death. I obtained video and still footage, three sets of tissue samples and sent the samples off to three different veterinarian pathology labs for testing. (figure 17) Curiously, all three labs disagreed on what the cutting agent was.[37]

Dr. John Altshuler was convinced that high heat had been the cutting agent on the Hooper calf. I wasn't so sure. I called Tom Adams and mentioned the varying test results and he said, "That doesn't surprise me at all." (figure18)

In February 1998, a cow was found dead and mutilated on the George Giersch farm near Dawson Creek, British Columbia, Canada. The cow was discovered "lying in a pool of blood with its tongue missing, half its face stripped to the bone and a deep slash to its chest." Remote Dawson Creek is located in northern British Columbia about 733 miles northeast of Vancouver. Giersch told reporters, "I've never seen anything quite like this." The jaw cut "was too precise to be caused by a predator." No tracks were found in the surrounding snow.

A local investigator suggested to Giersch that he leave the cow's carcass in place for a few days to see what would happen. "No animal came near until the fifth day, when birds began to land on it. That's odd. It's a large coyote community here," Giersch noted.

According to the *Ottawa Sun*, "RCMP and Alberta officials have concluded that cattle are dying natural deaths and becoming food for predators... But Fern Belzil, a farmer in the St. Paul area of northern Alberta and a part-time mutilation investigator, wrote that most of the 50 cattle killings reported by Alberta and Saskatchewan farmers in the past three years weren't done by animals."

Last June (1997) Laura Afdahi found a dead Charolais cow on her farm in the Pincher Creek area of southern Alberta. "The cow's teeth were missing, as were its sex organs and teats." 'I can't tell you how sick I felt when I looked at it,' Afdahi said, adding that the coyotes and magpies had no interest in feeding on the carcass." Pincher Creek is just east of the Alberta/British Columbia provincial border, and located 655 miles east of Vancouver.[38]

Also reported in February 1998 was the discovery of 20 dead dolphins, over a three-week period, on the Languedoc-Roussillon beaches in France, near the Spanish border:

They all had a six-inch wound, in exactly the same place on their throat, cut with a precision, which ruled out a natural predator, or disease. There was no sign of them having been entangled in nets, so accidental death from encountering a trawler, or death at the hands of fishermen, was also ruled out. One theory is that they had been trained by the US Navy to carry out surveillance, and when they outlived their usefulness their signal collars were exploded by radio control.[39]

On Sunday, May 3, 1998 a cow was found dead and mutilated in a remote mountain pasture 10 miles southeast of Questa, New Mexico.

[The cow] which had been dead for about a day... was missing its eye and its tongue and suffered massive hemorrhaging. John Paternoster, District Attorney for Taos, NM, said authorities are investigating the case as a cattle mutilation—the latest in a series of cases of unexplained animal deaths that have occurred in New Mexico over the past 25 years. "Samples of the cow's tissue, blood and organs will be analyzed at an Albuquerque laboratory", Paternoster told reporters "No apparent cause of death was immediately visible... I'm not certain what we're looking for, but we have since the beginning been taking these deaths seriously."

A team of law enforcement officers visited the crime scene in the Moreno Valley—east of Taos—along with former New Mexico State patrolman Gabe Valdez, an agent for the National Institute for Discovery Sciences, a privately-funded Las Vegas, Nevada organization that investigates paranormal phenomena.[40]

The UK Needs More Investigators and Researchers

I must remind you that this appears to be a global phenomenon. All through the nineties, mutilation reports were being filed by UK farmers. I would say that an entire book (or more) could be written covering mutilation cases in Great Britain alone.

Besides Tony Dodd, there are a number of unsung UK researchers who have been investigating unexplained animal death cases for over the past 30 years who are little-known in the U.S. Among them are David Cayton, veterinarian pathologist Tony Freeman, Philip Hoyle and his team of researchers at the Animal Field Pathology Unit and relative newcomer Richard D. Hall. All have unsuccessfully campaigned to get UK government disclosure on what they know concerning the many cases of unexplained livestock deaths.

Richard Hall made the following observations at the 2010 "The Wake Up Call" Conference concerning official UK government run-around that private investigators face concerning the subject of animal and human mutilation cases:

"The only actual statement from the government that we know of, ever, on this subject was in 1998. BBC Manchester was doing a piece on it, so [they] got in touch with the government [who] obviously thought 'we've got to say something if the BBC [is] involved.' All they said was":

> The series of animal mutilations has been very distressing for the farmers involved and the majority of these incidents have been reported to the police as very serious offences and are being dealt with at the present. As a result, it is not for the Ministry of Agriculture, Fisheries and Food to pass comment on these incidents, as they are being handled by the relevant authorities.[41]

After that point in time there has been both a media blackout and a government blackout—no one has ever spoken about it publicly, but the incidents have continued from the 90s onward until now—they're still happening now.

> [Hall's conclusions are that the animals] …are being used as incubators of anti-bodies or other biological agents…What I think is happening is: you've got an animal that you want to grow something inside. They inject the animal with whatever agent it is—a virus, whatever—they then tag that animal because at some point in the future they need to find that

animal after it's grown the relevant antibodies. So they tag it in the jaw with an implant, or in the ear; they then leave the [animal] three months, six months. Later on, they use that tracking device to find that animal. They then kill the animal, cut the tongue [out] and then use the tissue of the tongue to test to see if it's got what they want... they test the tongue, they say yes, it's got what we want; they examine the blood, take the organs that they want. And the last thing they do before they leave is strip the jaw off to remove the implant, or [remove] the ear, (depending whether the implant is in the jaw or the ear, they don't want to leave any evidence of this advanced tracking device). And then they just leave the carcass there because they know no one will figure it out...It is just a theory, I'm not saying that this is what's definitely happening, I'm saying it kind of explains the evidence.[42]

He then showed a map of the UK that he feels indicates the areas of highest activity, or incidence of mutilation reports, in the UK. North in Oswestry, southwest to Rhayader, east to Radner Forest (west of Shrewsbury), east to Leominster, south to Brecon Beacons (Tony Dodd human mute site) and way west to St. Brides Bay where many reports of USO (Unidentified Submerged Object) activity have been generated.

In a June 1999 issue of George Filer's *Filer's Files,* it was noted that a South Dakota mutilation report had been forwarded to Nancy Talbot from BLT Research.

[The] 1,800-pound bull was found lying impaled on a barbed-wire fence and mutilated a month ago. Ten days later, a neighbor located only half a mile away found [another] mutilated cow. They also reported seeing "columns, or shafts, of light" coming down from above. There was no discernible source where the light could be emanating. Ted Phillips reports that Missouri residents were also seeing "puddles" of light, which illuminated various areas of their fields. However, they had not seen a column or shaft of light coming down to the 'puddle' of light. Again there was no obvious source of the illumination. I'm getting weird stories from all over the world including a lot of crop circle activity in Canada. I phone people all over the world and never mention UFOs, but after collecting some facts they volunteer they are seeing them.[43]

They've Abducted an Elk?

The following preliminary summary of their findings to date was submitted jointly by UFO researchers Peter Davenport and Robert Fairfax. The following appeared in BJ Booth's "UFO Casebook:"

Location—Cascade Mountains, Near Mt. St. Helens, Washington, United States.

On Monday, March 01, 1999, the National UFO Reporting Center (NUFORC) received a call over its telephone Hotline from an individual who identified himself as an employee in the forestry industry in Washington State. The individual left a message, in which he reported that a team of forestry workers allegedly had been witness to an incident on Thursday, February 25, 1999, during which time an elk was lifted off the ground and carried away by a very peculiar, disc-shaped object.

Peter B. Davenport, Director of NUFORC [National UFO Reporting Center], contacted several of the individuals whose names and telephone numbers had been provided by the first contact. Based on those telephone conversations, he elected to initiate a preliminary investigation of the incident. Because NUFORC traditionally does not serve as an investigative body, Mr. Davenport contacted Mr. Robert A. Fairfax, Director of Investigations for the Washington State Chapter of the Mutual UFO Network, which does conduct investigations of alleged UFO sightings.

Davenport and Fairfax traveled to the location of the alleged incident, and jointly have been conducting an investigation of this elk abduction case since Friday, March 5, 1999. Their investigation to date has included a trip to the site of the incident, an interview of three of the alleged fourteen witnesses to the actual abduction, and several conversations with individuals who work with the eyewitnesses.

In addition, the investigators inspected the carcass of an adult elk, a pregnant cow, which was found dead beside a logging road on March 1st by other forestry employees within a few miles of the principal event. The investigation and collection of facts surrounding the case will continue.

Incident Summary:

On Thursday, February 25, 1999, at just a few minutes before noon, three forestry workers, who were planting seedling trees in the mountains of Washington State, witnessed a small, disc-shaped object slowly drift over a nearby ridge to their south, and descend into the valley to the north of their position. The object descended silently with what seemed to the witnesses a purposeful manner, exhibiting a slight "wobble" to its flight. The three workers at first thought the object was some kind of parachute that was drifting and descending, but they quickly realized that their initial impression was not correct. Hence, they shouted to their eleven co-workers nearby, who were working on the north-facing hillside, and all fourteen members of the work crew watched the object for an estimated 3-5 minutes.

Within seconds of their first observation of the object, the witnesses became aware that the object was traveling generally in the direction of a herd of elk that they had been watching all morning. They continued to watch as the object proceeded toward the herd until it succeeded in getting quite close to the animals. The animals apparently remained unaware of the object's presence until it was within a very short distance of the herd.

Suddenly, the animals bolted, most of them running up the slope to their east. However, one adult animal was seen by the witnesses to separate itself from the herd and run or trot to generally to the north, perhaps along a logging road.

The witnesses report that at this point, the object quickly moved directly above the lone elk and seemed to lift it off the ground, although no visible means of support of the animal was evident to the observers. The witnesses added that shortly after lifting the elk off the ground, the object seemed to begin to "wobble" to a more pronounced degree than it had exhibited earlier. In addition, as the object appeared to increase its altitude, the elk, which was suspended upright below the disc, rotated slowly beneath it and appeared to be getting closer to the ventral surface of the disc. They also commented that the object seemed to increase in size slightly after it had picked up the animal. With the elk suspended below it, the object began to ascend slowly up a clear-cut slope to the east. However, the witnesses watched it apparently brush the tops of nearby trees to the east, at which point it reversed its course and proceeded to the west. It executed a 360-degree turn to the left and may have gained some slight altitude in the process, the witnesses thought.

After the object had completed its turn and was once again proceeding in a generally easterly direction, it began ascending very quickly at what seemed to the witnesses to be a rather steep angle. It continued to ascend, and simply disappeared from sight of the witnesses.

The witnesses stated that once the object had started to ascend and had climbed to an altitude above their vantage point, they no longer could see the animal suspended below the craft. Their presumption was that the animal had somehow been taken into the craft, although the witnesses could discern no "door," or any kind of aperture through which the animal might have been conveyed into the craft.

The witnesses also stated that following the incident, the herd of elk remained in the same general area, although remained more closely huddled to one another than had been the case earlier in the morning. The workers added that they, too, had remained closer to one another until their departure from the area at the end of the workday. [44]

Cats, Bulls, Cows and Ohio Joins the Fray

On June 29, 1999 north of Columbus, Ohio in the Richwood area, rare Ohio mutilations had occurred on the Tom Issler farm. In all, four cows and one goat had been targeted and mutilated over the past 14 months "The five animals all had holes punctured in their uterus. The goat also had both eyes removed." Issler recalled that the first case occurred in October 1997 and the most recent attack had been on June 12th. Local veterinarian Louis Levan, DVM, examined the first cow.

Later in 1999, Linda Howe was sent a copy of *The Independent* (Sunday, August 1, 1999 edition) which had a three-page article entitled, "The Cat Flap" by Richard Askwith. The article, sent by UK mutilation David Cayton, included additional headlines from other papers: "Serial Cat Killer Cuts Up 100 Pets" (*The Mirror*) and "Ritualistic killers stalk family pets" (*The Sunday Telegraph*).[45]

The following report was filed by South Dakota MUFON investigators:

> On September 16, 1999, a farmer reported a suspicious cattle death to the Hutchinson County Sheriff. He had found one of his bulls dead in the pasture. The bull was lying on its back on top of the fence, its reproductive organs removed. The wounds were clean and did not appear to have been caused by predators. There was no blood, no sign of a struggle and no obvious cause of death.
>
> After examination, the animal was left to lie in the pasture. Even after several days of 90-degree weather, decomposition was minimal and the carcass was untouched by flies and scavengers.
>
> That same night another man was driving home and spotted lights in a field near the farmer's field. He pulled into a road (an access road for tractors and such) and drove toward the lights to investigate. He was chased out of the field by the lights and drove to a friend's house who also saw the lights. There is a discrepancy here—a coworker of my husband insists that Fred told her that the lights came from above but our neighbor says they were ground-based spotlights.
>
> On 8-23-99, Tuesday, another farmer (of Menno) also reported a suspicious cattle death to the sheriff. His was a heifer, found dead with the reproductive organs removed. I don't have any other details about that one.
>
> Farmer #1 lives about two miles from us—Farmer #2, about three fourths of a mile. Most of the farmers around us have cattle but the farms are small and can be easily protected from coyotes by a good dog—and everyone has dogs. There is a sort of coyote "highway" that follows a natural drainage from the highway to our place and farther northwest. We've seen coyotes traveling that way several times and that's were the hunters find them in the fall.
>
> It has been unseasonably hot and dry for the last six weeks; water

holes are dry and small animal populations seem to be down (rabbits, coons and such). It is possible that coyotes are starting to raid pastures out of necessity for food and water. Although how a coyote or a pack of coyotes could drop a bull on top of a fence is beyond me.[46]

They've Gone to the Dogs

Much to her credit, Linda Howe has relentlessly documented claims of outbreaks of unexplained pet deaths as well as the better-known livestock variety. Her earth-files.com website is the go-to clearinghouse for all unexplained animal death. This next example of inexplicable pet deaths was reported in Woodleak, North Carolina:

> Eight dogs died and [a] ninth were attacked... between May 9th and May 27, 1999. All eight of the dead dogs had quarter-inch wide puncture wounds in their neck, back and chest. The Rowan County Animal Control Center did not call for a necropsy by a veterinarian until the eighth dog was found dead early on the morning of May 24th.[47]

Linda has also reported on other field investigator's cases (including many of mine) over the 30-plus years she has been actively pursuing the mysterious animal surgeons. An unsung hero who investigated reports up in Canada, Fernand Belzil, submitted the following cases to Howe. By the end of the 1990s, Fernand had investigated about 40 unusual cattle deaths reported in Alberta and other western Canadian Provinces. According to Howe's earthfiles.com:

> One [mutilation] on June 6, 1999 was in Speers, Saskatchewan east of North Battleford on the Wendy and Trent Foster ranch. They phoned me [Belzil] and I went out there right away the next day. I'm about 225 miles from there. This was a six-year-old cow. She had died close to three days before I got there, so again, I couldn't do the necropsy. But I made a lot of soil and grass samplings for W. C. Levengood, the bio-physicist in Michigan.
>
> [Howe] called and spoke with Sergeant Investigator Altemueller about the most recent heifer calf found at the Filippini's Badger Ranch on June 14, 1999. The calf was last seen alive around 6:30 PM the evening before by the owners whose family [has] ranched in Battle Mountain since the 1940s...[48]
>
> Another Alberta case [occurred] on July 6th, 1999... only a few miles east of St. Paul and about ten miles from Belzil's spread on the Ken Cooknel farm. This was a Hereford Simmental cross herd bull. When the farmer got into the field to check the cattle that morning, the cattle were very excited. And this was a very quiet herd, very docile. And that morning, they were very frustrated. He thought it was unusual, so they

figured something was going on. They finally found the bull in the bush among willows and poplar trees. The rancher and his son estimated that the bull had died about 24 hours before they found him. And then they called [Belzil] and [he] went over the same afternoon and took some soil and grass samples.[49]

The last case that Belzil investigated in 1999 was the mutilation of a 1,700-pound herd bull found on October 29th in Spedden, Alberta—located a few miles west of St. Paul.[50]

Thus ended the decade of the nineties. By this time, the average person with a casual interest in so-called paranormal, or ufological, phenomena was probably unaware that the "cattle mutilation" phenomenon was alive and well—or should I say dead—out on the range. As we have seen, cases continued to be reported around the west however word of these cases seldom made it out of the locale where the reports were filed. Researchers remained absolutely flummoxed. Some of them simply gave up.

Old hands at the mute game continued to fall by the wayside. The last time I saw Tom Adams was in December 1999. He and Gary Massey were visiting David Perkins in Santa Fe, and I remember bringing a case of Lone Star beer down from Colorado to pay off my bet with Gary. I bet him that by 2000 someone (someone, anyone) would be charged with perpetrating a cattle mutilation. I was dead wrong. Gary and I had made our bet in June 1993—the very day I first met David, Tom and Gary up at the Libré community's 25th anniversary bash. After that December 1999 day in Santa Fe, David and I would never see Tom again. He disappeared after Y2K into the æthers of Texas never to be heard from again by anyone in the mute research community! To this day, no one seems to know where he is or what he has been up to for the past 13-plus years. Tragically, Gary blew his brains out while burning his house down around himself a couple of years ago. I wonder what happened to all of Gary and Tom's files. A warning to you aspiring mutologists: "mute investigation" is not a user-friendly pursuit. It's sad to note: many are called, few are chosen and most eventually burn out.

Finding that case of Lone Star beer to pay off the bet was hard—Colorado liquor stores do not carry Texas beer... OK, so I lost the bet. If I knew in '93 what I wouldn't know in 2013, I would never have bet on any aspect of the unexplained livestock death phenomenon. Or bet on when someone will turn their back on this tricksterish subject and walk away forever!

The first couple of years into the 2000s would quickly remind the remaining mute investigators that this is a *global* phenomenon and North America is not alone when it comes to reports of unexplained livestock deaths. A huge, still ongoing wave of mutilation reports continues to blister South America—mainly Argentina, but also Brazil, Uruguay and elsewhere. The South American wave started soon after the start of the millennium and the discovery of "hoof-and-mouth disease in South American cattle herds. Foot-and-mouth indeed....

Chapter Eight: Sources and References

1. Dodd, Tony, *Alien Investigator,* 1999, Headline, London, UK
2. *ibid*
3. *Fortean Times,* July 1992; Jan-Ove Sundberg; Tony Dodd
4. Dodd, Tony, *Alien Investigator,* 1999, Headline, London, UK
5. *ibid*
6. *ibid*
7. Press Release, Ted Oliphant/Fyffe, Alabama Police Department
8. *ibid*
9. Linda M. Howe/earthfiles.com
10. O'Brien, Christopher, *The Mysterious Valley*, St Martins Press, New York, New York 1996
11. *ibid*
12. *ibid*
13. *ibid*
14. Dodd, Tony, *Alien Investigator,* 1999, Headline, London, UK
15. O'Brien, Christopher, *The Mysterious Valley*, St Martins Press, New York, New York 1996
16. *ibid*
17. *ibid*
18. David Perkins Interview with Larry Gardea
19. Linda Howe; David Perkins
20. *ibid*
21. Dodd, Tony, *Alien Investigator,* 1999, Headline, London, UK
22. *ibid*
23. *Strange Universe,* Fox, *Enter the Valley*/O'Brien
24. Interview w/ Rio Grande County undersheriff Brian Norton
25. O'Brien, Christopher, *Enter the Valley*, St Martins Press, New York, New York 1999
26. *ibid*; David Perkins
27. *ibid*; *Denver Post*
28. O'Brien, Christopher *Enter the Valley*, St Martins Press, New York, New York 1999
29. *ibid*; Art Troil
30. *ibid*; Dale Spall; David Perkins; Phaedra Greenwood
31. Linda M. Howe/earthfiles.com
32. *ibid;* WC Levengood/BLT Research
33. *ibid;* Phyllis Budinger
34. Knapp, George & Kelleher, Colm, *Hunt for the Skinwalker,* Paraview, New York, New York 2005
35. *Florida Today,* "A Sci-Fi Whodunnit With Many Suspects," Billy Cox, April 19, 1997
36. Dodd, Tony, *Alien Investigator,* 1999, Headline, London, UK
37. O'Brien, Christopher *Enter the Valley*, St Martins Press, New York, New York 1999
38. *Ottawa Sun*, 3-15-98; Dr. Diane Landry; *UFO Roundup*
39. Dodd, Tony, *Alien Investigator,* 1999, Headline, London, UK
40. *Albuquerque Journal*, 5-4-98; Bruce-Knapp/UFO Updates; *UFO Roundup Vol. 3, #19*
41. Transcript of a statement from MAFF RE: Animal Mutilations, faxed to BBC Manchester TV December 11, 1998
42. From the Press Office: Stuart Dobbs
43. Nancy Talbott; *Filers Files*

44. UFO Casebook; National UFO Reporting Service; MUFON
45. Linda M. Howe/earthfiles.com
46. South Dakota MUFON
47. Linda M. Howe/earthfiles.com
48. Linda Howe; NUFORC; Washington State MUFON; UFO Casebook
49. Fern Belzil; Linda M. Howe/earthfiles.com
50. *ibid*

Figure 1
UK Police officer/paranormal investigator Tony Dodd. (credit: shelf3d.com)

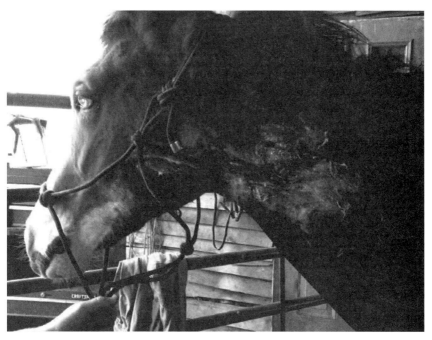

Figure 2
Horse slashing damage. (credit: Philip Hoyle/APFU)

Figure 3
Seal mutilation. (credit: dailymail.co.uk)

Figure 4
SLV's Valley Courier logo. (credit: alamosanews.com)

Figure 5
Hematologist/pathologist Dr. John Altshuler. (credit: TMV Archives)

Figure 6
Mutilated steer found in a locked potato barn. (credit: Eagle Valley Enterprise)

Figure 7
Vigil bull mutilation. Chama Canyon, Colorado. (credit: TMV Archive)

417

Figure 8
Eagle Nest, New Mexico rancher Eli Hronich. (credit: TMV Archive)

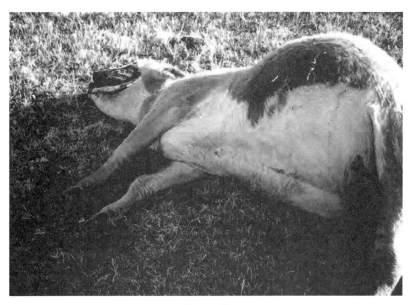

Figure 9
Harr mutilation. Silent chopper was seen over the house the night before.
(credit: John Harr; TMV Archive)

Figure 10
l to r, Rancher John Harr being interviewed by *Jane's Defence Weekly's* Nick Cook.
(credit: TMV Archive)

Figure 11
David Perkins & Christopher O'Brien. (credit: TMV archive)

Figure 12
Rio Grande County Sheriff Brian Norton. (credit: pueblochieftain.com)

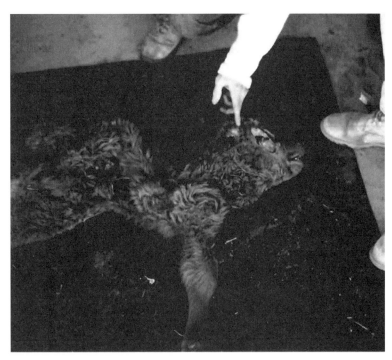

Figure 13
Del Norte, Colorado calf mutilation. (credit: Ed Burke; TMV Archive)

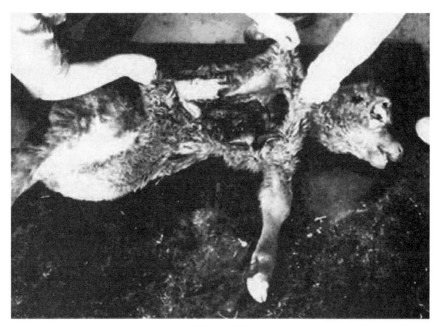

Figure 14
Del Norte calf mute. My strangest case. (credit: Ed Burke; TMV Archive)

Figure 15
Laffing Buddha—my bandmates somehow put up with my investigative work.
(credit: Gary Atencio;TMV Archive)

Figure 16
Hooper case—rare winter mutilation. Weird blue lights seen the night before.
(credit: TMV Archive)

Figure 17
Hooper case found in a pristine snow covered pasture. (credit: TMV Archive)

Figure 18
l to r Christopher O'Brien, John Alshuler and Tom Adams.
at "Crestone II" conference, 1993

Chapter 9
The 2000s

Y2K passed into history with barely a whisper on the mutilation front. Western culture appeared to be preoccupied with fears of computer system failure on a mass scale as the dot-com revolution drove Internet startups into the stratosphere. It was a Silicon Valley version of the Wild West and yet, out on the western plains, there were few reports worth noting on the mute front. The initial reports of the year uncharacteristically began that spring in the Pacific Northwest.

Millican Valley is a remote area in central Oregon located about 25 miles southeast of Bend. The terrain is rugged and for the most part inaccessible to vehicles. The region is mostly covered in high desert plant life—sagebrush and juniper pine—and cattle are forced to forage far and wide to find what little grass is available.

On March 18, 2000, Kimball Lewis, a Deschutes County Sheriff Deputy, received a report from a local rancher who had discovered four dead, *skinned* calves on the free-range land on which they had been foraging. The calves were found in two groups about a quarter mile from one another, and to compound the mystery, the following day, *eight additional calves were discovered dead and four of these had also been "skinned the same way."* This is a strange case that didn't make sense to the rancher or to investigators; you could say these were anomalous anomalies.

Puzzling over the lack of tracks and blood on the ground, Kimball Lewis

decided to call in a veterinarian to do necropsies to see what the calves looked like [on the] inside. Lewis has worked sixteen years on animal abuse cases, first in Colorado. Then in 1996, Lewis was appointed by Oregon's governor to be one of the state's four commissioned agents specializing in large animal abuse and neglect. But he had never seen anything before like the skinned calves.

Only one year ago in March 1999, fourteen other dead calves and a pig with its legs cut off had been found only a couple of miles from this new batch of dead calves...[1]

Horse slashing cases continued to be reported but this time the "sexual deviates" (as they were called in a *Calgary Herald* article) targeted horses in the Calgary, Alberta region. The first report occurred in late 1999 and then Guy Elford made two additional horse-slashing reports in the fall of 2000. RCMP officials were called in to investigate two more Calgary cases that occurred the night of April 9th 2001. Linda Howe noted on her earthfiles website:

> Over the past 20 years, there have been at least a dozen similar equine attacks in the Spy Hill [area] of Calgary. Yet, despite the suspicions that a sexual predator is on the loose no person has ever been arrested and arraigned on a horse slashing charge.
>
> Hundreds of other horse slashings and deaths have been reported in Europe since the early 1990s. In Sweden more than 200 horses and cattle had been slashed by 1992. No arrests were made. Britain's Hampshire and Buckinghamshire Counties in 1992 suffered attacks on thirty horses, including ones whose "genitals had been shocked with electricity. Other stallions and geldings have been rectally assaulted, flogged and stabbed."[2]

These sick horse-slashing cases are more prevalent than one would think. As we have seen, some person (or group) in western Washington State was responsible for over a dozen cases in the late '70s and early '80s in and around Pierce County and reports have ebbed and flowed in the UK for decades. And now the slashers continued their unholy escapades in the 2000s.

Spring 2001 brought an unwelcome surprise for Missouri farmer James Roy. On June 5th he discovered a mutilated Charolais bull calf on his ranch near Dadeville. He described the calf's condition to Linda Howe:

> "I could see how he had been mutilated. His testicles had been cut out and his rear end had been cut out and his tongue was half gone (deep in the throat) and his ear was gone and one eye was plucked out. And his penis was gone. No blood. There wasn't a drop of blood nowhere around him."[3]

Sure sounds familiar. If you haven't noticed by now, this language is interchangeable with hundreds of other quotes over the past 50 years (and throughout this book). The above quote sounds like a sports interview with a baseball player who has learned all the well-worn clichés. In my mind, this cannot be by accident. There is something going on *culturally* regardless of who is culpable.

As we have seen, the vast majority of cattle that are reported mutilated are most often also reported deceased, and there is most often no apparent cause of death. The Swedish *cattle slasher* cases are an anomaly. Horse slasher cases often feature horses that survive, but not so with cattle; they are most often found dead with extreme prejudice—missing various parts.

The following report is a rare example of a calf that apparently survived a mutilation attack. And, as a result of this anomaly, scientific analysis was brought to bear on the case. After being alerted in a timely manner, two National Institute for Discovery Sciences (NIDS) field investigators and a veterinarian were dispatched to ascertain the injuries, and establish the cause of disfigurement:

> On May 20, 2000 NIDS was alerted to a two-year old Charolais cow that had been mutilated near Cuba, New Mexico, three days previously but the animal had survived. The animal was recovering at a nearby veterinary clinic. On May 22, 2000 the NIDS veterinarian plus two NIDS investigators arrived to examine it. The animal's left ear had been removed completely, its right ear was substantially removed and the animal's lips appeared to have been injured or degraded. A search for needle marks was negative.
>
> Both veterinarians concurred that there was no evidence whatsoever that the animal had been attacked by predators or scavengers. Rather, they concurred that a sharp instrument had likely been used to remove the ears. Multiple blood samples, a small tissue biopsy and fecal samples were taken and analyzed.[4]

The idea behind NIDS back in the mid 1990s was (potentially) a groundbreaking step forward in the right direction toward the discovery of truth. Robert Bigelow is a very rich man who was willing to put up the money it takes to conduct peer-reviewable science. What a concept! It should be obvious by now that the government is absolutely not interested in becoming involved *publicly* in a way that could be taken as "official" acknowledgment of unusual livestock death reports. We, the people, had our chance with Condon, Flickinger and Rommel—tough luck, folks, nothing to see here. We had to find private sources of funding. Well, perhaps Robert Bigelow gave it his best shot, perhaps he didn't, but regardless—he is sitting on an impressive pile of data.

My personal process has ebbed and flowed over the past 20 years and funding for my investigative efforts has relied on my so-called disposable income. I happened to be in the right place at the right time and innocently put a few hypotheticals in the ear of Laurance Rockefeller, and he financially supported my efforts for a number of years. But it really takes the deep pockets of a well-heeled, up-to-speed, connected, willing capitalist to create a structure within which scientific work can be properly conducted without fettered expectation and with transparency. Unfortunately, Mr. Bigelow pulled the plug on NIDS in 2005; I would like to acknowledge whatever altruistic inclinations he may have had in sponsoring the work of NIDS. The published reports related to cattle mutilations and other phenomena are no longer available for download, but they are highly important, in my estimation. If you dig hard enough, many of them have survived on other websites as cached versions, and I recommend you study every one of them. You will see in them the potential for a proper study and presentation of fieldwork and analysis in their papers. Thank you Mr. Bigelow and the NIDS team for all your efforts in this regard.

In a book such as this, you can barely scratch the surface of such an extremely complex and challenging sociological subject. But what separates the 'mutes' mystery from other subjects is its decidedly visceral nature. One thing that must be stressed is that this mystery is *grounded in biology*. This is an important, but mostly overlooked, analysis made by David Perkins years ago. Later in the unraveling process in our next book, David and I plan to tackle this subject (and other hidden elements) ducking behind the mystery.

As we push into the middle of the second decade of the 21st century, this protoscientific field of "unexplained animal death" research requires a new crop of courageous, up-to-speed volunteers ready to help us tote the "rock" down the field. It also requires Bigelow-level cash for all the lab work, logistics, gear, etc., and the time needed from veterinarian and other scientific professionals to perform the necessary work it will take to continue the complex process of unraveling this mystery.

The Cases Continue (They Never Went Away)

As noted above, the dawn of the new millennium passed through with barely a whisper on the 'mute' front. The SLV was thankfully serene, New Mexico appeared to be relieved and other areas around the country seemed quiet. Few reports were logged in North America during 2000.

Spring 2001: Burleson County—north of Houston, Texas. Officials claimed to have experienced mutilations every spring (since the 1980s) and by 2000 law enforcement and the ranching community were stumped. Every year around Easter and sometimes Halloween a rancher or two would invariably report a mutilation. This had been rumored to be going on like clockwork since 1994. As with a vast majority of these types of reports over the years, no crime scene evidence was left behind by the mutilators, and ranchers—like the cops—were unable to explain away these deaths as mundane. Word of these cases did not extend beyond the regional community. In a July 2001 article, the Burleson County sheriff was quoted by the *Bryan-College Station Eagle* saying: "It is a mystery to me." The *Houston Chronicle* in 2001 also covered these cases that appeared to be targeting "prize bulls."

The prize bulls of Burleson County are dying. The troubling questions are how and, more importantly, why. Some ranchers talk of a cult that drains the blood of the animals for use in satanic rituals. The sheriff believes most of the animals are dying of natural causes but admits he is perplexed by some of the circumstances.

An investigator for a cattlemen's association chalks some of the deaths up to thieves stealing body parts, rather than meat. Whatever the cause, cattle have been turning up dead under what ranchers consider "mysterious" circumstances at almost predictable intervals— once or twice a year, around the time of Halloween or a religious holiday, such as Easter—for nearly a decade.

"I don't know what it is," said Johnny Lyon, who lost a valuable Charolais bull last Easter. "It could be a prankster, but if it is the other (a cult) it could be pretty dangerous."

These kinds of stories have been told in cattle country for as long as cattle have been dying. Sometimes the stories grow outlandish. Rarely is there evidence to back them up. Nevertheless, ranchers in Burleson County believe there is something more than storytelling going on there. When Lyon found his bull at the rear of a 300-acre pasture, its abdomen had been split open and its genitals removed. He said that has been a consistent pattern in previous incidents.

Another rancher, whose family has lost several head of cattle in recent years, is so convinced that a cult is behind the deaths that he would only speak anonymously. There were no signs—claw or teeth marks—to suggest that his cow had been killed by a coyote or other predator and "there was not a drop of blood on the body or the ground," the rancher said.

Not all cattle deaths arouse suspicion. In some cases, the cause is obvious. Lyon recently found an angus cow that died after breaking a leg. "I didn't report that one," he said.

Those in the mysterious category, however, share similarities. Like Lyon's Charolais bull, the cause of death was not apparent; body organs and, sometimes, tongues were removed while the valuable meat was untouched. In most cases, the genitals were removed. And, Lyon said, it appeared in each case that the blood had been drained from the bodies.

"The buzzards don't even go up to them," he said. Scavenger birds, he said, do not feed on bloodless carcasses.

429

Burleson, a hilly and wooded county about 75 miles northwest of Houston, is home to several small ranches where cattle often graze in thickets away from highways or other public vantage points. Often, a carcass is not immediately discovered, which has made investigation difficult.

"I don't think it has anything to do with a cult," said Sheriff Thomas Gene Barber. "Some are natural deaths. But, some are very unusual… the removal of the organs. You wonder if any animal could do that."

He said it is also "strange" that most of the cattle whose deaths seemed unusual "were the best animals they had," not the weakest or sickest.

In the past 10 years, Barber said, the "unusual" deaths have occurred about once a year, sometimes twice, and in one year—1994—there were four clustered near Halloween…[5]

As we saw earlier, Cascade County, Montana was particularly hard hit in the mid to late '70s, but cases continued to be reported all through the '80s and '90s and for two months between June and August 2001 seven additional reports were filed with the authorities. Most of these reports centered around the Dupuyer, Conrad and Fort Shaw area and two ranchers, Don Reishus and Karl Rappold recalled that these cases were eerily similar to cases in the area 25 years before. Rappold told Linda Howe that he had discovered his huge, five-year-old, 2,000-pound bull alive but missing its tail about "six inches from the base of the spine." He observed that the cut was smooth "like you would take a circular saw through it, but [there] was no blood, no fluid of any kind… completely dry."[6]

The end of August and beginning of September 2001 found the mutes continuing in Conrad. Rancher Gerald Miller reported a mute on August 31st and then Jim Vandenbos reported a case on September 24th that featured an interesting twist. Deputy Sheriff Dan Campbell told Linda Howe:

> [I]t looked like the hide had been burned pretty severely on it. The cow was laying in a little grassy area that was like too rocky to plow around out in a grain field. But it was laying on the only grass. The hair was all gone on quite a bit of the carcass. The face was skinned out. Same as the others as far as how much was cut on… it just looks like the hide, all the hair has been burned off or scraped off. It gives the appearance from the jaw, the hide is gone from the face and then you get to the neck and brisket, there's no hair on it. I mean, it's down to the bare hide itself… it looked barbecued, like it caught on fire.[7]

Let's Support Public Sector Science

Three additional reports were filed from the Conrad area in late October. The rancher noted that one of the apparent mutilations attracted scavengers after the animal had been discovered, but the other one remained untouched. A third "classic" case was reported on the Lettenga ranch and NIDS was notified:

> Ranchers in Dupuyer and Fort Shaw have reported four cattle deaths in which portions of the animals' faces were cut or peeled off and eyeballs and genitals were removed. The animals had not been shot, and investigators say whoever is responsible left few clues behind
>
> Dan Campbell, a deputy with the Pondera County Sheriff's Department, believes humans are responsible, but their motives remain unclear. "I don't believe in little green men," he said. "I think 500 people have asked me, 'Well, what's doing it?' If I knew, I would get it in the paper."
>
> Colm Kelleher, deputy administrator of the National Institute for Discovery Science in Las Vegas, confirmed Tuesday that the sheriff's office contacted the institute for help. "They'd heard about some of our previous research from a retired deputy sheriff in that area," he said. The group [NIDS] describes itself as a research organization that studies a variety of unconventional scientific theories.
>
> NIDS investigated the 1970s cattle mutilations in Montana, and Kelleher said its research found a correlation between the animal killings and UFO sightings around Malmstrom Air Force Base.
>
> "Just because we found a statistical linkage between UFO sightings and animal mutilation, we are not drawing a direct link," he said. "We are completely undecided as to the perpetrators of these mutilations."[8]

As we have seen, NIDS had conducted field research into unexplained livestock deaths that were being reported in the United States and Canada. They hired field investigators to alert them of any fresh cases that were reported in a timely manner, and if at all possible, made arrangements with local veterinarians to conduct field necropsies on the animals. Then forensic samples were analyzed. One case that was reported on Halloween 2001 is particularly noteworthy. Dr. Colm Kelleher filed this report that appeared on rense.com:

> NIDS was contacted on October 31, 2001 by a rancher to report the possible mutilation of a nine-month old Red Angus cross steer. The animal had been found dead the previous evening at feeding time. NIDS alerted our Utah investigator who in turn alerted the Cache County deputy sheriff who investigated the mutilation and provided NIDS with his report. At the same time, NIDS also contracted a local veterinarian to conduct a necropsy on the animal. The necropsy was successful and samples of vitreous fluid from the animal's eye, liver and a vial of blood were collected by the veterinarian at NIDS's request. The samples were shipped overnight to NIDS.

The animal's scrotum had been removed in what the veterinarian termed a circular pattern. The bowel was visible protruding from the opening. Surprisingly, the entire penis and urethra had been skillfully removed through the small opening (shown in the full report). The incisions also cut through abdominal muscle layers.

NIDS spoke with the veterinarian following the necropsy and after the x-ray analysis of the animal's head was complete. The veterinarian confirmed his remarks made earlier to the deputy sheriff concerning his mystification about the surgery. It is noteworthy that the veterinarian was impressed with the surgical skill in removing the penis and the urethra in a series of bloodless incisions. X-ray analysis showed an otherwise normal brain with no sign of a bullet or anything metallic. Therefore it was concluded that the animal had not been shot.

Multiple chemical analyses [IR, extraction, gas chromatography mass spectrometry(GCMS), etc]. were conducted on the blood, liver and vitreous fluid from the animal's eye. NIDS has begun to develop a subtraction procedure in which GCMS analysis of eye-fluid from a mutilated animal is compared, molecule by molecule, with the GCMS analysis from eye-fluid obtained from an animal that has been left to decompose for a few days and serves as an 'unmutilated' control.

Table III in the full report on the [now defunct] NIDS web site comprises a direct subtractive comparison of the GCMS analysis of the eye-fluid from the mutilated animal in Cache County in the left hand column versus GCMS analysis of the eye-fluid from the control animal in the right hand column. The molecules in the eye-fluid are presented in ascending order according to GCMS retention time.

As can be seen from Table III in the full report, the GCMS analysis yielded an enormously complex chromatogram, comprising over sixty separate molecules. A careful comparison between the left and right hand areas of Table III shows what appears to be multiple phenolic compounds in the eye-fluid from the mutilated animal that were not in the eye-fluid from the control animal.

The 'mutilation specific 'molecular entities include, but are not limited to: 3-Methoxy-2-methylphenol, 5-Methoxy-2,3-dimethylphenol, 4-(2-phenylethyl)-phenol, 2-Methoxy-4-methylphenol, 3,5-dimethoxyphenol.

Whether this family of phenolic compounds, none of which were found in the control animal are breakdown products from narcotic substances (see for example Table IV in the full report), or simply metabolic decomposition products from the animal has not been determined. However, the range of multiple phenolic compounds is suggestive. It is therefore speculated that the excess phenolics could originate from decomposition products of drugs and/or controlled substances. Many of

432

these substances have similar phenolic functionalities as part of their structures. The phenolic structures suggested by the MS analysis are singled out and shown along with a few drugs and controlled substances having structural similarities in Table IV of the report.

NIDS cannot, however, be definitive that these compounds are not decomposition breakdown products, even though they were not present in the control animal. Such a conclusion can only be derived from multiple additional analyses as well as a much more sophisticated research database of the complexity of ruminant decomposition (ruminant decomposition being much more complex than human decomposition).[9]

In the mid 1990s, I was contacted by Alberta rancher Fern Belzil who became one of the NIDS field investigators/bird dogs. Fern had a ranch in the St. Paul area that had been victimized by the mutilators in the '80s and '90s. He was attempting to bring himself quickly up to speed on the mystery and soon he became the "go-to" private investigator of mute cases in southern and central Alberta. By the beginning of 2001, he had investigated around a dozen or so cases, and was working closely with the RCMP. He also became involved with BLT research—through Linda Howe and Nancy Talbott—and he doggedly logged thousands of miles traveling to sites where Canadian mutilation cases were being reported.

A soft-spoken, kindly man, Fern was quite a help to distraught Canadian ranchers who were experiencing the loss and fear that one feels when the mystery cattle surgeons paid their ranches unwelcome visits in the night. Linda noted in her earthfiles.com website an interesting case that Belzil investigated that was included in Levengood's "Bovine Excision Site" study:

> September 7, 2001 St. Paul, Alberta, Canada— Rancher Fern Belzil of St. Paul has been investigating unusual cattle mutilations in Alberta for the past several years. On October 16, 2000, the Royal Canadian Mounted Police called him about the eerie death of a 2200-pound bull found at the Saddle Lake Indian Reserve on October 12th about fifteen miles southwest of St. Paul in a rural area called St. Brides. The bull was a seven-year-old Simmental, a robust blood line from Europe, owned by rancher Marshall Kiziak.
>
> In addition to the dry, bloodless "cookie cutter" excision of the scrotum, the ear had been cut off, the tongue was excised from deep within the throat and a circle of hide had been removed from around the rectal area. Oddly, the penis had been stretched out of the abdomen towards the rear legs and three of the bull's four small nipples had been excised, leaving a triangular pattern of small red marks near the penis.
>
> The bull's rear was lying on grass and soil only about eight inches from a clump of willow trees. Biophysicist W. C. Levengood of Grass

Lake, Michigan had asked Fern to collect grass and soil samples for study from the mutilation site. Recently, the findings were released in a report by Levengood and analytical chemist, Phyllis Budinger, *confirming the third case of pure, dried hemoglobin at an animal mutilation.* More than a dozen cattle mutilations were reported in Montana's Pondera, Teton and Glacier Counties in 2000. [my emphasis][10]

September 2001 featured the worst 'attack' in U.S. history when two planes slammed into NYC's World Trade Center on September 11th resulting in the first three steel skyscrapers to ever be brought down by fire—collapsing at free-fall speed. September 2001 also found our mystery mutilators avoiding the U.S. and returning north of the border to British Columbia in the Falkland area. BC ranchers had reported cases to officials in the 1980s. CBC Radio covered these reports that received little notice in the United States. British Columbia investigator Brian Vike noted the following detail from the CBC coverage:

> The area where this took place was between, Fulton and the Chase area in British Columbia. Some horseback riders had found the carcass of the animal (cow) and had contacted the farmer and the RCMP were also contacted. There was only one set of tracks leading to the animal. These tracks were left behind by the farmer as he inspected the dead animal. No other tracks were found around the area, leading in or out. After an inspection of the dead animal, there was "no" blood remaining in the animal, no blood found around the scene whatsoever, also I was told that a rectal core was taken from the animal. The udder was removed, and sexual organs were also missing.[11]

Eldorado Springs, located nine miles south of Boulder, Colorado is the site of the next report from 2001. On October 2nd, MUFON field investigator Lou Ashby discovered what appeared to be a mutilated heifer on the Hagan Ranch. A ranch hand claimed he had seen the heifer alive the day prior. Another case on the ranch that occurred ten years earlier is one of those atypical cases that pop out from time to time. The rancher told Ashby about the unreported 1982 case, and Ashby contacted Linda Howe and provided earthfiles.com with a description of the crime-scene. She noted the unusual circumstances:

> [Hagan] lost a cow… [in 1982] and he said when he found that dead cow, *it was lodged in a stand of trees and it was lodged so tightly they had to cut down trees to get the body out.* What Mr. Hagan said to me was that he saw these excisions on the body of the animal, "You could tell it had been done with a laser." [12] [my emphasis]

This Boulder-area incident appears to be the single, stand-alone case from the first week of October, 2001 all the way through the early spring of 2002. I feel that it should be noted that mutilation reports appear to have ceased completely during the fall and winter of 2001. As I pointed out in Chapter Four, it may be when the culture heats up and is sidetracked by important events that we see the mute meme take a vacation. After the horrific events of 9/11 it appears that the mutilations abruptly stopped for almost nine straight months. *I think this may be an important clue.*

I was told by the Sheriff of Conejos County of a SLV case in December 2001, that featured a landed object and bright "blue and red lights" but the witness refused to officially report the mutilated cow found in the field where the lights were seen the night prior.

Daylight mutilation cases are extremely rare. They have occasionally been reported as we have seen with the 1999 Sherman Ranch Case, but the vast majority of these killings and disfigurements are conducted under the cover of darkness. This did not hold true on Fritz Morrison's ranch near Sand Springs, Oklahoma—just outside Tulsa—in May 2002. Tireless Linda Howe fielded this report that is another puzzler. Who *are* these guys?

That day, Fritz had been at the water pump at 12:30 p.m. and his bull was laying beside the trough chewing his cud, seemingly well and content along with several cows. But when Fritz returned only three hours later to do more work at the pump, this is what he found.

> "His testicles had been cut off and his butt had been cut out. And I'm sure the blood was completely gone. There wasn't a drop of blood anywhere he had been cut out. And his penis had been pulled out from inside. The skin had not been cut from his testicles up to where it comes out in the belly. It had been pulled out from the inside and was hanging out and was real fresh, like maybe I'd interrupted something again. I don't know…
>
> I go out there every day and kind of look at him. He's never been eaten on. There were no flies on him. Nothing touched him, but the cows every night seemed to gather around him about 5 or 6 o'clock and just stand there awhile before they go off and eat, at least for a week after he died."[13]

Hoofin' Footin' the Mouth South of the Border

The U.S. had enough on its meme-plate after 9/11, and the culture became understandably sidetracked into a Middle/Near East fixation that manifested with retribution and a questionable agenda for economic hegemony. The ranching community in North America had other things on their plates. The ones that noticed probably thanked their lucky stars they didn't have to deal with what suddenly emerged in South America and the UK during the first year of the new century.

In early August 2000 a nasty virus *Aphthae epizooticae* broke out inexplicably in cattle herds in Argentina, Brazil and Uruguay, and the stage was set for the nightmare that would unfold in 2001. Called foot-and-mouth disease (FMD) (or hoof-and-mouth disease) this is an extremely infectious and sometimes fatal viral disease that can infect cloven-hoofed animals and wild bovines such as buffalo, bison, and other domesticated animals like sheep, goats and swine. We will visit the devastation the disease brought to South America in detail in a moment.

FMD probably has *the greatest economic impact of any disease on global livestock production.* The virus infection causes symptoms that first appear as a high fever that lasts for two or three days. The infected animal then develops blisters inside its mouth and, if the disease continues unchecked, blisters develop on the feet that can lead to lameness. This attack on the mouth and feet led to the name. Highly infectious, FMD can be a death knell to ranching communities.

> FMD has severe implications for animal farming since it is highly infectious and can be spread by infected animals through aerosols, through contact with contaminated farming equipment, vehicles, clothing or feed, and by domestic and wild predators. Its containment demands considerable efforts in vaccination, strict monitoring, trade restrictions and quarantines, and occasionally the elimination of animals.[14]

In February 2001, FMD decided to break out in the United Kingdom—initially in an abattoir in Essex. The infected animals had come from Buckinghamshire and the Isle of Wight. During the next several weeks, additional cases were reported in Devon, Cornwall and southern Scotland, where it bloomed into a full-blown outbreak. In case you've forgotten: on February 24, 2001, a worldwide ban of UK exports of livestock, meat and other animal products was called for by the European Union. By the end of March upwards of 50 new cases per day were being reported in the UK. The disease spread to other western European countries, but was quickly dealt with by culling and burning between 80,000 to 90,000 head of livestock per week until over four million animals had been destroyed. The outbreak was declared over by October 2001.[15]

How the disease was introduced in the UK is in doubt, but some officials placed blame on infected South American animals and/or meat products. The following is an overview of the South American FMD outbreak that started in 2000. It was published on a website devoted to training veterinarian students:

> In 2000, Argentina, Brazil, and Uruguay reported outbreaks of FMD with both the type O and the type A viruses. FMD types A and type O were reported in Argentina, where 124 premises were eventually involved. Twenty-two facilities were affected in Brazil, with 12 confirmed as type O, and three farms were infected in an adjacent part of

Uruguay. All three countries conducted depopulation ('stamping-out') campaigns and, by the end of 2000, believed the viruses to be eradicated. However, in February 2001, Argentina reported the first cases of a massive FMD outbreak that would eventually affect all three countries. This virus, a type A, spread rapidly and explosively through the central and eastern part of Argentina, although a special control region prevented the epidemic from extending into the south. Despite extensive depopulation efforts, the disease had affected over 2,000 premises by the end of 2001 and was still out of control in Argentina. Brazil reported its first outbreak with this virus in May 2001, in the state of Rio Grande do Sul.

On April 23, 2001, FMD type A appeared in Uruguay, apparently spread from Argentina. The first infected farm was reported in Palmitas, Soriano Department (state). Palmitas is approximately 70 km from Uruguay's border with Argentina, the Uruguay River. Thirty-nine of the 430 cattle on the affected farm had signs of FMD. Lesions were not seen on the farm's 640 sheep. The affected and exposed animals were killed the following day. On April 26, FMD was found on a neighboring farm, which had a mixed population of cattle, sheep, and pigs. At the same time, several infected premises were found in adjacent Colonia Department, 25 km from the Uruguay River and 40 km from the first cases. The zone where the outbreak first occurred is economically integrated with the adjacent region of Argentina, which was experiencing FMD outbreaks, and the virus is assumed to have spread from this region via fomites or people.

Quarantines were immediately placed on both affected departments and, the following day, the remaining affected and exposed animals were destroyed and buried. In total, 5,093 cattle, 1,511 sheep, and 333 pigs were culled. Three days later, the government was forced to suspend the stamping-out procedure because of strong resistance by local farmers and the discovery that the disease had spread to other areas of the country. Authorities learned that, a few days before the first cases were recognized, cattle had been sold at auction and delivered to other parts of Uruguay. The movement of people, agricultural equipment and machinery, and milk and beef trucks are also thought to have contributed to the spread of the virus...

From April 23 to August 21, 2001, a total of 2,057 farms or facilities in Uruguay were affected by FMD, a number similar to the farms affected by the epidemic in the U.K. However, Uruguay was able to eradicate its extensive outbreak solely by restrictions on livestock movement and the vaccination of cattle, in spite of having a large and fully susceptible sheep population in close contact with the cattle. The total direct cost of eradication was estimated at $13.6 million. Vaccine purchases accounted for $7.5 million, with the remainder used for compensation payments to farmers, cleaning and disinfection, and operating expenses. The $13.6 million does not include some expenses incurred by the Army, which collaborated by controlling illegal livestock movements in border areas and providing other support. Argentina and Brazil also managed to control their epidemics, in part by vaccination.

The loss of export markets and a pronounced decrease in livestock prices associated with the epidemic were costly for Uruguay. The estimated losses as a result of the closing of external markets to Uruguayan farmers exceeded $200 million. Financial losses to meat and dairy producers, in particular, had a significant negative impact on the national economy. In addition, movement restrictions on the entire livestock sector affected many workers and associated industries such as packing plants. Losses associated with closed packing plants, as well as the return of 380 containers of meat that were in transatlantic transit at the time of the outbreak, added approximately $30 million in costs. In total, the epidemic cost Uruguay approximately $243.6 million, a much smaller figure than the approximately $10 billion in losses to agriculture, the food chain, and tourism during the outbreak in the U.K. In addition, approximately 6,900 animals were culled in Uruguay compared with the more than four million animals killed in the U.K. As of September 2009, Uruguay was recognized by the OIE as "FMD free where vaccination is practiced.[16]

The South American epidemic was finally declared over at the end of May 2002. As the outbreak fizzled out, *early spring reports of cattle and other livestock mutilations began to be reported to officials in Argentina*, which had been devastated by the FMD pandemic. In my mind, this cannot be a coincidence.

The South American cattle mutilation wave that began as the last cases of FMD were eradicated may have commenced near the Pampan town of Rancul in the province of Entre Rios, located north of Bueno Aires near where Brazil and Uruguay border Argentina. By the fall of 2002 an estimated 400 cases had been reported. All through the South American outbreak from 2002 through 2008, Scott Corrales and the Institute of Hispanic Ufology collected newspaper articles and investigator reports from the hardest hit areas of Argentina and Brazil. Many of these stories were translated by Corrales and appeared in his excellent online publication *Inexplicata* and re-published by George Filer in his weekly *Filer's Files* report. Many thanks for their hard work and dedication—please visit their sites and support their tireless efforts and fine work.

The mystery in Argentina grows with a wild boar added to the list of cows, horses, guanaco and sheep being mutilated. The wild boar is highly distrustful and detects—through their sharp olfactory system—the presence of strangers. An eight-month-old boar was found mutilated. While the mutilation count is now reaching 170 and the cases recorded extend to nine Argentinean provinces. This is the 6th species found with mutilations, lack of blood and with geometrically perfect incisions and missing the anus, tongue and jaw. To the surprise of the rancher and the farmhand escorting him, the animal was still soft in spite of the -14 C temperature. "It's impossible that an animal could remain in this condition after it's dead and after the cold."

A mysterious situation also occurred to the north of the Pampan town of Rancul at the "Los Caldenes" ranch, where a cow had died of natural causes in the afternoon only to be found with incisions on its jaw and missing its tongue the next day. The province of Entre Rios has also the epicenter of these events: in a field, a rancher found a 170 kg heifer and a 500 kgs milk cow some 800 meters from each other, both presenting the notorious incision marks.

Strange dwarf like midgets have been reported wandering the backyards of many neighborhoods in General Acha. [my emphasis] A short, green entity that runs away with haste when detected, has been reported. These reports tied with UFO reports and mutilations have the area in an uproar. The stories have been reported in the news and on radio stations. Red intense lights, as though from a laser, moving very quickly across the countryside are being reported. Veterinarian Omar Fernando Lopez also observed a new case that involved a pregnant cow found in the fields of Juan Carlos Robilotte, showing the same incisions, with the difference that the cow was about to give birth. "There was a circle [on the left flank, above the udder] through which half of the calf's body was protruding." A racehorse belonging to the Quarter Horse breed, belonging to stables near the town of Choele, was found dead with strange mutilations: "It was as though it had been hollowed out from within," reported police sources in describing the stud horse, of considerable economic value. Veterinarian Carlos Montobbio, who certified the case, reported that the horse was missing an eye and tongue, but no incisions on the maxillary had been performed. It had also been castrated and a significant part of its small intestine and rectum had been removed...

"We have great fields and a lot of cattle in Patagonia. In April gauchos found some cows dead with perfect mutilations with eyes, jugular vein, nipples and genitals removed. Virtually the same parts were cut and cauterized in a perfect way. The mutilated animals seem to be dropped from the air. Cults were ruled out because the bodies do not have any cult marks or symbols. There are no footprints and carrion [eaters] do not eat the dead body"[17]

Cows Found Stuffed Inside a Water Tank

Corrales also posted the following interesting information that stumped ranchers and investigators alike:

> Perhaps even more astounding is the *sudden disappearance of water from reservoirs and tanks during the night.* [my emphasis] Frogs were found dead in reservoirs where one hundred thousand liters of water disappeared over night. Obviously frogs can live for long periods without water, so their death may be a clue to the mystery. Argentina does not have sophisticated tools or advanced equipment to do research.
>
> Argentinean health authorities concluded that a small carnivorous mouse known as "red muzzle" (hocicudo rojizo, in Spanish) was responsible for the mysterious mutilations found in recent months in over a hundred cow carcasses in different rural sectors of the country. The lifeless bovine bodies, which were largely found without anuses and missing parts of the mouth and genitals, and around which no tracks or traces could be found, gave rise to a wide array of speculation ranging from Satanic rites and UFOs to little green men. Bernardo Cané, president of the National Health and Agro-alimentary Quality Service (SENASA), brought the mystery to a close today and pointed out that the party responsible for the mutilations is a mouse that dwells in rural areas and whose nutritional habits have changed due to the scarcity of worms and insects it normally feeds on, turning into a scavenger. This was the conclusion reached by scientists from the Universidad Nacional del Centro. The study promotes the belief that the animals died from malnourishment and Magnesium deficiencies, with the presence of parasites and metabolic shortcomings.[18]

The newspaper *El Diario* published this amazing story in July 2002 as translated by Scott Corrales:

> On the last Friday of June 2002, an event of truly strange characteristics took place in a field of the locality of Suco, located to the west of Rio Cuarto, very near the border with San Luis Province. In the Cordoban locality, a well-known livestock producer respected by all for his responsibility and honesty, found 19 dead animals within an Australian-type water tank. Nine of the bovines were dead, according to subsequent medical-veterinarian examinations due to asphyxiation through immersion. The rest were alive, but affected by the low temperatures and near dead due to freezing.
>
> The news not only spread like wildfire throughout the area: it was confirmed by police officials of Regional Unit 7, headquartered at Rio

Cuarto, who took over the investigation of the case employing personnel from the Sampacho District Sheriff's Office, located 50 kilometers west of Rio Cuarto on National Hwy. 8. What no one could explain is how the 19 animals could have entered the enormous water tank, bearing in mind that they first had to cross an electric drover [sic], then a 1.50 meter tall fence, and finally, "jump" over the tank wall…

[T]hese repeated events do away with the efforts aimed at explaining the events and which lay the blame on both "red-muzzled mice" and "carnivorous bees" and "cattle rustlers."[19]

The debunkers' blanket assertion that *all* of these hundreds of South American cattle died from malnutrition sounds highly implausible to me. As with the mutilation reports in North America, they appeared to unfold in waves, starting and stopping unexpectedly, and instead of the mystery helicopters—as seen in the U.S.—we have dozens of apparent UFO reports. These red muzzle mice—if they are responsible for the mutes—must be particularly mighty mice to be able to chase, take down, kill and then disfigure a 300 to 2,000-pound bovine, or carry a herd over fences and deposit them in a water tank.

I assume that media induced misidentified scavenger action may have prompted some erroneous reports, but not all of these cases can be debunked with this tired, one-size-fits-all excuse—something or someone has been (and still is) involved in killing and disfiguring livestock—all over the world. I assume I've illustrated this point effectively over the past couple hundred pages.

Space constraints do not allow for a complete examination of these waves of mutilation claims that began at the turn of the new century in the Southern Hemisphere. Reports from Argentina, Brazil, Uruguay, Paraguay, Chile and Peru form a huge story, largely unknown in North America. I intuit that this extensive wave of South American livestock mutilations—that continues today—is an investigators "mother lode." I sincerely hope there are dedicated investigators still on the case monitoring the largest cattle herds on the planet. An entire book should be written examining this little-known, ongoing South American mutilation phenomenon.

For further information on the South American unexplained livestock death cases, a collection of over 50 translated, in-depth articles is available for researchers at rense.com/Datapages/argentinedata.html, and there are dozens of articles translated and reprinted at Scott Corrales' South American clearinghouse, inexplicata.com.

Back North Stateside

I have seen countless reports that involve the discovery of dead livestock that have had various body parts removed, but seldom have I run across a report where body parts have been found—especially in the middle of a big city suburb.

What do you make of this following news report from the *St. Louis Post-Dispatch*? Who is watching whom?

> When Adam Comer's children ran screaming into their house in Ferguson on Tuesday night, it didn't take him long to see why. There were 13 eyeballs staring back from the rear yard. Just eyeballs.
>
> Puzzled police gathered the grisly find in plastic bags and shipped them off to St. Louis County Medical Examiner Mary Case, who offered relief with the news they weren't human. But forensic science went no further to explain how the eyeballs—apparently from cows— ended up in the Comer's yard and three others along Elkins and Trask drives, where Ferguson meets Dellwood.
>
> "They looked like meat," said Comer, who described how he nudged one with his foot. "I couldn't believe it was an eyeball." Comer said he called over a neighbor who was outside barbecuing. The man, an avid hunter, had no explanation either. That's when Comer called Ferguson police. Officers with rubber gloves collected 18 eyeballs in all, and left a few behind. "I had to pick them up and throw them away," Comer said.
>
> The experience scared his children and left Comer distressed about who left the remains in his yard. "That's the freaky part," Comer said. "I don't have any idea where they came from." Ferguson and Dellwood police continue to investigate.[20]

After an apparent lull in activity for almost seven years, the mutilators made a surprise visit to the SLV during the spring of 2005. Although rumors of other cases have circulated around the SLV over the previous few years, no official reports of unusual livestock deaths had been filed until this latest case. Other reports surfaced in Alberta, Ontario, British Columbia and Colorado during the spring of 2004 and 2005.

A rancher reported a head of mutilated livestock found south of Monte Vista, Colorado near the Wildlife Refuge and Rock Creek Canyon. Another case may have occurred the prior month near Jaroso, Colorado when a motorist chased an "'orange light" and returned to the site two days later and found what he described as "a mutilated cow." According to a small article in the *Valley Courier:*

> The Rio Grande Sheriff's Office is investigating a cattle mutilation discovered in the county Friday morning. Rio Grande County Sergeant Jon Gonzales said the sheriff's office received the report on the mutilation, which was found in a field off County Road 29, at 9:57 a.m. Friday April 22, 2005. "The facial area of the cow was removed from the back of the jaw to the front of the nose by the eye line," Gonzales said. Gonzales said the cut seemed precise, but there was a small amount of blood.

Gonzales said a person convicted of the mutilation could face cruelty to animals and trespassing charges.[21]

Other cases were being reported that spring as well. This time the report came from up in the Province of Winnipeg, Canada:

An Arborg, Canada cattle farmer made a horrific discovery when he found the partially skinned carcass of one of his animals that was missing its tongue and apparently drained of its blood... Arborg is 75 miles north of Winnipeg...

"The whole thing has turned out to be more sinister than I thought," said Yvonne, a neighbor, who examined the mutilated animal. She asked not to have her last name used to protect her family. "What sort of weirdos have we got traveling in our neighborhood?"

Gordon, who would only allow the *Sun* to print his first name, said he discovered the carcass on his farm Monday afternoon. "I don't really want to speculate on what happened. I know what I saw," he said, adding he is still shaken up by the find.

The mutilation happened Saturday or Sunday night, Gordon said. No one heard anything. He's heard of several cow mutilations in the area over the past few years, Gordon said. He called the RCMP, reporting that the animal had been attacked by a predator. He has since changed his mind about the cause. "It was definitely a sharp object used," he said.

Arborg RCMP Cpl. Glenn Syme said he has never investigated an instance of cattle mutilation. The RCMP did take a call this week about a cow being attacked by a predator, likely from Gordon. The animal was found with an incision under its chin. The skin had been pulled from the face, exposing the teeth. "It's not the gore, we've seen that before, it's the evil behind it," Yvonne said. The tip of the animal's tongue, cut from its root, was placed in the mouth, she said. "There's not a drop of blood in that animal. The only way you can drain an animal of blood is (to cut into it) with the heart still pumping," Yvonne said. The cuts were very precise, as if made by a surgeon, she said. "You don't know whom you're dealing with...the average wild and woolly neighborhood brat wouldn't be capable of doing it," she said.

Gordon and Yvonne called Fern Belzil, an Alberta-based investigator of unexplained deaths who has been studying cow mutilations for eight years, for help. Belzil has studied 100 cases, two-thirds of which remain unexplained. "I'm not saying it's aliens ... a lot points towards aliens but there is no proof," he said. Belzil said he has never encountered any evidence pointing to who or what is killing cows. "It's a real mystery," he said.[22]

Another Arkansas Wave Begins

Since her introduction into the perplexing field of unexplained livestock death investigation in the late 1970s, Linda Moulton Howe has been a clearinghouse of information about these claims from ranchers and law enforcement officials. Linda has also kept an ear open for reports of pets being abused and/or killed. Almost single-handedly during the eighties and early nineties Linda kept the subject alive and actively investigated new reports and networked with officials and ranchers. The following account describes a disturbing outbreak of domestic pet killings.

April 21, 2006, Hot Springs, Arkansas:

The worldwide animal mutilation mystery that I've investigated since the fall of 1979 is most commonly reported for cattle and horses. But wild animals such as deer and elk have also been found with their rectums cored out and sexual organs removed along with jaw flesh, tongue, eye and ear—with no signs of blood. In addition to cattle, horses and wild animals, every kind of farm and domestic animal has also been affected, including house pets such as cats and dogs. Those cases are especially terrible because the pet owners are devastated to find a beloved dog or cat dead with its paws cut off, or head cut off, or even skinned.

Now, comes news from Garland County, Arkansas west of Little Rock, that since November 2005 into this spring, a cow and three pigs have been cut open, as well as puppies and cats cut up strangely, and a beagle dog was literally skinned alive. Concerned residents in Hot Springs, Arkansas and animal activists from People for the Ethical Treatment of Animals, (PETA), raised $21,000 reward money for information leading to the arrest of the perpetrators. Predictably, local young boys and teenagers are suspected by the Garland County Sheriff's Office because at least one bragged about killing the cats and skinning the dog. Yet, so far no person has been arrested or arraigned for any of the assaults.

This week, I talked with Garland County Sheriff's Capt. David Ray Shoptaw about the animal attacks and deaths—especially two dogs with bloodless holes in their heads. Their respective rectums were also cored out in deep, bloodless holes which the veterinarian said must have been done with a cauterizing instrument. Capt. Shoptaw has worked in the Sheriff's Office for 24 years and now heads up the Criminal Investigation Division. He told me he has never seen anything before in his law enforcement career in which animals have been attacked like this.[23]

Eads, Colorado is situated about 40 miles from the Kansas border and is the location of Chuck Bowen's sprawling 13,000-acre cattle ranch. The second week of May 2006 brought an unwelcome surprise when Bowen discovered two of his cows mutilated. "Both of them had the skin sliced off the left side of their faces in exactly the same pattern…The grass around their legs was still upright, still tall. When an animal dies it usually thrashes around and disturbs the ground. This was like the cows had been gently laid down in the grass. Like they'd been lowered." His wife Sheri told *Denver Post* reporter Rich Tosches "The cut was a perfectly straight line. You could tell it was done with a knife."

When asked who or what he thought was responsible and did he think it could have been 'aliens,' Bowen replied, "You would think they'd have something more important to do." Tosches then went on to observe an interesting fact about the location of the Bowen spread:

Oh, and there's this little tidbit that jacks up the spooky meter another notch in Bowen's head: The ranch, originally owned by his grandfather, sits on the site of the infamous Nov. 29, 1864, Sand Creek Massacre, in which some 200 Cheyenne and Arapaho Indians were killed by U.S. Army soldiers. Bowen and his wife, Sheri, have spent decades sifting through the dirt, uncovering about 3,000 artifacts of that horrible day. Everything from cannonball fragments to metal arrowheads to soldiers' uniform buttons.

In February and again in April [2006], not far from that main battlefield and down by the towering cottonwood trees that stood even back then, Bowen found the dead cows…

And yet Bowen wonders what on earth could have killed his Angus cows and surgically removed the skin from the same side of both cows' faces, leaving the carcasses otherwise intact in the undisturbed grass of the sprawling ranch…

Kiowa County Sheriff Forest Frazee and deputies examined both carcasses. Frazee said a veterinarian told him an eagle might have sliced the skin from the cows' faces. And that the brittle winter grass around the bodies had not been stepped on.

"That grass breaks. It's easy to see a footprint. No one came anywhere near those cows," Frazee said. "So I don't really know what happened. I do know that I don't believe in the boogeyman."

The Bowens—seemingly about as regular and ordinary as people can be—live about 30 miles south, in Lamar. They run about 90 cows on the family land, and the two deaths have left them rattled.…Chuck's metal detector, the one we use to find artifacts, it gave a reading of foil over the entire body. Aluminum foil.

"I've heard all the stories, but I have a little trouble with the alien thing. Aliens killing our cattle just doesn't make any sense…Both cows had the exact same patch of skin taken from the same side of their face," she said. "And to be honest, it's a little creepy."[24]

A farmer near Paradise Hill, Saskatchewan discovered what was described to investigators as a "classic mutilation," on June 16, 2006, and he immediately contacted the Saskatchewan Provincial Paranormal Research Centre who have conducted some research into mutes in the past. Spokesperson Barb Campbell told investigators that the animal "shows all the classic signs of being a mutilation—eyes gone, ears gone, certain incisions in the body— all of which are very suspicious."

There were evidently 55 head of cattle in the herd, and after taking some forensic samples and investigating the scene, Campbell concluded that the animal's condition cannot be attributed to a predator. The incisions appeared to be "very fine cuts," and the carcass had its "back legs totally behind her, and her whole spine is twisted. There's no sign of a struggle—it appears she was just dropped from the air." There were no vehicle marks, human tracks, or predator markings nearby. Campbell mentioned that the rest of the herd, including the dead cow's calf, would not go near the mutilated cow.

Cattle mutilations were reported to authorities in Manitoba, Canada on ranches near Lake Winnipeg during a month-long flurry from July 8 to August 9, 2007. Komarno rancher Sheila Vigfusson told Linda Howe:

> "It's just so weird to me. What gets me is that I have ten animals dead and I don't know what they died from. And I've never seen this (dead animals) with no blood. We've been farming a long time and have quite a lot of cattle. I've had dead animals before, but I've never seen them like this, you know? And then Greg (Wotowich) lost his bull and just recently, Lois and Steve Matis lost one of their cows. The teats on theirs was cut off in circles just like mine."[25]

On July 29th, "only a couple of miles down the road from Sheila's place," a prize bull was discovered dead and disfigured, and Howe was told of another case in the area that was reported on August 9, 2007.

The following year, in April and May 2008, Esterhazy ranchers—located west of Regina, Saskatchewan—reported fresh unexplained livestock death cases. As you can probably imagine, more mutilations were rumored to have occurred around the west through the end of the decade and up to the present day. In a *Denver Post* article in December 2009, Jason Blevens described his visits with southern Colorado ranchers who had quietly been experiencing mutilations over the prior ten years. His article "Colorado cow mutilations baffle ranchers, cops, UFO believer" was published on December 9, 2009:

> "I have no idea what could do this. I wish I did," [Tom Miller] says.

Four calves all killed overnight…

"A lion will drag its kill. Coyotes rip and tear flesh. These were perfect cuts—like with a laser or like a scalpel. And what would take the waste—all the guts—and leave the nice, tender meat? …No tracks. No blood. No nothing. I got nothing to go by. They don't leave no trace."

…Colorado Brand Inspector Dennis Williams came out and looked at Miller's calf. He lives next door; the calf would be the last of three strangely mutilated cattle that he would investigate in March of this year.

"I've heard about it. It was weird, to say the least. Totally unexplainable. To me, it looked like that calf had been dropped from a high distance, the way its hips were dislocated and all its broken bones," Williams says.

That same month, ranchers had called Williams to grisly scenes northeast of Aguilar and west of Weston [Colorado] to investigate mysteriously mangled cattle that had been seen healthy the day before.

To add to the weirdness, [Manuel] Sanchez, [Tom] Miller and Mike Duran, who found a sliced Red Angus cow near Weston in March, have all experienced similar mutilations before. Sanchez lost cows in 2006 and 1993, Miller in 1997 and 1980, and Duran in 2000 and 1995.

"It's weird and unexplainable," says Duran, who lost a healthy 27-year-old Red Angus cow on March 8th, [2009] her udder and rear end removed with what he describes as "laser cuts, like when somebody cuts metal with a torch…"

[According to] Las Animas County sheriff's Deputy Derek Navarette, who investigated the Miller and Duran calves. "We can't come up with anything… We've seen these before and they are all the kind of the same… Northern New Mexico has had some of these same cases, and in those cases they never got any further than we did."[26]

My Last Mute Field Investigation

An apparent SLV cattle mutilation was discovered off State Highway 285 by a passing motorist and passenger on June 19, 2010. The animal was located just north of mile marker 398 on the west side of the highway. The motorist was able to contact me, and I went to the scene with investigator Saundra Marsh to document the report. I happened to be visiting the SLV for the San Luis Valley Camera Project—installing the first surveillance camea of a proposed seven camera set-up around the area. Because of time constraints, I was unable to conduct a thorough investigation of the report, but made a cursory 20-minute examination of the site and reported the case to the Conejos County sheriff's office. This latest potential case brought the total of reported unexplained livestock deaths and disfigurements in the Greater SLV to 12 cows, two horses and one goat since November 2009.

The cow was lying on its left side, facing north, about 100 feet off the roadway, and was missing the flesh on the right side of its jaw. The cut was very precise and appeared to have been made by a sharp knife or scalpel. The denuded jawbone seemed unusually pale. There was clear evidence of cut hair follicles present on the backside of the mandible excision, and the topside of the mandible cut had unusual evidence of cut hair that alternated with 1/2 inch patches of uncut hair. I have never seen this type of alternating cut/uncut hair evidence before. No other organs were apparently excised, however a small coring of the female reproductive tract was evident as were bubbling body fluids in the wound. Abrasions were noted on the front right hock above the dewclaw and high on the left rear hock. The dewclaw on the left rear leg was missing. The unusual presence of uncoagulated blood was evident on the leg abrasions, and tufts of hair were noted lying near the legs and belly of the cow.

Both Saundra and I suspected that the cow had been lifted by a harness and dropped. The cow had smashed down 'chico' bushes and sage that were splayed out around the hips from the impact. There was also what appeared to be an abrasion on the animal's back above the right hip. The cow's own tracks were not present and we did not note any globules of hemoglobin on or around the carcass.

The animal was still bloated, and blowfly maggots appeared to have hatched earlier that day which would place the probable date of the death and disfigurement to between June 12th and 15th. Scavengers had not touched the carcass; small birds we observed were reluctant to linger on the carcass for more than a couple of seconds and only a couple of small bird droppings were noted on the carcass. No evidence of magpies, crows, ravens or possible raptors was noted, which is highly unusual for the SLV.

A cursory examination of the entire area around the cow revealed no predator or scavenger tracks, but a faint set of tire tracks were present. They approached to within 15 feet of the animal from the south. Two sets of footprints were noted (probably the initial witnesses who reported the case) but no footprints from the occupants of the vehicle were observed. The animal's ear tag was intact which indicated that the rancher may not have been the occupant of the vehicle. (Ear tags are routinely taken off dead livestock by the rancher in order to document the animal that has died.) The immediate area around the cow appeared to be drier than the surrounding pastureland. This may have been due to mundane environmental conditions, but this observation is worth noting.[27]

In August 2012, the mutilators revisited the scene of many earlier crimes since they were first reported in 1975, descending on the Cochetopa region—located on the Continental Divide—east of Gunnison, Colorado. As word spread about the mini-wave of reports, *Denver Post* reporter Nancy Lofholm spoke with several of the affected ranchers:

In recent weeks, a horse was shot and had its head skinned at the

LeValley Ranch property, which is part of the Esty Ranch holdings about eight miles east of Gunnison. The horse also had its tongue and anus removed.

Less than two months ago, a prize heifer in the same heavily traveled area just off of Colorado 50 and Colorado 114 had its tongue, lips and anus removed.

"To me it looks like a ritualistic issue. Either that, or they are high on drugs. There is just no logical explanation for it," said Esty Ranch owner Mike Clarke. Two other incidents took place on other ranches in that vicinity in May and July.

The four mutilations have prompted the Gunnison County Stockgrowers Association to offer a $500 reward for any information that will lead to a conviction. The Colorado State Patrol has also been alerted to watch for strange activities in that area. The Gunnison County Sheriff's Office, the agency investigating the mutilations, did not return phone calls asking for comment.

Clarke's ranch foreman, Allen Roper, told the *Gunnison Country Times* that the mutilated animals appeared to be shot, but no bullets were found and that the mutilations were done with knives and were not a result of predators…

In 2009, a San Luis Valley rancher found four calves with their tongues sliced out, udders removed, eyes cored and faces skinned. Those cases were never solved and there was no blood nor tracks around those animals.[28]

Meet Chuck Zukowski

Clarke suggested to Lofholm that if the mutilations continued people shouldn't be surprised if "the ranching community will really be up in arms." He voiced the feelings of the local ranchers, "What concerns us is what they are going to do next?" Fortunately, it appears they stopped soon, in September, although there is always the possibility that further incidents occurred and ranchers covered them up.

Paranormal investigator Chuck Zukowski has investigated at least two-dozen Southern Colorado mutilation reports since 2008. Several of these claims were located in the San Luis Valley—in Costilla County—some further to the east near Trinidad and others further north up the Front Range of the Rockies.

An article written by Nick Bonham and published by the *Pueblo Chieftain* on July 14, 2013 observed that ranchers in the region were experiencing mutilations all through the years up to the present day and it would appear that these unexplained livestock deaths have never completely gone away—they seem mostly invisible today but they are omnipresent.

[It] wasn't until 1999 that [rancher] Tom Miller said he started looking at the animal deaths differently, not as the product of twisted mischief or the feeding scraps of predators.

"At first I thought it was a prank, but there were no tracks, no blood. It looks like the carcass is peeled off, and it happens overnight...There are just so many things that happen that doesn't seem like it's human. I know people think you're crazy, but there are so many things people can't explain."

Since 1999, six cows and calves have been mutilated on Miller's ranch northeast of [Pueblo, Colorado]. Two calves were mutilated in May [2013] and the day after meeting with a *Chieftain* reporter and photographer this week, he found another mutilated cow on his property. Miller thinks the seventh death happened in the last week.

Chuck Zukowski has been investigating UFO sightings, paranormal cases and animal mutilations throughout the United States for 28 years. A California native who lives in Colorado Springs where he makes his living designing microchips...

In his cases, he's found little evidence to suggest human intervention or natural predators. "You don't see any predator markings at all—bite marks, claw marks—and if you did, it would be a clear giveaway," Zukowski, a former volunteer sheriff's deputy said. "I don't see blood stains on the hides, which is ridiculous... Why would an animal carve and cut a perfectly round circle on one side of a head? Why would a scavenger do that? The lack of blood, unusual cuts, and there's no human evidence there—no foot prints, no tire marks."

Not everyone subscribes to the thought of extraterrestrial life. For some ranchers in the San Luis Valley they believe the deaths to be the work of the bloodthirsty "Chupacabra," a creature of Hispanic lore that preys on livestock.

Zukowski said some ranchers have seen black military helicopters hover over their cattle and later find a mutilated carcass. Some may think Satanic cults are to blame, or such was the case in some of the earliest publicized mutilation cases in the 1960s and '70s. Whatever the thought or theory, mutilations continue to happen and the culprit(s) remain at large. And Zukowski, who volunteers his time to investigate, has linked commonalities that he says points to aliens.

"I believe, without a doubt, that there is life outside of the planet," he said, adding that the mutilators are "a highly intelligent predator."

"In the cases I investigate, there are no signs the animal struggled. In some cases, it looks like (the animal) was dropped there," said Zukowski, whose investigations can be found on his website, ufonut.com

He's found animals inside a depressed ring and in one out-of-state case, found a mutilated animal inside a fresh crop circle. Zukowski collects soil both inside and out of the rings and has the samples tested at Colorado State University-Fort Collins. "I'm seeing some kind of nutrients being altered in the soil. The soil inside the depressions is less soluble than outside the ring."

In one of the May [2013] cases at Miller's ranch, Zukowski said he picked up high radiation readings around a carcass found beside a tree. Above the carcass, Zukowski said, he found broken limbs in the tree, which leads him to think the animal was dropped from above. "I had some unusual radiation readings in a field at Tom Miller's place, and you could see where branches were broken where the carcass was found," he said.

While some ranchers may be scared, Miller said he's not, only more concerned for his herd. Years of drought have taken a toll and, looking down at the remains of a mutilated calf, he says: "That could've been $800... There's just so many questions no one can answer."[29]

Margie Kay in the "Show Me" State

Missouri became ground zero during the summer and fall of 2013. A total of six separate cases were filed with authorities.

Rancher Casey Hamilton called Northland, Kansas police on Saturday, January 5, 2012 to report a mute. He had been treating a sick cow and when he left on Wednesday night, she was standing on her own and eating. When he returned the following morning—12 hours later at 6:30 A.M.—she was dead and mutilated, missing her udder and rear end. He checked for gunshot wounds and found none. Where she lay was on grounds that abut the runways at Kansas City Airport. Interesting to note that she was fairly close to the traffic control tower. Hamilton told KCTV-Channel Five News, "For somebody to get a 1,200 pound cow down and do that, they had to know what they were doing with a tranquilizer."

According to Aaron Brisbane, the veterinarian who examined the animal, "There was no legitimate reason for the surgical procedure the animal underwent. The way the cuts were done, someone had to have done this before... It was too clean to have been done with a knife or a box cutter... You lose cattle, it's part of the business, and you see when coyotes get a hold of them, and tear them up." MUFON Assistant State Director for Missouri Margie Kay visited the Hamilton mute site with friend, police officer Geremy Pierce in an on-site investigation. The following quote is from the November 2013 *MUFON Journal* cover story.

Geremy and I noticed immediately that the hard, dry ground was indented where the cow had been found, appearing as if the animal had been dropped from above. The outline of the animal's body was clearly visible. We took soil samples inside and outside the area and mailed them to MUFON's Deputy Director of Animal Mutilations Chuck Zukowski. Chuck had the samples analyzed at a lab in Colorado along with samples taken from a recent investigation he completed. Both soil samples indicated that the soil was non-water soluble, meaning that it had been exposed to extreme heat.[30]

Another Missouri case was reported on July 10, 2013 in Henry County on the Lyn Mitchell ranch, located west of Warrensburg. This time it was a healthy six-year-old Angus cow. The poor animal was missing the udder, anus, an ear, and the tongue appeared to have been excised. Margie Kay and investigator Larry Jordan visited the site and immediately noticed something strange about the death scene:

> [A] strange, black, burnt-looking outline [could be seen] around where the cow had been laying on the ground. No samples were taken from the cow, which was badly decomposing and had been moved to a different location... On July 19th, Lyn Mitchell called me to report that yet another of her cows was found dead... A rancher in Gasconade County, Missouri found a dead and mutilated cow on his 200-acre ranch on the morning of September 6, 2013... The animal had severe wounds: a large cut-out section of the left jaw and cheek with gum tissue removed, the tongue was cut out below the esophagus, the vaginal area was cut out and part of the udder removed... [H]er calf which had been nursing, was found suddenly blind without any signs of pink eye or other health problems.[31]

There were so many outbreaks with reports and potential cases from 2000 to 2013 that I wouldn't know where to begin to attempt to put together a well-researched overall case history for this time period. I have presented a mere smattering here. Thousands of reports may have occurred over the decade down in South America. Perhaps someone will get motivated to take up the mantle and drive this bus a bit further down the road; but then again, maybe not.

As I go to the printer with this book, I am reminded that this is a global phenomenon and cases still are reported that defy explanation. Case in point as covered in a January 9, 2014 huffingtonpost.com article:

> The carcasses of almost a dozen cows have washed ashore in Denmark and Sweden, puzzling police in the Scandinavian countries. Since Dec. 29, 2013 eight dead cows have been found by people strolling on beaches in southern Sweden and three in Denmark. All the animals had parts of their ears cut off. Investigators suspect this was done to remove the identification tags used to trace the cows.
>
> Danish and Swedish police said Thursday the cows were probably

dumped from a ship in the Baltic Sea. They are trying to pinpoint which livestock transports have passed through the waters separating the two countries in recent weeks. Dumping livestock like that is illegal in both countries. It's unclear, however, whether the cows were thrown overboard in Danish, Swedish or international waters.

Some of the cows had their back legs tied together with a blue rope, Danish police officer Boje Joergensen said, adding it was probably done to be able to lift the animals up with a crane.

Veterinarians in Sweden found no traces of disease in the animals washed ashore there, Swedish police said.[32]

I have attempted as best I could to provide you with an objective recounting of documented unexplained livestock death mutilations, as the phenomenon appears to have unfolded since 1606. I welcome your help, comments, critiques and analysis of my effort. If we're ever going to solve this perplexing conundrum, we'll need all the help we can muster from every quarter. But for now it's on to the weirder side of the mystery, and then on to the influence and role of the "media"—the perpetrators behind the dissemination of this vexing puzzle....

Chapter Nine Sources and References:

1. Linda M. Howe/earthfiles.com
2. *ibid; Calgary Herald*; 4-11-00
3. *ibid*
4. NIDS Report, 6-26-00; rense.com
5. *The Houston Chronicle* 7-31-01; Rense.com
6. *Op. cit.,* Howe
7. *ibid*
8. foxnews.com, 8-8-01; rense.com
9. rense.com 6-26-00
10. *ibid*
11. Brian Vike HBCC
12. Linda M. Howe/earthfiles
13. *ibid*
14. Canadian Food Inspection Agency—Foot-and-Mouth Disease Hazard Specific Plan
15. UK Dept for Environment, Food & Rural Affairs, "Origin of the UK Foot and Mouth Disease Epidemic," 2001
16. Center for Food Security & Public Health, "Emerging Diseases of Animals," cfsph.iastate.edu
17. Scott Corrales, Institute of Hispanic Ufology/Inexplicata; Filer's Files
18. *ibid*
19. *El Diario* del Sur de Cordoba-Villa Maria, 7-9-02
20. *St. Louis Post-Dispatch*, 5-23-02
21. *Valley Courier*, 4-23-05
22. *Winnipeg Sun*, 5-1-04

23. Linda Howe/earthfiles.com
24. *Denver Post* 5-24-06
25. Linda Howe/earthfiles.com
26. "Colorado cow mutilations baffle ranchers, cops, UFO believer," Jason Blevins/The *Denver Post*, 12 09-09
27. Brendon O'Brien; Saundra Marsh/Christopher O'Brien, Field investigation
28. "Livestock mutilations shake up Gunnison ranching community," Nancy Lofholm/Denver-Post.com 08-12
29. chieftain.com/mobile/mnews/1470804-123/zukowski-carcass-miller-animal; ufonut.com/archives/6343
30. Margie Kay; MUFON Journal, No. 547, November 2013; KCTV—Channel 5
31. *ibid*
32. huffingtonpost.com/2014/01/09/dead-cows-beaches-denmark-sweden_n_4569434.html

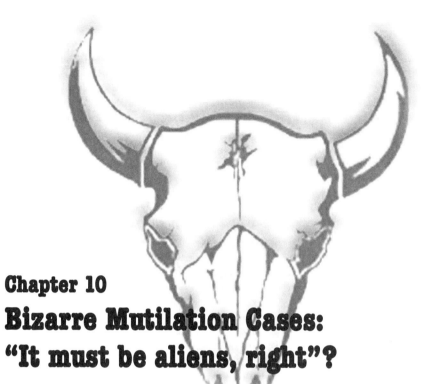

Chapter 10
Bizarre Mutilation Cases: "It must be aliens, right"?

C attle mutilation theorists can be divided into five main groups. 1) Those who suspect a government or quasi-governmental program monitoring the spread of "mad cow" disease and/or conducting a sampling of cattle for unknown purposes that may be related to establishing the level of environmental effects on livestock. 2) Those who suspect that non-terrestrial beings are targeting cattle for unknown purposes that may be related to some kind of genetic experiments or hybridization program. (Howe). 3) Proponents of the exotic perpetrator theory; ultra-terrestrials or other dimensional beings (Keel); prophetic tulpoids (Bearden); materialized psychisms from the collective unconscious (Jung); and the tricksterish nature spirit elementals (Vallee and Hynek). 4) The small number of researchers who cite rare reports of what appears to be some sort of ritual cultist activity often referred to as Satanism or "black magic." (Ellis); 5) The "it's all scavenger action" deniers. There is a body of circumstantial evidence that both supports and negates all five of these theories, and it is clear that there is no one-size-fits-all answer that can adequately explain all true unexplained livestock death cases that appear high-strange in nature.

The Blood Sucking Scorpion Crab Thing

Enter a sixth theory: crypto-creatures (odd, unknown animals) have gained some

limited notoriety in mute circles as a result of an article at the *Journal of the Bizarre* (JOTB) that notes a strange claim made by a Baptist minister in an interview on Linda Howe's July 15, 2007 earthfiles.com podcast. The following is synopsized from the May 12, 2012, JOTB article.

Around 1992, John Click, an ex-marine (at the time, a delivery truck driver), was taking a truckload from Campbell to Upland, Nebraska, located south of Grand Island and east of Lincoln. He was traveling on State Highway 4 when he looked over into a pasture and claimed he witnessed:

> [a] strange creature on the back of a cow. He described the creature as a football-shaped animal with hairless, yellow skin, which looked like a cross between a crab and a scorpion. It had attached itself to the back of a cow, which was bellowing in pain, and Mr. Click observed a red fluid passing through the creature's tail, as if the animal was sucking the blood of the cow. Mr. Click also observed a white-yellow ball of light near the creature, leading to the speculation that the mysterious creature was extraterrestrial in origin.[1]

The JOTB article goes on to describe another strange event that features a new species of subterranean giant crayfish that was discovered in November 2011 by Nicholas Bianco, an amateur spelunker while exploring a small cave in central Pennsylvania. The *Journal* article quotes Bianco describing his unusual find:

> "When I came across a small cave I decided to check it out, in the event that it may have been the legendary lost silver mine." By crawling on his hands and knees, Bianco was able to enter the cave about five feet until the opening narrowed to a foot-wide gap. "The sound of running water was very discernible and seemed to be coming from the narrow gap," says Bianco. "I reached my arm into the gap, expecting to feel water, but grabbed a chunk of ice instead." Trapped inside the ice was a partially-decomposed animal which, at first glance, appeared to be part reptile, part crayfish, and part scorpion.[2] (figure 1)

Bianco took the specimen to a local biology teacher who wrote the JOTB the following letter:

> I received the specimen from Mr. Bianco on the evening of November 29, which was sealed in a clear plastic bag in an attempt to prevent further putrification. Mr. Bianco explained that after melting the chunk of ice, the soft tissue remaining on the skeleton began to decompose rapidly. Since the specimen's tissue was too far putrefied, preventing any useful study, I informed Mr. Bianco that I would need to remove all remnants

of decayed flesh so that I could examine the skeleton. Mr. Bianco gave his consent.

On December 3, I removed last remnants of soft tissue and measured the specimen, which measured approximately ten inches in length. The specimen's most noticeable feature was a long thick bony spine featuring raised osteoderms (not made of bone but of a chitinous protein similar to the exoskeletons of crustaceans and insects), which culminated in a tail that was curled, much like that of a scorpion. The specimen's tail was devoid of the venomous telson consistent with scorpions; however the specimen's telson most closely resembled that of a crayfish, its long tail ending in a caudal furca replete with resial ramus and lateral ramus. I believe that the specimen's curled tail is an example of Batesian mimicry, an evolutionary adaptation used to scare off predators. However, since the creature had been allowed to evolve for millions of years without the presence of predators in its subterranean habitat, the lengthened tail could have been an evolutionary adaptation that aided the creature in navigation and locomotion.

The specimen's head is virtually indistinguishable from that of a crayfish, except for under-developed eyes and a lack of pigment commonly associated with cave-dwelling animals. The bones of the skeleton are somewhat flexible and have the feel and appearance of chitin rather than true bone, which may possibly suggest that the specimen had evolved from a sarcopterygian or crossopterygians during the late Devonian period...

...Strangely, the specimen has hind legs and crude front legs/arms, which implies that this animal falls somewhere on the evolutionary scale between sarcopterygians and tetrapods. The flesh of this specimen probably featured a lateral line that aided the animal in finding food; a feature found in many species of fish and amphibians... Perhaps the most interesting aspect of this specimen are the hind legs, which are similar in skeletal structure to the hind legs of a modern bullfrog. The specimen's femur, tibia, fibula, astragalus, and calcaneum appear similar to the common bullfrog; however, there are some peculiarities. Instead of having a frog's phalanges and metatarsals, the specimen's "feet" are nearly identical to the pereiopods of modern crayfish. This may indicate that the legs and feet of modern amphibians evolved from the pereiopods of crustaceans. Specimen lacks the swimmerets (pleopods) found in most crustaceans. Since the swimmerets are used for swimming, the lack of pleopods suggests that this creature was not adapted for swimming but, instead, depended on its hind legs for locomotion.

Another strange skeletal feature appears near the creature's chelae (claws). In modern crayfish, the dactyl and propodus of the chela are joined to the carpus, the carpus is joined to the merus, and the merus is joined to the basioischial segment. Oddly, this specimen's merus appears to be part merus and part radio-ulna, and is attached to a humerus, which resembles that of a frog… The specimen appears to have a movable neck, which is an important feature. In early amphibians, the cleithrum/clavicle complex allowed neck movement. However, the cleithrum disappeared in the early stages of reptile evolution. The lobe-finned fishes also feature a cleithrum. This indicates that the specimen first lived before the appearance of reptiles, and may have been one of the first amphibians…

It is my opinion that the specimen had existed for millions of years as a much smaller freshwater animal, living beneath underwater rocks. At some point the creature's ancestors began to inhabit subterranean rivers and streams, much like amblyopsidae fishes. A lack of predators allowed this creature, heretofore unknown to science, to grow to its large size. However, a geological event such as an earthquake must have closed off all possible exits, trapping the creature in its subterranean habitat where it was allowed to evolve uninterrupted for millions of years. During this period of unhindered evolution, the creature no longer required its pleopods for locomotion, due to its shallow water habitat. This led to the development of hind legs, much like those found on amphibian species. It is possible that this creature possessed the ability to "walk" on land, though it probably spent most of its life in water. Its long tail, when not curled up, allowed the animal to swim when necessary. On land, the tail provided the animal with balance, and a means to "scare off" predators through Batesian mimicry. The animal probably hopped with its powerful hind legs, while using the tips of its claws to drag itself over obstacles. Its amphibious nature allowed the animal to scavenge food on land and in water, which would have been an evolutionary necessity because of the lack of food in a subterranean environment.

It is also my opinion that the specimen discovered by Mr. Bianco had been alive up until September or October of 2011. During this period, much of Pennsylvania experienced record flooding due to a lengthy period of heavy rainfall. This surely led to a rise in the water level of the underground river, allowing the animal access to the surface for the first time in several million years. Unfortunately, its large size prevented it from squeezing through the cave's narrow passageway, where it may have gotten stuck. As a result, the creature probably died from starvation, or as a result of entombment in ice.

The remoteness of the area in which the specimen was found causes me to believe that this specimen is indeed authentic, and I believe that with more exploration, several living specimens of this animal may be obtained from the subterranean stream in Lebanon County.[3]

Could these two creatures (one witnessed and the other discovered) be of the same species? Based on Click's description and the specimen that Bianco discovered in the cave, there are remarkable similarities. Personally, I find it highly improbable that these creatures are solely responsible for mutilating cattle, but JOTB speculates that these strange-looking apparent predators could somehow be responsible for cattle mutilations. They point out that there are cave systems in many (but not all) regions where cattle have been found in a mutilated condition and suggest that the bioluminescence could be responsible for eyewitness reports of yellow-orange lights that have been reported at mute sites. But this doesn't account for sightings of these lights that appear to be airborne. Unless these creatures can fly, they could not be responsible for sightings of aerial light phenomena. The article continues:

> The Pennsylvania cave creature may also provide an explanation of the "ball of light" which was witnessed near the creature Mr. Click saw in Nebraska. Bioluminescence is the emission of light by a living organism (such as glow worms and fireflies), and bioluminescence has been observed in many species of animals that live in dark habitats, such as cave-dwelling organisms and deep-sea marine life. Bioluminescence has also been observed in crustaceans, such as the ostracod. Since both of our mystery creatures have distinct "crab-like" features, these unknown animals may possibly be related to bioluminescent animals in the class of *crustacea*...
>
> Bioluminescence is produced when a molecule known as luciferin chemically reacts with oxygen and an enzyme known as luciferinase. An article published by *Scientific American* magazine in 2009 states that 80 to 90 percent of deepwater life has evolved to produce light, because it is necessary for survival in the dark environment. Scientists now believe that bioluminescence has evolved at least 40 different times across the animal, fungal and bacterial kingdoms. Bioluminescence is used by animals to attract prey, or to repel a potential predator.[4]

Personally, I find the Click account extremely intriguing but the JOTB theory falls far short as a blanket explanation for the unexplained livestock death phenomenon.

Animals Found in Trees

Over the years, rumors of livestock mutilations being discovered in trees have surfaced from time to time. New Mexico State Patrolman Gabe Valdez claimed he had investigated a case of this ilk. Other stories I heard during my years in the SLV mentioned this, but I was never able to locate any photographs or other evidence that would bolster these claims. Several of these claims were from the Sanford, Colorado area near the Rio Grande River. Over the years other investigators have also mentioned claims of animals being found in trees. The only case that I have been able to document was found south of Alamosa.

August 6, 1996, Estrella, Colorado: Not all "unusual animal deaths" involved bloodless incisions and missing soft-tissue organs. The following report comes from an August 7, 1996 *Valley Courier* article written by former editor Greg Johnson.

> …A large Morgan draft horse was found wedged in the fork of a large tree in Estrella, (Colorado) about seven miles south of Alamosa near Highway 285, apparently dead. (figure 2) Officials for Alamosa County, said the horse… may have eaten some loco weed, or may have been trying to jump through the fork of the tree for some unknown reason, but fell short. Haddock said he is treating the incident as a freak accident, and that he didn't know what would motivate a (twelve to fourteen hundred pound) horse to jump in a tree.[5]

Reading this strange account, and looking at the photograph of the huge horse with all four feet off the ground, I searched my files for a similar event. I found one from west of Sedona, Arizona.

Tom Dongo has been investigating reports of the unusual around the Sedona region for over thirty years. He has witnessed many unusual events, and he described the following incident involving terrified horses in the book *Alien Tide* (co-written with rancher Linda Bradshaw).

> During an eight-month period at the end of the summer, 1994, I was investigating a number of reports from a ranch outside of Sedona. Several Bigfoot sightings occurred around this time, and the owner of the ranch told me of an ordeal involving one of their horses. Well, I went and saw the spot where this happened, and it was pretty strange. The rancher told me that one of his horses became wedged between two large branches on a good-sized tree near the house. It had evidently been trying to escape from something and became wedged while on a dead run. It was so stuck, they had to cut the two branches to get it out. Fortunately, it lived.…
>
> Just prior to the horse getting stuck, we had a near encounter with a Bigfoot. It was dark, and we were staking out the property. We heard something grunt real loud on the other side of the apple orchard opposite the house. It wasn't a lion or a bear. Well, when it grunted, six horses in a nearby corral went wild. They were racing around and literally scream-

ing. The next morning we found Bigfoot tracks near where we had heard the grunt, and they had a thirty-five to forty inch spread between strides! Whenever the Bigfoot was around, their horses were literally terrified.[6]

Now, I'm not suggesting that the SLV draft horse was being chased by a Bigfoot, but in light of the time proximity with "mutilations" to the south, I wonder, what could have terrified the animal enough to prompt it jump off the ground into the crotch of a tree?

Investigator Thomas Peay moved to the San Luis Valley in 1996 and immediately began to notice odd objects flitting about the airspace over his Mesita ranch perched in the rarified valley air. He also began to keep his ears open for unexplained livestock death cases in Costilla County where he now resided. As we have seen, Costilla is one of the most targeted counties by mutilators in the country. Thomas and I have dovetailed our efforts over the years to investigate the strange goings-on in the SLV and he is a top-notch sleuth. In 2000, Peay was headed up a back road toward Alamosa when on a hard, 45-degree hairpin turn—a few miles south of town—he noticed something in a tree that was located just to the west of the road. He pulled over and was startled to discover a young, mutilated javalina about seven or eight feet up in the branches of a leafless tree. (figure 3)

First off: javalinas are not found in Colorado or near the San Luis Valley. They are found at lower altitudes in the hot deserts of Arizona, southern New Mexico and southern Texas.

> Javelinas are commonly found in dense thickets of prickly pear, chaparral, scrub oak, or guajillo in the brush country south of San Antonio, and over wide areas of the Edwards Plateau and the Trans-Pecos. They can also be found throughout Mexico and Central America and well into South America.[7]

Second: what in the world was this poor animal doing up in a tree in a mutilated condition? Either someone has a very sick sense of humor, or this poor animal was very hungry—obviously it was extremely unlucky.

Another strange claim was reported to me by the brother of a hunter who, along with another hunter, allegedly found a mutilated deer in the crotch of a tree. The deer was located about four to five feet off the ground with no obvious signs of how it had ended up there with all four legs and hooves off the ground. The hunters were in the Rio Grande National Forest in November 1996 during a wave of UFO sightings and cattle mutilations. They estimated that the animal had been there a short time as it had snowed that night and there was no snow on the deer. (figure 4) They pulled it down out of the tree and immediately noted its reproductive organs had been pulled out of its rear end like a plug, and there was a small hole drilled from one tear duct through the nose to the other tear duct. They carefully checked around the site and were unable to discover any tracks or indication how the animal had died and become lodged off the ground in the tree. Go figure!

It Must Have Been el Chupacabra

Chupacabras (Spanish for "goatsucker") are said to be alien-looking creatures that prey on small to mid-sized animals, like chickens, goats and sheep. These animals are apparently, according to witnesses and law enforcement officials, attacked, killed and then drained of blood. Some household pets such as cats and dogs have reportedly been victimized, but generally it's small farm animals on isolated small farms that are targeted. Chupacabras are a relatively new crypto-creature and are almost exclusively a Spanish-speaking country phenomenon. There is some evidence to suggest that a few cases of a similar nature were reported in the mid- 1970s, but it wasn't until the mid-1990s that waves of animal deaths were reported and blamed on chupacabra-like creatures. Since the onset of the first reported "official" cases in 1995, in Puerto Rico, the chupacabra phenomenon has swept through Mexico, Central and parts of South America.

In the late 1990s a few cases were reported north of the American border in Texas, New Mexico and California, but this is primarily a rural Latin American mystery. It is interesting to note that the original descriptions of the Puerto Rican creatures seemed fairly consistent, but as the phenomenon spread, descriptions of the creatures began to vary widely from region to region. It appeared to some investigators that the phenomenon was actually multifarious, with several types of mystery "goatsuckers" running amok around the jungles and even deserts of Latin American countries.

Scott Corrales' book *Chupacabras and Other Mysteries* is considered the go-to work examining strange outbreaks of goatsucker reports. According to his research, the first reported attack attributed to chupacabras occurred in mid-March 1995 in Puerto Rico near the centrally located towns of Orocovis and Morovis. Eight sheep were discovered mysteriously dead by their owner, Enrique Barretto. The sheep each had two puncture wounds on the chest and appeared to be completely drained of blood. Because the deaths were highly strange and unexplainable, he immediately called law enforcement authorities to file a report. Two officers were dispatched to Barreto's and while investigating, one of them noticed a strange creature peering at them from the shadows. What they described was a humanoid-looking 'thing' that was "three to four feet tall, and had orange-yellow eyes. The police officer ordered his partner to stop the squad car they were in, jumped out, and pursued the creature. Immediately he was engulfed by a sense of nausea accompanied by a pounding headache. He was rendered so helpless that his partner had to come to his rescue."[8]

Later, on March 26th, another event occurred on the Barreto farm. An amateur ufologist, Jaime Torres, claimed he encountered a "round-headed creature with elongated black eyes, a fine jaw, and a small mouth…resting on a tree limb not far from his position. (figure 5) This unusual thing had a chameleon-like pigmentation, alternating from purple to brown to yellow, while its face was a dark, grayish color. According to the lone witness, the creature made a curious gesture. It moved its head from side to side and produced a sibilant hissing sound that caused him to feel faint. Overcoming the sensation, he managed to see the creature drop from the tree limb and rush off into the dense foliage." To complicate matters, there are descriptions of chupacabras that have noted bat-like wings and the apparent ability to fly.

Puerto Rican comedian Silverio Perez came up with the moniker "chupacabras" in one of his stand-up routines soon after the first incidents were reported in the press. The name stuck, and soon reports began to spread first to the Dominican Republic and then to Mexico, Central and South America—ending up with alien-looking canines spotted in Texas. In his book, Corrales has compiled a good textbook quality definition of the chupacabra:

> The most common description of Chupacabra is a reptile-like being, appearing to have leathery or scaly greenish-gray skin and sharp spines or quills running down its back. This form stands approximately three to 4 feet high, and stands and hops in a similar fashion to a kangaroo. In at least one sighting, the creature was reported to hop 20 feet… It is said to hiss and screech when alarmed, as well as leave behind a sulfuric stench. When it screeches, some reports assert that the chupacabra's eyes glow an unusual red [that] gives the witnesses nausea.[9]

> I should point out that a sulfuric scent is reminiscent of devil/demon encounters down through history and there are numerous accounts and claims of this olfactory element in reports of unusual encounters. Maybe witnesses are being overpowered by chupacabra exhaust?

> Still other cases (mainly in Texas) mention strange-looking hairless canines that authorities dismiss as coyotes with mange. (figure 6) After several years of reports, chupacabras seemed to have taken a hiatus.[10]

> Then in April 2006, inexplicably, reports began to surface in, of all places, Russia. If you believe the Russian press, villagers began experiencing unexplained animal deaths the year before and it was reported that thirty-two turkeys had been attacked and drained of blood. Also reported were 30 sheep that were killed and also drained of blood. Witness descriptions of the creature thought responsible were of a classic chupacabra-looking animal. What are these goatsuckers? Escaped "genetic experiments" as has been suggested?

According the earliest accounts, the livestock attacks began shortly after Hurricane Hugo passed over the island. Rumors started that the Chupcabra escaped from a damaged secret United States military lab, where genetic experiments were allegedly being carried out. Soon after, the sightings spread to Central America, Mexico, South America and finally the southern United States. To date, none of the 'supposed' attacks on humans have been fatal.[11]

The Varginha Case

What about the strange events of January 20, 1996 in Varginha, Brazil? Although no mutilations are directly tied to this case, the rumored death of a soldier and the bizarre claims by witnesses are worthy of mention. To this day one of the most intriguing and perplexing "alien" sighting cases, Varghina features over 35 witnesses, alien autopsies, government misdirection, alleged NASA involvement and possibly the death of a Brazilian soldier or fireman (depending on the version) during the capturing of at least one alien.

In 1996 I was invited to speak at the Missouri MUFON "Show Me" conference where I spoke at length with fellow presenter Dr. John Carpenter, who had recently returned from Varghina. He was convinced that this could be one of the best cases of a supposed UFO crash and subsequent alien capture ever reported. The primary events unfolded over several days, but reports of a strange, red-eyed creature seen lurking about the outskirts of town were filed by several witnesses over the next several months. There are still some who wonder if an alien is on the loose around Varginha.

> The incident that made this town a hot spot in the intergalactic search for intelligent life started quite innocently. On a Saturday afternoon stroll in January, a trio of young women decided to take a shortcut home through a vacant lot. In a clump of weeds, the three said, they encountered a creature like nothing they had seen before. (figure 7)
>
> "It wasn't a man or an animal—it was something different," said one of the women, Katia Andrade. The being had oily, brown skin and rubbery limbs, she said. Three rounded protrusions sprouted from its oversized head. Standing out in a different way was the creature's odor: One ghastly whiff weakened the knees. As for the stranger's demeanor, the women unanimously, if tactlessly, agreed: It was "muddle-headed." When the creature wagged its big noggin dizzily in their direction, the three women ran off.[12]

I've compiled a thumbnail sketch of the Varginha events from various sources, reports and a personal conversation with Dr. Carpenter. It seems that in the city of Varginha, in the central Brazilian state of Minas Gerais, several persons witnessed a UFO crash, seeing a cigar shaped craft heading for the ground. In other parts of the town there were many anomalous lights reported. On the same day, three girls saw a creature of the following description: "brown, soft skin ('like a heart'), large, red, bulging eyes and visible veins."

According to veteran investigator Bob Pratt, who investigated the Varginha case, these events were part of the biggest UFO wave ever reported from Brazil:

> Eurico de Freitas, was awakened by the sounds of his cattle. He glanced at the alarm clock, hence the exact time. [his wife] Oralina opened the window and saw the cattle were very agitated and stampeding all over the pasture three hundred to four hundred feet away. Then she saw a cigar-shaped object just above the cattle. There was no moon but the craft gave off a faint light. Oralina called out to her husband, Eurico, forty, and he rushed to the window. "My God!" he cried. "There's a submarine above my pasture."
>
> They could see gray smoke or vapor coming out of the back as it moved slowly, in a sort of rocking motion, only fifteen to twenty feet above the ground. Neither Eurico nor Oralina ventured outside, but stood at the window watching as the object took forty five minutes to pass ever so slowly out of sight over a ridge about two thousand feet away, heading in the direction of Varginha.
>
> They had the impression that it was having difficulties of some kind because of the very slow way it was moving. If the UFO was making any sound, the bellowing of the cows drowned it out. All this time the cattle remained panicky and frightened but the couple's four dogs, although awake, showed no reaction. Eurico and Oralina's four children, aged twelve to twenty, slept through it all.[13]

I discussed the incident in my last book *Stalking the Tricksters:*

> During the following few days, alien beings [as many as six, according to some estimates] were allegedly spotted by other witnesses, trying to escape, as they were being hunted and even fired upon by the military... One of the alien bodies was allegedly recovered and autopsied at the local hospital, then taken away to another location. Its hairless body was not more than five-feet tall and dark brown, as though it had oil on its skin. It had two large, red, pupil-less eyes, a small mouth and nose and a big, brown head with three rather rounded horns.
>
> Revelations on Varginha Case are aired on Brazilian TV and reach the rest of the world. In May, 1997 a scientist accused of having autopsied the alien(s) states at a conference he will be able to speak on the subject sometime in the future. Also, added to the mix were reports of missing animals from the region that may have helped spread the story beyond the region.

On June 1997, 15 witnesses allegedly confirmed involvement of dispatched soldiers in the alien capture. Another witness reports that he was offered money to keep his mouth shut. Press and TV journalists joined ufologists in a six-month-long hunt for additional information about the fate of the two surviving aliens, providing fodder for conspiracy theorists that resulted in revisions of the number of witnesses and their stories, including varying claims as to the number of aliens.

The latest version claimed that five ETs were flushed out of hiding in the Jardim Andere, a park on the north side of Varginha. John Carpenter said that he was impressed by what he has learned so far. "There are at least 35 first-hand witnesses to the presence of the strange beings. This includes audiotaped interviews with several military participants. There is the possibility of a UFO crash, but there is little doubt about the existence of five or six strange beings resembling a cross between the Little Greys and the Chupacabras. Some were shot or died, others captured alive," he said.[14]

There were rumors that a U.S. government scientific team arrived shortly after the capture and spirited the body away to an unknown destinations. Is it too much to suppose that your tax dollars may be involved in covering up paranormal events in other countries?

Brazil Cow and Sheep Mystery

In 1975 a mutilated cow was found near death on a farm near Santa Victoria in the state of Rio Grande do Sul—located in southern Brazil. Its udder was gone and, impossibly, *the veins near the udder had been removed, all with perfect surgical technique.* This occurred within 250 feet of the farmhouse and no noises were heard that night, nor did the normally vigilant dogs bark. There was no blood found on the ground or near the animal. The unfortunate cow died soon after being discovered. This was the latest in a series of events that had plagued the region.

On the same farm two years earlier in 1973, more than 300 sheep were found dead or dying. All of them eventually expired and they all had puncture marks in the necks. This is where the story gets bizarre:

The first sheep found was surrounded by a circle of her own blood. The farm manager decided to barbecue one of the animals since the body was still warm but when he hung it up and sliced it open he found no blood in the animal. In the same area many circles of burnt grass were found.

During this time one of the farm owners, a lawyer, heard noises and thought someone was using a truck to steal sheep. He and two nephews took their guns and ran out but what they saw was a UFO, a disc with many rotating lights, going up. This was about the same time as when the sheep were killed. After the sheep died, circles of burnt grass were found. This was in winter, probably June or July.

The state's Secretary of Agriculture went to the farm and he and his aides thought wild dogs were responsible but no teeth marks were found on the animals. After this, a group of farmers who jointly owned the sheep took police dogs and guns and stationed themselves around the flock one night. They didn't see or hear anything—but in the morning two sheep were found dead. They happened to be the fattest sheep in the flock. One pregnant sheep almost ready to give birth was found one morning with a *circular hole in her side and the fetus was gone.*

On the same farm in 1973 a calf was found dead with a piece of its tongue cut off and no blood in the carcass. The face looked as though something had suctioned off all the blood through the face. Near Pelotas, Rio Grande do Sul, a number of pigs were found with holes in their necks and elsewhere. They were dead and there was no blood. It was assumed wild dogs were responsible but none were ever seen. And, in perhaps 1975, an ox was found with burns on it. *The burns grew and eventually the animal weakened and died.*[15] [my emphasis]

Human Mutilations

Over the 20 plus years that I have been involved with investigating unexplained livestock deaths I have often been asked if human mutilation cases have been reported. My stock answer is: Most, if not all warm-blooded animals have been found in this horrific condition—including humans. The most famous report of this type has become known as the Guarapiranga Reservoir Case from Brazil that allegedly occurred in 1988. The autopsy photographs were leaked to Brazilian researchers and the case became a sensational news story in late 1992. It is important to note that the case did not have any apparent UFO activity tied to it and this stand-alone case has never been solved.

On December 10, 1992, a public message written on Prodigy, a national computer network, discussed a human mutilation being shown to a group of UFO researchers at a UFO conference in Las Vegas, Nevada. According to this individual, a professor, A.J. Gevaerd of Brazil presented seven photos of the human mutilation to researchers at the conference, which was similar to the cattle mutilations. UFO researchers were trying to associate this human mutilation with the UFO phenomenon just like they have done with the animal mutilations. The Prodigy member said, "The deceased had the skin cut away from one cheek/jaw, cut very precisely (surgically), exposing the bone/teeth underneath. The photos also showed the absence of various parts – ears, eyes, lips, and certain unmentionables…I suppose this could be a deadly hoax, but the similarities to the cattle mutilations are startling.[16]

Early the following year, G. Cope Schellhorn published a sensational article that documented the particulars of the Brazilian case. He quoted from the attending coroners and released to the public the horrific autopsy photographs that can be found all over the Internet:

> Encarnacion Garcia learned from her friend, Dr. Rubens Goes, that he was in possession of some rather "odd" photos [that] had been given to him by his cousin, police technician, Rubens Sergio. These were official photos of a body [*GRAPHIC* Figure 7] that had been found near Guarapiranga reservoir on the 29th of September 1988, of an unnamed male who was, however, later identified. The name of this man has been withheld from all media investigators, including UFO investigators, at the request of his relatives.
>
> After studying the photos, Encarnacion Garcia was impressed with how similar the wounds of the body were to those found on the carcasses of so many UFO-related mutilated animals, knowledge which the original investigating police officials and medical doctors involved with the case did not possess. Surprisingly, Dr. Cuenca, head of the primary investigation, offered his files on the case. This is the stroke of luck which I previously mentioned and for which we can all be thankful. These included the all important autopsy description to which I will momentarily refer.
>
> The initial police report, however, was not extraordinary in nature except for the recognition that the body, although extremely mutilated, had not met with unusual violence; that is, there were no signs of struggle or the application of bondage of any kind.
>
> It was the autopsy report itself which was most revealing, especially when we compare the remarks made there with what we have learned from animal mutilation cases elsewhere. It is imperative to remember, as I have stated previously, that the individuals conducting the autopsy had no knowledge of similar animal mutilation cases. This makes the official remarks of the report all the more revealing in retrospect.
>
> Encarnacion Garcia received copies of seven photos. I have included the five most revealing ones here with a description and commentary. The work of the perpetrators of this atrocity: the kinds of cuts made, the precision of the cuts, the removal of whole internal organs through small apertures, the lack of bleeding, the failure of the body to smell or decompose rapidly— all these are hallmarks of UFO-related animal

mutilations. These peculiarities would seem to rule out Satanists, revenge-seekers or casual mutilators and go beyond even the capacities of a modern Jack the Ripper…

[Excerpts from the autopsy report stated] "The axillary regions on both sides showed soft spots where organs had been removed. Incisions were made on the face, internal thorax, abdomen, legs, arms, and chest." As Garcia observed, the doctors stated that these wounds were quite uncommon. The report also observes, "Shoulders and arms have perforations of 1 to 1.5 inches in diameter where tissue and muscles were extracted. The edges of the perforations were uniform and so was their size. The chest had shrunk due to the removal of internal organs."

In other words, internal organs were removed or sucked somehow through these small circular incisions. Why such a technique? Some doctors today are using a similar method to remove diseased tissue and organs from their human subjects - but this kind of procedure injures those organs in the process. Did the "surgeons" who worked on this victim care whether the organs were injured or not? What kind of specimens were they looking for? What kind of research is this?[17]

I have elected to reproduce a now-famous image from the series of autopsy photos, but I must warn you it is graphic. These photographs have been on the Internet for almost 20 years and they are fairly well known. The images are disturbing, and although Schellhorn titles his article to insinuate that this human mutilation case was somehow "UFO-related," there is no evidence whatsoever that any UFO activity had been reported in the region during the time period when officials think the murder and disfigurement occurred.

After hearing rumors of human mutilation cases, longtime ufologist and former publisher of *UFO Magazine,* Don Ecker, researched the subject back in the late 1980s. In 1993, after the release of the autopsy photographs from the Guarapiranga case, Ecker wrote an article titled "The Human Mutilation Factor." Today ex-police officer Ecker is the host of the popular radio program *Dark Matters* and I asked him if I had his permission to re-publish his article. He agreed to the reprint and told me that he had "hit a brick wall" with his investigation into the subject. Here is Don's article:

In the last forty years of UFO research, one of the most baffling questions that has plagued researchers has been "Is the UFO Phenomenon dangerous to humanity?" Over the years, there have been numerous cases where the phenomenon has figured into human deaths, but as a rule, most cases have been officially ruled accidental. When speaking of cases where death has resulted, usually most assume cases where military pilots have died as a result of "chasing" the phenomenon. One of the most famous of these military chases that is discussed whenever the subject of death and UFOs is raised is the famous "Mantell Case". This case is so well known that I will not discuss it here, but there are many others. In one of the less well-known cases, during the mid 1950s, a military jet interceptor was observed on radar being "absorbed" into a UFO over the Great Lakes. No trace of pilot or aircraft was ever found. In another case reported in the excellent work *Clear Intent* was the case of the "Cuban MIG Incident". In this case a Cuban MIG was locking on his weapons radar when the aircraft exploded in midair. The wing man was certain that the UFO had fired some type of weapon, but other than the jet exploding, no other smoke, flame or other obvious weapon firing was observed.

The matter of either overt or covert hostility on the part of UFOs has always been treated warily by serious researchers. On the one hand, if the enigma is hostile, then several questions must be faced. What if anything should the powers in authority tell the public? Is the government capable of handling a threat of this type? Is the public ready to face an issue as potentially terrifying as a "possible threat from somewhere else?" Other than incidents involving military involvement, have there been cases where civilians have been injured or killed during some type of UFO encounter? Is it possible that the reported cases of UFOs and their occupants abducting unwilling humans for some type of medical or genetic experimentation could be true? Now, if any of this is factual, then what ramifications does the Human Race face in light of the above…?

…While researching several stories for *UFO Magazine*, I interviewed a number of prominent UFOlogists, over the last several months, and in each case, the question of human deaths, in connection with animal mutilations, invariably was raised. Most readers of this text will be familiar with Mr. John Keel, who many regard as the last of the great UFOlogists. From the earliest days of modern UFOlogy, Keel has been a force to reckon with. The author of numerous books that address various aspects of UFOlogy, and magazine articles too numerous to mention, Keel has a unique slant on the subject that most will never experience. According to Keel, the phenomenon has always had an unexplained hostility towards humans that has led to untold numbers of deaths. While Keel will be the first to explain that he rejects the ET hypothesis, he does not doubt the phenomenon a bit. In what many UFOlogists consider as one of Keels best works, *The Mothman Prophecies*, E. P. Dutton & Co., Inc. 1975, Keel related report after report of animal mutilations involving cattle, dogs, horses and sheep, and also related what were called "vampire killings" of four humans in Yugoslavia, here the victims were "mutilated and drained of blood"…

…After growing up in an age where the entire human race can be decimated by nuclear, biological and chemical weapons, the human race somehow manages to keep slogging on. I have seen more people "panicked" over a shortage of gasoline than imminent nuclear holocaust, yet somehow when the subject of UFOs crops up, the government doesn't want to panic anyone. It really makes me wonder what they know, that I should. I really don't think that they are going to talk to anyone soon, as you shall soon see.

In January 1989, it came to the attention of the MUFON State Director of Idaho, Mr. Don Mason, that cattle mutilations had occurred once again in the southeastern section of Idaho. After an investigation by a MUFON investigator, the facts were as follows. The animals (two cattle, same night, but each owned by different ranchers) were "somehow" killed, sexual organs removed, body fluids drained, patches of hide "surgically" removed. All the appearances of what is today considered to be a classic case of animal mutilation. As of this date… the final lab reports are not back yet, but already the Sheriff's Department has labeled it a "cult killing." No tracks, tire or human, around the animals even though it had just rained, no unusual activity reported by the ranchers that evening, and one animal was found next to an occupied house. One of the ranchers admitted that this was the second time he had been "hit" by the mysterious mutilators. The last incident had only been a bit over a year previously, and they were worried enough that all had their "deer rifle" within easy reach.

After having been personally involved in an investigation of cattle mutilations as a police officer back in 1982, I was very familiar with the "cult" theory of perpetrators. The Idaho Department of Law Enforcement drags it out every time there is a new rash of mutilations. The problem is, and every one is aware of it, that no one has yet been brought to trial, or arrested yet for these crimes. Out here in the west, people know that you are flirting with a rancher's bullet if you are caught fooling around with the rancher's cattle. They are his livelihood, and he will defend it. Yet, the mutilations keep occurring, and no one is any the wiser, or are they?

…Now I must explain that I had very mixed feelings about whether I wished to attempt to explore this subject any further, or allow sleeping dogs to lie. On the one hand, I wanted more than anything to discover just what was occurring, and on the other, I realized that this had the potential to backfire on someone that disturbed the status quo. I was familiar with reports of human abductions and mutilations that had surfaced in the last several years in reports such as the Lear documents, Grudge 13 reports and others, but yet I was not sure what I believed, or even if there was anything to believe.

I ran across a friend that was still employed with a police department in this area who was a detective. I had mentioned to him the recent cattle mutilations, and what I suspected in the above-mentioned case of a human that had been mutilated. Scot had also been involved in the last several years with several cases of mutilations that he had been called upon to investigate, always with negative results. He was as curious about this phenomenon as I was, and since he was still an active duty police officer, he had access to the department computer, to access the NCIC system that is maintained in Washington D. C. by the FBI.

After giving Scott the criteria for a search of unexplained human deaths, that involved factors of mutilation, I asked that the search go back to at least 1973, involving this area of the Northwest. Scott (not his real name) ran the request through the department computer. As he mentioned at the time, he had expected to get reams of reports back that we would have to wade through, to get to the reports that would be our further study. Scott ended up requesting that the inquiry be run back to 1970, and involve not only Idaho, but also Utah, Nevada, Oregon, and Washington states. Because of the magnitude of this search, Scott stated that it would take about one week to get the results back into his department. As a side note, for anyone that is not familiar with the NCIC system, it is a national data bank for Law enforcement agencies all across the United States. It is maintained and controlled by the Federal Bureau of Investigation, at FBI headquarters, in Washington D. C.

On the 14th of February, Scott contacted me in person, and appeared very troubled. His exact words were that "something is really screwy, Don." "I got the request back from NCIC on Monday, and there has gotta be something wrong. They told me that they had NO unsolved murders at all, zero, that met that criteria. That any further requests will have to be made by voice, telephone call, with the proper authorizations. Somebody is sitting on something, big as Hell." I also knew that something was as screwy as hell. After all, anybody that has had any dealing with law enforcement knows about the "Green River Killer" in Washington State. This serial killer is credited with at least 30 to 40 murders of young women, and to this date, the case is as big a mystery as ever. Many of the killings showed some types of mutilation, and if nothing else, at least some of these homicides should have shown up.

Once more, as a side note, I had been warned by a prominent UFOlogist, that there was a lid "screwed down tighter than you would believe in regards to human mutes." I also was warned that in order to break through the secrecy, it was going to be a long and sometimes weary job, but that if enough persistence was applied, then it was possible to get to the bottom of this facet of the UFO enigma. Do I think that this can be solved, along with the rest of the puzzle? Yes, I do, because I think that the secrecy can only be maintained for so long, and then no longer. I also believe very strongly that only if the entire UFO community works in concert will this be accomplished, and the infighting and arguments must cease for the good of us all.[18]

Hitting a Brick Wall

Over the years I have also heard mention of human mutilation cases and attempted to dig around for more information. These cases, if real, are undoubtedly some of the most disturbing reports investigated by law enforcement. It would stand to reason that they are probably the least likely cases to get any publicity due to their horrific nature.

In 1996 at a book signing in Taos, NM, I was told by an "ex-intelligence" worker who lived in Taos, that he had heard of a young teenage girl that had been found mutilated "just like the cows," down in the Silver City, NM area. He gave me the name of a state patrol contact to call. The officer vehemently denied the story. Something in his voice told me that even if it had been true, he would never admit the case had occurred. Several phone calls later, I had a strong hunch that I would be unable to confirm this claim no matter how deep I dug. I was right.

Back in 1994, I remember hearing about a claim made by researcher Bill English concerning a downed B-52 in Vietnam that appeared to have been set down in the dense jungle. When rescuers arrived on the scene (in another version it was a "combat photographer"), English claimed that the crew were found strapped into their seats, but they had all been horribly mutilated—again, just like the cows.

There have been other claims of this sort over the years—none of which has any accompanying documentation or corroboration:

> In 1956 at the White Sands Missile Test Range, an Air Force major reported that he had witnessed a disk shaped flying object kidnap Sgt. Jonathan P. Louette. Louette was missing for three days when his mutilated body was found in the dessert near the test range. Louette's genitals had been removed and his rectum cored out with surgical precision. Like many cattle mutilations, Louette's eyes had been removed and all of his blood was missing. The Air Force filed a report stating that Sgt. Louette had died of exposure after being lost in the desert.[19]

Another intriguing claim comes from well-respected researcher Len Stringfield, who specialized in chasing down stories involving UFO crashes and possible retrievals. This account from an article written by Tim Swartz, also features the war in Southeast Asia—this time Cambodia:

The late Leonard H. Stringfield, a former Air Force intelligence officer wrote in his self-published book, *UFO Crash/Retrievals*, Status Report No. 6, about the testimony given by a "high ranking Army officer" whom Stringfield says he has known for several years and who is allegedly a "straight shooter." The officer claimed that while he was in Cambodia during the Vietnam war, his Special Operations group was involved in a firefight with aliens, whom the soldiers came across sorting human body parts and sealing them into large bins. Subsequently the unit was held for several days and interrogated under hypnosis. The officer claimed that he and his men were given cover memories which only began to surface years later.[20]

Swartz has also uncovered another claim of the discovery of an alleged human mutilation—this time from Idaho:

In 1989, the mysterious death of a man a decade earlier came to the attention of the MUFON State Director of Idaho, Don Mason. According to the report, in 1979, two hunters in the Bliss and Jerome area of Idaho stumbled across the almost nude body of a man that had been hideously mutilated. The body's sexual organs had been removed, its lips were sliced off, and the blood had been drained. Although the body was found in very rugged country, it's bare feet were not marked, and no other tracks, animal or human were evident. After the police were notified, an intensive search was mounted and the man's possessions were recovered miles from where the body was found. No one knows how the body ended up where it was found, or even more importantly, what happened to him.[21]

Another Idaho report investigated by Swartz involves a claim that numerous mutilated victims had been found by authorities and (if true) covered up:

In 1978, I had a Deputy Prosecuting Attorney friend. He had many associates connected to law enforcement and other areas of investigation. He once came to me because he was having terrible nightmares, and he felt that maybe I knew of something or someone that could help him.

Reluctantly, he began to tell me a story that he swore was true. He said that for months law enforcement was finding dead bodies up around the Rathdrum Idaho area, [just east of Spokane, Washington] a place notorious for witchcraft and Satan worship. They hadn't found just a few; there were numerous unidentifiable bodies. He said that at first he thought the bodies were involved in some kind of ritual. In fact, someone had seen strange lights, went to the area where the lights had been seen and stumbled onto a few bodies. It wasn't until he was invited to take a look at some of them in the morgue that he was overwhelmed with horror.

The bodies were mutilated exactly the same... and they had no idea who they were, because they barely had a face left. He described them in detail to me and explained that the medical examiner was totally at a loss for explanation. He said there was nothing at that time that even came close to instrumentation made by humans and the expertise in dissection methods were far beyond medical know how in those days. I had forgotten about his story until I found the one above. The amount of bodies and what had actually been done to them was never revealed. Where had all of them come from, and what did this?[22]

While attending the International UFO Congress in 2010, I was told by a Native member of the San Carlos Indian Reservation that there were rumors whirling around the Rez that someone had been discovered dead and horribly mutilated and that knowledge of the case was quickly suppressed by authorities. Again, I made several calls and again came up blank.

Are human mutilation cases occurring? I certainly hope not, but it would not surprise me if there are real cases occurring. Need I say, humans are capable of being the most heinous, vicious and cruel life forms on this rock spinning in space.

There are accounts from Africa that would suggest there are more than a few ritualistic human murders and disfigurements taking place. But apparently word about many of these cases does not filter out beyond the rural communities where these alleged events are said to be perpetrated. There are exceptions however— as with this 2013 CNN report from Yaounde, Cameroon:

Michele Mbala Mvogo, a 17-year-old high school student, left home to go to school one morning, and she never came back. On Friday, police found Michele's corpse with four other bodies dumped outside a kindergarten school. Fighting back tears, Deborah Ngoh Tonye described what was left of her sister's gruesome corpse. Someone had removed Michele's genitals, tongue, eyes, hair, and breasts.

Michele's bizarre murder is believed to be part of a wave of killings linked to occult rituals that has triggered panic in Yaounde, the capital city of more than 2 million people in the West African nation of Cameroon. In the past two weeks police have found 18 bodies dumped along the streets. Authorities said all of the bodies had been mutilated. Officials have not said if the female victims among the 18 bodies had been raped.

State security officials said Tuesday the bodies have been identified. The victims, who are between the ages of 15 and 26, are mostly Yaounde high school students, police said. They said a number of suspects have been arrested in the case, but so far no one has been charged. State intelligence officials have launched an investigation to track down the killers, said Communications Minister Tchiroma Bakari.

In some regions of the country, traditional healers claim eyes, genitals, tongues and other organs have mystical powers. Some occultists believe such organs hold the keys to gaining wealth and other good fortune...[23]

Some theorists have postulated that cattle may be a ritual substitute for preferred human victims and that these human cases do occur. I can't say that this is true, for (thankfully) there is no unequivocal evidence of this being the case—at least here in North America.

I could go on and on listing strange, bizarre, inexplicable examples of unnatural deaths and disfigurements of warm-blooded animals on the planet, but let's move on and continue examining cattle and the implications of their presence in our environment. There are even more horrific implications for us to ponder, believe it or not.

Chapter Ten Sources and References:
1. Linda Howe/Earthfiles.com
2. *ibid*
3. *Journal of the Bizarre 5-12-12; Linda Howe/earthfiles.com*
4. biolum.eemb.ucsb.edu; Scientific American
5. *Valley Courier,* 8-7-96
6. Dongo, Tom & Bradshaw, Linda, *Alien Tide*, Hummingbird Pub, Sedona, AZ 1990
7. Schmidly, DJ, *The Mammals of Texas*, University of Texas Press, Austin, TX, 2004
8. *Chupacabras and Other Mysteries,* Scott Corrales, Greenleaf , Murfreesboro, TN 1997
9. *ibid*
10. *ibid*
11. elchupacabra.com
13. *Wall Street Journal*, 7-12-96
14. Pratt, Bob, *UFO Danger Zone,* Horus House Press, Madison, WI, 1996; bobpratt.org/varginha
15. O'Brien, Christopher, *Stalking the Tricksters,* AUP, Kempton, IL, 2009
16. *Ovni Documento* Jan/Mar-1980, Rio De Janeiro, Brasil; Dr. P. Edwards, *Stigmata*, 1980
17. Project Stigma
18. "UFO-Related Homicide in Brazil," GC Schellhorn, *International UFO Magazine*, 1993
19. "The Human Mutilation Factor," Don Ecker, *UFO Magazine,* 1993
20. "Are UFOs responsible for mysterious human mutilations?" Tim Swartz, 1997
21. *ibid*
22. *ibid*
23. *ibid*
24. cnn.com, Tapang Ivo Tanku, 1-22-13

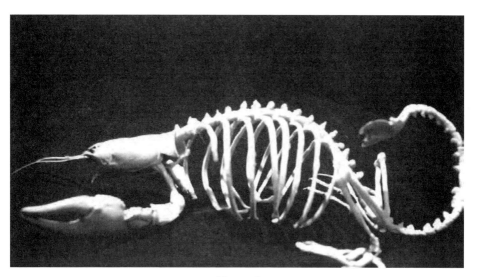

Figure 1
Pennsylvania cave creature. (credit: *Journal of the Bizarre*)

Figure 2
Morgan draft horse found dead in the crotch of a tree horse. (credit: *Valley Courier*)

Figure 3
Javelina found mutilated in a SLV tree. (credit: Thomas Peay)

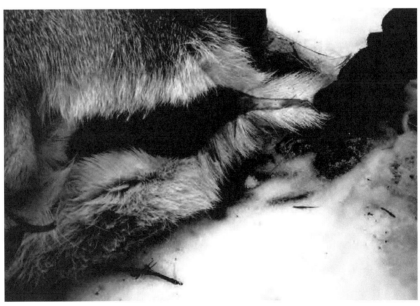

Figure 4
Deer found by hunters mutilated in a tree. (credit: Judy DeBon; TMV Archive)

Figure 5
Rare alleged photograph of a Puerto Rican chupacabra up in a tree.
(credit: hauntedamericatours.com)

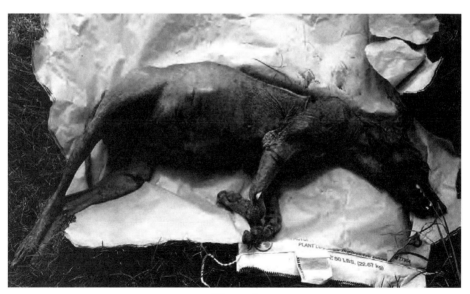

Figure 6
Mangy coyote-style chupacabra from Texas.(credit: sciencebuzz.com)

Figure 7
A drawing of the alleged "Varginha alien." (credit: ufo.se)

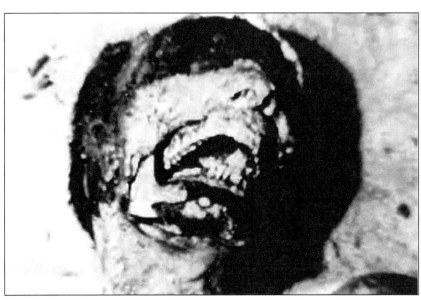

Figure 8
The infamous Guarapiranga Reservoir Case. (credit: G. Cope Schellhorn)

Chapter 11
Mutes and the Media

The role of language and how we communicate with each other contextualizes and defines our consensus reality. This especially holds true with dissemination of the unexplained livestock death phenomenon out into the culture. Specific words, phrases and terms and the manner in which they are used have a tremendous influence in programming the message being communicated.

I realized this fact early in my investigative process and have always watched what I say, but perhaps more importantly how I say it. I feel labels and buzzwords wield tremendous subliminal power and influence, and I wondered if perhaps this "mute" mystery needed a voice. And I thought: let's re-think the very term "cattle mutilation," redefine the term, and then perhaps investigators of this "serial crime spree of all time" might get some notice, respect and scientific and academic help. Perhaps this basic element represented a blind spot of sorts? The very term "mutilation" is harsh—perhaps too harsh.

It should be obvious by now that language and the role of the media has inexorably shaped the public's perception of the cattle mutilation mystery. I'll go one step further and suggest that this media-derived influence may be an extremely important key in the tool kit, which we will need to unravel the mystery. And it should be obvious by now that pop culture, media-derived education concerning any "inexplicable" subject is a fertile ground for societal manipulation. This particular mystery's impact on pub-

lic perception has been tainted by the media's inability to ask appropriate questions of the principles involved—let alone determine unequivocal answers and convey them clearly to the public.

The following are examples to show how public perception of the cattle mutilation phenomenon has been manipulated by the press. These are only a sampling of many possible scenarios that I have discovered over the years of pondering local, regional, national and international media coverage of the cattle mutilations.

The Terms We Choose: The Role of Languaging

As I realized early on and suggested in my first three books, the San Luis Valley could be considered a near-perfect, textbook example of a sociological Petri dish giving birth to a powerful new meme within our increasingly dysfunctional western culture. We have the birth of the cattle mutilation meme with the Snippy case, the first case to gain international media coverage. Then the Iowa rustling wave in the early '70s, followed by the 1975 SLV outbreak that started with atypical, high-strange (unpublicized) cases, which then morphed into initial cases where the cattle were *shot with firearms*—then all hell appeared to break loose across the western United States.

When I began researching the 1975 SLV wave, several elements of the local SLV media coverage stood out. Most importantly, only one person wrote the *Valley Courier* articles during the height of the "flap" period—a reporter named Miles Porter IV. Porter's descriptions of the carcasses in his many articles all had a similar tone. Descriptions attributed to ranchers and law enforcement officials all shared a similar quality. Case upon case revealed identical descriptions of the mutilations and the surrounding "crime scene." There were even identical verbatim quotes from one article to the next!

I had heard identical descriptions of unknown anomalous lights during the New Year's Eve party that previous January when I began my research project. And I couldn't resist diving into the hypothetical realm of the Jungian "archetype." My gut told me it was no accident that these witnesses apparently perceived these unexplained livestock deaths and UFO-type events in very similar ways from witness to witness, case to case, and used similar terminology to describe their experiences.

Premier ufologist/meta-logician, Dr. Jacques Valleé has long insisted that UFOs appear to be a conditioning or thermostat-like control mechanism in culture. By 1994 I had read every Valleé book I could find and his theoretical concepts rang true for me on a deep level of understanding. I could see his insight into the UFO phenomenon applied to my perception of the cattle mutilation mystery as well.

One of my early hunches centered on the initial outbreak of mutilation reports in a given area and how they were communicated out to the public in the media.

I instinctively intuited that initial cases in a particular wave or outbreak of reports, and how they were languaged by the media, might be the most revealing. I had a feeling that these first reports could dictate the way the general population viewed the flap that unfolded. This cultural lens supplied by the media coverage is tremendously influential and so are the very *terms we use to describe and communicate "the inexplicable"* out into the culture.

Here is a personal example of my thinking and how I attempted to communicate my analysis to the "experts." In April 1995, I attended the Ozark UFO conference in Eureka Springs, Arkansas where I networked and compared notes with several dozen investigator/researcher types at the now infamous "Lone Star Bar" and conference hospitality suite. This two-bedroom suite at the hotel where the conference was held became legendary for its raucous, "let your hair down" atmosphere and highly charged party-on atmosphere. I met some of my best investigator friends at the Lone Star Bar and the events that transpired there over the next 10 years became the stuff of legend.

Over the years I have attended dozens of conferences around the USA but seldom have I attended any of the featured lectures. Sitting on a hard chair in a large hall with several hundred "true-believers" is not my idea of fun. Sitting and squirming, guffawing, fidgeting and trying to stay awake is also not my idea of fun. Sure, occasionally there would be a lecture, speaker or subject that I would be intrigued enough by to sit through an entire presentation, but most of the time I spent talking with other investigators and networking outside of the conference hall. Such was the case in '95 at the Ozark conference when I was asked to provide the conference with a quick 20-minute speaker's slot on Sunday morning, the last day of the conference. But it was Saturday night: Lone Star Bar, schmoozin, movin' and groovin' time and I bounced an idea off Linda Howe.

Much to the chagrin of Perkins, Adams and Massey, the prior several months had found me questioning the efficacy of the very term "cattle mutilation." I was convinced this term was not only wrong, it was ineffectual as a "PR buzzword." I would passionately argue with them as I tried to convey my thinking that the term "cattle mutilation" was a turnoff to most people. I argued that this very term, on its own, might be responsible for a lack of quality involvement by the mainstream press, academic and scientific communities. I suggested using the more neutral term Unusual (or Unexplained) Animal Death or "UAD" that I introduced in my first book *The Mysterious Valley.* Izzy (as David Perkins is known to his investigator friends) was right: it would never catch on. I observed that these so-called "mutilation" cases were not, by literal definition, "mutilations." To me, this term suggests a hacking, uncontrolled, haphazard process of disfiguring flesh. These unexplained livestock deaths, I pointed out to my betters, seemed much more controlled and methodical—more akin to a careful excision process or experiment conducted by experts. The very term "mutilation" in general is repelling, repugnant and abhorrent to most people. As I quickly discovered, this was not a popular idea and my fellow investigators, some to this day, disagree with my analysis of the term "mutilation." Perkins thinks the term accurately denotes a shocking in-your-face phenomenon, which is impossible to ignore. Both Adams and Massey said the term had already been historically established. All concerned preferred the more sensational term versus the watered-down PC version. I tried to convince Linda that night in the Lone Star and I was NOT successful.

As I've suggested, prior to the Snippy case, no notable documentation exists that effectively coalesced the "mutilation" meme into widespread public perception. Sure, we have Fort's citations, obscure regional or local news stories and rumors of more ancient accounts, but until Snippy, *the mystery as now defined did not exist.* With the establishment of this meme in the mid to late 1970s the mystery gained a public face—a terminology and a cultural focus that the media still utilizes when cases are reported. As time passes, and last year's reports fade from the headlines—only to rear up again—it appears that competing theories as to the responsible parties has taken a back seat to the sensationalism and market-driven titillation. Usually, in the local coverage, "if it bleeds, it leads," but when it comes to unexplained livestock deaths in the regional and national viewing markets, they still don't know exactly how to handle "mutilations," so they leave it on the cutting room floor, out of sight, out of mind.

Here is a case in point: ABC's Dave Marish's censored *20/20* story on the cattle mutilations in 1980. Perkins was extensively interviewed and looked forward to seeing even-handed coverage of the mystery. The show never aired because, as an ABC producer later told Perkins, "they were afraid they might end up with egg on their face." The Rommel report had just been released and it appears the network got extremely cold feet.

There are many examples of slanted media coverage of the "mutilation" phenomenon as it raises its ugly head in the U.S., South America, and the UK from time to time.

Having said this, any attempt to try to explain away the mystery as "mass hysteria" by simply placing the blame on sensational local news coverage is an example of knee-jerk nearsightedness, in my opinion. The skeptics have been citing this scenario for decades and it accomplishes nothing except to further muddy the waters. To further complicate matters, it appears that badly briefed reporters and their harried news directors pick up on manifestations of the real phenomenon and then editorially slant their coverage in an effort to simply sell papers and attract more readers/viewers. This is not helping matters either. In my estimation, this subject has not been adequately addressed by researchers and investigators of the "cattle mutilation" mystery, and how mutilation reports are handled by the local media may hold another crucial key to understanding.

Do Reporters Fan the Flames of Hysteria?

Kagan and Summers in *Mute Evidence* place the blame for so-called mass hysteria of the mid-70s solely in the lap of the media. They chastise the media's coverage of alleged mutilation cases and also blast the investigative community's hardworking, proactive proponents—most notably Tom Adams and Gabe Valdez. They also suggest that a pivotal role was played by reporter Dorothy Aldridge, who wrote a series of sensationalized articles for Colorado's *Gazette-Telegraph.* She tied Front Range Colorado UFO activity directly to the wave of mutilation reports that occurred in 1975 as noted in *Mute Evidence*:

> This was the person whose UFO articles had almost single-handedly fired the start of the mutilation phenomenon in Colorado in 1975. This was the person whose sensationalistic, shallow and naïve articles had been the prime source of information about cattle mutilations for thousands of ranchers in the region. This woman, who constantly said, "oh, I'm not a very good investigator" (clearly she knew her limits), sat, all wide-eyed surprise and befuddled, calmly assuring us that the UFO buffs were on the right track. But her lack of journalistic skill had suddenly mattered a great deal when she had been turned loose on the cattle mutilations. She had almost single-handedly caused a statewide panic with her coverage. Apparently, the editors of the *Gazette-Telegraph* did not care about accuracy, as long as it sold newspapers.[1]

What happens when the reports continue, and the regional media catches on and identifies that a wave of activity is underway, and the story becomes a sensationalized national/international news headline? All bets are off. Then it appears that the phantom helicopter reports become news and are tied into the mutilation reports. There appears to be a cycle of reportage that spins through this perception in the media. Gail Olson from the *Rio Grande Sun* was targeted by Rommel as one of the chief promulgators of the sensational aspect of mutilation press coverage in northern New Mexico. David Perkins observed that her investigations and articles were well researched and accurately written.

Our examination of the *publicized* aspect of the unexplained livestock death phenomenon started with Snippy the horse in 1967 and this bellwether case set the standard for sensationalism that still echoes through the years into the 21st century. Nellie Lewis' assertion that "flying saucers killed my horse" in the *Pueblo Chieftain* and the convenient misnaming of the horse had a tremendous impact on *how the case was perceived by a startled public*. "Snippy" had, and still has, a much more relevant ring than the lackluster "Lady," and the fact that the owners never set the record straight to reporters covering the aftermath of the case, is a perfect illustration of meme creation and rudimentary myth making.

As we have also seen in our scrutiny of the early 1970s cases in the upper Midwest, reporters were quick to jump toward the most sensational-sounding explanations for who was responsible for the initial cases reported in Minnesota and Iowa. Obviously media outlets attempt to maximize interest by slanting coverage in such a way that the direct result is more newspaper sales and higher television viewership—often sacrificing accuracy. Early skeptical reaction to these trumpeted claims was quickly seized upon by critics of the "mystery," who discounted rancher and law enforcement claims that this is a *true* mystery.

A Hoax About a Hoaxer?

The following is an interesting observation in Kenneth Rommel's infamous *Operation Animal Mutilation* report (1980) explaining how his team surmised when the cattle mutilation hysteria had begun. In the report, they cite the early days of the publicity surrounding the wave of reports that swept through the Midwest from 1975 through 1978, and mention a May 14, 1976 *San Francisco Bay Guardian* article written by stringer Burton J. Wolfe. Wolfe proposed that the early media hysteria about the possible involvement of "satanic cults" and "UFO creatures" around the subject was inadvertently jumpstarted by a Minnesota radio show host hoaxing his listening audience during a broadcast sometime in 1974. Rommel's report notes this alleged correlation and the report suggests that the emerging mutilation "myth" then propagated quickly in the subculture, and this ultimately resulted in the media's full-blown hysteria from 1975 through 1979. The report cites Wolfe's final conclusions after he debunked insurance scams as a potential motive to explain the mutes:

> Although the profit motive cannot be entirely discounted, the livestock mutilation phenomenon is much too complex to be explained solely on this basis. Another possible explanation is offered by Burton Wolfe (1976) in an article entitled "Demystifying all the Satanic Conspiracy Stories on the Cattle Mutilations," which appeared in the May 14, 1976 issue of the *San Francisco Guardian* [sic]. Wolfe attributes the cattle mutilation phenomenon to a hoax originally perpetrated by an astrologer named Dan Fry, host of a radio program in Minnesota called the "Cosmic Age." According to Wolfe, about two years ago Fry announced on his program that cattle were being mutilated "either by some weird satanic cult or supernatural creatures arriving on the range in UFOs." Fry, apparently intending his comments as a joke, was alarmed at the impact they subsequently had on ranchers and farmers.[2]

OAM goes on to quote the Wolfe article as evidence that mass-hysteria was prompted by a simple hoax that created public perception that livestock mutilations were a real phenomenal mystery:

> Suddenly, farmers in Minnesota accustomed to finding dead cows with parts severed by predators began attributing the scavenging to Satanists

and UFO creatures. Through the mass communication media, including the *Associated Press* and such esteemed newspapers as the Houston *Post*, the story was disseminated to millions of people in hundreds of Midwestern cities. Reporters began to vie with each other for the most sensationalized version of how mysterious creatures from UFOs or stealthy night figures from satanic cults were mutilating cattle. Alarmed by the results, the astrologer appeared on a number of radio and television shows "in an effort to abort his prank before the press created still more mass hysteria with it."

'Man, there weren't any cattle mutilations,' Fry explained in a typical appearance on a Texas television talk show in March 1975. 'I just started these rumors as a joke' (Wolfe 1976).[3]

Naturally, I dug into Wolfe's story and could find no supporting research that confirmed his radio show claim. Someone named "Dan Fry" (not to be confused with Daniel Fry, the infamous contactee from the 1950s) did have a radio program called "Cosmic Age," but I can find no other source that mentions his on-air prank involving cattle mutilations. Did Fry actually make these statements or was Wolfe himself making them up? If Wolfe fabricated this scenario, we have a hoax about a hoax. Readers of my last book *Stalking the Tricksters* will undoubtedly appreciate this potential tricksterish irony!

Whether or not you accept Wolfe's explanation for the origin of the mutilation phenomenon, his (and Rommel's) observations about the role played by the media are quite revealing. Similarly, my own investigation has clearly shown that the media helps create public perceptions and promotes both the unexplained livestock death phenomenon and the lore surrounding the mystery.

Obviously, like almost all popular subjects, the media *does* play a crucial role in the propagation of cultural memes. We have Lindsay Lohan, Honey Boo Boo and a myriad of other examples—some less appealing than others. But in the business of hard news reporting, where does pure reporting end and the programmed slant begin, and why? As mentioned, early reports from the upper Midwest did have the implied UFO and/or cultist slant, whether deserved or otherwise, and this did lead to a rapid spread of ill-informed hyperbole and speculation by all concerned—reporters, ranchers—even law enforcement officials and ultimately the politicians.

While researching this chapter on the media's role in this mystery, I reread Rommel's report and was reminded of the Wolfe article. Something about the tenor and slant of his piece seemed dismissive and too conveniently pat, and this piqued my suspicions. So, I did a background check on the author, Burton J. Wolfe, and was I startled at what I uncovered!

Burton J. Wolfe, a longtime San Francisco/Bay Area writer, has an interesting past. He's covered everything from the flower power generation (*The Hippies*, published by Signet Books in 1968) to musings on Adolph Hitler. In 1963, he was publisher of the tabloid newspaper *The Californian* and at some point, while taking notes on the psychedelic San Francisco scene of the mid '60s, he met and befriended Anton LaVey. Bingo! LaVey was the infamous founder of the Church of Satan (COS). Evidently, this was not a casual relationship. In the late 1960s, Wolfe and LaVey apparently became business partners for a short time. Wolfe joined the COS in 1968, and he actually wrote the introduction for LeVey's *The Satanic Bible* published in 1969 where he described the role of Satan worship in modern society:

> In *The Satanic Bible*, Anton LaVey explains the philosophy of Satanism better than any of his ancestors in the Kingdom of Darkness, and describes the various rituals and trappings that have been devised to create a true church of flesh-worshippers. It is clear, from the interest in Satanism that erupted in 1968…that there are many people who would like to know how to start Satanic cults and ritualize black magic. This book shows them how to go about it and fills that need. It is also clear that there is a place for the formulation of teachings that constitute the antithesis to the repressive, inhibiting, antimaterial dogma of Christianity and other antiquated religions. *The Satanic Bible* also fills that need.
>
> Perhaps the most important social value of this book is its challenge to other religions: Deal with carnal desire and the flesh in a logical, rational manner or lose the struggle not only for men's bodies, but also their souls.[4]

Wolfe was a professional writer and he covered a variety of topics and stories for regional publications. When a drive for unionization of the newspaper industry occurred in the mid '70s Wolfe is credited with soothing tensions; he helped avert potential labor strikes with a series of pro-management pieces now considered classics in 'anti-labor' speak.

What's wrong with this picture? Here we have an avowed Satanist who is also a crack journalist with a record of penning extremely persuasive pieces of writing that play a key role in manipulating a target audience. In his *Guardian* article, he debunks the notion that "satanic cultists" and "UFO creatures" are involved in the mutilation mystery, and asserts that it all started out as a joke-gone-wrong. Now knowing what I know about the man, it comes across to me as a well-crafted disclaimer for the Satanist crowd—accomplished by casting attention on an obscure radio show remark in an effort to divert attention away from his support of a controversial cultist group of believers acknowledging "the dark side." Wolfe's article was picked up by the wire services and had the apparent effect of further dampening mainstream national acceptance of "cattle mutilations" as a true mystery worthy of note. I am not surprised that no one has seen the importance of this crucial 1976 article, and the effect it still plays on the public's perception of this memeplex.

Sensationalizing the Sensational

I found the following example of blatant, sensationalistic "cattle mutilation" meme propagation re-posted on the website Squido in late 2011. Originally written by Minister Gary Stearman for *Prophecy in the News*, the quoted article provides an embellished third-hand reprint of the reports gathered originally by Linda Moulton Howe. Stearman presents the case while contributing not a shred of additional information, tangible scientific evidence, or other corroborative witnesses:

This account [from *Glimpses of Other Realities* by Linda Moulton Howe, 1989, pp. 167, 168] involves an event in which 27-year-old Timothy Flint describes his own abduction from a Portland apartment. He appears to have been taken *for the specific purpose of being allowed to witness a cattle mutilation.* [my emphasis] While resting in his apartment, he was transported to a dark field out in the nearby countryside, where he was allowed to see a strange spectacle. He describes a domed, bluish glowing disc that hovered over a grazing cow:

"This thing went down the hill a little bit off to my left and hovered above the brownish-red cow. The cow was still eating and didn't even know that the domed thing was there, I guess. All of a sudden, this light beam came down from the blue base of a round, lighted object in the sky, a kind of milky white light that I could see right through. And it came down and surrounded the cow, and the cow started to levitate. The cow went stiff and its head popped up and its eyes were wide open and its tongue was sticking out. And it went up."

"At the top of the beam, the cow hung there, and to Timothy's horror, began to be dissected. He heard a sound, which he described as, 'a high-pitched zinging sound, like the sound of a power saw cutting wood."

"At the same time, the cow uttered a series of blood curdling screams. As the operation continued, the cow was rotated feet up. The unwilling witness became extremely disturbed:

"I could clearly see that the right side of the cow's face was gone. There was no ear, no eye and the tongue had been removed and it was down to the bone on the jaw. The meat had been removed right down to the bone."

"Young Timothy, now himself *a victim of interdimensional kidnapping*, had for some reason been allowed to witness an event that is *often seen by ranchers in their waking state*, but for obvious reasons, seldom reported by them. For fear of being branded crazy, they remain stolidly closemouthed. *This was true in the case of ranchers who saw things in the "Snippy" case, and it is true today.* [his italics]

Howe describes the way Dwain Wright of Grants Pass, Oregon, recounted his meeting with a rancher east of Bend, while on a hunting trip. He got into a conversation with the old cowboy, who lived in a dilapidated travel trailer near the area where his cattle grazed. While talking, their conversation turned to UFOs. The cowboy asked the hunter an unlikely and riveting question, recorded in the following conversation:

"Do you believe in flying saucers?' And I said that I did. And he said, 'Well, they come across the desert here at night. I want to show you something.' He took me to another area and there was a dead bull pressed into the ground as if it had been dropped from a great height.

"'How far into the ground?' I asked.

"'About half way. The cow was heavy to begin with, but it has to have been dropped a couple of hundred feet. And what I noticed about it is that certain parts of it were missing: ears, eyeballs, sex organs were missing, its anus was also cut out.' And the cowboy said, 'This is not the only one. There are lots of them like this.'

The cowboy went on the describe glowing saucers that came by night and floated cattle off the ground, later dropping them, bloodless and in a mutilated condition.

In this region, ranchers report that *it is not uncommon to see cattle in the treetops, hanging twisted, torn and bloodless.*[5] [his emphasis]

This is a textbook example of how slanted, sensationalized third or fourth-hand reporting is seized upon by other writers looking to maximize the impact of a case, or account, and in the process warp it further over-the-top into a new version that further feeds a hungry readership that is ill-informed and eager for titillating coverage of this perplexing mystery. Howe's account is slanted enough to begin with, but Minister Stearman takes it far over the top with absolutely unfounded hyperbole and embellishment. And the memeplex continues to propagate. The italicized portions were added by Stearman and are not true and accurate. To the average interested reader who hasn't done his or her homework, these embellishments intensify a false sense of the actual reality of the mutilation phenomenon and places it firmly into the realm of creative science fiction. In my estimation, this penchant for questionably-motivated sensational reportage *is one of the most frustrating roadblocks* to acceptance by most mainstream science and academia who still refuse to entertain the possible reality of the mutilation phenomenon—or any number of so-called paranormal phenomena or conspiracy theories.

Careful What You Wish For: The BBC Boys

Here is one of my favorite examples of your average, "big-time" city-based reporter heading out to ranching country to report on this mystery. The following is from my 2007 book *Secrets of the Mysterious Valley* and is a perfect illustration of how an unsuspecting big-city media-person can be blindsided by the reality of the unexplained livestock death mystery—up close and personal.

The winter of 1996-1997 passed by like a whisper. The uncharacteristic mild weather and record snow falls relieved 1996's dry conditions and the region's ski areas profited handsomely. Spring arrived and the cattle death cases began in earnest, first just north of Taos, then in the heart of the San Luis Valley.

It was early in the March morning when the rancher discovered his prized breeding cow dead in the pasture, about 500-yards from the front door of his ranch house. He couldn't believe the animal's condition; left eye carved out, and the left-side mandible neatly "sliced off." He muttered to himself when he realized her young calf would probably die as a result of losing its mother.

The rancher had been hearing about area "mutilations," and had watched videotape taken by a nearby neighbor of another strangely slain cow, less than a mile from his spread, in southern Alamosa County. He had not been convinced by the video that the animal had been killed and mutilated. He told his neighbor that it may have been a "cat" [mountain lions are rare out in the valley, over twenty miles from the foothills]. He couldn't explain the lack of any tracks or the slightest indication of a struggle that is usually present after a predator kill or another death by attrition. Like all ranchers, death in the pasture is a part of life and his neighbor's loss seemed unusual but he blew it off, not aware that in a few short days, he'd lose a cow under similar circumstances.

Angry, he placed a call to the sheriff's office to report the unusual livestock death. The investigating deputy (aware of my on-going investigation) sensed something strange about the crime scene and the animal's unexplained demise. He attempted to obtain my phone number from Richard Gottlieb at the Narrow Gauge Bookstore in Alamosa. Richard immediately called me and told me of the deputy's request and asked me to call the sheriff's office right away.

A fresh one, less than eight hours old! I set up a rendezvous at the crime-scene with the deputy and rushed down with a musician-friend, Barry Monroe. The three of us examined the grim scene in the diminishing light. It was deathly still out but cold, and to my amateur eye, it looked "The Real Thing," a true high-strange case. I made arrangements to return the following morning, meet the rancher, gather plant, soil and forensic samples and conduct a full investigation of the crime scene. The temperature would be just above 35 degrees, and the animal carcass would stay in a pristine condition overnight.

Meanwhile, two weeks prior, your media-magnet San Luis Valley investigator had finished up a television shoot with England's British Broadcasting Company (BBC) with an extracted promise to let Louis Theroux's *Wild Weekends* BBC crew know if we had any "fresh cases." The day they were finishing their shooting trip in Arizona, I called with the grim news. They rushed back to the San Luis Valley to tag along and film the investigation that would be included in the BLT Research "Bovine Excision Study." They arrived early the following day and headed to the ranch located just south of the Alamosa airfield.

Louis, the urbanized correspondent, began the questioning as we drove the several miles south around the airport toward the site, (this is a verbatim transcript off the BBC raw video audio track):

"So, what's the story Chris?"

"I received an interesting call yesterday. It seems the [Alamosa County] Sheriff's Office received a couple of reports, over the last four days, of 'cattle mutilations.' The investigating deputy asked me to come down and check one of the cases out."

"Have you already been to see it?"

"Yes. I wouldn't have called you out, Louis, unless I suspected a report worthy of gathering forensic samples and conducting an investigation."

"What kind of animal is it?"

"It's a four-year-old cow with a calf, about three-and-a-half months old. It was part of a large herd of about one hundred and ten animals. Fifty-five cows and their calves. The rancher came out yesterday at five in the morning and found it 'mutilated.' Its mandible's been excised and an eye was carved out"

"NO way!"

"Way...you'll see."

"Is it the real deal?"

"Based on my amateur eye, it definitely looks bizarre, Louis. Strange."

"Has it got a name?" I grimaced and tightened my hands on the steering wheel, "I don't know Louis, I just call them all 'Bessie.'" He chuckled.

A fierce wind ripped across the bleak pasture (within sight of the south end of the Alamosa Airport) as we arrived at the site, cameras and investigative tools in hand. We approached the tarp-covered animal and I pulled the tarp off. Louis took his first look at the animal and I commented, "*That* is not natural!"

"Oh check it out!... the eye socket! Chris, the eye socket is bubbling!" Simon, behind the camera muttered "Oh my God..."

"Chris, how come the eye socket is bubbling?" Louis asked,

"Well it's pressure from the fluids in the body going to the lowest point [of the carcass]. You'll have a certain amount of activity [and settling] until all the blood coagulates. The fact that the blood isn't coagulated is interesting." Louis' cavalier demeanor had rapidly faded. He stared at the carcass with a rather grim look on his face as I walked back to get my tool-bag and gloves. Louis asked, "You're putting gloves on so you don't get gunk on your hands?"

"Several cases in the last two years have had people getting their hands really burned after touching one of these."

"No!" Louis wrinkles his nose as the wind changes. "It smells a bit."

"Louis, you wanted to help? Here, put this tape measure as close to the head as you dare. That's right—right on the nose."

"On the nose? Do you want me to actually tuck it in the mouth?" I began the process of measuring out a five foot, ten foot, twenty-five foot, and fifty foot mark for gathering soil and plant samples north/south/east and west. Louis, the glib London reporter had lost a bit of his normal lighthearted demeanor.

"How does this figure as far as mutilations go, or mutes, as you call them? How does this rate? Is this an extreme one, an average one...?"

"I'd say it's average for this part of the San Luis Valley. Over the last three years, we've had a number of intact rear-ends."

"Rectums?"

"Yeah Louis, as you can tell the rectum hasn't been cored out. Further south in New Mexico, in all their recent cases, the rear end has been taken. I don't know if that's a trend, but this appears to be a typically average case." Louis momentarily rediscovered his English-style humor and opined, "Maybe rectums aren't a hot commodity anymore...?"

"Uhh right Louis, maybe now it's lip and eye stew, instead of udder-rectum soufflé. So Louis, what do you think, now that you've seen one?" I clapped him on the shoulder in a cold manly embrace.

"Well-l-l, it's pretty repulsive seeing the eye-socket bubbling like that!" We took the rest of the tarp off, revealing the intact rear-end. Louis almost loses his cookies. "Oh, oh-oh-oh MAN! Is-is-is that normal?!" He starts to cough and retch. "It's rectum... is... bubbling!" I started laughing and patted him on the back, "I know it's tough Louis, but you can handle it..."

"Is that normal?! Why is it bubbling?!"

"Well, it's natural. The animal had probably eaten a lot. When it died, the vegetable matter all fermented and created gas. So what you're seeing is the process of that gas bulging out and bloating the animal."

"But why is it bubbling out of that little hole right there?"

"There is so much pressure, it split the animal's uhh, soft-tissues."

Louis tells Simon the cameraman, "Get in close on that bubbling rectum."

"Oh-h, man! YOU fuckin' get the fucking close-up!" Simon, the cameraman is not having fun. Louis looked down at the animal's missing mandible flesh around the jaw and comments, "Well, at least it died with a smile on its face." I laughed, "You're pretty sick, man." I started to videotape downwind, "Oooo wee, geez Louise. That's the problem with these things…"

"What's the problem?"

"The problem is the smell downwind. You just don't want to get downwind." Even though the animal had lain in a pristine, refrigerated environment, my well-exposed nose caught a whiff of cadaverine.

Louis coyly suggests, "Let's go downwind and get a good sniff! Come on Chris, let's do it! It's good TV, come on-n-n. Come on Chris—as a favor to me!" He pulled at me insistently, trying to get me to move downwind for a video shot. I declined, just as the rancher arrived in his pickup bouncing over the pasture to the site. Sternly, he slowly climbed out of his truck accompanied by his son and a couple of their alert blue-heeler ranch dogs.

Louis regained his journalistic composure and asked, "Chris, what are the characteristics of this animal carcass that mark it as a possible mutilation, and make it mysterious?"

"Well, first of all, Louis, the cut around the jaw and snout area is peculiar. The cut obviously starts here and goes around in this direction. And the eye was apparently carved out. It wasn't plucked out, like from a bird, the whole socket has been reamed out around the orbit. You can see the fluids bubbling up in there from the pressure… It is kind of gross!"

OK, I told myself, enough of this. It was getting colder and the wind had picked up. It echoed the stone face of the rancher who stood surveying the scene. The dogs darted purposefully around the perimeter, their alert senses on high alert as the sun sunk below the line of clouds on the western horizon.

"Let's go gentleman, I'm going to get some samples here." After the rancher and I gave a quick analysis of the unusual cuts for the camera the Brit's eyes bulged as I started the forensic sample gathering procedure. I carefully cut into the animal's hide and flesh. Louis lost it completely and started making strange gagging noises. His hands were steepled in front of his face and his face was screwed up and turning a cold purple. He almost upchucked his lunch. "Oh God! I don't think viewers can watch this, it's-it's too dis-disgusting!… Don't you think?"

"I can't believe *I'm* doing this, Louis. It does take a little bit of getting used to." Louis regained his composure and tried his lighthearted approach.

"Chris, shouldn't you get a sample of the eye juice?"

"No, I'll let the vet do that, I can't have all the fun." I looked at the mandible cut closely and noticed hair follicles that appeared to have been cut during the original excision. I cut into the mandible flesh for the second sample and told him, "you get used to it after a few dozen of them." I finished the tissue excising and began gathering the final plant and soil samples tested later by W.C. Levengood at the Pinelandia Biophysical Laboratory in Michigan for the "Bovine Excision Study."

Back at the mutilation site, the wind had become gale force and it sucked the moisture out of the thin, freezing air. I started gathering plant and soil samples ten feet from the carcass in the rock-hard ground. I was busy digging away with my back to the carcass, when just behind me, I heard Louis gag and moan, " OOHHHH!!!"

I turned just in time to see the rancher's dog furtively licking the quietly oozing blood and fluid from the upside, excised eye-socket. The rancher gave the pooch a casual kick and put his hands back in his pockets. "Oh, OOHHH, Ohhhhhh, Ohh, the-the-the dog is licking the juice from its eye-socket!" The rancher scratched his head—he didn't know what to make of these BBC boys. I did; welcome to the bloody wild-wild west, blokes.

I looked at the rancher and said to Louis "they do that. They're dogs. You should see what a pack of coyotes would do to this thing…" I asked the rancher, "right?" He didn't answer. Louis kept repeating, "…the dog was licking the juice from the eye-socket of a mutilated cow…"

"Louis, you are really funny, man! So you almost lost your cookies again, huh?" He repeated, "the dog was licking the eye-socket of a mutilated cow!"

"It's a natural thing."

"I'm never going to forget that image." He turned and stepped away from the carcass and said to me: "You've got a FUN job." I pointed to the rancher and responded, "Owning a cow that's had this done to it is no fun. What do you think?" I asked the rancher for his opinion. He stood and looked down at the cow. "It's very suspicious… I've never seen one like this, in over thirty years of ranching. I see dead cows all the time, but I've never seen one that's cut up like this. Or been cut at all!… I've never seen an animal that's been cut on like this!" Louis was still amazed by the dog. "Have you ever seen a dog licking an eye-socket before?"

"Yeah probably, and other parts too." He turned away from the BBC boys, "This is very strange, Chris. This animal has been cut on by a sharp knife or high-heat, or something. Normally, if a cow just dies that cheek patch wouldn't be missing and the eye-socket would still be there."

"So what do you think did this?" Louis asked. The rancher paused a second before he answered, "I wish I knew… That's why Chris is here, maybe these samples will enlighten us."

Louis asked, "Do you think it's UFOs and aliens?"

"I guess it's possible. Either that, or we have some real strange individuals in this country that would get a sick thrill out of this. This is our livelihood. There's been too much of this going on. It's not happened to me previously, but [this] one's quite enough… It's happened to my neighbors."

Louis, again re-discovering his journalistic demeanor quips, "I've read accounts that say this is just predator damage. Vultures, maggots and what-not…" The rancher looked off and his jaw tightened before he disagreed, "Totally impossible. Vultures, predators, varmints; they did not do this. This was done by some… it may have been a varmint, but it's of a two-legged kind. It's not animals. This is not an animal kill at all, if it was, they'd be around the backside of the animal. That's where they always start. I've hunted all my life; I butcher my own beef. To do that kind of work up there on the jawbone where the skin's extremely tight, you'd have to have a lot of experience, or a very good instrument. They did this in the dark. We live less than 500-yards away; the dogs never barked. It's very unusual! *That* cow was healthy prior to her death and there's no visible indication of how the animal was killed. There's no sign of a struggle, or anything else… This cow never did anything to anybody! Why her? Why me?! Why my neighbors? We need answers to who, what, and why this is happening. I don't care to have any more."

The mood had turned somber, I felt uneasy. The rancher was actually a bit choked up over the loss of his cow, and I could tell Louis and Simon were uncomfortable at the rancher's anguish. I know I felt uncomfortable. We covered the animal with the whipping tarp as the cold San Luis Valley wind tore fiendishly at our clothing and further chilled the darkening scene.

Before leaving I thanked the rancher for coming forward and reporting the case. The BBC boys were quiet and lost in their thoughts as we drove the few miles to the Alamosa airport. Gone was the lighthearted banter and glib attitude. I dropped them off at the airport, bid them *adieu* and headed home mulling over several explanations for these perplexing animal deaths.[6]

Occasionally investigators get lucky and are able to get on-site before the victim animal becomes too necrotic for post-mortem testing. In this case, the cold weather kept the animal pristine long enough for forensic sample to be obtained.

These tissue samples—along with the plant and soil samples—were sent to Levengood at the Pinelandia Biophysics Lab as part of the BLT Research Bovine Excision Site study.

David Perkins noted the results of the test conducted at this particular mutilation site in his article "High Heat," published in the May 1998 edition of *Western Spirit* magazine:

> In 1996-97, the tiny magnetic beads that had been noted in crop circle formations, started showing up at animal mutilation sites. Imbedded beads of magnetite were found in plants near a mutilated calf in Red Bluff, California. The magnetite concentration around the animal was about 10 times higher than the control samples. A similar case in Papoose Meadows, California revealed "higher concentrations within proximity of the excision points around the animal." In April 1997, researcher Christopher O'Brien sampled a mutilation case in Colorado's San Luis Valley. The magnetite sphere concentrations around the dead cow were the highest yet recorded (over 500 times greater than what would be expected from normal soil). In a January 1997, mutilation case investigated by Jean Bilodeaux, the magnetite particles clustered in higher concentrations "within proximity of the excision points around the animal."[7]

A couple of months passed before the BBC sent me a copy of the show. I cringed as I watched Louis tear into a Nevada militia group that has been formed to protect the aliens after they land and poke fun at the two owners of competing crash sites in Roswell. Then my segment came on. In light of his sobering experience at the mute site, I was not surprised that Louis and Company presented my investigative efforts as a straight, fairly serious news story on their popular BBC reality show—*Louis Theroux's Weird Weekends*.

This is NOT a Funny Subject!

This was my only foray into the realm of mainstream comedy trying to make jokes about the unexplained livestock death phenomenon. Over the years I've noticed that cattle mutilations have attracted mainstream humorists, but only on rare occasions, and, for years, I've declined all media inquiries from known comedic shows or personalities. When David Letterman's people contacted me in 1999, I was understandably excited, but made the mistake of proposing a bunch of one-liners and ideas for set-up pieces. My booking and flight, etc., fell through. I didn't have to give a second's thought when John Stewart's *Daily Show* contacted me the following year. I remember telling the producer that he must *really* think I'm crazy if he thought I'd agree to let Stewart's zany Comedy Central roving reporters loose on me and my "serious" investigative work. Aliens coming to Earth to gather cattle parts for lip-'n-eye stew? …yeah, sounds tasty, but that's a bunch of bull—udderly ridiculous—people would have a cow if it were true!

Sources and References

1. Kagan & Summers, *Mute Evidence,* Bantam book, NY NY, 1983
2. *Operation Animal Mutilation,* K. Rommel/NM District Attorney Eloy Martinez, 1980
3. *ibid*
4. LaVey, Anton, *The Satanic Bible,* Avon, NY NY, 1969
5. Minister Gary Stearman for *Prophecy in the News*; squidoo.com/cattle-mutilation-modern-sacrifices-to-evil-gods
6. O'Brien, Christopher, *Secrets of the Mysterious Valley,* Adventures Unlimited Press, Kempton, IL, 2007
7. "High Heat," David Perkins, *Western Sprit*, May 1998

Chapter 12
Mad Cows and Angry Ranchers

The subject of cattle mutilations and any objective in-depth look at this mystery can leave one bewildered and bereft of a grounded point-of-reference. This is where the rubber leaves the tarmac. There are innumerable cases that potentially validate and support almost every potential hypothesis to explain what is going on, and this chapter is where we put this mutilated holy cow subject into a current cultural and environmental context.Before diving into cattle and human health concerns, I should mention that I am *not* a vegetarian with an axe to sharpen or a hide-skin drum to bash. I have always loved bison, venison, elk and beef steaks, hamburgers, T-bones, lamb chops, chicken, turkey, lobster, crab, trout, salmon, sushi, and the occasional bacon and egg breakfast. I'm a red-blooded American who puts real cream in my coffee, loves all kinds of cheese (even the stinky ones), and was raised on bloody red, white, and blue meat. "Rare as you dare," I like to tell waiters. But honestly, after researching this chapter, I am having second thoughts about my love of bloody red meat and I'm now reminded of the following research whenever that primal carnivorous craving arises.

I'm now certain that there are several important factors involved in the unexplained livestock death mystery that, until now, have not been adequately addressed by researchers, investigators and theorists: first is the role of cattle and human religious belief, second is the role of cattle and modern human health and third is the

undercurrent of political/cultural/agricultural manipulation. I suspect that these are key factors and there are clues hidden within these three arenas that can help us unravel the cattle mutilation mystery.

David Perkins, a true pioneer thinker into this particular rarefied realm of cultural pathology, has reminded me over the years that, for every theory you can come up with to explain the "cattle mutilation meme," there is an overwhelming data set that can be used to successfully nullify any one-size-fits-all theory offered to explain the mystery. After reading all the case histories that have been documented since at least 1605, what do *you* think? Who, or what, is responsible for the "real" cattle mutilation cases—those that were perpetrated with intelligence and appear to be agenda-driven and not the result of mundane scavenging? Having asked this, where are we at this point in the process of analyzing all this bewildering data?

I have presented this historical overview of apparent mutilation cases as objectively as I have been able to, and now that I have done this, I'm embarrassed to say that I may be more confused now than I was back in 1993—at the beginning of this investigative work. Is it the U.S. government? Possibly… But, playing the trickster here, I propose that while the government *does* appear to have some knowledge of what's going on—i.e., apparent choppers and the close proximity to military bases—it is doubtful that government agencies could be behind the perpetration of all of these events. How can that hypothesis account for the many inexplicable cases characterized by state-of-the-art, cutting-edge forensic medical knowledge? Or all the strange flying object sightings; or the Montana, Colorado and Missouri Bigfoot reports; or the groups of robed and hooded figures in Colorado, South Dakota, Idaho, Texas, Arizona and Montana? How could occultists be responsible for all of the above? Is there some sort of well-financed blood sacrifice conspiracy, and if so what would be its source? Is it big beef muscling in on small ranches in a political grab for commercial domination? Any of these? None of these?

Over the years some in the media and law enforcement communities have proposed various theories, but none of them seem capable of accounting for the daunting, mind-warping, high-strange cases that remain beyond prosaic explanation. Even the proposal that the waves of mutes suggesting that a (quasi?) government environmental monitoring program is underway, encompassing a possible multi-national agenda, cannot account for the high-strangeness cases.

A Self-Negating Mystery

So, where does this leave us? I have said for years that I suspect "there are multiple groups with various agendas at work and play" out in the pastures of the world. Perhaps *all* the theories are true! Or perhaps *none of them* are true. Whoever is responsible for these many thousands of real and unexplained livestock deaths is likely aware of how the collective human psyche processes such deeply entrenched cultural memes back out into the modern culture-at-large. Usually, if "it bleeds it leads," but not if a mystery calls into question our collective addiction and carnivorous love of red meat.

Some of you are probably still scratching your heads thinking, "so, it's aliens, right?" Sure, anything is theoretically possible; we definitely can't rule them out, but do we have enough data to rule them in as the sole perpetrators behind the mystery? Again, I don't think so. As ironic as this might sound, the "alien" answer may be far too simplistic. What about all the hundreds of apparent helicopters in and around mute sites—located in many areas featuring military bases? If extraterrestrials *are* behind the mutilations as some investigators insist, it would seem that the government/military power structure is allowing these experiments and disfigurements of livestock to occur right under their noses. If this is true, it appears to be by design, and by sleight of hand. We need to ask what could possibly be the "aliens" motivation for disfiguring and removing soft-tissue organs from livestock. If they were after "genetic material" (for whatever hypothetical reason) why not raid the nearest abattoir or rendering plant? There are more than enough supplies of blood and other fluids there.

It appears to me that we are dealing with a netherworld of shadowy characters that are acting upon and maintaining overlapping agendas that reverberate on deep archetypal levels within Western, Christian culture. This process of "mutilations" appears to exist within a cultural feedback loop of denial—even outright dismissal. This pattern of cultural dismissal and/or denial is exacerbated by the sensational popularized interpretation that "cattle mutilations" are an "alien" harvest.

When I first became involved investigating, researching and pondering this most challenging of mysteries, I immediately had a gut feeling that there was far more going on than appeared on the surface. My first personal investigation—of the Sutherland bull mutilation, 13 years after it had taken place—featuring the yellow whirlybird flying over my house, which *changed my inside-the-box perspective* and perfectly illustrates the high-strange complexity of the mutilation mystery. This high-strangeness realm is where you'll find the "trickster" lurking.

Through the seventies into the nineties, law enforcement and forensic crime scene investigators were picking up and establishing a definitive fact: many mutilations were misidentified scavenger action, but *not all cases* reported could be due to simple scavenging and other natural processes. The local/regional media was also picking up on something ritualistic and occult-tinged, and their slant over the years has provided a sensationalized spin to the mystery. Media coverage has enflamed the mysterious nature of the emerging modern version of this meme.

The true-believer crowd winks knowingly at each other and they only tout the cases where so-called "evidence" or at least anecdotal stories suggest that alien interaction with planet earth has been manifested in the unexplained animal mutilation phenomenon. (figure 1) But it has been established that there are more mundane "real" cases that feature the skillful use of old-fashioned scalpel technology, etc. And around and around and around we go.

As we have seen, it doesn't matter what theory you propose—from outright skeptical dismissal to the other extreme—the extraterrestrial hypothesis (ETH)—there is *more evidence out there to negate all theories than there is to support any conclusion.* And this especially holds true for the skeptical argument that *all mutilations are simple scavenging action.*

If I had to choose an overriding hypothetical motivation for perpetrating the mutilations, I would agree with David Perkins's original 1979 assessment that this is somehow related to "environmental testing." But something else might also lie at the heart of the mystery. For the past 20 years I have pondered all of this and come to the conclusion that we must start at the beginning to fully understand our species' profoundly sacred relationship over millennia with proto-cattle and cattle, as recounted in the first chapters of this book. Experience and ideation developed in the beginnings of human civilization, essential to the strength and survival of our species over millennia, must reside in the human collective unconscious. I feel this is an important key to understanding developments in the modern world including the increasing commodification of cattle and the bizarre and horrifying cattle mutilations of the last 45 years. Today, in the modern world, a critical ancient covenant is being violated by powerful forces—fed by our primal carnivorous desire for "beef," that protein-of-status—and manifesting in our cultural perceptions of and responses to the mutilation phenomenon. Our Western, Christianized version of the "sacred cow" has become a simple line entry on the latest profit and margin report. Millions of cattle are being unceremoniously slaughtered, rendered, packaged, and sold as Big Macs, White Castle Sliders, Whoppers, insulin, human blood replacement, drug capsules, industrial cleaners, cement blocks, sexual lubricants, explosives and other products for sale every day.

One disturbing aspect to this unholy scenario is being demonstrated by the industrialization of livestock as a processed source of protein. Unless we become fully aware of the implications of this industrial 21st century, high-tech view of cattle, and the implications this mindset may have on exacerbating our troubling relationship with bovines, we may have set ourselves up for potential health consequences that are unimaginable.

Where's The Beef?

Let's contemplate the facts and consequences of our species' current exploitation of cattle. Currently, it is estimated that there are 1.37 billion cattle on the planet in 2014 taking up about 25 percent of the planet's landmass. (figure 2)

With only five percent of the world's population, the U.S. consumes about 25 percent of the world's beef. The average American eats 65 pounds of beef per year. Americans consume twice the amount of daily protein recommended, far more than the body can even absorb...

A recent study of air quality in the Los Angeles basin revealed that meat is the number one particulate in Los Angeles' famous air...

Over 70 percent of the grain produced in the U.S. is fed to livestock. This means a cow produces less than 50kg of protein from consuming over 790 kg of plant protein...

It takes an average of 185 acres a year to sustain a cow on fragile Western BML [Bureau of Land Management] and FS [Forest Service] land. A cow eats for about eight hours a day and consumes 700-800 pounds of vegetation per month...

More than 260 million acres of U.S. forests have been cleared specifically for livestock— an area the size of Texas and California combined. Of the remaining U.S. forests, over 63 percent is used as pasture...

Over 100 million acres of healthy and diverse land have been turned into a "cow burnt" and denuded wasteland. In the past 200 years, human activities have depleted 75 percent of U.S. topsoil, about 85 percent of this due to the feet of livestock or the production of livestock feed.

Ninety percent of the surface water on Western public land is significantly polluted, with livestock being the leading cause. Livestock production accounts for more than 70 percent of all the water consumed in the 11 Western states.

Seventy percent of the 11 Western states is "open range" managed for livestock ranching. Of this grazed 70 percent, 58 percent is publicly owned land. The vast majority of this publicly owned 30 million acres is administered by the Bureau of Land Management (BLM) and the Forest Service (FS).

Grazing permits are granted to these "welfare" ranchers at roughly 20 percent of their fair market value. Thus, about 30,000 ranchers (less than two percent of U.S. cattlemen) are the unfair beneficiaries of big-time taxpayer money. [It has been] estimated that this amounts to a total tax loss of roughly one billion dollars annually, if all impacts of public lands ranching are considered. Among the many "improvements" to public lands taxpayers have paid for, or heavily subsidized, are 600,000 miles of livestock fences (mostly barbed wire) and over 500,000 miles of ranching roads carved into these same delicate public lands.

According to the Arizona Game and Fish Department, 97 percent of the state's original riparian habitat has been lost, primarily to livestock grazing. In Colorado, 90 percent of the 5,300 miles of riparian habitat managed by the Bureau of Land Management (Bureau of Livestock and Mining as some call it) was listed in "unsatisfactory condition" in a 1988 General Accounting Office report.[1]

Forests, particularly the rain forests of Central America and the Amazon (which are considered the "lungs of the planet") are being burned and cleared to make way for more livestock grazing lands. Since the early 1960s, more than 25 percent of the Central American forests have been irrevocably lost due to increasing levels of beef consumption by the West. It is estimated that for every quarter-pound fast-food hamburger made from Central American beef, around fifty square feet of tropical forest, including 165 pounds of potentially unique species of plants and animals, are destroyed and possibly lost forever. Many scientists and environmentalists are worried that unknown viruses, hidden for thousands-of-years in the equatorial rainforests, are now, due to rampant deforestation, being released into an at-risk global environment.

Today, the world's cattle are stripping vegetation and compacting and eroding soil and are rapidly creating deserts out of grasslands. More than 60 percent of the planet's rangelands have already been adversely impacted by rampant livestock overgrazing during the past half century. In the Western United States, for instance, it has been determined that cattle have done more to damage the environment than all the highways, dams, strip mines, and power plants combined.

Cattle production is a major cause of water and air pollution. In the United States alone cattle produce nearly one billion tons of organic waste each year. It is estimated that cattle and other livestock account for a significantly high percentage of pollutants in rivers, lakes, streams and aquifers since raising beef-based protein requires staggering amounts of fresh water. Nearly half the water consumed in the United States is used to water and grow feed for cattle and other livestock. The overall global effect of water usage for livestock has yet to be determined as the planet's precious stores of fresh water continue to dwindle away at an alarming rate, with no end in sight.

The world cattle-complex is also contributing to global climate change. This is a major environmental issue that will be unavoidable in this new century. It has been determined that cattle are a significant factor in the adverse generation of three of the major gases—carbon dioxide, methane and nitrous oxide—that are largely responsible for global warming. Cattle, and cattle grazing, account for more ozone-depleting gases than any other natural source (with the possible exception of termites). The burning of the world's forests to create additional cattle pasture is also releasing billions of tons of CO_2 into the atmosphere. The world's 1.37 billion cattle (whose belching and flatulence drive methane skyward an average of twice per minute per animal) and other ruminant livestock, emit 60 million tons of methane from their digestive systems into the atmosphere each year. Producing feed crops for cattle often requires the use of petro-chemical fertilizers, which emit vast amounts of ozone-depleting nitrous oxide. These gases are quickly building up in the atmosphere, blocking heat from escaping the planet—which is thought to exacerbate climate change.

Cattle and beef production is contributing significantly to the dramatic loss of bio-diversity, including rampant species extinction occurring across the globe. In all major cattle producing countries wildlife habitat is being destroyed to create more cattle pasture (as with the rain forests of Central America), and the growing cattle population worldwide is destroying habitat and using up forage and water needed by impacted wildlife. In the United States and Australia cattle ranching practices have also resulted in the purposeful mass extermination of predator and "nuisance" species—a virtual war on predators and scavengers. In Africa millions of grazing and browsing wild animals have died of thirst or starvation after finding their migratory paths blocked by fences built to contain growing cattle herds.[2]

Beef is the largest income-producing sector of U.S. agriculture. This is a *really big* business. Last year the Agricultural Statistics Board published statistics that showed there were 29.3 million beef cattle and 9.2 dairy cattle in the United States. This is the lowest inventory since 1952, which may be an indication that a sizeable number of beef cattle are being raised overseas by multinational corporations. Many of those herds are located in India (buffalo), and in Argentina and Brazil (beef). Of course most of the buffalo and beef end up as ground meat that is sold around the world by the fast-food chains and supermarkets.

Here are the beef industry's own figures from 2012:

- 2012 Cattle inventory: 89,299,600 (USDA NASS)
- Economic impact: $44 billion in farm gate receipts (USDA NASS)
- Number of herds: 742,000
- 29.3 million beef cows
- 34.3 million head calf crop (2012)
- *90 percent of cow-herds have less than 100 cows (avg. 44 head)*
- 2012 beef exports: $5.51 billion (up two percent from 2011), 1.13 million metric tons (USMEF)
- Top export markets: Canada, Japan, Mexico, South Korea and Hong Kong

More than 50 percent of the total value of U.S. sales of cattle and calves comes from the top five states: (January 1, 2012 USDA Cattle Inventory Report)
1. Texas
2. Nebraska
3. Missouri
4. Oklahoma
5. South Dakota

Cost of production: from 1990-2003, feed yard cost of gain was $261/head; in the past four years, feed yard cost of gain is $494/head

Average producer age: 58, up from 56 in 2002 (USDA 2007 Ag Census)

33.6 million head of cattle harvested under USDA inspection (2011).

43.4 billion pounds of beef harvested under USDA inspection. Average live weight 1,277 pounds.

Total cash receipts: $62.9 billion (2012 Agricultural Statistics Annual)

Per capita spending on beef in 2009: $261.90 (47.8 percent of per capita spending on all meat)[3]

Although the average amount of meat consumed every year by Americans has been on a slow decline (since 1975), the emergence of other formerly third world countries' middle-classes has driven worldwide demand for beef products upward.

Exports are big business for the U.S. beef industry, which shipped a record $5.4 billion worth of beef abroad last year (2011).

Last year, 14 percent of the beef produced in the U.S. was shipped overseas. Measured in both sales and volume, exports saw growth of more than 20 percent according to the U.S. Meat Export Federation.

Four countries, Canada, Mexico, Japan and South Korea, accounted for 65 percent of last year's beef exports. Here's a look at them and other top buyers:

- CANADA imported 191,047 metric tons of U.S. beef in 2011, a 25 percent increase over 2010. (One metric ton equals nearly 2,205 pounds). It was worth $1.03 billion, up 41 percent from 2010.
- MEXICO imported 256,938 metric tons, a four percent increase. It was worth $985 million, up 20 percent. Mexico is among the major buyers of variety meats—pieces Americans disdain including tongues, livers and other organs. Last year, it was the number two importer of variety meats by volume at 100,410 metric tons worth $223 million, and number one measured in dollars. Mexico would continue imports with safeguards it has had in place for eight years to keep mad cow cases out.
- JAPAN imported 158,646 metric tons, a 27 percent increase. It was worth $874 million, up 37 percent. Cow tongue is a delicacy that fetches high prices in Japan, one reason it is the number three buyer of variety meats as measured in dollars. It imported 19,732 million metric tons worth $116 million last year. As a safeguard against mad cow disease, Japan limits its imports of U.S. beef to cows of 20 months or younger. Many countries limit imports to meat of 30 months or younger.
- SOUTH KOREA imported 154,019 metric tons, a 37 percent increase. It was worth $686 million, up 32 percent. South Korea's 40 percent tariff on beef is being phased out over the next 15 years under the new U.S-Korean free trade agreement.
- EGYPT imported 147,833 metric tons, a 30 percent increase. It was worth $236 million, up 33 percent. Egypt's was the number one importer of variety meats by volume — 113,953 metric tons worth $141 million, and number

two in dollars. It is the top buyer of U.S. beef in the Mideast.
- RUSSIA imported 72,797 metric tons, a 27 percent increase. It was worth $256 million, up 68 percent. Russia imported 24,514 metric tons of variety meats worth $39 million, ranking it number three in volume and number four in dollars.
- HONG KONG imported 50,705 million metric tons, up two percent. It was worth $237 million, up 50 percent. Mainland China remains mostly closed to U.S. beef imports, however.
- VIETNAM imported 44,643 metric tons, up three percent. It was worth $192 million, up 17 percent.[4]

The lucrative overseas markets are understandably skittish because of the fear of mad cow disease, growth hormones and other risky U.S. big agro practices. To protect these potential emerging growth markets, it wouldn't surprise me in the least if the powerful beef industry controllers have managed to obtain control and/or at least influence over media coverage concerning beef safety in U.S. cattle herds. They have much to gain and a lot to lose if and/or when word gets out about any outbreaks of bovine, swine, or poultry diseases. I would venture a guess and say that big media and big agro have been winking and nodding at each other to protect their profit margins, advertising revenues and big beef's emerging overseas markets.

Did You Know?

But we're only talking "beef-as-food." What about other uses for cattle? Not all non-edible cattle parts are simply disposed of, for there are many additional uses that we have for all those leftover cow parts. Non-food use and the utilization of cattle by-products is a subject that is not well known by the average person munching on a Whopper or Big Mac—with a burger patty that McDonald's admits could contain meat parts from up to 100 different bovines. The actual number may go as high as 1,000 animals![5] I love a good hamburger. Here's one that is touted as "a heart attack" burger (figure 3).

In case you didn't know, the list of products that utilize spare cattle parts is huge. Here is just a partial sampling of these products and categories: (figure 4)

Deodorants, shampoo/cream rinses, detergents, shaving cream, doggie chews, soaps, fabric softeners, textiles, floor wax, toothpaste, glue, upholstery, insecticides, violin strings, gelatin for drug capsules, Insulin – treatment of diabetes, Heparin – prolongs the time needed for blood to clot, Corticotrophin – used in the treatment of allergies, rheumatoid arthritis, rheumatic fever, and respiratory diseases, Thyrotropin– stimulates the thyroid gland, hormone – used to treat parathyroid deficiencies, Thrombin – promotes coagulation during surgery, Glucagon – treats hypoglycemia (low blood sugar) Sodium levothyroxine – thyroid replacement therapy, Fibrinolysin – treatment of blood clots within the cardiovascular system, Pancreatin – treatment of infants with celiac disease (gluten intolerance) and related pancreatic deficiencies, Thyroid – treats myxedema (metabolic disease caused by deficient action of the thyroid gland) in adults and cretinism (deformity and mental retardation in children, Parathyroid hormone – used to treat parathyroid deficiencies, asphalt, car polishes and waxes, rubber tires, hydraulic brake fluid, textiles for upholstery, animal feed, industrial cleaners, cement blocks, personal lubricants, explosives, molds for plastics, fertilizers, printing ink (and the list goes on and on…)[6]

Modern Beef is What's For Dinner

As you can see, we have found many uses for "Bessie's" various parts. But when addressing the subject of meat and the role it plays in the human diet and on human health, we must realize that the subject should be addressed from two perspectives—what we *know* is in our meat and what *may* be lurking in this portion of our human food chain. First let's take a look at what we know:

Nearly all meat in America is contaminated with such man-made carcinogens as dioxins, a family of chemicals related to Agent Orange and DDT, the notorious chemical that was banned domestically over [35] years ago but that remains in the ground (and will remain there, unfortunately, for thousands of years to come) and therefore in the crops fed to animals. Crops grown for cattle feed are permitted to, and almost always do, contain far higher levels of pesticides than crops grown for human consumption. About 80 percent of pesticides used in America are targeted on four specific crops—corn, soybeans, cotton and wheat—that are the major constitutes of livestock feed. Since animals store pesticides and other toxic substances in their fat, they get their most concentrated doses of these carcinogens when they eat other animals. And we in turn get even more concentrated doses of carcinogens when we eat them.[7]

We have all heard how eating red meat promotes higher risk for cardiovascular disease by clogging your arteries with fat-derived cholesterol, leading to a higher chance of cardiovascular disease and increased risk of heart attack and death. The statistics are staggering when you really look at them: one out of every two Americans will be impacted by and suffer from heart attacks caused by cardiovascular disease brought on by atherosclerosis (or clogging of the arteries). It is a well-established fact that the single biggest cause of this condition, in fact *all* this cholesterol clogging the arteries, comes from the fat of animal products.[8]

Combine the higher risk of heart attack and known carcinogens stored in the fat of animals bred and raised for food consumption and you have a double-headed beast bearing increased risks for cancer and for heart disease. In 1971 Richard Nixon declared two "wars:" one on drugs, the other on cancer. At the time, about one in five Americans developed cancer during their lifetimes. That figure today has risen dramatically to one in three. And it will continue to rise as America continues to battle ever-more-resistant weeds with more and more powerful chemically derived weed-killers. It is obvious by now that Americans are rapidly becoming more and more unhealthy, and much of this is due to diet and lack of exercise. We have already solidified our dubious distinction as the most obese nation on earth due to high fat, low fiber, fast food and processed food in our diet in general.

Here is a perfect illustration of how a national diet can adversely affect health: the Japanese, as a direct result of their low meat diet, have significantly reduced rates of heart disease, but when Japanese move to the United States and adopt an American-style diet, their rate of heart disease skyrockets as much as *tenfold.* Arguments that genetic predisposition accounts for heart attacks appear mostly unfounded: risk of heart attack is directly predicated on the amount of animal products, including chicken, fish, eggs and dairy consumed, which significantly increase your risk factors for cardiovascular disease and heart attack. Medical studies have shown time and time again that vegetarians have a greatly reduced risk for cancer and heart disease:

> Not only is a vegetarian diet the best preventative medicine for our hearts, it may also help us finally to win a war we've been losing since it's been declared: the war on cancer.
>
> The German Cancer Research Center conducted a study of over 1,900 vegetarians, and found that rates for all forms of cancer were only 56 percent of the normal rate. The…study of Seventh-Day Adventists men also found that this group, about half of whom are vegetarian, and who eat on average about 50 percent more fiber than the general population, suffers 55 percent less prostate cancer than other American males. Similarly, a ten-year study of over 120,000 Japanese men reported that vegetarian men had a lower incidence of prostate cancer than meat-eaters. The Association for the Advancement of Science reported: "Populations on a high-meat diet are more likely to develop colon cancer than individuals on vegetarian or similar low-meat diets."
>
> An investigation by the National Cancer Institute correlated the incidence of colon cancer with over 100 specific foods. All types of dead animals fared the worst. "Risks of beef, pork, and chicken all rose with frequency of use, and the composite picture suggest an underlying dose-response relationship." [A] 36 country study reported a strong and direct correlation between consumption of dairy and animal fat and the incidence

of prostate cancer, colorectal cancer, lung cancer and breast cancer.[9]

Auntie Biotic's Abuse

Now that we have established that eating meat—especially beef—leads to health problems, let's have a look at what factory farming operations are putting into your meat. The Union of Concerned Scientists concluded in a 2001 study: "Estimates of Antibiotic Abuse in Livestock" (*UCS,* 2001) that at least "70 percent of all antimicrobials used in the United States are fed to livestock." This roughly translates into 25 million pounds of antibiotics annually, which is almost nine times the amount used to treat human diseases.[10]

Now, just 13 years later, estimates of the percentage of antibiotic use in cattle have risen a staggering 10 percent to 30 million pounds. There appears to be no end in sight as levels of use continues to spiral upward. But other meat is being impacted as well:

> [In 2013] members of Congress and the U.S. Centers for Disease Control have escalated warnings addressing the growing danger of antibiotic resistant pathogens emerging from farm animals, which consume about 80 percent of all antibiotics in the U.S. *The Atlantic* reported last summer that medical specialists are seeing a spike in women with urinary tract infections caused by antibiotic-resistant bacteria, likely transmitted by chicken meat.
>
> More stark was the proportion of microbes identified that were resistant. Of all the salmonella found on raw chicken pieces sampled in 2011, 74 percent were antibiotic-resistant, while less than 50 percent of the salmonella found on chicken tested in 2002 was of a superbug variety.[11]

This is an alarming, hidden public health issue that all of us need to be educated about. Over the past 25 years, health care professionals have seen a dramatic increase in resistant bacteria partially due to farming practices of feeding low-dose antibiotics to livestock to protect them from infection in their unhealthy, unsanitary feedlot environments. This continual low dose usage has led to resistant bacteria strains which are becoming more and more difficult to combat because of their acquired resistance, and, again, this resistance is largely due to overuse and abuse of antibiotics fed to consumable animals.

> More than half of samples of ground turkey, pork chops and ground beef collected from supermarkets for testing by the federal government contained a [bacterium] resistant to antibiotics, according to a new report highlighting the findings.
>
> The data, collected in 2011 by the National Antimicrobial Resistance Monitoring System — a joint program of the Food and Drug Administra-

tion, the Agriculture Department and the Centers for Disease Control and Prevention—show a sizable increase in the amount of meat contaminated with antibiotic-resistant forms of bacteria, known as superbugs, like *salmonella, E. coli* and *campylobacter*…

These little-noticed tests found that supermarket meat samples… harbored significant amounts of the superbug versions of salmonella and Campylobacter, which together cause 3.6 million cases of food poisoning a year [in the U.S.].

A significant contributor to the looming superbug crisis, according to scientists and health experts, is unnecessary antibiotic usage by factory farms that produce most of the 8.9 billion animals raised for food in the U.S. every year. Industrial livestock producers routinely dose their animals with pharmaceuticals, mostly administered with limited veterinary oversight and frequently without prescriptions, to encourage faster growth or prevent infection in crowded, stressful and often unsanitary living conditions.[12]

The statistics from the above-mentioned study are alarming. Antibiotic resistant bacteria were detected in "39 percent of chicken breasts, wings or thighs, 55 percent of ground beef, 69 percent of pork chops and a sobering 89 percent of ground turkey."[13] Today in the early 21st century almost every known strain of staphylococcal (staph) infection in the United States is resistant to penicillin and other newly-developed antibiotics as a result of overuse. This is a major, little-discussed public health concern and there are other public health concerns that are being kept from the American public as well.

An estimated two-thirds of all U.S. cattle raised for slaughter are injected with growth hormones. Six different hormones are used on beef cattle, three of which occur naturally, and three of which are synthetic. Beef hormones have been banned in the European Union since the 1980s. The European Commission appointed a committee to study their safety for humans. Its 1999 report found that residues in meat from injected animals could affect the hormonal balance of humans, causing reproductive issues and breast, prostate, or colon cancer. The European Union has prohibited the import of all beef treated with hormones, which means it does not accept any U.S. beef.

Recombinant bovine growth hormone (rBGH) is a genetically engineered, artificial growth hormone injected into dairy cattle to increase their milk production by anywhere from eight to 17 percent. The FDA approved rBGH in 1993, based solely on an unpublished study submitted by chemical giant, Monsanto. Canada, Australia, Japan and the European Union all have prohibited the use of rBGH.

Approximately 22 percent of all dairy cows in the United States are injected with the hormone, but 55 percent of large herds (500 animals or more), such as those found on factory farms, use rBGH. Its use has increased bacterial udder infections in cows by 22 percent, thereby increasing the need for antibiotics to treat infections.[14]

The Politics of Modern 21st Century Beef:

The major beef corporations have slowly become sensitive to increasing levels of consumer concern and have started looking for workarounds to these ever-increasing levels of growth hormones and antibiotic use. Girls in the U.S.—some as young as age nine or 10—are prematurely entering puberty. Is this an unintended result of residual growth hormones, acquired through consuming hormone-laden beef, milk and other dairy products? If I had to venture a guess, I'd say yes.

The pharmaceutical giant Merck & Co. has developed a new drug product called Zilmax, and a rival drug called Optaflexx has been produced by Eli Lilly; both belong to a new class of drugs called beta-agonists. Originally developed to treat asthma in humans, beta-agonists were discovered to produce an interesting side effect—putting bulk on livestock, thus requiring fewer animals to produce the same amount of meat.

The original beta-agonist drug that increases protein synthesis, called Ractopamine, was enlisted for livestock use when researchers found that the drug made laboratory mice more muscular. This reaction to the drug reduces the overall fat content of the meat. But since its introduction a decade ago, some food experts have expressed concern over this class of drug's use in bulking up consumable meat animals. The agro-giant Cargill resisted for six years buying cattle that had been supplemented with Ractopamine drugs. They finally relented in June 2012 and began accepting treated animals for slaughter. The Food and Drug Administration's official policy toward a new drug is predictable. They stated the following when approving Zilmax in 2006: "We have deemed beta-agonists safe both for farm animals and for human health. No animal safety concerns were described in any of the studies performed."[15]

Ractopamine is currently used in about 45 percent of US pigs, 30 percent of ration-fed cattle, and an unknown percentage of turkeys are pumped full of this drug in the days leading up to slaughter. Up to 20 percent of Ractopamine remains in the meat you buy from the supermarket, according to veterinarian Michael W. Fox.

Since 1998, more than 1,700 people have been "poisoned" from eating pigs fed the drug, and Ractopamine is banned from use in food animals in no less than 160 different countries due to its harmful health effects. Effective February 11, 2013, Russia issued a ban on US meat imports, slated to last until the U.S. agrees to certify that the meat is Ractopamine-free. At present, the US does not even test for the presence of this drug in meat sold commercially. In animals, Ractopamine is linked to reductions in reproductive function, increase of mastitis in dairy herds and increased death and disability. It's also known to affect the human cardiovascular system, and is thought to be responsible for hyperactivity and may cause chromosomal abnormalities and behavioral changes. Where it's banned: 160 countries across Europe, Russia, Mainland China and Republic of China (Taiwan).

The U.S. Department of Agriculture allows beef produced with beta-agonists to be labeled hormone-free, antibiotic-free and "natural," as the drugs do not fall into the same class as either growth hormones or antibiotics.[16]

As with most drugs, the beta-agonists produce apparent side effects. During the first week of August 2013, at a Beef Industry conference in Denver, Dr. Lilly Edwards-Calloway, an animal health auditor for the beef industry giant JBS, U.S., presented a video showing clips of beef cattle having trouble walking and showing other signs of distress. *This is also a sign of advanced mad-cow disease!* JBS wanted other beef producers' feedback and it was stated that beta-agonists may have been a contributing factor to these clear signs of dysfunction in the animals shown in the video. That same day another agro-meat giant Tyson Foods, Inc., announced that it would no longer accept cattle that had been administered the most popular of this class of drug, Zilmax. Coincidence? The drug was cleared for use by the FDA in 2007 and has gone on to be a real moneymaker for Merck. Tyson said that they had noticed problems in their operations with cattle that showed similar signs of ambulatory distress and equated this condition to use of this new class of drug.

It is obvious to me that this almost rubber-stamp mentality by the FDA and the introduction of new drugs into the food chain is a very dangerous and steep-pitched downward slope. Corporate power and influence over public policy is illustrated by the naming of the newest deputy commissioner of the Office of Foods for the FDA, Michael R. Taylor. Back in 1990 Taylor was the deputy commissioner on policy for the FDA, then left to become Monsanto's Vice President of Public Policy. During the years he was at Monsanto, before returning to the FDA, Monsanto developed the controversial growth hormone rBGH, discussed earlier. Now he's back, this time in charge of packaging and labeling guidelines. Can you spell conflict of interest? But that's not all. Commercial predators are overseeing the FDA, our guardians of the safety and quality of our food supply.

Also tied up in the rBGH debacle are Margaret Miller and Susan Sechen. Miller, the deputy director of the Office of New Animal Drugs at the FDA, and a former Monsanto scientist, helped develop rBGH. Sechen, a data reviewer in Miller's department, worked as a graduate student on some of the initial bovine drug studies. [T]hese studies were conducted at Cornell University and were financed by none other than Monsanto.

Other Monsanto alumni include Arthur Hayes, commissioner of the FDA from 1981 to 1983, and consultant to Searle's public relations firm, which later merged with Monsanto. Michael A. Friedman, former acting commissioner of the FDA, later went on to become senior Vice President for Clinical Affairs at Searle, which is now a pharmaceutical division of Monsanto. Virginia Weldon... became a member of the FDA's Endocrinologic and Metabolic Drugs Advisory Committee, after retiring as Vice President for Public Policy at Monsanto.[17]

Of course, in response to the predictable criticism by government watchdogs and public health advocates, Monsanto issued several press releases denying any nefarious influence within with the government regulatory agencies. It stated that conspiracy theories relating to the FDA "ignore the simple truth that people regularly change jobs to find positions that match their experience, skills and interests."[18] Doesn't that make you feel warm and fuzzy, safe and sound knowing the very people that helped develop the growth hormones jacking up our meat animals have been the same ones responsible for testing and their rapid rubber-stamped certification. Not to mention the deceptive labeling guidelines guaranteeing their former employers billions of dollars in profits. And who says we don't live in a red-meat plutocracy?

> Our misguided industrialized corporate farming practices and the undue influence of these agro and chemical corporations on public food safety policy and regulatory oversight have set in motion a vicious cycle that will not be contained. The results of these unregulated experiments to manipulate and monetize unnatural processes in our food may be wrought with catastrophic implications. Genetically modified organisms (GMO) patented and owned by Monsanto are escaping containment and hybridizing themselves with "heirloom" seed strains and Monsanto is actually suing organic vegetable farmers, because GMO plants are showing up in their fields—the seed introduced by the wind and water run-off. Monsanto sends out investigators who look for violators of their stringent contract for usage and target legally those farmers that refuse to pay for GMO seeds and would rather grow vegetables the old fashioned, healthy way.[19]

This mad scenario of manipulating nature is sitting at the threshold of a brazen new world. Advanced genetic experiments on humans have undoubtedly steamed full speed ahead now that mapping of the human genome has been accomplished. Horrific visions of the "Island of Dr. Moreau" have the potential to become science fact. Mother Nature developed natural systems over millions and millions of years and these evolved systems work splendidly for the most part. If it ain't broke why are we trying to change it? Short answer: the profit motive, greed, and perhaps a sick sense of curiosity. "Let's do it and see what happens."

When we upset the natural balance of our food and environmental ecosystems it is nearly impossible to fully anticipate and plan for the potentially catastrophic consequences of our meddling with nature. Here is a clue for you herd stalkers. We are meddling with human and environmental health in the name of money, market share, profits and greed. Antibiotics and their use in meat animals are a direct result of unhealthy industrial farming practices. Herds of cattle numbering in the tens-of-thousands, all crammed together in hideously filthy feedlots are being given increasing levels of growth hormones. Along with the unsanitary conditions, these practices are giving rise to opportunistic bacterial infections. These unnatural living conditions necessitate more aggressive antibiotic use by the corporate pushers of meat-derived protein. It's a vicious cycle.

> *Every day in the United States*, roughly 200,000 people are sickened by a foodborne disease, 900 are hospitalized, and 14 die. [my emphasis] According to the CDC more than a quarter of the American population suffers a bout of food poisoning each year. Most of these cases are never reported to authorities or properly diagnosed. The widespread outbreaks that are detected and identified represent a small fraction of the number that actually occurs…Although the rise in foodborne illnesses has been caused by many complex factors, much of the increase can be attributed to recent changes in how American food is produced…[T]he nation's industrialized and centralized system of food processing has created a whole new sort of outbreak, one that can potentially sicken millions of people.[20]

This increasingly centralized system of processing food, genetic manipulation and the escalation of the unnatural manipulation of food genetics cannot continue for much longer. Invariably, a superbug will emerge that is completely resistant to all known antibiotics, or even more ominous, *a new strain of bovine disease may arise and invade the human food chain* to race through the populace with unchecked fatal fury.

> This erosion in the confidence of the food system carries serious implications. It financially threatens large corporations if long-established food brands come under prolonged and severe public questioning. It threatens economic performance if foods deemed "safe" become scarcer and thus

more expensive. And it is potentially explosive politically if too many people lose confidence in the professionalism of the food regulators who are supposed to be protecting us from tainted food, and encourages folks to exit the public food system for [a] private solution...[21]

Another sobering fact concerning GMOs, antibiotics, growth hormones and increasing pesticide use is what these chemicals are doing to our nation's water supply. Rainwater run-off is leaching these unnatural substances directly into our drinking water, down the streams and rivers into the ocean. As time passes, more and more of these toxic substances are being concentrated into freshwater aquifers. The companies who make these chemicals appear to be in denial:

Monsanto, Dow, Tyson Foods, and Johnson & Johnson, among others, have been known to dump all kinds of carcinogenic chemicals in our rivers, streams, oceans and municipal water supplies. Furthermore, Monsanto and other GMO corporations plant genetically modified crops that are supposed to stand up to RoundUp chemicals, but the soil runoff damages our water. We end up drinking the poisons they spray our plants with like an afternoon cocktail. Water contamination due to corporate greed and lackadaisical political policies that don't adequately police corporate infractions, or make sure these companies pay fines to clean up their messes are harming our water supply. There are hundreds of chemical contaminants in our water now.

The EPA, a government institution that has been given the responsibility of protecting our food and water supply has said that there is a "healthy" level of contamination, but it seems clear from the declining health of our ocean life, and through observing our own health crises, that there isn't an 'acceptable' level of toxic dumping that should be allowed.

The following is a partial list of some of the chemicals in our water supply that cause everything from an increased risk of cancer, to debilitating nervous system collapse, eye and nose irritation, asthma, stomach problems, anemia, increased heart disease, intestinal polyps, intestinal lesions, skin diseases, kidney and liver failure, thyroid disease, bone disease...

Inorganic Compounds: Compounds that typically do not contain the element Carbon. They can become dissolved in water from natural sources or as the result of human activity.

Dissolved Gases: (oxygen, carbon dioxide, nitrogen, radon, etc.)—no appreciable health effects, except for dissolved radioactive gases like radon...

Organic Compounds: These compounds all contain the element Carbon. Although there are many exceptions, naturally occurring organic compounds (sugars, proteins, alcohols, etc.) are synthesized in the cells of living organisms, or like raw petroleum and coal, formed by natural processes acting on the organic chemicals of once living organisms.

Synthetic Organic Chemicals: Organic chemicals can also be synthesized in laboratories and by chemical companies. A growing number of these synthetic organic compounds are being produced. They can include pesticides used in agriculture, plastics, synthetic fabrics, dyes, gasoline additives like MTBE, solvents like carbon tetrachloride {MCL=0.005}, and many other chemicals. Many synthetic organic chemicals, like benzene {MCL=0.005} carbon tetrachloride, and vinyl chloride {MCL=0.002}, vaporize easily in air and are grouped under the category of volatile organic chemicals (VOCs). Methyl tertiary butyl ether (MTBE) is a common synthetic organic chemical used for a number of years as a gasoline additive [MCL=Maximum Containment Level]. In January 2000 it received national notoriety on CBS' 60 Minutes because of its ability to contaminate water supplies after leaking from storage tanks...

[T]hese are not nice chemicals to have in your water, many of them are presumed to increase the risk of various cancers in humans, often after many years of low-level exposure, others may affect the nervous system. Some researchers are reporting that yet other synthetic chemicals can cause hormonal disruptions. Most laboratory tests of the effects of these chemicals are done using a single chemical, but there may be several organic contaminants together in a water source. Scientists are just beginning to realize that exposure to multiple organic chemicals seems to increase the risk of health problems much more than any of the chemicals would separately.

Trihalomethanes {MCL=0.1} There is a class of organic compounds that is important because their formation and presence in drinking water is a direct result of the most common and economical process used to kill harmful pathogens, chlorination. This chemical group is the trihalomethanes (THMs). THMs are formed when the chlorine that is added to the water interacts with organic material also in the water, like leaf fragments, etc. The level of THMs in water is usually greater in water systems where surface water is the source, and levels typically vary seasonally with the organic content of the source water supply. Chloroform is usually the most common THM, and in Denver for instance, it varies from about 10 micrograms per liter in the winter to about 50 micrograms per liter in the summer with an average around 20-25 micrograms per liter. These levels are well below the EPA's Maximum Contaminant Level (MCL) of 100 micrograms per liter, but as you will see from some of the journal abstracts, referenced here even drinking water with THM levels below 100 microgram per liter over a 40-50 year period might increase the risk of certain cancers.

[I]t is important to understand that a fairly large percentage of people in the United States and in other countries that chlorinate their water are *drinking small quantities of chloroform and related substances on an ongoing basis.* [my emphasis]

Pathogens: disease-causing organisms. I need to mention here that exposure to the disease causing organisms discussed below (*E. coli, cryptosporidia , giardia,* etc.) can come form sources other than one's drinking water. Exposure, for instance, can come from eating contaminated food, or from swimming in contaminated water…

Bacteria: years ago cholera (caused by *Vibrio cholera*) and typhoid fever (caused by *Salmonella typhi*) were responsible for epidemics (caused by drinking contaminated water) that killed many thousands of people. Today, in most parts of the world, because of chlorination and other water purification processes, we do not usually hear about cholera outbreaks unless an accident or natural disaster has disabled water purification plants. Today in the US, the pathogenic bacterial contaminant most often encountered is fecal bacteria or E. coli {MCL=0.0 bacteria}, which enters the water supply from human or animal wastes…

Protozoans: *Cryptosporidia* and *giardai* {MCL=0.0 oocysts}. These are one celled organisms, both of which form dormant cyst stages that are resistant to typical levels of chlorination, cause gastrointestinal disease, and are prevalent in the environment. According to EPA 811-F-96-007, May 1996:

"*Cryptosporidium* has been found in nearly all surface waters that have been tested nationwide. As water systems monitor for *Cryptosporidium*, the likelihood exists that it will be detected occasionally at low levels in finished water derived from surface water sources. Cysts are very resistant to disinfection, and even a well-operated water system cannot ensure that drinking water will be completely free of this parasite."

According to the Centers for Disease Control and Prevention: "*Cryptosporidium parvum* has been recognized as a human pathogen since 1976. In people with normally functioning immune systems, *Cryptosporidiosis* is manifested as an acute, self-limiting diarrheal illness lasting seven to 14 days and it is often accompanied by nausea, abdominal cramps, and low-grade fever." For people with compromised immune systems an infection can be fatal.

Asbestos and other suspended solids: Unless the materials in the water are themselves dangerous, suspended solids are typically a nuisance rather than hazardous. Suspended materials in the water, however, can interact with the disinfection processes making them less effective. Water professionals also use turbidity of the finished water as an indicator of its quality. If the purification process is letting enough solids through that the water is cloudy, there is a chance that some of the "stuff" contributing to the turbidity is harmful.[22]

Add to this stew of ingredients the run-off from cattle and swine feedlots downstream into the water table and aquifers. This is the water that can potentially be consumed by humans and animals and used to water our vegetables, fruits and nuts and grains.

Meet the Meat Monster:

How much do you know about industrialized livestock farming? Do you have any idea what needs to take place in order for that steak, ground beef, package of chicken breasts, or slab of bacon to end up sitting on Styrofoam under plastic wrap in your supermarket? Have you ever wondered what is entailed in this out-of-sight/out-of-mind industrial process? This is a dark, closet subject lurking in our culture. Ignorance about this subject is indeed blissful, but we need to talk about it as we continue stalking what is stalking the herd.

Do you really know what is in your average fast-food hamburger? Beef, right? Well, yes, but there is more to a burger than beef. A typical fast food burger (7.5 oz (214 g) total weight with the bun and trimmings) contains the following amounts of calories, fats, salts and protein: We won't even mention other potential chemical ingredients that may be added:

- 539 total calories
- 261 calories from fat
- 29 grams of fat (45 percent of recommended daily allowance)
- 10 grams saturated fat (50 percent of daily allowance)
- 1040 mg of sodium (43 percent of daily allowance)
- 45 grams of carbohydrates (15 percent of daily allowance)
- 3 grams of fiber
- 9 grams of sugar
- 25 grams of protein

Recently a study was conducted to ascertain what exactly constitutes an American fast food hamburger. It's a nasty mix! These are eye-opening statistics:

Americans consume somewhere in the ballpark of five billion hamburgers a year. To keep up with this demand, just over 4,100 cows are slaughtered every hour in the U.S. That's a lot of dead cows! When 68 cows a minute are slaughtered you can bet that mistakes are made or parts are shifted into the wrong areas. A study published in the *Annals of Diagnostic Pathology* helped to discover just how much "shifting of parts" is really going on.

The study presumed that most hamburgers are composed primarily of meat. Eight different popular fast food hamburger brands were tested using histologic methods. The burgers were evaluated for water content by weight and then microscopically to verify tissue types. An additional test known as *Glial fibrillary* acidic protein staining was used to test for brain tissue. We'll give you the good news first; none of the eight samples had brains in them. [This could potentially be a very important finding] Unfortunately that is as good as it gets.

The mean water weight of the burgers was about 50 percent. Now for the strange part, actual meat content in the burgers ranged from 2.1 percent to 14.8 percent. That's right; the product that you are expecting to get is only 2 to 14 percent of what you really think it is!

What made up the rest of the burger you ask? Well a variety of fun and interesting tissue types were found. The tissues found other than skeletal muscle tissue a.k.a. meat, were connective tissue, blood vessels, peripheral nerve, adipose tissue, plant material, cartilage, and bone. That's not all, also found in some of the burgers were intracellular parasites known as *Sarcocystis*. An animal is infected with *Sarcocystis* when it ingests material contaminated with the infected feces of another animal.[23]

One unsettling subject that has not been effectively integrated into the western beef-eating cultural zeitgeist is the bait-and-switch tactics of unscrupulous suppliers of meat sold for human consumption. We have all heard about an occasional Chinese restaurant being closed by health departments because of cat (and other meat) being substituted for conventional meats such as chicken and pork. These examples are probably only the proverbial tip-of-the-iceberg when it comes to industrialized meat production. In a recent news item that failed to gain much notice in the West, we have the following news item from China regarding "fake beef:"

This week, [September 15th 2013] police in Xi'an province reported that they had found and seized more than 22 tons of fake beef at a local factory. Get this: the "beef" was actually made from pork (which is considerably cheaper than beef) that had been treated with chemicals including paraffin wax and industrial salts to make it look like it came from a cow. Shanghiist reports that the factory sold more than 3,000 pounds of the fake beef to local markets at around 25 to 33 yuan ($4 or $5) per kilo. Six workshops that were producing the fake beef have been discovered and shut down.

This isn't the first instance of fake meat being sold in China. In May of this year, *Medical Daily* reported that 904 people were arrested in China for "meat-related offenses" over three months at the beginning of 2013. Included in these arrests was one gang of meat crooks who made over 10 million yuan ($1.6 million) by selling rat, fox, and mink meat at markets.[24]

And now comes breaking news that the Chinese conglomerate Shaunghui has been approved to acquire the world's largest pork producer, Virginia-based Smithfield Foods. (figure 5) After a four-month delay, the sale was approved by the US Treasury Department. Predictably, the sale was rather contentious and was only approved after Congress deliberated over potential national security issues surrounding foreign ownership of a major U.S.-based food processor. This five billion dollar corporate sale and takeover is the largest purchase of an American company by a Chinese buyer.

Smithfield's ability to mass-produce hogs has made it the largest pork producer in America. But its high level of technology in genetics, production and food safety is why China's largest pork producer Shaunghui wants to buy the company.

China has major food safety problems, starting with pork. Last spring, thousands of dead pigs were simply dumped into the river that supplies Shanghai with drinking water. Two years ago a Shaunghui subsidiary was caught putting a banned chemical into pig feed to make the animals lean... Some in Congress, and many in the town of Smithfield, are asking if the Chinese are buying Smithfield to learn America's food safety secrets or to cut corners... Shaunghui has told investors it's not changing Smithfield's safety practices.[25]

As you fry up your next pan of bacon strips for breakfast, doesn't that make you feel comfortable? It appears that the Chinese have found a safer, more viable way to "bring home the bacon" to their masses and one can only wonder about corporate shortcuts that could be introduced by Smithfield's new owners.

After researching the subject of food safety and becoming more fully aware of the adverse impact *processed* meat has on human health it suddenly dawned on me: what if eating meat became a privilege, not a right? Let's say you needed to obtain a license to buy meat, much like a license to drive a car. I'd be willing to bet that if there were a required three-day course that educated the applicant in the entire industrialized livestock process: birthing, raising, feeding, slaughtering, rendering, processing, packaging and transporting raw meat, (and disposing of the millions of tons of waste), immediately *a sizeable percentage of the U.S. population would become instant vegetarians*. This idea is suggested partially in jest—such a system would obviously be impossible to legislate, administer, and monitor—and our hypothetical law would stand absolutely no chance of ever passing through our "red-meat" U.S. congressional herd. But I think I've made a relevant point here.

This industrialized meat production process—kept hidden by the most powerful economic force within the U.S. agricultural juggernaut—is beyond unappetizing; it is horrific and inhumane, and the potential health implications of continued meat-as-a-protein source constitute a loaded powder keg that could explode with potentially catastrophic results. The bottom line is: we appear to be setting ourselves up for a health crisis of untold magnitude, and it may be too late to stop the emergence of pandemic food-borne disease(s). I remember that fast-food commercial back in the 1980s with the tag line shouted by the little old grandmother: "WHERE'S the BEEF?" Well, in 2014, we've got our beef—don't "beef" about where it comes from or what it contains.

Space limitations and better judgment dissuade me from a more probing, in-depth look in this book at what could be described as the entrenched industrialized consolidation and political power of the meat industry. Oprah was able to afford the million dollars she spent on a cattlemen's lawsuit (probably aided by a building's worth of lobbyist lawyers in Washington D.C.) for simply saying on national TV during a show on 'mad-cow' disease that she'd "never eat another hamburger." A February 27, 1998 *Washington Post* article noted Winfrey's elation when the verdict was announced:

> The jury of eight women and four men decided that Winfrey, her Harpo Productions Inc. and Howard Lyman, a guest on her show, did not hurt four Amarillo ranching families and their cattle companies with an April 16, 1996, show on mad cow disease. The plaintiffs claimed that comments made during the program, including Winfrey's disgusted vow that she would never eat another hamburger, caused cattle prices to plummet, costing them about $11 million.
>
> "My reaction is that free speech not only lives, it rocks!" Winfrey said, pumping her fist in the air as she emerged from the federal courthouse here, surrounded by lawyers and bodyguards. Lead plaintiff Paul Engler vowed to appeal the verdict. "From the word get-go, there was never anything frivolous about this suit," he said.

There have been quite a number of mostly overlooked books written that address the subject of industrialized beef protein and the implications this process carries for human health and our future as the "keystone" species on this planet. Unfortunately, this is one of those subjects that most people tend to instinctively shy away from: Ignorance is bliss to those in denial. See the bibliography for a listing of sources that I have cited in the overview I've just provided if you are interested in learning more about industrialized meat protein production.

Most of this subject of industrialized food boils down to convenience and acceptance of the inevitable lack of healthy alternatives. One of the prime moving societal forces fueling this industrialization process is the rise and consolidation of corporate "fast-food" restaurant chains that make a lot of money for their shareholders. They provide time-crunched customers (especially lower-income customers) who are unable to prepare their own meals because of time constraints or other concerns. The lower cost of fast food provides what is perceived as a viable, convenient source of nutrition. This is a huge, important topic that deserves serious analysis.

The history of the U.S. beef industry in the 20th century is an often-overlooked part of our cultural heritage, and the powerful beef industry has managed to stay out of the public eye for decades while wielding and exerting tremendous political clout over our culture. This was not always the case. Back in 1890 the first comprehensive "anti-trust" legislation, the Sherman Anti-trust Act, was formulated and passed to not only break up the oil trust, the sugar trust, the steel trust and the consolidation of other emerging industries, it was originally created to bust up *big beef* and the stranglehold the meatpacking companies had on their captive marketplace. Back in the final decade of the 19th century there were concerted attempts to break up these monopolies, but for over 25 years this effort was unsuccessful when it came to 'big beef.' It wasn't until the public outcry that ensued after the release of Upton Sinclair's sensational and horrific 1906 expose of the Chicago "meatpacking industry," *The Jungle,* that Woodrow Wilson and Congress were finally motivated to create a Federal Trade Commission inquiry into the big beef/meatpacking industry:

> The FTC inquiry concluded that the five major meatpacking firms [Armour, Swift, Morris, Wilson and Cudahy] had secretly fixed prices for years, had colluded to divide up markets, and had shared livestock information to guarantee that ranchers received the lowest possible price for their cattle.
>
> For the next 50 years, ranchers sold their cattle in a relatively competitive marketplace. The price of cattle was set through open bidding at auctions. The large meatpackers competed with hundreds of small regional firms. In 1970 the top four meatpacking firms slaughtered only 21 percent of the nation's cattle. A decade later, the Reagan administration allowed these firms to merge and combine without fear of antitrust enforcement... [L]arge meatpackers gained control of one local cattle market after another. Today the top four meatpacking firms—ConAgra, IBP, Excel, and National Beef—slaughter about 84 percent of the nation's cattle. Market concentration in the beef industry is now at the highest level since record keeping began in the early 20th century... Over the last 20 years, about half a million ranchers sold off their cattle and

quit the business. Many of the remaining 800,000 ranchers are fairing poorly… [T]he growth of the fast food chains has encouraged consolidation in the meatpacking industry. McDonald's is the nation's largest purchaser of beef. In 1968, McDonald's bought ground beef from 175 local suppliers. A few years later, seeking to achieve greater product uniformity as it expanded, McDonald's reduced the number of beef suppliers to five.[26]

When skeptics point out the fact that only small, private ranching operations are targeted by the mutilators, I should remind them that these cattle deaths are not necessarily due to bad ranching practices and misidentified scavenger action, but may be (partially) due to attempts to scare smaller beef raising operations into selling out and ceasing cattle raising operations—aiding the further consolidation of the industry. Potential intimidation of small ranching operations and possible efforts to drive small ranching operations out-of-business has never been suggested as a motivation of some of our mystery mutilators. This is a complicated hypothetical scenario that deserves at least a mention.

The consolidation of the cattle industry also includes the relatively new practice of "captive supplies," meaning the establishment of huge unsanitary feedlot operations where hundreds-of-thousands of cattle are sent to be fattened up unnaturally on grain before being unceremoniously slaughtered by a blood-thirsty industrial process that has been formulated for clockwork efficiency to maximize profits and exploit workers' efforts. These so-called "captive supplies" allow the consolidated large beef concerns to completely manipulate the marketplace. If the price of cattle goes up, they simple slaughter extra animals to flood the market with meat and drive the price back down. If the price goes down, they hold back supplies driving the price upward. To my understanding there are no effective checks and balances in place with the deregulation of the beef industry and the 'beef trust.' At this time, corporations appear to have complete, unregulated control of the market price for beef and other meat products.

I Know, It's Just a Coincidence, Right?

Conglomerate ConAgra (figure 6) owns and operates the world's largest meatpacking complex located just north of Greeley, Colorado in Weld County. *Weld County coincidentally is one of the hardest hit counties by the cattle mutilators.* In order to keep the slaughterhouse operating and producing product, ConAgra has located two monstrous feedlots nearby. Each of them can hold upward of 100,000 head of cattle all jam-packed together in a foot deep ocean of cattle feces and urine. Cattle have evolved their marvelous multi-stomach digestive systems to gain nutrients from grasses. Here, in the feedlot, they are fed rich grain for three months to fatten them up for slaughter. It's ironic that over this three-month time period a typical cow is fed 3,000 pounds of antibiotic and growth hormone-laden grain to add a mere 400 pounds of body weight before slaughter. There are around two billion starving people on the planet and "*...we could feed an additional two billion people worldwide if grain fed to livestock was diverted to human consumption.*"[27]

> The transition of world agriculture from food grain to feed grain represents a new form of human evil, with consequences possibly far greater and longer lasting than any past wrongdoing inflicted by men against their fellow human beings. Today, more than 70 percent of the grain produced in the United States is fed to livestock, much of it to cattle.— Jeremy Rifkin, Los Angeles *Times*, 27 May 2002

If you have ever traveled in the American Midwest and had the misfortune to suddenly realize you are downwind from a feedlot or slaughterhouse, the first thing that you notice is the assault on your olfactory senses from the horrific smell. Sometimes spreading miles downwind, the smell can be a combination of a fetid greasy odor with a hint of burning hair and the overpowering stench of rotten eggs, which is the hydrogen sulfide gas that wafts up from the wastewater lagoons. These sewer lagoons sometimes overflow from torrential rains or flood conditions or are compromised by leaks so that they leach into the groundwater. On occasion, this bacteria-laden water is accidentally discharged into irrigation systems where it can inadvertently be sprayed onto vegetable crops that may lead to *E coli* outbreaks and massive recalls of leafy vegetables. (figure 7)

Again, space limitations won't allow me to give you a blow-by-blow description of the horrendous fate that awaits the millions of cattle destined for your next hamburger, but here is a brief overview of the process to enliven your day:

> Knocker, sticker, shackler, rumper, first-legger, knuckle dropper, navel boner, splitter top/bottom butt, feed kill chain—the names of job assignments at a modern slaughterhouse convey some of the brutality inherent in the work. Meatpacking is now *the most dangerous job in the United States.* The injury rate in a slaughterhouse is about *three times higher* than the rate in a typical American factory. [my emphasis] Every year about one out of three meatpacking workers in this country—roughly 43,000 men and women suffer an injury or work-related illness that requires medical attention beyond first-aid. There is strong evidence that these numbers, compiled by the Bureau of Labor Statistics, understate the number of meatpacking injuries that occur. Thousands of additional injuries and illnesses most likely go unreported.[28]

Because cattle come in all shapes and sizes, unlike (what are still known as) chickens that are now of a genetically-modified uniform size when slaughtered, cattle must be killed, rendered and processed by the skillful, overworked brutal hands of meatpacking plant workers. The assembly line operation has changed little in the past 100 years and there is no substitute for sharp knives expertly wielded. Some job positions on the 'dis-assembly line' make upwards of 10,000 knife cuts per eight-hour work shift. The process has developed into a well-honed ballet of bloody mayhem. Back in the days of the 1906 exposé novel *The Jungle*, (which focused on the plight of immigrants working in the Chicago meatpacking industry), about 175 cattle were processed an hour. Today, in these monstrous factories of death, upwards of 400 cattle an hour meet their unceremonious demise. This translates into about six animals every minute and that is in one factory. (figure 8)

I don't think it is a coincidence that methamphetamine use is said to be rampant among the work force and 'speed' is a real law enforcement problem in the surrounding communities where these factories are located. Because the jobs in these plants are so dangerous, it is difficult to hire and retain a skilled workforce willing to work in such nightmarish conditions. Often illegal aliens—mostly Mexican—and other low skill laborers are hired for the most demanding, dangerous positions. Union membership in the meatpacking industry has gone from 46 percent in 1980 down to 16 percent in 2003. Most employees have no say in the labor practices, line speed, or safety precautions and they are under the constant threat of replacement by other unemployed illegals eager to earn ten times what they could earn back home.

Supervisors are on bonus plans that often include incentives for reporting the fewest injuries, which in turn translates into injuries not being reported to management. This disregard for workers' health and welfare has become a vicious cycle of unreported injuries and abuse by line managers, a truly abominable situation enabled by the Reagan administration's gutting of the Occupational Safety and Health Administration (OSHA) in 1981. OSHA, formerly empowered to require conformity with safety and health standards in America's factories and workplaces, has since 1981 been forced to adopt a policy of "voluntary compliance." Currently, all OSHA regulators are required to do is review the injury logs submitted by the factory. If the numbers are at an average or below average level, no factory walk-throughs are made by OSHA inspectors. There are countless documented examples of falsification of injury statistics by meatpackers, demonstrated in law suits filed (and won) by injured workers and revealed in the Congressional inquiries that have uncovered duplicate sets of injury logs, lack of worker safety training, sanitary violations, inhumane slaughter practices—not to mention the impact on the health of human end use consumers. (figure 9)

Who Knows What Outbreak Lurks?

Cattle diseases have plagued ranchers for thousands of years and will continue to do so as long as we herd them together in close proximity to one another. One of the ten plagues in Egypt described in the *Bible's* Book of Genesis was a cattle plague. In 31 B.C., the Greek poet Virgil mentioned a plague that swept through the herds of northern Greece in his book *Georgics* stating that, "wild beasts and cattle met an equal death [and] each pool, each pasture, felt the poisonous breath." About 700 years later in Ireland the *Annals of Clonmacnoise* referred to a plague in ominous terms: "There was a great morren [def: to utter or emit low dull rumbling sounds] of cattle throughout all England."[29]

Then in the 13th century, all hell broke out in Eastern Europe when the herds following Genghis Khan's 'Golden Horde' introduced a new disease. Called rinderpest it is "an acute infectious viral disease of ruminant mammals (such as cattle) that is caused by a *morbillivirus* (species *Rinderpest* virus) and that is marked by fever, diarrhea, and inflammation of mucous membranes and by high mortality in epidemics."[30] When I began researching this chapter in the fall of 2012, I had never heard of this disease. It can infect domesticated buffalo, large antelopes, deer, wildebeests and giraffes and is an extremely infectious ungulate malady similar to human measles, rinderpest has a three-to-fifteen- day incubation period during which the infected animal shows no symptoms and is able to pass along the virus exhibiting no outward signs of sickness. The animal's bodily secretions become infected and harbor the virus; saliva, nasal discharge, tears, urine and feces all carry the disease making it extremely easy for the virus to pass from one head of cattle to the rest of the herd in a very short time. Rinderpest can sweep through herds like an unbridled wildfire killing literally millions of cattle in a dramatically brief time period. After the outbreak of full symptoms, the animal usually dies on the sixth day of the infection, but not before infecting other animals in the herd in a domino effect. One British witness in the 19th century described the symptoms:

> After the fourth day [after the fever is first observed] the constitution is thoroughly invaded. Then ensue the urgent symptoms—the drooping head, the hanging ears, the distressed look, the failing pulse, the oppressed breathing, the discharge from the eyes, nose and mouth, the eruption of the skin, the fetid breath, and other well-known signs of the disease. During the sixth day there occurs a great diminution of the contractile force of the heart and voluntary muscles, the pulse becomes very feeble and thready, the respiratory movements are modified, and the animal sometimes shows such weakness in the limbs that it has even been thought that some special paralytic affection of the spinal nerve must exist. The temperature now rapidly falls, and signs of a great diminution in the normal chemical changes in the body appear.[31]

Rinderpest is thought to have originated in the Far East. It wasn't until infected Mongol cattle were introduced into Hungary and Austria around 1240 that the disease appeared in Europe. The disease swept westward and southward through

Europe infecting millions of animals and exacting a terrible toll on a superstitious populace. The scourge arrived in the British Isles in the mid-14th century shortly after the Black Plague had decimated millions.

> [R]inderpest has been a rolling horror for Europe's bovines, with outbreaks periodically annihilating herds across the [European] continent. It struck England in 1348-1349, when the human population was still reeling from [bubonic plague] the 'Black Death.' The herdsmen, dead or simply too frightened of returning to blighted pastures, let their cattle roam free, spreading the plague across the countryside. From 1480 to 1481, Germany and Switzerland lost an entire third of their cattle to the disease. In the 19th century, it struck Napoleon's baggage animals during his invasion of Russia, a disaster that likely helped convince him to turn tail for Paris. But as bad as these historical outbreaks certainly were, no one imagined the scale of the catastrophe that lay ahead.[32]

Outbreaks in England continued through the 18th century from 1709-1720, and during the lull between the 1742 to 1760 outbreak, a new deadly livestock affliction— scrapie— struck English sheep herds in 1732. This was first known outbreak of prion disease in nature—or "mad" sheep disease, if you prefer. We will closely examine "mad cow" and other forms of deadly prion disease later in the chapter. There was another European outbreak… between 1768 and 1786.[33]

In 1865, following an approximately 75-year lull in rinderpest outbreaks in England, an unscrupulous cattle trader knowingly imported at the Hull docks, a herd of Eastern European cattle that he suspected had become infected with rinderpest and sold the animals off quickly before the onset of full-blown symptoms. It was May of 1865 when these animals were auctioned off and were dispersed across England. By November, upwards of 6,000 new cases of rinderpest were being reported weekly and the outbreak proliferated with a vengeance. British authorities were at a loss to explain how the disease was being spread, and by the time the outbreak had run its course nearly a half million cattle had died of the disease in the UK alone. It was estimated after the 1865 rinderpest outbreak had subsided that the outbreak in Europe had killed over two million head of cattle.

Fifteen years before Louis Pasteur developed the first vaccine for cholera, in 1865, veterinarian John Gamgee, a proponent of the newly proposed "germ theory" for disease, pleaded with the government not to ship infected cattle that were being slaughtered and sold as food around the country. He was certain that the prevailing theory of "occult atmospheric condition" as the casual element spreading disease was incorrect and that the disease was being spread by close contact of infected animals and also through consumption of infected meat products. It took nearly a quarter century for the British beef industry to recover from the devastating outbreak of 1865-66. But rinderpest wasn't quite finished targeting the world's domesticated cattle herds.

India, land of the "holy cow," could not escape the scourge. Mongols raiding the northeastern part of India also brought with them herds infected with the dread disease:

> [Rinderpest], according to medical historians, probably got introduced into India through the northeastern route from Mongolia/China around the mid-18th century. Efforts to control it can be traced back to the establishment of the Indian Cattle Plague Commission in 1868. In 1871, the commission, headed by J.H.B. Hallen, carried out a detailed study of the murrain across the country based on farmers' reports and identified it as identical to the one prevalent then in Europe. Like elsewhere in the world, in India, the continuing wide prevalence of the disease and the impact it had on the agro-based economy led to the initiation of veterinary research in the country, with the establishment of the Imperial Bacteriological Laboratory in Pune in 1889 and the Indian Civil Veterinary Department in 1891.[34]

Africa managed to escape a complete pandemic with a brief outbreak in Egypt in 1841 that killed 665,000 head but the disease failed to spread into Ethiopia and the Masai herds to the south. However, in 1885, Italian troops inadvertently introduced diseased cattle in the port city of Massawa—located in Etrea—and the disease raced through East Africa and headed south forever changing the ancient symbiotic relationship and political power of the Masai. As we saw in chapter one, cattle have been the life-blood of every aspect of Masai culture and the devastation of their livestock forever reduced their cultural and political power in East Africa. As the disease killed off the all-important oxen draft animals that were the transportation system of the day, the entire culture began to collapse. A French missionary noted the utter devastation experienced by local African people during the outbreak of 1897:

> [Rinderpest] mowed down the whole bovine race in its passage. Hundreds of carcasses lay here and there, on the roadside or piled up in fields… the carrion lay there, putrefying everywhere. More than 900 wagons, loaded with merchandise, without teams or drivers, stood abandoned along the road. Never in the memory of man has such a thing been seen.[35]

India has also suffered through repeated outbreaks of rinderpest and over the decades has marshaled all available resources to eradicate the dreaded disease. These sacred Indian cows have been "officially" delivered from further outbreaks after years of aggressive attempts at complete eradication of rinderpest.

Rinderpest was endemic throughout India until the mid-1950s, with about 8,000 outbreaks a year that affected on an average about 400,000 bovines, killing about 50 percent of them... After sustained campaigns of mass immunization and surveillance followed by diagnostics, serious surveillance and focused vaccination efforts in endemic regions, India was finally declared rinderpest-free in May 2006 by the World Organization for Animal Health (OIE).[36]

Anthrax

Another nasty, lethal scourge that can strike down bovines is our unfriendly buzz-word-disease "anthrax." Anthrax spores have been documented as *living up to 70 years* in the environment and are found on all continents, even Antarctica.

Throughout history, anthrax infections have killed countless thousands of animals and people around the world each year. In 1881, French scientist Louis Pasteur developed the first vaccine for tuberculosis and due to his discovery of the vaccination process, worldwide animal vaccination programs have rendered anthrax outbreaks rare in domesticated animals. Only a few dozen cases are reported each year.

German physician and scientist Robert Koch, is credited with being the first person to identify the bacterium that caused the 'anthrax' disease. Working diligently in 1875, his groundbreaking work in the late 19th century demonstrated that diseases are caused by germ cells. In a series of experiments, he uncovered the life cycle and means of transmission of anthrax, and his experiments were among the first to demonstrate the role of microbes in causing illness during a time when spontaneous generation was the prevailing theory of disease. Koch went on to win the 1905 Nobel Prize for Medicine for his discovery of the bacterium causing tuberculosis. Thank the cattle and science marches onward.

Anthrax elicits visions of weaponized germs used as a biological weapon spread by madmen—as in 2001 when five people died and 17 others became infected by a weaponized version of anthrax called the Ames strain. This strain is one of about ninety of the anthrax bacterium (*Bacillus anthracis*). This particular strain was first identified from a 14-month-old Texas Beefmaster heifer that died of the disease in 1981. The strain was isolated by the Texas Veterinary Medical Diagnostic Laboratory and sent to the U.S. Army Medical Research Institute of Infectious Diseases (USAMRIID) at Fort Detrick, Maryland.

Fort Detrick had been the epicenter of America's biological warfare program since 1943. When bio-warfare programs were banned by President Nixon's Executive Order in 1969, Fort Detrick's mission changed to developing defensive measures for potential bio-warfare attacks. In 1972 the U.S. signed the Biological Warfare Convention that prohibited its signatory nations from developing, producing or stockpiling biological weapons. An exception was made for countries to possess small quantities of toxic agents for "prophylactic, protective or other peaceful purposes."

In the wake of the 2001 "black valentine" letters, Fort Detrick immediately came under scrutiny as a known possessor of the Ames strain. In an article for *Science* (12-7-03), Gary Matsumoto quotes bio-defense specialists who called the Ames strain in the letters "weapons grade" and marveled at its conversion into a cutting edge aerosol… a diabolical advance in biological weapons technology."

Only Dugway Proving Ground would admit to having made aerosols with the Ames strain spores. It was determined that Dugway had begun experimenting with the Ames strain in 1994, in what the Army called "bioprofiling", an effort to "establish a library of information." Dugway officials insisted that all anthrax used there had been accounted for. They maintained that they were merely trying to develop an "effective bioaerosol collection."

Suspicion then turned to the Batelle Memorial Institute. It was known that Batelle possessed the Ames strain and had the ability to aerosolize it. According to Matsumoto, Batelle had made regular anthrax powders "for use by the Army and U.S. intelligence agencies, but rarely for Fort Detrick that specializes in vaccine development."

The FBI polygraphed scientists working at both Dugway and Batelle and found no "person of interest." The anthrax letters are still a hotly debated topic in the biodefense community. We might recall that in the weeks following the letter attacks, the Bush White House pushed hard to pin the attacks on Saddam Hussein. One conspiratorial school of thought suggests that this was a strategy to provide more pretexts for invading Iraq. U.N. weapons inspector, Scott Ritter, who was quite familiar with Saddam's arsenal, hotly disputed that Saddam was responsible. According to Ritter, the only anthrax possessed by Iraq was the Vollum strain. Iraqi scientists had obtained the strain by simply ordering it from American Type Culture Collection, a U.S. company that made various germ cultures available commercially.

> The Vollum strain was isolated in 1935 from a cow in Oxfordshire, UK. This is the same strain that was used during the Gruinard bioweapons trials. A variation of Vollum known as "Vollum 1B" was used during the 1960s in the US and UK bioweapon programs. Vollum 1B is widely believed to have been isolated from William A. Boyles, a 46-year-old scientist at the U.S. Army Biological Warfare Laboratories at Camp (later Fort) Detrick, Maryland, USA (precursor to USAMRIID) who died in 1951 after being accidentally infected with the Vollum strain.[37]

Although Fort Detrick scientists still dabble with anthrax, strictly for making defensive vaccines you understand, this was not always the case. The facility's colorful and lurid history has come into greater focus with the gradual release of previously classified documents. During its heyday in the 1950s and 60s, it was the scene of events that seemed to provide the fodder for bad science fiction movies or second-rate spy novels.

One of the most dangerous but fascinating characters in this little shop of horrors was a Bronx-born and Cal Tech-trained chemist named Sidney Gottlieb. He joined the CIA in 1951 and quickly rose to head the chemical division of the Technical Services Staff (TSS). In this capacity he worked closely with the Army's Chemical Corps' Special Operations Division at Fort Detrick. At the time, the Army scientists were working furiously to weaponize virtually every disease known to humanity. Gottlieb's job was to take the finished products back to the CIA and figure out how to use them against "the enemy". Gottlieb tackled this task with fiendish glee. Around the labs he was affectionately called "the Black Sorcerer" and "the Dirty Trickster".

For Gottlieb, 1960 was an especially thrilling year. He and his TSS merry pranksters were unleashed to focus on assassinating foreign leaders. Gottlieb personally flew a vial of anthrax to the Congo to pull the old poison toothbrush trick on Prime Minister Patrice Lumumba. The plan had to be aborted.

Next, Gottlieb tried the ever-popular "poison handkerchief" caper on Iraq's Prime Minister Qasim. He soaked the handkerchiefs in *Clostridium botulinum* (Botulism) and had them sent from India to Qasim. Again the plot failed.

Looking for easier targets, Gottlieb focused on Fidel Castro. This time it was the classic "poison cigar and wet suit" gambit. Again, no cigar. Gottlieb's previous plot against Castro had been the "dose the leader with LSD" stunt, always a crowd-pleaser. The idea was to spray Castro's TV studio with LSD just before he was to give one of his four- hour speeches. Thus, the Cuban people would watch as their fearless leader had a complete meltdown and presumably would overthrow him for being a nut case. No luck on this *Get Smart* scheme either.

Sidney Gottlieb is probably best known for heading Project MKULTRA, the CIA'S LSD-infused mind control research operation. He was convinced that he could "develop techniques that would crush the human psyche to the point it would admit anything." Toward this goal, Gottlieb explored nearly every mind-altering substance and technique imaginable. According to Gordon Thomas' book *Secrets and Lies* (2007), Gottlieb launched another program called Project MKOFTEN in which he set out to "explore the world of black magic…and harness the forces of darkness." For this effort he enlisted the aid of "psychics, demonologists, witches, wizards and Satanists." We may never know how much success Gottlieb and the CIA had with that project.

Apparently all was not doom and gloom for the good doctor. Though he was a stutterer and had a clubfoot, Gottlieb was an avid folk dancer. Oddly enough, Allen Dulles, his boss at the CIA was also a stutterer with a clubfoot. It's unlikely that the two ever danced at the same time but it must have made for some interesting meetings.

Sidney Gottlieb retired from the CIA in early 1973. Richard Helms, CIA Director at the time, ordered him to shred all the records of MKULTRA before his departure. According to Gordon Thomas, Gottlieb destroyed about 80 percent of the files but "inexplicably" left 130 boxes of files in the archives. The shocking files are now available to the public.

With his anthrax toothbrush glory days behind him, Gottlieb and his wife moved to India to run a leper hospital. Was this penance? Did he finally see the light after 200 self-administered LSD trips? Is this evidence that even the coldest of Cold Warriors can have a change of heart? There's always hope.

We should re-remind ourselves that Anthrax is a naturally occurring bacterium that infects domesticated livestock who ingest the spores from infected grass and soil. Outbreaks in nature are rare, but they do occur. Fifty head of cattle died from anthrax on a Sterling, Colorado ranch the first week of August, 2012 and two weeks later, ten people were stricken and one died of anthrax in the Russian Altai Mountain region. As we've discussed the region around Sterling was probably the hardest hit cattle mutilation region in the mid-1970s.

Mad Cow Disease: Is it Loose in the Food Chain?

Anthrax is nasty, but it could be described as a mild cold compared with Mad Cow Disease. We have all heard of it, but most of us are oblivious to what this "100 percent fatal" affliction actually is, how and why it is caused, and when and where it originated. Mad cow, or bovine spongiform encephalopathy (BSE) is the bovine variant of prion (pronounced pree-on) disease, or transmissible spongiform encephalopathy (TSE). Dr. Stanley Prusiner won the Nobel Prize for Medicine in 1997 for discovering this aberration. It is thought to appear spontaneously in one out of a million cows. It may appear spontaneously in deer, elk, sheep, pigs, cats and humans. It is designated by different names based on the animal type that develops symptoms i.e., mad cow (beef), chronic wasting disease (deer and elk), scrapie (sheep), Cruetzfeldt-Jakob and *kuru* (humans). But all of these types are variant forms of the alarming scourge dubbed TSE.

According to the Centers for Disease Control (CDC) TSEs are caused by prions, which are now considered the smallest life forms yet discovered by science—a thousand times smaller than the next smallest life form, a virus. Until recently, there have been no tests developed that can detect prions in a living host. The disease can only be detected post-mortem after the host has died and its brain tissue is examined. Scientists using the discarded appendices from appendectomy patients have perfected a test for prions that has yielded alarming results.

TSEs are a family of rare progressive neurodegenerative disorders that affect both humans and animals. They are distinguished by long incubation periods, characteristic spongiform changes associated with neuronal loss, and a failure to induce inflammatory response.

The causative agents of TSEs are believed to be prions. The term "prions" refers to abnormal, pathogenic agents that are transmissible and are able to induce abnormal folding of specific normal cellular proteins called prion proteins that are found most abundantly in the brain. The functions of these normal prion proteins are still not completely understood. The abnormal folding of the prion proteins leads to brain damage and the characteristic signs and symptoms of the disease. Prion diseases are usually rapidly progressive and always fatal.[38]

Although considered a life form because they can induce abnormal folding of other proteins and spread, or in a sense, procreate, *prions are virtually impossible to kill*. So are they alive? Being a 'life-form' means you can be somehow killed, right? In the case of prions, they can also survive in the soil for years, survive in bone ash from diseased animals that have been cremated in which some of the misfolded proteins still remain infectious. Able to withstand chlorine and heat upwards of 2000+ degrees, prions redefine resilience. Once the misfolded proteins spread through the patient's nerve tissue, death from the resulting degenerative symptomatic disease *is 100 percent certain.*

[CJD and its variants] are thought to [spontaneously] occur worldwide at a rate of one in one million people, meaning some 300 Americans can be expected to develop it each year. But a Swiss surveillance team recently revised that number to three in a million, based on improved recognition of the disease in their country.[39]

This figure has changed and has been revised as a result of a 2006 UK study. Now, the statistic stands at *1 in 2000 people.* According to an official government website in Canada: collectionscanada.gc.ca "The appearance of bovine spongiform encephalopathy (BSE) followed by new spongiform encephalopathies and variant Creutzfeldt-Jakob disease (CJD) in the United Kingdom indicates that these diseases may be linked."

As is widely known, a devastating outbreak of mad cow disease occurred in southern England in 1985-6, and after 13-years of battling the rapidly spreading outbreak in UK herds, the government was forced to call for *the complete eradication* of all cattle in the British Isles—at the time about *4.5 million animals.* (figure 9) The animals were slaughtered and incinerated. There should be more controversy concerning what was done with the tons of bone ash left behind. One unconfirmed source in late '90s mentioned infected bone ash had been innocently sold to over 70 countries—mainly in the Third World.

Epidemiological activist Patricia Doyle, M.D., has asserted that much of the bone ash is being secretly stored in WWII-era "blimp hangers" in the UK. Out of sight, out of mind I suppose. After a history of battling rinderpest and now mad cow, the media, the public, and government officials should be concerned that this potentially emerging cattle-borne disease may have the ability to jump the species barrier and create an pandemic in meat-eaters and vegetarians exposed to infection from still viable prions. As an indication of the high level of concern about the potential spread of TSEs, if you spent more than six months total in the UK since 1980, you not allowed to donate blood to the American Red Cross.

Why all the fear surrounding tiny misfolded proteins? What is mad cow disease anyway, and why should we care about it one way or another—or bother to educate ourselves? When and where did this scourge originate?

A good place to start is 250 years ago when the first outbreaks of "scrapie," were noticed in English sheep herds. Scrapie is a form of prion disease that has been detected in sheep since the first known outbreak in early 1732 in England and is considered the first manifestation of TSE identified in nature. It is still a mystery to science why TSE disease is thought to have spontaneously emerged in nature.

The name scrapie is derived from afflicted sheep's extreme discomfort, as they often attempt to madly scrape against fence posts and tree trunks in an effort to scrape or itch their hide, thus the name scrapie. In England the disease was first recognized to be a distinct disease in 1732, and the earliest outbreaks were confined exclusively to the Suffolk breed of sheep. When the highly transmissible, highly infectious nature of the disease was established in the 18th century, British wool was one of the most important and vital commercial products of the time. The government was understandably alarmed at the potential adverse economic effects of this newly emerging disease and much effort was undertaken to isolate and destroy animals that exhibited signs of infection. It is thought that scrapie might have been inadvertently introduced into the United States through contaminated sheep parts imported to Wisconsin mink ranches as feed from Great Britain in 1947. This outbreak among mink that were fed the scrapie-infected feed is considered to be the first outbreak of prion disease identified in North America.

While the outbreak in Wisconsin was initially considered to be a simple neurodegenerative infection, after further unexplained outbreaks on five Wisconsin mink ranches, it was determined that tainted feed was the causative agent. All five ranches shared a single source for mink feed. The as yet undefined prion disease was thought to have been successfully eradicated by destruction of all possible infectious carriers of the disease.

Initially, during the 1947 UK outbreak, scrapie was exclusively reported only in the Suffolk breed of sheep, but since then it has also been diagnosed in a Cheviots, Border Leicesters, Corriedales, Dorsets, and a number of other crossbreeds of the Suffolk breed. Although spontaneous outbreaks in nature are rare, scrapie continues to rear its ugly presence from time to time and has never been successfully eradicated. It is now fairly well established that these misfolded proteins called prions hang around for many years.

Scrapie in sheep, like all TSEs found in nature, is a 100 percent fatal disease. One epidemiologist observed that prion infection made "AIDS look like a bad cold." After an animal is infected with the activated misfolded proteins, prions invade the lymphatic system traveling to the lymph nodes and eventually migrate throughout the nervous system where they lodge in nerve and brain tissue creating holes in the tissue. These holes enlarge and begin to interfere with synaptic function and as a result, the animal develops the now recognized symptoms of prion disease; twitching, shaking limbs and the inability of inflicted animals to stay on their feet. The animal then slowly dies from the resulting brain degeneration and synaptic dysfunction that impacts the entire metabolic and respiratory process, leading to certain death.

Since the supposed identification of the prion in the mid-1990s, scientists have exhausted all efforts to develop a live animal test for prion disease..

Cattle, sheep and many other animals have developed a unique third eyelid called a nictitating membrane. This eyelid is drawn horizontally across the eyeball as added protection against adverse environmental conditions. This unique physiological adaptation was developed as a way to keep the animals' eyeballs moistened in dry, windy or particulate-filled air. Reptiles, birds, sharks, and some mammals have evolved this additional membrane that is part of the conjunctiva, a mucus membrane. At rest this membrane is found in the corner of the eye and in humans nictitating membranes are permanently folded there. They are those little pink nubs located next to the tear ducts. The breakthrough was announced in USDA Release No. 0161.98, 4-09-98:

> USDA scientists have discovered that sheep eyelids hold the key to an easy, relatively inexpensive test for diagnosing scrapie, a fatal brain disease in sheep, Agriculture Secretary Dan Glickman announced today.
>
> This [Pullman] test will allow producers and veterinarians, for the first time, to easily detect scrapie in sheep before the animals show signs of the disease," said Glickman. "Until now, scrapie could only be confirmed by examining the brains of dead animals. Clearly, this is an important step toward controlling this disease."

Now comes news that a second live animal test has been developed by the Animal and Plant Health Inspection Service that focuses on the other end of the animal. This time the test was developed to test mucosal lymphoid tissue from the rectal area. *It's interesting to note that eyes and rear ends are the organs that are most often reported as the body parts found missing.* Researchers in Norway and Scotland have modified the eye-lid test and use lymphoid tissue in the lining of the animal's rectum. The rectal biopsy is a quick painless test that allows for the detection of prion infection. A *Dairy Goat Journal* article "Scrapies: Rectal Biopsies May Hold Clues to Eradication," in 2009 announced this development.

"Rectal biopsy also allows for more repeat samples from an individual animal when needed," state microbiologist Katherine O'Rourke, a member of the scrapie research team that includes APHIS Veterinary Services and Wildlife Services, the National Park Service, Colorado State University, and the Canadian Food Inspection Agency.

Another form of prion disease—in humans—was identified by researchers in New Guinea, in the mid-1950s, and it may be related to other emerging human variants. I have researched first contact scenarios between Europeans and the South Forè tribe of the Okapa District of the Eastern Highlands of Papua, New Guinea (where a human variant of prion disease called *kuru* was first identified by Australian authorities in 1953) to try to establish a connection with the 1700s scrapie outbreak in Suffok sheep herds in the UK. Is there a link between the earliest outbreaks of scrapie and early European exploration of New Guinea? Although this link has not previously been proposed (let alone proven), it is possible that the initial scrapie 1732 infection in the UK may have migrated from the South Pacific?

So, what is kuru and how does this variant manifest? With up to a 40-year incubation period, kuru is a fatal degenerative human form of prion disease that probably developed from the practice of ritualistically dismembering and (on occasion) eating the brain and muscle tissue of recently diseased family members. The term "kuru" is derived from the Forè word *kuria* ("to shake"). A major outbreak of kuru occurred between 1953 and 1960 that killed upwards of 1000 tribespeople. (figure 10) This prompted Australian medical personnel to begin studying this horrific disease that causes uncontrolled twitching of limbs and outbreaks of uncontrollable laughter and facial grimaces in its victims and other symptoms similar to those observed in livestock afflicted with prion disease. Because of the strange symptoms of "manic laughter" and frozen manic grins, the disease acquired the nickname "the laughing sickness." It has always been tough going in the wilds of New Guinea and for 50,000 years, no food source was wasted—even grandpa.

> Upon the death of a Foré individual, the maternal kin were responsible for the dismemberment of the corpse. The women would remove the arms and feet, strip the limbs of muscle, remove the brain and cut open the chest in order to remove internal organs.
>
> Shirley Lindenbaum, one of the early kuru researchers, states that kuru victims were highly regarded as sources of food, because the layer of fat on victims who died quickly resembled pork. Women also were known to feed morsels—such as human brain and various parts of organs— to their children and the elderly.
>
> It is currently believed that kuru was transmitted among the South Foré through participation in such cannibalism, although opportunistic

infection through wounds when removing infectious tissue from the corpse can be assumed to be another cause, as not all cases can be explained by ingestion of infectious tissue.[40]

Lately, I've wondered why we have seen an upsurge in popularity of cannibalistic "zombie" stories. Cultural trappings of this current interest are readily found. The zombie-laden *Walking Dead* on AMC is one of the most popular shows on broadcast television and I can't help but think that there is something lurking just out of sight in the culture that might tie into a kind of prescience of horrors to come. *World War Z*, indeed. Perhaps we are on the verge of a horrific malady, plague, or genetic mutation where life could be setting itself up to imitate "art"? I sincerely hope not!

Kuru was first identified and researched by the late Daniel Gajdusek from samples obtained in New Guinea by medical field explorers Michael Alpers and his co-worker anthropologist Shirley Lindenbaum. Gajdusek obtained samples of brain tissues of infected Foré tribes people, injected them into the brains of chimpanzees and established this disease's transmissibility across the species barrier. In 1976, Gajdusek was awarded the Nobel Prize for Medicine for identification of the cause of the disease. Twenty years later Dr. Stanley Prusiner won the Nobel Prize for Medicine for his role as the first clinician to identify and name the infectious misfolded protein he named the "prion."

Although the Lindenbaum and Alpers' research indicates that the disease may have spontaneously arisen around 1900 from a single Foré tribesperson who developed what is now known as Cruetzfeldt-Jakob disease. Then the unexpected might have occurred after imported samples of the disease were introduced into United States' biological laboratories in the 1960s. First, in Maryland at Ft. Detrick as inoculation experiments with monkeys and then into Colorado and Wyoming biology laboratories where scrapie experiments were taking place. It seems possible that the as yet unknown, undefined prions could have escaped quarantine into the neighborhood and emerged as a new variant of the disease in Eastern Slope Rocky Mountain deer and elk herds.

The most extensive outbreak of CWD began west of Ft. Collins, Colorado in early November 1997 and has since spread eastward across the continent inflicting deer throughout most of the eastern United States. As an interesting coincidence, this spontaneous outbreak occurred within the same time period as the inexplicable blow-down of upwards of two million trees on the Continental Divide. This rare atmospheric event occurred *in the same region* where the CWD outbreak bloomed and then subsequently spread across the Eastern half of the United States. According to the Centers for Disease Control, "As of November 6, 2013, there were 128 counties in 18 states with reported CWD in free-ranging cervids [deer, elk and moose]." Did you know this? What about the many big game hunters who bag and tag thousands of cervids in North America every fall—do they know that CWD has been detected in animals where they hunt? How about the many family members, friends and buyers of this meat? Is there a need for them to be made aware of the potential hazard in the pot of venison stew? Looking at the anemic attempt by government to educate the public and (in the case of Colorado) the $82 million windfall generated by hunting licenses in 2006, in light of the revenue potential I would assume there is a veneer of "ignorance is bliss," at work and play. Financial concerns tend to trump public health concerns, it would seem.

In the early 2000s, microbiologist Colm Kelleher (at the time working for the National Institute for Discovery Sciences) uncovered a number of disturbing facts while working with a scientific team stalking our mutilated cattle. Kelleher's investigation is documented in his important (but largely overlooked) 2004 Paraview book *Brain Trust* (figure 13):

[A] prion catastrophe occurred in the United States. It likely began with the routine importation of dozens of kuru brains from New Guinea by Charleton Gajdusek and Joseph Smadel beginning in 1957. Subsequently, there were large-scale inoculations of that kuru material into dozens of species of animals in the middle of a wildlife refuge at Patuxent, Maryland, from 1963 until 1970. 'They even inoculated alligators' is a phrase that sums up their indiscriminative approach… The importation of dozens of kuru-laden brains from the wilds of New Guinea into Maryland may have been the first step in the spread of infectious prions into the wildlife population in the United States. The second step was the frantic, widespread, but inadvertent amplification of prion diseases through multiple species…

Did the prion disease [that threatens] our wildlife originates with these inoculations? …The disease appeared in mule deer in the wildlife research facilities at Ft. Collins, Colorado, and its sister institute [Sybille Wildlife Research and Conservation Education Unit, 45 miles northeast of Laramie] Wyoming in 1967, possibly as a result of scrapie-infected sheep being housed in the same facilities. But the disease may also have erupted from the contaminated wildlife in the area around the facilities [and] it is difficult to refute the fact that the Colorado and Wyoming wildlife facilities subsequently became the epicenter for an epidemic of chronic wasting disease, which rapidly spread into neighboring states, beginning with Nebraska and spreading into the rest of Wyoming.[41] (figure 14)

Inquiring Minds Want to Know!

Over the past 40 years there have been few scientific studies that have objectively studied the cattle mutilation mystery in an attempt to establish a motive for perpetrating these animal deaths. Given the fact that most veterinarian pathologists are highly dubious and skeptical of claims that any of these cases are of a high strange nature, it stands to reason that they might have become convinced ahead of time that all mutilations can be explained away with mundane explanations. There have been published exceptions to this, as we have seen.

As noted earlier, Operation Cattle Mutilation coordinated by ex-FBI agent Kenneth Rommel appeared on the surface to be a serious look at mutilation claims arising from New Mexico ranching communities along with law enforcement assertions that someone (or something) was mutilating cattle. However, like the now-infamous "Condon Report," (which claimed to objectively study UFO reports) Rommel's attempt to study the mutilation mystery appeared to be slanted toward a pre-conceived mundane conclusion, and the report had the evidently desired effect of "officially" debunking the mutilation mystery. Armed with a broad brush of plausible deniability, Rommel dismissed the mutilation phenomenon and it became beyond a moot point. But inexplicable livestock death and disfigurements still continued to be reported to authorities—as recently as November 2013.

Two fairly extensive scientific papers have been published that detail biophysical study results that indicate there is evidence of cutting instruments being used in some cases. In W.C. Levengood/BLT's 1993-1997 *Study of Bovine Excision Sites*, it was noted that heightened concentration levels of magnetite were detected at a number of mute sites—including a case that I was directly involved with (with the BBC tagging along documenting my field work). Potentially, these suggestive findings are alleged to have been duplicated at UFO landing trace sites and in crop circles. David Perkins noted this in his article "High Heat" published in *Western Spirit Magazine* May 1998:

> In 1996-97, the tiny magnetic beads that had been noted in crop circle formations, started showing up at animal mutilation sites. Imbedded beads of magnetite were found in plants near a mutilated calf in Red Bluff, California. The magnetite concentration around the animal was about 10 times higher than the control samples. A similar case in Papoose Meadows, California revealed "higher concentrations within proximity of the excision points around the animal." In April 1997, researcher Christopher O'Brien (author of *The Mysterious Valley*) sampled a mutilation case in Colorado's San Luis Valley. The magnetite sphere concentrations around the dead cow were the highest yet recorded (over 500 times greater than what would be expected from normal soil). In a January 1997, mutilation case investigated by Jean Bilodeaux, the magnetite particles clustered in higher concentrations "within proximity of the excision points around the animal."

A surgical pathologist colleague of William Levengood examined tissue samples from the large black bull and found "evidence of heat cautery artifact and 'blistering' of the epidermis at the edge of the tissue." In 1991, tissue samples from a mutilated steer found near Portland, Oregon, were analyzed by the Veterinarian Diagnostic Laboratory at Oregon State University. The lab concluded that the tissues exhibited "a band of coagulation necrosis consistent with a heat-induced incision, such as an electro-surgical unit."

Dr. John Altshuler, a doctor of pathology and hemotology in Denver, has examined tissue samples from more than 40 "excised" animals since 1989. He has concluded that the cutting was done with "high heat." Dr. Altshuler has consistently observed "cooked hemoglobin" indicating "high heat as in laser surgery...probably above 300 degrees F."

If these scientific findings are real, they may be offering us a clue to help us determine potential casual energetic forces at work at these sites. Since the mid-1990s Levengood's scientific work has been controversial but (in my opinion) represents a positive step in science.

Another paper worthy of mention was published by The National Institute for Discovery Sciences in 2003 entitled: *Unexplained Cattle Deaths and the Emergence of a Transmissible Spongiform Encephalopathy (TSE) Epidemic in North America.*

NIDS and the Mad Cow Paper

In the abstract of this important position paper, the NIDS team—headed by Dr. Colm Kelleher—concluded that there appears to be a link between cattle mutilations and the hypothetical monitoring of the possible spread of "mad cow" disease. This proposed link, if real, may be a major clue to the identity of perpetrators of (at least some) unexplained cattle mutilations that have occurred in North America. I have reprinted the following proprietary information (that is easily available on the Internet) acknowledging their important contribution toward the public welfare, and I applaud aerospace entrepreneur Robert Bigelow for putting his money where it should have been spent when it comes to stalking the herd. *Everyone should be paying attention*—especially if you like beef, like I do—this is a public health issue that may have profound implications:

> "[NIDS] present evidence that a correlation exists between reports of animal mutilation and the emergence of a Transmissible Spongiform Encephalopathy (TSE) epidemic in North America.
> • We show that sharp instruments are used in animal mutilations. Our data contradict the conclusions of the 1980 Rommel Report that claimed predators and scavengers could explain reports of cattle mutilations.

- Using data obtained from a NIDS nationwide survey of bovine veterinarian practitioners, we show that certain organs are preferentially removed during animal mutilations.
- We focus attention on the temporal and geographical overlaps between the animal mutilation and TSE epidemics in NE Colorado. The most highly publicized TSE epidemic in North America, chronic wasting disease (CWD), emerged in NE Colorado in the late 1960s.
- We show evidence that patterns of animal mutilations conform to covert but classical wild life sampling methodologies for infectious diseases.
- We show evidence in support of an epidemic of prion disease that is both subclinical in cattle and clinical in deer/elk in North America.
- We describe evidence from two laboratories that a number of prion diseases in humans are misdiagnosed as Alzheimer's disease and therefore currently escape detection.
- The historical record shows that high levels of infectious TSEs were imported from New Guinea into research facilities at Fort Detrick and Bethesda, Maryland after 1958 and were used for intensive cross-species infectivity experiments.
- We hypothesize that animal mutilations represent both a TSE-disease sampling operation on domestic animals AND a graphic warning that *the beef and venison food chain is compromised.* [my emphasis]

"Overall, the evidence suggests that animal mutilations are a long-term, covert, prion disease sampling operation by unknown perpetrators who are aware of a substantial contamination of the beef and venison food supply. Although this paper presents evidence in favor of a motive for animal mutilations, there is still insufficient evidence to identify the perpetrators.

"The hypotheses described in this paper yield a number of testable predictions. Examining these predictions in the coming months and years is increasingly urgent because they have considerable public health implications. Secondly the recent (May 2003) announcement of a case of mad cow disease in Alberta, Canada has brought the issue of the contamination of the human food chain into sharper focus.

NIDS Conclusion, Hypothesis and Predictions

"The primary conclusion of NIDS paper is that the animal mutilation epidemic of 1970-2003 was and is a monitoring operation for an infectious agent that is spreading through the human food chain (cattle, sheep and wild & farmed deer/elk). In North America (Canada and United States) the infection comprises a full-blown CWD epidemic in deer and elk and a sub-clinical BSE infection in cattle. The infectious agent, unlike all known viruses and bacteria, is almost indestructible and the symptoms in people appear very difficult to diagnose pre-mortem. In short this TSE agent is the perfect stealth killer. If the hypothesis is correct, animal mutilation operations are carried out by a knowledgeable group that is cognizant of the biochemistry and infectious potential of prion diseases and their fatal spread. How difficult is this knowledge to come by?

"Beginning in 1958, Dr. Carleton Gajdusek began mailing kuru brains from the wilds of New Guinea to the central neuropathology facility at NIH in Bethesda and Fort Detrick. Hence, these fatal neurodegenerative diseases have been known in the United States, but not highly publicized, since the late 1950s or early 1960s. Only recently, due to the intensive prion research carried in the past two decades has the extent of prion replication become obvious in the eye, tongue, anus/large intestine and reproductive organs of animals. If these specific tissues are indeed removed during animal mutilation for the purpose of prion monitoring, this implies an intensive knowledge of prion physiology, biochemistry and infectiousness, involving research results *not published until relatively recently*, on the part of the perpetrators of animal mutilations. [my emphasis]

"The identity of the mutilators remains unknown, but in addition to knowledge of prion infectiousness research, a high level of technology, surgical skill and stealth has been a feature of animal mutilations. [my emphasis]

[The above statement is important. It would appear that the level scientific knowledge exhibited by the mutilators predates official scientific understanding by at least 20 years. Whoever is responsible for mutilating cattle appeared to have *advanced knowledge of prion disease*, and this knowledge may be behind perpetration of the mutilation phenomenon.]

"It is a recurring theme in law enforcement circles that not a single person has been caught or charged for the crime of animal mutilations in the 30-year history of the epidemic."

Why Leave the Body?

"This question has plagued investigators ever since the first well-publicized investigations of mutilations began back in the early 1970s. As any reader familiar with the animal mutilation topic will agree, a plethora of hypotheses have sprung up about the perpetrators and their motives for animal mutilations.

"One of the most quoted hypotheses involves a government operation to monitor radiation or biological warfare testing. But the question "why leave the body?" has never been adequately answered by these hypotheses. The government can just as easily test their own herds, the counter-argument goes, or obtain carcasses from a slaughterhouse if they wish to covertly monitor radiation. Thus, for this and many other reasons, the evidence points away from the government as perpetrators of animal mutilations." [End of NIDS Paper]

To me the answer to this question of "why leave (or return) the animal" is obvious: if they take the animal it's larceny and an official report would be filed with law enforcement. Leave the animal "mutilated" in the pasture with none of the good parts missing and there will always be plausible deniability. Blame it on weirdos with scalpels or Wile E. Coyote tricksters and his bird friends and be done with it. The twisted beauty of these nuanced parts of the mystery is a perfect example of a true conundrum—one that is able to self-nullify the reality of its true nature. Everything renders everything else into the land of moot.

Paraphrasing the rest of the NIDS conclusions, Jacques Vallee and F.W. Smith [Author of *Cattle Mutilation: The Unthinkable Truth*] point out that leaving the cow carcass on the ground appears to be a deliberate message being sent to parties as yet unidentified. But I would ask who is sending whom a message? In the NORAD case, was one faction of the military sending another faction of the military a message? Is big agro-business involved on some level? Are aliens truly concerned about our environment? Did prion experiments get away from biologists?

There exists an abundance of down-to-earth scenarios, hints and possibilities of subterfuge and suggestions of slight-of-hand intrigue unfolding, which needs to be addressed before we throw our hands up to the sky and pronounce, "it must be aliens."

I think it's very likely that some sort of message is being sent that *appears to place* the onus on possible "off-planet" ET culprit(s). I would call this an example of societal manipulation of belief. This hypothetical message being conveyed involves an admonishment that persistent human-generated degradation of our planetary environmental biosphere is detrimental and "others" are concerned. If the Others are real, could it be that we are placing *these perpetrators at risk* with our unfettered degradation of the environment and this is why the message is being sent through cattle and other means? And if this is so, then the possibility exists that *the "ETs" are as terrestrial as we are*. It would make sense that they would be highly concerned if they lived here as we do.

With the rampant environmental damage that has been taking place since the dawn of the nuclear age, it will only be a matter of time before we are faced with a catastrophe. Oh yeah, then there is Fukushima… I know, we can't factor any hypotheses in, but we sure don't want to factor this particular one out! This is a highly complicated scenario that deserves far more chapters than this first book is able to provide. David Perkins and I have a lot to say about this and many other subjects and this would require an entire book's worth of analysis for the various theories and we will need room to explain how each one of us have arrived at our present thinking—not to mention our synthesis. But, I would suggest that we heed Kelleher's warning:

"We suggest that attention is being deliberately focused on the mutilated animals. Further, we suggest the warning is that the human food chain is compromised, probably with a prion-associated infectious agent that still remains mostly undetected."[42]

I must mention that Colm Kelleher traced the history of prion disease from its first discovery i.e., scrapie and kuru, up through the UK mad cow outbreak that ended in 1998 on to 2004 when he pointed out the hidden health crisis that was unfolding around the potential misdiagnosis of Alzheimer's and dementia deaths. In case you were unaware, Alzheimer's is considered the sixth leading cause of death in the U.S. and in 2010, there were 83,494 officially-attributed deaths to the disease.[43] In the past 20 years, Alzheimer and dementia deaths skyrocketed and in *Brain Trust* Kelleher suggests that the real cause of this dramatic increase is misdiagnosis of CJD (and the rarer variants, vCJD and nvCJD) symptoms. Alzheimer's and dementia victims often exhibit mental deterioration, and other initial signs and symptoms also shared by victims of CJD. These symptoms typically include:

• Personality changes
• Anxiety
• Depression
• Memory loss
• Impaired thinking
• Blurred vision
• Insomnia
• Difficulty speaking
• Difficulty swallowing
• Sudden, jerky movements[44]

As the debilitating disease progresses, synaptic function becomes further impaired. Most patients eventually lapse into coma succumbing to heart and/or respiratory failure—pneumonia or other infections are often cited as the actual cause of death. The disease usually runs its course quickly—within six to 7 months, but after the onset of full-blown symptoms only a few people are unlucky enough to live over one to two years after their diagnosis.

As with death by dementia, the end can be horrific. Patients diagnosed with the vCJD death sentence, begin to slowly exhibit psychiatric symptoms such as the loss of the ability to think, to reason, and descend into an unfathomable cavern of dream-like existential nightmares. Autopsies are not required if a death is officially declared as the result of Alzheimer's or for "dementia" and escalating tens-of-thousands of deaths are not being firmly ascertained as to the actual cause of death. *Many of these cases may be due to prion infection.* This is a huge subject that should be addressed in-depth in the mainstream scientific and health care communities.

Dr. Colm Kelleher published a short article in February 2005 in which he pointed out that cattle have a history of passing along other potentially fatal diseases into the food chain besides mad cow.

> Bovine tuberculosis, which includes *Mycobacterium bovis* and *M. avium-intracellulare* or *paratuberculosis*, is and has always been the most prevalent threat to the cattle industry, and the USDA reports that between 20 percent and 40 percent of US dairy herds are infected with paratuberculosis alone.
>
> The health risk for milk tainted with M. bovis has been known for decades and there was a time not so long ago when "tuberculin-tested" was printed on every milk container. Schliesser stated that meat from tuberculous animals may also constitute a significant risk of infection. At the turn of the 20th century 25 percent of the many US deaths from TB in adults were caused by M. bovis. Dairy products aside, when past and present meat consumption are factored in, there is *three times the risk of developing Alzheimer's in meat eaters* as opposed to vegetarians. [my emphasis]
>
> The investigation into the causal trail for Creutzfeldt-Jakob, indistinguishable from Alzheimer's except for its shorter, lethal course might have grown cold where it not for [scientists] who linked mad cow in cattle with M. bovis and related paratuberculosis on clinical, pathologic and epidemiological grounds. The southwest of the UK, the very cradle of British BSE and CJD outbreaks, saw an exponential increase in bovine tuberculosis just prior to it's spongiform outbreaks.
>
> All of this brings up the unthinkable: that Alzheimer's, Cruetzfeldt-Jackob, and Mad Cow Disease might just be caused by *eating the meat or dairy in consumer products or feed*. It is only appropriate therefore to explore the role of bovine TB and the atypical mycobacteria in Alzheimer's, JCD and Mad Cow disease and develop better serological surveillance for these pathogens.[45] [my emphasis]

The NIDS paper and *Brain Trust* lay out a thought provoking case that at least some of the "real" livestock (and wildlife) mutilations are being performed by someone or something in an attempt to covertly determine the potential spread of "mad cow" or prion disease in North American herds.

And we should also factor in the potential effect of radiation on natural and introduced pathogens into the environment. Although this explanation and NIDS's proposed evidence might explain some mutilation cases, I suspect that not all true mutilations are due to unknown parties monitoring the food chain. This is a complex scenario that appears to feature multiple groups with independent, overlapping agendas.

Where Does That Leave Us?

As we dig deeper into the belly of this mystery, the complexities and nuances gain lives of their own. Sometimes the effort to remain objective is lost in enthusiastic theoretical speculation, and at other times it is swamped in pure frustration.

Since the early 1990s few ranchers around North America, to my knowledge, have actively networked and attempted to collectively dig deeper into this perplexing phenomenon, and over the years, the reoccurring phenomenon of animal mutilations has left behind numerous burned out ranching community casualties along the way. Ranchers who have been victimized over and over again usually reach the point where they are silenced by their own volition and go out of business, but a few are outraged enough to talk about their experiences.

The same goes for law enforcement. They have always been back on the heels of their Tony Lama cowboy boots and they have pretty much given up as well. Can you blame them? I would guess that countless cases are still occurring and because of this sense of resignation nothing is being done by law enforcement. Maybe if we don't investigate it they're not really there—out of sight out of mind. County sheriffs and local cops have been rendered impotent in the situation and this fact of law enforcement nullification may be an important clue to revisit during our extended analysis of the mystery in the follow-up book to *Stalking the Herd*.

Over the past 40 years, only a handful of investigators have somehow managed to stick to the task of stalking the perpetrators of the unexplained livestock death mystery. Most have fallen away from the subject, some with extreme prejudice. Tom Adams was working on a book when he dropped off the map in 2000, never to be heard from again; Peter Jordon hasn't publicly commented on the subject in almost 10 years; Gary Massey blew his brains out; ex-police officer Ted Oliphant has asked not to be contacted any further for his comments on this troubling subject; Gabe Valdez, Tony Dodd, Bob Pratt and John Keel have passed on. Gail Staehlin and Fern Belzil no longer actively investigate cases to my knowledge. Philip Hoyle in the UK is on an extended hiatus—the list goes on and on.

Besides reliable trooper Linda Moulton Howe, Colorado's enthusiastic Chuck Zukowski and Margie Kay in Missouri, only a few out there are courageous (crazy or willing) and knowledgeable enough to chase these particular tricksters. Honestly, I've always hated being around dead cows. My last case was unexpected with an ad-hoc "investigation" and I do not care to ever repeat the experience again in my life. (figure 15) My longtime investigative associate Thomas Peay would rather not field calls asking him to go out on occasional mutilation claims in the SLV—flying humanoids, yes, dead cows, well, no. He's also patiently setting up a network of Native American-style "medicine wheels" to honor important sites located around the perimeter of the world's largest alpine valley in south central Colorado—that's cool—dead cows on the other hand…

I'm sure it's readily apparent that this is not a subject that attracts the curious weekenders or those who are not ready to go "all out" in their attempt to actively investigate the mystery. I know, it's a tired cliché, "many are called—few are chosen." One thing should be clear: we need more troopers like Linda, Chuck and Margie and the others walking the walk down into bloody trenches. These are minefields through darkening pastures with their mushroom growing cow pies—watch your step in the trenches.

Debunking Common Theories About Cattle Mutilations

Some researchers who have studied the cattle mutilation mystery suspect a link to the U.S. government because helicopters have been seen consistently in regions reporting a high rate of mutilation reports. According to some skeptics this turns out to be mere coincidence because many military installations can be found in and around areas of high mutilation activity. What a coincidence! The link between the government and cattle mutilations would be moot if these events occurred exclusively in places where helicopters are seldom seen, but this is unfortunately not the case. For instance: Northeast Alabama—mute central—is home to two military bases, Anniston Army Depot and the famous Redstone Arsenal. Ground Zero in central Colorado is home to six military facilities, including four Air Force bases (Buckley, Lowery, et. al.); Ft. Carson; the Piñon Canyon maneuver site; NORAD and the Air Force Academy. All of these military facilities are located in close proximity to the locations of where major cattle mutilation outbreaks have taken place. Helicopter activity in northern Arkansas can be attributed to Arnold AFB in Tennessee, just across the Mississippi River. Fort Indiantown Gap is only about two miles away from the Pennsylvania cave where the mystery crab/scorpion-like creature was discovered in 2011.

Over the decades the stealth exercised during the perpetration of hypothetical military-style operations against livestock (without alerting ranch dogs and their vigilant owners) has been beyond amazing to ranchers, farmers, and investigators. "Murphy's Law" suggests that at some point in the operational process something invariably should have gone wrong *once* over the decades. Remember the Iranian hostage rescue mission and the recent assassination of Osama Bin Laden, where helicopters and their operators kissed Murphy on the lips? If even one helicopter crew messed up and was caught, or brought down, the resulting legal implications and class action suit would be unprecedented. Therefore, the goal must be important enough to justify all that risk. The apparent ease and intricacy of operations exhibited by the perpetrators, bolsters skeptics' arguments that this cannot be an organized human effort. The apparent absence of errors, miscalculations or human and/or equipment failure on the part of the mutilators is still a major theoretical hurdle for law enforcement and independent civilian mute investigators who suspect human perpetrators.

It is highly questionable that the helicopter crews (and/or the potential ground-site personnel) have the requisite high-precision surgical skills and training to perpetrate possibly thousands of attacks—*and never experience a breakdown, run out of gas, crash or experience other mistakes.* It is interesting to re-note: With the single exception of the UK Edalji Case in 1903, to my knowledge, *no person has ever been charged, convicted and sentenced* for the crime of livestock mutilation.

Some believe that cults and devil worshippers may play a part in the mutilation mystery. We've been sacrificing animals to the gods for thousands of years—this must be somehow involved, right? I've always wondered why some humans still offer up blood sacrifice to the gods and why livestock mutilations are only reported in Christian countries. Some proponents of this cultist theory are quick to point out that pharmaceuticals have been allegedly found in the bodies of mutilated cows.

Of course we can't forget those hairy giants that seem to lurk about regions where rustling, mutilations and other phenomena are being reported. Remember our Lawton Wildman with the seventies-style pants "two sizes too small?" Or, other creatures associated with animal mutilations around the world? David and I both agree that many of these hairy humanoid cases are to be found, along with a correlation to outbreaks of other weirdness. There is no substitute for an *informed* opinion.

As you probably realize there are too many questions to address and analyze in a few pages at the end of a book like this. I originally planned to offer an extended analysis of the information in this book. I now realize that a full, quality analysis will be possible only after factoring in all the potential, circumstantial evidence and other attendant phenomena. And that takes time and space, which I don't have in this work.

MuteSpeak: Stalking the Stalkers
So, how should we go about creating an objective, fully realized analysis of the unexplained livestock deaths based on what we know, what we don't know, and what we don't know we know, etc.? I have already gathered almost 100 pages-worth of interviews with mute investigators, affected ranchers, law enforcement officials and journalists, position papers from veterinarian pathologists and law enforcement officials (both pro and con)—the range of differing viewpoints and opinions is voluminous. Perhaps a good way to cover all the available information and hypotheses would be for the other thinkers/experts/theorists to share their expertise in one place. All of their opinions are relevant and

valuable on many levels. Because this book was expanded into its present long-form scrutiny of the mystery, I literally don't have the room to include all of the opinions and theories expressed in the many sources I gathered for the end of this book.

So, I've decided to quickly follow up *Stalking the Herd* with a second book that is an analysis of the entire data set—in as complete and objective a fashion as possible. I discussed this idea with David Perkins after several long weeks of hard-core meme investigation and urged him to consider co-authoring a follow-up book entitled: *MuteSpeak*, or (his idea) *Stalking the Stalkers...* David and I have long been colleagues and collaborators in the cattle mute field and others, and he has agreed to co-produce the follow-up to this book.

The bottom line is: we need dedicated researchers willing to take the calls, follow up leads and do The Work. There is no substitute for making the necessary investigatory phone calls, interfacing with law enforcement, logging the data and helping to monitor newly reported cases *in your region.* Whether as a result of age, attrition, frustration or dismay, most aspiring mute investigators have stuck it out for no more than a few years before fading into the background noise of history, so be careful what you may invoke. This ain't ghost hunting, it's thousands of pounds of rotting flesh and being relegated to a low social status flavored by cadaverine and formalin.

Some journalist with a know-it-all attitude once quipped that cattle mutilation investigators represent "the bottom-feeders of the paranormal." That's a bit harsh and a misinformed pejorative, in my humble opinion. David Perkins wryly observed that "the bottom is where you find the rich nutrients" and we both agree that this closet subject may have profound implications for the planet—regardless of what deniers need or want you to believe.

And everyone has a theory—some more informed and evolved than others. Here's an analogy: this perplexing mystery resembles a central room with many dim passageways leading off into the darkness toward The Answer. Some of these passageways undoubtedly join up somewhere, but they all initially take off in their own unique and limited direction. In order to simultaneously entertain several provisional theories one must cultivate a radical openness to ambiguity. Easier said than done.

My interviews, conversations and research suggest that each individual investigative pathway has been colored by the researchers' bias (whether conscious or unconscious) that has been formulated by the circumstantial evidence and their interpretation of the data. The expectations of the investigator can become validated by the synchronistic data that the phenomenon provides. This makes for an interesting data stew to ponder, pull apart, fold, spindle and mutilate.

One thing is for certain: as soon as you think "you" have solved the mystery, remember—the data you haven't seen yet can supply more than enough ammunition for any devil's advocate session to slam dunk your thinking back in your face. The cattle mutilation mystery is like a monochromatic 1,000 piece puzzle with several extra misshapen pieces thrown in for good measure. This mystery can easily erase your own particular theory back off the blackboard into cloud of chalk dust, accompanied by a good smack upside the head by your latest teacher. The eight-second bell just rang and this cowboy is on to the next rodeo. So round-up them rank bulls...

Chapter Twelve Sources and References:

1. "The Trouble With Cows", David Perkins, 1999, *Beyond Beef,* J. Rifkin, Dutton, NY, NY 1992, *Food, Inc.,* Karl Weber, Persseus Books, NY, NY 2009
2. *Beyond Beef,* Jeremy Rifkin, Dutton, NY, NY 1992, *Beef,* Rimas, Fraser, Harper/Collins, NY, NY, 2008*; Food, Inc; Fast Food Nation*
3. beefusa.org/beefindustrystatistics.aspx#sthash.6QZCK109.dpuf
4. foxnews.com/us/2012/04/25/us-beef-industry-profits-from-fast-growing-exports/#ixzz2byGS-uD2
5. macdonalds.co.uk/ukhome
6. USDA, Ag in the Classroom, forces.si.edu/main/pdf/6-8-BeyondTheBeef.pdf
7. *Mad Cowboy,* Howard Lyman, Scribner, NY, NY 1998
8. *ibid*
9. *ibid*
10. Union of Concerned Scientists, Estimates of Antibiotic Abuse in Livestock," and "Food and Environment: Antibiotic Resistance," *UCS,* 2001, 2003
11. Environmental Working Group, 2-5-13, *New York Times,* 4-16-13
12. *ibid*
13. *ibid*
14. *Food, Inc.* Karl Webber, Public Affairs Books, NY, NY 2009
15. Reuters.com, 8-113-13
16. realfarmacy.com; Mercola.com; Reuters.com
17. IVN.com, Edward Bonnette, *Civil Rights, Drugs, Economy, Electoral Reform News,* 2-11-13
18. *Ibid*
19. *Food, Inc.,* Karl Webber, Public Affairs Books, NY, NY 2009
20. *Fast Food Nation,* Eric Schlosser. Houghton-Mifflin, NY, NY, 2001
21. *Waking Times,* David Gumpert, 8-13-13
22. dwb4.unl.edu/Chem;National Science Foundation statistics
23. realfarmacy.com/fast-food-burgers-only-7-meat/#sZbkpo0Bculix9XK.99
24. firstwefeast.com/eat/20000-kilos-of-fake-beef-seized-in-xian-china/ 10-16-13
25. cbsnews.com/8301-18563_162-57593188/many-concerns-as-china-eyes-largest-u.s-pork-company/
26. *Fast Food Nation,* Eric Schlosser. Houghton-Mifflin, NY, NY, 2001
27. "Can We Continue to Feed the World?" Jeffery A. Schneider, Ph.D., SUNY Oswego, 2003
28. *Food, Inc.* Karl Webber, Public Affairs Books, NY, NY 2009
29. *Beef,* Rimas & Fraser, Harper, NY, NY 2008
30. *Webster's Dictionary*
31. *Beef,* Rimas & Fraser, Harper, NY, NY 2008
32. *ibid*
33. "Cattle Plague in Eighteenth-Century England" Broad, J. Agricultural History Review, #2 1983

34. *Frontline* magazine [India] Volume 28 #15, 16 July 2011
35. *Beef,* Rimas & Fraser, Harper, NY, NY 2008
36. *Frontline* magazine [India] Volume 28 #15, 16 July 2011
37. *Boston Sun,* "Army harvested victims' blood to boost anthrax" 6-8-09 UCLA Dept. of Epidemiology
38.Centers for Disease Control and Prevention, cdc.gov/ncidod/dvrd/prions/
39. *New York Times,* 1-27-04
40. *Kuru Sorcery: Disease and Danger in the New Guinea Highlands,* Shirley Lindenbaum, Mayfield, NY, NY, 1979
41. *Brain Trust,* Colm Kelleher, Paraview NY, NY 2004
42. NIDS paper, 2003
43. CDC.gov/nchs/faststats/deaths.html, 2010
44. mayoclinic.com/health/creutzfeld-Jacob disease/
45. "Alzheimer's, CJD & BSE—Losing Your Mind For A Burger Thinking The Unthinkable," Colm Kelleher, 2-15-05

Figure 1
Cow abduction lamp—makes a perfect gift! (credit: dudeiwantthat.com)

Figure 2
In the 1860s cowboys were busy punchin' doggies. (credit: *Harpers Weekly* 1867)

Figure 3
Here's a burger from the "Heart Attack Grill."
(credit: commonsenseconspiracy.com/heartattackgrill.com)

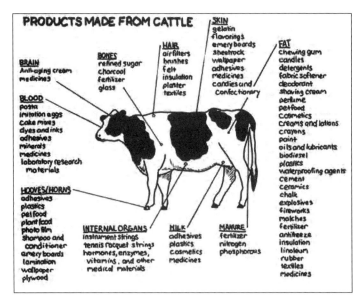

Figure 4
We utilize cattle for hundreds of products and usages. (credit: agricultured.org)

Figure 5
The Chinese now own and operate Smithfield Farms, world's largest pork processor.
(credit: smithfieldfoods.com)

Figure 6
Corporate Food Giant ConAgra has many processed food products
for your consumption. (credit: conagrafoods.com)

Figure 7
Cattle shoot to slaughter—burgers anyone? (credit: sodahead.com)

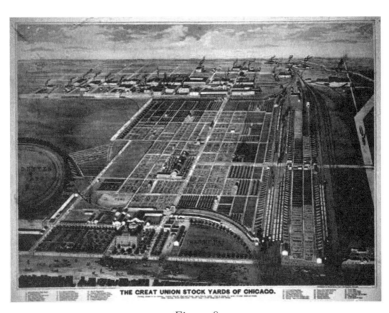

Figure 8
The Great Union Stockyards of Chicago—75 acres; 50 miles railroad tracks; daily capacity 25,000 head cattle, 160,000 hogs, 10,000 sheep—1878 (credit: Library of Congress)

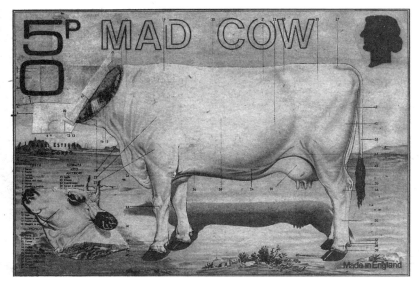

Figure 9
An artistamp that commemorates the scourge of Mad Cow disease when
it was destroying the livestock in UK beginning in 1986.
(credit: Michael Thompson/wikimediacommons.org.

Figure 10
East Highland New Guinea natives.
(credit: twodifferentgirls.com/author/omillett/)

Figure 11
D. Carleton Gadjusek, won the 1976 Nobel Prize for Medicine
for his discovery of kuru disease. (credit: nndb.com/people)

Figure 12
Stanley Pruisner won the 1996 Nobel Prize for identifying prions.
(credit: bioch.ox.ac.uk/)

Figure 13
l to r: Journalist George Knapp and NIDS biochemist Colm Kelleher
at MUFON lecture for their book *Hunt for the Skinwalker.*
(credit: abovetopsecret.com/forum; johnnyAnonymous)

Bibliography

Adams, Thomas R., *The Choppers, and The Choppers,* Project Stigma, 1980

Balter, Michael, *The Goddess and the Bull,* Free Press, NY, NY 2005

Bearden, Thomas, *Excalibur Briefing,* Walnut Hill Books, San Francisco, CA 1980

Blackman, W.H., *Field Guide to North American Monsters*, Three Rivers Press, NY, NY 1998

Bishop, Greg, *Wake Up Down There,* Adventures Unlimited Press, Kempton, IL 2000

Bishop, Greg, *Project Beta,* Gallery Books, NY, NY, 2005

Blann, Tommy, *Unmasking the Enemy,* Unpublished, 1993

Brandon, Jim, *Weird America,* Dutton, NY, NY 1978

Carlson, Joseph, *Voodoo Killers,* Futura, London, England, 2011

Cavendish, Richard, *The Black Arts,* Putnam, NY, NY 1967

Cis Van Vuure, *Retracing the Aurochs*, Sofia, Bulgaria, Pensoft Publishing, 2005

Clark, Jerome, *Unexplained*, Visible Ink Press, Detroit, MI, 1993

Clark, Jerome, *The UFO Encyclopedia Vol 3,* 1979, Omnigraphics, Detroit, MI 1996

Conrad, Jack Joseph, *The Horn and the Sword*, EP Dutton, NY, NY 1957

Cole, Leonard, *Clouds of Secrecy*, Rowman and Littlefield, Totowa, NJ, 1988

Coleman Loren, *Mysterious America,* Faber & Faber, Winchester, MA, 1983

Condon, Dr. Edward U., "Scientific Study of Flying Saucers," Director/CSU/USAF, 1968

Cooper, DJ., *Mithras,* Samuel Weiser, Inc., York Beach, Maine, 1996

Corrales, Scott, *Chupacabras and Other Mysteries,* Greenleaf Publications, Murfreesboro, TN, 1997

Dodd, Tony, *Alien Investigator*, Headline, London, UK, 1999

Dolan, Richard, *UFOs & the National Security State—1941-1873,* Hampton Roads Pub, VA, 2002

Dolan, Richard, *The Cover-Up Exposed 1973-1991* [UFOs & the Nat. Security State Vol II] Hampton Roads Pub, VA, 2002

Drake, Frank & Sobel, Dava, *Is Anyone Out There?* Delta, McHenry, IL,1994

Eberhart, George, *Geo-Bibliography of Anomalies,* 1980, Greenwood, Westport, CT

Eisnitz, Gail, *Slaughterhouse,* Prometheus Books, Amherst, NY, 1997

Ellis, Bill, *Raising the Devil,* 2000, University Press of Kentucky

Fawcett & Greenwood, *Clear Intent,* Prentice Hall Press, NY, NY 1984

Fort, Charles, *Lo!,* Kendall Publishing, NY, NY, 1931

Fort, Charles, *Wild Talents,* Kendall Publishing, NY, NY, 1932

Frazer, Sir James, edited by: T. Gaster, *New Golden Bough*, Criterion Books, NY, NY 1959

Garcia, Nasario, *Tales of Witchcraft & the Supernatural in the Pecos Valley,* Western Edge, Santa Fe, NM 1999

Girard, Rene, *Violence and the Sacred*, John Hopkins Press, NYC NY 1972

Glemser, Kurt, *The Saucer Phenomenon,* Kitchner Publisher Ontario, 1970

Godfrey, Linda, *Real Wolfman, True Encounters in Modern America,* Penguin Group, NY, NY 2012

Good, Timothy, *Alien Contact,* Random Century Group, London England, 1991

Guiley, Rosemary, *Atlas of the Mysterious in North America*, Checkmark Books, NY, NY 1995

Guiley, Rosemary, *Guide to the Dark Side of the Paranormal,* Visionary Living, CT, 2012,

Guiley, Rosemary, *The Djinn Connection,* Visionary Living, CT, 2013

Hansen, George, *The Trickster and the Paranormal,* Xlibris Corporation, 2001

Hastings, Robert, *UFOs and Nukes,* Author House, Bloomington IL, 2008

Howe, Linda Moulton, *An Alien Harvest*, Linda Moulton Howe Productions (LMH),1989

Howe, Linda Moulton, *Glimpses of Other Realities, Vol. I: Facts and Eyewitnesses*, (LMH), 1994.

Howe, Linda Moulton, *Glimpses of Other Realities, Vol. II: High Strangeness*, (LMH), 1998

Howe, Linda Moulton, *Mysterious Lights and Crop Circles*, (LMH), 2002

Hyde, Lewis, *Trickster Makes This World*, Farrar, Straus, Giroux, NY, NY 1998

Hynek, J. Allen, *The UFO Experience,* Henry Regnery, Chicago, IL, 1972

Kagan & Summers, *Mute Evidence,* Bantam, NY, NY 1983

Keel, John *Mysterious Beings,* Fawcett Publications, NYC, 1970

Keel, John, *Strange Creatures From Time and Space,* Fawcett, Inc, NY, NY 1970

Keel, John, *The Mothman Prophesies,* Saturday Review Press, NY, NY 1975
Keel, John, *The Eighth Tower,* Signet, NY, NY 1977
Kelleher, Colm, *Brain Trust,* Paraview, NY, NY, 2000
Kelleher & Knapp, *Hunt for the Skinwalker,* Paraview, NY NY 2005
Lindenbaum, Shirley, *Kuru Sorcery: Disease and Danger in the New Guinea Highlands*, Mayfield, NY, NY, 1979
Lhote, Henri R.U, *The Search for the Tassili Frescoes,* Hutchinson, London, 1960
Lyman, Howard, *Mad Cowboy,* Scribner, NY, NY 1998
Marrs, Jim, *Alien Agenda,* William Morrow, NY, NY 2000
McKenna, Terence, *Food of the Gods*, Bantam, NY, NY, 1992
O'Brien, Christopher, *The Mysterious Valley,* St Martins Press, NY, NY 1996
O'Brien, Christopher, *Enter the Valley,* St Martins Press, NY, NY 1999
O'Brien, Christopher, *Secrets of the Mysterious Valley,* Adventures Unlimited Press, Kempton, IL, 2007
O'Brien, Christopher, *Stalking the Tricksters,* Adventures Unlimited Press, Kempton, IL, 2009
Oliphant, Ted, "Dead Cows I have Known," The Anomalist #6, Charlottesville, VA 1998561
Paragamian & Vasilakis, *The Labyrinth of Messara,* Heraklion, Athens, 2002
Perkins, David, *Meet the Mutilators,* Animal Mutilation Probe, Gardner, CO 1979
Perkins/MacAdams/Clark, *Altered Steaks,* Am Here Books, Santa Barbara, CA 1982
Perkins, David, *The Mysterious Valley,* (Foreword) St Martins Press, NY, NY 1996
Perkins, David, *Enter The Valley,* (Foreword) St Martins Press, NY, NY 1999
Perkins, David, *Secrets of the Mysterious Valley* (Foreword) AUP, Kempton, IL 2007
Perkins, David, *Stalking the Tricksters* (Foreword) AUP, Kempton, IL 2009
Perkins, David , *UFOs 1947-1997,* "Darkening Skies, 1979-1980" John Brown Pub, London, England 1997
Perkins, David, "The Ranch From Hell," *Spirit Magazine*, Vol.#10, #1 1997
Perkins David, "High Heat," *Western Spirit Magazine,* May 1998
Perkins, David, "Tangling With the Trickster," *Magonia* #80, London, England 2003,
Purdy, Mark, *Animal Pharm,* Clairview Books, East Sussex, England, 2007
Radin, Paul, *The Trickster*, Schocken Books, NY, NY 1972
Rampton & Stauber, *Mad Cow U.S.A.,* Common Courage Press, Monroe, ME, 2004
Redfern, Nick, *Final Events,* Anomalist Books, Charlottesville, VA 2010
Redfern, Nick, *Keep Out!* New Page Books, Pompton Plains, NJ 2011
Redfern, Nick, *The World's Weirdest Places,* New Page Books, Pompton Plains, NJ 2012
Redfern, Nick, *Monster Files,* New Page Books, Pompton Plains, NJ 2013
Rhodes, Richard, *Deadly Feasts,* Simon & Schuster, 1997
Rifkin, Jeremy, *Beyond Beef*, Dutton Books NYC, NY 1992
Rimas & Fraser *Beef*, Harper Books, NYC, NY, 2008
Ring Kenneth, *Germs Gone Wild*, Pegasus Books, NY, 2010
Roberts & Gilbertson, *The Dark Gods,* Panther Books, London, England 1985
Rokosz', M. "History of the Aurochs in Poland," journals.cambridge.org/ 1995
Rommel, Kenneth, *Operation Animal Mutilation, New Mexico District Attorney Eloy Martines, 1980*
S., Acharya, *Suns of God,* Adventures Unlimited Press, Kempton, IL, 2004
Schlosser, Eric, *Fast Food Nation,* Houghton-Mifflin, NY, NY, 2001
Singer, Charles, *From Magic to Science,* Dover Pub, NY, NY, 1958
Smith, F.W., Smith, *Cattle Mutilation: The Unthinkable Truth* self published, 1976
Smoley, Richard, *Supernatural,* Penguin Group, NY, NY, 2013
Steiger, Brad & Sherry, *Conspiracies & Secret Societies,* Visible Ink Pres, Canton, MI, 2013
Steiger, Brad & Sherry, *Real Encounters, Different Dimensions & Otherworldly Beings,* Visible Ink Pres, Canton, MI, 2014
Teller & Blackwater, *The Navajo Skinwalker, Witchcraft & Related Phenomena,* Infinity Horn Pub, 1997
Valdez, Greg, *Dulce Base,* Levi-Cash Publishing, Albuquerque, NM, 2013
Vallee, Jacques, *Passport to Magonia,* Henry Regnery, Chicago, IL 1969
Vallee, Jacques, *Messengers of Deception,* And/Or Press, Berkeley, CA, 1979
Vallee, Jacques, *Anatomy of a Phenomenon,* Ballantine, NY, NY, 1987
Vallee, Jacques, *Dimensions,* McGraw-Hill, NY, NY 1988
Vallee, Jacques, *Confrontations,* Ballantine Books, NY, NY 1990
Webber, Karl, *Food, Inc.,* Public Affairs Books, NY, NY 2009
Yam, Philip, *The Pathological Protein,* Copernicus Books, NY, NY 2003

About the Author:

From 1992 to 2002 Christopher O'Brien investigated and/or logged one thousand paranormal events reported in the San Luis Valley—located in South-central Colorado/North Central New Mexico. Working with law enforcement officials from five counties, ex-military, ranchers and an extensive network of skywatchers, he documented what may have been the most intense wave of unexplained activity ever seen in a single region of North America. His ten-year investigation resulted in the three books of his "mysterious valley" trilogy, *The Mysterious Valley* (1996) *Enter the Valley* (1999), and *Secrets of the Mysterious Valley* (2007). His field investigation of UFO reports, unexplained livestock deaths, Native American legends, cryptozoology, secret military activity and the folklore, found in the world's largest alpine valley, has produced one of the largest databases of unusual occurrences gathered from a single geographic region. He is currently working with a team of specialists installing a high-tech video surveillance and hard-data monitoring system in and around the San Luis Valley. His last book *Stalking the Tricksters* (2009) distilled his years of field investigation and research into an ingenious unified paranormal theory that looks at the "trickster" mechanism in culture.

O'Brien is an entertaining, thought-provoking speaker and has been a guest on *Coast-to-Coast*; developed, supplied footage, field-produced and appeared in four segments of the Paramount television program *Sightings*. Ten episodes of *Ancient Aliens* and he has provided visual elements and appeared on *UFO Hunters, Inside Edition, Extra, Showtime's Sci-Friday Chronicles*; the TBS documentary *UFO: The Search*; the BBC2 program Louis Theroux's *Weird Weekends*, Nippon TV's *Special Research 2000*, the Discovery Channel's two-hour documentary, *Billion Dollar Secret* with *Jane's Defence Weekly's* Nick Cook, the TV series *Unexplained Files, Exploring the Unknown, The Unexplained, Secrets of:, Profiles in Ufology, Unexplained Mysteries, Weird or What* and in the English documentary film *Mutilation Files* plus others. At home in front or behind the camera, O'Brien has field-produced and directed television segments for the nationally syndicated paranormal news-magazine *Strange Universe*. O'Brien also produced *History, Mystery and Greed*: the story of Snippy the Horse, and co-produced *Dead Whisper*. He is also a consulting producer and writer/researcher for Ronald James Films—a Los Angeles-based video production company. Chris has co-written an action/adventure film screenplay, *Heavy Waters*, inspired by his field-research that was judged Honorable Mention in the Southwest Screenwriter's Guild Contest.

Since 1993, he has written articles for *Fate, UFO Universe, Leading Edge, Cyber-West, Western Spirit, World Explorer's Club Magazine, Crestone Eagle, Phenomena,*

Zeitgeist and *UFO Encounters*. His investigation and research have been featured in the Denver *Post*, Pueblo *Chieftain*, the *New Mexican*, the *Rocky Mountain News*, the Albuquerque *Journal*, the *Deseret News*, the *Red Rock News*, *Phenomenon*, (France) *OVNI* (Spain), *Borderline* (Japan). He has appeared on dozens of regional and national radio stations and was a perennial guest lecturer at Adam's State College. O'Brien has captivated conference and seminar audiences around The USA with his unique insight into some of our culture's last remaining mysteries. He hosted his own regional Colorado/New Mexico radio show, *Mysterious Valley Report* (1996-1999), and published the bi-monthly *Mysterious Valley Report* (1993-2000). Since 2010, O'Brien has served as co-host of the nationally syndicated paranormal radio show, *The Paracast*.

A keyboard player/music-producer, digital artist and videographer, he makes his home near Sedona, AZ.

You can visit his webpage: ourstrangeplanet.com, or stalkingtheherd.com